A SA GRAY, the leading Amei
of the nineteenth century, was tne center
of a network of botanical exploration,
handling collections both from western
North America and from American overseas expeditions. First as the junior colleague of Dr. John Torrey in New York,
and later by himself in Cambridge, Massachusetts, Gray stimulated collectors in the
field, sold their specimens, and published
the scientific results. He helped to raise the
standards of science in America not by
competing with Europeans but by co-
operating with the greatest of them. He
reported American results to Europe and
interpreted Europeans to America.

The most persistent and effective pro-
tagonist in America of Charles Darwin's
views, Gray was also a creative member
of Darwin's inner circle of scientific
friends. At the same time that he was trying
to get a fair hearing for Darwin in America
he was trying to convince Darwin that
there was no inconsistency between natural
selection and natural theology. Although
Darwin rejected this view, he and Gray remained close collaborators on botanical
experiments until the end of Darwin's life.

Based on original sources, largely letters,
this book presents the first full-length interpretation of Asa Gray. Written for the
scholar and the layman alike, it will appeal
to a wide variety of interests. In addition to
botany, it deals with the history of science,
American intellectual and social history,
philosophy and its relations to science,
theology, the history of higher education,
the New England scene, explorations,
geology, and zoology.

A. Hunter Dupree, a graduate of Oberlin
College and Harvard University, is now
Associate Professor of History at the University of California, Berkeley. He is the
author of *Science in the Federal Government: A History of Policies and Activities
to 1940* (Harvard University Press, 1957).

*The flower which appears on the jacket
is Lilium Grayi, named after Asa Gray.*

A Belknap Press Book

ASA GRAY

Asa Gray in 1838. Crayon portrait by Sir David McNee, P.R.S.A., now in the possession of the Royal Gardens, Kew.

ASA GRAY

1810–1888

A. Hunter Dupree

THE BELKNAP PRESS OF
HARVARD UNIVERSITY PRESS

Cambridge, Massachusetts

1959

Distributed in Great Britain by
Oxford University Press
London

Library of Congress Catalog Card Number 59–12967

Printed in the United States of America

FOR
BETTY, MARGUERITE, AND ANDY

PREFACE

This book is a biography of Asa Gray. As such it tells a personal story. Yet the life of a man who spent most of his waking hours working at science and thinking about science includes in the personal story much that belongs also to the history of science. Asa Gray was a Yankee and a resident of New England, but as a regional study his biography must concern itself with the Southeast, Texas, the Rockies, California, Latin America, and the whole Pacific basin. Asa Gray was an American, and his career is inseparable from the social and intellectual history of the United States from his coming of age in the late 1820's to his death in 1888. Yet a national setting is not wide enough for him. He was an actor on a trans-Atlantic stage, taking part in the transit of knowledge across the ocean. His role in science must be described partly in terms of institutions, for he shaped the pursuit of botany in America for a long generation. Yet at a crucial moment in the development of scientific ideas he was one of a handful in the world who had both the preparation and the access to information to play a creative part.

Because of the varied paths through which the subject led his biographer, any reader who limits himself to one of the themes will find the book tailored to his needs only part of the time. The botanist must put up not only with definitions of terms he knows well but must also suffer the discussion of questions which normally belong to intellectual and even religious history. The nonbotanist will insist on considering some of the issues as technical and should not resent the suggestion that he can get something out of these parts without being able to visualize every last flower which can, after all, be designated briefly only by its Latin name. The student of American civilization must accept botany as a part of his proper subject and at

vii

the same time be willing to wander geographically from Japan to Vienna and up the Nile. The historian of science must accept taxonomy as a subject worthy of his attention and the United States in the nineteenth century as a locale of some possible interest. The student of Darwinism must face the fact that the same man can be important to his story and remain an orthodox Christian. The most fortunate reader will be that rare person uncommitted to any special interest who nevertheless has the desire and patience to meet a man whom he perhaps has not known before, a man who used his talents and was fortunate in his time and place.

This book may see daylight during 1959, the hundredth anniversary of the publication of Charles Darwin's *Origin of Species*. The year is also, for reasons closely associated with Darwin's achievement, the centennial of the most exciting, stimulating, and creative year of Gray's life. Hence the festive timing of publication is entirely appropriate. Nevertheless, I cannot take full credit for this happy conjunction. The impending centennial played no part in stimulating this biography. Indeed, if, when I first conceived this work in the eighty-ninth year after the *Origin,* someone had remarked that it would be published in 1959, I should have been plunged into the depths of gloom.

Over the past decade I have incurred debts to more people than I can ever hope to list here. The few I feel impelled to mention must stand for that host of librarians, historians, botanists, secretaries, and friends who have, by helping me to find the trail of Asa Gray, made historical research one of the most pleasant of occupations. The first eight chapters of this biography served as my doctoral dissertation at Harvard University, where I had the privilege of working under the direction of Arthur M. Schlesinger, Sr., who has continued to allow me the use of wise counsel and friendship after my student days were over.

The Gray Herbarium and its staff have rendered me essential aid, not only by allowing me access to the key collection of Gray manuscripts and to a library based on Gray's personal collection, but also by giving me a botanical education in an atmosphere still flavored by Gray's presence. When I first went there to work, M. L. Fernald and Charles A. Weatherby were still active on the *emeritus* staff, almost bridging the gap to Gray's time, and they both proved willing to help an unknown young man. Reed C. Rollins, director of the Gray Herbarium, has, from the first day I arrived to the present, gone out of his way to assist my researches in every way possible and to allow me the use of all sorts of facilities. My work was especially aided by an appointment to the staff as a research fellow in 1952–53, 1953–54, and 1955–56. Vera Campbell has contributed much to the successful completion of this work by her kindness, her concern, and her innumerable services. I am also indebted to other members of the staff, including Bernice G. Schubert, R. C. Foster and three successive librarians—Ruth D. Sanderson, Margaret Stone, and Lazella Schwarten.

Members of the Gray and Loring families have helped with reminiscences and manuscripts. Mr. and Mrs. Joseph Robbins welcomed my wife and me when we visited Sauquoit, New York. General Harris Jones made an important group of letters available. Mrs. John Noble showed us the Loring summer home at Pride's Crossing. Mr. Patrick Tracy Jackson told me of his memories of Dr. and Mrs. Gray. Mrs. Nathaniel Clapp allowed us to examine a large collection of Loring family manuscripts.

An early climax in our personal interviewing came in May 1949, when we spent a morning with Liberty Hyde Bailey at Ithaca, New York. Dr. Bailey, who was well worth interviewing in his own right, was the only survivor of those who had known Gray professionally, and he also put me on the trail of an important group of letters. Andrew Denny Rodgers III shared with me his extensive knowledge of the whereabouts of the manuscripts of American botanists. My footnotes do not adequately indicate the role which he and his books played because, if I have checked and therefore cited original sources, I was nevertheless often led to them in the early stages of the work by Rodgers.

To Elizabeth Cook Rochow, I owe a special debt for her services on this book in 1955–56. I owe an unrepayable debt to the late Richard A. Studhalter of Texas Technological College, who taught me early in life to look upon botany as a great science and who showed me the treasures to be found in Gray's target area, the Sangre de Cristo Mountains.

PREFACE

At several stages I have had financial assistance. The people of the United States through the GI Bill of Rights helped in the early years. The American Academy of Arts and Sciences, through a grant from its Permanent Science Fund, made possible the resumption of research in 1952. Major financial assistance, which made the difference between continuing and abandoning the research, came from my parents, George W. and Sarah H. Dupree. But money was only a counter for their real contribution, which was a faith in scholarship and a belief in the importance of this work.

At one time or another a number of qualified people have read all or part of the manuscript and given me valuable suggestions. I wish here to thank especially Reed C. Rollins, Paul C. Mangelsdorf, I. Bernard Cohen, Lincoln Constance, and Conway Zirkle. Sole responsibility for all the conclusions resides nevertheless completely with me.

Finally I wish also to thank my wife. Her handwriting on many note cards is evidence of her assistance, especially in copying documents. But she has also given Dr. Gray a welcome and honored place in our family circle for a decade and has given me the kind of support and encouragement which cannot be measured.

CONTENTS

LIST OF ILLUSTRATIONS

ASA GRAY

EARLY YEARS

DURING the long winters in central New York, young Asa
Gray had plenty of time to read. The bulky *Edinburgh
Encyclopaedia* could well occupy a seventeen-year-old youth, for the
article on botany surveyed in 343 double-columned pages the study
of plants beginning with the Greeks. Great names followed one another down the centuries—Theophrastus, Dioscorides, Brunfels,
Camerarius, Bauhin, Ray, Tournefort. In high relief stood Linnaeus,
whose system the writer applied to his impressive catalogue of the
genera and species of plants. Here was an epitome of past knowledge. Here was the record of learned men who devoted their lives to
examining the infinitely varied tangle of vegetation about them.
Among the scholars with their weird ritual of Latin names appeared
adventurers of bolder stamp, like Sir Joseph Banks, who helped
Captain James Cook explore the South Seas and brought back the
curiosities which lived in *Terra Incognita*. Such is the stuff from
which any boy can make wild dreams.[1]

However little he understood the science, Asa must have grasped
some of the meaning of one passage, which brought adventure to
him right here less than ten miles from the Erie Canal.

In proceeding . . . to give some account of the progress of discovery in
North America, it will not be necessary to enter into much detail. The greater
part of this vast region, with all those stores of vegetable life, utility, and
beauty, which it must necessarily contain, is yet to be explored. Nor can we
ever say with truth, that our information, with respect to the flora of these
districts which have already been examined, is by any means so extensive
and satisfying as we might have been naturally led to expect; a circumstance
which is probably to be accounted for, in part, from a fear inspired by the
neighborhood of the Indians, and the difficulties with which the inhabitants
of the United States have had to contend in the infancy of their government.[2]

In this paragraph Asa Gray met two ideas which made the work of a lifetime. An immense continent with an infinitely varied covering of chaotic vegetation awaited a comprehending mind. Botany, still a young and groping science, had developed sufficiently to be effective. Here the worker found his task and his tool. Although Gray could not recognize the import of the moment, his life had found a theme. During his years both the knowledge of the North American continent and the knowledge of the nature of life would expand and change, and he would henceforth be a part of both streams. Ahead on one of them lay the *Flora of North America*. Ahead on the other lay Charles Darwin and the theory of evolution.

Primary among the resources which at seventeen he already possessed for his great undertaking was his Yankee heritage. His grandparents were among the first to arrive in the valleys of central New York just after the Revolution, during which the Iroquois had vanished from their ancestral home. Yankees just starting the long road that led to Oregon left the uneasy hill country of New England and sought better land on the Mohawk. Central New York was still the frontier when Moses Wiley Gray and Joseph Howard, each following his separate path, turned south from the river at Utica and ascended one of the small tributaries. With its rippling water and high-shouldered green hills the Sauquoit Valley could pass for the promised land.

Moses Wiley Gray was of the first generation of his family born in America. His father, Robert Gray, had been among an early group of Scottish Presbyterians who emigrated from the north of Ireland. This particular colony, landing in Boston in 1718, soon settled in Worcester, Massachusetts. The New Englanders who had recently founded the town did not take kindly to the strangers, called them Irish, and tore down their meeting house. Most of the outraged immigrants left to join some of their own kind in Pelham, New Hampshire. But the Grays, perhaps showing a family trait of flexibility in difficult social situations, remained in Worcester as farmers. Robert married Sarah Wiley, one of the colony, about 1729, and spent the rest of his life in Worcester.[3]

Moses Wiley Gray, who was born in 1745, felt so much at home among the better established settlers of English origin that he married Sally Miller, whose family had been in America for well over a century. But as Moses Wiley was the eighth of ten children he made soon after his marriage a first short move westward and lived in Templeton, Massachusetts, during the Revolution and the trying years just afterward. Although called out with the militia for two short tours of duty at the time of Lexington and during the Burgoyne campaign, he was still in Templeton when his own eighth child, Moses Gray, was born February 26, 1786. The plight of the hill country which had aroused the Shays rebellion urged the Gray family to move on, and about 1787 they went to Grafton, Vermont. Here Sally died in 1793, and Moses Wiley, left with ten children, looked westward again to the Mohawk Valley. Before another year had passed he was clearing a hilltop farm near Sauquoit.[4]

Joseph Howard's people had lived in Ipswich, Massachusetts, since 1636, but his tribe showed much the same restlessness as the newcomer Grays. Probably not long after his birth in 1766, the family moved to Pomfret, Connecticut, its first ephemeral stopping place. Joseph married a Connecticut girl, Submit Luce, but by the time his daughter Roxana was born March 15, 1789, he was living in Longmeadow, Massachusetts, just south of Springfield. Four years later he went west to the valley of the Sauquoit. Here, true to the genius of New England, he first appears trying to duplicate one of its characteristic institutions, the Congregational Church. He was the clerk of a society which in 1795 unsuccessfully attempted to provide the village of Sauquoit with a place of worship.[5]

Even in New York the mining frontier sometimes led the farming frontier, and it was the promise of profits in iron that bade Joseph Howard stay in the valley. About 1800 a company was formed to build a forge at Paris Furnace Hollow, two miles up the creek from the village of Sauquoit. Members of the group were important enough to have honorific titles. Judge Eliphalet Sweeting as the founder evidently supplied the technical supervision, while Colonel Gardner Avery managed sales and finance. Deacon Howard had the misfortune very early in the undertaking to forge off three fingers with the trip hammer, which "appears to have qualified him to be the clerk in charge, or manager, of the office and store." In erecting a brewery as a side enterprise, he did not in the least lower himself

3

in the estimation of his devout neighbors, true descendants of the early Puritans.[6]

Meanwhile the Gray family had hard luck. Moses Wiley Gray had remarried, and three sons and a daughter were born in Sauquoit, which with Sally Miller's ten children brought the number to fourteen. But in 1803, when after years of labor at clearing and farming he might have looked forward to increasing prosperity, he was killed by a falling tree. Young Moses was at this time just over seventeen, and the event must have forced a decision concerning his future, for he soon afterward went as an apprentice to Mr. Gier, the tanner and currier in Sauquoit. One of the older brothers must have taken the farm, for Moses continued as a helper at the tannery even after he reached twenty-one. He probably had considerable responsibility for the younger members of the family, especially for a brother named Asa who had consumption. But his energy and quickness made him acceptable as a suitor to Roxana Howard, and they were married July 30, 1809.[7]

The couple set up housekeeping temporarily in a small building that had once been a shoeshop as a part of Gier's tannery, snug against the hill at the eastern edge of the village. Sauquoit is really two parallel streets, the Methodists living on the eastern side of the creek, and the Presbyterians on the west. Thus the Grays were removed from their own people, for although not church members they had close ties with those who were just then forming a church in the west part of the village. Joseph Howard was one of the trustees of the Union Society, founded early in 1810, which was the forerunner to the Presbyterian Church. Moses and Roxana Gray merely bivouacked until they could make some better arrangement.[8]

Their first child was born on Sunday, November 18, 1810. The parents perpetuated the name of the ailing brother by calling the boy Asa. He began life with bright prospects indeed. The Grays were respected members of a promising community in which they intended to stay. Their finances could only get better, and with their New England belief in education they would give their son any advantages central New York offered. Although the Mohawk Valley might seem isolated in 1810, something in its clear air produced not only ingenious religious experimenters but also many more than its quota of scientists. It is true that Asa Gray was born back of the tannery, that his father was still but a journeyman, and that the hills enclosing the valley seemed to shut out the wider world—a modest background if measured against that of a lad near two years old in England. Charles Darwin counted physicians, a philosophical poet, and a fabulously successful potter among his forebears. But Master Darwin had an exact contemporary in Kentucky who was to become the prototype of all those who start life humbly in a cabin. Asa began his pilgrimage several steps ahead of Abraham Lincoln.

The family did not tarry long among the Methodists of Sauquoit. Within a few months after Asa's birth, Moses Gray set up a tannery of his own at Paris Furnace, where he could be a part of the small nucleus of industries and Roxana Gray could be near her parents. The move probably came before May 1811, when Asa, the brother of Moses Gray, died at Paris Furnace. Here the boy formed his first impressions of a world of trees and green fields. The valley of the Sauquoit was and still is superbly beautiful on a sunny spring day. Asa's playmates were Howards and Averys, for the Grays were socially, if not yet financially, members of the managerial class which was leading the community's iron forge in a fleeting day of economic glory. Tanning was a considerable industry in New York at the time, and Moses Gray had a more than local market, for he shipped hides to Albany by wagon. Asa early worked in the bark mill, which was turned by an old horse. The Grays were soon able to build a house and settle down with an increasing family.

The few positive bits of information that have survived concerning his early years support the tradition that Asa was an avid reader. He himself gives the age at which he started to school as three. Since the Lancasterian, or monitor, system was then the prevailing method of instruction in the district schools of New York because of a lack of teachers, the older children who taught as well as learned could easily take a youngster in tow. The tales that he and others remember of spelling matches reflect the emphasis of the schools, for reading, writing, and figuring must have been the sole concern during each of the several years that Asa attended. His early aptitude for reading shows most clearly in a scheme for pooling book resources in the village. There was "a little subscription library at

5

Sauquoit, the stockholders of which met four times a year, distributed the books to the highest bidder (maximum, perhaps, ten or twelve cents) to have and to hold for three months. . . ." Although young Asa had "no great choice in my early boyhood . . . History I rather took to, but especially voyages and travels were my delight." [9]

A religious element entered Asa's early training. He spent at least one year in a private school taught by the son of the village pastor, and for a period he lived at the house of his grandfather, Deacon Howard, while working in the office of the furnace company. His parents showed unhurried sympathy with the Sauquoit church, which from its joint status as a union society was drifting toward Presbyterian dominance. Roxana Gray became a member in November 1816, and on the following Christmas Day her three children, Asa, Roxana, and Elsada, were baptized.[10] Moses Gray was not yet a church member, and religion did not mean a narrow restraint on Asa. He was quite free, for instance, to read novels, although he could only lay his hands on Miss Porter's *Children of the Abbey* and *Thaddeus of Warsaw*. The sum of all his childhood religious training probably amounted to a rather vague acceptance of an unexciting Presbyterian Church.

In the early 1820's the economic base of the community around Paris Furnace was changing. During 1824 Colonel Avery sent his son Eli with a wagon down into Pennsylvania to get a load of anthracite coal, hoping that it would make harder plow points than did charcoal. This experiment symbolized the danger which threatened the whole cluster of industries. Wood was running out. Not only was the forge dependent upon charcoal, but the tanning process used large quantities of wood and bark. The largest tanneries of the state were congregating around the Catskill Mountains where lumber was plentiful. Moses Gray was both astute and forehanded in meeting the shift, for he saw that lumbering in the area around Paris Furnace left the land ready for agriculture. Using the profits from his hides and shoes, he bought up good farms as they were cleared. About 1823 he sold the tannery and moved back to Sauquoit village where he became farmer Moses Gray, who, finding his new occupation agreeable, increased the capital he brought to it.[11] He even had a small surplus to apply to the education of his bright and eager eldest son.

Nine miles over the hills northwest of Sauquoit lay Clinton, the seat of one of the four colleges in the whole state of New York. When the Hamilton-Oneida Academy became Hamilton College in 1813 it left room for a preparatory school, which took the form of a rapid succession of teachers conducting classes in Greek and Latin under the name of Clinton Grammar School. Colonel Avery's brother, Charles, had tried his hand there for a couple of years after his graduation from Hamilton College in 1820. Orlando Kirkland had taken over in 1822, but the Grays must still have felt some personal connection with the school.[12] Asa probably began his two years of attendance in the fall of 1823. He lived at Clinton except for the summer months, when he helped with "the corn and hay-field" at home.[13]

Looking across a great many years, Asa Gray did not think highly of his schooling under Orlando Kirkland. "I was drilled after a fashion in the rudiments of Latin and Greek for two years. . . ." This estimate, probably justified in itself, somewhat obscures the crucial importance of an introduction to classical training, the great dividing experience which produced an educated man. For young Asa would soon find Latin not only a mark of cultivation but also a practical necessity. Nearly all plant descriptions and many of the standard works of botany were written in that language. The universal tongue of the Middle Ages had not completely lost its function as a means of communication between scientists who spoke different vernaculars.[14] Although the Latin of the botanists was modeled on Linnaeus and not on Cicero, Asa would soon have plenty of use for some case endings when he first tackled a *Flora*. Poor as the training probably was, it gave him his first papers toward becoming a scholar and a gentleman.

Even a stronger school than the one at Clinton could hardly have held very much of Asa's interest, particularly after he found Sir Walter Scott. "One Sunday afternoon, of the first winter I was at Clinton, I went into the public room of one of the two village inns, where half a dozen of the villagers were assembled; and one was reading aloud 'Quentin Durward.' " That summer he read *Rob Roy*, and the next fall he hit upon a source of reading matter which greatly broadened his range. Some Hamilton College students ate at the house where he lived. "One of them, seeing my avidity for books, introduced me to the librarian of the Phoenix Society of the college, which had a library strong in novels, which I was allowed, one by one, to take home for reading. I suppose that I read them every one."

Since the Hamilton College Library, like most of its contemporaries, took little responsibility beyond the classics and theology, the students who wished to read modern literature had to provide it for themselves through their societies. Hence these groups played a far larger part in college life than mere social clubs. An eager prep school boy who was after books that were interesting could not have done better than to seek out the Phoenix Society. It is at least possible to infer some of the books which came Asa's way.

The college boys were avid for Scott's works and added them to their collection as soon as new books came out. They had *Tales of My Landlord, Third Series* in 1820, within a year of its publication in England. They had *The Fortunes of Nigel* and *Quentin Durward* in 1823, and *Redgauntlet: A Tale of the Eighteenth Century* in 1824. Surely Asa read them as soon as he could get them. He probably read Tobias Smollett. He may have met Tristram Shandy and the Scottish Chiefs, Tom Jones and Gils Blas. *The Spy* and *The Pilot,* written by a man over in Cooperstown named James Fenimore Cooper, may have given Asa some idea that all novels did not come from England.

Many of the novels Asa read at Clinton were not destined to be enduring literature, and perhaps some of the more obscure ones entertained him and formed his thoughts quite as much as those whose titles are familiar in the twentieth century. He had plenty of opportunity to imbibe both manners and morals from Susanna Haswell Rowson's *Rebecca, or the Fille de Chambre,* from Mrs. Ross's *The Bachelor and the Married Man, Or the Equilibrium of the Balance of Comfort,* and from *Hesitation: Or, to Marry, or, Not to Marry?* With all these delights to occupy him Asa probably never saw Erasmus Darwin's *Botanic Garden* or the scientific works which lay within his reach at the Phoenix Society. But his interest in a good story at least introduced him to the world beyond the Mohawk, and subconsciously he was becoming familiar with some facets of the thought of his time.[15]

The ceremonial opening of the Erie Canal in the fall of 1825, which made a profound impression on the people of central New York, stood out in Asa Gray's memory especially since he saw for himself the barge carrying Governor DeWitt Clinton and his party. The canal meant a profound change to the villages founded by New Englanders on the tops of hills, for the life blood of the region now flowed between the towpaths. Little Fairfield high up on the edge of the Adirondack wilderness could be proud of its academy and the College of Physicians and Surgeons of the Western District of the State of New York, but its prospects were at best somnolescent. Asa was fortunate that he came there no later, for a few years still remained for a golden age. He remembered well that during his first fall in the academy he and his classmates went down the seven miles to Little Falls on the canal to see the splendid barge as it passed just at sunset.[16]

Asa's parents sent him to Fairfield because Charles Avery, the erstwhile teacher of the Clinton Grammar School, became principal of the academy. Business connections between the Grays and the Averys back in Paris Furnace undoubtedly had something to do with the decision, for Asa's board was paid for by products from the forge. Charles Avery "was sharp at turning a penny in various ways; among them, he for the first year and more jobbed the board of his nephew Eli and myself, who were chums, paying for it in cooking-stoves and the like from Paris furnace."

Academies were the mainstay of the educational system of New York in the early nineteenth century. Although most were secondary schools, many of them aspired to be colleges and some, like Hamilton, gained the promotion. Others felt free to compete with the higher institutions while retaining considerable flexibility and educational daring. Fairfield Academy was founded in 1808 to bring learning to a region where New England ways were beginning to penetrate the earlier scattered German settlements. From its very beginning the school envisaged a curriculum which emphasized the sciences and English letters. In 1808 the courses posted with the

9

Regents of the University of the State of New York showed the third year of study as consisting of composition, oratory and history, astronomy, philosophy, mensuration, geometry, trigonometry, surveying, navigation, botany, chemistry, materia medica, and the general principles of the military art. The bent of the school was even more evident when in 1809 medical lectures began, and in 1812 the Regents granted a charter to the College of the Physicians and Surgeons of the Western District of the State of New York to be located at Fairfield in connection with the academy, which continued its work as a preparatory school.[17] Since Asa planned to go to college, he probably studied the classics and mathematics in his first year. But the shrewd principal Avery did not arouse much enthusiasm in his pupil. "I cannot say that I owe much to him, even for teaching me mathematics, which was his forte. My capital memory allowed me to 'get my lessons' easily, and that sufficed; and I had none of the sharp drilling and testing that I needed."

The lack of academic inspiration lends a certain color of probability to the type if not to the content of the stories that have grown up about Asa's cow-painting and chicken-stealing escapades.[18] At fifteen he was by no means a serious scholar, but his education progressed in other ways as in the rural academy he could spend much time out of doors in intimate if uncritical touch with nature. Maple sugar expeditions often took the boys deep into the woods, and Asa could always recall that he learned to identify trees by their bark. This easy familiarity with the ways of living things gave a naturalist an advantage that no formal training could replace. Of course Gray did not roam the woods seeking solitude, for he was above all gregarious. He joined almost immediately the Calliopean Society, where with the guidance of the Muse of eloquence the young gentlemen debated the topics of the day, such as "Are Secret Societies Beneficial?" and "Does the Stage Promote Morality?" Asa was at least more successful than his friend Eli Avery in keeping clear of fines for breaking rules. The society also owned many of the few books in Fairfield. Indeed one of its major projects was the serial purchase of the *Edinburgh Encyclopaedia* from William Williams, the printer at Utica.[19]

After one year in the academy Asa abandoned his plan to go to

college by switching to Fairfield's medical school. He himself explained the change in terms of his father's wishes. "It was intended
that I should go to college, and my father could have put me through
without serious inconveniences; but he was buying land about this
time, and he persuaded me to give up that idea and to go at once at
the study of medicine, which I did in the autumn of 1826 . . ." Asa
hoped to go to neighboring Hamilton College,[20] and since a year
there actually cost less than a sixteen-week term at Fairfield medical
school, the explanation on financial grounds needs some elaboration. The fact that Hamilton was in grave difficulties which would
soon in effect close its doors must have weighed heavily on the
Grays' decision.[21] With the college at Clinton temporarily in eclipse
they probably saw Yale as the nearest college which would meet
their wishes.[22] The additional fees and travel expenses in going to
New Haven would have made considerable difference to Moses
Gray just when he was hard up for cash. Had Hamilton been flour-
ishing in the late 1820's, his decision might have gone in that direction. As it turned out he probably did his son little disservice, for
physicians had attained the rank of gentleman without the necessity
of the A.B. degree, and Fairfield medical school was at its height
both in prestige and resources.

The greatness of the College of Physicians and Surgeons of the
Western District lay in the men who taught there. Familiarly called
the Fairfield medical school, it had neither money nor location to
recommend it as an institution. But for a few years the itinerant
doctors who had begun as teachers in the Dartmouth and Berkshire
medical schools moved west with the trend of population. They
used Fairfield as their headquarters before drifting on to Geneva,
Buffalo, and Cleveland. Lyman Spalding, the first president, came
directly from the Dartmouth medical school, and, although he left
after a few years to edit the first *United States Pharmacopoeia,* a
strong staff had by Gray's time attracted 145 students. Most of the
faculty resided elsewhere and came to Fairfield only for the sessions.
James Hadley, the professor of chemistry and materia medica, was
the only one who made his home there.[23]

Lectures began on the first Tuesday of each October and lasted
for sixteen weeks, into January. The faculty converged on Fairfield

from their various homes, often from teaching at other medical schools. The students, who presumably spent the rest of the year understudying some older doctor, bought tickets for each course, the money going directly to the professors. The lectures were the same each year, and after a student had attended the course twice, he could come free thereafter if he thought he could get something out of it. Nothing required a person to attend the required two sessions consecutively. For instance, a pious young doctor named Marcus Whitman attended in 1825–26 and again in 1831–32, practicing medicine in the meantime.[24] Even the degree of doctor of medicine depended less upon the schoolwork than the apprentice system, for the regulations stipulated that students should have "studied medicine and surgery, for the term of three years after the age of sixteen, with some physician duly authorized to practice his profession" in addition to being twenty-one years of age and to attending two courses of lectures.[25]

The school gradually accumulated some equipment and resources. In 1839, the year before it closed, it listed among its assets a museum of human and comparative anatomy, "one of the most splendid and valuable collections of Minerals to be found in the country," chemical apparatus, specimens to illustrate materia medica, and a library of 1400 volumes. The state gave the college the right to demand from the authorities of the state prison at Auburn "and to receive from them . . . the dead bodies of any convicts that may die in said Prison . . ."[26] With such attractions enrollment was increasing rapidly, and although larger ticket sales might raise the professors' incomes, this put nothing into the coffers of the college. But the influx of students led the school to erect in 1825 a four-story stone building, which proved to be the ultimate undoing of the whole enterprise. The addition so exhausted the finances that after 1828 operations could continue only because the professors were willing to pay running costs out of their private receipts. Most of the school's scientific collections fell within the responsibility of Dr. James Hadley, and the full measure of his devotion may be gathered from this report of the trustees. "Incidental expenses of the current year have been defrayed by the Professors and chemical

12

apparatus to the amount of $1000 has been procured at the expense of the Professor of that department." [27]

In Dr. Hadley, Asa Gray immediately found his ideal. The other professors must have received his respectful attention, but only the teacher of chemistry genuinely stirred his interest. Tradition has Gray in his student days giving little promise as a physician,[28] perhaps because, like Darwin, he was squeamish when confronted with anatomical dissections.[29] Even if he was slightly miscast as a doctor Hadley became his "earliest scientific adviser and most excellent friend." For in the early nineteenth century the medical profession was dividing from its main body workers interested in sciences independent of medicine. Hadley was typical of the transitional period of the physician-turning-naturalist. To chemistry he added mineralogy as an interest which had little enough to do with medicine. From materia medica, a study which must include useful plants and herbs, he progressed to a more general curiosity about botany. Hadley's interests had changed consciously, for he went to New Haven to study sciences in 1818, the year Benjamin Silliman founded the *American Journal of Science and Arts* there. A religious attitude toward nature was an added spur to his interest in science. "Infinite variety is expressed on the face of vegetable existence. Whether we regard the magnitude or minuteness of herbage, the forms, the colorings, and beautiful arrangements, we recognize an act of creative power and consummate wisdom." [30]

Such a feeling that all nature evidenced the handiwork of a supreme Creator was almost universal among the naturalists of the early nineteenth century.[31] It led to their catholic interest in all the artifacts and phenomena of the natural world. For instance, a single scholar, clergyman by profession, considered it quite proper to work simultaneously at physics, chemistry, geology, botany, and meteorology. But this universal delight did not mean a universal science. Irreversible jumps divided the various branches of science. Animals, plants, and minerals belonged to different kingdoms, and even in the brain of one man the study of each kingdom had its separate discipline with its own rules and history. In practice the naturalist chose a few congenial and convenient fields and specialized in them. If he taught chemistry all week and liked to get out in the air of a Saturday, he would gather plants and rocks on his weekly walks, thus becoming a naturalist although his special fields of interest were less than universal. He had nothing against the insects and weather data which some of his brethren collected, but he just did not have time to get around to everything. As a body of scientific knowledge grew, he found himself able to master adequately fewer and fewer of the aspects of nature.[32] James Hadley limited himself to chemistry, mineralogy, and botany, and Gray followed in his footsteps.

"I had a passion for mineralogy in those days, as well as for chemistry," wrote Asa of his first session at Fairfield. He spent the spring and summer of 1827 in Sauquoit in the office of a Dr. Priest and in the fall returned to Fairfield. Still following the pattern of Hadley's career he allowed his thoughts to wander toward botany, although it was now winter and he was "out of reach either of a greenhouse or of a potted plant." His only recourse was to some book, and the *Edinburgh Encyclopaedia* was very nearly the fount of all knowledge and inspiration in upstate New York.[33]

The article on botany in the *Encyclopaedia* was a full and leisurely attempt at a compendious view of the whole scientific study of plants. After presenting a rather elaborate account of the history of the subject and an extensive glossary with both English and Latin definitions, the author discussed vegetable physiology and classification. Although he gave most attention to Linnaeus's artificial system of arranging plants into orders by a mechanical counting of the male and female parts of a flower, he also treated briefly a natural system of Antoine Laurent de Jussieu based on the general relationships of plants. The article, lengthy though it was, left Gray in ignorance of many things. Written in 1811, it gave little hint of the great developments brewing in plant physiology. The passage concerning the state of the science in North America which must have inspired Gray left out of account many workers who had recently entered the field.[34] Asa himself probably could not explain the spell which botany cast over him, but from this point onward the study of plants became his business, his delight, his ambition.

Since it was still the middle of winter, he bought a copy of Amos

Eaton's *Manual*,[35] "pored over its pages, and waited for spring."
This book was the only one available to him which contained a
guide to the plants he would actually encounter. Eaton, the old
schoolmaster down at Troy, was indeed a well-known figure in New
York state, and Gray no doubt heard of him through Hadley. But
the mere fact that Asa used the manual does not establish him as a
student of Eaton's, whose role in Gray's education was limited to
having produced the manual.

When the spring of 1828 finally did arrive, Asa was serving his
medical apprenticeship at Bridgewater, just nine miles south of his
home at Sauquoit, under Dr. John Foote Trowbridge. This was
the usual country practice with its continual rounds for childbirth,
tooth extractions, backache, and an occasional cut or broken leg.
Dr. Trowbridge met the ills of the populace with plasters and emet-
ics, paregoric and unidentified pills. Whether the rarity of bleeding
in his lists of treatments was the result of extraordinary enlighten-
ment can only be surmised. He was indeed a man of some education, being a graduate of the College of Physicians and Surgeons in
New York. Not only were his fees modest—twenty-five cents for a
visit and four dollars for an accouchement—but his pay often came
in the form of small pigs and shrunken wheat.[36] Since the practice
covered a considerable area around the headwaters of the Unadilla
and over into Gray's own Paris township, the apprentice was often
out of doors when spring came to the hills about Bridgewater. "I
sallied forth one April day into the bare woods, found an early
specimen of a plant in flower, peeping through dead leaves, brought
it home, and with Eaton's Manual without much difficulty I ran it
down to its name, *Claytonia Virginica*. (It was really *C. Carolini-
ana*, but the two were not distinguished in that book.)" Soon he began a herbarium "of shockingly bad specimens."

Collecting plants was Gray's first sustained effort in science. Since
he had open to him no formal course in botany, this was a good way
to begin. By gathering and naming the plants around him he could
gain not only a rough knowledge of local flora but also some sense
of which plants were common and which were either undescribed
or imperfectly understood—"interesting" the botanists loved to call
such oddities. Also, the duplicates of local plants could be used to

good advantage in trades with other workers, serving as the currency which bought wider horizons in the form of books and specimens from distant places. Plants pressed between blotters until dry and mounted in some convenient way form a permanent record and are thus an essential part of the apparatus of botany. Each worker prided himself on his herbarium, as the collections are called, and attempted to add as many plants as possible. Such specimens were even in 1830 comparatively easy to send long distances wrapped in small parcels or even folded in newspapers.

Gray hardly missed formal classes in botany, for he had the help and encouragement of Dr. Hadley from the beginning. But there was a limit to the direct instruction that Hadley with his few months' training in New Haven could give. He performed a far greater service to Gray by putting him in touch with the more active workers. "At Professor Hadley's suggestion I opened a correspondence with Dr. Lewis C. Beck of Albany, the leading botanist of the region."

Dr. Beck, who sometimes gave a course of summer lectures in botany at Fairfield, was one of a number of men interested in science in the neighborhood of Albany. He had at one time taught with Amos Eaton at Troy and was in 1830 teaching at the Albany Academy.[37] Gray probably began sending him plants in 1829 and received in return both specimens and the names of plants about which the inexperienced collector had doubts. In May 1830, Dr. Beck wrote to Gray at Bridgewater, "Your plants have interested me very much & I should think your locality a fine one. I wish you would take up the mosses of your region." Mosses were not flashy enough for a very young man, but Beck furnished some food for thought on other unsolved problems, one of which stayed with Gray for the rest of his life. "Solidagos & Asters vary so exceedingly that I hardly dare pronounce on many of them. They do not appear to have been well studied by any of our botanists. . . ." Thus Gray had found the great family of the *Compositae* and began to gather the experience with its unusual complexities which ultimately made him an authority on it.[38]

Since he spent most of the time he could spare from medicine on botany, Gray did not take long to catch up with Dr. Beck in output if not in experience. The naturalist, amid his galaxy of separate sci-

16

ences, was breaking down under sheer weight of work. Beck with the best of intentions nevertheless had to stall in furnishing aid. "I hope you extend your charity to me for seeming neglect, when I state that . . . I have been incessantly occupied in lecturing & in superintending the publication of a Manual of Chemistry which is just completed." [39] Gray was on the lookout for new friends and new opportunities.

In the summer of 1830, Dr. Trowbridge needed medical books and in sending his apprentice on the errand he gave Asa his first glimpse of New York City. He drove in a wagon, "with my own horse, ninety miles to Albany, thence by steamer to New York over night; one night there, and back next day by boat to Albany, and so driving back to Bridgewater. . . ." Stopping at the Albany Academy he saw Dr. Beck and also "a grave-looking man who I was told was Professor Henry, who had just been making a wonderful electro-magnet." Both Joseph Henry and the magnet would make a mark. In New York, fortified with a letter of introduction from Dr. Hadley, Asa called to see one of the foremost American botanists, Dr. John Torrey. But it was a false dawn, for the good doctor was away from the city, and Gray could only leave his letter and a parcel of plants to be named.

When John Torrey returned home in the fall he saw in the quality of the specimens left by Gray the work of a collector able enough to be an ally. To encompass the flora of North America presupposed a network of field men sending in plants from every locality, and Torrey, much to his distress, had not even been able to cover such a settled and accessible region as upstate New York. With the parcel of plants left by the medical student Torrey's hopes rekindled. "I thank you for this gentleman's correspondence," he wrote to Dr. Hadley, "for I hope he will materially assist me in my endeavours to elucidate our northern vegetation." [40] Gray had evidently prepared his specimens well, for Torrey invited further exchange. Gray had reached a man who could bring him into close touch with the scientific world.

When in the fall of 1830 Gray came to Fairfield for a fifth session of medical lectures, no one thought to ask him if he had reached his twenty-first birthday. Before the end of December 1830 he had passed his examinations and returned to Bridgewater ready to start practice. His thesis on "gastritis" probably diverted him from his botanical interests only a little. In January 1831 the College of Physicians and Surgeons of the Western District of the State of New York conferred on him the degree of doctor of medicine, one of a class of forty-four.[41]

With graduation from Fairfield Asa Gray completed his formal education. Although he lacked a bachelor's degree and a gentleman's mastery of the classics, he had at least a nodding acquaintance with *Arma virumque cano*. He had some knowledge of chemistry, mineralogy, and especially botany, and at Fairfield he had found friends with whom he could discuss these sciences. In Hadley he had the inspiring teacher and unselfish adviser found near the beginning of most great scientific careers. He had the honorable title of Doctor and a profession by which he supposedly could earn a living. These were solid accomplishments for a young man of twenty.

Whatever Gray's personal preference, the next step in his career could only be the practice of medicine. The society in which he lived knew not the calling of botanist, and even if a few far-sighted friends like Hadley had ambitions for Gray as a naturalist in a broad sense, they did not dream of his making a living at it. He could pursue the sciences alongside his proper business as a doctor, and perhaps later he could teach. For the present he went back to Bridgewater.

∽ II ∽

FROM MEDICINE
TO SCIENCE

ALTHOUGH the village of Bridgewater was a modest one, Dr.
Asa Gray found it congenial. The young physician measured his prosperity by the ills of the populace. "It is somewhat
sickly & I had some good buisness of late." In his cures he showed
a certain experimental tendency, as in the treatment he discussed
with one of his Fairfield classmates, N. Wright Folwell, who lived
near the Finger Lakes.

I have tried your Scotch snuff plaster in a number of cases of croup &
Bronchitis of children—sometimes with fine success. (it makes a devil of a
sore occasionally). In a few cases it produced little or no effect, & I was
obliged to resort to my old prescription—viz ground Mustard & black pepper,
mixed up with vinegar—which is a glorious thing by the way. I suppose the
difference in its effect arises from the snuff being of different degrees of
strength. You must take it from the old womens boxes just as it comes.—On
the whole I am pleased with it.

Such a remedy, traditional art rather than science, is not a complete measure of Gray's medical horizon. Dr. Trowbridge, the medical preceptor, used the coming of his protégé as an excuse for a
vacation, and when he returned he brought with him a choice collection of books, which were at Gray's disposal. "Abercrombie on
Brain, Williams on the Lungs, Bichat, Gen. Anatomy. Colles, Surg.
anatomy, Beclard, General Anatomy. Velpeaux, Topographical
Anatomy, 2 very large volumes with splendid plates, (a present
from Dr. Rhinelander of N.Y.) Travers on Consti[tutio]n[al] Irritation. Martinet Therapeutics . . . &c. &c. I mention only the
best." [1]

Gray really gave these works serious attention. He thought Abercrombie "very valuable" and considered that Williams "gives the most rational view of the principles on which the use of the stethoscope is founded I have seen." But he was not impressed with writers who pressed their ideas "to a devil of a length. . . . [W]e must learn [the] substantial and matter-of-fact part of every work and not be carried away by doctrines and dogmas." The novice was thus a part of medicine's struggles to become a science. But the book which made the deepest imprint on his mind was Sir William Lawrence's *Lectures on Physiology, Zoology, and the Natural History of Man, Delivered at the Royal College of Surgeons.*[2] "That Lawrence is a grand fellow,—a strong and aggreable writer. I wish you to read whenever you can obtain it. He is a materialist—after my own fashion precisely—Don't attempt to form an opinion on such matters until you read it." [3]

Lawrence indeed posed some very leading questions, such as, "[t]ake away from the mind of man, or from that of any other animal, the operations of the five external senses, and the functions of the brain, and what will be left behind?" To theologians in Great Britain, who were attacking him with the protection of the courts, he replied with great gusto that "the odium theologicum is the most concentrated essence of animosity and rancour. Let us not open the fair garden of Science to this ugly fiend; let not her sweet cup be tainted by the most distant approach of his venomous breath." Having ruled theology out of science, and the soul out of physiology, he asserted a sweeping credo of the freedom of inquiry. "The assent of mind to any proposition cannot be forced;—it must depend on the weight of evidence and argument." He included academic rights. "Without this freedom of inquiry and speech, the duties of your professors would be irksome and humiliating; they would be dishonored in their own eyes and in the estimation of the public." Since one of the criticisms against him was his reliance on the great French scientists such as Cuvier, he held up as an ideal international cooperation. "Science, the partisan of no country, but the beneficent patroness of all, has liberally opened a temple where all may meet." [4] From this rather disputatious source Gray became familiar with some of the highest ideals of eighteenth-century rationalism.

Knowing the impression which Lawrence's book made on Gray allows the identification of at least one source of three basic positions which at this impressionable age became a part of Gray's permanent equipment. The first concept was the materialist and empirical tenor of the whole work. The second concept was the assumption that man was a part of nature as a whole, amenable to the same physical laws which governed the functioning of other organisms. The third concept was Sir William Lawrence's strong assertion of the unity of the human species. He was one of the early advocates of the point of view that all the human races belong to one species and hence are genetically connected with one another. Gray's own explicit and contemporary confession of the impact of this book is not the only evidence that eighteenth-century rationalism as worked out in these three concepts entered Gray's mind. They all had a future in his later thought.

Another set of ideas, scattered through the book which young Gray so much admired, was the stuff of which Charles Darwin a few years later would construct a biological revolution. Lawrence pointed to geographical isolation as a mechanism leading to new varieties. He saw the great differences which men could introduce in domestic animals by selection. He applied this concept of selection to the human species. "A superior breed of human beings could only be produced by selections and exclusions similar to those so successfully employed in rearing our more valuable animals." He recognized at least dimly the analogy between the breeder's selection and selection in a state of nature.[5] Gray no more than Lawrence himself saw these ideas in the same pattern which Darwin was to use. No one can even say that Gray agreed with them or remembered them. Later, however, when arguments concerning artificial selection, natural selection, and their application to man became supremely important, Gray was dealing with concepts he had seen before in a book he had admired tremendously.

Materialist ideas did not arise in a vacuum, for Bridgewater had its small circle of *philosophes,* the leader of whom was

Dr. Trowbridge. Gray fitted in well, and over port and a game of whist he could discuss the peril threatening the community from the plots of the orthodox, who "have the impudence to talk about the finger of the *Almighty* being in the business. While any rational man can perceive nothing but the *Paws of the Priesthood*—and grasping paws they have." He could flaunt his knowledge of literature. "In this town it is managed by a few of the 'unco good' (as Bobby Burns so appropriately terms them)—who have much more zeal than wisdom, and . . . seem to think that the better part of valour is *impertinence* not as Sir John Falstaff would say—discretion." How clever must his fellows have thought the young doctor's answer to a delegation of the "unco-pious" who solicited a subscription "to pull down an old meeting house . . . and build a new one." He told them he had "scruples of conscience about aiding and assisting in building meeting houses, but would willingly give a small sum toward pulling the old one down." [6]

Before he had been many months in the pleasant and worldly atmosphere of Bridgewater, Gray's ambitions wandered from medicine back to his love of botany. "It is a very healthy time with us. I have only a small business in the medical line for which I am very thankful as I want all the time I can get. Dr. Tro will be at home in a week or two when I shall be even more at leisure." Meanwhile his correspondence with Dr. Torrey flourished. "He promises to send me a first rate microscope &c—." Nor had Dr. James Hadley forgotten his prize student. For some years Hadley and Dr. Lewis Beck had given a summer course at Fairfield, charging six dollars per pupil for a series of chemistry lectures and four dollars for similar instruction in botany. In the summer of 1831 Beck could not be there and Gray received his place through the influence of Hadley, a young doctor named William Mather taking the chemistry. Gray occupied himself the whole spring in blocking out the thirty lectures and "preparing plates, etc." He also industriously lined up some among his Fairfield classmates as students. He wrote to Folwell, "you must collect plants like the Devil and all—. I expect you to bring 150 species at least. . . . Montgomery, Willoughby, Field, Miller, & *last but not least* N. W. F. would make a fine body guard for me. They would truly be *l'esprit du corps*." Here at the very beginning of his career Gray thought of scientific work not as an isolated individual enterprise but as a cooperative undertaking, and even now he unconsciously assumed that he himself was a leader, taking both honor and responsibility.[7]

Going up to Fairfield in the latter part of May, Gray gave his series of lectures at the usual price. Whomever he finally rounded up as students, he at least cleared forty dollars. The course, no doubt beneficial as a first start in teaching, could hardly serve as an opening to a career, for the medical school's days were numbered. Within a decade James Hadley would with heavy heart give up "the attachments formed by a residence of many years" and go elsewhere because there was no hope of continuing the College of Physicians and Surgeons of the Western District. Dr. William Mather, who shared the summer school with Gray, chose to cast his lot with Fairfield and spent the rest of a long life faithfully teaching in the academy and giving itinerant lectures on electromagnetism.[8] Asa Gray's summer course was his last formal connection with Fairfield, and although it remained the center of many of his friendships he avoided being entombed in its fall.

With forty dollars and some hospitality along the way he managed a collecting trip to western New York. "Halcyon days," he later described these, "when I have little to do and plenty of time to do it in." [9] From Niagara Falls and Buffalo he turned back to visit his mother's brother, a "well-to-do country merchant." He then spent a week or two collecting with "my chum, Dr. Folwell" at Lodi, Seneca County, which lies between Seneca and Cayuga Lakes. From Ithaca a stagecoach brought him back to Bridgewater. It was a modest journey when compared to his plans to visit Ohio and Michigan, but he had made a short start at the wandering which is an essential part of a naturalist's business, and he had enjoyed a pleasant time besides.

The fall of 1831 was neither prosperous nor happy for Asa Gray. Thanks to the euphemism of memory he claimed in later years that "I hardly know what I did [that] autumn and winter. . . ." But at the time he was not so casual. Medicine, never more than a means of livelihood, had lost even that attraction. "Notwithstanding colds, &c.," he wrote to Folwell, "it is very healthy and Doctors have fair prospects of starvation. There is not at present $\frac{1}{2}$ as much business as one man ought to do in this place." This was part of a general complaint of the times that medicine was overcrowded, and for Gray it required drastic action. "I shall leave Bridgewater next summer, *for good,* as the saying is. What I shall do and where I shall take up my abode—the D——l only knows." He asked Folwell to "cogitate a little upon these affairs & try your skill at scheming for me." [10] All his interests pointed to science, and while he assumed he should become a well-rounded naturalist, botany alone really caught his imagination.

His chances of becoming a botanist, or even a naturalist, with superficial claims to several branches of knowledge, depended not only on his own desires but on the state of the scientific institutions in the United States. With his bare hands he could do little in science. For example, to classify a single new species of plant was a complex operation which required many aids. In the first place, the classifier had to have the leisure and the means of going out in the field at just the proper season, or he must hire someone to do it for him. Either alternative implied that society must yield him considerable sums above mere subsistence. In the second place, after he had examined the plant under a microscope not easy to come by, he had to check a large number of books to see if someone else had described the plant before him. To be absolutely sure required not merely standard works but also the latest periodicals from both Europe and the United States. Sometimes he could not be certain just what his predecessors, fallible humans all, had been talking about, so he had to consult the original dried specimen from which the old master, say Michaux, had described some closely similar plant. This required not only large herbaria but also the very same collections that had been used in the previous classification.

Having satisfied himself that he had a new species, the botanist had still accomplished nothing unless he could inform other workers. He had to describe it and give it a name and, if possible, make an illustration by which it could be recognized. Not only was publication a necessity, but the paper had also to reach the people competent to judge and use it. Asa Gray, whose activities were still limited to the collecting phase, was fortunate in being neither the founder nor the father of American botany. The United States had already provided many facilities for the scientist.

The characteristic research institution of the early Republic was the learned society. The American Philosophical Society and the Academy of Natural Sciences perpetuated Philadelphia's preeminence in colonial culture, which had in the eighteenth century been represented in botany by the careers of John and William Bartram. Boston also paid allegiance to science by founding the American Academy of Arts and Sciences. New York, slower to organize, had formed her societies under the aegis of Dr. Samuel Latham Mitchill. He stressed the uses of science and succeeded in making science fashionable in a practical and intellectually unfavorable environment. The New York Lyceum of Natural History, which grew from his influence, served as a focal point for men whose tastes ran to science. The movement penetrated even into Gray's own county, for the Utica Lyceum of Natural History, founded in 1823, lasted into the 1830's.

Each of these societies in varying extent furthered science by providing a place to pool information, books, and collections. They often afforded a means of publishing papers, and they helped to organize a qualified scientific reading public. But all the societies were in fact, if not in name, local clubs of amateurs. Since they drew members of varied scientific interest, mostly doctors, lawyers, clergymen, and teachers, they were severely limited in the projects they could undertake. Their efforts remained diffuse because of the many different fields of science cultivated. Since all the members made their living in some outside profession, young men without means had almost no opportunity to seek a career under a society's auspices. Further, their collections, the main tools of research, remained largely in the private hoards of the members. The preserving of dried plant specimens for future reference was left to the discretion, and often the whims, of individual collectors. The societies, which had kept science alive during the early Republic, had resources too weak and sporadic both financially and scientifically to meet rapidly changing situations.

Educational institutions bore a share of the support of research. Harvard by the 1830's had a wide variety of equipment, even a botanic garden, and several faculty members spent most of their time teaching some science if not conducting much original research. Silliman at Yale, active in both instruction and research, had in the *American Journal of Science* the sole organ with both a nationwide circulation and an audience in Europe.[11] In New York and Philadelphia medical schools served as centers of scientific instruction. Men like Hadley and Amos Eaton provided a stimulus in the rural districts.

But the appointments which would allow both teaching and research were few. Even those which paid enough and left sufficient leisure made no provision for a man to coordinate his classroom work with his special studies. John Torrey and Chester Dewey, although they taught sciences, were quite as nonprofessional in their botanical studies as they would have been preaching, practicing medicine, or engaging in trade. Torrey wrote that "I must attend to Chemistry, because I get my bread by it, and I love it very, *very* much. Yet I love Botany more if I may judge by the comparative zest with which I pursue the two studies. Perhaps, however, if Botany were my task, and Chemistry were my *play,* matters would be reversed." [12]

If the societies and colleges had maintained a static monopoly of science, Asa Gray, without means of his own, could hardly have hoped to become a professional naturalist, much less botanist. But the many changes of the 1830's exerted pressures on the scientific institutions as on political and social institutions. For one thing, the country's increasing wealth and prosperity yielded added support to science through the existing channels. Also, the reform movements of the Jacksonian period in demanding education for all helped to open new ways for science to reach more people. Since the belief was widespread that science was a boon to the common man, legislatures, elected now by manhood suffrage, showed an increased interest in using this new tool in the service of their constituents. States began to authorize surveys of natural resources, with a staff of experts, each responsible for a separate science. Here was opportunity with pay for many specialists.

Inside botany, forces were also working for change. Not only were the separate sciences breaking away from one another, but within them subdivisions were developing. Linnaeus in the eighteenth century had erected the necessary framework of rules for great advances in taxonomy—the science of classification. During the first half of the nineteenth century it was enjoying a great boom, and most European botanists were, above all else, classifiers.[13] Thanks to the spread of Europeans over the world, they were studying in a comprehensive way the plants of the whole earth. Americans, who lived near great unexplored areas, had more classifying at hand than they could attend to, and the European scientists, far from being jealous or contemptuous, urged that local men work out their own flora to a much greater extent than they had.[14]

Other lines of investigation were also opening up. New systems of classification required botanists to look more closely at the form and structure of plants—morphology was thus separating itself from taxonomy. The great advances in chemistry led similarly to fresh insights into the functions of plant organs—physiology was coming of age. After 1825, when the new achromatic microscopes made possible the observation of plants on a new scale, investigators wasted no time in following a path that would soon lead to the cell theory. Americans, limited as they were in equipment and already overburdened with taxonomic problems, could not at once join in the new and exciting pursuits. But if they wished even to be classifiers they had to find out about the new discoveries and apply them in their own work. The branches of botany, while they had become separate, were still interdependent. One great theorist of the day wrote that "nothing is so contrary to progress of any one of the branches of botany, as to isolate it from all the others. . . ." [15] Americans did not degrade themselves when they chose taxonomic problems for research. The epithet "mere classifier" was wide of the mark, since taxonomy was beginning to take all the plant sciences into consideration. Provincials were rather to be judged on how well they applied all the new resources to the investigations they did take up.

In 1830 equality with Europe in botany—the ability to cooperate fully—was far from a reality. On a technical level, the backwardness stemmed from American botanists' long lag in adopting a new method of classification which Europeans had used for some time.

In the eighteenth century Linnaeus's artificial system of classification, based on the rather simple procedure of counting the male and female parts of a flower, had done essential service to botany by making possible the organization of an immense number of plants into a coherent body of knowledge. But it soon degenerated into the kind of fascinating game now indulged in by stamp collectors, and the enthusiasts tended to lose sight of the plants themselves.

Through the work of Antoine Laurent de Jussieu and Augustin-Pyramus De Candolle the French escaped this particular dead end and developed on an alternate tradition from Linnaeus what they fondly called the natural system, which aimed at classification on the basis of general similarities. A rough analogy may illustrate the difference. The Linnaean system would classify furniture by placing all four-legged pieces in one group. The natural system would consider the legs as only one of many characteristics and by weighing several factors place all individuals of a kind, say tables or chairs, into one group. The new scheme, although it did not question the constancy of species and was not "natural" in the sense of establishing kinship between different groups, nevertheless opened new avenues of morphology as the whole plant became the object of study instead of arbitrarily selected flower parts. The systematists who developed the natural method managed to convey, at least to an outsider, a sense of the unity and interrelatedness of the whole plant kingdom. Ralph Waldo Emerson, visiting in Paris, saw in a display arranged by Jussieu one key to his all-embracing conception of nature.[16] But American botanists, left far behind, clung to the artificial system even after Great Britain, herself a laggard, had abandoned it.

Two men who had already come within the knowledge of young Asa Gray epitomized the stresses that were changing American botany and its institutions. John Torrey was trying to catch up to Europe while Amos Eaton clung to the older way. The school-teacher of Troy above all wanted to reach the masses of Jacksonian America. "I have had more than two thousand students in botany—among them some are very correct; all have considerable taste for books of Natural History. More than 2500 of my own books on botany . . . are now in the hands of as many persons." [17] To disseminate his science so widely he had to reduce it to the simplest terms, and any great change which caused complications filled him with consternation. The artificial system was a keystone in his instruction, and he built up a case for it as the proper elementary exercise in botany even though advanced students might shift to a natural system. "[N]one but adepts in Botany can dispense with the Linnean Artificial system." [18]

On the other hand John Torrey had published in 1824 a *Flora* [19] covering the United States north of Virginia on the Linnaean system. As one in touch with the currents of world botany, he came under increasing pressure to change to the natural method. In his descriptions compiled of the plants of the Long expedition in 1826, he switched to the new way. Once he had made the change, Torrey faced a complete rearrangement even of the material he had already published, a formidable task of several years at the least. Since he depended on others for collections and aid in special groups, he had to carry the whole of American botany with him to the new way. To further this he edited John Lindley's new *Introduction to the Natural System of Botany.*[20] The very fact that this work appeared in America within a year of its London publication indicates a shortening time lag in the Atlantic crossing.

With his practice dying away in the winter of 1831–32, Gray kept up his spirits by scientific activity. He struck up a correspondence with Chester Dewey, clergyman and scientist of many interests then living in Pittsfield, Massachusetts, where he taught a high school for boys. In botany Dewey wisely confined his efforts to one genus of plants—*Carex,* or the sedges—which is quite extensive and complicated enough to keep a botanist busy.[21] Torrey also kept up his interest and began to give Gray advice. He sent a microscope, no doubt a simple one, saying that little "can be done in philosophical botany without such an instrument, for the knowledge that is acquired by mere superficial examination is scarcely worth possessing. . . ." Torrey took his role as correspondence teacher seriously enough to point out shortcomings. "I regret that you closed your botanical labours for the season before collecting the Asters and Solidagos."

For all his botanizing Gray was trying also to be a naturalist. He

wrote Torrey asking about books on entomology.[22] Fossil animals—
"trilobites . . . a variety of bivalve and a few univalve shells, etc.,
both in lime rock and greywacke"—attracted his attention in the
surrounding countryside, and he offered a set to Torrey or the Lyceum of Natural History. Professor Hadley, ever his friend, sent him
minerals. In some way he had added French to his linguistic attainments and was embarking on Spanish.[23]

Short, slight of build, quick in his actions, Gray was extremely
sure of himself and impatient with slowness in others. When one of
his Fairfield buddies indicated he might come for a visit at Bridgewater, Gray wrote that ". . . (*entre nous*) I do not wish to see him.
He probably means to ransack my herbarium, but I have already
confered [*sic*] more favours of that kind than he will ever be able
to repay. . . . It is like *casting pearls before the swine*." [24] Yet no
evidence exists that the young Asa Gray exhibited undue malice in
his dealings with his fellows. On the contrary his assurance came
from an attractive countenance, an abundance of physical energy,
and a mental alertness which made his horizons much broader than
the hills surrounding Bridgewater. That he should settle down and
become a country doctor is hard to imagine.

As the collecting season of 1832 approached, he began making plans desperately, the more spectacular the better. "I am
young, . . ." he wrote to Torrey, "without any engagements to
confine me to this section of the country, and prefer the study of
botany to anything else." Possibly thinking of his namesake Asa
Gray and urged by his friends "to spend a few years in a milder climate, our family being predisposed to phthisis" he looked for some
warm winters. "I have thought of the Southern States, but I have
for some time been inclined to prefer Mexico, both on account of
the salubrity of its climate and of its botanical and mineralogical
riches, which so far as I know have never been very thoroughly explored." Having no illusions that repayment would come in money,
he planned to "combine the study of natural history with the professional business which will be necessary for my support." He
would collect in New York state during the summer and head for
Mexico about September. It is worth noting that in 1832 the present
southwestern United States belonged to Mexico, and Gray may pos-

sibly have had a slight case of Texas fever. Had his plans come to fruit he might have anticipated by fifteen years many of the discoveries his own collectors later made, or he might have broken himself against the hard life of scientist in Mexico as a young Swiss named Louis Berlandier had just done.

Society had a way of laying some claim on Gray whenever he started to leave it for the wilderness. Hardly had he formed his plan to explore Mexico when a place for a naturalist opened in Utica, New York. Dr. Fay Edgerton, famed teacher of science and a disciple of Eaton, died, leaving Dr. Charles Bartlett's Utica Gymnasium without an instructor in the middle of a term. Gray, being recommended, "made an arrangement for one year; took charge of a class in botany and mineralogy on 20th May. . . ." [25]

The Utica Gymnasium, formerly called the High School for Boys, was just then enjoying a period of prosperity. Dr. Bartlett's aims, modeled on George Bancroft's Round Hill School and Eaton's Rensselaer institute, were progressive.[26] Because he was assigned to teach chemistry, botany, mineralogy, zoology, and geology, Gray needed all his attainments in several sciences.[27] His salary was three hundred dollars a year in addition to "room, board, washing, fuel, and all other expenses of the kind, for the whole year, or as much of the year as I choose to remain here." The choice was a rather free one, since he taught only until July 1832, and then had off until January 1833. Dr. Bartlett evidently provided too rich a fare for his young paragons to partake continuously. To Gray the attractions of the place were "leisure and the means of a comfortable income. . . . I am now advantageously situated for the collection of plants, etc., as, if I choose, I can travel every year with a class who will defray my expenses." [28] He also made an acquaintance who would serve him well in later years. S. Wells Williams, son of the Utica publisher of the *Edinburgh Encyclopaedia,* had just finished his studies with Dr. Bartlett and instead of going to college was preparing to leave for China as a printer for missionaries in Canton. Among his promises was one to collect plants for his friend Gray. The young teacher also knew by reputation a recent graduate named James Dwight Dana, who had gone on to Yale.[29]

With his class as helpers Gray set out to make a definitive collection of the plants about him in the vicinity of Utica. One of his students long afterward could remember the teacher, "his flashing eye and his cry of exultation as he bounded forward to seize a new plant which he spied at a distance, while botanizing with his class in the Oriskany swamp." [30] A local *Flora,* one of the basic building materials for any great regional study, was his projected contribution to science. Although the work was wholly collecting and identifying, merely the first step in complete classification, it was a necessary beginning. Gray encouraged his students to form herbaria and rapidly built up his own collection.[31] The large number of grasses and sedges he gathered in this period show his first special interest in a particular group of plants. They offered special challenges in that the large number of species tended to shade off into varieties among which the differences were inconstant and barely perceptible.

As the term at Utica Gymnasium closed in July 1832, cholera struck viciously in upstate New York. Brought first to Canada, it spread with the transportation routes westward, along the Erie Canal and the Ohio River. Doctors, completely unprepared, had each to struggle with it as best he could. Conscientious young Fairfield graduates like Marcus Whitman found it a time of tribulation. Asa Gray years later remembered that the disease was "very fatal in Utica," but he saw nothing odd in saying that "about the time [the cholera] made its appearance in New York I started off from Bridgewater, taking a little country stage-coach down the Unadilla to Pennsylvania. . . ." He would no doubt have been amazed had anyone suggested that he had a duty as a physician, for unconsciously or not he had completely turned his back on the profession. He was now a naturalist, and his proper business was to collect plants, not to struggle with diseases he did not understand.

Down the Unadilla lay new wonders of nature. At Carbondale Gray collected calamites (a genus of fossil plants) and fossil ferns. He continued to "Sussex County, N.Y., collecting minerals; thence to . . . Orange County, N.Y., collecting spinelles, etc., as well as botanizing." But his most fruitful findings were men. Detouring to Bethlehem, Pennsylvania, he paid his respects to Lewis David von Schweinitz, an administrator of the Moravian Church as well as one of the few American botanists with a broad grasp of both European and American plants.[32] Although only fifty-two, he was ill now and seemed "old Bishop Schweinitz" to his young visitor. Gray's Yankee world contained no one to match him. Although the young visitor remembered that "I . . . gave him a Carex which he said was new, but I told him it was a Carex livida, Wahl. (and I was right)," he was actually much more respectful. At the time he admitted that he had "never seen a description of C. livida" and wanted Schweinitz to "favour me with your opinion of [the specimen]." [33] Gray could hardly have failed to see science in a slightly broader dimension through Schweinitz.

In New York early in September Gray for the first time met Dr. Torrey. As a tryout for each other they went on a "little expedition together down to Tom's River [New Jersey] in the pine barrens, and back to New York in a wood-sloop." The choice of the area was significant, for as a plant region it formed "a long wedge of the Carolina coast . . . thrust up northward quite to New York harbor, bringing into a comparatively cool climate many of the interesting low country plants of the south. . . ." [34] Not only did Gray see plants growing here which were new to him, but he also had his first experience with a region that had already been extensively studied. The pine barrens were becoming "classic ground." Gray as a collector evidently measured up well, for Torrey soon proposed to hire him for the next summer to collect extensively in New Jersey.

Gray returned to central New York, and, although he did not teach during the fall, he spent most of his time in Utica. The busy summer, his first as a real naturalist, gave him much to work on, and he was not long in producing his first publication, "A Catalogue of the Indigenous Flowering and Filicoid Plants Growing within Twenty Miles of Bridgewater (Oneida County), New York." [35] It was a modest work, a simple list of species without description, locality, or comment, undoubtedly based in large part on his collections of the Utica Gymnasium period from May to June of 1832. Not having perfected the classifying operation, he listed a few plants simply by the generic name, for example, "Ophioglossum, N. sp.," or with question marks, as "Erysimum officinale, n. sp.?" Inability to consult the literature and good herbaria prevented him from reaching the authoritative decision necessary to publish a new species. But he had no great love for his position as a "mere" collector who had to depend on others whenever any real problem arose. "I am confident my leisure time would be employed to greater advantage if I was situated so as to have access to good libraries and extensive collections." [36]

This first publication was arranged into larger groups according to Lindley's *Introduction to the Natural System of Botany*. Before Torrey's edition of 1831 the natural system would have been out of Gray's reach. The natural system was trickling down from the "favored few" who could afford and understand the works of Jussieu, Robert Brown, and De Candolle to an ordinary botanist. A question which might well arise in Andrew Jackson's United States was which one of these methods would be most widely applicable to the education of the great masses of the people. Amos Eaton, while admitting in his *Manual* that the "Natural Method *is the grand climacteric in Botanical science,*" insisted that "the Artificial System is the *brightest epoch of its youthful pilgrimage.*" He thought the Linnaean method necessary to give a "taste for natural history" to the masses.

On the other hand Asa Gray showed clearly that in the winter of 1832 he understood the problem and had made his choice. Writing to Torrey of the Utica Gymnasium, he complained that "the principal wishes to retain too much of the Eatonian plan to suit me." Whether or not the artificial system was the whole of the "Eatonian plan" which Dr. Bartlett favored, it certainly played its part. Gray willingly credited Torrey with the idea that the "natural system was not much longer to remain, here and in England, an esoteric doctrine, confined to profound botanists, but was destined to come into general use and change the character of botanical instruction." [37] But Torrey, a busy man who always had more fires going than he could tend, left the execution of this educational reform to Gray.

Except for a spring vacation Gray put his students through their paces from January to July of 1833. For the first time in his life he taught chemistry. Finding that chlorochromic acid of his preparation set "alcohol, ether, spirits of turpentine, etc., on fire," he promised he would "prepare it again in a few weeks for class experiments." [38] It is doubtful if he realized that this kind of demonstration, so ununsual at that time in a secondary school, was a part of the Eatonian method bequeathed to him by his predecessor.

By this time Gray had hit upon another means of increasing his scientific capital. He found that it was no great trick to bundle up some dried plants and send them to European savants. "Botanical presents are like gifts among the Indians. They always presuppose a return. . . ." [39] His first essay was with a French army officer and naturalist named J. F. Solierol, who, although stationed in Metz, had collected in Corsica. The results were most gratifying, for Solierol sent a parcel to Gray that "contained 650 species of which 585 were new to me, bringing collection up to 2562." [40] This enormous 25 per cent increase in the number of different plants in his herbarium definitely demonstrated that trading was more profitable than depending wholly on personal collecting.

He also wrote to Professor J. G. C. Lehmann at the botanic garden at Hamburg. Although a year elapsed between Gray's original letter and Lehmann's answer, the parcel of New York plants pleased the German professor, who sent in return "about 500 species of dried plants." Lehmann was quite as interested in hearing from America as Gray from Europe.[41] The young American, reveling in the newest books of German origin, thoroughly understood the reciprocal advantages and responsibilities of these exchanges. "I shall continue my correspondence with Lehmann and shall take great pains to send him books, plants, etc. hoping to receive 7 fold in return." [42]

During the spring recess Gray visited a doctor friend in Watertown, New York, named J. B. Crawe. Together they rambled through Jefferson County and into St. Lawrence County in the very north of the state. Crawe's great interest was minerals, and the pair collected industriously, identifying all the rocks they could find. Their efforts were modest, but with a sure sense that work in science, as elsewhere, must be known if it is to be effective, they managed to insert into the *American Journal of Science and Arts* a five-page account of their explorations.[43] Some of their information came from the proprietors of iron forges, whose shop talk Gray no doubt knew from boyhood.

When the Utica Gymnasium closed its term on the first day of

August 1833, Gray lost no time in taking a packet on the canal for Albany, where he tarried a few hours before going on to New York and New Jersey. Torrey had arranged to pay Gray's field expenses in exchange for a half share of the collections. Although he was still merely a "weed-puller" his station was a bit higher than it had been when he was the authority on the plants of Bridgewater, for now his work fitted into a larger scientific enterprise. Torrey had in February gone to Europe, ostensibly to buy scientific apparatus for New York City University but mainly to consult the European herbaria which contained the original collections of North American plants. Five weeks of his visit he spent in Glasgow with William Jackson Hooker, the Regius Professor of Botany at the University.[44] Not only as one of the able scientists and botanical teachers of Great Britain but as the organizer of a major project in North American exploration, Hooker was the connecting link between the best of Old World science and the brightest of New World hopes. His collectors had ranged to the farthest outposts of the Hudson's Bay Company, bringing back plants for a *Flora Boreali-Americana,* of which the first part was nearly through the press in 1833.

The specimens which Gray delivered to his employer found their way into the stream of scientific exchange. These plants "went to B. D. Greene and his brother Copley." These New Jersey plants were thus the first indication to anyone in Boston, Massachusetts, that Asa Gray existed. Benjamin D. Greene, Harvard class of 1812 and a son-in-law of Josiah Quincy, was a perfect example of the gentleman amateur. The essential contribution of men such as he was to interject into the barter economy which characterized botanical exchange a trickle of hard money.[45]

John Torrey's large plans for North American botany were continuously threatened by his heavy engagements as a chemistry teacher. He needed intelligent help so badly that he was willing to pay his young collector a small salary to extend activities from the field to the herbarium. On November 2, 1833, Torrey wrote in his last letter to the dying Schweinitz: "Did I tell you that I had made an engagement with Dr. Gray (of Utica), to aid me in my botanical & chemical labours? He lives in my house, & is now working daily at my herbarium. My whole collection will soon be arranged according to the Natural method." Torrey probably could not afford a full-time assistant, for "Dr. G. will devote part of his time to his own concerns. . . ." [46] The plans for this spare time throughout the fall show two very important advances over any work Gray had done before. In the first place, he now looked at each group of plants in continental rather than local terms. In the second place, he was in a position to work his own findings through the entire operation of classification and to write up the results. With Torrey's herbarium, library, and friendly counsel, Gray had all the advantages of a junior officer attached to headquarters.

The shift to New York was for Gray no less crucial personally than it was scientifically. As a doctor of medicine he was socially acceptable, and by moving in with the Torrey family he found a companionship altogether new to his experience. About fifteen years older than Gray, Dr. Torrey was thirty-seven in 1833. Besides the restless energy which drove him to transcend the limitations of a naturalist, he had many strong convictions. As a patriot he was proud of membership in the Order of the Cincinnati. The remark he once made to Gray that he would "rather have a new Yankee grass than a new palm from any of the Mexican states," [47] while not precisely accurate, indicated his attitude for the world at large. His nationalism led him to feel a deep sense of responsibility for the standards of science in the United States. "We must do all in our power to put an end to quackery in our land—& every man must feel so jealous of his own particular science as to refute all pretended discoveries." [48]

John Torrey's religion was as definite as his patriotism. He was a Presbyterian and found the New School branch of the church most congenial. [49] During the Plan of Union days, when at each new hamlet in the West such as Sauquoit the Presbyterians and Congregationalists joined in a single church, the New Englanders, themselves affected by liberal Unitarianism, had substantially softened the hard doctrines of the older Calvinism. The resulting New School theology believed in a benevolent God, and its followers had a marked tendency to participate in the burgeoning reform movements of the time. [50] Torrey took an active and solicitous interest in the religious state of his colleagues. Of Joseph Henry he once wrote, "I don't like the idea of his removing to Philadelphia, for I think the men of science there will have an unfavourable influence upon his spiritual welfare." [51]

Torrey's social position in New York was entirely acceptable. He could even expect the rich people of that very commercial city to patronize his popular lectures. His prestige was a boon to his protégé from the very beginning. Not that Gray was ever a bumpkin. With enough education to get along, he had already seen something of the Middle states. A scientist who knew the young botanist at a little later period denied that Gray showed any "awkwardness or rusticity. . . . In fact I doubt whether I had any suspicion that he was not city bred. . . ." [52]

The really overpowering impression that the Torrey family made on Gray came not so much from the doctor as from his wife. Eliza Shaw Torrey was such an extraordinary woman that her personality and intellect rose above the limitations of ill health and the ornamental position of her sex. How she appeared to Asa can be inferred from the impact she made on his younger brother George a few years later. "She has an interesting countenance & is sprightly. And she has a large heart full of kindness. She is a real lady & has from childhood been in the best society, & has visited Europe. But withal she would be nothing without her piety." Furthermore "she is a scholar, reads Latin, Greek, etc. has written sermons *that have been preached* & wrote the preface to Dr. Grant's book on the Nestorians." [53]

As Mrs. Torrey's quick sympathy attached Gray to the family, he became a beloved older brother to the three young girls. After he had left the next spring Torrey wrote him that "the children often talk about you. They say they do not have such pleasant rides on your back as they used to have." [54] Close and affectionate personal ties had been lacking in Gray's life since he left home for Fairfield eight years before, and their renewal gradually had a profound effect on his outlook.

The scientific fruit of his first season in New York was the first part of a work on grasses and sedges called *North American Gramineae and Cyperaceae*. It consisted of sets of one hundred specimens of plants from these families mounted on large folio sheets and bound into a book. Printed labels and a foreword gave the collection the appearance of a published work, and while it contained no formal descriptions several new species were included. It was dedicated to James Hadley "by his former pupil and much obliged friend." The continental aspect of the work was mainly a hope for the future, for the plants came from New York and New Jersey, and with a few exceptions were all of Gray's own collection. The five dollars for each set was important, for further parts depended on "adequate encouragement" as did a similar project on mosses, an indication that Gray had by this period given some attention to the lower plants.[55] The form of publication itself showed a dependence on wealthy amateurs with small herbaria, for in a later day with huge collections specimens bound together could not be filed in any intelligible manner.

His sojourn in the city ended early in 1834 when the young naturalist, his sophistication a bit ruffled by a drunken stagecoach driver, returned to his post at the Utica Gymnasium. While he taught chemistry, mineralogy, and geology, he laid big plans for the coming season. Major John LeConte, an insect-seeking friend of the pine barrens, was attempting to get the young botanist attached to a cavalry expedition to the West.[56] A journey to Georgia beckoned still. As usual, however, these large ideas had to give way to more pressing and remunerative duties near at hand. James Hadley, always solicitous for his prize student, had an opportunity to get him a temporary position at the newly rejuvenated Hamilton College. The Fairfield doctor had served as a part-time professor during the period of reorganization and was now on the point of resigning. Hadley hoped that if Gray taught there for the summer he would be in line for a permanent appointment.[57] At the moment two hundred dollars for the summer course looked almost providential, and a permanent professorship at eight hundred a year seemed by no means uninviting. To Torrey, Gray wrote that "the college has now one hundred students, is situated in a beautiful village nine miles from Utica, has the best college buildings of any in the State, has a good faculty, etc." [58]

Teaching at Hamilton College was mildly interesting. "I am lec-

39

turing here to a small but quite intelligent Senior class, twenty-six in number, just enough to fill three sides of a large table, and time passes very pleasantly." He felt he was gaining some good experience, especially by "lecturing in mineralogy, in which science I am becoming somewhat acute." As it was a cold, late spring, and Clinton was not a good place to botanize, there was time to turn again to the problem of elementary instruction in botany, and Gray found new cause for enthusiasm about the natural system. "I have nearly finished De Candolle's *Théorie Elementaire*.[59] I have devoured it like a novel. It ought to be translated that it may be more generally read in this country, where something of the kind is much needed." This work could give to Gray an enlarged view of the relation of taxonomy to science in general. Since it was not in itself a manual which could be used in America, Gray still sought a good text. "By the way," he continued to Torrey, "as soon as you receive Lindley's new elementary work, I hope you will set about preparing an American edition." [60] Certainly Amos Eaton satisfied Gray less than ever.

The prospects for a permanent appointment at Hamilton did not develop. Gray early found that the fund "for the support of this college will, I think be secured, but the trustees do not act in concert with the faculty, and it is rumored quarrel among themselves. . . ." [61] More important to his own future, he discovered a rival for Hadley's place already ahead of him. The erstwhile Fairfield Academy principal Charles Avery himself, an alumnus and sly as ever, had been in Clinton since early spring, and he may have helped solicit donations for the college.[62] Such claims the trustees could not deny, and Avery became the new professor of chemistry and natural philosophy. In retrospect Gray considered he had received a favor. "I wonder if I should have rusted out there if I had got the place." But at the time even a friend like Hadley did not see that temporary failure to get a good job left Gray more leisure for research than most of his naturalist contemporaries had. If he could starve through a few years he could do more work in botany than many were doing in a lifetime of evenings and holidays.

Asa Gray had ended his formal teaching career in upstate New York when he reported that "I have just finished at Hamilton Col-

40

lege a long tedious course." Continuous collecting in the late summer brought no immediate cash returns, making Gray count heavily on his assistantship for the winter. But the chronic bickering among the medical factions in New York weakened Torrey's position. Gray lamented that "the appointment of Dr. Rhinelander has raised the D——l in the N.Y. Med. college." The professors "will have to retrench as much as possible and as a consequence my little purse will suffer correspondingly." In his distress he went "out to Fairfield to see & consult Dr. H. . . . Had I anticipated all this trouble I should have obtained more work this summer. I have retrenched many expenses. But 'nil desperandum' is my motto." The uncertainty of his income made him feel that he must "work very hard this fall and winter,—much harder than ever. How I should like to have 2 or 3 weeks of absolute leisure. . . ." [63]

Once Gray reached New York, enthusiasm for botany swept away his doubts about finances. He and Dr. Torrey went off almost immediately to Philadelphia, the scientific capital of the United States. Here they could make definitive comparisons with older collections. "We spent our time mostly over Muhlenbergs Herb'm in the American Philosophical Society and Nuttalls Baldwins [64] and the late Mr. Schweinitz at the Academy of Nat Science." But plants were not the only attraction, for during the week "I made acquaintance with most of the Philadelphia naturalists and also had time to look about the city a little." The city of brotherly love was a community with a long tradition of civic enterprise and ingenuity, and at the moment it was in the storm center of Andrew Jackson's war on the bank. Gray saw much of it—"the waterworks at Fairmount on which the Philadelphians pride themselves and well they may. The Penitentiary. Girard College buildings are now going up, the U.S. Bank the Mint, etc. etc." He already had the eyes of a New Yorker. "In public buildings Phil. is far beyond N.Y. But our new Custom House will almost equal anything in Phil—, that is when it is builded [sic] for it has not rose above the surface of the ground. Our private residences . . . however taken as a whole are superior. . . ." Thus the bustling life of America which went on around him did not escape his matter-of-fact observation. But he shared few passions with it. Science to him had nothing to do with the quarrels of parties. "I have been so entirely removed from the political atmosphere that I do not know or care much about the matter." [65]

After collecting during September in New Jersey, Gray moved into his old place in Torrey's house for the winter. Meanwhile the reliable three hundred a year from the Utica Gymnasium was no longer a prospect. Gray wrote his father to "call as soon as possible at Mr. Bartlett's and get all the boxes that remain there. . . . I wish you to be sure to take them away for I learn that [he] . . . is insolvent and I do not know how long he will remain there." Moses Gray acted in the nick of time, for a fire soon finished Bartlett's hopes in Utica. Although the medical class was so "slim" that he had no salary at all, he was again Torrey's assistant with his time "divided between Chemistry and Botany, and as Chemistry must have the preference I shall get along but slowly." He had no lack of confidence. "I shall . . . be able by systematic economy to live through the Winter and trust to providence or luck as the case may be for the future." [66] His plan was simple—use the spare time which accompanied his lack of income to build up his fame. He sought his goal first by corresponding with anyone, the more eminent the better, and second by publishing. In Professor Hooker, Gray had a strategically placed ally who was willing to be an agent as well.

For a publication Gray decided on a complete treatment of a small genus of beak rushes called *Rhynchospora*. This group offered several advantages. As part of the family *Cyperaceae* it fitted in well with Gray's earlier studies. Also, the comparatively few species were found mostly in North America, and the original specimens on which earlier work had been done were, for a wonder, all available in the United States. Moreover, the group was in such a mess that the bright young man who reduced it to order could pose with some justification as a giant-killer. He also described some new plants from western New York. Gray's papers, read before the Lyceum in December 1834,[67] mark his coming of age as a botanist, for they show that he could carry through the complete operation of classifying a plant.

The papers also show that Gray now fully grasped the principle that the work of the headquarters scientist depended more on bringing together the collections of many people than on his own field excursions. He considered his opportunities "highly favourable for arriving at correct results" not because of his sojourns in the pine barrens but because with "a liberality that does honour to the cause in which they are engaged, my botanical friends have placed their collections at my disposal or permitted me to examine them. . . ." Between Torrey's collection and those in Philadelphia, Gray had an inclusive view of past work, upon which incidentally he did not hesitate to improve. A recent specialist honors Gray's "Rhynchospora" as the "first treatment of the genus to be done in the carefully documented, modern style. . . ." [68] The young scientist had come in from a field regiment and had made good on the headquarters staff. He had mastered the tactics of the classifying botanist.

Regardless of the approbation he may have received from members of the New York Lyceum of Natural History, Gray's financial resources continued to dwindle. His whole income during the winter seems to have come from the sale of his grass book. The demand for the first part was great enough that he made out some additional sets of those species before going on to the second hundred. In spite of difficulties he was able by April 1835 to send to Professor Hooker a copy of Part II, together with three copies of the whole two hundred to sell in Europe in Gray's behalf. Even though the plate of illustrations was still lacking, the American also sent the loose sheets of his "Rhynchospora." It impressed Hooker quite as much as had the first work, and he undertook to publish it in Great Britain.[69] But hard luck accompanied this success, for fire—the scourge of wooden New York in the 1830's—destroyed the American printing before it was distributed, and Gray had to wait another year to get his paper into the hands of the profession. In spite of the gains in reputation he began to find genteel poverty tedious. "My time is spent here very profitably, and I am advancing in knowledge as fast as I ought to wish, but I make no money or scarcely enough to live upon." [70]

Dr. Torrey, powerless to pay anything, recognized both his assistant's talents and the discomfort of his position. "I should be very sorry to have him leave me,—but he will have to be in some public institution one of these days." Trying to make a place for him at Princeton, Torrey wrote to Joseph Henry,

43

Gray (my assistant) would be a great acquisition. . . . He is a *first rate fellow*, & is good both in Chemistry & Natural History. He would do great credit to the college, for he must make a noise in the world—& he will be continually publishing. He has just prepared for publication . . . two capital botanical papers. He is a good scientific and practical mineralogist. Keep your eye on him.

When this letter produced no results, Torrey returned to the subject, saying Gray "has no superior in Botany—considering his age—& any subject that he takes up he handles in a masterly manner." Although Torrey was genuinely solicitous for this "uncommonly fine fellow," he, like James Hadley, conceived of Gray's future in terms of his own career—a naturalist whose energies spread thinly over several sciences. "How would it do for Gray to be a Tutor or assistant in Chemistry?" Indeed the young man had good claims on a job as a naturalist, for he "has a capital Herbm. & collection of minerals. He understands most of the branches of Natural History well, & in Botany he has few superiors." [71] But Princeton offered no job, and in spite of his theoretical qualifications as a naturalist Gray remained in practice a research botanist.

Just at this moment when he had attained scientific maturity Asa Gray took a step which profoundly altered his whole view of life. Torrey's firm faith, his wife's warm understanding, and the social attractions of their family circle had their result. The memory of Bridgewater waned, and early in 1835 Gray joined the Bleeker Street Church. Its pastor, the Reverend Erskine Mason, who had in the 1820's led a group called the Associated Reformed Church into the Presbyterian General Assembly, was one of the leaders of the New School forces then locked in battle for the control of the whole denomination.[72] The religion Gray accepted, while still within the bounds of a kind of orthodoxy, had considerably altered the Calvinistic idea of predestination. The young scientist looked to a "God who is both able and willing to save all who come unto him. . . ." [73]

The conversion which led Gray out of his "dark delusion" was an extremely orderly one, for "the tone of my mind and the whole tendency of my education and habits of thinking does not incline me to credulity, or subject me to the influence of fanaticism." However completely he might reject the modes of expression of his Bridgewater days, the spirit of rationalism remained intact. In trying to help his old friend Folwell, who still remained in outer darkness, Gray revealed his own views. "All that I ask is that you would quietly examine the subject for yourself with a single and sincere desire to know the truth and I have no fears for the result. . . ." All the difficulties vanish at once. "Divested of all human speculations your course is very clear. Do not wait for any super-natural convictions nor for any excited state of feeling, for religion does not consist of these things." He found even the method of science applicable. "Leave all theological speculations alone and investigate the plain elementary truths, examine them as you would those of any other science without prejudice or bias, carefully distinguishing between fact and opinion." This was the kind of rational religion which had flourished in the eighteenth century. Even the demands of scripture were made to the mind. "Recollect that if there were not another Christian in the world, your duty would [not] be the less obvious nor the claims of the bible less peremptory." [74]

In fact Gray's espousal of religion was in no way a retreat from science. Bridgewater had been an isolated and doomed outpost of eighteenth-century deism, and Dr. Trowbridge was one of the last of the faith of Jefferson. "I have just heard," wrote Gray a little later, "of a cheering revival of religion in Bridgewater (the wickedest place I know) of which the two lawyers of the place and several other men of influence are subjects. Some have been infidel for years. Dr. Tro. still holds out and says they are all crazy." [75] Gray had left this backwoods enclave far behind. The great men of American science with whom he now associated were all religious. Torrey's piety and standards of scientific accuracy went hand in hand. Joseph Henry was of orthodox faith, as was Benjamin Silliman. To speak of a conflict between science and religion would have been to them absurd. To probe nature was but to discover God's design. In Gray's case the Calvinistic doctrine of a calling heightened his determination to be a scientist. Up to now he had pursued the way of a naturalist because he liked it, and a large factor in the imbalance of his career in the direction of botany came from his sheer joy in plants. Now science was raised, or reduced, to a duty. "Indeed I am not interested in [botany] . . . myself as I once was. I continue in these

45

pursuits because science is now my profession, & I have become disinclined to the practice of medicine. I am fond of these pursuits and take much delight in them. But I am no longer ambitious as I once was." Botany had become his Christian calling. "Whenever I see clearly that my duty calls in any other direction I shall throw up science as a profession, if not without a sigh, yet without a moment's hesitation. Meanwhile I feel that the labor of years would be wasted if I did not now turn the knowledge I have acquired to the greatest account." [76]

Religious orthodoxy, definitely on the rise in America in the 1830's, was but a part of a great shift of opinion that occurred throughout the Western world. The romantic literature which Gray had been reading since childhood—Scott and Bobby Burns—prepared his mind for a change in climate. Some of his correspondents in Germany, C. G. Nees von Esenbeck, for instance, had taken science as a platform for the speculations of an elaborate *Naturphilosophie*. Johann Wolfgang Goethe's ideas of the metamorphosis of plants had profoundly impressed sober scientists. In America, Emerson would soon publish his *Nature*. A design was still as evident in the universe as it had been to the deists, but now God pervaded all nature and spoke intimately to man in beautiful and cloudy mysteries. Young Asa wrote in his sister's album some stanzas from Horace Smith's "Hymn to the Flowers,"

> There, as in solitude and shade I wander
>   Through the green aisles, or stretched upon the sod,
> Awed by the silence, reverently ponder
>   The ways of God,
> Your voiceless lips, O Flowers! are living preachers,
>   Each cup a pulpit, every leaf a book,
> Supplying to my fancy numerous teachers
>   From loneliest nook.[77]

But Gray was a mature and practicing botanist, and science has a tough central stalk not easily swayed by variable breezes of opinion. Only the persistent trade winds of fundamental social change gradually bend it in a new direction. Even in the depths of Germany the wildest speculations of *Naturphilosophie* did not prevent precise scientific work. Gray's respect for the *facts* about *Rhyncho-*

spora was unchanged. He still held the ideals of the freedom and independence of science he had found in Sir William Lawrence's *Lectures.* Dr. Trowbridge and Folwell, unconverted, remained his friends. Although Gray's conversion was sincere and complete, it did not interrupt the flow of his scientific thinking, and eighteenth-century rationalism stayed on as an essential part of his mental equipment.

The Presbyterian Church formed for Gray a renewed bond with his family in Sauquoit, the first real interest they had held in common since he had immersed himself in science. "They were not people who talked much" [78] about such things, but Moses Gray had joined his wife in the Sauquoit church in 1826, a time of great religious excitement. The Utica Synod was subsequently a center of New School opinion.[79] Asa down in New York was in a position to send his parents the latest religious literature. "Tell mother I have for her a copy of Barnes's 'Notes on the Gospels,' but I want to read it myself before I send it up. . . . I think you will all be very much pleased with it." That Albert Barnes, the very symbol of the New School, had emerged from the same Fairfield-Hamilton College background as Asa Gray emphasizes the essential congeniality of this brand of religion for a central New Yorker of that period. Moses Gray's closer relations with his son took more forms than just religious sentiment, for Asa, harassed by debts, could now call on him as a patron of science for a loan of fifty dollars.[80]

As the spring of 1835 progressed, Gray's future was even more uncertain than before. Torrey could not keep him, and even help from his father could not save him from debt indefinitely. He spent his time "busily but quietly at work at botany and . . . studying plants in the right way, the only way in which one can make satisfactory progress." He examined one group after another. "When I have finished a family thus I feel that I know something about it." As the weather grew warmer, he dreamed again of Georgia. It was high time to begin his great explorations. By some chance he fell in with the agent of a French company in Mexico. "The account he gave me of the vegetation of that region made me for the time a little crazy. . . ."

Since traveling took money, he had to content himself with vi-

47

carious journeys by packing up bundles for Lehmann, for Nees von Esenbeck, for K. S. Kunth of Berlin, and for two botanists in St. Petersburg. These would no doubt bring in rich returns of books and plants, but nothing to live on. Around the whole horizon only one project appeared likely to produce some income. Gray's opportunity sprang as usual from Torrey's inability to do everything at once. The young man confided to his friend Folwell that "Prof. Lindley has published a new elementary work which will probably supply a desideratum long felt in this country. We expect soon to receive it and if it is the kind of work we wish, I shall myself if any publisher pay me pretty well for my labour prepare an American edition with all speed." [81]

When Dr. Torrey moved his family to Princeton where he lectured in the summer, Gray, left without board or employment in the city, retreated to his father's house in Sauquoit nursing the ambition to enter the elementary textbook field. Gradually he formed an audacious resolve. The idea of editing Lindley's textbook he rationalized away along with all other European works because of "those best adapted to our purpose some were much too large, others were illustrated with expensive engravings, or contained a considerable quantity of matter which did not seem to require a place in a mere elementary work." [82] He would be satisfied with nothing less than an original book of his own, an American Lindley or De Candolle. It was for him a personal declaration of independence. Amos Eaton, his protégée Mrs. Almira Hart Lincoln Phelps, and J. L. Comstock had turned out botany books which were American enough, but their quality was too inferior to impress the world. Gray hoped to challenge the European masters with their own standard of excellence.

Torrey, though approving, was apprehensive. "You have a more serious task before you.—but it will be quite within your power to finish it in three months, & perhaps in a shorter time. However, to write a regular *tome* from the *preface* to FINIS;—including 300 or 400 pages—is not mere play & cannot be done in so short a time as some people imagine. . . ." Asa himself had misgivings. "Nothing but the stimulus of dire necessity could induce me to undertake it." His pride of being "pretty familiar with the ground [,] perhaps rather more so at the moment than any other Botanist in the Country" was tempered by fear that he could not "put A G to" his work. "I write for money yet I would not sell my reputation for money." He implored Folwell not to mention it, "for in case . . . I have to abandon the project I would not like that any should know I had been thus engaged." [83]

Throughout the summer he wrote. De Candolle's *Théorie élémentaire* and *Organographie* were within reach, as were also the plants of the Sauquoit Valley. When the confinement became too close to bear, he got outside to "take severe exercise almost constantly." His observation of plants broadened as he looked at them with a new eye for form and function. "I have just now a mania for examining and preserving the roots and fruits of our plants." He probed into the "vascular and woody bundles" in the stems of *Smilax rotundifolia,* and he tried to distinguish roots from rhizomes (underground stems) in many plants.[84] He was gaining a general understanding of all branches of botany, not merely taxonomy.

As September approached, panic clutched him. The book was far from finished; he had neglected collections during the flowering season; no job appeared for the fall. The United States, unprecedentedly prosperous, offered him no opportunity. The very lack of openings had contributed to Gray's concentration on botany, so that now he seemed hopelessly overspecialized. He couldn't continue this way forever. Why not throw the whole thing up and go after some money?

In his despondency he turned to the original source of his love for science, his "steadfast friend." Dr. James Hadley for a second time held in his hands the future of Asa Gray. The country medical professor's career has been so completely overshadowed by that of his son, a great professor of Greek, and his grandson, a distinguished president of Yale, that memory of him has faded almost to genealogy. But in the space of a few days Hadley rendered great and essential service to science in America. Gray went over to Fairfield. "About that time I was in deep discouragement and just ready to abandon dearly beloved science and to betake to some other business even if it be necessary the peddling of pills." [85] When he came down out of the hills he had put Satan behind him. "One thing is

pretty certain," he wrote to his father, "after thinking over the matter quite seriously, and consulting with Dr. Hadley, who is my firm
friend in all these matters: I am determined to persevere for a while
yet before I give up all hopes from science as a pursuit for life."
Science was his calling. "I have now, and expect to have, a great
many discouragements, but I shall meet them as well as I can, until
it shall seem to be my duty to adopt some other profession for my
daily bread." [86]

Gray went on down to New York, where the "scientific atmosphere" helped him accumulate a "stock of perseverance, or obsti-
nacy, I don't know which." [87] In a boardinghouse at 286 Bleeker
Street he worked hard at his book, seldom stirring out except to go
to Dr. Torrey's. The only distractions were enticing bundles of
plants, the result both of his correspondence and of his newly found
religion. He forced himself to lay aside the parcel from his Utica
friend S. Wells Williams, now in China, but some dried plants from
the Reverend John Diell, chaplain of American seamen in the Sandwich Islands and acquaintance of the great British collector David
Douglas, required immediate attention, not that he had any interest
in such exotic flora directly, but rather because it would be "of more
interest to people on that side of the water than to us." Gray certainly saw by this time his opportunities as a middle man between
collectors on the fringes of American expansion and the centers of
learning in Europe. Meanwhile his hopes for an income rested on
the three hundred dollars he expected to receive for his book. A little later he began to look forward to a job as curator at the Lyceum
of Natural History, which would bring in three hundred a year as
well as the advantage of "the best scientific library and cabinet in
the city, [and] a couple of fine rooms to live in." [88]

Religious life offered some diversion. Gray spent busy Sabbaths
teaching a class of black boys at Sunday school and listening to the
latest preaching attraction among the Presbyterian ministers, the
Reverend Thomas H. Skinner, fresh from Andover Theological
Seminary. The young scientist also continued to furnish his family
with religious literature. "The Observer and the Evangelist are both
excellent papers and I hardly know which to choose. I would send
the Evangelist did not Mr. Leavitt fill it up too much with anti-

slavery." [89] This comment did not mean that Gray was proslavery but simply that he was not as much interested in the issue as was the *Evangelist,* which indeed soon went over to the Congregationalists. Asa Gray was not one to become unduly excited about reforms.

The grand objective of the new textbook was to supplant Eaton's type of instruction. In 1835, ten of forty-two academies of New York State used Eaton's *Manual,* and twenty-two used Mrs. Almira Hart Lincoln Phelps' text in some edition. Mrs. Phelps, the sister of Emma Willard, taught in Troy, New York, and pioneered in a remarkable series of science textbooks suitable for women. Her botanical information came directly from Eaton. The remaining ten schools scattered their choices among Beck, Comstock, Jacob Bigelow, or Peter Parley.[90]

These elementary works, whose success was a measure of the need they filled, aimed to give boys and girls enough polite learning in botany to recognize plants and to form a herbarium for their own pleasure. The emphasis fell heavily on identifying and naming plants by means of the artificial system. Structure and functions of plants received more attention from Mrs. Phelps than from Eaton, but her discussion of physiology was far from exact. For instance, she glossed over the complicated and then imperfectly understood function of pollen with the statement that, swelled "with the moisture which it finds [on] the [stigma] each little sack of the pollen explodes, and the oily substance which it contains is absorbed by the stigma, and passes through minute spores into the germ." The real attraction of Mrs. Phelps' *Familiar Lectures* was, as with Eaton's work, its belligerent democracy. Although "Europe may boast of many stars which irradiate her firmament of letters, shining with brilliant lustre amidst the surrounding darkness of ignorance, may we not justly feel a national pride in that more *general diffusion of intellectual light, which is radiating from every part, and to every part of the American republic.*" [91]

Gray opened direct battle—his first great scientific controversy— even before his book was published. In November 1835, the old schoolmaster of Troy came down to New York, and when the fray, which took place at Torrey's house, was over, Eaton could only sputter to his host. He recalled their great friendship in the past. "But ought you to have countenanced Mr. Gray in his vituperation and consummately impudent course with me? I will not call him a conceited upstart, because he has obtained your patronage." It was hard for an old man to take. "Had *he* told me that my erroneous views would be discouraging to *his* efforts—had he questioned me in his pedagogue-like style, &c. under any other circumstances he would have *met his reward."*

With due allowance for Eaton's persecution-haunted frame of mind, his description nevertheless evidences Gray's cocksureness. "I was questioned by him in lofty style, like a poor trembling urchin, cringing under the birch." Torrey's scientific views were quite as far from Eaton's, but the old affection still bound those two together. No such consideration either deterred or protected Gray. Eaton could not be "brought to resent any thing from Mr. Gray, after he had given me a small specimen of his urbanity. Contempt was my highest emotion for him *personally*; though I was disposed to set a high value upon him; as my students well know." Eaton's request for aid in preparing a sixth edition of his *Manual* was the match which touched off the row. "Several times I repeated, that I desired to keep pace with *published discoveries*. Mr. Gray (unasked) interfered, as if he—though he said we—held the destinies of the science in his hands, and that the ground whereon he stood was Holy." The old man heard the voice of youth. "Take thy shoes from off thy feet, and put on the sandals of the Natural Method, and *we* will begin to hear you." [92] Eaton here touched on the crux of Gray's position. The younger man knew, as did of course Torrey, that the natural system was coming in America, for the simple reason that it had already arrived in Europe.

Gray's *Elements of Botany,* however much it opposed Eaton, did not challenge the ideal of a democratic science. Beginning with the proposition that botany was useful not only to doctors but also to farmers, Gray implied that Americans deserved the very best available science from the first day of their training. He sought, besides "a popular form and a familiar style," the most "rigid perspicuity and philosophical accuracy." In addition Gray asserted that the natural system was actually easier for the beginner than was the artificial. He pointed out that the botanist who merely counted stamens was helpless when those parts were missing, or when, as is often the case, their number varied from species to species within a genus, or even among individuals.[93] Poor Eaton would have been heartbroken to see a letter which one of his beloved students wrote to Gray. S. Wells Williams out in China had run into an Englishman who had worked with Robert Brown. "He has paid much attention to the natural orders, and can detect an unknown plant by those affinities with which the disciple of Linneus is entirely ignorant. I find, by a little intercourse with him, what a precious little Eaton at Troy knew about botany, notwithstanding all his pretensions." [94]

Gray's espousal of the natural system went deeper than mere ease of collecting. He was attempting to get students to understand plants, and he felt that the "whole science of Botany rests on the foundation of vegetable organography and physiology." Hence the student should "in the first place direct his attention to the study of plants as organized and living beings, and become familiar with all the ordinary forms of structure." The first four of his six chapters treated morphological and physiological subjects. A fifth surveyed the much neglected flowerless plants, emphasizing Gray's desire to include the whole plant kingdom. Only in the last chapter did he cover succinctly the actual systems of classification, relegating to an appendix instructions for collecting. Thus he presented botany as a balanced science, with the forms, the functions, and the classifications of plants equal and mutually supporting frames of reference. Although he did not treat them in the book, he also recognized the importance of applied botany—agricultural, medical, economical— and of *"Geographical Botany,* which attempts the investigation of the circumstances regulating the distribution of vegetables over the earth's surface." [95]

From De Candolle, the great Genevan master of all fields of botany, Gray took his main arguments, for example, his warm admiration for Goethe's ideas of the metamorphosis of leaves into flowers. The *Théorie élémentaire* had read like a novel the summer before, and many of its ideas reappear. De Candolle argued in favor of starting students on the natural system and, of course, strongly urged a balanced science. Most important was De Candolle's idea of a species. He carefully considered the claim of some naturalists who "deny the existence of species and say that closely related groups may come from the same source." While granting that this might be true in a few cases, he held that the "hypothesis of nonpermanence is less workable than the other for with it we would know nothing." He then defined a species "the collection of all the individuals who resemble one another more than they resemble others; who are able, by reciprocal fecundation, to produce fertile individuals; and who reproduce by generation, such kind as one may by analogy suppose that all came down originally from one single individual." [96]

Gray, adopting this definition almost precisely, defended it. "The fact that botanists often differ in opinion as to what are species, is no evidence against the existence or nonpermanence [*sic*] of species, or the correctness of our definition." But he was already considerably impressed by the problem posed by less stable forms which he called varieties, following De Candolle in attributing them in part to variable local environment and in part to hybridization. Thus species were permanent, and varieties were not, but to tell them apart required "much experience, combined with close observation, and a just appreciation of the value of characters." [97] Gray here had consciously chosen to reject the evolutionary ideas of Jean Lamarck in favor of the dominant belief in the constancy of species. But both De Candolle and Gray faced the issue without a trace of religious horror, and they based their conclusion on scientific reasons.

Throughout the fall and winter Gray pushed his book through the press. New York publishing houses were in the 1830's just emerging from among the booksellers, who served as informal post offices and meeting places as well. G. & C. Carvill and Company, who published the *Elements,* had the reputation of being "the lounging place of the literati." To help him read proof, Gray was most fortunate in falling in with a lovable but lugubrious Englishman named John Carey. Twelve years older than his young friend and a man of considerable botanical attainments in England, this cultured gentleman had come to America a widower in 1830. When his sons were old enough to enter Columbia College in 1836, he moved to New York and spent his life dabbling ably in business and botany, too greatly occupied with his own sorrows to push through any great projects in either sphere. Since he had a vivid style of his own and a happy faculty for riposting Gray's incisive botanical tirades with good-natured repartee, Carey added much to the clear, crisp, businesslike prose which distinguishes the *Elements*.[98]

At last in April 1836, Asa Gray signed the preface. He wrote jubilantly to Folwell that he had "worked harder indeed than I intend to again very soon. . . . My 'Elements of Botany' is in the hands of the binder, and will be published in 10 or 12 days. It extends to about 420 pages, closely printed,—so that job is off my mind." He was free to "go to studying plants again, having done scarcely anything that way for almost a year." But he felt he had spent his time well. "This preparatory training . . . has prepared me most thoroughly for future progress, and if I happen to pursue Botany undividedly for a little time I shall (entre nous) be soon the best botanist in this country." [99] Strong boast for a young man just over twenty-five, but who could gainsay him?

As an embryo recapitulates rapidly the evolutionary history of his race, Gray in changing from doctor to scientist passed rapidly through the primitive stages of botany. The physician-naturalist turned into the teacher and collector. From the field he entered the library, herbarium, and laboratory to become a specialist in classifying. He was then ready to examine the broader bearings of botany, reduce his ideas to a book, and with it enter the competitive lists of the textbook market. At each stage he accumulated valuable baggage. Always he would be able to recognize the value of the amateur, the local collector, the elementary teacher. A naturalist's catholic interest in all the sciences never left him. Both the precision of the monographer and the necessity for the surveyor's view became part of his scientific standards. Through the whole process an increasing abundance of opportunity for organized work coupled with the lack of any paying and demanding job made Gray a professional botanist in a country where there had been few before. Chester Dewey, naturalist of the old school, wrote to Torrey that "Dr. Gray is working well. . . . It seems to me he is a noble Botanist.—When he sent me his Carices . . . , I wondered at his judgment—& told him so—but he had some better help than you or I had for a long time." [100] At twenty-five he had scaled the heights on which the preceding generation stood and was ready for new adventures.

GOVERNMENT
AS A PATRON

THE New York Lyceum of Natural History was at the height of its prosperity in 1836. The young men who had founded it in 1817 discovered as the years went on that the "cost & difficulty to an individual of procuring the requisite means of study, the necessity as well as pleasure of sometimes conferring and comparing observations with others similarly occupied" had "kept them together to the present time, and enabled them to collect a valuable library, and a numerous cabinet of specimens." As the focus of scientific interest in the city, the Lyceum's list of supporters, studded with Rhinelanders, Verplancks, Rensselaers, and even a few commercial names like Tappan, seemed to assure its prosperity. Now in its own quarters it was ready to invite the public to participate "upon terms of mutual advantage." [1] No wonder that Asa Gray, soon after his appointment as librarian in February or March 1836, remarked with elation on the "elegant new building in Broadway near Prince St." He was accepting also "the situation of Superintendent or Resident Curatory,—and have a fine apartment in the building." Since he would have entire charge of the books and collections, he thought that in spite of a very small salary "it will be a fine situation for scientific pursuits and I think I shall be pleased." [2] Gray had landed one of the few paying jobs in the country offered by scientific societies.

With a position of much prestige and some income, Gray nevertheless had plenty of time to pursue his own work, arranging in his herbarium "the accumulation of three years." Torrey too came forward with a scheme for him to prepare monographs on which to base sections of the *Flora of North America* in return for three hundred dollars a year. Whatever his motives (possibly a desire to save Torrey the money) Gray was reluctant, and immediately Torrey made a new offer, more risky financially, which in effect raised the younger man to substantial equality in the work. Gray would get a share of any profits, and Torrey would give him "due acknowledgement of the aid you afford me—not only in general matters, but in indicating several of the families for which you are responsible." Gray would spend part of his effort on monographs published independently, which Torrey would quote in putting "the matter into a synoptical form." [3] This arrangement evidently proved satisfactory, for Gray began on the *Flora* about this time. Torrey was just then accepting a commission as botanist of the Natural History Survey of New York, which would, whether he realized it or not, again compromise the time which he might otherwise have spent on his own project. Gray, although not yet an equal partner, was in a fair way to become one simply by doing most of the work.

The state of New York, with Governor William L. Marcy himself hiring naturalists for the survey, was rapidly opening opportunities for the scientific community, and an atmosphere of confidence and expectancy prevailed. One day in July, Gray met Dr. James E. De Kay in the street in New York. This European-trained physician, a specialist in zoology and a leading member of the Lyceum, was on his way to Albany to join the survey. Even more interesting to Gray was the fact that De Kay had "partly offered Reynolds to go on the South Sea expedition in case he concluded not to engage in the State Survey."

This news was exciting, not only because the South Seas had all the lure of another world, but because Jeremiah N. Reynolds was the harbinger of a new patron for science in the United States. "I understand," wrote Gray, "the 'old General' has given Reynolds power to engage a full scientific corps, and to offer as high as $2,000 per year, no small inducement." [4] The United States government under Andrew Jackson was at last sponsoring a scientific enterprise of the first importance.

The idea of a national expedition to the Pacific Ocean went back at least as far as the first annual message of President John Quincy Adams, who suggested the exploration of the "whole northwest coast of this continent." When embodied in a Congressional resolution, the survey had expanded to other parts of the Pacific.[5] The Antarctic also came in for a share of interest from the followers of Captain John Cleves Symmes, whose theory that the earth was open at the poles naturally led some to wish to sail into the holes and see the concentric spheres and other delightful things inside. Jeremiah N. Reynolds, a landsman from Ohio, began his public career as the foremost of these enthusiasts. By his tireless efforts he induced Adams's Secretary of the Navy Samuel L. Southard to order an expedition south with the hope "that we shall add something to the common stock of geographical and scientific knowledge." [6] When these plans collapsed, the promoter, determined to go anyway, shipped in a sealing vessel for the southern seas, where he stayed until 1834.[7]

On Reynolds's return, interest again revived, this time with the Jackson administration's blessing. Now well seasoned at sea, the Ohioan, having learned enough to jettison Symmes's theory, stressed the need for protection and navigational aid for whalers. He had also found tropical islands like the Fijis more attractive than high southern latitudes. But science remained a prominent aim, natural history as well as geography. It formed a part of Reynolds's many appeals to patriotism—that America should compete with the Old World in adding to knowledge.[8] This combination of nationalism and science was constant in all exploring expeditions since Cook and Bougainville, and Reynolds was by no means betraying science in linking the two. As a matter of fact he had labored hard, if humbly, at collecting plants, bird's skins, eggs, shells, minerals, and insects while on his cruise to the south.[9] Congress definitely contemplated the triple objective of military protection, surveying, and scientific observation when in May 1836 it authorized a "Surveying and exploring expedition to the Pacific Ocean and South Seas."

Reynolds immediately went to work gathering information and opinion concerning the proper conduct of the expedition. Not only public men such as James K. Paulding and Thomas ap Catesby Jones, a Naval officer, favored him with recommendations, but also scientists. Benjamin Silliman outlined a detailed plan for all the departments he considered essential. Dr. James De Kay offered the services of the New York Lyceum of Natural History. Dr. Asa Gray furnished a plan for the expedition's botanist.

Gray was interested like Reynolds in "national honour," but he emphasized that the surest way to impress the world scientifically was by "enlightened liberality." Hence he insisted that the botanist should collect at least twenty-five specimens of each species, and that these be distributed freely to learned societies and even "to the most eminent scientific individuals, both in this country and in Europe." He thought the botanist should be much more useful than "the mere collector of ornamental plants," for he dreamed of discoveries of valuable woods, cordage, new dyestuffs, and drugs. The man selected must know "vegetable chemistry" and have equipment to test "on the spot, the nature . . . of various vegetable products." This was a direct extension of the principles on which he had based his *Elements of Botany*.[10]

In spite of his summer's activity and seeming authority, Reynolds's position as the "old General's" agent was not secure. Mahlon Dickerson, Secretary of the Navy, gradually began to show signs of activity. He dispatched Lieutenant Charles Wilkes to Europe to buy instruments, and toward the end of August, too late for a possible sailing in 1836, he asked the American Philosophical Society and other organizations to prepare a scientific plan for the expedition. He was thus belatedly collecting in a formal way the information Reynolds had been gathering unofficially. The various societies, forewarned, were able to compile extensive replies rapidly, the Philadelphia Academy incorporating in their report the suggestions of the New York Lyceum of Natural History. Dickerson had asked for recommendations of scientists qualified to fill the various posts, and while the societies themselves refrained from mixing in the business of appointments, there was no lack of applicants.[11]

Gray had spent the month of August showing Torrey some of his old haunts in central New York, but by the middle of September he was in the midst of the negotiations for places. As Reynolds was in New York the young botanist was in a position to get firsthand news. Charles Pickering, the New Englander who as a curator of the Academy of Natural Sciences of Philadelphia had by far the best claims on a zoological post, wrote to Gray about the various schemes of organization. In touching lightly on his own ambitions he suggested that as "I have pretty much concluded on going, will you have the kindness to ask Mr. Reynolds whether it would not be proper for me to make application direct, to the Secretary—" Gray himself was having the same thoughts and evidently Reynolds instructed his chosen scientists to apply, for on October 3 the Secretary of the Navy, impressed by the *Elements of Botany* and letters of recommendation, wrote to Gray that as "soon as the scientific corps of this expedition shall be detailed you will hear from me." [12]

Three years in the South Seas! Gray wrote his parents of his prospects—five ships including a frigate, comfortable quarters, pay of twenty-five hundred dollars a year. Since he had been able to advise Reynolds, the scientists would be "mostly my personal friends: two of them at least having been recommended at my suggestion." One of his protégés was James Dwight Dana, the erstwhile pupil of Dr. Bartlett who had had some sea experience and was doing well at mineralogy in New Haven. They might even get away during the winter, but surely by the spring of 1837. So far was Gray in his expectations from the starving days of 1835 that when some poor college down in Jackson, Louisiana, offered him a professorship at fifteen hundred dollars a year he declined with a brusque "I do not like the Southern States." [13]

Difficulties almost at once began to interfere with the dreams based on Reynolds's cozy arrangements. News began to reach New York that politics was playing a part. Although Jefferson's instructions to Lewis and Clark set a precedent which allayed most constitutional scruples, the government had never before undertaken to organize a corps of professional scientists for an expedition, and counsels as to proper procedure were many and divided. Richard Harlan, a member of the Academy's committee in Philadelphia, wrote hinting darkly that Dickerson was a mere clerk and that "men of real merit, must wait to see if the President has friends to serve!" Gray and Pickering were secure in their places, but they would be joined by another chief botanist, whom "no one knows as a botanist," and three other chief zoologists, in spite of the fact that *"four persons qualified . . . do not exist in this country."* Reynolds, in an ambiguous position as a professional lobbyist standing for the best scientific applicants, had had "the impudence" to seek to be director of the whole corps, but the authorities, "fearful of his having the expedition in Symes's hole," would give him a lesser position. Harlan ended with the suggestion that, if too many political favorites were added, the "real *horses* of the expedition may decline working in the same team with the 'asses'." [14]

Gray was so alarmed by this news that in telling Professor Hooker of his prospects he warned that the expedition "may be so marred by improper appointments," that he would not go. William Darlington, politician, banker, botanist, and sage of West Chester, Pennsylvania, wrote that William Rich, the proposed political botanist, was an *"amateur* of the science, rather than a *connoisseur."* Darlington had written the Secretary in behalf of Gray and Pickering, but hesitated to do more because "I am not considered *orthodox* by the present administration." [15]

Here was a beginning of bickering, jealousy, inefficiency, and delay. It is impossible to trace in detail all the crosscurrents of bitterness and misunderstanding which plagued all connected with the expedition. Gray himself thought the "stories are too long to relate." Amid all the accusations, however, a pattern emerges which shows some of the difficulties with which Gray had to deal.

The villain turned out to be not the "great unerring one," Andrew Jackson, but rather the Secretary of the Navy. Reputedly the President was astonished when in October 1836, he learned that little progress had been made. The expedition's naval commander, Thomas ap Catesby Jones, a crusty old sea dog who carried in his shoulder "a lead-mine" of British ball, made a reasonably good impression on the scientists, but had a hard time establishing his authority with his own kind. Dickerson's excuse at this period was that the recruiting of the crew was lagging. Later he assigned part of the equipment to another survey, leaving the exploring expedition with the ugly choice of leaving its instruments behind or waiting until they were again free. Finally, he appointed a commission to review the vessels assigned to the expedition and cut down their number.[16] Whether or not the Secretary really meant to scuttle the expedition, his actions gave that impression.

To the scientific corps, left in great uncertainty and not yet on the government payroll, these delays were particularly irksome. In November, Dickerson wrote Gray that it would be two or three months before the crews were ready, but that he planned to call six or eight of the head scientists together in Washington to make plans and allocate duties. In January 1837 Gray was still waiting, momentarily expecting formal appointment and a call to Washington, high in hopes of sailing by late spring. Rumor had it that only the direct intervention of President Jackson forced Dickerson to issue the scientists' commissions. But by February Gray believed that a "strong attempt is making to break" the expedition. He evidently feared that "the naval influence" and Dickerson wished to change or abolish the civilian scientific corps.[17]

Finally in March 1837 the inauguration of Martin Van Buren seemed a propitious time to appear in Washington, orders or no. Gray, Pickering, Reynell Coates (one of the zoologists), and presumably Reynolds went there, each paying his own expenses, "which were not small." Dickerson had wanted the scientists to submit lists of needed equipment for their departments, but this they decidedly refused to do until they should be officially convened— that is, put on the payroll. In spite of the fact that the Secretary had continued in the new administration, a different court of appeal always inspires hope, and Reynolds lost no time in putting his case to Van Buren. For two hours they looked at charts "of the great theatre of our future explo[ra]t[io]n—the Feejees and all." The promoter urged the necessity of organizing the scientific corps, the need of all the ships including the frigate, and "touched gently upon our difficulties with the Secretary." Van Buren, who was new to the problem, seemed sympathetic.[18]

By April, in spite of the "abominable management & stupidity (if not something worse) of the Secy. of Navy," Gray left the employ of the Lyceum of Natural History and soon afterward gave up his rooms. His "fondness for roving of old" returned with all its force. There was a possibility—the Secretary promised Reynolds—that several scientists would go in advance to Europe for books and equipment, but Gray placed "so little confidence in his promises that I shall suspend my belief until I see the order." He hoped to get away by May or June, or at the latest by July when the main expedition was scheduled to sail.[19]

Nevertheless, "many of the wise ones" in Washington were already predicting that the expedition would fail. The outbreak of open hostilities between Reynolds and the Secretary was evident by April, and by midsummer it was blazoned in the press. Gray and the other scientists, excepting of course political appointees like Rich, were undoubtedly in full sympathy with Reynolds, and he often seemed to voice their criticisms.[20] The summer and fall wore on in rage, and the sailing date receded indefinitely. At some point Gray participated in a scheme, which came to nothing, to take the whole affair out of the hands of the Navy. But some improvement did come, for by November Gray was drawing his pay and sending his gear aboard one of the vessels which lay in Brooklyn Navy Yard. Perhaps they would sail within a month. This time Commodore Jones fell ill, with "little probability that he will be much better ever," and he resigned his command in an exchange of correspondence with the Secretary which exhibited "throughout a want of . . . respectful courtesy." [21] Without a commander and with the Secretary as uncooperative as ever, the expedition fell into a welter of demoralized confusion. Gray faced a second year of uncertain waiting.

He had of course not idled in the long interval since he had engaged to enter the government service. His *Elements of Botany,* favorably reviewed,[22] had reached all corners of the land and made him something of a personage who found "that reputation is on the whole pretty well paid for by the increased cares &c. which attend it." His correspondence with American botanists multiplied rapidly, and many of them wrote him high praise of his book. Dr. Charles Wilkins Short, a pillar of medical education in Kentucky and a distinguished local collector, added his admiration and support—approbation more significant because he had formerly favored the Linnaean system and as a Westerner had a lively appreciation of Eaton's service in spreading "a general knowledge of the plants of North America" through his many students to the farthest outposts of the frontier.[23]

In a paper in the *American Journal of Science* Gray entered into the role of interpreter of European science to American botanists.

His *Elements* had already shown a broad grasp of the problem of fertilization by pollen. Now, translating by main strength rather than by any previous knowledge of German, he presented a paper on the impregnation of the ovules of the *Coniferae* by a young European named A. J. C. Corda. Already he found himself able to guide his more isolated colleagues to the latest discoveries made in Europe. Although Gray himself was not adept at drawing, he provided a very acceptable illustration for the article done by Lieutenant Jacob Whitman Bailey, a young instructor at West Point who had been a student of Torrey's and who was already making a name as a microscopist.[24]

Occasional articles occupied little of Gray's time compared with his steady systematic work on the families which he and Torrey would soon treat in the *Flora*. From these efforts came two papers published in the *Annals* of the Lyceum. One is particularly interesting because he attempted to apply the new researches on plant embryos, especially those of Brongniart, to a problem in classification.[25] Later Gray felt embarrassed by this article, saying that he had rushed too hastily into print with erroneous ideas. The other paper, which stood up better under his examination when he was older, was a perfectly safe formal treatment of a family, written wholly in Latin.[26] Having mastered the technique, Gray stacked up large quantities of organized information which would fit into the *Flora,* even writing some sections himself.

Meanwhile by early 1838 the expedition was in a complete turmoil in Washington, as one senior naval officer after another refused the command. Gray chafed not only because of the delay but because in his uncertainty he could scarcely leave the city. Benjamin D. Greene's invitation to spend a week in Boston had to be refused.[27] It is not surprising that Gray began to think of some other job and doubtless let it be known that he would entertain offers.

Although the Panic of 1837 rendered the time unfavorable, stirrings in the West gave hope not only of more jobs for scientists, but also of institutions in which science would occupy a new and controlling place. The state of Michigan had just entered the Union, and its young governor was full of zeal for education. Stevens T. Mason, whose father had stood for Jacksonian ideals in the Michigan Territory, was a thorough enthusiast for a university and a scientific survey. The men around him in these enterprises had already made impressive contributions to knowledge. Both Henry R. Schoolcraft and Zina Pitcher, who had participated in western explorations, were correspondents of Torrey, as was Douglass Houghton, the director of the geological survey. By March of 1838 Asa Gray's application for a professorship lay before the board of regents, which was beginning to make definite plans to build the state university.[28]

John Torrey's aid was a great asset to Gray, for not only was he acquainted with the men on the board, but he had the year before arranged for them the purchase of a cabinet of minerals. The regents clearly indicated their scientific cast of mind by entertaining applications from both Gray and Joseph Henry, and had their plans worked they would have boasted a staff of specialists unrivaled in the country. But it was still a paper university, and the Board felt its "unprepared state" prevented them from making appointments immediately. Gray could only have been tantalized by this further uncertainty.

About this time the expedition began showing signs of life. Contrary to Gray's expectations, "this nasty administration" would not let the laurels of discovery go uncontested to the rival French and British expeditions now making up. Mahlon Dickerson found it convenient to become ill and resign from the cabinet. The affairs of the expedition fell into the hands of the Secretary of War, Joel Roberts Poinsett, who had an entirely fresh outlook on the problem. He soon appointed Charles Wilkes, a relatively junior officer, as commander.

On the surface the new regime meant a defeat for Reynolds and his group of scientists. In the course of his newspaper controversy with Dickerson, the promoter had bitterly criticized Wilkes's purchases in Europe on the ground that he had spent all the funds for surveying instruments and nothing for microscopes and books for naturalists. By fighting for a frigate Reynolds had also insisted on a strong military show in behalf of the whalers.[29] Poinsett's course would defeat all this, and Gray probably expected the bickering to go on undiminished.

In April, however, he received word from Pickering of a shift in the wind. "I do not know whether [Reynolds] has told you," the zoologist wrote from Washington, "that I had gone over to the Enemy. . . ." After dining with Wilkes he felt "many of his ideas not bad, and though rather hasty in his conclusions and in danger of running against a few posts, if he takes time I have reason to believe he will bring up about right." Pickering stressed the futility of trying again to organize the expedition outside the Navy and told Gray "that the Administration stands pledged that an *honourable station* be assigned to our friend R." [30] With one of the key scientists supporting the new arrangement and Reynolds provided for in some measure, the chances rose for sufficient harmony to put the expedition to sea.

Gray was now in a quandary. Should he continue to count on an expedition which in spite of its bright prospects had offered only continued disappointment? Or should he switch his allegiance to a potentially great university which was as yet a mere idea? No one could say which would fail and which succeed. The state of Michigan indeed seemed anxious to get Gray. Douglass Houghton offered him a position on the state survey, and Governor Mason, when he was in New York in May, made an even bolder statement. He proposed to buy Gray away from the expedition by informally promising that the board of regents of the university would give him a position which would repay him for the "sacrifice you may otherwise make in accepting the offer of Dr. Houghton." [31]

As Mason went over the details of the offer with Gray, one inducement doubtless had a particularly powerful attraction. The university needed an agent to go to Europe to purchase books and equipment, an opportunity which almost any scientist in America would have seized.[32] The great centers of learning of the Old World had always lured an American youth of scientific leanings, and Silliman's journey in 1808 had set a pattern for new professors spending a year doing a scientific version of the grand tour. Torrey had managed his short stay as an agent of New York University. Joseph Henry, after nine months in France and Great Britain, made a point of calling on Gray when he returned in November 1837. In the space of a few months the young botanist could hope for training and inspiration unobtainable at any price in America.

More especially, a sojourn in Europe would allow Gray to continue as Torrey's colleague on the *Flora of North America* and solidify his position as an equal partner, for they continually encountered difficulty because the original collections of North American plants were in European herbaria. To make their work worthy of international respect required that they see the material preserved abroad.[33] For Gray to join an expedition which left both civilization and North America far behind meant an indefinite setback to the *Flora*. Michigan's offer seemed perfect for furthering its progress. In a very different way from the South Seas, Europe appeared a paradise to an American scientist.

Throughout June, Gray vacillated, but on July 10, in spite of Michigan's continued uncertainty, he submitted his resignation to the expedition, "or rather requested to be left out of the new arrangement." But Secretary Poinsett, not one to lose a good man easily, summoned Gray, along with Dana, J. P. Couthouy, and Pickering, to Washington to try to "remove my present dissatisfaction." Since the young botanist fully appreciated that "their new plan has the advantage of leaving home all the blockheads and taking the best fellows," he feared the Secretary would ply him with such strong reasons that he would relent. The absence of definite word from Michigan also raised the specter that he "should get nothing satisfactory for a year or two," but he went to Washington determined to stay by his resignation.[34]

The Michigan board of regents acted on July 17, 1838. Gray had evidently communicated to them his intention to resign from the expedition, and through C. W. Whipple, the secretary of the board and an old friend of Torrey's, he had promised to come to Detroit during August. The board in appointing him professor of botany and zoology made him the first permanent paid professor in the history of the university. Curiously, the copy of the resolution sent Gray omitted the words "and Zoology," and Gray found himself "hereby appointed, Professor of Botany in the University of Michigan." The board seems to have fallen in with the abbreviation, and Gray thus received an appointment to the first chair devoted exclusively to botany in any American educational institution.[35] It was a new step in the progress of specialization and the culmination of the breakdown of the naturalist.

Michigan had outbid the United States government. Gray wrote his father on August 6: "I have resigned my place in the exploring expedition! So that job is got along with. I have been long in a state of uncertainty and perplexity about the matter; but I believe I have taken the right course." [36] Never one to brood over past decisions, Gray put the expedition out of his mind and headed for Detroit. Strongly fortifying him was the knowledge that just off the press had come the first part of volume one of the *Flora of North America,* and on the title page, fully equal to John Torrey, was the name of Asa Gray.

His friends Pickering, Dana, and Couthouy cleared Hampton Roads on August 19. The political appointee William Rich, bolstered by the addition of W. D. Brackenridge as horticulturist, had charge of botany. Lieutenant Wilkes, now the Commodore, having surmounted the difficulties of getting started, would be equal to his task at sea.

The conclusion is difficult to avoid that Gray made a mistake in abandoning the expedition just as it was about to make scientific history. Certainly the work of the corps suffered. Had excellence in botany matched the great work of Pickering and Dana, the results would have been fuller and more balanced. Gray's energy and ability to ask questions of nature might have yielded discoveries which eluded the expedition completely. His pertinacity in pushing books through the press would have served well in the period immediately after the return of the expedition. His shoes were already much too big for William Rich to fill.

Gray personally suffered a great loss of opportunity. Exploring expeditions were the graduate schools of the early nineteenth century for many of the best scientists. Robert Brown, Alexander von Humboldt, Darwin, T. H. Huxley, A. R. Wallace, Joseph D. Hooker, even James Dwight Dana, founded careers in their long wanderings in the far places of the earth. These men, for the most part borne by naval vessels, saw so much of nature in a few intense months that great comparisons and generalizations dared to emerge. Gray's field of action would have grown immediately from eastern North America to the greater part of the world. His interest in the geographical distribution of plants, already hinted at in his *Elements*, might well have blossomed into a spectacular contribution to nineteenth-century science before he reached his thirty-fifth year.

Potential discoveries missed are mere idle speculations, but from another point of view Gray's loss was definite and measurable. Although he put the expedition out of his mind, it came back to haunt him. However much he might rationalize that he stepped aside to let Rich go in his place, he knew in advance that Rich was no botanist, and for that knowledge he paid his price. During a whole decade, long after the expedition's botanical accomplishments should have stood complete in tidy volumes, Gray burned the midnight oil trying to make some sense out of the scanty, disorganized, and ill-preserved collections which had long lain in chaos.

So understandable were his reasons for resigning that he came under no open criticism, but in an indirect way his reputation suffered. From his early years he had yearned for adventure, for scientific conquest in a distant field. He had, in his small early opportunities, showed that strength, energy, love of the wilds, and keen scientific ability necessary for a great explorer. In passing up his chance he labeled himself forever as a "closet botanist," a man who studies nature second-hand in the garden and herbarium. The faint aura of pedantry—unjust though it is—which still clings to his name would never have formed about a shellback of the United States Exploring Expedition.

As Gray hurried west to Detroit through his well-loved hills of central New York, his thoughts went only ahead: to the great interior of North America, to its *Flora,* and to Europe beyond. The new professor hurried to Michigan not only to get his instructions but also to help shape them. Because of the fast-spreading network of steam transportation he could hope to reach Detroit from New York in four days—rail to Utica, stage to Buffalo, and lake steamer the rest of the way. But flesh could not stand such a pace, and Gray, fatigued by the excitement of the past few weeks, had to lay over a day in western New York to recuperate. As he would not travel on the

Sabbath, he spent another day in Cleveland, Ohio, "which will ultimately be a very pleasant place." On Monday the New Yorker resumed by ship his journey to Detroit, a town which for all its ostensible concern for education was a focal point for the roughest elements of Western population. They were there hoping to take advantage of the current unrest in Canada to stage a border incident.[37]

Since his appointment was already settled, Gray immediately gave his full attention to urging a policy for the university which would give a central place to the sciences. The original act had envisaged professorships in chemistry, geology, botany, fine arts, civil engineering, and architecture as well as the usual ancient and modern languages, philosophy, moral philosophy, and natural theology. This broad framework offered the possibility of giving the sciences an emphasis unique at that time in American higher education. Although Gray's detailed plan has not survived, he clearly wished to have his friends Torrey and Joseph Henry appointed to two of the places, to design the buildings of the university specifically for their needs, and to buy a good stock of books and equipment on his journey to Europe. This platform was essentially and simply the scientist's Elysian dream of an ideally equipped laboratory, brilliant and congenial colleagues, and the freedom that stems from ample support. Although he expected some opposition, he had faith, not misplaced, that the board would consider his views sympathetically.[38]

His first acquaintance in Detroit was C. W. Whipple, a friend of Torrey's and a "downright clever fellow in both the English and Yankee senses of the term." Although not properly a voting member of the board, he was its secretary and was in line for appointment as chief justice of the state. The botanist, sizing him up as the "moving spirit of the whole," cultivated him accordingly. They called on Dr. Pitcher and Dr. Houghton, the leading scientists already on the ground, before paying respects to Governor Mason. At a meeting of the board, unfortunately without a quorum, Gray met other members, with whom he attended an examination at the local branch of the university, really a secondary school. This was a danger signal which Gray in his enthusiasm failed to recognize, because the branches were draining money away from the parent institution even before the latter was born, and the "stupid" examinations gave an index to the level of preparation of the students immediately available. His hosts showed their professor all the sights and entertained him royally. There were broad hints, completely ignored, that the handsome Easterner would not remain long unmarried here. The oft-repeated fare of roast pork made Gray remark that Charles Lamb would "riot in his favorite dish," but the city fellow had no taste for the "wretched stuff" nor for losing his heart in the country.

On a trip alone to Ann Arbor, Gray had the more serious purpose of viewing the university grounds, a bit too level for one accustomed to Hamilton College. He had "contrived a plan" for their arrangement which had met with favor. Since his hopes depended in part on convincing Torrey and Henry to come West, he was especially interested in the houses for the professors, to be built separate from both dormitories and classroom buildings. Hence he put much thought on providing an adequate water supply for the second stories of the houses, hinting rather obviously that such a convenience would please his dear friend Mrs. Torrey.

After several days of conferences Gray felt much encouraged about his plans. He was too impatient to leave to await their official adoption. The board still lacked a quorum, and the architect, Alexander Jackson Davis, one of the most prolific designers of his time, would not arrive for several days. Gray, although aware of having gained much influence since arriving, knew that he endangered his position by departing before he had appropriations for his salary and for purchases in Europe. As he had a rather low opinion of Davis as an architect, he doubtless expected trouble from that source. With the *Flora* and plans for sailing urging him on, he arrived back in New York by the end of August. Before leaving Detroit he must have prepared lists of scientific books and equipment to be purchased abroad. The proportions he had in mind are evident from a request that Henry furnish recommendations of physical apparatus to the value of three thousand dollars and also titles of books on his subject. Torrey would furnish a list of chemical apparatus. Since Gray could not have forgotten botanical books completely, he had in his imagination already spent on the sciences alone the whole five thousand dollars allowed by the board.[39]

The months of September and October after his return from

Michigan were frantically busy. Gray and Torrey pressed to finish a second part of the *Flora* before his sailing date on November 1. He also gave much attention to the plans for the university buildings and took a prominent part in trying to secure for the staff not only Henry and Torrey but also the even more eminent Silliman. Naturally, arrangements for his voyage also took time. His friends—especially Torrey, Henry, and Carey—showered him with letters of introduction. Since a "private hand" was the most trustworthy method of transporting delicate and valuable instruments and supplies, each American scientist who went to Europe was well laden with miscellaneous orders from colleagues for every conceivable shopping errand from books to microscopes. Gray was generous in offering to do these favors.[40]

Meanwhile in Detroit the drafting of Gray's instructions fell into the hands of those who, although his friends and supporters, were much nearer to the problems of starting a university in a new land. The board appropriated five thousand dollars for a library and fifteen hundred dollars as both a year's salary and personal traveling expenses. But the library should consist of "Standard English Works in history, biography, voyages and travels, poetry, statistics, science, and one copy of the most approved British Annual Register." The board also wished a formal report of his observations while in Europe.[41] Gray probably never saw a copy of the instructions prepared by the board. Governor Mason came to New York in October to try to forget a major scandal and to get married.[42] He gave the substance of the instructions to Gray, explaining gently that the board considered as "premature" the exclusively scientific library which Gray envisaged, but giving permission to purchase any specialized works which might be hard to get later. He suggested that Gray's report discuss the "literary institutions of Europe" in connection with the University of Michigan. Zina Pitcher had urged Gray to throw his "best efforts into" this phase of his journey.[43] In spite of the title of professor of botany, Gray thus found himself the general agent of an unspecialized college. Had he construed his instructions as they seemed to be intended, he would have toured Europe examining the universities in much the same manner as Horace Mann would soon observe and report on the elementary schools. Instead he adopted

72

a policy of cheerful conformity to the letter of his orders while bending all his thought and energy to his own botanical objectives.

In the space of two years Gray had sought a living as a botanist from three sources. The private society in the form of New York Lyceum had barely kept his body and soul together. The federal government had offered to pay well and to provide unprecedented experience, but delay and confusion had nearly worried him to distraction. Now the state government with its ideal of a university for all the people was giving him an unusual chance.

ENVOY TO EUROPE

As the packet ship *Pennsylvania* moved through the Narrows on November 9, 1838, Asa Gray wrote a last note to his mother by the pilot boat and prepared for a "fine time to rest." Fortunately the ship had delayed for several days because of weather, because only by working day and night had he been able to complete his packing. His mid-Atlantic twenty-eighth birthday found him smooth-shaven with a face still boyishly slim. But he was no mere graduate student seeking crumbs of knowledge from the great. Professor Hooker, now Sir William, had assured him a welcome as an "excellent Brother Botanist." Joseph Henry even warned him of the heady effects of discovering that those "we have long considered almost more than human" are "but men inferior perhaps in some respects to ourselves." [1] Nor was he a mere book buyer for a possible university. Rather he was both a promising botanical author in his own right and the chosen colleague of Torrey, who had the best European reputation of all American botanists. The first part of the *Flora of North America* had preceded its junior author and the second was on its way.

Gray's objective was, first, to wrest from Europe control of the source material on North American plants by resolving disputed points of nomenclature and establishing the *Flora* as the authoritative base for future work. Second, he wished to establish channels of continuous communication so that a botanist in America could know enough of what was going on in the world to do first-rate work, and when he had done it to gain recognition everywhere. William Starling Sullivant, a wealthy amateur in Ohio who had commissioned Gray to buy a microscope for him, felt that his mission was "exactly what was required for the botany of this country." [2] John Torrey was confident that his young friend, embarked on a diplomatic mission in behalf of all American workers in botany, would "make a good impression wherever he meets with men who are capable of appreciating him." [3]

When he landed at Liverpool on Saturday, December 1, 1838, he tarried only long enough for a lonesome Sabbath before becoming an indefatigable tourist. On visiting Chester, which according to his guidebook had been founded while "Ahab governed Israel," he made a circuit of the walls before breakfast and had all the proper emotions when reflecting on "the vestiges of Roman occupancy." Everything in view he assiduously compared with New York. The ferryboats were inferior, and the elaborate docks would be unnecessary "as we always have plenty of water," but the profuse ivy and a "coach and four with postilions" impressed him. To remove any possibility of a provincial look he ordered a new coat, which after the fashion of the day had a high collar. By the time he had his land legs he was off for Glasgow to see Hooker, for "no one else abroad is so rich in North American botany or takes so much interest in it." [4]

Living at the Hookers' "truly hospitable mansion" Gray felt quite at home. Joseph, the son of twenty-one years who was just then pushing to qualify as a surgeon on an exploring expedition, was at home studying botany.[5] Gray ignored the sights of the city and with scarcely a moment away from the herbarium worked for twenty days beside Sir William, "one of Nature's noblemen."

The young American was in Scotland only in body, for his mind ranged constantly to the great western reaches of North America which were represented in Sir William's collections. Before Gray left New York he and Torrey had studied the plants brought back from the transcontinental wanderings of Thomas Nuttall, the erstwhile lecturer at Harvard, and through these specimens they had glimpsed a botanical empire in the Rocky Mountains, the Oregon country, and California. Hooker not only had received most of Nuttall's plants in various trades, but had a great accumulation of specimens from his own collectors in western North America. For instance, Torrey and Gray had named but not yet published the new genus *Nuttallia,* a shrub found on the Columbia. They had

75

seen only Nuttall's specimen and an earlier imperfect one.[6] Now in Glasgow Gray found the same plant in the collections of David Douglas, Dr. M. Gairdner, and in a group of specimens from the Snake River collected by John McLeod and sent by the Hudson's Bay agent at Fort Nisqually (Puget Sound), Dr. W. F. Tolmie.[7]

This collection was an indication of the strategy necessary for further botanical exploration. The Hudson's Bay Company territories, the Missouri and Columbia rivers, and the coast of California had been explored by several collectors. But the Great Basin, the Colorado Plateau, and all the southern Rockies were almost wholly unknown. The plants of McLeod which Dr. Tolmie sent, one of which Hooker called *Grayia,* came from the Snake River and as far inland as the old trappers' rendezvous on the upper Green River. Sir William had seen that they opened a new territory and with international impartiality urged the men of the "Hudson's Bay and American Companies" to spend their leisure in collecting.[8]

Gray, besides being quick to grasp the potentialities of the unknown center of western North America, also found impressive the financial support which Hooker arranged for his collectors. Specimens seemed to have a good market value in Europe. Accordingly he called on Torrey for quick action, urging that Dr. Peter Knieskern, a local collector and old Fairfield graduate, "make the excursion to Santa Fe in the coming spring." Since regular annual transportation with the traders was possible, a collector could reach the heart of the southern Rockies quickly. It sounded very easy, and Gray was confident that if Knieskern worked hard "he will make $1000 clear of expenses!" But from Woodside Crescent in Glasgow, distance blurred the harsh realities of the wilderness. No mere excursion would wrest many plants from the bastion of North America.

Gray set out from Glasgow by stage, skirting the highlands through Stirling and Perth to Kinross, where Hooker's colleague G. A. Walker Arnott awaited him. His old love for Sir Walter Scott came back to him in Rob Roy's country, but he was ever the American traveler. "If 'Jessie the flower of Dumblane' lived in one of these comfortless and wretched hovels I'll warrant her charms are much overpraised." Although he had no use for "dirty Scotch villages," ruins of all kinds impressed him, and he never tired of seeing the numberless places in Scotland associated with the "lovely and ill-fated Mary Queen of Scots."

After a few days spent "very pleasantly indeed" with Arnott, Gray approached his first real European center of learning. Edinburgh, with its long record as a mecca for Americans seeking advanced training and its strong Presbyterian flavor, was a good place to start. In fact, Gray had long breathed this very same intellectual atmosphere, for example, from the *Edinburgh Encyclopaedia*. Well armed with letters of introduction, he planned his campaign carefully, first calling on the botanist R. K. Greville, who insisted on his being a house guest. Here he felt quite comfortable among a family of "much true Christian feeling and simplicity"—precisely the environment he always sought in strange places. With congenial headquarters and a host to arrange calls, dinners, and social breakfasts the visitor met the other botanists of the city—Robert Graham, William Nicoll, and J. H. Balfour, who was about Gray's own age. Since the Edinburgh collections contained few North American plants, he was free to attend lectures at the university. He sampled everything from Christopher North Wilson on the association of ideas and Dr. Thomas Chalmers on "Scripture criticism" to Sir Charles Bell on surgery and James Forbes on natural philosophy. It rather amazed Gray that Forbes, only thirty years old, had long since beaten out the encyclopedist Dr. David Brewster for a professorship. Not all that he heard pleased him. Robert Jameson's "dull, doleful" lecture was just like the table of contents of a book, and "I may add just as interesting." The chemistry experiments he saw were "few but rather neat."

As he "ran about the streets," Gray tried not to miss a monument worth seeing or a person worth meeting. He had "pleasant conversation with all," and doubtless made a good impression by being alert and courteous. Even here in his first real experience with European learned men he showed neither a parochially closed mind nor indiscriminate adulation.

From Edinburgh Gray took a stagecoach through Scott's country, visiting Abbotsford and Melrose Abbey, which was "just in that state of dilapidation in which it appears to the greatest ad-

vantage as a ruin. . . ." He felt himself identified with Scott's characters, crossing the Tweed "where the White Lady frightened the
Sacristan in the Monastery." So close was his feeling of personal intimacy with the novelist that in his journal he described at length
the troubles of Scott's last years. Since Gray's business was not romantic reverie, he hurried on, passing by several ruins, to New-
castle. Pausing just long enough to visit the natural history society,
he arranged for correspondence with the Michigan State Survey—
probably a routine request he made whenever he came upon geologists.

At the great cathedral city of Durham, Gray visited Professor
James T. W. Johnston, a chemist. The asperity of his remarks about
Durham University indicates that, after leaving Edinburgh, Michigan's observer had already made up his mind not to waste much
time on institutions of higher learning. "I can't express . . . the
profound contempt I feel for the English University system of education." Although promising in some respects, Durham had
"adopted the monkish system of Oxford and Cambridge to the fullest extent." Most of the professors were clergymen, and the curriculum included "nothing but classics, a little mathematics, and less
logic." The professor of natural philosophy never lectured, and no
one had to attend the classes of the poorly paid teacher of chemistry,
mineralogy, and geology. Gray's educational philosophy was fundamentally a simple desire for more and better science at all levels of
schooling. This had been the basis of his plans while in Detroit,
and the Old World in no way influenced him.

On January 16, 1839, Gray arrived at London, "this modern
Babylon," stopping at the White Bear, Piccadilly. Following Torrey's tracks he immediately looked up Dr. Francis Boott, a member
of a new dynasty of Massachusetts capitalists who found it congenial to practice medicine in London and study sedges on the side.
Gray could depend on him as a fellow countryman to ease the
strangeness of the great city. Throughout his stay he called regularly at the Boott home and found the doctor's mother, wife, and
three daughters always cordial. Acceptance in this household meant
pleasant evenings in London, but its more profound importance
stemmed from the Boott family's standing in New England, where

they were closely allied in business with the Lowells. Gray here came within the notice, limited but favorable, of Boston society.

His first day in London he could not let pass without seeing the greatest botanist in England, Robert Brown. Far from feeling abashed at the prospect, Gray showed his *savoir faire* by the speed with which he sensed that Brown preferred Mr. to Dr. as a title. On arriving at the British Museum the young American found not only "the man himself" but with him Sir William Hooker and Joseph, down from Scotland, along with the Arctic explorer Sir John Richardson. When the Glasgow professor immediately took Gray in tow, it was the beginning of a two months' whirl through a great scientific capital.

Gray's years of close study of plants now paid dividends. He had reached a plane on which he could take for granted a knowledge of the fundamentals of his science and concentrate first on meeting men, second on studying unique material, and third on learning directly of recent researches. With Sir William to guide him to the true sources of botanical information immediately, Gray wasted no time in false starts and never failed to get entrance to a library or herbarium through lack of an introduction. In the early part of his stay he was constantly in the company of Joe Hooker, with whom he now became really acquainted. The Ross expedition to the Antarctic was in the air, and young Joseph was planning to win his spurs as Darwin had on the *Beagle.*

Robert Brown, heir of Sir Joseph Banks, held court with a very select company at the British Museum, and while nobody forgot for a moment that Humboldt had dubbed him *Botanicorum facile princeps,* he ruled by brilliance rather than great labor.[9] Young Gray found him "very fond of gossip at his own fireside," amusing with his dry wit, and as to botany "he knows everything!" Quick to size up a "peculiar" fellow, Gray realized that he could not "ask him directly any question about plants," because Brown was "the driest pump imaginable." Undiscouraged, the American undertook by "coaxing and careful management" to get information. Not only did he succeed in obtaining some very acute judgments on taxonomic questions, but he also induced Brown to go over his old notes on the development of the embryo. Thus while the great botanist "read his newspaper and cracked his jokes" his visitor was gleaning pearls. Before Gray left, he had Brown toying with the idea of a journey to the United States.

George Bentham, a much more comfortable acquaintance, was hardly less instructive. He was the son of Sir Samuel Bentham, who as naval architect, soldier of fortune in the service of Catherine II, and a British representative to Russia during the Napoleonic Wars was worthy of the colorful times in which he lived. George had preferred the tradition of the family represented by his Uncle Jeremy, and he not only received legal training but also wrote an ambitious treatise on logic before giving his whole attention to the botanical interests bequeathed him by his mother. Now financially independent, he and his wife lived quietly in Jeremy Bentham's elegant house in London when not traveling on the Continent. In his own notable herbarium he gathered authoritative collections on the families of which he prepared monographs.[10] January 1839 marked not only his first acquaintance with Gray, but also the effective beginning of a friendship with Joseph Hooker. He thought his American visitor, ten years his junior, "a zealous botanist, and of a good deal of talent." [11] Gray could step into a cosmopolitan's drawing room which had recently known Jeremy Bentham as the host, drink Assam tea, and appreciate the dinner as a "beau ideal of taste and simple elegance." Gray and George Bentham were close enough in age and temperament to fall quickly to working long evenings together. Bentham was studying plants collected by Theodore Hartweg, who had penetrated far into North Mexico, thus bracketing Gray's no man's land of the Rockies on the south.

John Lindley, whose books had meant so much to Gray in his earlier days, appeared a "rather difficult person to deal with," and the visitor determined to let the older man make the advances. Somewhat to Gray's surprise, Lindley obliged handsomely, inviting him to spend a day at his house in Chiswick. The host proving "certainly very civil," Gray looked over his collection. A few days later Lindley was able to confer a real favor by arranging access to Thomas Walter's eighteenth-century collection of Carolina plants, then still in private hands. The rules for handling specimens were so informal that the American was allowed to snip off characteristic parts of the original specimens to take home with him. This practice enabled Gray to carry part of Europe's superiority to America in small envelopes.[12]

Of other botanists Gray saw a great many, learning what he could from each. David Don, A. B. Lambert ("the queerest old mortal I ever set eyes on"), Conrad Loddiges, and John J. Bennett helped him cordially. N. B. Ward, who had invented a case for preserving live plants, entertained the visitor repeatedly, since he "seems to have taken a fancy to me." Two aged men linked Gray directly to the eighteenth century. Archibald Menzies had seen the northwest coast of America with Captain George Vancouver in 1792. Now he was a "pleasant and kind-hearted old man" who had the young American come to dinner. At Kew Gardens, Gray found Francis Bauer, botanical illustrator to George III, still hard at work at eighty-five making drawings "beyond comparison excellent."

In a less comprehensive way Gray met some scientists besides botanists. J. E. Gray, the zoologist at the British Museum, gave him tickets to a lecture by Michael Faraday at the Royal Institution. The subject of electric eels gave this modest and "pleasant man" full opportunity to impress an American both as a "most elegant lecturer" and a "brilliant and rapid experimenter." Gray dined with Peter Mark Roget, who was a scientist and secretary of the Royal Society as well as author of the *Thesaurus*. Charles Lyell he met, but evidently with no real continuing spark of friendship. Much more impressive at the time was Sir Astley Cooper, fabulously popular surgeon and lecturer on anatomy.

One morning Gray and Joe Hooker went to the College of Surgeons to see the great Hunterian Museum, which was the best the American traveler had seen. Their primary object was to pay respects to Professor Richard Owen, but in the course of the visit they "there met Mr. Darwin, the naturalist who accompanied Captain King [*sic*] in the Beagle." The heavy-browed young explorer made small impression compared with Owen, a "profound scientific scholar," whom Gray thought "the best comparative anatomist living, still young, and one of the most mild, gentle, childlike men I ever saw." Twenty-one years later Olympian thunder would have accompanied a meeting of Darwin, Owen, Hooker, and Gray. The native of Sauquoit felt no foreboding that these men would mold momentous issues, nor had he any inkling that Darwin would one day seem the giant.

In his general sightseeing Gray was fortunate that Sir Francis Palgrave, Sir William Hooker's brother-in-law, took him in hand. The "great antiquarian and Saxon scholar, Keeper of the Records, of whom I have read so much in the 'British Review,' " showed him the Domesday Book and other breath-taking documents, such as "the original papal bull sent to Henry VIII, constituting him 'Defender of the Faith.' " In repayment Gray set Sir Francis straight on the definition of that strange Americanism, locofoco. Besides guidebook stops at inevitable places, St. Paul's and Westminster Abbey, the tourist sooner or later attended sessions of the House of Commons and the House of Lords. Both were notable bodies only seven years after the great reform crisis. He heard Lord John Russell, Sir Robert Peel, and "others too tedious to enumerate." Everything that came into his view he assimilated easily, still maintaining a balanced attitude, neither blasé nor naïve.

On Sundays, however, Gray dropped completely out of the brilliant society of the rest of the week, and sought out dissenting church services as best he could. He regretted that he had not brought letters of recommendation to "some pious people and ministers here." Failing to find his own denomination, he resorted to the established church, where he waxed enthusiastic about Baptist Noel, whose sermons were the "most thoroughly evangelical and earnest I ever heard from an Episcopal pulpit." Although willing thus to experiment with the Church of England, he made his most sincere pilgrimage to the chapel of the great colonial revivalist, George Whitefield. It recalled to him "more interesting associations than Westminster Abbey or any vast and splendid cathedral."

Toward the end of February, Gray began to work steadily at the various herbaria containing North American plants. Housed in London, the herbarium of Linnaeus, who had his own network of correspondents in the colonies, was very important to Gray. The British Museum also had many early collections, such as that of John Clayton, on which Gronovius based his *Flora Virginica*. Sir Joseph Banks's herbarium, in addition to its plants, gave Gray many ideas on mounting and storing dried specimens. Lambert possessed the collections of Frederick Pursh, whose earlier *Flora of North America* set important precedents. Gray examined the plants, taking careful notes and revising his own judgments on names and classifications.

The commission from Sullivant of Ohio to buy a microscope led to his association with yet another group of scientists who contributed greatly to his education. William Valentine and Edwin J. Queckett gave him detailed demonstrations with their instruments, as did, of course, Robert Brown. By the time the young botanist had attended a few "microscopical parties," he was able to discriminate between the lenses of the various makers, and he learned much about the many discoveries resulting from the recent development of the achromatic microscope. Since he always tried to reciprocate in any way possible, he gave to his hosts some specimens which Lieutenant Bailey of West Point had fortunately prepared for him. Gray never thought of himself as a mendicant seeking Europe's knowledge for nothing. His aim was to set up a free exchange even though he could not yet repay full value.

As Gray found his way about scientific London, he gained considerably in that sophistication which can only come from acquaintance with timely and authoritative professional gossip. For instance, Nees von Esenbeck, hitherto a valued German correspondent, enjoyed none too high a reputation in England, partly because "although very old and terribly ugly he contrived to run off from Bonn with some fellow-professor's wife!" Of more direct consequence was the discovery that Corda's *Memoir,* which Gray had labored hard to translate, "turns out to be mere humbug." Henceforth the provincial would have friends to warn him of the pitfalls even in formally impeccable literature.

Visiting these opulent British botanists also confirmed Gray's hopes for the exploration of western North America. He was now certain that a collector who went into the unknown southern Rockies could make both his expenses and a profit by selling specimens. "I know how all this should be managed now." The field man should continue Gray's grass book and others like it. In addition, he should make up fifty sets of all his plants, publishing monographs on them to assure priority as he distributed them to subscribers. Doubtless Gray hoped not only to put Knieskern into the field but ultimately to go himself.

Gray made one friend in London who performed for him providential service. All the enthusiastic botanical study and palaver left almost no time for the considerable job of shopping for general books for the University of Michigan. The second part of volume one of Torrey and Gray's *Flora* was due in London at about the same time as its junior author at the office of Wiley & Putnam in Paternoster Row. George Palmer Putnam, younger than Gray and like him a Yankee who had made good on his own in New York, was then opening the London end of a notable transatlantic book trade.[13] After one or two business parleys the two visited the House of Lords together, and in the latter part of Gray's sojourn their friendship quickened. Before the botanist left London he had arranged with the bookseller to keep his eye out for titles suitable for a college library. By the time Gray had spent several months on the Continent the purchases would be almost complete. In this way the traveler not only freed himself for his important scientific work, but also secured for the university an agent admirably equipped by omnivorous reading and a thorough knowledge of the international book trade.

When on the nasty, rainy morning of March 14, 1839, Gray, far behind on his sleep, boarded a grubby channel steamer for Boulogne, he had accomplished many of the essential purposes of his tour. Besides studying the North American plants in British herbaria, he had arranged for his purchase of books. Even more important, his hosts, among the most distinguished botanists of Europe, had placed themselves lastingly at his service. Dr. Francis Boott, still enough of a Yankee to consider Gray his compatriot, wrote to Torrey that the young man had "left a bright remembrance behind in us all. His simplicity and integrity of mind with fine great insight to all he does" was evident to the doctor. "I pray God he may live long to build up a reputation honourable to our country." [14] Behind was solid accomplishment; ahead lay the "semi-heathen" shore of the realm of Louis Philippe.

In Paris, Gray repeated his London routine. His ardor was at first somewhat dampened by the strange language, because he was able only to produce "such French as has not been heard since the days of King Pepin." He continued to keep his appearance "rather spruce" as in London, although he found that "gentlemen in Paris dress anyhow." By consistently refusing many invitations he preserved his Sundays, but he was enthusiastic about his hosts the other six days. Only when he visited services at Notre Dame and St. Sulpice did a note of rancor enter his thoughts about the French. Generally he was much more flexible and friendly in his attitude than was Joe Hooker, who would make the same sort of botanical sojourn six years later.[15]

Gray's most useful acquaintance in Paris was P. Barker Webb, a wealthy Englishman who after much travel had settled in France to work on a natural history of the Canary Islands. Webb was a "polyglot," speaking French, Spanish, Portuguese, Italian, modern Greek, and "I know not what besides his mother tongue." In addition to talk of botany and an immense herbarium, the young visitor could always find at the Englishman's house a good cup of tea, a bachelor's party, and a great deal of help with linguistic problems.

Among the French botanists Gray made the rounds, managing friendly intercourse even when there was no common spoken language. At the Jardin des Plantes, Joseph Decaisne, a quiet scientist only a little his elder, was a most pleasant and helpful working partner. Adrien de Jussieu, bearer of a great name, was also a cordial friend. Gray also met many others, and some, such as Benjamin Delessert, placed the great private collections of Paris at his disposal.

Shopping for microscopes again gave opportunities for lessons in plant physiology. J. F. C. Montagne, retired army officer and now a moss expert, showed the latest and best instruments made by Charles Chevalier. Since the building of microscopes was still an individual art, Gray's increasing ability to distinguish the best points of the products of each maker was a necessary accomplishment. More important, he was able to meet Charles P. B. Mirbel, who explained to the young American his views. The veteran plant physiologist patiently and clearly described "how the curious thickening . . . of the walls of cells takes place by the development of new cells within the old." He gave Gray a paper in which he "has completely upset the new-fangled views of Schleiden, Unger, etc." Although M. J. Schleiden had published the year before the "Beitrage zur Phytogenesis," the young American first heard of these researches only second-hand from Mirbel and Robert Brown. So strong was Gray's initial impression that even in later years he gave Mirbel more credit than Schleiden for the elucidation of the cell theory.[16] Certainly in the welter of confused and often erroneous ideas out of which this great scientific discovery came it was not easy to spot the particular interpretations which would later gain general acceptance.

In studying the North American plants preserved in Paris, Gray indulged in a small piece of bravado. Among the collections of the French explorer, André Michaux, who journeyed through the southern United States between 1787 and 1807, Gray found a specimen which was after all the intervening years unclassified. On examining it carefully he decided it was a new genus. "I claim the right of a discoverer to affix the name." Since it came "from near Kentucky, it shall be christened Shortia," after Dr. Charles Wilkins Short.[17] This little discovery, besides incidentally showing that Gray worked over the North American plants at Paris more carefully than had the French themselves, dramatized to him another "great unknown region, the high mountains of North Carolina." The southern Appalachians, like the southern Rockies, stood out as a region ripe for botanical conquest.

When Gray boarded the mail coach for Lyons at Paris in mid-April, 1839, he was striking into completely new territory. Up to this point he had followed pretty much in Torrey's footsteps. Now, with only instructions from George Bentham to guide him,[18] he began a grand tour of southern France, Italy, and Austria to Vienna, where he would again take up botany. All along the way were scientists and gardens to visit and microscopes through which to peer, but few North American plant specimens. The real business of this leg of his journey was culture. With a copy of Byron and Samuel Rogers's *Italy* at hand Gray saw antiquity through romantic eyes. As an American abroad, he was as reverent if not as reflective as an Emerson, as scholarly if narrower in his interests than a George

Bancroft, as appreciative as any of the many Harvard-trained Lowells who made the family tour of Europe.

At Nîmes, a favorite spot of Thomas Jefferson's, Gray, standing in the amphitheatre, found it required "no great stretch of the imagination to repeople [it] . . . with the ancient inhabitants . . . and to fill the arena with savage beasts tearing each other in pieces. . . ." At Montpellier, where he visited Bentham's mother, he saw at the once great university one of the oldest botanic gardens in Europe. But in a fit of homesickness he became impatient and pushed on to his next stop, Italy.

Genoa, Leghorn (with a side trip to Pisa), Civita Vecchia by sea, and then he reached Rome, where his enthusiasm fully returned. Guidebook [19] in hand he missed none of the sights. With an ailing English clergyman as companion, he saw not only the glories of antiquity but also "Popery in its true colors," disapproval of which did not keep him from being profoundly impressed by St. Peter's. Viewing the Apollo Belvedere, the Laocoön, and the Dying Gladiator, Gray compared the originals with the descriptions in *Childe Harold*. He left Rome with the feeling that he had been close to one of the wellsprings of civilization. Still, it was good to find on his way back to Florence an American ship, which took aboard two hats for Dr. Torrey and many engravings of the old masters for the rest of the family.

In Florence, Gray called on the great microscopist, C. B. Amici, who had charge of the grand duke's observatory. By this time, however, the wandering American had become a sophisticate in the matter of microscopes. Amici thought his instruments "unrivaled, but I don't." Gray also considered that while the Italian was a good observer "his anatomical or physiological notions are in some cases very wide of the mark, and quite surprised me." From time to time the traveler allowed himself reflections on European government, and he found the regime of the grand duke of Tuscany despotic but paternal, much more to his taste than what he observed in the Papal States or the lands of Austria. He paused to reflect on Machiavelli, and on Galileo and the Inquisition.

By land Gray crossed rapidly from Florence to Venice. At Bologna, "a city famous for its university and its sausages," he found "the former decayed almost to nothing, the latter still in great demand, diffusing their abominable garlic odor from every table." At Padua he saw the botanic garden, "the most ancient in Italy." That Venice from a distance reminded him of New York "as you approach from Amboy," showed that he was still an American. But by now he thought the best education for a family would be this "peripatetic way." It would be best "for those who have time and means sufficient . . . to study the history of each place on the spot with all its monuments and relics around them."

After reaching Trieste by boat, Gray had a long journey to Vienna, its tedium relieved only by seeing a fete at the Adelsberg grotto and by the company of a young American painter named Philip, who knew some German. Stephen Ladislaus Endlicher, "extremely good-looking," who although only six years older than Gray had already begun a comprehensive *Genera Plantarum*, received his visitor cordially and in English. Under his friendly guidance Gray spent a pleasant twelve days seeing all the collections and gardens of the city and meeting the botanical lords of an earlier day, J. F. von Jacquin and Karl Hügel. By chance he met A. J. C. Corda, visiting from Prague, and found the young man mainly occupied with the study of fungi. Time enough was left over for sightseeing and hearing the band led by "the most celebrated musician here, Mr. Strauss. . . . It was the best music I ever heard."

By degrees Gray was becoming more polished, more at home in strange places, more able to put local differences in the background while recognizing the international brotherhood of science. But his travels changed his fundamental outlook little. Vaguely aware that his religion remained strait-laced compared with the easy ways of the Continent, he pleaded fatigue when Endlicher invited him to an opera, remarking that "I suppose it would be perfectly impossible to make him understand how one could have any scruples against this amusement." In a more profound way Vienna really shocked him into pausing to appreciate after all the easygoing American indifference to science. Americans had long since developed the dual attitude toward science. On one hand democracy militated against patrician support. On the other hand republican institutions gave science freedom and a unique opportunity. Gray found that every book had to be submitted to a censor "who knows as much about it as if it were written in Arabic, and who certifies to each portion that it contains nothing offensive to the emperor, to religion, etc., and more than all, that it is good science." Endlicher himself had fallen afoul this rule when he had used the natural system before Jacquin, the censor, had switched from the Linnaean. Gray now saw more clearly the necessity for freedom of thought and action governed only by the ethics of the profession itself.

After ascending the Danube to Linz he took a horse-drawn railway to Gmünden, then on to Ischl in the Austrian Alps. Stopping over a day he climbed the Zeimitz, "the highest in the neighborhood," and, besides a magnificent view, "imagine my pleasure at collecting alpine plants for the first time, some of them in full blossom under the very edge of a snowbank." Both the mountains and the "kindhearted simplicity of the people" in these regions pleased him, but it was already June, and he was again so restless to be moving toward home that he hurried through Salzburg and on to Munich.

Each of Gray's major stops was carefully designed for some botanical purpose. Munich's university and library would scarcely have attracted him had not a great authority on the plants of Brazil been there. C. F. P. von Martius, although weighed down by a professorship and duties as director of the botanic garden "for which he is most miserably paid," nevertheless did the honors handsomely. As a special treat he invited Gray to a picnic celebrating the birthday of Linnaeus. Working in the herbarium the young botanist at least glimpsed the forests of Brazil.

In a completely unplanned and unexpected way Gray first touched at Munich one of the elements which would eventually find a place in his greatest piece of scientific theorizing. No *a priori* reason directed an American's attention especially to the flora of eastern Asia, nor would Gray have tarried in Bavaria in the hope of gaining knowledge of Japan. Yet here he met J. G. Zuccarini, who had assisted the traveler and scientist Philip Franz von Siebold work up the plants of Japan. Always on the alert to contribute a bit of knowledge where he could, Gray named Zuccarini's American *Cyperaceae* and in return received the offer of the *Flora Japonica,* "which is an expensive work, but it is very desirable for us to have, though it will be rather difficult for me to give him an equivalent." Perhaps after all Gray was seeing as much of the world as his friends on the expedition.

At Zurich, Switzerland, the traveler, sending his trunk ahead, became a hiker. With "my knapsack on my back, the Guide to Switzerland in one pocket, and Keller's excellent map in the other, I set out on my travels in search of the sublime." Except for the occasional aid of a lake steamer or other conveyance he walked, sometimes at the clip of thirty miles a day. Over the Rigi and the Joch to Meiringen, he continued to circle into the high peaks to Grindelwald. Mountains were just coming into their own both as scenery and sport, and Gray had the delicious feeling that he was among their discoverers. Of the valley of Engleberg, "the most beautiful and picturesque I have seen," he thought it probable that "I am the first American that has visited it." After a Sunday in the snow of the Grimsel, "perhaps the wildest and grandest pass across the Alps," he rapidly descended to the Valais, the broad smiling valley of the Rhone. Finally on reaching Geneva he returned again to the world of scholars. Augustin-Pyramus De Candolle and his son Alphonse welcomed the wanderer into their home. "You cannot know how pleasant it is, after being jolted about in the rude world for months, to get again with a pious family."

By working through the De Candolles' great herbarium as far as they had carried their great inclusive *Flora* of the world, the *Prodromus,*[20] Gray saw a great many important type specimens. The father, who remembered well the Paris of the Directorate and also America's earlier gift to science, Count Rumford, was nearing the end of a most distinguished career. The son, only a little older than Gray, was just reaching the professional stature necessary to carry on the tradition of a great scientific family.[21] In seeing the herbarium specimens which formed the basis of the *Prodromus* Gray had an authoritative introduction to one of the great monuments of nineteenth-century scholarship. As the Hookers, father and son, were to be Gray's most intimate and useful British friends, the De Candolles were his most important acquaintances on the Continent.

As the traveler left Geneva his thoughts turned insistently toward home. For the University of Michigan he depended on Putnam to pull him through adequately. But in addition for himself he had "blocked out, in my mind, scientific labor for several years to come. . . ." With some of these works he definitely planned to attract a wider audience than the few professional and amateur scientists in America. To Putnam he claimed facetiously that as "Murray's fame is derived from Byron, so shall you be immortalized and known to all posterity as the publisher of the celebrated Dr. Gray!!!" [22]

The lamp of science and culture still burned brightly enough so that he conscientiously turned eastward, visiting botanists and the proper sights on his way through Switzerland and Germany to Berlin. In Freiburg he heard the organ. In Tübingen he spent a morning with Hugo von Mohl. In Dresden he saw Professor H. G. Reichenbach and thought the picture gallery "deserves to be called the richest out of Italy." After a day in Halle he reached Berlin where he settled down for nearly a month. There he spent most of his time secluded in the Royal Herbarium at Schöneberg, which was far enough from the city to escape the disturbing presence of "loungers." A "transient illness" kept him down for a week, but J. H. Klotsch, the keeper of the herbarium, took good care of him. Among the collections he saw was that of Humboldt, in the herbarium of K. S. Kunth. Abandoning a plan to see Lamarck's herbarium at Rostock, Gray returned westward to Hamburg for a few days with his old correspondent Lehmann before sailing to London. [23]

In England, "from which there are but two steps home, on board a ship, and off again," Gray worked furiously to complete his book purchases for the Michigan library. With the aid of Putnam he was successful in buying a "large collection." The many botanical works he had picked up on his travels were all on his own account, and the university's books were truly a general library. [24] Gray went down to Portsmouth on the last day of September and on October 1 stood to sea in the ship *Toronto*. He was somewhat disappointed that the steamer *Great Western* passed them on the way, making her passage in less than half the thirty-five days required under sail.

On November 4, through "the favors of a kind Providence, my journey is safely brought to a close." [25]

Personally Gray's year of travel was a great success. He had met a large and brilliant group of European scientists and won their respect. Not only did he round out his education looking through microscopes and ransacking herbaria, but he broadened his horizons in the Louvre and the Pitti Palace. Besides feeling the spell of nature in Switzerland, he gained new insight into the spirit of his time by considering the works of Scott and Byron in their original settings. He returned in many ways quite unchanged—his basic ideas, his religion. Even his manners were only somewhat improved, for he had become no foppish George Bancroft kissing astonished clergymen on both cheeks in the Continental manner. But from this point he had every claim to be considered a learned man of the world. The graduate of a country medical school who had never gone to college was henceforth a *savant*. The few in America who might have challenged him in breadth of culture and experience claimed him instead as their peer.

In the cause of science Gray solidly accomplished his objectives. The United States now possessed for the first time a botanist so familiar with the North American material housed in Europe that he could do authoritative work. This comprehensive view was no accident. No amount of travel or amiable intercourse with botanists could have prepared Gray as his journey actually did. Through his preliminary work on the *Flora* he knew what he wanted to see, and he went after it systematically. Also European botanists now recognized that the United States had a competent team to whom they could apply with confidence for information on North American plants. In accepting Gray as a colleague they received his and Torrey's enterprise into the organization of international science. The ambassador had effected an unwritten trade treaty good for many years which established in the eyes of the world America's right to explore its own plant life.

LAST YEARS
OF UNCERTAINTY

ALTHOUGH Gray landed in New York expecting immediate instructions from the University of Michigan, he soon learned that troubles there made his services unwanted. The depression begun by the Panic of 1837 had discouraged even the exuberant promoters at Detroit, and Gray's friend Governor Mason received most of the blame. The branches had drawn off assets, and most of the cash available to the regents went into interest on a debt to the state. Gray while still in Europe had sensed that some of his hopes were unjustified when Torrey and Henry failed to hear anything concerning professorships. He had, it is true, received during the previous summer a second year's salary as an advance for buying books on his own account,[1] a drain of fifteen hundred dollars which no doubt impressed the regents. In hard times a scientist was a luxury, and the university could have little use for a botanist when the prospects of even opening its doors were dim. Hence the regents did not invite Gray to report for duty, and in April 1840, they wrote asking their first professor to "assent to a suspension of his salary" for a year.[2]

Gray, who cared more for research than money, agreed, sending the library books on to Ann Arbor. A committee which examined the purchases—Schoolcraft, Pitcher, and George Duffield—reported that "the trust committed to Dr. Gray has been executed in a manner which reflects much credit upon his judgment and discrimination in selection and cost." The purchases consisted of thirty-seven hundred volumes "embracing the various departments

of history, philosophy, classical literature, sciences and arts, juris-
prudence, etc." An average cost of one dollar and twenty-five cents
a volume was indeed reasonable for "works which could not be obtained in America and many of the editions are scarce and rare in
Europe." [3] The regents were so harassed that they probably had no
more desire to read a report on European higher education than
Gray had to write one, and the whole idea dropped quietly out of
sight. When the year's suspension of salary was over in the summer
of 1841, Gray simply heard nothing from Michigan and thus continued in unpaid limbo.

New York offered plenty of botanical opportunities. On the surface Gray's life settled into a routine not unlike that of the years
before 1837—hard work on science which yielded him reputation
but no pay. A friend saw him as always happy. "There is no ingenious combination of disagreeable circumstances that can de-
press your whale-bone sinews & your gum elastic spirit." Witness
"your little den in the medical college; all alone, hot hard coal fire
in a dirty box stove, surrounded by dead and decaying vegetable
matter, making no money, working like a dog, no pretty wife, no
sweet little ones—and yet *credat Judaeus,* who so happy as thou?"
Although he had spent most of his government money on publishing the *Flora* and most of his Michigan earnings on books and
traveling, he had enough to live on for a while. Because the "financial state of the whole country is very bad, and almost everything
stands still" [4] Gray could see little chance of another job.

But in some ways his position had changed. Torrey was as usual
occupied with the "lecturing business," and in addition to studying
the plants and writing the *Flora,* Gray undertook three new regular
functions which were a part of his increasing eminence as an
American scientist. The first, of course, was the continuation of the
friendly relations he had established in Europe. Second, he took
over from Torrey the main burden of recruiting American botanists
to contribute to the *Flora.* Third, he gained an abiding place in the
pages of the *American Journal of Science,* both to introduce new
literature appearing in Europe and to appraise the works of American botanists.

The benefits of his journey of 1838–39 now became more evident. Thanks to "books and specimens, as well as valuable notes I find that I can work with much better advantage," [5] and he regretted having published any of the *Flora* in 1838. Constant correspondence with his European friends, such as Sir William Hooker and Bentham, afforded him good counsel on taxonomic problems, and he even borrowed a whole section of Hooker's herbarium—the large and complicated family of *Compositae*. Gray discovered that free exchange could not supply him with everything he needed— "often do I wish to be within reach of your herbarium and library"—and in spite of the advent of steam nearly three months could go by without a transatlantic mail.[6] Gray kept up the American end of the trade not only by letters and parcels of plants but by the promise of the *Flora*. In the spring of 1840 volume one was complete, and by March 1842 he had progressed to page 392 in volume two.

Some of the subjects Gray had found of great interest in Europe were tempting to pursue at home. In another age he could have with profit followed up his introduction to microscopy and plant physiology. Even more inviting were problems in geographical botany. Alphonse De Candolle wrote him asking about the effect of the destruction of the forests in America on the climate. Although Gray recognized the question as "still unanswered," he feared that for "a year or two I shall not be able to pay any attention to these subjects except to collect materials." Since Gray was working for nothing anyway, economic limitations were no bar to plunging into geographical botany. He was prevented instead by the fact that the basic job of classification had not yet been more than started, much less brought under control. The *Flora* had to come first. "By the time this work is completed we shall have settled somewhat accurately the geographical range of our plants, and have laid a good foundation for the comparison of our flora with that of other regions, etc." [7] Although he here stated precisely both the immediate task and the range of problems he hoped ultimately to consider, he would be ten times the two years in reaching the second stage.

On the domestic front Gray largely took over the direction of Torrey's team of collectors. Even if one of the leaders could be called a professional, the rank and file were still the miscellaneous group of doctors, schoolteachers, clergymen, army officers, and merchants who as a side issue studied the botany of their own locality. By June 1840 seventy-eight Americans, living or recently dead, had sent "plants of particular districts, accompanied in many instances by valuable notes and observations. . . ." [8] They were distributed geographically as follows:

Northeast		*West*	
New England	10	Tennessee	1
New York	14	Kentucky	4
Pennsylvania	3	Illinois	1
Total	27	Indiana	1
		Ohio	4
South and Southwest		Michigan	3
Virginia	1	Wisconsin Terr.	1
North Carolina	3	Canada	5
South Carolina		Rocky Mountains	2
& Georgia	7	Total	22
Florida	9 [9]	Grand total	78
Alabama	3		
Louisiana & Arkansas	6		
Total	29		

Of the three major sections of the United States proper, the Northeast furnished twenty-seven contributors to the South's twenty-nine for a much larger area. Many both in the South and West owed their interest in science to having lived or studied in the Northeast. Hence the welfare of the *Flora,* if it was truly to cover North America, depended on increased activity south of Pennsylvania and west of the Appalachians.

Gray personally took the field in conquest of the South. He wanted to penetrate the high mountains of North Carolina, partly perhaps to confirm his handiwork in naming the genus *Shortia.* Moses Ashley Curtis, Yankee clergyman whose love of learning took the form of collecting the plants of the rural sections of the Carolinas where he lived, warned the New Yorker that "you will be obliged to travel on foot or horse back along intricate cattle paths, and put up with accommodations on the way, *such as you never dreamed of."* When Gray asked for letters of reference, Curtis replied that none would be needed, since "as to several of those mentioned in my former letter, I doubt if they can read." [10]

Leaving New York on June 22, 1841, Gray with John Carey and one James Constable ascended the Valley of Virginia, where they hired a wagon with a single horse and a driver who "proved entirely wanting in the skill and tact necessary for conducting so frail a vehicle over such difficult mountain tracks." They spent most of their time collecting around Jefferson, Ashe County, North Carolina, climbed Grandfather and Roan mountains, and were at times across the line into Tennessee. Gray was still enough of a doctor to spot a local snakebite cure as a holdover from the days of the doctrine of signatures, the plant's root happening to look something like a snake. In late July the party left for New York by way of Raleigh and Richmond. Since they were in the field only a month, the resulting collections were startling neither for novelty nor completeness, but Gray in his report showed a marked interest in the geographic range of various species of plants over large areas of the country, and to deal again with living nature was both refreshing and instructive.

During 1840 Gray picked up a friend who greatly strengthened botanical science in the West. George Engelmann, son of a schoolmaster of Frankfort-am-Main, had had a thorough medical and scientific education in various German universities and at Paris. As some members of his family had joined the incipient migration to the Mississippi Valley, it was natural that he should come to Illinois to look after the land investments of an uncle. At the end of three years traveling about Missouri and Arkansas he settled down to practice medicine in St. Louis. After returning to Germany in 1840 to marry, his interest in science led him to look up Asa Gray when he landed in New York. The Yankee made suggestions about plants Engelmann might find on his way west, and a correspondence sprang up between them. Even the young German doctor's first letter indicated that St. Louis was not just another local station, for he spoke of the plants of Joseph N. Nicollet collected up the Mississippi. Engelmann was in a position to be gatekeeper for all scientists going to the wilderness. Within a year Gray had a working agreement with him to send back notes on specimens of the families currently under study for the *Flora*.[11]

For the present Gray had little or no knowledge of the great stretches west of the organized territory of the United States. Although cactus is an obvious feature of many Western landscapes, Gray had only a few species from along the Missouri and reported that "farther south on both sides of the mountains, Cactaceae doubtless occur in considerable numbers: but on account of the extreme difficulty of preserving and transporting specimens, it is almost impossible to obtain materials for their study." For the whole western half of the continent Gray had only two sources besides what he had seen in Europe. Edwin James, who accompanied Major Stephen H. Long's expedition across the plains to the Rockies, had submitted a small collection of plants to Torrey. Far more important was Nuttall's work. This diffident Yorkshireman had based his principal early travels on Philadelphia in the years before he went to Harvard as curator of its botanic garden in 1823. Ten years later he resigned to make a prodigious journey to the Pacific coast with Nathaniel J. Wyeth. Returning by way of the Hawaiian Islands, the California coast, and Cape Horn, he settled in Philadelphia to study his collections. Here Gray visited him in November of 1840.[12]

Nuttall's eccentricities perhaps led the confident Yankee to misunderstand one of the greatest field explorers of that generation, and the results of their meeting do not make a pretty chapter in the story of American botany.[13] In discussing the disposition of Nuttall's specimens Gray wrote to Sir William Hooker that the collector "ought to send all these to you, but his *amor pecunia* is rather strong." Some such sentiment must have reached Nuttall, who replied tartly with a lecture on transportation—"the *whole distance* of the continent, and then . . . round Cape Horn. . . . If a *pint* of New England rum which costs 12 cents, has to be charged *3 dollars* in the mountains, some idea may be formed of the value of other things dragged on horseback over double such a route."

Gray's visit to Philadelphia happened to come between the delivery of two papers by Nuttall on his *Compositae* before the American Philosophical Society. Since the New Yorker was working on that family throughout this whole period and knew the bibliography of prior studies better than Nuttall, he could point out what he considered earlier names for several genera which the explorer was publishing as new. When the printed version reached Gray's hands, he found that, although some of his suggestions had been followed, he received no credit for them. Nuttall, while halfheartedly apologizing that "your letter came to hand after my paper was printed off and there remained no opportunity of making the acknowledgment you required," clearly thought little of the complaint. When Gray refused to be satisfied, Nuttall defended himself on sundry detailed taxonomic points and went further to accuse Gray of shutting him out of Torrey's herbarium, entry into which "I had thought, in consideration of what I had done, *not in the closet* but in the *field,* entitled to expect." Gray not only denied this indignantly but, unmindful how insufferable it is to be right too often, bored in unmercifully on the taxonomic injuries he claimed Nuttall had done him. The explorer's last letter to Gray continued the discussion, but it was obviously written by a man under great emotional strain, and a paragraph which he immediately reconsidered and struck out states clearly the real drift of the controversy. He requested Torrey to return the set of his plants from the western expedition. "I have sold everything I am able to keep out of debt . . . [and] having given away one set . . . it is as much as I owe to a *country* that never patronized or assisted me in anything and to explore wh I have sacrificed much money and spent nearly my whole life."

Within a few months Nuttall left America to accept a small legacy in Northern England which required him to stay on the estate for nine months of each year. Although he once revisited the United States, he did nothing further in the remaining eighteen years of his life for North American botany. Gray in his published accounts of the plants in question stated his own case in such a way as to conceal his animosity to Nuttall, and their meeting in 1848 was cordial. In 1844, while paying tribute to the explorer in the field, Gray nevertheless hinted that he still disapproved of Nuttall.[14] Although Gray's attack was not the moody collector's only source of trouble and cannot have been a deciding factor in his self-banishment from North American science, still a young man's insistence upheld a minor point of courtesy at the cost of discouraging a valuable worker in science. Upon reaching eminence, Gray in his every action affected both men and professional standards, and while he never looked back at such episodes, he did not again allow himself to be drawn into a full-fledged controversy for the sake of personal credit.

Another aspect of Gray's increasing responsibility appears in the pages of the *American Journal of Science*. As he did before his journey to Europe he contributed occasional long articles and reviews. In 1840 he published notes on orchids.[15] The next year he recounted in an interesting manner what he had learned of European herbaria containing North American plants. Also he undertook the "somewhat ungracious task" of evaluating the work of the weirdly brilliant Constantine S. Rafinesque, who in forty incredibly energetic years had published thousands of new genera and species of plants and animals. These names still clutter scientific literature.[16]

Since Gray felt with most other scientists of that generation that Rafinesque's "passion for establishing new genera and species, appears to have become a complete *monomania,*" he did not deal patiently with the results of these prodigious labors. Some of Rafinesque's views have given him some fame as a precursor of Darwin. The proposition that "both new species and new genera are continually produced by the deviation of existing forms" Gray rejected completely. Nevertheless, the really noteworthy feature of the review is Gray's fairness to work he obviously abhorred. Even though he considered that all the later writings deserved no consideration by scientists (here senior editor Benjamin Silliman, adding a note of confirmation, explained that he had barred Rafinesque from the *Journal* in 1819), he attempted to list them so that "future writers can correct our opinion wherever they think we have done the author injustice." Thus the scorn which led Gray to accuse the strange wanderer of classifying genera and species of thunder and lightning did not blind him to his responsibilities even to eccentric predecessors. In later years he continued to collect Rafinesque's fugitive writings and to recognize his prior nomenclature whenever possible.[17]

In 1840, under the heading of "Miscellanies," the *American Journal of Science* printed a series of short paragraphs called "Bibliographical Notices.—Brief Notices of Recent Botanical Works, Especially Those Most Interesting to the Student of North American

Botany. (Communicated)." [18] A list of some of the authors reviewed strikingly resembles the names appearing in Gray's European journal—De Candolle, Endlicher, Hooker, Arnott, Zuccarini,
Lindley. Some of the notes merely indicated the contents of the
work, but others Gray expanded into short essays. This was the first
of a series which appeared in the *Journal* for an unbroken span of
forty-seven years. Here Gray introduced the botanical research of
Europe to American students. Here too he set the standards for
home-grown works by subjecting them to judicious and often severe criticism. In this way Gray wielded the power of the press both
to mold opinion and to instruct. The Sillimans evidently allowed him
a free hand. No other business, however pressing, tempted him to
lay down this somewhat onerous burden, for he had a tool with
which to shape the whole course of American botany. [19]

His department in the *Journal* also filled a personal need. The
trend in science throughout his lifetime had been toward greater specialization. Even inside the bounds of botany he had found it necessary to limit himself largely to tasks impinging directly on the
work of the *Flora*. But within him still beat the heart of a naturalist
who took all nature for his province. In these informal reviews
dashed off at odd times—sometimes scarcely more than reading
notes—Gray could again roam widely over botany if not over the
whole of science. He approached chemistry in commenting on the
woody tissues of plants. In reiterating his smoldering interest in
plant geography, he anticipated clearly conclusions amplified nineteen years later, for in commenting on Siebold's *Flora Japonica* he
noted the "striking analogies" between the plants of Japan and
North America and promised that on "some future occasion we
hope to make a somewhat extended comparison between" the two
floras. [20]

Gray's first serious venture at criticizing an American botanical
work in his columns struck a familiar note. Amos Eaton had supervised a textbook written by his sister-in-law, Laura Johnson, called
*Botanical Teacher for North America, in Which Are Described the
Indigenous and Common Exotic Plants Growing North of Mexico.*
Gray called the second edition a "ludicrous jumble" and concluded
that "when young ladies write, and learned professors supervise such

books as that before us, we are reminded of a chapter, we believe in Fielding, 'showing that an author writes all the better for having some knowledge of the subject of which he treats.' " Eaton wrote furiously to ascertain the author of these "belchings." Benjamin Silliman was sincerely grieved to have offended "an early friend of the Journal and I feel kindly to him having been in fact the means of bringing him forward from his prison gloom," but Benjamin Junior turned the complaint over to Gray, saying he "thought it was so well known who was the author of the botanical notices . . . that it was perfectly understood by all" and told the botanist to "stick to your proverb 'fiat justitia ruat coelum.' " Gray answered immediately and with such spirit that Eaton complimented him "for your *courage* and *military gallantry* in daring to offer . . . to give further unprovoked abuse to an old man of three-score-six. . . ." [21]

On May 10, 1842, soon after publishing a defense of the *Botanical Teacher* in the *Journal,* Amos Eaton died, and with him went a whole point of view on science and the last serious opposition to the natural system in America. Gray had just started a second department in the *Journal* called "Botanical Necrology" in which he surveyed briefly the work of those who had died in the past year, but he delicately left the task of memorializing Eaton to Chester Dewey. This old-school naturalist had already attempted to defend Eaton's point of view, claiming that "the Nat. Method takes Botany from the multitude, & confines it to the learned." [22] Although Gray denied in theory such a charge, he faced the embarrassing fact that inexpensive and well-written textbooks arranged according to the natural system were not available.

His own *Elements* was long out of print and its publishers out of business. Nor did it completely meet the needs of practical collecting, which was after all an inevitable part of elementary instruction as long as the only laboratory available was the woods. A typical complaint came from Moses Ashley Curtis in North Carolina. When asked to recommend a book on botany for schools, he "could do nothing but say, get Eaton's Manual or Gray's Elements, according to what he proposed teaching. At the same time I called all Troy books quackery, & urged the claims of the Elements." He considered it "high time that Eaton, Lincoln, Comstock, &c. should meet

their deaths." [23] Eaton in spite of his shortcomings had always labored to bring science to the masses in America, and unless the advocates of the natural system could fill his place, the charge that
they were fostering undemocratic science would soon be true.

Hence Asa Gray in 1841 began, in spite of the *Flora,* to prepare
a new textbook. He could scarcely have posed much longer as solely
an advanced researcher in any case, for Gray's economic resources,
without succor from the University of Michigan, were dangerously
low. Americans, even those interested in botany, did not buy enough
copies of the *Flora* to make it pay. Its reviewer John Carey, who
may well have been speaking for the authors, noted that it "may
seem extraordinary, that his undertaking which has attracted so
much attention amongst European naturalists, should have excited
so little comparative interest amongst those of our own country, for
whom it is more especially designed." Since botany was widely
taught in the schools, he blamed "the *low standard* adopted by our
professors. . . ." [24] By writing a new textbook Gray could at once
make some sorely needed cash, reach students until now served
only by Eaton and his followers, and nourish a class of botanists
capable of using and incidentally of buying the *Flora.*

For ten years he had by a combination of frugality and luck been
able to earn enough not only to exist but to spend most of his time at
research. Although he had at times drawn an adequate salary both
from the exploring expedition and from the University of Michigan
—new and untried sources of scientific patronage—neither feder-
ally financed research nor state education had proved stable enough
to give him security and continuous employment. Dr. Bartlett's
school and the Lyceum of Natural History paid too little and were
too uncertain as employers to become vehicles of a great scientific
career. Meanwhile, with the glacially unhurried pace of an institution confident of enduring forever, Harvard University had been
preparing a place for a botanist.

America's oldest and most famous college had just completed
two centuries of steady instruction, much of which differed only in
degree from secondary school drill. Yet Harvard was dimly aware
of a larger function. According to President Josiah Quincy, the "interests of society demand, that . . . the greater seminaries of sci-

ence . . . should be highly endowed, and so constituted as to become, if possible, the common centre of action to those minds of great power, which in every passing period exist in a community." [25] Research activities were getting underway on an ambitious scale in some fields by 1840. An astronomical observatory had large public support, and Jared Sparks was making Harvard a center for American history.

A group of leading Boston citizens in 1805 founded the Massachusetts Professorship of Natural History. Foremost among its duties was to "form and care for a botanic garden" and to show it to people who wanted to use it. Second, the professor "shall read lectures on Botany & Entomology to such of the Students of Harvard College as may be induced to attend thereon." He might also lecture to the public. The rules finally enjoined him to collect specimens of minerals and form a cabinet, so that the term natural history meant at that time zoology, botany, and mineralogy. [26] While linked with the college, the establishment was a community project. The first professor was to be elected by the subscribers, and only his successors were to be chosen by Harvard. William Dandridge Peck (A.B., 1782) became the first and only Massachusetts Professor of Natural History. Peck traveled in Europe to prepare for his task, and the botanic garden of about eight acres was soon afterward underway on the site in Cambridge it was to occupy for one hundred and thirty years. In 1810 a roomy two-story house was built, tastefully decorated in the style of the day with white Roman Ionic pilasters and an oval fanlight. Peck quietly but industriously carried out his duties until his death in 1822. [27]

Colleges have always had difficulty making botanic gardens a success, and Harvard began to have trouble by the time Peck died. The original subscribers, feeling their work complete, gave no money for upkeep, and the $30,000 of original endowment dwindled steadily. The President and Fellows of Harvard, who now had the choice of the professor, attempted to economize by leaving the chair vacant and appointing Thomas Nuttall as curator of the garden at a small salary—a device which not only saved money but also brought to the college a botanist and ornithologist whose reputation was already outstanding. He was so retiring in his ways that he never became a part of the Cambridge community, and like many great travelers felt ill at ease in the settlements. His ten years at the garden left no permanent mark except to keep it alive, not a small feat in itself. Continuing his collecting trips, he was often absent from Cambridge.[28]

Because of the stimulus of young scholars like George Ticknor who had studied in Germany, Harvard was in the 1820's broadening its curriculum to include the Romance languages and to a certain extent the sciences in a way faintly suggestive of the elective system. After 1825 natural history shared in this expansion, and Nuttall, under the title of "Curator of the Botanick Garden, and Lecturer on Botany and Zoology," undertook instruction "for those who wish to attend." Of a senior class of fifty-three, thirty-one chose to recite to Nuttall lessons learned from Smellie's *Philosophy of Natural History,* an eighteenth-century treatise really limited to zoology which had been brought up to date by John Ware, a Boston physician.[29] In addition, Nuttall gave lectures in botany, attended by twenty-one seniors and one junior. This same organization of the department and about the same interest from the students continued into the 1830's. The tuition for these classes was collected separately, Nuttall receiving in 1825 a total of $210 for his teaching. Since his salary as curator was probably $500, a rather distinguished scientist was performing a professor's duties at the bargain rate of $710 a year.[30] But the work stimulated him to publish in 1827 an elementary botanical text for his classes.[31]

In spite of everything the funds of the professorship steadily drained away. By 1834 this had dwindled to less than $9000. Early in that year Nuttall could no longer resist heading for the wilderness, the Cambridge ice dealer Wyeth having offered him a place on his second expedition to the fur country. Resigning his place at Harvard, he was off on the greatest of his journeys.

To save the garden endowment from complete extinction, the Harvard authorities sold a half-township of land in Maine belonging to the professorship for $15,000 and left only a gardener in charge of the land and buildings. For instruction the college relied on the temporary services of local naturalists. Thaddeus William Harris, the college librarian, finished out the year 1833–34. Augustus A. Gould, a Boston physician with a strong interest in zoology, taught for two years, and in the fall of 1836 Harris again took charge of the department. However, relief was in sight for natural history at Harvard, a study now in effect limited to botany and zoology since mineralogy had joined geology in an entirely different line of development. In 1833 a doctor of Beverly, Massachusetts, left $20,000 for a professorship.[32]

After adventures as a surgeon on a privateer during the Revolution, Joshua Fisher (1740–1833, Harvard, A.B., 1766) settled down in Beverly, practicing medicine and investing his money. Since he was a second cousin of Fisher Ames and a close friend of George Cabot, his lively interest in politics centered around the hopes and fears of the Federalists, among whose more admirable qualities was a deeply felt responsibility for the institutions of civilization. Natural history and especially botany was an appropriate interest in the home territory of Manasseh Cutler, and Dr. Fisher, although never publishing anything, was always devoted to its study. He lived until 1833, but his gift to establish a professorship sprang from the same climate of opinion as had the original subscriptions of 1805. The Fisher fund remained separate from the Massachusetts Professorship, and the college chose to let its proceeds accumulate for several years, until the endowment would entirely pay a standard salary of $1500 or more.[33]

Thaddeus William Harris would have dearly loved to spend his life teaching natural history at Harvard. He had been a student under Peck and was so confident of succeeding him that he even prepared a course of lectures before Nuttall's appointment dashed his hopes.[34] After several years as a physician, he came a little nearer his goal by securing the librarianship at Harvard, at that time a post of very light duties and pay. During the period of his teaching on a temporary basis, 1837–42, he was engaged in a notable piece of research in entomology for the Massachusetts Survey. While his recitations in Smellie were extreme examples of a drillmaster technique, he showed great interest in taking his students on expeditions into the countryside around Cambridge.[35] An active natural history club among the students had his support, and he had an enthusiastic following for his optional Friday evening lectures on entomology. Probably least advanced in botany, he still taught the Linnaean method of classification. Although the author of the text he used in plant physiology had relied on De Candolle and was, according to George Bentham, "remarkably well informed on a great variety of subjects," any book which began by saying that botany is "a science particularly adapted to Switzerland" could hardly be exciting to American students.[36] But at least some he taught felt that in "him there lived for us the very spirit of Linnaeus, or whatever name best represents the simplest and purest type of naturalist." [37]

By 1838 Harris, anxiously eying the Fisher fund, began to fear that the President and Fellows of Harvard did not want him as the professor. "If a *first-rate botanist* be wanted in that office," he wrote, "the corporation must look further for a suitable candidate." He considered himself rather "a teacher of the elements of Natural History . . . who, by zeal & ardor . . . might eventually make up any deficiency in his previous qualifications." [38] In fact the presence of the garden had suggested the desirability of a botanist in the professorship. A group of Bostonians offered to make up an additional endowment if Francis Boott, the London doctor, were appointed, and the place was offered him. But he refused, ostensibly because he would take no responsibility for teaching zoology, and the friends withdrew their offer.[39] The matter stood thus until late 1841, when the size of the Fisher fund, now nearing thirty thousand dollars, began to call for a more active policy.

Although Gray had never been to Boston, his nationally prominent position in botany had enabled him to build up a certain acquaintance among scientists there. His friendship with Benjamin D. Greene was longstanding, and of recent years it had become stronger because both were close to Sir William Hooker. In 1837 Gray had become a corresponding member of the Boston Society of Natural History. His European journey had brought him into Francis Boott's circle. He was in regular correspondence with William Oakes of Ipswich, the most active local collector of the region, and he probably exchanged publications with Harris. In 1841 Gray and Torrey furnished letters of introduction for Edward Tuckerman, a young Bostonian of many different educations who was leaving for Europe on a scientific journey.[40] These scattered but increasing connections with Boston people culminated in the fall of 1841 in the election of both Gray and Torrey to the American Academy of Arts and Sciences. Thus Gray was recognized in Boston as one of the country's leading botanists, and should he need them he could muster friends there.

In December 1841, while writing to Greene about some plants collected in Chile long before by J. N. Reynolds, Gray added a few paragraphs inquiring about Harvard. "Some friends of mine," suggested he apply at Harvard. Who the friends were he did not say, and his referring to botany only indicates he was not fully familiar with the possibilities at Cambridge. He even fancied "lectures on Botany could be introduced as a component part of the instruction in the medical department, as it is in every medical school in Europe." Such an idea, which looked more to the past than to the future, had little relevance at Harvard, whose medical school had upon moving to Boston become almost independent of the college. Gray also wanted information "as to the duties and emoluments" of the place, and "under what terms it was offered to our good friend Boott." In another place Gray intimated that the rumor had come through some friend from President Josiah Quincy himself, and the botanist had considered for a week or two before writing his seemingly casual inquiry.[41]

Greene was the right man to consult, since he immediately inquired of President Quincy, his father-in-law. He could then tell Gray of the unique nature of the offer to Boott and describe the status of the Fisher legacy. He disposed of the medical school idea by quoting Dr. Jacob Bigelow, who "told me he thought a small class might be obtained from the medical students for a course on Botany, but I doubt whether it would be easy to persuade the profession to engraft botany as a necessary portion of the studies of the medical student." Greene cordially suggested that Gray visit Boston, for "by applying nearer the fountain" he might get more information.[42]

In January 1842, Gray for the first time saw the dome of the State House in Boston. A native of the hill country who did not reach the Athens of America until his thirty-second year, he might well have been awed. Boston held no terrors for one familiar with

Paris, London, Rome, Vienna, and Berlin. As a New Yorker, he was accustomed to urban living. He stayed at Greene's house, and although he modestly asserted that his host was his only acquaintance there, he had no trouble meeting the proper people. At Cambridge he dined with President Quincy, who included a representative inspection committee from the faculty. William Oakes came in from Ipswich, and the botanical talk at the Greene house in Boston often lasted far into the night. This rustic collector enlisted, perhaps unintentionally, the man who had decisive influence in selecting the professor.[43] "I saw G. B. Emerson when at Boston last Thursday, & made him promise to call on you at Greene's." [44] Schoolmaster and botanist, George Barrell Emerson as president of the Boston Society of Natural History was the official head of the scientific community of the city.

After his conferences in Boston, Gray probably determined his conditions for accepting the place. If "freed from other engagements, I would like the botanical part of the professorship, but not the zoölogy: and . . . the former, with the charge and renovation of the Botanic Garden, would be quite enough for one." [45] On his return to New York he could only await the next step, far from confident of success. And the local competition in a society normally less aware of outsiders than of its own members was indeed formidable. Harris not only had present possession of the department but had claims which became stronger by having been denied so long. Gossip also placed in the contest Jeffries Wyman, a most promising young anatomist who had just been to Europe and was the curator of the newly founded Lowell Institute. There he worked under John Amory Lowell, a member of the Harvard Corporation.

A few days before the regular March meeting of the President and Fellows of Harvard, who as a governing body are often called informally the Corporation, Quincy sought through Greene to get George B. Emerson's opinion of Gray as a prospective professor. It might have been an embarrassing request, for both Wyman and Harris were important members of the Boston Society of Natural History. But Emerson spoke for Gray unhesitatingly. He thought the parts of the *Flora* written by the junior author "bear comparison, most favorably, with the corresponding portion of the Prodro-

109

mus of the late De Candolle, unquestionably one of the best botanists that have ever written." To illustrate the skill with which
Gray "communicates a knowledge of the elementary principles of
the science" Emerson cited the "excellent 'Elements of Botany.'"
Although he had seen the New Yorker "but once and then only for
a short time[,] [t]hat interview left upon me the most agreeable
impression of his manners and kind feelings." Lastly, he observed
that Professor Silliman "thinks very highly both of his character as
a botanist and of his qualifications as a teacher of Natural History." [46] This letter, written by one whose judgment was quite free
from personal bias, was both a powerful endorsement of Gray to
the Corporation and a measure of his accomplishments in the first
thirty-one years of his life.

Present at the meeting of the Corporation on March 26, 1842,
were President Quincy, Treasurer Thomas W. Ward, and Fellows
Joseph Story, John Amory Lowell, and James Walker. Of the two
absentees, Charles G. Loring had a greater personal stake in this
appointment than had any of those present, but he could hardly
know that the Corporation was choosing him a son-in-law. They
voted that "the President, Judge Story & Mr. Lowell be a committee to open a correspondence with Dr. Asa Gray with a view to his
being appointed to the Professorship of Natural History." [47] Thus
these eminent men approved in principle Gray's selection and gave
the president formal power to conduct negotiations.

In his letter to the candidate Quincy outlined a plan which since
has become so commonplace that its boldness in 1842 is hard to appreciate. Briefly, the offer was a salary of $1000, two-thirds of the
yield of the Fisher fund, and in return Gray could confine his work
*"to instruction and lecturing in Botany and to the superintendence
of the Botanic Garden. . . ."* This unusual feature—that Gray
could confine his attention "to the branch, in which you have already attained such eminence and celebrity"—was only a part of
the attraction. The appointment would also "leave you time, to pros-
ecute the important work, in which you are engaged. . . ." Leisure
for research was so fantastic in American education that Quincy felt
obliged to explain that an "arrangement of this kind is not new, in
our seminary; and is in point of amount and terms precisely similar

to that, on which Professor Sparks now holds the Professorship of Ancient and Modern History." Although research time had its price in the substandard salary, still, even one-half of Gray's paid duties dealt more with research than with instruction, for the botanic garden had "since the decease of the former professor been maintained in a state rather of preservation than progress; and the corporation hope that under the influences you may introduce it may become more productive and useful." [48]

Behind the formal exchange of letters the reasons for Gray's appointment are fairly clear. The fact that neither of his competitors was primarily a botanist told greatly in his favor, for the garden did require attention. His dislike of zoology was also an asset, since he was willing to be paid for only a part of the professorship. Although he had done little teaching, his reputation for research completely outclassed both Wyman and Harris. A few years earlier this eminence might have helped him little, but by the 1840's Harvard was groping toward research as part of its function—witness the observatory and the work of Jared Sparks. Finally, old Josiah Quincy was a shrewd judge when it came to choosing men, and Gray not only had a pleasing personality but a way of showing immediately the deep enthusiasm which motivated him. The erstwhile mayor of Boston may also have seen that, while Harvard and New England would gain nothing new in the appointment of Harris or Wyman, they would by winning Gray immediately gain parity with New York and completely outstrip Philadelphia as a center of the study of botany.

Genuinely taken by surprise, Gray immediately answered Quincy that "the situation would place me in such favorable circumstances for the prosecution of my favorite science, and for contributing as far as my ability extends to its advancement in this country, that I am disposed to accept the proposal." Quincy then requested a definite answer by the end of April. Although Gray immediately sent his resignation to Michigan he was slow in getting an answer. Judge Whipple attempted to keep him on as a professor while allowing him to accept temporary employment elsewhere, a gesture which showed Gray still in the good graces of his friends in Detroit.[49] But the board, recognizing their own "embarrassed condition," accepted the

111

resignation, happy to know that Gray's accomplishments "have been appreciated by one of the oldest & most valuable of our American Colleges." Before he heard of Michigan's action Gray sent his acceptance to President Quincy.[50]

Meanwhile, Harris, belatedly sensing his danger, attempted to marshal his forces in Boston. He was particularly hurt by word that the Boston Society of Natural History seemed to favor Gray. Having waited twenty years, during several of which he had borne the actual burden at very low pay, he now saw his life's ambition snatched from him by a complete stranger. Many honored names in Boston—Parkman, Frothingham, Perkins, Francis C. Gray—appeared in his list of supporters. His view of his own qualifications was still soundly based on the old naturalist's ideal of a well-rounded teacher. "By the way," he asked a friend, "is it known that both botany & zoology must be taught by the Professor? The instruction in Zoology will probably have to be increased—that being the largest branch, & also the most favorite one with young men." Certainly Harris's policies had favored such an emphasis. "How will this suit Dr. Gray? Do you suppose he would qualify himself to be an acceptable teacher of zoology? Hitherto he has been nothing but a botanist." [51] Harris was too late, both because the Corporation had already acted, and because the broad naturalist virtues had now less market value than specialist precision in one field. Since the old Federalists had money and were willing to give it for science, Harvard could be among the first to bid in the new market, and the botanic garden meant that animals must for the moment give way to plants. Harris's tragedy was not that Gray got his place, but rather that America provided no other position for an able and deserving scientist.

The Corporation formally appointed Gray to the Fisher Professorship of Natural History on April 30, 1842. In telling Gray of this meeting Quincy explained that the Board of Overseers, "constituted of some of the highest minds & influences in our state," must give final approval, but that Gray could have "full confidence, that no other consideration interferes with their approval except, unquestionable inadequacy or moral delinquence." [52] Had other considerations than Gray's scientific fitness entered into Harvard's calculations, he would probably not have received the appointment. Not only was Harris a native son already on the ground, but religious controversy was bitter in Cambridge. The Unitarians of Harvard were under attack by the Congregationalists,[53] and Gray as a Presbyterian could only be classed with the orthodox. But the question of his religion never even came up.

The New England botanists were jubilant at the news. William Oakes immediately wrote to Gray congratulating him, considering it "among the best appointments they ever made there." But he also knew the Harvard community, and he ventured a friendly warning. "I only hope that you will escape the benumbing effects of the Cambridge atmosphere, which has often subdued the energies of the most active men, & which assisted a little perhaps by old age, has even tamed the indomitable Mayor of Boston, Josiah Quincy." [54] Although their good wishes were slower in arriving, Gray's other botanical friends on two continents saw not only his personal advancement but also better opportunities for science and especially for completing the *Flora*.[55]

Since the president allowed him to choose his own time for reporting, Gray continued to work in New York on his new botanical textbook. Now he had an added incentive, as he himself needed a good text for his classes. Quick to appreciate the community he was about to join, he singled out the most eminent botanist of Boston and inscribed the book "to Jacob Bigelow, M.D. . . . Professor of Materia Medica in Harvard University; Author of the Flora Bostoniensis, and of the American Medical Botany." [56] As usual, Gray underestimated the time necessary to write a book, and instead of going to Cambridge early in June as he first planned, he finally made it late in July, still in plenty of time to get settled before taking up his duties in September.

Gray's only remorse at the change was that he would leave the vicinity of the Torrey home—his social and scientific headquarters for almost a decade. The improvements far outweighed his loss, for he could still collaborate regularly with Torrey on the *Flora*. Thanks to a half-century of active local interest, there were more botanical books in Boston than in New York.[57] The New England city was actually much nearer to Europe because of the regular service of the

Cunarders, while New York still depended mostly on sail. Even the loss of the daily use of Torrey's herbarium was a blessing in disguise, since it would force Gray to build up his own collection, creating two great centers of reference instead of one. Above all, the new position gave Gray direct responsibility for a stable botanical establishment whose endowment, slight though it was, made it unique in America.

Gray's coming to Harvard was a turning point in his own life because it meant the end of uncertainty. Ever since he left Dr. Bartlett's school, his place in society had been obviously insecure. The continuing growth of science in America had specialized the man before it had changed the institutions. By concentrating on botany alone Gray had had no regular job and no reliable income for any long period. Both the federal government and a state university had failed to give him financial security with scientific opportunity. But by good fortune he had been able to specialize anyway, which in part accounts for his having completely passed the field of part-time workers in such a few years. Finally, at Harvard the demands of science and the rewards from society balanced.

But the appointment was less a fulfillment of the past than a promise of the future. Although Jared Sparks's research, to which President Quincy compared Gray's, may have been only a false dawn of the critical study of history, the Fisher professorship marked a real beginning of a continuous scientific study of botany at Harvard. Gray now commanded more resources for the science than did anyone else in the United States, and the trust he took up would be with him until death.

THE PROFESSOR
AT CAMBRIDGE

O N Friday, July 22, 1842, Asa Gray arrived in Boston, a town somnolent in midsummer because people of quality were at the seashore. President Quincy left for Portland that very day, and the newcomer enjoyed the hospitality of Benjamin D. Greene's empty house in Pemberton Square. Undaunted by the quiet, Gray went at once about his business calling on botanists and inspecting the various libraries. On Sunday he did not hesitate to show his preference for the Congregationalists over the Unitarians by attending Park Street Church even though King's Chapel was but a step down the street. When he came out he met George B. Emerson, who observed that Gray was "of Orthodox faith," remarking that "he was very glad of it, although not altogether of that way himself." Within two or three days the young New Yorker was entering into the spirit of the Athens of America, telling the Torrey girls of "a learned lady of these parts . . . who hears the boys' recitations in Greek and geometry at the ironing-board . . . reads German authors while she is stirring the pudding, and has a Hebrew book before her when knitting. . . ." [1]

Within a week the new professor had, with Greene's aid, arranged living quarters in Cambridge. Located conveniently "off the main road, about halfway between the colleges and the Garden," Deacon Munroe's house on James Street provided for the rent of three dollars a week three rooms, "one pretty large, one moderate (of which I shall make a bedroom), a small nearly dark bedroom which I shall shelve and use for my herbarium, and three closets. . . ." By a path through the garden (now part of Radcliffe Yard) he could quickly reach his boarding house, owned by the widow of William Dandridge Peck, late Massachusetts Professor of Natural History. Although some called Mrs. Peck "the pudding stick" as "she was fond of going about and stirring people up," and although she had very little interest in her husband's science, she liked Gray and tried to ease his bachelor's existence with motherly attentions.[2]

Cares of the flesh did not occupy Gray long, nor did the leafy languor of a Cambridge summer dull his sense of the greatness of his opportunity. As Sir William Hooker wrote him, "I am sure that you will have both the *power* & the *will* to render essential service to American botany there." The new professor saw the garden, so long untended, as the core around which to build a botanical empire. He did not lose a day in broadcasting the news to the South, the West, and to Europe. "I have just come on to Cambridge, to take possession of the Botanical Professorship, and of the Botanic Garden, which we hope to renovate and make creditable to the country and largely subservient to the promotion of botanical science." [3]

Besides calling for seeds and roots from his many correspondents in the United States and Canada, he also proposed to take to the field himself to gather hardy plants. Although another journey to the mountains of North Carolina was too ambitious for the fall of 1842, Gray did manage to get to the White Mountains with Edward Tuckerman, just returned from Europe. Setting out from Conway, New Hampshire, in a one-horse wagon, they botanized up Crawford Notch. As well as enjoying this short escapade into the wilds, Gray made "a fine collection of living plants, which was the chief object." On his return in the middle of September he found Harvard coming to life with the return of the president, which opened the way for an official and comprehensive plan of action.[4]

In his letter to President Quincy, Gray was careful to stress the local uses of the garden. He hoped to exhibit "the more interesting exotics, especially those which will live in open air, those most interesting for their economical, medicinal, and other uses. . . ." He recognized a possible source of revenue in "ornamental plants which may be sold to greatest advantage." But the key of his plan was to build a large reservoir of the plants of North America, with which he could then open a regular international trade. "There being no public botanic garden in this country except our own (which is nearly forgotten abroad)," a great opportunity existed for an "institution like ours, with a botanist at its head, who is willing to undertake the labor and trouble" to "monopolize this business and be placed at once in advantageous correspondence with the public gardens of Europe. . . ." The Harvard Corporation fell in with the scheme, authorizing the use of $300 for the "introduction of indigenous plants and maintaining a correspondence with the Naturalists of Europe. . . ." [5] Perhaps more important than the actual money was the fact that John Amory Lowell became one of the committee to supervise its use.

The apparently simple plan of trading plants with Europe implied more than even Gray recognized at the time. Not only must he exploit his friendship with Europeans such as Hooker at Kew and Lehmann at Hamburg, but he had to secure American plants from somewhere. John Torrey was quick to point out that the professor himself could not collect enough live plants in occasional holidays to provide a steady or a sufficiently varied supply. Gray had to resign himself to the closet and spend his time "imploring correspondents in every part of the country to send me all they can." [6] In spite of the difficulties and disappointments involved in the precarious business of shipping live plants over great reaches of sea, the garden and the trade supporting it became the core of Gray's central research organization.

But his new interest and responsibility did not remove the shadow of the incompleted *Flora*. Since he had no classes to teach in the fall, Gray had opportunities to return to New York twice to continue his work, and in February 1843 another number, which completed the gigantic order of *Compositae*, came off the press. Many a botanist still joined William Darlington in hoping that the epoch-making work "may be completed in my life-time. . . ." However, a nagging doubt soon overtook Gray when he contemplated the fate of his "labor of love" from his changed position. "I heartily wish," he wrote, "the *Flora* could have been finished before I accepted this place; as there is here more work than one can attend to. I feel constantly *driven,* which is uncomfortable. I am of course liable to more interruptions here than formerly in New York." [7] Although it was never far from his thoughts, no more of the *Flora* would see the light of day for thirty years. Gray's period of quiet, unhurried, exhaustive research was over. He was hereafter like a statesman—the molder and prisoner of events.

The move from New York to Cambridge at first rather depressed Gray in spite of his new work. John Carey wrote that "I did not expect that you would feel snug & at home, all at once, as you must needs miss your friends and associates, more especially the good Dr. T. & his family. . . ." [8] And, because he had seized the Fisher professorship from the grasp of a locally well-known man, he faced the possible hostility of an old, settled, and highly articulate community.

Any transcendental flowering of genius which may have been adorning the New England of the early 1840's meant little to Gray. Ralph Waldo Emerson and Henry David Thoreau did not cross his path. Bronson Alcott's aspiring vegetables had no place in the professor's herbarium. Tilling the Botanic Garden was both a more serious and a less practical business even than Brook Farm. Of all the great literary figures of the area only Oliver Wendell Holmes had directly common interests with Gray, and the botanist's correspondence shows no particular awareness of these great names in the early years of his life in Cambridge. Henry Wadsworth Longfellow was an early acquaintance, but as a faculty colleague and a neighbor who wanted evergreens for his garden rather than as an intellectual influence.

Gray's whole life in New England centered rather around the Yard of a Harvard where Emerson was already *persona non grata.* On the horizon loomed only commercial and financial Boston— whence periodically emerged such worthies of the Corporation as John A. Lowell and the lawyer Charles Greely Loring. The Harvard community of 1842 was not without its distinguished veterans, like Justice Joseph Story, the Dane Professor of Law. "The Unitarian Pope," Andrews Norton, continued from his nearby retreat at Shady Hill to set the theological tone. His relatively conservative position added to his dislike of denominational lines allowed him a warm friendship with the new natural history professor even though Gray had the unthinkable originality to be a Presbyterian. Richard Henry Dana, Senior, "father of 'Two Years before the Mast' Dana," was eminent enough to impress the matter-of-fact New Yorker on a first meeting. Gray steered his way amiably and unobtrusively through the dignitaries both in Cambridge and in Boston, where he soon was attending the inevitable "soiree at Mr. Ticknor's." Although he had long since retired from the faculty at Harvard, George Ticknor's influence was still felt there in the vestiges of an elective system.[9]

But these were the last leaves of an earlier summer of Harvard glory which reached its solstice in the Kirkland administration in the 1820's. Gray found as his contemporaries both in age and appointment many of the men who would set the tone and direct the policy of Harvard through the middle years of the nineteenth century, a period in many respects undistinguished in the college's history.[10] Jared Sparks, C. C. Felton, and James Walker would each serve a short term as president. Benjamin Peirce, Gray's senior by only a year and already a foremost mathematician, was joining with the astronomer William Cranch Bond to make the observatory a great research institution. Longfellow still had charge of Romance languages and *belles lettres*. A young Greek who had probably had a hand in naming himself Evangelinus Apostolides Sophocles managed in 1842 to catch on as a tutor despite a rather enigmatic journey in life from Thessaly to Mount Sinai to Amherst, Massachusetts. These men would be Gray's friends, associates, and sometimes superiors through most of the next thirty years.

Harvard was so predominantly Unitarian that the claim could be made, although with some lack of justice, of its being a sectarian institution. In addition, fresh in the minds of most Cambridge residents was the bitter strife which attended the separation of the orthodox Congregationalists, led by old Abiel Holmes, from the Unitarians, who triumphantly retained the church property. Although most Harvard professors continued to attend the services in the college chapel, thus casting their lot with the Unitarians, the orthodox church gradually gained a place in the Cambridge community. After Abiel Holmes's retirement, John A. Albro, "our good pastor," headed the congregation. Even though technically a Presbyterian,

Gray had no trouble in choosing the church most congenial to his own beliefs. Parting from most of his colleagues at the college, he became a member of Albro's Congregational church in Cambridge on December 30, 1842, transferring his membership from the Bleeker Street Presbyterian Church in New York.[11] Thus the new professor took the risk of reaffirming his orthodox religious beliefs. But his lack of dogmatic assertiveness and the long habit of tolerating other opinions, which went all the way back to Dr. Trowbridge in Bridgewater, enabled him to avoid friction.

The same friendly sincerity smoothed his first arrangements with the college authorities. Attractive terms offered in the heat of a negotiation do not always stand up under daily realities. Harvard hired Gray strictly as a botanist but made no provision for instruction in zoology. Since it was impossible to keep Harris on in his old subordinate role, someone else had to teach elementary natural history to freshmen. Although President Quincy offered Gray about $200 extra to take these classes, it soon became clear that "this pay would come from the funds of the Garden, let who would perform the duty." Gray therefore volunteered to take the job, "but to receive no pay for it." He was conscious that this "little piece of generosity in a small way" impressed John A. Lowell, the member of the Corporation who by appointment, family, and avocation naturally took greatest interest in botany at Harvard.

Lowell placed a semiofficial stamp of approval on the newcomer by inviting him to give a course of lectures in the newly founded Lowell Institute. Although frightened, Gray saw that "it is now neck or nothing . . . ; to decline the offer, coming from one of the most influential of the corporation of the college, would have had an unfavorable effect on my prospects, which moderate success will greatly advance." [12] If he could pass muster with those who attended his lectures, he would be secure in Cambridge and Boston. The Lowell Institute hoped to attract not only such leading American scientists as Silliman, but also such as Faraday and Lyell from abroad. An appointment to Gray made him seem their peer. Because of the work involved, Gray was lucky that his lectures would not begin until early 1844.

Since science was by far the most important thing in Gray's life, it is not surprising to find that he formed his social bonds most enduringly with the lively group of scientific men in the Cambridge-Boston community. This had long been his position in New York, where the Torrey home had been his headquarters, and where one friend claimed that "you only value men for their Botany." [13] In New England, Gray became only moderately intimate with individual colleagues, but he entered into the local scientific organizations with enthusiasm.

Since the Boston Society of Natural History had already made Gray a member, he needed to wait for no invitation to enter into its activities. He had been in Cambridge scarcely three weeks when he gave the Society a copy of this new textbook and some miscellaneous scientific pamphlets. Within five months he was twice on the program, reviewing literature received from Europe and giving a demonstration with a microscope. Two years after his arrival Gray had the honor of delivering the Society's annual address, "an abstract of the recent progress and present state of Vegetable Physiology," which was "listened to with profound attention by a numerous audience." [14]

Gray saved his best efforts for the more general and more venerable American Academy of Arts and Sciences. With his extensive acquaintance in Europe he quickly found himself in the post of corresponding secretary.[15] Here he could not only further the Academy's relations on a great scale but also had a vehicle for some of his own exchanges of information and publications. He felt a particular duty to attend its meetings regularly regardless of "any winter storm." The great men of Boston supported the Academy with their presence as well as their money, and Gray by knowledge and service became one of them.

Although formal societies were more important in the 1840's than later, even then they did not satisfy the desire of scientists to meet informally for shop talk on a broader scale than was possible in day-to-day work. Asa Gray, who felt this strongly, did not hesitate to do something about it. He helped to found a scientific club made up mainly of the college faculty. Of course it included Thaddeus Harris, Benjamin Peirce, Joseph Lovering, and Daniel Treadwell, who could be considered professionals. Science was still so largely amateur that everyone welcomed the membership of President Quincy, historian Jared Sparks, lawyer Simon Greenleaf, theologian James Walker, philosopher Francis Bowen, and classicists Charles Beck and C. C. Felton. Outside the faculty, Cambridge furnished the schoolteacher Epes S. Dixwell, the lexicographer Joseph E. Worcester, Lieutenant Charles Henry Davis of the navy who was working at the observatory, and Dr. Morrill Wyman. The club met twice a month, each member entertaining in turn and giving a paper which touched off discussion. Gray could regularly match his wits and ideas with some of the best intellects in Cambridge.

The club had its worldly side. They sat down "to a hearty meal of chicken, tongue, ham, pastry, fruit, Scotch ale & two or three kinds of wine." This was much too elaborate and convivial for the taste of President Edward Everett. "If they partake of them—what are they fit for the next morning; if they do not, why have them?" He finally resigned, asking, "How can I inculcate temperance on the young men while I belong to a club which once a fortnight has an elaborate supper with wine of five kinds?" [16]

With these manifold activities to occupy him, the first fall and winter in Cambridge slipped by, bringing Gray before he realized it face to face with his first classes. He had been working steadily toward this goal, especially on the problem of providing drawings for his lectures. The Corporation voted $100 to provide him with "an adequate number of illustrative figures &c. to be used in his lectures, and in recitations in Natural History. . . ." [17] Nevertheless, because he had not taught since his summer at Hamilton College nearly nine years before, he approached his duties with trepidation. That President Quincy would attend the first class was not frightening, for "he is said always to fall asleep on such occasions, and to be very commendatory when he wakes." But the slight hesitancy which already marked Gray's speech robbed him of complacency.

For the recitations in Smellie's *Philosophy of Natural History* he divided the freshman class into four sections, hearing each once a week. Harvard was at that time in the clutches of a vicious system known as the "scale of merit," which by requiring a teacher to give a grade on each student for every meeting of the class forced instruction into a strait jacket of rote drill. Gray at first feared that the recitations, for which he received no pay, would be "a great bore," but after a few days he had them "well in progress, and am quite interested in it." He fancied himself "pretty good at questioning," and took pains to "give them plenty of illustration, explanation, and ideas not in the book." In one section he gave "a sort of lecture, two hours long!" to which they "listened well; for I gave them, or those who chose, the opportunity of going at the expiration of the regular hour, but not one of them budged. . . ."

Although such enthusiasm in both instructor and freshman seemed to augur a new era in Harvard education, the very same lecture produced an episode casting doubt on the college's readiness for the millennium. Gray, turning his head "at a fortunate moment . . . caught one of the fellows (a rather stupid fellow, a boarder with me last term), throwing his cap to his companion or playing some trick." The new instructor was not so inexperienced in iniquity as to let the matter pass. "You know how I can scold. So I gave him about half a dozen words that made him open his eyes wide; and I do not think that he, nor any of that division, will venture anything of the kind again very soon." [18]

Scattered evidence of Gray's early years of teaching indicates that he gradually accommodated himself to the prevailing puerility of the institution. While he continued to bring his experience as a botanist to bear in his beginning classes—telling them of "the proper method of forming an herbarium"—he was not an overwhelming success as a director of recitations. The flattering but secondhand reports of a young Lowell are more than offset by a diarist's frank assertion that while "the matter was very good . . . the manner was positively shocking. I never saw a person more awkward in delivery." [19] In fact Gray conducted recitations in an extremely routine manner. One student, admitting that he "did not study much on my Botany," left a clear record of his procedure. "The way that I and in fact by far the greatest part of the class do is to read their lesson over once and get it in the recitation room." Gray would call on them in a fixed order, and "as we can tell about on what part we shall be taken up, we can get that part perfectly and thus make a squirt." It was even safe to read Charles Lamb during class.[20] Edward W. Emerson later told the same story, and James K. Hosmer even ascribed to Gray a positive philosophy of refusing to disturb the immature and recalci-trant.[21]

The young gentlemen of the 1840's, just beginning to sprout beards, used their abundant excess energy to make life miserable for the college authorities, especially Old Quin and his successor Edward Everett. Professor Gray came in for his share and perhaps more. "In the Botany recitation some of the second division threw some torpedoes which exploded with a terrible noise. Prof. Gray was quite enraged and dismissed the class." Somewhat more serious was the time "a number of fellows . . . met in one corner and during the whole recitation did what they could to disturb the lecture. They stamped, whistled, and made as much unnecessary noise as possible without being discovered." Gray, after several times requesting them to be still, "at length commenced with Allen and went on in alphabetical order asking if he had made the noise. Allen, did you? No, Sir. Bailey? No, Sir, and so on, every one either answering No, Sir or Oh, Sir." The professor, remarking "that some of us must have had the satisfaction of lying to him, . . . went on with the lecture." But when such tactics proved ineffective, he reported the class to the president, whose threats finally quelled the troublemakers.[22]

Although Gray decided to accept the system rather than to reform it, his unaffected good spirits never completely abdicated before the duties of taskmaster. In the years when he taught in Holden Chapel, that Georgian gem which had long since been put to profane use, the students had to crowd through a narrow entry. When "Gray keeps the first division over their time, the two divisions meet *accidentally* with great confusion, and Prof. Gray rushes out through a side door with great vim—pulling out the combatants one by one —seeming to enjoy the fun highly." [23]

The lectures in botany to seniors offered the new professor a better chance to teach his subject maturely. Even if the students could not wander much from the set curriculum without being penalized in the scale of merit, an elective system of sorts allowed a heartening thirty-seven students to appear for Gray's first lecture. Armed with his large illustrations, he experimented with his method of delivery, a rather painful aspect of the business. "I am convinced that for lectures with much illustration I must have only heads and leading ideas written; for others, I will write nearly in full." [24] Although designed for seniors, the lectures were not at first an advanced course. Gray in all his theories of botanical education insisted on a thorough grounding in plant physiology as the basic step toward a mastery even of collecting and naming specimens. In his first lectures he seriously took up only this introductory study of the functions and structure of plants.

From the point of view of the undergraduate, the Fisher bequest, the botanic garden, and one of the country's most promising professional scientists added up to no more than an elementary course in botany. But in the long view of scientific education it was an achievement, not a failure, and is but a measure of the effort required for such a seemingly simple accomplishment.

If the students at Harvard had a new opportunity in Gray's courses in botany, it was less because of his questionable forensic abilities than because he was the author of the *Bontanical Textbook,* which now supplanted Mrs. Marcet's *Conversations.* While the *Elements of Botany* of 1836 had given him good experience, the *Textbook* was virtually a new beginning. Gray, taking seriously the need of a practical work to replace Eaton's *Manual,* used a great deal more space on the systems of classification which a beginner could use in identifying specimens. At the same time he did not abandon any of his earlier emphasis on plant physiology as the proper basis for the study of plants.

As soon as Gray had survived a year of teaching and come to understand the problems of presenting his own course, he began either consciously or otherwise to shape the curriculum for natural history, called in the president's *Reports* the Department of Zoology and Botany. If Thaddeus Harris, now resigned to his increasingly heavy duties as librarian, ever paused to contemplate the trend of affairs in the department he had once tended, he doubtless gasped to see Gray blithely putting zoology away and giving all training, required or not, in botany.[25] In the spring of 1844 the freshmen still studied Smellie, but in 1845 they pitched immediately into plant physiology in the *Botanical Textbook* for their required recitations. This allowed Gray to move his lectures up a notch in complexity, taking up structural and cryptogamic botany with forty students from the higher classes. The next year he advanced even farther, lecturing on systematic and geographical botany to forty-five students. His effort, perhaps perfunctory, to return to zoology for sophomores was "necessarily abandoned after the delivery of three Lectures, on account of the failure of the Professor's health." In 1847 and 1848, while no semblance of zoology appeared, Gray pushed on toward advanced training in botany, giving a month of "particular instruction in botany, with microscopical illustrations," [26] at the Botanic Garden. Thus between five and twenty students attained the equivalent of a laboratory course six years after Gray took up his work. The determination to specialize in botany regardless of the claims of zoology had enabled him to make modest but significant progress in introducing advanced instruction. Even more years lay ahead before many fruits of these labors would appear.

Boston in the 1840's was a center for scientific lectures which would have cheered the heart of old Amos Eaton. The popular desire for adult education which existed everywhere in the country found a powerful ally in the old Federalists with their ideals of stewardship of science and their belief in the duty to lead the masses to higher things. Lectures served both as entertainment and instruction. The estimate that 13,500 persons attended twenty-six courses during a single season in the city gives an index to their appeal.[27] Such an audience no scientist in that day could afford to ignore. Indeed men like Silliman had almost built a career on lectures. Since Gray's invitation to give a series for the Lowell Institute provided him a perfect opportunity to win a name in this great arena, the event loomed ever larger on his horizon as February of 1844 approached.

Of all the schemes for the popular diffusion of knowledge in the country, the Lowell Institute displayed its lecturers with the greatest *éclat*. Only nine years before Gray stepped to the rostrum, John Lowell, Junior, while using the last of his ebbing strength to collect Egyptian antiquities, had made a notable will, which had the primary object of providing for "lectures to be delivered on the historical and internal evidences in favor of Christianity." But he also felt that "my native land, New England, which is sterile and unproductive, must depend hereafter, as it has heretofore depended, first on its moral qualities, and secondly, on the intelligence and information of its inhabitants. . . ." Hence he wished lectures on "physics and chemistry, with their application to the arts; also, on botany, zoology, geology, and mineralogy, connected with their particular utility to man." [28] John Amory Lowell, the sole trustee of the Institute, had assumed the management of the funds with all the energy and shrewdness of a lord of industry, at the same time devoting to the choice of speakers the discrimination of a highly educated man.

Silliman had opened the first season in 1840 with twelve lectures on geology. John Gorham Palfrey had given a series on evidences of Christianity, and since the trustee was an amateur botanist Thomas Nuttall's appearance in nine lectures was not surprising. These first lectures, addressing a general though highly intelligent audience, set a standard of excellence which compared favorably with college courses. The good people of Boston rose to the occasion, breaking in the window of the Old Corner Bookstore in quest of tickets and forcing a repetition of several of the lectures. By the fall of 1842, when he engaged Gray, John A. Lowell's ambition had heightened with success. He hoped to get orthodox as well as Unitarian theologians for the lectures on the evidences of Christianity (Gray guessed one would be President Francis Wayland of Brown, but Mark Hopkins of Williams appeared instead). In the sciences his securing Charles Lyell made him look beyond the Atlantic toward Faraday and Richard Owen. Although these two never came, Lyell returned, and soon Louis Agassiz would make the journey.[29]

One reason for the unparalleled distinction of the Lowell Institute was the regal scale of fees paid to the lecturers.[30] John A. Lowell offered Gray $1000 for twelve lectures, or the equivalent of his year's salary at Harvard. If he repeated the series he received an extra $200 to $500. The trustee was willing to engage him for two or three years, "but I told him he had best wait to see how I succeeded." [31] For Gray this doubling of income in 1844 marked an epoch financially. No longer was he living at a loss, making ends meet by borrowing from his father. Now, even though science cost him heavily in the form of books and specimens, he was in a position not only to repay his debts, but to help his family directly. The starving times were over forever.

As Gray prepared his lectures, he came to realize that even Boston had limited facilities for making scientific illustrations. "The Institute will pay for full illustrations," but where to get them done? Gray's first impulse was that of a colonial, asking Sir William Hooker to sell the illustrations he had used at the University of Glasgow. America, Gray felt, could not possibly provide the pictures he needed. But because Hooker wished to save his drawings for his son Joseph he evaded a commitment.[32] Gray, in reconciling himself to trying to find local talent, added a humble but important amendment to America's declaration of scientific independence. By using the services of Miss Susan Quincy, eldest of the president's famous daughters, he began to supervise botanical drawings which would ultimately add much to the value of his scientific work. These first efforts produced a set of large paintings six to eight feet high. Incidentally, Miss Susan Quincy talked a great deal about a botanist that season.[33]

Early in 1844 a settled panic descended on Gray. The preceding November he complained that he had "but just found time to commence the preparation of my course of lectures . . . which will give me plenty of labor and anxiety before they are over." [34] With the "time of trial" drawing near and a "pretty brisk application for tickets" he quailed to think that his "last two lectures are not even *blocked out upon paper.*" Nevertheless, "strange as it may seem, my spirits are rather on the rise. . . ." He was proud to have "contrived a diagram illustrating the cycle of relations of three kingdoms, which I think is capital (as it is quite original). . . ." [35] Sometimes he worried that he would not have an opportunity to use his illustrations. In general, whenever he thought of botany he quickened to his task, but whenever he thought of standing up before the audience horror struck him.

For subject matter Gray "restricted myself to physiological botany only,—tak[ing] up only great leading views. . . ." Since he had already covered the ground thoroughly in his textbook, he felt that the success or failure of the series depended on his delivery— the weakest part of his equipment. As he went along he reported to

Torrey in New York how he was faring. In his first he "said plainly what I intended to say and delivered it not very well indeed, but well enough to satisfy me I could do *well* with practice." On his second evening he tried "the experiment of lecturing by the general guidance of my notes only (which indeed were but partly written out). So with long pole in hand to point at the pictures I set at work, and talked away for an hour and 10 minutes." He felt like "a person who can hardly swim, thrown into the river . . . and had to kick and strike to keep my head above water." But in spite of all his misgivings about repeating himself, leaving important things out, and having to break off in the middle, he thought "the whole was probably more spirited in appearance than if I had followed my notes." [36]

As he reached the real meat of his subject Gray gained confidence. He pleased himself with the lecture on "the anatomy and physiology of leaves, and exhalation and its consequences." The high point of the course was on "food of plants, vegetable digestion, and the relations of plants to mineral and animal kingdoms." Gray was at his "very best . . . and secured the most intense attention on the part of the audience for a hundred minutes." Out of the welter of anguish over his delivery emerged the intense, almost arrogant, self-confidence which really characterized his view of himself and his fellows. It would be, he wrote to Torrey, "mere affectation to pretend not to know—as I well do—that it is one of the best scientific lectures that have ever been delivered in Boston." Here he took the measure not only of Nuttall and all the local talent, but also Silliman and Lyell.

No doubt he was aware that the scientists in his audience praised him highly. "I think I should be an unhappy, discontented, unthankful person not to be gratified with . . . success. . . . But it is not likely to turn my head." [37] To so great a personage as Sir William Hooker he admitted that his "Lowell lectures have succeeded beyond my most sanguine expectations." [38] John A. Lowell stayed by his original offer to engage Gray for additional series. He appeared again both in 1845 and 1846, continuing beyond plant physiology to systematic and geographical botany.

Gray's experience as a public lecturer thus had two sides. On the one hand, excruciating self-consciousness and worries about his delivery made each appearance an ordeal. On the other, the opportunity to speak on his beloved science with an enthusiasm which penetrated all difficulties brought him acclaim and the satisfaction of spreading scientific understanding. Ordinary members of the audience had a correspondingly mixed reaction. Mrs. James Freeman Clarke wrote that "yesterday I went to one of Dr. Gray's botanical lectures. . . . Botany, with him, is a different thing from the dry arrangement of plants according to the number of their pistils or stamens which used to repel the interest we might have taken in the study. Dr. Gray is a poor speaker, but his facts are very interesting, & his illustrations by paintings are beautiful." [39]

The amount of time and trouble which Gray devoted to the lectures raised a strategic problem which faced all scientists in the 1840's. The demand for popular education was so insistent and the rewards so immediate that the easy way was to follow the path of Amos Eaton and Silliman. Even those like John Torrey who were temperamentally unsuited to the lecture platform often spent more time and energy there than they themselves realized. Torrey, ever solicitous for Gray's welfare, could see the dangers for his friend if not for himself. Gray felt obliged to defend himself in terms of Christian duty. Although he recognized that the lectures "will probably tend to advance my interests, as I certainly wish [they] may," he insisted that his "high and honorable" object was "to benefit the science of this part of the country." [40]

Hiding behind the cloak of duty, Gray did not in 1844 admit to Torrey that his services to botany in New England and his heightened position in the eyes of the public and of John A. Lowell had serious drawbacks in his lack of flair for the business and the great amount of time it took from research. But after he finished his three series he appeared no more at the Institute, leaving the rewards to perennial lecturers such as Agassiz, Silliman, Joseph Lovering, and Josiah P. Cooke. Nor did he accept other lectureships except on very rare occasions. This was another road not taken in his career, and like so many other decisions its real significance appeared only dimly at the time. He had avoided one more hazard on the long journey to a professional and specialized science.

Although Gray's first years of teaching at Harvard showed no revolutionary success, they were far from a failure. A poor lecturer with no interest in making sluggards transcend themselves, he had without departing from the rigid frame of Harvard instruction built modestly but well toward a department of botany which could give mature instruction. Plant physiology on an elementary level, lectures on systematic and geographical botany, and the beginnings of laboratory exercises at the garden made it theoretically possible for Harvard in 1848 to train a botanist. This had not been true in 1842. That virtually no one had used the opportunity in these early years indicates that Gray as a teacher was slightly ahead of his contemporaries. Just as he was a lone professional among amateurs in his research work, he had to be content that few yet wanted really advanced training. It would be another decade before advanced students would flock to him and make him into a renowned teacher.

Of all his educational activities writing the textbook bore most fruit. Difficulties in lecturing did not hinder him here, and the unseen audience accepted his high standards of excellence more readily than did Harvard boys. He could serve science and at the same time do his duty by the public much more readily on paper than on the platform. The *Botanical Textbook* gave the United States an opportunity to learn the best of a science which had not existed before. If Gray retired from lecturing and complained of the confinement of the classroom, he never flagged in keeping the public supplied with his books.

VII

THE PATTERN
OF A YOUNG MAN'S
THOUGHTS AND DEEDS

As Gray's life in Cambridge settled into a routine, he had to face the fact that even though teaching occupied only part of each year he always had "work enough lined up for two men." [1] In addition to the tasks he deliberately sought, others arose from the logic of fundamental aims—the *Flora,* interchange between America and Europe, the professorship, and now the garden. Each of the new responsibilities jostling for a place in his day emphasized inexorably the drive toward specialization which had given direction to Gray's career from the beginning.

A tacit confession that the ideal of the naturalist had passed from his life beyond recall appears in Gray's outright gift to Harvard of a "valuable collection of the rocks and minerals of the States of New York and New Jersey, with several from other places." [2] Since he had not, of course, worked at these for at least seven years, he had long before lost any claim to the title of mineralogist. But that he kept the cabinet indicated he had up to now felt that someday, when the work eased up, when there was more time, he would return to the pattern of Beck and Hadley and to the catholicity of Amos Eaton. No such view opened from the chair of the Fisher professorship. Ahead lay not simply more work than one man could do, but the vision that the heights of science were accessible up a single narrow ladder.

Gray's picture of himself as a field collector died much harder.

Exploring had been the part of science first to grip his imagination, and although he had relinquished his opportunity to go on the Wilkes Expedition, he had continued to hope to see actually growing the plants he studied. Not only had his vigorous, active body always stood well the rigors of an outdoor life, but his spirits lifted even to a few days in the open, such as his short journey to the White Mountains in 1842. After his first year of teaching he was able to break away for a more ambitious attack on his unfinished explorations in the southern Appalachians. By going late in the season and making his aim live plants for the garden, Gray could use money appropriated to the Botanic Garden. Also he arranged to join forces with W. S. Sullivant, the banker and capitalist of Columbus, Ohio, who had shown more than usual aptitude as a correspondence student of Torrey's and Gray's. The microscope investigations in Europe had been partly for his benefit, and with the instrument Gray ordered he had become steadily more proficient, centering his attention on the mosses. The Ohioan had visited Gray early in the summer of 1843, when they tentatively agreed on the excursion.[3]

Sullivant had grandiose ideas of zigzagging back and forth across the mountains, taking ship from Charleston to "touch at various points on the eastern coast of Florida . . . and on the northern coast of the Gulf of Mexico—at N. Orleans—thence up the Miss." Gray, not being a big businessman, was less ambitious, suggesting they "trace the more westerly ranges of the mountains down to North Carolina and Tennessee, to revisit my old ground in Ashe County, etc., and to continue our journey farther south into Georgia, coming out at Augusta. . . ." [4] His itinerary was approximately the route they took.

The expedition was not altogether a failure. Seeds and roots added considerably to the number of plants growing in the garden. Sullivant had collected enough mosses to publish them in prepared sets with Latin descriptions written in part by Gray.[5] This work put the Ohio amateur well on the way to becoming a foremost moss expert, one to whom Gray could turn in all things relating to these obscure plants. But in other respects this journey, at a cost of much money and time, had produced rather slim botanical results—much scantier in fact than would have three months' work at home. Although the distance to remote areas and the difficulties of travel were a factor, the essential drawback was that Gray alone possessed the experience, the skill, and the communication facilities to be a headquarters man, while many could go out and dig up plants. Not the rigor of the field but the demands of the closet kept him tied to his working table for the next thirty years.

In the summer of 1844 Gray improved not only his living quarters but his scientific facilities by moving into the house at the Botanic Garden. Built in 1810 for Peck and occupied by Nuttall, it had passed to nonscientific hands when the college rented it to Dr. James Walker. The Corporation included the house as a part of Gray's salary when they gave him the full duties of the Fisher professorship. Spacious rooms and broad windows were a contrast to his makeshift quarters at the Munroe house. To match the splendor of his new mansion Gray spent over $500 on furnishings, glassware, dishes, and linens. These domestic activities were so intense that they gave rise to a rumor, quite unfounded, that the bachelor professor was to be married.[6]

The move to the garden meant even more than gracious quarters handy to his flower beds, extra rooms to use for hothouse plants, and a means of keeping his younger brothers while they went through college. Gray's herbarium, his collection of dried specimens, had remained small as long as he was in New York because he could use Torrey's. Cramped into a cubbyhole in the Munroe house, it was still "temporarily arranged in loose ordinary paper." Now, permanent quarters made it possible to preserve the specimens as Gray had seen it done in Europe, by gluing them to half sheets of thick smooth white paper. The various species of each genus could then be filed in a heavy brown paper folder.[7] Because of their durability and ease of shipping, herbarium specimens were then and would long remain the most trustworthy way of transporting plants for scientific study. The herbarium edged its way in as one of Gray's most important enterprises. He was fortunate to get space and a system for it before the explorations of the 1840's and '50's inundated him with collections.

By 1843 the drive toward specialization had done its work with

Gray. He was not only a botanist, but a herbarium botanist. One of the dangers of specialization is that it relieves the scientist of the duty of asking big questions, of facing up to the philosophical implications of his work. If science remained a static pursuit, Gray might have been spared further philosophical reflection for the rest of his life. Gray, the dedicated specialist and religious man, had reached a philosophical equilibrium in 1843 which matched the comfortable specialization of his research. Little evidence exists that he thought about philosophical problems in a systematic way during this period. Nevertheless, a pattern emerges from scattered hints which suggests the development of a definite philosophy which guided the young man's mind.

Before his conversion Gray had been a materialist after the fashion of Sir William Lawrence, an admirer of eighteenth-century rationalism. His conversion might conceivably have led him away from this orientation. He might have yielded to the intellectual currents which were sweeping other young Americans along and moved through various theological positions to transcendentalism. The romanticism of his literary interests, Byron and Scott, could have provided an avenue here. And idealism in natural history might have helped. De Candolle had familiarized him with Goethe and the metamorphosis of plants. Some of his German correspondents like Nees von Esenbeck might accentuate the pattern.

Every bit of evidence, however, indicates that any temporary drift in the direction of German idealism either in religion or botany after his conversion died aborning. Mention of Goethe dwindled and disappeared from his textbooks. In 1837 he took the momentous step of disassociating himself from the idea of an over-all pattern for the plant world in a great chain of being, "a regular gradation, by a single series, from the most perfect and complicated to the most simple forms of existence." [8] This was an idea "once so strongly insisted on by poets and metaphysicians." In disguised form the sweep of the great chain of being still held sway in many forms of idealism. In a review in 1841, Gray was careful not to associate himself with a book under review which "affords a good idea of that tendency to transcendentalism which thoroughly pervades the German mind, and has found its way into physical as well as psychological science." [9] Gray could be converted to Christianity without changing his philosophy to some form of idealism.

As to religion, no doubts exist about Gray's institutional alignment. "I am an orthodox Presbyterian as my fathers were." He did not say he was so because of the beliefs of his fathers, and indeed the record points to Dr. and Mrs. Torrey rather than his parents. He never referred to Calvinism in any of its more rigorous forms. Yet he maintained his orthodoxy in the face of the strong Unitarian influences which surrounded him, a token of the strength and sincerity of his commitment to a faith which can be called evangelical. This term described not only American Presbyterians. It described the dominant faith of the Victorian England which was then achieving its greatest vigor and prosperity. It was a belief in the Gospels, in the sinfulness of man, in the need of God's Grace, in the necessity of conversion, in redemption through faith. The climate of these ideas was, however, cool and rational, fitting well the utilitarianism which flourished alongside evangelicalism in England. Gray's conversion had been a temperate, almost scientific affair, stemming from the same source as his inspiration to go on in botany.

A literal belief in the Bible was no part of his version of evangelical religion. He did not even resort to symbolic interpretations to reconcile science and the Scripture. No need for reconciliation existed. Science was one of the things which, as he remarked to his brother George, the Bible did not teach. The Bible was simply not a textbook in science. Significantly, he went back to a minor writer of the eighteenth century for a rationalization as to the place of the Scriptures as evidence. He agreed with Soame Jenyns that the "Scriptures are not revelations from God, but the history of them: The revelation itself is derived from God; but the history of it is the production of men, and therefore the truth of it is not in the least affected by their fallibility, but depends on the internal evidence of its own supernational excellence." Soame Jenyns had been a deist, and his reconciliation of Christianity with the religion of reason had been so ingenious as to lead to some doubt of his sincerity.[10] Gray too had been a "materialist" in his Bridgewater days under Dr. Trowbridge. On his conversion he had taken over the main structure of eighteenth-century rationalism into his religion.

The transference of the rationalist and materialist ideas of his early anticlerical period into his evangelical Christianity was easy for Gray. This very combination was widespread in nineteenth-century America, and the symbol for it was the work of William Paley. This eighteenth-century divine's *Natural Theology* was being used as a text at Harvard by President James Walker as late as 1845–55.[11] Paley was, after all, the high priest of those who pointed to material evidence in nature as the proof of God's existence. Paley permeated the school systems and churches of New York State. Paley's watch, found on a desert path, implied a designer. As important as his inference of the existence of God was the empirical approach and his utilitarian exploration of adaptation in nature. It was the hand and the eye—exquisite mechanisms both—which implied a designer of nature. They showed that the designer had adapted their structure to the purpose each was to serve. Thus Paley's doctrine was at once utilitarian—nature's usefulness to man proved the existence of God—and an explanation of adaptation. He was in the same current of utilitarianism as was Jeremy Bentham, with the added attraction of summing up eighteenth-century rationalism in a form superficially palatable to nineteenth-century orthodox Christians.[12]

Asa Gray had imbibed the doctrine of design ever since he first heard of natural history under the tutelage of James Hadley. He taught it to the Torrey children in the 1830's. His references to it, although infrequent, span the whole of the 1840's and the early 1850's.

As an adherent to the doctrine of design and Paley's general scheme of ideas, Gray was close to being a materialist. His belief in God stemmed directly from his observation of order in nature. The general prevalence of this orientation is proved at length by the *Bridgewater Treatises,* published in England in the 1830's, which expanded Paley's arguments and brought them up to date.[13] That Hume had knocked the underpinnings from Paley before the latter ever wrote his book, by showing that the argument ultimately reduces the deity to a mechanic,[14] may appear obvious to a twentieth-century philosopher. But in the 1850's Paley was a symbol for a live system of ideas widely diffused, strongly felt, thoroughly in tune with the traditions of science, and thoroughly accepted by evangelical Christianity.

Above Gray's religious beliefs stood his philosophical orientation, even less explicitly defined but nevertheless quite clear. He was an empiricist in the great British tradition extending from John Locke through Hume to Jeremy Bentham and John Stuart Mill. His sympathy with Paley was one instance of his indebtedness to this stream of thought. The most important source of his empiricism and its British cast arose in his intimacy with British botanists. The Germans he kept up with, such as Von Martius, tended to be the plodding professors who would write him long letters about taxonomy and nothing else. After the death of Augustin-Pyramus De Candolle in 1841, his son Alphonse was the only major continental influence on Gray. In contrast, his working intimacy with the Hookers and Bentham grew continuously.

Gray nevertheless had a low opinion of "pantheism" and "deist rationalism." He had a device for keeping the universe of Paley from becoming a mere machine. It was a seldom-expressed belief in vitalism, which itself had a long history closely connected with that of natural history.[15] Again Gray's orientation goes back to A. P. De Candolle, who made the firm distinction between organized and unorganized beings. Organization, the essential characteristic of all living matter, was the product of a vital force, of which there was more in a large tree than a small one. Gray used the word force advisedly, never equating vitality with a chemical substance or a fluid. "Surely" if matter and force "stand in any relation of cause & effect, *matter* is not the *cause* of *force*—But rather, *force* of matter." [16]

The neat equilibrium of science, philosophy, and religion which Gray had attained by 1843 was almost immediately disturbed by questions emerging from the confluence of several deep currents in the scientific thought of the West. For the fundamental questions— What is life? Where does it come from?—tugged restlessly at many minds. To consider it from the point of a single science—for instance, botany—was impossible, because physics, chemistry, geology, and zoology as well groped for facts which most men had earlier left largely to the philosophers and theologians. The natural system had produced a vivid picture of the living world, suggestively placing species in groups related to one another in structure. Where the relation originated and what caused it were matters that the botanist, even by the most careful comparisons of all the organs of two plants, could not fathom. The assumption that species were the separate creations of some supreme being who had arranged the relation of plants and animals according to his plan, was not only deeply ingrained in the thinking of Christians, but was the best guess that the scientists of the day could make from their own data.[17] Gray was convinced of its probability not because of Genesis, but because every scientific influence upon him, at least since he had read De Candolle's *Théorie élémentaire,* had considered and rejected the idea that one species grew out of another.

Also Gray's own observation seemed to confirm the views he learned from his elders. In the first place he always saw "oaks producing oaks, and never pines, animalcules giving rise to animalcules, and not to fish or quadrupeds. . . ."[18] In the second place, his strain of vitalism made him feel very strongly that living things were essentially different from the nonliving. Some active force organized inert matter, changing it and causing it to behave under different rules. Such a vital force at work in the living world was eminently compatible with some kind of divine guidance. Yet as a student of sedges and *Compositae* he knew that the Maker did not always distinguish between His creations as clearly as one might wish. Above all, his ear for scientific news from Europe brought him to lines of thought which raised great difficulties for the views he found so comfortable.

As Gray built his fires for the first cold days of the winter of 1844, snug in his new quarters, his philosophical colleague Francis Bowen called upon him to summarize for the readers of the *North American Review* several books which reflected far-reaching revolutions in science.[19] The concepts of chemistry were beginning to produce large results when applied to plants and animals, thus breaking down supposed boundaries between the organic and inorganic. If the laws of chemistry which applied to minerals would fit equally well for living matter, there would be little place left for a vital force peculiar to life. Friedrich Wöhler had made urea, a product of vital forces. Justus Liebig had by 1840 presented in fairly precise terms the elements used in plant food and the way in which they derive from the air rather than from the soil. Gray, picking his way carefully through the polemics which then raged around Liebig and using material he had prepared for Lowell Institute lectures, managed to give a balanced account of the new view of plant nutrition and to weigh several items of the current literature.

Gladly he accepted the researches of J. Dumas and J. B. Boussingault. Courteously he acknowledged the practical applications to agriculture made by his old friend at Durham, James F. W. Johnston. But the book [20] by an English-born chemist at New York University, John W. Draper,[21] was an entirely different matter. Not only did Gray, always anxious to raise American science in the eyes of Europe, object to the "very paltry and feeble philosophizing," [22] he also refused to go along when Draper jumped all the way to the conclusion that "those all-pervading forces which . . . chemists recognize" are the direct sources of "elementary organization." In Gray's eyes this was "atheism."

Gray, although giving credit for occasional bits of real research, pointed out extensive borrowings from other writers and took issue with many specific points concerning the action of light on plants. And he roundly attacked Draper for a chemist's propensity "to explain almost every thing in the animal and vegetable economy upon chemical principles," which resulted in Draper's denying the existence of a vital force. This position of Gray's, incidentally shared at the time by many of the founders of organic chemistry, was to remain dominant in science for at least another decade. Gray hit strongly at Draper's lack of new evidence, and his substituting for vital force the "true nervous principle" of plants, derived from the rays of the sun. "Some modern physiologists have been vainly searching for the traces of a nervous system in the plant itself. They should have looked to the sunshine; unless, indeed, moonshine would do as well." He let his contempt come to the surface even more when he compared Draper's work to an "*omelette soufflé* of which Dumas & Lavoisier have furnished the egg,—Cuvier, Humboldt & Lyell—the salt and spices—Draper the *sugar* and *wind!*" [23]

Gray's penchant for sarcasm should not obscure the essential base of his criticism of Draper. The numerous outbursts of "bah," "Whew," and "pssha" which line Gray's review copy are matched by many notations of "good," "Dumas," "Lavoisier," "Cuvier," "Brongniart," "Henslow," "Müller," and "Boussingault." Gray showed he was perhaps even more familiar with the literature of the new science than Draper, whom he accused of parading things "all very true, & extremely trite" as new and revolutionary discoveries. His attack on Draper's ultimate conclusion came not from fear for vitalism but from scientific skepticism about his methods.

In New York, Draper raised such a howl about Gray's "wickedly assailing him" that John Torrey and others felt they should defend their friend's *"credit and good name."* Gray, however, wrote the whole thing off as amusing, saying that Draper had "no recourse except to abuse, or to decry motives, or to charge ignorance." And he felt his criticisms would stand before the only people about whom he cared—scientists. "If any competent persons do not see the true state of the case, they must be *asses,* and it would be throwing away powder to attempt to enlighten them." Considering Draper, "a man who can introduce such rigamarole into a scientific treatise," as "nearly past cure," he admonished Torrey, "pray keep cool!" [24] The controversy dropped from public notice and perhaps from the consciousness of both men. If in later years they both became evolutionists, they became so not from any personal esteem or connection, nor by parallel processes of thought.

Out of the battle Gray emerged as strong a vitalist as before. Echoes of the confused struggle then centering about Liebig on the Continent occasionally attracted his notice, especially a book by the Dutch chemist, G. J. Mülder, which found its way into an English translation.[25] Here not only were laws of inorganic chemistry applicable to living things, but the line of thought completely bridged the mineral and the living world, opening a door for the revival of the ancient concept of spontaneous generation. "The idea of an ovum is thus reduced, in truth, to that of an organic molecule. . . . In the same way . . . the general vital force is reduced to molecular forces." This threatened the orderly divisions of the natural system even more than the mechanization of life, for it brought into question the Maker in the very act of creating. Again, however, Gray did not engage in blanket condemnations but followed the same line of approach he had just used on Draper. Although Mülder was "very ingenious," he "has not . . . advanced our knowledge a particle, and . . . his generalizations are unsound." Especially were his "conclusions as to equivocal generation . . . non-constat from his own premises." [26]

From another direction, geology, disturbing ideas were also assailing scientists in the 1840's. When Charles Lyell published his *Principles of Geology* in 1830 he popularized two concepts. The first, developed from fossils found in various strata of rock, greatly extended the time span during which the earth's crust was formed and had been inhabited. The second, uniformitarianism, accounted for these changes far back in the geological past by the same forces of wind, water, and volcanoes which could be observed at present. A homely illustration which Gray had no trouble visualizing was Lyell's calculation that the Niagara River was of sufficient strength to cut the seven miles of channel from Lake Ontario back to the present rim of the falls in about 33,000 years. "If such events can take place while the zoology of the earth remains almost stationary and unaltered, what ages may not be comprehended . . . during which the Flora and Fauna of the globe have been almost entirely changed!" [27]

The lines of thought which Lyell advanced produced epic conflict within geology. On the one hand, it required an adaptation if not the abandonment of the deluge of Noah's time as found in Genesis. By the 1840's virtually all responsible thinkers had reconciled themselves at least to interpreting the Scriptures broadly on this point and to assuming a great antiquity for life on the earth. The more fundamental problem concerned those schools of geology which saw the progression of organisms revealed in the various strata as the fulfillment of the great chain of being, the development of a progressive idea. To explain the discontinuities in the ladder of beings through the ages as shown by the breaks between strata, these idealists became also catastrophists. Lyell's uniformitarianism cut across both the catastrophes and the unfolding of a progressive idea. [28]

Gray's philosophical orientation made Lyell's position so congenial that he never recorded a conversion to it; he neither fought nor celebrated it. When in the winter of 1845 Lyell himself was lecturing at the Lowell Institute just before Gray began his series, the botanist attended regularly, seeing "him and Mrs. Lyell now and then—chiefly at the lecture room." Although he was not to Gray's mind a "good lecturer at all," he had a "fine audience throughout. They have been so much interested in his later lectures occupying— though under a rather different aspect the ground I am to take up . . . on Geographical Botany &c—that I feel quite emboldened to go on with them." [29] Thus by 1845 Gray had effortlessly absorbed Lyell's geology, or at least its point of view.

About this time a book fell into Gray's hands which had gathered up these strands of thought and speculatively projected them into a comprehensive picture of the past history of the earth, bringing into the open deep antagonisms. The anonymous author of the *Vestiges of the Natural History of Creation*,[30] starting with the nebular hypothesis of the origin of the solar system, moved through the successive geologic eras, showing wide reading and an amateur's understanding of scientific literature. He prudently kept his identity secret. To him the inorganic world merged into the organic by spontaneous generation as a preliminary to the progressive development of one species from another, it having "pleased Providence to arrange that one species should give birth to another, until the second highest gave birth to man who is the very highest." Although extremely pious and deferential in his language, he was careful to exclude any supernatural tampering after the first act of creation. All was ruled by comprehensive law after the initial impulse— gravitation in the inorganic world, and the organic, "the other great department of mundane things, rests in like manner on one law and that is,—DEVELOPMENT." [31]

As Gray read the book his pencil stabbed indignantly. When the author claimed his scheme was actually in harmony with Genesis, Gray noted that the Mosaic account "is in harmony with what there is of truth in your scheme." To the idea of creation by law he retorted that "rule is not opposed to the idea of *direct, immediate* creation." To the contention that the same laws govern organic and inorganic matter he "Denied absolutely that there is anything in mineral matter tending to produce ligneous fibre." To the farfetched argument that some mineral crystals resemble trees and shrubs he snorted, "Stuff. What is to be inferred from such remote analogies of external form. . . . Hardy assumptions and doubtful facts are all equally fish that come into his net." To the argument that Wöhler had synthesized urea, Gray dodged that it was "not a fact. Wöhler probably made something like *urea*. [It] is a product of decomposition, even if it were formed from Carbonate of Ammonia—it would prove nothing."

To the argument that spontaneous generation had recently slacked off because the world was nearly full, Gray asked, "Why should it not keep at work? Laws are absolute. The spinning jenny & loom once set in motion can not stop to calculate whether the state of the cotton market makes it worth while to go on producing." The report of experiments that small plants had been observed generated in places where there were no seeds made Gray sarcastic—"Denied outright. But we will give you *air* in plenty." The absurd contention that "flowers which bear stamens on one stalk and pistils on another, can be caused to produce both . . . by having a sufficiency of nourishment supplied to them" brought from him a curt "not so!" And when the author claimed that Africans who "in the United States . . . have enjoyed a within-door life for several generations, assimilate to the whites amongst whom they live," Gray was reduced to a flabbergasted "!!" This easy and inexact use of environment to alter species led Gray to claim that the work of the French naturalist Lamarck "contained essentially all your book!"

Gray was not alone in having both his scientific and his religious complacency ruffled by the *Vestiges*. Boott wrote of the excitement in London and the speculation as to who the author might be. In Boston a geologist named Henry Darwin Rogers took the lead in espousing the new ideas, and the Harvard faculty began to choose sides. Gray, who just at the moment was giving his Lowell Institute lectures, had an opportunity to put his views forward and become the leader of the opposition. Benjamin Peirce, at first "rather inclined to favor Rogers," came over "sound and strong." That Gray saw religious implications in the controversy is clear from the fact that he read his lecture in advance to Mr. Albro, pastor of his church.[32]

It is possible to identify with confidence some manuscript notes for Gray's lecture. Significantly, the point of which he was most critical is the *Vestiges'* reliance on spontaneous generation. He examined cases in the seed plants and also discussed *infusoria,* coming to the confident conclusion that spontaneous generation does not take place.[33] Not only was the author of the *Vestiges* on dubious ground in the light of the evidence. In general the simple, single series progression of organisms from inert matter to man envisaged by the author of the *Vestiges* was theoretically abhorrent to Gray, who had already denied the chain of being in a single series and had pointed to the multiple relation of organisms as described by the natural system.

Although extremely anxious to get into print on the subject, Gray did not immediately succeed. Francis Bowen, doubtless using scientific data from his botanical colleague, himself took up the cudgels in the *North American Review,* laboring the *Vestiges* as a return to Epicurus's fortuitous concurrence of atoms. Gray felt this "long winded article" would keep him from "touching it there." [34] The *American Journal of Science* noted the book only briefly and noncommittally, James Dwight Dana preparing the paragraph from some notes of Silliman without ever having seen a copy. Since this was something of a victory for the *Vestiges,* Gray's remonstrances drew from his good friend Dana, a geologist perhaps as well qualified to review it as any scientist in the country, the admission that "I regret that the few words said were not of a more conservative character but still think that no permanent injury will result from the wide distribution of the work." [35]

In 1846 the author of the *Vestiges,* goaded by the "shaving he did get on both sides of the waters," published an answer to his many critics called *Explanations: A Sequel to "Vestiges of the Natural History of Creation."* This gave Gray his chance. Again his pencil flew furiously as he read. And the way was now open for a long article in the *North American Review.*[36]

He left no doubt that he considered the idea of the transmutation of species instead of special creation most objectionable both theologically and philosophically. He saw the "unity we perceive in nature" to which "sound science has ever delighted to point, as the proof that all is the direct handiwork of a single omniscient Creator." He saw law operating in the universe, to be sure, but the regularity with which species reproduced their like impressed him "that they not only *had* a Creator, but *have* a Governor." He felt that "abler pens than ours have shown, that the agencies now in operation will not account for the origin of any created thing." To Gray, creation did not need to limit itself to the beginning of time, and, while admitting that land animals did not appear until a late geologic era, "we are still to be convinced that they were not *then* created as perfect as they are now." The direct creative agency of the Deity was "the only cause, so far as we yet know, which will account for the facts." Those who "adopt the other view, and carry the principle *nec Deus intersit* to this length, are bound to show that natural agencies are competent to produce such results as these. The burden of proof rests upon them."

The easy way out for those who, like Gray, subscribed to the Protestantism of nineteenth-century America was to fall back on the authority of the Scriptures and cite the story of the creation in Genesis. But the core of Gray's position in the controversy rested precisely on the fact that he tacitly but steadfastly refused to take such a course. Bibliolatry being no part of Gray's religion, he could confidently test ideas abhorrent to his theology by scientific truth, which "we must receive . . . if proven, and build up our religious belief by its side as well as we may."

Actually Gray considered the *Vestiges* an attack on the integrity of science quite as much as a disturber of religion. In the first place, the claim that all the theories were new irritated Gray, as always conscious of the continuity of science. "To the *savans* they have not the charm of novelty." Especially was the "development scheme . . . just that of Lamarck, with the modifications of St. Hilaire, sustained now and then by special arguments, which we allow, these veteran naturalists never dreamed of." The author by his claim of novelty thus, according to Gray, by-passed such devastating refutations of Lamarck as that of Lyell. But more important than his repudiation of his predecessors was the author's rejection of his contemporaries' judgment. Faced with the undoubted fact that *"nearly all the scientific men are opposed to the theory of the Vestiges,"* the author neutralized "the natural effect of his admission" by doubting "whether the *savans* understand science." In the increasing specialization which Gray's career so well illustrated the author could charge that scientists were incapable of the over-all view necessary to deal with the fundamental problems of the origin of life.

Gray answered with a spirited defense of scientists, not only in their own special fields, but also because one "deeply versed in a single department, is much better qualified to judge of the whole scheme, than one who, like our author, professes to possess only a superficial acquaintance with any branch of science whatever." Great comprehensive views had always come from men of research. "Did Newton, Herschel, Laplace, Cuvier, Davy, De Candolle, or Humboldt, give to the world mere naked facts, the germs of great views that had to fall into other minds ere they were developed or grew fecund?" Scientists opposed the idea of transmutation of species not out of hypocritical fear for their positions, "but because it is really as repugnant to their reason, and contrary to their observation, as it is to the common sense of mankind. . . ."

Although weighted with sarcasm and occasionally overconfident in slashing at particular errors of fact, Gray's review adds up to a comprehensive demonstration of the shortcomings of the *Vestiges*. The later acclaim of Darwin should not obscure the very good reasons why his supposed forerunner failed of acceptance. In the first place, Gray pointed out that although the simplest animals appeared in the lowest geological strata and became progressively more complex in the higher, there was no explanation forthcoming of a necessary connection between the strata. In the second place, the analogy—that "tricksy companion"—of the development of the embryo with the progress of animal life established no causal relation between the history of the individual and the history of life. Nor was there any way around the observed fact that species usually breed true. Nor was refuge in an "internal impulse" sufficient explanation for the direction of evolution. That life followed a "law" did not prove anything as to its origin. Spontaneous generation had never stood up to a reliable experiment. The clear statement of questions is of the utmost importance in science, and even if few grasped the significance of this aspect of the review, it at least set Gray's own mind in order. When some genius should come along to supply "probability and proof" on these critical issues, he would be ready. In the meantime he would do credit to his scientific acumen by joining not only Agassiz and Richard Owen but also Huxley and Darwin in condemning the *Vestiges*.

At only one point did Gray close a door he would in time have to reopen. He freely admitted that if the transmutation theory were established *"there must be a complete revolution in the view which is generally taken of the relation to the Father of our being."* His friend Dana immediately pointed out to him an alternative. The geologist, whose work on the exploring expedition corals had brought him close to the junction of animal and plant life, had "never been afraid of" the *Vestiges,* "although I have not doubted that it would make some infidels." He reasoned that man needed "the principles we as Christians believe, and this fact will not be modified by any view of our creation. We are sinful beings and no other plan could restore us." Hence he assured Gray (and also published in the *American Journal of Science*) that *"should the* theory *prove* true, it would not affect the truths of religion." [37] If Gray ever faced the terrifying necessity of accepting the transmutation theory, he might wish to reconsider his prediction of revolution.

The agitation of this "whole series of subjects"—Draper, Mülder, and the *Vestiges*—changed Gray's outlook in important ways. The natural-system equilibrium of the early 1840's had at least been jostled. His religion and his science worked together as well as before, but now he was conscious of the joint where they met. He was looking for a new synthesis to take the place of that of the old-time naturalist. Now, in place of the old grouping around the naturalist's collecting, a new pattern was emerging of sciences oriented to the problems of life—botany, zoology, geology, organic chemistry. Gray could no longer look even at his everyday tasks without seeing the intrusion of new and insistent questions. When reading the *Vestiges* he had remarked, "Who knows but *he* made many primary individuals of a species. All that we maintain is that *He* made them." [38] This problem was unsettled in any cosmogony. Did species descend from a single pair as in the story of Noah, or from many pairs independently created? The question nagged.

Not the least important effect of his controversies was the fact that Gray became a leader of scientific opinion in Cambridge with more than *ex officio* weight. The *Vestiges* became directly involved in faculty politics in 1846 with the vacancy of the Rumford professorship in the application of the sciences to the useful arts. Henry Darwin Rogers, who, with his brother William Barton, had long had his eye on Boston as a site for a polytechnic institute, was trying hard to get the appointment, which would then have furthered the plans of a remarkable family. Gray, considering him a "Lamarckian Vestiges" heretic, took "prompt and decided action" with the Corporation.[39] Even an alleged recantation by Rogers was of no avail, and Eben N. Horsford, whose candidacy Gray had helped in various ways, received the job. This erstwhile student of Amos Eaton's and more recently of Liebig's was an asset to Harvard, but Rogers's coming might very well have changed the history of science in Boston in important ways. For Gray this was at best a questionable victory.

In a more positive way he set out to attract to Cambridge outstanding scientists, especially in the fields which were beginning to bear on the problems of life. Since James Dwight Dana would have strengthened Harvard in geology immeasurably, Gray tried hard to get a place for him, but the result was a generous balancing offer which kept him at Yale. The old dream of working with Joseph Henry again appeared briefly. More successful was his part in getting a first-rate zoologist. When old Dr. John Collins Warren, long the Hersey professor of anatomy at Harvard Medical School in Boston, retired, the friends of Jeffries Wyman saw their chance. They would persuade the Corporation to split the Hersey fund, allowing Oliver Wendell Holmes to give the lectures in Boston and setting Wyman up in Cambridge to teach anatomy and physiology to the college students. Gray had known and liked this young scholar, who had been curator of the Lowell Institute. As soon as he "understood the divorce project" [40] Gray aided in securing the appointment.

Wyman, a careful observer and experimenter, enriched Gray's scientific surroundings in Cambridge greatly. As an anatomist he could complement the department of botany and zoology on the side which Gray completely neglected, for among his early duties was teaching the elementary natural history of animals. Even more important was the fact that, without presuming to speculate on the larger issues, he conducted research on many specific zoological points which had a place in the discussions of the big questions of the development of life. He designed careful experiments on spontaneous generation.[41]

Overshadowing all these steps to make Harvard a scientific center was the arrival of a true giant. Louis Agassiz, only three years older than Gray, had already an established reputation as a protégé of Humboldt, a brilliant successor of the comparative zoologist Cuvier, and an ingenious and speculative thinker on glaciation.[42] On the recommendation of Lyell, John A. Lowell engaged him for the Institute for the fall of 1846, and Agassiz, in financial difficulties, came to America to give them and remain for a short visit. The spell of undeveloped possibilities for science and the receptiveness of the large lecture audiences convinced him by stages that he should stay permanently. Not only his attainments but his remarkable personality created a sensation among the local scientists.

Asa Gray had every reason to rejoice at Agassiz's coming. Since he had accepted so much hospitality in Europe, his desire to reciprocate reinforced his enthusiasm for a man who, among many other things, had been a student of his friend Von Martius and who was a brother-in-law of the botanist Alexander Braun. Since Agassiz wished to visit as much of the country as possible, he struck off immediately for New York, stopping off at New Haven to see Silliman, "the patriarch of science in America." Gray was waiting to join him at Torrey's house in Princeton to take him to Washington. They spent four days in Philadelphia and made the rounds of the scientists at the capital. Gray left his charge at Philadelphia on the return trip. As a guide for American science he had done good work, for Agassiz, although appalled at the lack of institutions and leisure, was pleasantly surprised at what he saw. "I thought myself tolerably familiar with all that is doing in science in the

United States, but I was far from anticipating so much that is interesting and important."

Back in Cambridge in December 1846, Gray introduced various of his Cambridge colleagues at a dinner. Although Agassiz thought of Gray more as one who "with his indefatigable zeal . . . will gain upon his competitors " [43] than as a completely established leader, he was nevertheless most pleasant. To one inured to the comparative absence of sparkling scientific talk which prevailed in America the very presence of Agassiz was invigorating. He "gave to our club . . . a most excellent and spirited account of the mathematical arrangement of leaves." [44]

At this period Gray's brother George, an undergraduate at Harvard, was living at the garden. With the unscientific and unspoiled eyes of a country boy from central New York, he gazed out of the window of the garden house and described to his cousin a scene at which she "would have laughed finely."

Mr. Agassiz came here today & brought with him a friend of his, a Swiss or a Frenchman, who wears big whiskers & an odd sort of overcoat so as all in all to cut a most queer figure. They, and Dr. went into the garden after some specimens of branches. Not long after I looked out of the window. They were running about the garden each one loaded with branches, hallooing like schoolboys as one or the other found a branch at all peculiar; and that Frenchman had a great toad, carrying it by its leg, gently as if it were a lump of gold, & now & then raising it up to examine its peculiarities. The toad is now carefully laid aside; poor fellow it will soon have to be cut up to satisfy the Frenchman's curiosity.[45]

Agassiz, not long in giving bold answers to bold questions, "unsparingly & thoroughly cut up Lamarckian Vestiges theories." [46] When a group of scientists asked him to define a species, he answered—sententiously it seemed to Gray—"A species is a thought of the Creator." Even in the 1840's this was an extremely idealistic statement of special creation. To him the animal species of each geologic age were completely distinct from those that preceded or followed it.[47] The Lowell Institute gave him an opportunity to introduce his plan of creation. It was a dramatic performance. Lecturing "without notes & from a full brain . . . he has now got his English in well enough trim, and charms all, both popular & scientific." After introducing the subjects of comparative anatomy and the development of the ovum, he surveyed "the succession of species in time," and the "geographical distribution of extant and fossil species." [48]

Gray was more than just an interested listener, for he was acting as Agassiz's agent in arranging, through Torrey, for a course of lectures in New York. Since more than one interpretation could run afoul of Moses, the rumor-mongers there were busy spreading the word that Agassiz was "hostile to revealed religion," and many subscribers were "withholding their names without some . . . guaranty that their religious opinions shall not be assailed." Torrey wrote as if even he almost believed them. Gray's reports to Torrey, which thus had an important practical relation to Agassiz's success in America, unequivocally vouched for his new friend. The rumor arose, he thought, from the contention that "animals and plants were originally created in numbers occupying a considerable area, perhaps almost as large as they now occupy." In applying this to man, Agassiz did "not believe that the Negro & Malay races descended from the sons of Noah but had a distinct origin." [49]

As a devoutly religious man defending a friend Gray edged close to indignation. "The whole course was planned on a very high ground, and his references to the Creator were so natural and unrestrained as to show they were never brought in for effect." Agassiz soundly adhered to special creation of present species "at the commencement of the historic era—which is all we want to harmonize Geology with Genesis." He wrecked the *Vestiges* completely. His "admirable lectures on embryology contain the most original and fundamental refutation of materialism I ever heard." As to the tale-bearers in New York, Gray would "be glad to know that Dr. J. A. Smith in the whole course of his public teaching, has displayed a reverence for the Bible, equal to that of A." Gray spoke as one who had had opportunity to know. "I have been on the most intimate terms with him. I never heard him express an opinion or a word adverse to the claim of revealed religion."

When Gray examined the particular point at issue, he revealed a peculiar and crucial divergence from Agassiz. The European defended his views of the separate creation of Negroes and Malays not only on the general analogy of his studies of the lower animals but also by a rather ingenious piece of Biblical criticism, showing that "the sons of Noah (Ham with the rest) were fathers of the Caucasian races—races which have remained nearly unaltered from the first, and if any Negroes proceeded from Ham's descendants it must have been a miracle." Special creation and miracles were evidently two different things. Gray, the devout Presbyterian, admitted that Agassiz had "conclusively" proved his point from the Bible and then with a free conscience denied the conclusion! The reason, he cryptically told Torrey, was that "We should not receive it (rejecting it on other than scientific grounds, of which he does not feel the force as we do)."

Having left Agassiz's science unchallenged and having admitted his scripture, Gray heard the fire bell in the night. In the year of the Wilmot Proviso slavery was becoming a serious problem in the United States. The pro-slavery argument had its scientific side, and Gray was entirely aware of the work of men like Josiah Nott, who were trying to prove the Negroes inferior to the white race. He had himself developed a great abhorrence of slavery.[50] He did not take Agassiz's suggestion as any more than an "extension" of scientific principles. Therefore political convictions could count against them. As to religion, the spirit and not the words was important. Gray assured Torrey that "we may reject his conclusions but we cannot find fault with his spirit. . . ." Of the two men, Agassiz had much the more highly developed scientific position—more data, more positive answers. Gray had as yet nothing to say about the problem of the distribution of species, but he showed awareness of the religious storms boiling up without feeling panic, and he had an acute insight into the final political uses to which a scientific theory might be put.

At just this period another change affected the scientific institutions of Harvard. For the first time a large sum from the burgeoning profits of the cotton mills along the Merrimac came to their service. Abbott Lawrence offered $50,000 for the founding of a scientific school. A practical businessman whose companies faced complex technical problems, he visualized an education for "men of action. Hard hands are ready to work upon our hard materials; and where shall sagacious heads be taught to direct those hands?" He was quite aware that his gift might easily arouse the envy of the scientists who had struggled for years on a pittance. He hoped he would not draw donations from the observatory. "Nor do I mean to occupy the ground of another branch of science that will, I suppose, at a future time, present strong claims upon the public bounty. I allude to Natural History, now in charge of that accomplished naturalist, Dr. Gray." In order to preserve the "perfect harmony at Cambridge" he wished for, he proposed that instruction in the new school in "natural history and natural philosophy, be given by the present College Professors." [51]

When the gift was first announced, Gray, looking forward to a real change in his work, felt the importance of being "ready to teach practical botany." From a financial viewpoint he "would like it if our scientific school should bye & bye bring in a few botanical students." [52] For a moment the vision loomed up of Gray as a great pioneer in economic botany, horticulture, possibly agriculture, but the occasion almost immediately passed. The Lawrence Scientific School never went very far in applied science but became instead the means of bringing Agassiz permanently to Cambridge. Lawrence guaranteed his salary of $1500, and in April 1848 he began his first regular classes. The stamp of his personality and interests immediately obliterated all other ideas from the school, and Harvard's older college departments, although sharing somewhat in the Scientific School's instruction, continued to go their own way.

Gray, much too busy to be jealous, felt only intense satisfaction at having Agassiz for a colleague. He could gain strength from this master of several sciences and foe of infidelity. Joseph Henry, just moving into a wider sphere at the new Smithsonian Institution, was visiting in Cambridge in the fall of 1847. In a long evening at the Botanic Garden, he, Agassiz, and Gray talked with mellow affection. Homesick for his family, Agassiz read letters from Switzerland. The physicist told of his early boyhood in New York State. Asa Gray exulted, "It is not a year since I told Henry that he should have either Agassiz or Wyman at Washington, but that we must have one of them at Cambridge. Beyond all expectations we have them both!" [53] Harvard and Gray had added new dimensions in the past six years.

VIII

"WHERE PLANTS HAVE NO LATIN NAMES"

NEITHER teaching nor gardening nor philosophizing could account completely for the fury with which Asa Gray attacked his work in the late 1840's, "studying out something to save the world from ruin or the sky from falling." His brother George, watching him, said he "would like to have forty men at his command, one to hold his pen while he thinks, another to hand him books, another to hold his paper &c. &c. in a word he would keep them all busy & want a half a dozzen boys to boot; & yet work would not go fast enough for him." [1] The demon which drove him rose up from the smoke of campfires on plains and mountains, far from the complacently placid streets of Cambridge. Gray had committed himself to North American botany, whose scope was geared to American expansion.

Penetration of the trans-Mississippi West [2] and especially of the Rocky Mountains was nothing new. Many a mountain man, a bit down on his luck with the decline of the beaver trade, carried around in his head a marvelously accurate map of the whole West, and in his skill at hunting and woodcraft he possessed a sharp if rather uneven insight into the natural history of the region. The new factor after 1840 was the advent of science to the plains and Rockies. To the shadowy boundaries of Oregon and the Republic of Texas, to the somnolent provinces of northern Mexico, Americans were thinking of political integration under the flag of the United States. They needed knowledge of the region beyond the hearsay of the mountain men.

To explore in an orderly way required an elaborate outlay of men and equipment, all highly specialized. The effective botanical collector had to know enough science to give precious baggage space only to the most significant specimens. He had to have skill in the delicate business of drying and preserving plants. In addition, he had to be a good plains and mountain traveler, knowing not only how to handle a wagon, endure a steady diet of buffalo meat or much worse, and to live in the saddle or walk twenty miles a day; but also how to hunt and to fight Indians. Above all he had to be willing to live for months or years away from civilization without family, with only army men and trappers for company, with at best an uncertain hope of reward at the end. A man who could do and endure all this was not likely to have either the ability or the desire to study the collections, compare earlier literature, and write the descriptions which were sedentary necessities in completing the job of scientific exploring. Often the wanderer could not stand the rigors of civilized life at all after several seasons in the West.[3]

Since some of these men found their own way, their bundles appeared in the East, unassorted, unstudied, but full of new genera which had never before been described. Even plants which had appeared in other localities took on a new interest as the pattern of their geographical distribution emerged. These accumulations, calling to the botanists for action, found only three men in the United States able to answer. Engelmann, Torrey, and Asa Gray worked faultlessly together, yet each performed a somewhat different function.

Torrey, still in his late forties in 1842, had the advantage of the longest experience, the best herbarium, and a long record of working with the government on scientific problems. He was just now finishing his work on the New York state survey, which left him free to go back to his old love, the western explorations, which had interested him nearly twenty years before when he published the botany of the Long expedition. As the topographical engineers of the army, under J. N. Nicollet, began to make maps of the upper Mississippi in the late 1830's, Torrey received the plants. When Frémont took over the task of making a map of the California and Oregon trails—which might be considered the signal for the grand assault on the West scientifically—Torrey was the logical one to do the botanical work. Thus he was unofficially scientist for the plant side of government surveys. Although he farmed out certain families of plants, he kept control of these collections and published the result himself.

When Frémont returned from his 1842 expedition to the Wind River Mountains and sent his plants to Torrey, the botanist immediately saw a chance for even greater things in the future—seeds for Gray's garden, and possibly a chance for a collector to go all the way to the Pacific in 1843. When Gray received the Frémont *Compositae*, his favorite family, from Torrey to write up, he had dreams of botanizing "near the snow-line. . . . I wish we had a collector to go with Fremont. It is a great chance. If none are to be had, Lieutenant F. must be indoctrinated, and taught to collect both dried specimens and seeds." The reward would be glory; "he shall be immortalized by having the 999th Senecio called S. Fremontii. . . ." [4]

Frémont's bright promise for Western botany never fully materialized. In the midst of great uncertainty he left for the wilderness in 1843 without a collector. At St. Louis, George Engelmann "assisted him in his preparations and gave him instructions for geological & botanical researches. . . ." Thus Frémont handled his botany personally, and, although he promised Torrey to pay attention to what the botanists, "of course, consider the main object of the expedition," the commanding officer had both other interests and other duties while on the trail. Most of the collections from the second expedition were soaked in a flood on the Kansas River, and Engelmann, not allowed to dry out the specimens, complained that the lieutenant "appears to me rather selfish—I speak confidentially—and disinclined to let any body share in his discoveries, anxious to reap all the honour, as well as undertake all the labour himself." Gray, after he had tried in vain to get Jeffries Wyman a place on Frémont's third expedition, joined in this gloomy view. [5] Although the plants Frémont brought back were welcome, and Torrey liked the doughty officer, Gray and Engelmann were on the lookout for a more amenable explorer.

Since St. Louis was the funnel through which the nation flowed west, Dr. Engelmann had a unique opportunity to aid botanical exploration. This "center of North America, if not of the world and of civilization!—the great Focus for the west, and southwest" was a rough city for a learned man. "We burn $\frac{1}{3}$ of our steamboats, destroy $\frac{1}{10}$ of the wealth of our citizens in one night; kill $\frac{1}{10}$ by cholera—try our hand in burning again—all only to show how much we can stand without succumbing. . . ." [6] To Engelmann as a practicing doctor, the cholera especially meant months of exhausting toil, but after nine o'clock in the evening he found time for botany. In two ways he helped organize the explorations. In the first place he stood ready to help with outfits for plains travel and for collecting. Second, he could recruit any person who showed up in St. Louis with a yen for the business. As an immigrant he knew many of the university-trained Germans who for political or economic reasons had already wandered half around the world. The most promising manpower pool was here and not among feckless Harvard boys.

Engelmann's position, favorable as an advance base, also had drawbacks which made him call upon Gray as a partner. For final classification and publishing he had "neither the leisure, nor books, collections, etc., sufficient to do the work alone, or do it so well as to be creditable." [7] After numbering and ticketing the specimens, he would send them to Cambridge, where Gray made the final determinations and, through one of the local scientific societies, published the results. The *sine qua non* of all this activity was money. Gray with his large correspondence undertook to act as agent for selling the specimens by hundreds, ten dollars for those from the Rockies, eight dollars for Texas plants. Gray, Engelmann, and the collectors all hoped that the explorations would be self-supporting and that money advanced for the outfit would ultimately be repaid in plants. Gray felt this whole new activity as an intrusion on his well-laid plans, especially for the *Flora*, because "I excessively dislike to study special collections far ahead of my work. . . ." Indeed he was rather careful to promise to publish immediately only those families which already appeared in the *Flora*.[8]

Nevertheless the possibility of exploring the West had a strong hold on him. Ever since his visit to Sir William Hooker in Glasgow he had seen that great void on the map, the southern Rockies. Now he was not only receiving collections which came from that general direction but he pressed actively to send field men into the target area. "The interesting region (the most so in the world) is the high Rocky Mountains about the sources of the Platte, and thence south." This area was botanically unknown because it had not before been on the main-traveled routes. The very thing that repelled the average traveler made it beckon to Gray. He also had a tactical concept for the collectors which flowed from his strategy. To get the best plants, a man must climb, "get into high mountains, or as high as he can find, whenever he can." [9] Derived from his Carolina trips and his walking-journey in the Alps, this eminently sound scientific refrain must have irritated many a weary collector, held to a wagon train by threat of Indians, trying to get through the lowest possible pass. Generals are seldom popular, perhaps because sound strategy and tactics are not always compatible with the convenience of their troops. Part of the friction which sometimes developed between Gray and the collectors sprang directly from his tireless insistence that the southern Rockies were the target area, and that the higher one climbed the better the plants.

In 1842 Engelmann had available two men who might go West. Carl A. Geyer, a Dresden gardener who had come to America in quest of adventure, had gone out with Nicollet. Although Frémont would not have him, Engelmann thought highly of his collecting ability. Another young German, Friedrich G. J. Lüders, recommended to Gray by Lehmann of Hamburg and sent on to St. Louis, was also spoiling to get to the Rockies.[10] This first venture yielded the Engelmann-Gray partnership of exploring entrepreneurs exactly nothing. Lüders, far down the Columbia, upset his canoe, losing everything he had.[11] Discouraged by this disaster, he disappeared forever from North America. Geyer, on the other hand, began to feel independent in the mountain air. Oregon, jointly occupied by the Americans and the British, was still a target in Sir William Hooker's wide range of objectives. Geyer, finding the Hudson's Bay Company hospitality superior, soon wrote Engelmann that he would return not to the United States but to England. Sir William Hooker, although innocent of any connivance, was able to prolong his dominance of the botany of the Pacific coast by classifying the plants. Gray, lamenting how "shabbily" Geyer had "behaved," had to buy the specimens from Sir William, because it "is very important that there should be a set of these plants in the country, accessible to Dr. Torrey and myself, and I have concluded that I can afford to purchase them." [12] This experience not only left in Gray's and Engelmann's minds a most unpleasant impression of a field collector's trustworthiness, but it made them determined to control all work done in the West at least to the extent of keeping the collections in the United States.

In attacking the Texas frontier, the eastern approach to Gray's target area, the partners were much more fortunate. Indeed most of the details of their business arrangements came from their dealings with Ferdinand Jakob Lindheimer.[13] No plants of any significance had come out of Texas since Drummond and Berlandier had sent collections to Europe in the 1820's. But the revolution of 1836 had at once greatly increased communication with the United States, attracted a large number of immigrants, and provided a place for newly-arrived Germans to engage directly in pioneering. These new factors offered the possibility of renewed botanizing in Texas.

In 1842 Lindheimer sent Engelmann "a beautiful collection of plants from there—specimens as complete as you seldom see them. . . ." The next winter and spring—the same time Geyer and Lüders were going out—Lindheimer came to St. Louis, lived with Engelmann, and studied his specimens in order to have a better idea of what to collect. Since he was "to devote a few years entirely to the exploration of Texas and the collection of plants there, and intends to make at least his living by it," Engelmann proposed to Gray that the arrangement for studying the plants and selling sets of specimens be extended to these Texas collections. Gray agreed and included Lindheimer in his advertisement in the *American Journal of Science*.[14] The obstacles to collecting in Texas were immense. Although Lindheimer had his own wagon and lived by hunting, he was not able before 1845 to penetrate farther west than Drummond had before him. In 1844, joining a colony of settlers from Germany called the *Adelsverein,* Lindheimer pushed west of the Colorado River and helped found the town of New Braunfels. To him this was promising country where "the plants, I hope, have no Latin names." [15]

Since the years after 1842 were the period of his most strenuous attempts to build up the garden, Gray attempted a second enterprise with Lindheimer—to get him to collect live plants and roots to ship to Cambridge. Although the garden had little money to spare, Gray sensed a new source in John A. Lowell. Not only had he been generous as head of the Institute, inviting Gray to lecture and buying the best microscope in Boston for the use of scientists, but he had scientific interests of his own. "As Mr. Lowell expressed a desire to aid in this matter and as he is a cultivator, keeps a gardener, conservatory, etc., I asked him to eke out our poverty here at the Garden, by joining me in a remittance. . . ." They would pay Lindheimer $75, and $100 each year after the first for "*seeds, bulbs,* cacti (especially), tubers, and indeed roots of live herbs, shrubs." Mr. Lowell would get part of the plants for his own garden. Gray was elated that this wealthy man "begins to take hold of Botany with great spirit." [16] A new and important figure had entered the exploring business. The attempt to get live plants from Texas proved a costly failure. Gray had banked on the expectation that annexing Texas to the Union, of which he disapproved politically, would introduce better transportation.[17] But the precedent of having the capitalist advance money for botanical ventures might work with other projects.

In another way Gray was not satisfied with Lindheimer. Completely ignorant of the hardships of frontier life, he had trouble from the beginning believing that the collector was not lazy. Engelmann, closer to the scene of action, always backed Lindheimer, at one time advancing him $500, and this personal trust proved justified. Gray's doubts sprang in part from his strategic concepts. "As he gets more and more in the interior the species will be fewer like Drummond's, and like those of the southern United States generally." As the sales manager he had to consider the attraction of new genera, a few of which "will carry off a good many common plants." [18] Instead of moving faster toward the target area of the southern Rockies, Lindheimer moved ever more slowly, marrying and becoming a part of the German settlements in Texas. After

1852 he was to shift completely away from collecting to become the editor of a newspaper in New Braunfels. Had the frontier of Texas continued to move after the middle 1840's, he might have gone with it and found new collecting grounds. However, the advance of settlement was stalled for a quarter of a century. Lindheimer personally might be on "friendly terms with the Comanchees," but that fierce and warlike people, ranging far down from the strongholds on the high plains, kept all save occasional military expeditions at bay until the 1870's. Asa Gray, an American, couldn't wait that long.

Early in 1846, with the first part of "Plantae Lindheimerianae" off the press and no work to do on the departed Geyer's plants, Gray found enough time to return to his basic project of the *Flora of North America*. Indeed the special collections should fit into it rather than be described in messy scattered papers, as Gray well knew. He now made "preparations to take up the Flora again, and to stick to it *till done*." [19] But Americans could not wait for Gray either; it was the year of decision for the western country, and in a few brief months American expansion brought its weight to bear on Mexico from Texas to the Pacific. Gray, if he ever stopped to condemn the spread of slavery, did not let his political views blind him to scientific opportunity. When the war broke out, St. Louis swarmed with people, military and otherwise, who were heading for the botanist's goal.

On May 30, 1846, he wrote Engelmann that they "must have a collector for plants living and dry to go to Santa Fe, with the Government Expedition. If I were not so tied up, I would go myself." By getting the protection of the army and an advance of $200 or so from Lowell for an outfit, they could send a man into the field. Gray optimistically calculated—"sixty sets of five hundred plants . . . which, named by us, would go off at once at ten dollars per hundred"—a clear profit of twenty-eight hundred dollars for the season.

On June 25, Engelmann answered that "I believe I have found a young man." [20] Augustus Fendler was, like Lindheimer, and Geyer, a wandering German who had learned the ways of the frontier travel before getting interested in collecting. [21] Engelmann found him in St. Louis manufacturing fuel for spirit lamps and learning some botany on the side. The doctor talked him out of trying to sell plants from the oft-covered St. Louis area but helped him learn the technique. When the Mexican War came along Fendler was, after two stationary years, anxious to roam.

When Gray heard on July 3 that Fendler would go, he acted without hesitation. He used all his earlier experience, from the U.S. Exploring Expedition to Lindheimer, in making arrangements which were a model of prompt and efficient support. Sullivant would send $50 immediately against future collections of mosses. John A. Lowell agreed to his part and made an advance. Gray "immediately wrote to Marcy, the Secretary of War, and to Colonel Abert, the head of the Topographical Engineer Corps; asked the secretary to send anything he might be disposed to do to . . . St. Louis." Through Engelmann he sent instructions to Fendler. "His collection should commence when he crosses the Arkansas; his first envoi should be the plants between that and Santa Fe, and be sent this fall, with seeds, cacti, and bulbs, the former of every kind he can get." He must climb. "The mountains north of Santa Fe often rise to the snow-line, and are perfectly full of new things." He should get forty specimens of each plant. Engelmann was so "delighted to see with what promptness all acted, you yourself, Mr. Sullivant, Mr. Lowell, the Secretary and our quartermaster here" that he began "to hope a little more from this country for science!! " [22]

On August 10 or 11, 1846, just ten weeks after Gray first broached the idea, Fendler left Fort Leavenworth with "Col. Price's regiment of Cavalry." [23] While Engelmann worried about news of murders and insurrections in New Mexico and Asa Gray dreamed of ravishing high mountains, Fendler and his young brother, who went with him, waited out an uncomfortable and expensive winter in Santa Fe. Even when April came, he could not leave the neighborhood of the town. By July he was "sick with Scurvy and sick of matters . . . and wants to return." Inflation was so great that he had to sell even his watch and gun in order to live. At the end of the summer he turned his face toward Fort Leavenworth, thinking of the rich "gentlemen in the East . . . under the happy impression that the enjoyment of the fruits of my labour would soon compensate for all." [24]

Despite the handicaps Fendler's collections were notable. Engelmann reported that "they are beautiful, the specimens mostly splendid, and a great many new things amongst them. . . ." Both Gray and Sir William Hooker joined in this praise.[25] Gray, pushing much urgent work aside, had the "Plantae Fendlerianae" ready by November 1848. The bastion of the southern Rockies had yielded decisively.

Even before the gold rush Fendler wanted to go to California by way of Panama, and after the news from Sutter's Mill Gray could sympathize with his desire to shift objectives, for "he needs, with energy, certainly make more at digging gold than he ever can with plant gathering." But the over-all view showed botanists well stocked with California specimens and much still to do in New Mexico. "The place to collect now is about Taos,—and to get up Spanish Peaks, Long's Peak &c." After long negotiation, in which Gray refused absolutely any advances for a California expedition, he and Fendler finally agreed on a journey to Salt Lake. When only a short distance out onto the plains, the collector lost all his gear in a river "by foolish management of the commanding officer, Capt. Morris, a young officer of rifles, unexperienced in Prairie and Mountain life." Forced to return to the settlements, Fendler found everything he had left in St. Louis, including his own herbarium, had burned.[26] Although his collecting days were far from over, he never went West again. Gray allowed the advances to stand, departing for once from the rule that collecting specimens was a business. Engelmann remarked that "Mr. Lowell shows himself as a generous man, who knows how to appreciate the troubles of a poor naturalist." [27]

As Gray gathered experience, books, and specimens which enabled him to determine western plants authoritatively, he attracted some collections directly, sent through neither Engelmann nor Torrey. For instance, the American Board of Foreign Missions sent to the Presbyterian botanist "a pretty large and full collection of Oregon plants—complete and pretty well dried specimens" received from H. H. Spalding, "missionary on the Kooskooskie." Gray distributed them "after the way of the Lindheimer plants," reserving any profits for Spalding's mission.[28] The question of priority always bothered with such a collection containing just a few new things, whether to wait until a family could be surveyed comprehensively for the *Flora of North America* at the risk of having a similar specimen described by some second-rate or even first-rate European botanist. Gray worked some of the Spalding plants into the footnotes of "Plantae Fendlerianae." But since passive acceptance even of welcome plants never satisfied Gray, regardless of how pressed, he was on the lookout for a collector whose work and explorations he could directly control.

Charles Wright,[29] a native of Wethersfield, Connecticut, and a graduate of Yale, had wandered into Texas in 1837. When his first letter reached Gray in 1844 he doubtless appeared as an amateur who happened to live in an interesting region. Since Texas was one of his targets, Gray replied immediately with a "proposition," and Wright promised that "according to my ability I am ready to contribute my aid towards the advancement of any scientific undertaking."

Nonconformity stood out even in Wright's first letters. "I am no doctor or son of a doctor and neither have nor wish any handle to my name but plain Mr. I am graduate of Yale and so entitled to my A.B. if I want it and I seek no more." Only a year younger than Gray, he treated the professor with deference but without awe. "Neither of us can boast of the legibility of our penmanship—however having generally considered myself among the best in deciphering hieroglyphics yours gave me but little trouble." [30] For the collections he received Gray worked as a kind of errand boy. To buy a book on entomology, a Spanish dictionary, a microscope, a good supply of paper because Wright had "to buy newspapers out of the P.O. & pay the postage on them," was easy in Boston but difficult in Texas. Gray proved punctilious in this humble phase of his work, although he found answering letters promptly another matter.

After teaching for a while at a struggling East Texas institution called Rutersville College, Wright began to develop symptoms of the wanderlust, that disease so necessary to turn an amateur into a professional collector. The Mexican War, which had sent Fendler on his way and revealed Lindheimer as too sedentary to keep up with the scientific frontier, gave him his chance. In 1847 he wrote that as "my mind is fully made up not to stay here any longer than circumstances will require it of me, I shall equip myself for a frolic this summer." As soon as he got back to civilization in September he found a letter from Gray offering to make him curator for the winter at the garden to sort collections and incidentally to learn some advanced botany. Partly for the chance of visiting his family in Wethersfield he hurried North to spend the winter in New England.[31]

To meet a real weather-beaten collector face to face was a new experience for Gray, but they got on well together. The botanist once wrote, "you do not know what a helpless odd fellow he is— good for nothing but to collect & dry specimens—but one of the most unselfish & good natured men I know,—which good nature I test by *blowing him up* daily when he is here." From the beginning Wright wanted to go back to Texas. "There is still a vast field open here and if I were to consult my own taste I should prefer to be a collector." Gray, too, saw that he "prefers exploring to anything else —will go to Santa Fe, or wherever we choose to send him. He is used to roughing it, and long been in the woods and prairies." [32] By 1848 Lindheimer and Fendler had finished their best work in the West, but Wright was fresh, experienced, and ready to go. For his six years of hard work at Western exploration Gray could show not only significant results but an organization to complete the conquests.

As the collections came in from the field men, Gray felt more and more pressed to create a headquarters team which could turn out publications, a problem which involved much besides his books, specimens, and his personal knowledge of botany. He had already discovered in his teaching that illustrations were necessary, and since he himself was helpless, a botanical artist was as vital to the enterprise as the tough frontiersmen. Occasional aid from Miss Susan Quincy was not enough. Gray always considered that he was a lucky fellow, and his discovery of Isaac Sprague in 1845, the nick of time, must count among his strokes of good fortune. Sprague, born in 1811 in Hingham, Massachusetts, early began to paint birds and flowers from nature and in 1843 assisted John James Audubon on an expedition to Missouri. Professor C. C. Felton, who knew the artist in Hingham, introduced him to Gray in time for him to do drawings for the later Lowell Institute lectures and the second edition of the *Botanical Textbook*.[33] During the rest of Gray's career Sprague's competent illustrations provided seldom-mentioned but oft-seen support. He was much more than a mere artist who did what was set before him, for he learned to make his own analyses of flowers. Thus his work was scientifically correct without requiring Gray to check constantly. Indeed he often made discoveries by his close observation. To Sir William Hooker, Gray reported that "my artist has improved vastly in making analyses under the microscope, the drawings he is now making I know would please you greatly. He has a singular aptitude for this kind of work and the most exact eye, and conscientious as well as skilful hand." [34]

The German migration which brought Geyer, Lindheimer, Fendler, and Engelmann himself to America also helped strengthen Gray's artistic resources. A religious sect which came in a body from Germany and settled at Ebenezer, near Buffalo, New York, included a man named Joseph Prestele, who had worked for many years as an artist at Munich for Gray's friend Von Martius and others. Since he was highly skilled in drawing, painting, engraving, and lithography he wrote to Gray seeking employment.[35] Although he knew no English and would not leave his community to come to Cambridge, Gray gradually evolved a system which took advantage of Prestele's already fully developed talents. Sprague made drawings of plants which were growing in the garden and sent them to Ebenezer, where Prestele copied them on stone for lithographing. Thus in 1845 Gray brought together two superior workers in a very rare art. That many of his publications could match European standards physically stemmed from these men.

Gray, never one to let his team be idle, immediately began to hatch new projects which would rely heavily on illustrations. As early as 1843 he had a "plan to publish—from time to time—figures of rare or interesting N. American plants—chiefly those cultivated in our Gardens and those upon which I may throw some light." [36] Since all during this time seeds and roots were slowly reaching the garden, he would choose the most interesting ones each year, make a lithograph to be colored by painting, and publish them with a short description. In this way he could reap the triple advantage of furthering the knowledge of "new or scarcely known plants," advertising the garden, and often also the collectors. With Sprague and Prestele available Gray began to realize this dream in his "Chloris Boreali-Americana." [37]

Although Gray planned to publish a series of these illustrations, the first group of ten was hardly off the press when he had an even more grandiose idea for flower drawings. Since the *Flora* had bogged down under the weight of new material, it might be possible to choose a single species of each genus of the plants of the United States for description and an authoritative illustration. The first volume of the *Genera of the Plants of the United States* appeared in 1848.[38] This scheme involved immense labor, some of it Gray's and Prestele's, but much more of it Sprague's. Since the cost of the proposed ten volumes was far beyond anything Gray or anyone else in American botany had attempted, he did not expect to make money but was determined "to carry on the work to its completion . . . if the patronage received shall warrant the hope of a moderate remuneration of the artist." The *Genera,* which analyzed only one species of a genus, could not rival the *Flora* in scientific value, and Gray had foremost in mind the educational effect of the pictures— to turn "the ample and rapidly accumulating materials at my disposal . . . to useful account by prosecuting an undertaking which may . . . facilitate the more thorough study of Botany in this country. . . ."

Even with the best people of Boston, John A. Lowell in the lead, rallying behind the project, at least by subscribing for volumes, six modest dollars from great lords of industry like Nathan Appleton did not add up to very much after all. The total of $1000 was enough to go ahead with a second volume, but after that the work lapsed. The artist received $6 per plate which not only ate up $600 a volume alone, but "does not thus far pay Sprague day wages, he takes so much time and care with them." [39] The *Genera* joined the growing shelf of the incomplete works of Asa Gray. The *Flora,* the "Chloris," to a certain extent the "Plantae Lindheimerianae" and "Fendlerianae," trailed off in the mists even while prophesying more and better yet to come. In spite of his optimism Gray gradually began to recognize that "my great object and desire now is, to finish the work of various sorts in which I am now engaged,—and to take great care to engage in little more that will not *pay*." [40]

Just as Gray thought his cup was nearly full, a new attack came from a familiar quarter, which upset all his immediate plans and by implication threatened the whole structure of scientific organization he was building. Sometime in 1848 a man by the name of Alphonso Wood came to call on Gray in Cambridge. Although professing an interest in botany, his primary purpose was that of a teacher, to write as a textbook for secondary-school use a manual of the plants of the United States. Even if his original scheme was to get Gray to write such a book,[41] the busy professor's refusal is understandable, especially since he felt that his *Textbook* at least partly filled the need. Wood indulged in no Eatonian idiosyncrasies such as a weakness for the artificial system, professing to follow the "elaborate and highly authentic Flora of Drs. Torrey and Gray." [42] Yet little doubt could exist that he thought practical collecting rather than physiological botany the proper beginning course. Hence Gray's *Botanical Textbook* was his primary target.

Wood, who was just Gray's age and a New Englander teaching at an academy in New Hampshire, enjoyed the friendship and encouragement of Chester Dewey, but otherwise he didn't fit the pattern even of the amateurs like Engelmann or Sullivant, whose work Gray approved. He had published nothing and relied on his own rather haphazard collecting for herbarium specimens. Sullivant described a long call from Wood "just on his return from Indiana where he had spent 5 weeks (4 of them on his back with a fever) doing up all the Botany of the Western States. . . ." [43] Here was a teacher in the mold of Amos Eaton. Whatever his way with young people, he had not meshed his work with the main stream of science.

At first Gray took him very calmly. *"Wood* has called on me twice. He will I dare say produce something rather respectable— much better than anything of the Mrs. Lincoln school." The busy professor was even willing to appear magnanimous, admitting "that his work may do good, I dare say—though the better it prove, the more it will affect my own interest. But the field is freely open, and I wish him heartily all the success his book may deserve." [44] Wood was indeed violating Gray's cardinal principle that one "should be a complete master of a science, in order safely to teach its applications to practice. No idea is more fallacious, than that those who know little of a science may yet be qualified to write elementary books for those who know nothing." [45] Others had done just this. The length and complexity of the *Botanical Textbook* might lose it some customers in the lower schools, but generally it could take care of itself, especially in the new second edition of 1845.

When Wood's work actually appeared, Gray's complacency quickly evaporated. The damage went much deeper than the threatened income of the *Textbook*. For Wood, having disposed of anatomy and physiological botany in a scant hundred pages, relied heavily on a "Flora of the Northern Sections of the U. States, Particularly of New England and New-York." This was no mere list of families, as the *Botanical Textbook,* but a brief description in English of each species. Through the *Compositae,* about half way down the list of families, Wood could follow Torrey and Gray's *Flora.* But after that, having no guide, he "adopted those names which, in my own judgment, rest upon the best authority." [46] Here his work would be original, his judgments set precedents that, if adopted by most workers, Gray would have to follow regardless of his large collections and libraries. The schoolteacher was earnest and energetic enough to give the savants some twinges of conscience, but to allow his book to become the guide for the classification of American plants would have entailed a disastrous lowering of standards, a decline unnecessary because of the resources already gathered by Torrey and Gray.

The hard fact remained, however, that Gray's organization had put nothing forth which covered even briefly all the families of American plants. Charles Wright down in Texas was still using Eaton's *Manual.* Even good botanists would have to adopt Wood's new book as the best available. "Letters from Hitchcock [47]—and elsewhere—all point to the possibility that they will have to use his book (of which, by the way, he is preparing a second edition, which he cannot but improve), and ask me to prevent it by appending a brief description of New England or Northern plants to my 'Botanical Text-Book.'" With this encouragement Gray decided that the "great object is to keep the ground clear by running an uncompromising opposition against the threatening interlopers." As a builder of scientific institutions Asa Gray had a realistic grasp of power politics, and since he knew the strength of his position he made no apologies for declaring war.

He developed a scheme of action and a stand-by plan if the first one did not succeed. William Oakes of Ipswich, who had welcomed him to Massachusetts, had spent many years collecting the plants of New England for a regional *Flora*. "The man's preparations and materials are enormous!" Gray would provide the framework for Oakes to fill in "the specific characters and all that for New England plants." After adding "the characters of the (about 130) New York plants not found in New England," Gray proposed "to have a sufficient number of copies of this . . . bound up with the 'Botanical Text-Book' to meet the demands of the one-book system in New England and New York. . . ." To displace Wood he must offer it "at a price reduced to a minimum, so that nothing is to be made out of it, at least out of the first edition."

Oakes had already kept him "waiting and waiting" and now "something must be done at once." If the book was not complete by April 1, 1846, Gray had an "explicit" understanding Oakes "is soon to let me know, and to furnish me with New England matters, when I am to do, not exactly this, but a more compendious manual of the botany of New England, New York, New Jersey, and Pennsylvania, that is, the Northern States proper." Oakes soon proved unequal to the job, which forced Gray to adopt his stand-by plan in 1846, hoping to finish it by the spring of 1847. In this hectic and exasperating atmosphere of competition, Gray's most enduring systematic contribution was born. "It will be imperfect and hasty, but it will prevent Wood from fixing himself so that he cannot be driven out." [48]

Because of the reluctance with which Gray came to the task, it is easy to underestimate the resources he had. The herbarium, the library he had been collecting, the families unpublished but already elaborated for the *Flora,* and the continuous help of scores of botanists throughout the region,[49] all put power into his hands to do work which, even though provisional, would be authoritative. The *Flora* would have perhaps served better, but a *Manual* would be more widely useful. Since most of the field experience of his younger years lay within the range, he knew these plants not only as a closet worker but as a collector who had observed plants in all seasons, especially in New York and New Jersey.

Even more important was the team of experts Gray could call on for major contributions. The net of organization which he and Torrey had cultivated for so long now paid dividends. Oakes, of course, "who is far more intimately acquainted with New England plants than any other botanist," gave "essential aid." S. T. Olney, an old New York friend now living in Providence, also helped with New England plants. Sullivant took care of the mosses and liverworts. Edward Tuckerman worked up his specialty, the lichens.[50] Most important of all, John Carey came up from New York to live with Gray and work out the sedges and the willows. As usual, Carey had great personal sorrows, a fire in New York having killed his son and destroyed his herbarium, so that work for Gray was welcome distraction while anything he did for himself would only have reminded him of his losses.[51]

Since the elaborate Latinity of the *Flora* was impossible in a *"Pocket* guide," Gray had to make difficult decisions on scope and format. Carey feared he would be "between two fires"—formal descriptions on the one hand and "a mere synopsis" on the other. His recommendations that species be "well-defined, & closely approaching specs. must be *contrasted,* briefly but characteristically," were not far from the style of the finished work.[52] The accuracy of the *Flora,* the use of the vernacular, and complete coverage of all families, made the *Manual* the most immediately useful and at the same time most palatable work that Gray had produced. The necessities of battle had forced him down to a level where many Americans could profit by his work and put his knowledge to use while actually in the field.

By early 1847 he was driving ahead frantically trying to get through the press in April. Bulletins from the battle front spurred him on, for he now felt that Wood had been "shabby." On hearing that his rival was printing by what he considered an inferior method, Gray wrote, "I am glad he stereotypes,—but he is learning something, and if allowed to take the field another year without competition, I fear we shall not be able to dislodge him afterwards." As April approached the book swelled. The hope of binding it with the *Textbook* and of any idea of profits died as the work dragged on until fall. Finally on Christmas Eve of 1847, a year and eight hundred pages after he began, Gray signed the preface six days after Fendler's plants arrived from the West.[53] He well knew his work was imperfect, a "hurried *locum tenens*" that would need replacing very soon. But his multiplying labors drove Gray as close to bitterness as he ever got in his life. "I have worked like a dog, but my work laid out to be finished last July is not done yet. . . . As a consolation for my honest faithfulness in making it [the *Manual*] tolerably thorough, and so much larger than I expected it to prove, it is now clear that I shall get nothing or next to it for my year's labor." [54] Alphonso Wood doubtless had bitter reflections of his own.

On New Year's Day of 1848 Gray wrote, "To John Torrey, M.D., Corresp. Member of the Linnaean Society, etc., this volume is dedicated by the author, in grateful acknowledgment of the friendship which has honored and the counsel which aided him from the commencement of his botanical pursuits." [55] Gray, having reached the midpoint of his life, could see Torrey's shadow more clearly now because he had emerged from it. Still a cleancut youth in appearance, he had reached his full maturity in a society which had allowed few of his kind to develop before him. Through the various stages of increasing specialization, partly planned and partly a result of change, Gray had become a professional scientist in a sense that Torrey never was.

The appointment to the Fisher professorship at Harvard gave him the leisure and the physical facilities to create a personal, informal, but effective scientific organization to handle large problems and distant operations effectively. The collectors feeling their way toward the southern Rockies, the artists, the European correspondents, American correspondents, the herbarium, the garden, the *Flora,* innumerable notes in Silliman's *Journal,* the special studies of collections, the friendship with John A. Lowell, the *Manual,* the *Textbook* found in Gray an energetic organizer. As his mind groped around the edges of large philosophical problems, his net was gathering the knowledge he needed.

IX

THE PERSONAL
REVOLUTION OF 1848

WHILE performing botanical prodigies in the late 1840's, Professor Gray maintained a bachelor's establishment in the garden house. He was not, as local tradition reported his predecessor Nuttall to be, a recluse. A cook and a boy of all work kept the house in order and the table provided.[1] From 1845 onward, George Gray, Asa's younger brother, lived there while attending the College, and Joseph, a still younger brother, came over from Sauquoit in 1847. Moses Gray, ailing now, stayed at his son's house to get medical attention in Boston. Then, telling his boys good-bye, "with much earnestness," he "stepped into the carriage & was gone," as it proved forever.

These members of the Gray family gave a New York tinge to society at the garden house which was reinforced by other visitors who remained for periods long enough to become almost permanent lodgers. John Carey lived there for months at a time while working on the *Manual*. When Judge William Kent, son of the Chancellor, spent a year teaching at the law school he found the garden a congenial reminder of home. Philip Smith of the neighborhood of Sauquoit, down on his luck in Boston, knew where to borrow a dollar.

The house seemed almost New York itself when the Torrey family came to visit. "The girls are young ladies now," and good looking. Maggie "is a real good girl, Eliza a good & an excellent scholar. Jane more of a belle." George Gray, knowing himself to be susceptible, nevertheless "was not fascinated. Not because they were not fascinating, but because I had seen the mother, & to her the daughters are not to be compared." Mrs. Torrey, with her strong and scholarly mind, her radiant piety, and her angelic presence, was as capable as ever of taking a young man's breath away. Although both Asa and George successfully sublimated their feelings, the very presence of this paragon dazzled them. It was a common assumption around the house and the town that Dr. Gray would some day marry one of the daughters, but immediate action was held in abeyance by their mother's overwhelming charm and influence.

At the center of the household and the reason for its existence stood the boyish figure of Asa Gray. He still weighed only 135 pounds, and his rapid movements and half-running gait made him seem more like an undergraduate than a professor. His smooth-shaven face still had the general appearance of youth. Only a sprinkling of gray hair betokened his cares and his position. When Mrs. Torrey made him an academic gown, George was incredulous at "our brother looking for all the world like a bishop in full dress." The constant labors which shaped his domestic life made a profound impression on his companions. Hardly speaking except at meals, "Dr. has worked so hard that today he is almost ill."

George, when writing to the family back in Sauquoit, would always go through a little ritual with the Doctor.

"Well," say I, "Dr. I am writing to so & so?"
"Ah," says he, & he throws down his pen, straitens up & stretches himself.
"Yes," say I, "& what shall I say for you?"
"Oh," he bawls out, "Tell them my best &c &c." By this time he has finished yawning, & has got hold of his pen again.

Although he had long since laid aside "Asa" and virtually adopted "Doctor" as a first name, Gray appeared to his brother an excellent fellow, generous with money and considerate in remembering him with little gifts. High good spirits prevailed even in their arguments, as when the Doctor's "botanical Latin and that which I study do not agree very well."

John Carey, the only member of the immediate circle who dealt with the Doctor as a botanist also, saw a certain humor in the driving intensity of Gray's working routine. He was careful to save small questions for times when the lordly lion "is *not* lashing himself with his tail and foaming at the mouth." When giving Gray a sheaf of manuscript, Carey laid it "at the feet of the High Priest of the American worshippers" with "due reverence and submission." But if "when my package arrives, you should be in one of your ordinary (!) crusty snarly-cynical (study) humours—I forbid your cutting the envelope. . . ." [2]

Sundays accentuated the self-contained character of the household at the garden. George Gray, faithful to his Presbyterian upbringing in Sauquoit, had militantly orthodox views and dreamed of becoming a clergyman. He attended a little class of students, which had an average attendance of "only about eight," conducted by the Reverend John A. Albro of the Congregational Church. Estimating that more than half of his fellow Harvard students were Unitarians, he felt himself a part of a beleaguered minority, surrounded by these heathen, excellent fellows many of them, but few "consider the Bible as we do," something "safe & sure & certain" which "it is wicked to doubt. . . ." Looking up as he did to his older brother, he found much to admire in Asa's religion. "Dr. has taught me much. He is sound in his views & is a careful student of the bible & has showed me how to judge, in some degree I hope, what the bible teaches & what it does not teach." Perhaps George did not realize the momentous consequences of the admission on the part of the Doctor that there were some things on which the Scriptures were silent.

Since John Carey was an Englishman, he seemed to have more excuse than the local Unitarians to entertain strange religious notions. For he was a Puseyite, echoing the Oxford Movement which was by that time carrying a whole wing of the Anglican Church in the direction of Roman Catholicism. Instead of being shocked, the Grays found Carey a good foil for Sunday arguments. Eliza Torrey remembered the scene vividly even in her old age. The question was the way in which the Ten Commandments were binding upon Christians. Carey argued that their only claim "upon our obedience consisted in their having been reordained (endorsed as it were) by the Church." Dr. Gray "combatted this extreme church view warmly and cleverly. Both became pugnacious, amiably, as in their botanical fights." As the argument grew in warmth "the doctor showed his excitement in his characteristically self-forgetful way by moving or jumping nervously about the room, sitting on the floor, lying down

flat, and finally he had slipped under the sofa, all but his head. . . ."
In this position he was "laughing and sending sparks out of his keen
eyes, and plying his arguments and making witty thrusts all the
while." [3]

With the veil drawn around the garden by the New York atmosphere and the difference in religion, the rest of Cambridge seemed
to stand a bit off. George Gray brought in reports from the undergraduate world of rowdiness tinged with violence which made the
presidency a living hell for Edward Everett, that eminent and
strait-laced gentleman who had so recently been "doing business
with Queen Vic" as the American minister. Professor Benjamin
Peirce came up to the garden one time with a ten-year-old boy mathematical genius "to see if he can be educated." In 1846 George
began to observe "a foreign gentleman, one Agazez as it is pronounced" often at the garden. In spite of these occasional interruptions and the glorious visits of the Torreys, Dr. Gray's household in
George's eyes was a rather sombre place. "I can't tell whether he is
going to get married or not. I wish he would, for this living without
females as a part of the family is dull life, though it is an advantage
to one's studies, for he is driven to his books to drive away the
blues."

In May 1847, Dr. Gray came in and broke the news that he was
engaged. In his thirty-seventh year it was of course high time for it.
Nevertheless George was surprised. Although he had had some sus-
picions, he was deceived "by some things and some reports which
made me quite positive that if he married he would marry Eliza
Torrey. . . ." Poor Eliza, "she is a most lovely girl." And poor
Dr. Torrey would have to endure the mistaken congratulations of
many a botanist. The unknown fiancée who suddenly appeared in
their midst was not only from a Unitarian family but a belle who
moved "in the best, though seldom in the most brilliant circles of
Boston." [4]

Jane Lathrop Loring was more than equal to winning over her
prospective brother-in-law. George found she "has quite agreeable
features, though not beautiful, yet in full dress is really handsome."
She was quite slender and would have a pretty nose "if it were a little less pug." He did not think that she affected "the fine lady at all,

but seems womanly & good, laughs frequently & heartily as if she enjoys it." Had not the Doctor told him that she was twenty-six he would have guessed only twenty-two.

In her own eyes Jane was a "wild careless creature" who admitted she was "sometimes wanting in dignity; it is not in my nature; I am too democratic, & have too much of natural life and high spirits." When her father had taken her to a watering place, she wrote proudly, "I do enjoy most exceedingly talking with any sensible man who seems to consider me as equal to talking to him. . . ." She could not "even see any harm in occasionally *dancing* in the gaiety of one's heart." When stranded between coaches at a tavern with several strange men, she discussed with them "Martin Chuzzlewit, crops, gentlemen and ladies at a Shaker village, Puseyism, animal magnetism, love and courtship, imagination, and indeed almost everything." [5] One of the ladies' men of the class of 1844 at Harvard, James Gordon Clarke, had tried hard for her.[6] However, in the way of an early marriage stood the need of her twice widowed father for a hostess. Her sister Susan had already married Patrick Tracy Jackson and was raising a family of her own.

Charles Greely Loring, one of the leading lawyers of Boston, was at the height of a distinguished professional career.[7] Within two years he would be offered an appointment to Daniel Webster's seat in the United States Senate. He had been a member of the Harvard Corporation since 1835. Although not handsome "when his hat is off," he made both an agreeable and a powerful impression, and his future son-in-law accurately surmised that he was "in comfortable circumstances, but by no means at all wealthy." [8] In religion and political opinions Mr. Loring was a standard Bostonian of his class and period. He attended the West Church in Boston, where Dr. Charles Lowell had steered a conservatively Unitarian course. He had been a Federalist and was now a Whig. Although without sympathy for reformers and abolitionists, he quickened to the antislavery sentiment and would early become a Republican.

Back when he had graduated from Harvard in 1812 young Bostonians who entered law could not do better than to study under Judge Tapping Reeve, of Litchfield, Connecticut, a village which flourished for a while as a country center of learning somewhat like

Fairfield, New York. Besides the law school in Litchfield, the Misses Pierce school for girls helped make education a major concern. Charles Loring tied himself to this rural community more permanently than did most of the law students who, like John C. Calhoun, merely passed through on their way to fame or obscurity. But even after the young Bostonian had returned home to start his practice he remembered Anna Pierce Brace, the niece of the Misses Pierce, and in 1818 he married her.

Litchfield was above all things orthodox. No Unitarian heresies existed there. Lyman Beecher, the preacher in the village during these years, was beginning a fiery career as a new school Calvinist. His second wife's sister was the wife of John P. Brace, the new Mrs. Loring's brother and the leading schoolteacher and naturalist of the village. Perhaps because of some fear of eternal damnation implicit in her marriage outside the fold, Anna Brace Loring clung tenaciously to her country relatives, making sure that her four children knew Litchfield well. Jane, virtually under the guardianship of her great aunt Pierce "almost from infancy," felt that the village was her second home. When she was fifteen, her mother died, but even afterward she continued to spend most of her summers there. Jane's country Calvinist heritage through her mother's people was a godsend to Asa Gray when he tried to reconcile his own family and friends to his engagement. He even discovered that two generations of Pierces and Braces had corresponded botanically with Dr. Torrey.[9] Hence Litchfield provided a bond between Jane and Dr. Gray, a cultural climate in which both had deep roots and were completely at home.

Charles G. Loring saw, somewhat more quickly than the Bostonians who summered at such places as Nahant, the possibilities of the shore of Cape Ann beyond Salem. The railroad creeping down toward Portland brought within easy reach of Boston a picturesque area which up until the 1840's had been the farms of country New Englanders who for very good reasons placed no value on the rocky land immediately overlooking the sea. In 1844 Mr. Loring bought some twenty-five acres in Beverly, an ordinary farm except that it included the wasteland which dropped abruptly down to the sandy beach and tidewater.[10] George Gray, who had his first view of the

Atlantic here, described the farm as "uneven & full of rocks as big as small houses, half . . . covered with trees. . . ." The house was "no more than ten rods from the shore, nearly 50 feet higher than the water. You can hear the surge & can look out as far as your eye can reach upon the ocean. . . ." Across the island-dotted bay lay Marblehead. The great barn was almost more pretentious than the house, for Mr. Loring entered immediately and scientifically into the business of being a gentleman farmer.

Naturally a member of the Harvard Corporation felt free to call on the Fisher Professor of Natural History for advice about plantings around his new country place.[11] Naturally, too, Professor Gray after one of his lectures at the Lowell Institute had the pleasure of meeting Miss Loring.[12] By the spring of 1847 their friendship had so progressed that Dr. Gray took, in strictest confidence, the very proper step in applying to Mr. Loring for permission to seek the hand of his daughter. Although it was a somewhat formidable assignment for a mere botanist from the hinterland to approach a man of Mr. Loring's position and reputation, the answer which Asa Gray received could hardly have been more genial. There was "no person to whom I should with more trust and cheerfulness entrust the welfare of my daughter than yourself!—& I could not express a higher regard for you, as she is dearer to me than life." Jane's hand and affections were free and "your society is eminently agreeable to her. . . ." But her "sentiments on the subject of alliance are peculiar & may be affected by many other considerations." In short, you have to ask her yourself. Mr. Loring then very kindly removed the source of some of the peculiarity by assuring Gray that he by no means concurred in her "thought that her duty requires her to remain in her present position." [13] Even with this parental reassurance, it took Asa Gray two months to secure the lady's consent. The remainder of 1847 was full of joy even though the *Manual* was still unfinished and the printer was constantly calling for more copy. In the summer Asa went to Beverly at every opportunity, and in the fall he began going to Boston to the Lorings' house in Ashburton Place almost every other day. George was relieved that "*boys* are not alone in being foolish in such things. The grown-ups seem just as much infatuated." John Carey, who lost no time in recombining Miss Loring's name into Lady Jane, hopes that "she would not, like Lady Jane Gray, lose her head, although she had made Dr. lose his."

At first a fall wedding seemed in the offing. "Why waste time at thirty-six?" But even excluding the *Manual,* much had to be done. The Harvard Corporation entered into a scheme for building an addition to the garden house, which would provide a study with cases for books and specimens. Henceforth the four-square older part of the house would be entirely for domestic use. So confusion and carpenters reigned. Then Jane had a bout with jaundice. Then, as the New Year turned to 1848, a blow fell which tested their souls.

George Gray, junior at Harvard, young, witty, handsome, pious, came down with typhoid fever in December. When he seemed better, he got up and started home to Sauquoit for the winter vacation, but he had only reached Boston when he had a relapse. Taken into the Lorings' house, he came immediately under Jane's constant care. On January 9, after more than two weeks in bed, George said as Jane came into the room, "I scarcely thought in the night I should see you this morning." She sat down and read to him from the First Chapter of John: "In the beginning was the Word." He dozed and roused, his mind clouded somewhat, and then he sank peacefully away.[14]

The circumstances of George's death at the Loring house joined Asa and Jane in a common bond of sorrow. How insignificant were differences in denomination and of cultural background when, as Gray put it, "it pleased the Sovereign Disposer of events, to whom I bow, to remove him to a better world. . . ."[15] By the time the somber shadows cast by George's death had passed, spring had arrived again, and the wedding date was finally set for May 4. Since 1848 was a leap year, a full 365 days had elapsed since their engagement.

The two days before were rainy, but "Thursday was one of the brightest and finest days I ever knew." They were married at half past twelve, dined with all the Loring family, and "came out toward evening to our home, which Jane is very much pleased with indeed." No botany recitation that day, and after dark the Aeolian Choir, with Joe Gray for a guide, made its way to the garden for a serenade. In the still of the night, "the music sounded very well indeed."[16]

Asa Gray's report to his mother three days after the wedding fore-shadowed some of the basic conditions under which he and his bride would live out their long and happy marriage. "Jane," he said, "has been much worn down for the last week or two—much more than during the whole spring. . . . She is improving fast, but is not yet so strong as to be able to accompany me to church today,—which we both greatly regretted." [17]

Jane never joined the Congregational Church in Cambridge. Her devotion to Unitarianism, however conservative and indifferent to creed, remained strong. She continued to admire the Reverend Cyrus Bartol, her pastor in Boston, and in Cambridge she attended the Unitarian services at the College chapel.[18] By implication, the couple agreed to go separate ways in religion, but there is no evidence of the slightest friction on the subject. Such a solution must, however, have had its side effects. Asa Gray can hardly have avoided a broadening in his toleration of other sects and ideas. No doubt he also found additional reason to shroud his own religious opinions in reticence. To discuss theology was different from discussing the religious feelings on which there was an agreement to disagree.

Although it seemed transient in the beginning, Jane's poor health became distressingly permanent, at least for the 1850's and 1860's. As in many mid-nineteenth-century illnesses, no one could quite decide what the trouble was. Dyspepsia they called it, with headaches, dizziness, and other generalized phenomena thrown in. Mr. Loring had suffered thus, and Gray later likened it to the miseries of Charles Darwin. Although Mrs. Gray was never a complete invalid, her illness set the pace for domestic life at the garden. Dr. Gray was "the cheeriest & best of nurses, never caring for one's ups & downs, and taking pull backs as a matter of course." [19]

Another background fact which gradually became apparent and which shaped the nature of Jane's and Dr. Gray's relation was the absence of children. The routine which began in 1848 continued virtually unchanged for four decades, Jane devoting a larger share of her clear intellect to botany and botanists than could otherwise have been possible. Even though her intentions to become an amanuensis proved over-ambitious, she worked hard at the vast collection of autographs and photographs of botanists which eventually filled five great bound volumes. Perhaps because of the lack of children of their own, the Grays nearly always had a houseful of Jackson and Gray nephews and nieces either visiting, celebrating a holiday, or in the case of the Sauquoit relatives using the garden as a headquarters for Boston and Cambridge schooling.

Jane fully expected a curtailment in her standard of living. To move from her father's house in Boston to the Botanic Garden, nearly a mile beyond Harvard Square in Cambridge, was for her moving to "the country." The better class of servants "will always prefer the city, where there is more style, more servants are kept, where all the temptations without doors are more accessible." Besides, she knew what it meant to become a professor's wife. "When I married I knew I must always live economically, & laid my plans for the management of my family & style of living accordingly. . . ." Even later, when Dr. Gray became more affluent, she felt she "could not change that style without feeling I was doing wrong, & failing in my duty in the circumstances in which Providence had placed me & I had voluntarily chosen." Sometimes the yoke of Providence weighed rather hard. To break off a vacation in Beverly to come into the summer heat of Cambridge was a sore trial, especially when the purpose was to throw a commencement-time tea party for fifty people. Then "Dr. Gray did not approve of the oak wreaths . . . & I gave up the matter very quietly." When she borrowed candlesticks from Mrs. Dixwell, he borrowed others from Mrs. Parsons. As a host he put on a convincing show, "very agreeable, here, there, everywhere; & I guess they all thought he was housekeeper. . . ." Perhaps "I am too much of a Martha, anxious about many things." [20]

The shadows of vague illness, childlessness, and occasional irritation only heighten the effect of the light flooding into Asa Gray's life upon his marriage. For mostly Jane saw the Providence which had cast her lot there as benign. She was a great hostess, to the best of Boston society or to queer Charles Wright just in from Texas. When the sophomores came up for tea after the last lecture of the term, following "one another about so like a flock of sheep," [21] she gave her gracious best. Her husband's science, which subjected her to the duty of entertaining these awkward people, also brought within her doors representatives of the nobility and upper classes of three or four countries. A great share of the foreign intellectuals who always visited Boston on a tour of the United States either ate a meal or spent a night at the garden house. Some even tarried long enough for an excursion to Beverly. Jane adapted to the extended range of social life which botany imposed upon her with grace and enthusiasm.

In Cambridge itself, Dr. and Mrs. Gray now found a secure place and a multitude of activities. For instance, "we have taken up a new thing . . . reading Shakespeare aloud in parts—Miss Chandler, Mrs. Parsons' sister, & Mr. Treadwell are remarkably fine readers; Mr. Dixwell, Prof. Peirce & son are good too, & we get quite a number of us." When Dr. Gray's turn came around to entertain the Cambridge Scientific Club, the members were served in a style their well-developed taste approved—ham and canvas-back duck.[22]

Jane's presence at the garden began a general softening and lightening of the ponderous system of morals which Dr. Gray had taken over from the Torrey family. In 1839 in Vienna he had disapproved of opera. Now his wife went to Boston "by the Drs. special permission & heard Alboni." Mrs. Gray loved music, and although she felt "entirely cut off" from it after her marriage she did manage an occasional evening. If she had an objection to opera, it was because she found it "so unnatural to advance to the footlights & sing a bravura when pausing from gazing at a sleeping lover!" [23] Her husband imbibed some of her sunny outlook. The sombre phrase "if I live so long" occurs often in the letters of the young Asa Gray. After 1848 it becomes less frequent. Dread of death and any preoccupation with the sinfulness of man receded as the years went by, marked only by joy and love.

184

X

AN AMERICAN
IN WORLD BOTANY

I N JUNE 1848, Dr. Gray took Jane on a wedding trip to Washington, D.C., which, in addition to their personal pleasure,
marked a major turning point in his career. The spacious capital city
was beginning to have some interest for a scientific man, especially
one as important as Gray had now become. His old friend Joseph
Henry, attempting to make the new Smithsonian Institution into
something scientifically respectable, showed them around the patent
office. Lieutenant Matthew Fontaine Maury received them at the
observatory. They called at the White House on Mrs. James K. Polk.
However, the bouquet of pretty red cluster roses which Dr. Gray
brought his bride from Captain Wilkes's garden was the symbol of
the true business of the trip—the resumption of the burden of the
botany of the United States Exploring Expedition.[1] Despite his intentions when he had turned his back on Secretary Joel Poinsett and
had headed west for the University of Michigan in 1838, Gray had
never quite been able to put aside all concern for the nation's most
ambitious scientific enterprise.

William Rich had proved no more a botanist than anyone thought
him, but he had made collections, and the industry of Charles Pickering and the horticulturist William Brackenridge had added to the
haul. After many losses at sea, some damage in transit, and much
more in the unpacking, the collection had found its way to Washington. How was a collection, predominantly tropical and drawn
from the farthest reaches of the Pacific, to be elaborated in a town
without books and herbaria? Or worse, how was it to be studied in a
country in which not a single botanist had either knowledge or spec-

imens of the vast geographic area covered? Gray, always the internationalist, became involved in the problem because his friend, Sir William Hooker, wanted the collections. Young Joseph Hooker had just returned from the Ross Expedition with immense collections from many of the same areas visited by the Americans. To send the American expedition's specimens, except those from Western North America, to Kew, where unrivaled facilities existed, and have Joseph work up the two collections jointly, seemed like a sensible and scientific way of proceeding. The only result of Gray's good offices was a short-lived but violent quarrel between Sir William and Charles Pickering, who had charge of the specimens in Washington and who could see no way of sending them abroad.[2] The Hookers had to proceed without even a set of specimens for comparison, Joseph Hooker publishing the first part of his *Flora Antarctica* in 1844. In a review of this work in the *American Journal of Science* Gray criticized the American policy.[3]

Meanwhile, after a confused struggle in Washington over the custody of the expedition's collections, the Congressional Joint Committee on the Library took direct responsibility for publication of the results—one of the few times in American history that Congress has attempted the direct administration of a large scientific project.[4] The committee hired as their agent to supervise the publications Charles Wilkes himself, who soon laid out a plan calling for fifteen volumes and nine atlases. Some of the volumes, falling into competent and willing hands, appeared promptly. Gray was soon celebrating James D. Dana's *Zoöphytes* in the *North American Review*. Even here, however, he attacked the management of the enterprise. "Let our readers imagine their surprise and our mortification, when they learn that the edition ordered by the 'collective wisdom of the nation,' or the more concentrated intelligence of the library committee of Congress . . . is restricted to *one hundred copies!*" In private he referred to Senator Benjamin Tappan of Ohio, a leading member of the committee, as "the most obstinate, wrongheaded, narrow-minded, impracticable ignoramus that could well be imagined." [5] Gray's solicitude was for a policy which would glorify the nation by making the expedition results freely available to the international fraternity of science.

Wilkes naturally tried to get the botany volume done without any reference to Gray, turning first to the incompetent Rich. However, the cross-grained captain genuinely had the welfare of the publication at heart and made his decisions accordingly. When Rich had completed his work, Wilkes had the wit to reject a volume which had cost him over four thousand dollars, lest it bring disgrace on both the expedition and the author. By the end of 1847, William Brackenridge, the horticulturist of the expedition, was at work on the ferns, and John Torrey had agreed to do the Oregon and California plants. Sullivant was to do the mosses and Edward Tuckerman the lichens.[6] These last three were all close associates of Gray and members of his botanical team. Wilkes could find no one to take up the major part of the task. He had tried to get Torrey, but when the doctor proposed that the specimens be put out to monographers (doubtless most of them Europeans), the captain "pughed at the suggestion." Torrey's offer to go to Europe to do the work met the reply that on "no account would the expenses of a trip to Europe be paid by the government." Wilkes's botanical policy had clearly failed. Both Torrey and Sullivant insisted that if the bulk of the flowering plants from the tropical regions were to be studied at all in the United States, Gray would have to do it. Thus in June of 1848 Wilkes had to apply hat in hand to Gray, who went to Washington in a position to name his own terms.

Since it was a little too much even then to ask the Congress to condone, openly at any rate, the farming out of the specimens to Europeans to study, Gray centered his demands on a trip at government expense to do the work "in Hooker's, or Bentham's, or Garden of Plants herbarium." Also he determined the price for his work— $120 per month for five years, which he himself considered quite handsome pay for scientific work.[7] When Wilkes acceded without haggling, the contract was signed. Gray felt that besides the specimens which he would personally study he had the responsibility for overseeing all the botanical studies, such as those of Torrey, Sullivant, and Tuckerman.

Since Gray already had enough "other scientific undertakings which would most fully occupy all my best working years," it is not easy to see why he took up this heavy chore. He knew that the col-

187

lection, although running to 10,000 specimens, was of uneven quality and that its handling by Rich and others after its arrival in the United States had done it no good. He knew that years had already passed during which many new discoveries had already been anticipated by such publications as Hooker's *Flora Antarctica*. He was intimately familiar with the whole long history of administrative difficulty and frustration which had dogged the expedition from 1836 onward. He was a vocal critic of the publication policy. Why, then, should he tie himself to such a doubtful prospect?

The answer lay somewhat in the opportunity of a year's study in Europe and in the fact that Gray would actually get pay in money for scientific research. But primarily the reason for his acquiescence must be found in "a sense of duty to the science I cultivate & to the country." [8] It was a duty to science to bring this large collection from little-known regions into the orbit of usable botanical knowledge. Patriotism was involved because the United States Exploring Expedition was the greatest scientific effort yet attempted by a young republic. If the government could not succeed in publishing these results, those critics who believed that only a monarchy could effectively patronize science would be more certain of their opinion. Gray could not be the unofficial leader of American botanists and at the same time be indifferent to the fate of the collection, which so greatly expanded national horizons. His very prominence committed him to a concern for the state of botany in America and for the institutions which supported it.

The years between 1840 and 1850 were ones of rapid crystallization of new scientific institutions in the United States. The impending arrival of the Exploring Expedition collections had stimulated the abortive National Institute for the Promotion of Science. In 1846 the Congress finally honored the bequest of the Englishman James Smithson by creating the Smithsonian Institution, whose form and direction was largely determined by Gray's friend Joseph Henry. The founding of the American Association for the Advancement of Science in 1848 marked a new level of professional consciousness on the part of American scientists. Gray found that this new crop of scientific institutions on the American scene both gave him support and deflected his course. The AAAS he joined and, when it met in Cambridge in 1849, was a prominent local host. While he continued to put most of his organizational efforts into the ancient Amercian Academy of Arts and Sciences in Boston, he watched the newer institutions closely.

None of them interested him more than the Smithsonian. Because of his friendship with Joseph Henry, which went back to upstate New York days, he was an unofficial adviser to the Smithsonian from the very beginning. He was instrumental in the American Academy's endorsement of Henry's program in 1847. He soon found he could turn over to the Smithsonian at least part of the burden of keeping collectors such as Charles Wright in the field. Gray gave advice on the setting up of the institution's system of international exchange of scientific publications and began to use its agents in Europe extensively.[9] In return he and Torrey became a kind of department of botany for Henry.

When the Grays were in Washington in June 1848, Henry pressed his friend to undertake for the Smithsonian a study of the "economic and other uses of forest trees of our country. . . ." [10] This was a part of the Secretary's program to diffuse knowledge, and Gray's name would be a great help to the whole series. Henry's practical mind envisaged experiments on the strength of wood and research on the lumber industry and its methods. American science is reputed to be of a practical cast, diverting creative investigators from basic research, and this is an example of a pressure in that direction. Asa Gray had no eye for it, however. He would much rather have had Henry support his *Genera Illustrata,* and he envisaged a "Report on Forest Trees" as simple systematic descriptions with handsome plates drawn by Isaac Sprague. Had he been a practical genius, he might have put forestry on a scientific basis in America a generation before Charles Sprague Sargent and Gifford Pinchot.

Even though Gray should have known enough about himself and his other commitments to be wary, friendship for Henry, a desire to help the Smithsonian, and his usual overoptimism about the time required, led him into the report on forest trees. He signed a contract with Henry which plagued both of them for the rest of their days.[11] Added to the Exploring Expedition work, this project committed much of Gray's research time just when he was reaching the height of his powers as a botanist and as a man.

The immediate prospect, however, was a year in Europe. Gray spent most of 1849 making his preparations. Jeffries Wyman, whom he had been working into the instructional system at Harvard, would take over his courses to undergraduates, for the Corporation was quite willing to have him take a year for professional studies if he provided for the usual instruction in his department. The Smithsonian would supply some money for Charles Wright in Texas. John Torrey began to fear that Gray, making a perfect slave of himself, could never finish the work he had undertaken.[12] By some hook or crook he gave lectures, heard recitations, finished monographs, laid out work for Sprague to illustrate, set aside for future study a vast number of specimens, pigeonholed all the mail that was not absolutely urgent, and with Mrs. Gray made it aboard the sailing packet which departed Boston for Liverpool on June 11, 1850.[13]

The Europe to which the couple disembarked had changed in the eleven years since Gray had left those shores. Then Victoria had just come to the throne and the bitterness of the fight over the Reform Bill of 1832 was still a recent memory. Kew Gardens had meant little as a botanical institution. A. P. De Candolle had been the great botanist of the Continent, and the achromatic microscope still a new toy. Endlicher was one of the most promising of the younger men. In 1850 the Crystal Palace was going up in London to symbolize the wealth and glory of a Britain battening on free trade after the repeal of the Corn Laws. Sir Robert Peel came to his untimely end within four days after the Grays touched British soil. On the Continent order reigned after the revolutions of 1848, with only the exiled Kossuth to stir an echo of the recent violent passions. Endlicher had died a suicide in the aftermath of this upheaval. A. P. De Candolle was long since dead. Robert Brown and Humboldt lived on, but the young men, the contemporaries of Asa Gray, were now beginning to dominate scientific life.

It was an inspiring year to be in Europe, the beginning of the greatest period of the Victorian Age, the beginning of a decade in which scientific currents long underground would come out in the open.

Most of the summer of 1850 went to Jane's introduction to the Continent—Belgium, up the Rhine to Switzerland, Munich, Heidelberg, Cologne, the Netherlands. Alphonse De Candolle, now in charge at Geneva in place of his father, entertained them. Von Martius was as extravagantly and sentimentally hospitable as ever. In general, cathedrals and picture galleries filled their time.

Back in England in the autumn Gray settled down to the serious business of the Wilkes Expedition plants. George Bentham, who had escorted him about London in 1839, had now retired to Pontrilas, an estate in Herefordshire, whence a constant stream of papers showed him to be the most productive and discriminating of British taxonomic botanists. With a hospitality that received no repayment from the United States government, Mr. and Mrs. Bentham entertained the Grays for eight weeks while the two botanists turned through Exploring Expedition plants sheet by sheet. Bentham in his quiet way had handled many of the collections from the Pacific which the far-flung maritime activities of the British nation had continuously brought in. He had done several families on a world basis for the De Candolle *Prodromus,* and he had worked out special collections from such places visited by the Wilkes Expedition as the Fiji Islands. Gray thus received a concentrated education in tropical families, some of which were unrepresented in North America.

After their stay at Pontrilas House, Dr. and Mrs. Gray started for Dublin to visit Professor W. H. Harvey, the algologist who was one of the few European botanists with American experience and who eventually completed the elaboration of the algae of the Wilkes Expedition. As they boarded a steamer at Holyhead in the evening, Gray stepped over a hatchway and fell eighteen feet into a hold, suffering one of the worst accidents of his life. Yet in a week he went on to Dublin, and in four weeks he had returned to England, taking lodging near the Royal Botanic Garden, and was hard at work on plants in Sir William Hooker's herbarium.

Months of steady work at Kew were broken only by visits to the Crystal Palace exhibition, to Oxford and Cambridge which a younger Gray had by-passed in 1839, and to Paris. Robert Brown again showed himself more amenable to sharing his great store of

191

botanical learning with Gray than with most others. The two were alike in that they brought a lively interest in vegetable anatomy and physiology to bear on the problems of plant classification, thus heightening their awareness of the morphological characters by which species could be distinguished. In Paris, Adrien de Jussieu and François André Michaux as old men were connecting links to the late eighteenth century, when their fathers had been active.

But new currents were stirring and new names coming to the fore. Sir Charles Lyell in geology and Richard Owen in comparative anatomy were at the height of their powers and fame. Joseph Hooker came back to England in the spring of 1851 with new riches gathered during three years in India to add to his collections from the Ross Expedition. When Gray was having lunch one day at Kew with young Dr. Hooker, he met "a lively, agreeable person," Charles Darwin. Although their fleeting glimpse of one another back in 1839 was now forgotten, this meeting would not be. The actors were assembling who would make the 1850's a momentous decade in the intellectual history of the Western world. Within another four years Darwin would have completed his monograph of the *Cirripedia*, Hooker would be settled into a productive career at Kew, and T. H. Huxley would have established himself in London. In 1851 the curtain had not yet gone up, but both cast and audience were gathering.

Since Dr. Gray spent such long hours in herbaria his wife sometimes became lonely, especially when left in their plain lodging at Richmond, near Kew. She was, however, responsible for many of their meetings with Americans abroad. Abbott Lawrence, then minister to Great Britain, entertained them. The John Amory Lowells were in Europe, meeting the Grays at several points. Young Charles Loring Brace, a Connecticut nephew of Mrs. Gray's, reported to them from time to time with his traveling companions, Frederick Law Olmstead and his brother.[14] The chemist Josiah Parsons Cooke of Harvard turned up, ill at ease and seemingly unready for the title of Harvard professor which descended on him suddenly when Dr. John W. Webster was hanged for murder. From these travelers coming and going the Grays heard of the excitement in the United States in the wake of the Compromise of 1850, of the unpopularity of Mrs. Gray's idol Daniel Webster for his moderate position, and of Charles G. Loring's defense of a fugitive slave in the courts in Boston.

In July 1851, the Grays went to Ipswich to the meetings of the British Association for the Advancement of Science, an organization which, founded in 1831, was just coming into its own as the major market for the exchange of ideas in British science. At these particular sessions, some of them attended by the Prince Consort, T. H. Huxley, just back from his years in Australian waters on the H.M.S. *Rattlesnake,* read some papers and cemented his momentous friendships with Dr. Hooker and with a young physicist named John Tyndall.[15] Richard Owen was one of the great stars of the meeting, lecturing in the evening on "the difference or rather want of difference between the lower animals & vegetables." Much of it sounded familiar to Mrs. Gray because she had heard Agassiz, a much more agreeable speaker. Gray and Harvey whispered amusing "criticism & comments, especially when botanical matters were touched upon," until their neighbors grew annoyed and Jane had to hush them up.

All too soon the summer and the year were over. On September 4, 1851, the Grays were back at home, overjoyed to see the family and friends and the end of their ocean voyage. Their return also meant back to sordid reality, back to piles of plants, specimens, a rundown garden, heavy teaching duties, and, above all, back to a controversy that had arisen with Captain Wilkes.

While Gray was still in Europe, misunderstandings began to gather about the contract which had seemed so crystal clear back in 1848. The disputed matters had a trivial air about them. Wilkes thought the botanical volumes should follow the exact form and typography already adopted for the zoology. This involved, among other things, providing an English translation for the formal Latin descriptions. Gray and Torrey maintained that the discretion in these details should be theirs and that a simple translation of technical characters would serve no useful purpose, as would more extended discussion in English of the habit, locality, and peculiarities of the plant.

Nevertheless, tempers quickly rose, even across the width of the ocean. Wilkes tended to feel this was but another example of "whims and caprices" and of the "follies & conceits of those who confine themselves to one branch of science." At the same time, he insisted that the books were "intended for the benefit of the public" and hence should have the Latin translated. Shades of Amos Eaton and his arguments against the natural system as undemocratic. This work should be "for the people & not for any class of scientific man & I am truly surprised that Dr. Gray should venture at this day to express such an obsolete notion." [16]

The botanists on their side were appalled at having Wilkes address them "as he would a bunch of middies." Gray, while still at Kew, seriously considered throwing up the whole job and retaining his father-in-law to break the contract. To him the translation to English was silly, because technical botanical terms were equally incomprehensible to the general public in either Latin or English, and the English technical description would merely run up the printing bill, benefiting neither general reader nor naturalist. Beneath the particular points at issue lay Gray's insistence that the botanist should make his own decisions within his own specialty.

Viewed in this light, an obscure quarrel became a chapter in the struggle for the freedom of science in America. Sullivant was too sanguine when he urged Gray to ease off "and print in *Chicasaw* or *Choctaw*" if Wilkes wanted it, because everyone knew the whole expedition had been a series of blunders "from the beginning to present time." Instead, Joseph Henry applied his knowledge of Washington and his statesmanlike judgment to the problem and, after straightening Gray out on his tactics, arranged a compromise peace which admitted the principle of the freedom of science.[17]

In the summer of 1852, with the quarrel composed, Gray began to drive again at the Exploring Expedition plants and Sprague bent again over his drawing board preparing the illustrations. Others of Gray's team moved forward with their work on special groups. Sullivant, who did the mosses, ended up in as severe a controversy with Wilkes as Gray had ever had. Edward Tuckerman finished off the lichens promptly, but they waited long for printing. Jacob Whitman Bailey of West Point, who took the algae, and Moses Ashley Curtis, who worked out the few fungi, both felt the need of foreign assistance. Harvey became co-author with the former, and M. J. Berkeley, an English authority, with the latter. Although Brackenridge finished his book on the ferns, Gray and Torrey revised it thoroughly and translated the English descriptions into Latin. Torrey soon largely finished the Oregon and California parts of the collection.

By 1854 some progress was apparent. Brackenridge's volume appeared and also Gray's first volume of the flowering plants, each accompanied by an atlas of drawings. Gray's large volume, beginning abruptly without preface or introduction, moved about one third of the way through the systematic arrangement of plants as laid down by De Candolle, falling a few families short of his favorite *Compositae,* which had terminated so many of his special papers on western North America.

A curse hung over the Exploring Expedition and all who had anything to do with it. Twenty-one of the one hundred official copies of Gray's book were burned up in a warehouse fire in Philadelphia and never replaced. An unofficial issue, with which Gray hoped to spread the distribution to all botanists who were really interested, led to all sorts of embarrassment. Gray sold most of the edition to G. P. Putnam and took a note for $400, only to have his old London friend go onto the financial rocks and stop payment.[18] Poor Brackenridge lost most of both the official and unofficial issues of his volume to fire.

The unfinished portion was an even worse headache. Gray kept returning to it periodically in the years after 1854, and at every juncture of his career he found it haunting him. Publication difficulties in Washington were often a major discouragement. When in 1856 the Library Committee tried to curtail the unfinished volumes, Wilkes stood against it, this time siding with the scientists. Money kept running out, and the Civil War then stopped all publishing activity, although Gray worked on the plants of the "everlasting" expedition for a while in 1862.[19] In 1872 and 1873, he had to give more time to relieving Torrey of revising and publishing the Northwest American portions when his old friend was far gone in his last illness. This volume,[20] which included the papers on the lower plants also, was the last spasm of the effort which had occupied Gray and American science for nearly forty years.

Although the published parts of the work could play their part in the stream of science, the stack of handwritten manuscript pages—over 1700 of them—represent a severe loss.[21] It is a monument built of the life blood of a scientist—his time and skill. Of course Gray was paid, but $5,400 was modest in proportion to the labor, and less than he had expected in the beginning. What could Gray not have accomplished if these futile pages had never been written? Little wonder that he came to regard the government as a fickle and untrustworthy support of science.

How differently it all could have been done. Had he gone on the expedition in 1838 and pitched into his collections immediately after return in 1842, the whole work could have been before the world by 1846. Even had he not gone, some other botanist should have done the job long ere he took it up in 1848. But no other botanist did, because one did not exist in America. Gray here was paying a price for being an American, a price for the scientific immaturity of his country. He could not claim to be the best botanist in America if he shunned this job—so tied to the scientific reputation of the Nation. It was a trap from which there was no escape, and both he and the country suffered.

Nevertheless, the experience of working on the expedition's collections added a dimension to Gray's career which no amount of work on North American botany could have given him. By becoming a botanist with world-wide knowledge and interests, he escaped the tag of provinciality in the eyes of Europeans. John Torrey, for all his mastery of North American plants, could never take the international rank which Gray achieved through this forced widening of his horizons.

THE WAKING HOURS
OF AN OVERLOADED
BOTANIST

BETWEEN his fortieth and fiftieth birthdays, Asa Gray used his undiminished and well-sharpened powers so relentlessly that he often wore the aspect of a driven man. Besides the pressure of the contract with Wilkes, Harvard College was an even steadier drain on Asa Gray throughout the 1850's. His schedule went on much the same—work concentrated in one term, laborious recitations from the textbook, a few lectures approaching more advanced subjects. Wyman regularly taught the zoology—a great relief to Gray. A gesture toward student participation in research appeared in a "private course," in which students who had a particular interest in botany could go up to the Botanic Garden regularly from the middle of May until the end of the term in July. Ten or twelve students usually appeared. One student recorded in his diary for May 17, 1852, that he and three others "go to Prof. Gray's laboratory often now to study the analysis of flowers. He devoted three hours to us today." [1]

In these extra sessions alone did an enthusiastic student get a glimpse of Gray's real research interest and observe the actual technique of the science. Here if anywhere could a new botanist be discovered in Harvard. The hard fact is that Harvard produced no professional botanists in these years. In the first fifteen years of Gray's teaching career not a single graduate took up his profession even though he was continually looking for collectors, a herbarium curator, and a gardener. Teaching was a separate activity from research, not a source of personnel, for it served only as a distraction and a handicap.

James Kendall Hosmer, class of 1855, could well remember Professor Gray standing before him in Holden Chapel. "He would catch for his word often, reiterating . . . the article 'the-a, the-a, the-a,' his gaze meanwhile fixed upon the skylight, and a nervously gyrating forefinger raised high and brightly illuminated." He "soon established himself as a prime favourite among our lazy men" by following his remarkable practice of calling for recitations straight down the alphabet. The boys on the front row would put their feet on the rail in front of them. "The professor, withdrawing his gaze suddenly from the skylight" could see nothing but boots. "His face fell; his whirling forefinger, ceasing to gyrate, tilted like a lance in rest at the obnoxious cowhide parapet. 'Those boots, young gentlemen, ah, those boots,' he ejaculated forlornly, and, the boots came down with a mutinous clatter." He wasted no time beating botany into those who had no use for it, and the students had no idea that the man before them was in touch with higher reaches of science. "Abraham himself entertained his angel no more unawares than we, but gleams of fine radiance sometimes broke through even to our purblind perceptions." [2]

Harvard College, as a whole, was in the doldrums in the 1850's.[3] The presidents of the period, Jared Sparks and James Walker, were both estimable men, well-known to Gray and the others who had served with them on the faculty. They, like Edward Everett before them, were unhappy in a most unenviable job and fled rather than change the system. Although the rowdyism of the 1840's had abated somewhat with the rise of such sports as boating on the Charles, the student body was chained to the required curriculum and to the scale of merit. The president was usually occupied as Yard police chief while the faculty spent their main efforts keeping order, hearing recitations, and recording the daily grades. Most of them would probably have quit if they had had the money. Gray doubtless would have done so. Longfellow used his financial independence to carry out the threat in 1854, tired of "having great themes discussed by boys." [4]

The financial position of Harvard's botanical enterprises showed the same stagnation and lack of policy. That Gray had a desire for laboratory instruction is shown by a vote of the Corporation authorizing him to spend $72 for "several microscopes to be used by the Students of Botany." [5] This item stands almost alone. Gray's salary increased only slightly in the decade to $1,800 plus the use of the house, and the Fisher legacy stayed about the same.

Most of the financial difficulties of the department revolved about the garden. The capital fund eroded at the rate of $600 per year.[6] At the same time both the greenhouse and the fence, built forty-five years before, were literally falling down. Mrs. Gray, though fearful of being told to "stick to her needle," went the length of appealing directly to John Amory Lowell, both as a supporter of botany and as a member of the Corporation, to help "our poor garden." [7] The funds for refurbishing the conservatory and fence, however, came largely from private donors rounded up by Gray himself. The total was extremely modest—$3,885 for the greenhouse, which for Gray was all he expected "to require in our day." [8] The minute size of the fund and of Gray's expectations strikingly contrasted with Agassiz's regal plans for a Museum of Comparative Zoology, to which the Commonwealth of Massachusetts itself gave $100,000.

The shadow of Agassiz fell on other places as well. Since the Lawrence Scientific School had originated back in 1847 and since Gray's name regularly appeared as one of its professors as well as the College's, it is puzzling that it did not harbor a group of students with a particular interest in botany. Yet very soon after its founding the appointment of Agassiz had changed the engineering school envisaged by the donor into the professor's own personal image. Although some engineering persisted, most of the students came to study with Agassiz. He set the method and subject matter which were both highly individual. The Lawrence Scientific School was much more a laboratory and museum on the European model inhabited by the master and his apprentices than an American school in any sense. Gray merely sat on examinations and voted in faculty meetings. Agassiz's boys usually heard his lectures. It went no further. One student did come to Gray as a student in the Lawrence Scientific School, a man who was to play a significant and pathetic role in its history. Henry James Clark showed great promise as a microscopist and found in Gray a ready helper. Soon the spell of Agassiz came over him, too, and he shifted from plants to microscopic animals, becoming in time one of the most trusted of Agassiz's disciples.[9]

Only in 1858 did Gray get a student who was real timber for the profession. Significantly, Daniel Cady Eaton already had plenty of connections with botany. It is ironical that Gray's first student of promise was the grandson of Amos Eaton, the old foe of the natural system. The young man already knew systematic botany when he graduated from Yale in 1857 and was in touch with Gray, Torrey, and Sullivant. As early as his junior year at Yale he was working on a grand study of the ferns of the United States, taking up a group not covered by any of Gray's other specialists. Thus he was actually in a position to take graduate training in a period when such a thing was unprovided for in a regular way. He also wished to prepare to teach botany at Yale, where a position seemed ready to open up for him. Gray invited him to come up to Cambridge, stay at the garden house, and learn what he could "as to teaching, &c, if you can pick it up by yourself—which after all is the only way any thing worth knowing is obtained." He could register as a student or not, as he chose, because Gray would help him "as a *friend* and *fellow-worker*; but I cannot promise any special instruction, and shall take *no fee*." [10] Eaton chose to be academically correct, registering in the Lawrence Scientific School as a candidate for a Bachelor of Science degree.

Eaton's Cambridge training shows clearly Gray's lack of any concept of what a graduate school might be. The professor made no effort to push his student into the higher and more technical aspects of science or give him an over-all view of the field of botany. The degree requirements were for undergraduates and not well adapted for graduate work. He did nothing to attract Eaton to the science— that was already done by family environment. He did not have to worry about a job for him—that was already taking shape at Yale. If a man could provide his own motivation and basic training and look out for his own future, he found a plate, a bed, and a friend at the garden house.

Gray's and Torrey's network of botanical friendships provided the real institutional structure of the science in America during the 1850's. The two still worked closely together, Gray gradually becoming the more active of the two partners, partly because he was younger and more vigorous, ever widening his knowledge beyond the confines of the United States, and partly because he answered his mail more regularly. Engelmann performed prodigies of botany in St. Louis in the midst of his busy medical practice. His letters to Gray flagged only during cholera epidemics. The specialists in smaller groups were active—Sullivant on mosses, Tuckerman on lichens, Curtis on fungi. Nevertheless, it was hard to replace the men who dropped out. No algologist and microscopist took up the work left undone by the death of Jacob Whitman Bailey. No student of sedges took the place of Chester Dewey, who was getting old, or John Carey, who fled from his misfortunes to enter business in England. The rank and file of American botany were still the amateurs, with Gray as the lone regular holding the whole troop together.

The botanical network in the South is of peculiar interest in the 1850's because of the rapid development of a distinctive sectional consciousness. Gray's interest in the southern Appalachians was of course long-standing, and he had old friends there—Curtis in North and South Carolina, Lewis R. Gibbes in Charleston, Charles Wilkins Short in Kentucky, John Darby of Georgia, Alvin W. Chapman of Apalachicola, Florida, Henry Julian Ravenal of South Carolina. Others also began to send in specimens in the 1850's for the first time—Thomas M. Peters of Moulton, Alabama; the Episcopal clergyman Reuben Denton Nevius in Tuscaloosa, Alabama; H. M. Neisler of Columbus, Georgia. Obscure and often poor, struggling against rural isolation and lack of books and equipment, these gallant men were representatives of science in the South.

Gray's interest in the region, its plants, and its botanists existed in a separate compartment of his mind from his political opinions. In the deepening crises of the 1850's he was consistently antislavery, although not abolitionist, and early became a Republican. Before the year 1859, however, scant reference to his lack of sympathy with the trend of social and political thought in the South intrudes into the botanical correspondence steadily passing through the study of the garden house.

To keep his nationwide network of amateur botanists mobilized and functioning, Gray needed a stronger cement than even thousands of personal letters could provide. This he was forced to provide by writing textbooks. One of the foundations of the system was, of course, the *Manual of the Botany of the Northern United States,* which had been so hastily done in 1846 and 1847 that its revisions required both time and pains, a major harassment for several years. The second edition appeared in 1856—"*good* up to the end of the *Monopetalae,* &c.,—after that I fear poor,—yet better than old edition." [11] Because of the intellectual ferments of the 1850's, this work was not simply a chore but an important contribution to science, as a later chapter will show.

The other foundation of Gray's series was the *Botanical Textbook,* which he revised for new editions in 1850, 1853, and 1858, the last under the title of *Introduction to Structural and Systematic Botany.* Since this was essentially a college textbook which attempted to tackle the rapidly developing problems of botanical science, a great void existed to be filled by a simpler work. Most of the schools of the country, even the most elementary, made some gesture toward botany, and Alphonso Wood was still industriously reaping the profits with his series of books of which his proudest boast was their elemental simplicity.

Wood was not vicious—Torrey called him a "modest worthy man." What Gray and his friends objected to was his not being "a practical botanist—nor is he much acquainted with structural botany beyond what is contained in the ordinary text book." Moses Curtis pointed to the serious dilemma raised by Wood's success when he asked, "How is it, that the most *profitable* Text Books are prepared by sciolists?" Wood's methods were simple. According to Curtis, he "will make a four months' tour through the South,—in Winter too—take a rapid survey of a locality or two in each State— . . . pump every collector who will submit to the operation," thus giving his book "an appearance of singular authenticity." [12]

What could Gray do about this gap at the elementary end of the textbook series? After Putam's financial difficulties in 1854, Gray gradually shifted his books to Ivison and Phinney, publishers active in the textbook field. Under pressure from them he wrote *First Lessons in Botany and Vegetable Physiology* designed for high school use and published in 1857. Since even this was too advanced for a large segment of the market, the hours after dinner for the next year went into a still simpler work. The title, *How Plants Grow: A Simple Introduction to Structural Botany,* often appeared as "*How Plants Grow* Gray" on the outside cover, where it was rediscovered with delight by each generation of school children for almost half a century.

These little books differed from the big textbook only in complexity, not in content or mode of presentation. In all versions his essential pedagogical method was to state his propositions clearly and concisely, without frills. His single bow to the moralizing so prevalent in the texts of the day was a brief reference to the lilies of the field at the beginning of *How Plants Grow*. "Our Lord's direct object in this lesson of the Lilies was to convince the people of God's care for them." The rest was straight business—how plants grow from seed, the kinds of roots, stems, leaves, flowers, and fruits. While fewer technical terms appeared in the beginner's book, the young Americans of the 1850's still had to face the fact directly that a flower consisted of *Calyx, Corolla, Stamens,* and *Pistils*. They had to classify the margins of leaves as *serrate, dentate, crenate, wavy, sinuate,* or *incised*. They had to tell an endogenous from an exogenous stem.[13]

Gray was trying "to make *real science* as easy and simple as possible." The publishers often felt his emphasis too much on real science and too little on simple and easy. They had to push hard to get him down to the level of Alphonso Wood. In writing to his European friends Gray had an air of apology about this activity. To Bentham he wrote, "Forgive me for writing horn-books, and I am now done with that sort of work. There were several convincing reasons for doing it." [14] The testimonials, the publishers' reports, and the frequency with which these books turn up in old libraries indicate a steady sale and influence. Gray himself realized $500 to $600 per year during this period, most of it on a flat fee basis. In the steady expansion of American elementary education, Wood also continued to prosper.

This chronicle of Gray's activities in the 1850's has already accounted for many of his waking hours. Most of these activities—the Wilkes expedition botany, Harvard teaching, network of correspondence, and the writing of textbooks—were continuations of his tasks in the 1840's, now more insistent and more demanding. The botanical results of explorations were, however, the really dynamic factor with which Gray had to contend. These had flooded in continuously ever since the Mexican War, and as the federal government began to attack the problems of its newly acquired territories, the opportunities increased rapidly. Engelmann was still in his strategic position in St. Louis, and Torrey with his long experience was still the botanist to whom army officers with western collections usually turned first. Gray, besides doing his part with the other two members of the team in studying the collections, also had his own great collector Charles Wright in the field. American expansion westward shaped botanical exploration, which in turn shaped Gray's research career.

He was still pointing to the region "between El Paso & California & the Great Interior Basin" and, despite the frequent exchanges of indignation which passed between the two, Wright was rapidly becoming his most trusted instrument in the field. With a bit of assistance from the Smithsonian Institution, Wright fulfilled his desire for wandering in 1849 by returning to Texas. Traveling with an army supply train from San Antonio to the neighborhood of what is now El Paso, at the rate of a hundred miles a month, Wright made good collections of specimens among the plants and enemies among the officers. After a season wasted in Texas in 1850, an opportunity turned up in 1851 in the form of a commission to survey the boundary between the United States and Mexico, an aftermath of the treaty ending the Mexican War. Wright went out under the auspices of Colonel J. D. Graham, one of the commissioners. While he had to spend most of the time in the neighborhood of El Paso and even to serve on a surveying crew, he did penetrate New Mexico, and the northern part of the states of Chihuahua and Sonora.

After great tribulations in shipping bundles at the Texas end, and long hours of sorting sets and arranging collections in Cambridge, two considerable publications appeared which gave the team of Wright and Gray a commanding position in the study of the flora of the Southwest. *Plantae Wrighteanae* Part I, dealt with the 1849 collections and Part II covered the collections made with the boundary survey.[15] Both were incomplete in that they elaborated only those natural families through *Compositae* as arranged by De Candolle. This old stopping place meant that Gray did not publish many families included in the collection. His aim to combine the specimens of Lindheimer, Fendler, and Wright for these unpublished families only added one more task to those already hanging over his head.

The Mexican boundary survey was a confused affair, replete with false starts, rivalries among the commissioners, and an inefficiency that stretched its operations from 1848 to 1853 without conclusive results. Only when Lieutenant W. H. Emory, a topographical engineer who had earlier served as astronomer, became commissioner in 1854 did the organization unravel and finish its work. The period of confusion, however, gave opportunities to other botanists than Charles Wright simply because the rivalries of the authorities extended to the organization of the scientific corps. The British-born C. C. Parry, a medical student of Torrey's, made his appearance on the American botanical scene as chief botanist and geologist under Emory, who started the survey of the line from the California end. George Thurber, a self-taught botanist from Providence, Rhode Island, appeared with Commissioner John R. Bartlett at the Texas end of the line dressed, much to Wright's disgust, in broadcloth instead of deerskin. Dr. John Milton Bigelow, a friend of Sullivant's from Lancaster, Ohio, secured a post as surgeon. Too many botanists, certainly, for their own or the government's good. But their very numbers turned the Mexican boundary survey into a kind of graduate school for collectors. It was here, and not in the halls of Harvard, the botanists were really made in the 1850's.[16]

Besides Wright's plants, Gray published those of Thurber in his "Plantae Novae Thurberianae," which appeared in 1854. When

Lieutenant Emory secured an appropriation for publication by the government, all the collections were lumped together, Torrey taking the major part and Gray working out a few families. The huge volume finally appeared in 1859.[17] Bigelow felt keenly that Gray had anticipated him in publishing Wright's plants first, but this naturally disappointing situation arose because of delays on the part of Torrey and because of the vagaries of federal appropriations for publishing the reports.[18]

With the boundary survey collection under control by 1854, Gray even entertained the fatuous hope that he could go back to work on the *Flora of North America,* which had lain fallow for ten years, in the time he had been spending on western collections. "If I do not bring out the rest of vol. 2, I am sure I never will." But the knowledge which had stacked up in those ten years rendered the work of youth already obsolete. His task was further complicated by the great piles of collections of plants from families he had not yet studied. Here alone was enough work to occupy the prime of his life. "Last Saturday was my birthday; 44! Oh! Oh!" [19]

A mere botanist could not turn aside the forces of American expansion in the 1850's. Instead, he was their prisoner. The Mexican boundary survey was only the beginning of a great decade of activity by the federal government in studying the newly won domain of the West.[20] Settlement was already a fact in Oregon and California, making transportation a major problem throughout the area. The army, especially its corps of topographical engineers, was the dominant agency in the enterprise. Was it likely that the botanical exploration which had already established itself as a part of the army expeditions would cease to make its demands on Gray? He soon found the answer.

Hardly was he at work on the *Flora* "when Torrey swamped me by sending me a good part of Pope, Bigelow (Whipple's Expedition), Beckwith, &c—collections—to be worked up at once for Government Reports." [21] These specimens were the first fruits of the great railroad surveys of 1853 and 1854. Not only was a rail connection across the continent both a great need and a technical possibility, it was an integral part of the hottest political question of the day—the expansion of slavery. Hence Congress was willing to put up $150,000 in the hope that scientists and engineers could give an answer to the question of whether a transcontinental railroad should follow a northern or a southern route. The politicians would have been happy to have the scientific gentlemen answer this question. To Asa Gray it simply meant more collections from the West.

Secretary of War Jefferson Davis gave instructions to six different parties to survey parallel routes, the northernmost being along the forty-seventh parallel just below Canada and the southernmost along the thirty-second parallel near the Mexican line and taking advantage of the newly acquired Gadsden Purchase. Two of the parties directly assaulted the great bastion of the southern Rockies which Gray had so long considered the prime objective of botanical exploration in the West. In many respects Gray's responsibilities were lighter for the railroad survey botany than they had been for the collections of Lindheimer, Fendler, and Charles Wright in the 1840's. Torrey, still true to his specialty in the plants of Western America, took the lead as primary author or co-author of each expedition's report. The Smithsonian Institution cared for the details of equipment and supplies for the collectors. The army, on this occasion making exploration its primary business, both paid the collectors and directed the parties with an eye to maximum scientific results. The military officers also directed the preparation of the reports, with Congress paying the bill for publication. The heartaches of the United States Exploring Expedition had taught their lesson well, the twelve stately volumes rolling from the press in large printings, complete by 1859.

If Gray's responsibility was less exclusive, he and Torrey nevertheless turned out much western botany from these collections. The reports mark the end of the period in which the flora of whole regions of the West stood completely unknown. Of course these parties, like earlier ones, had moved rapidly, missing many plants which bloomed in other seasons or in inaccessible localities. But the major outlines were now drawn. No longer would collectors come in, as did Bigelow from the thirty-fifth parallel, with several new genera and more than sixty new species.[22] The results, applied to the problem of surveying for a railroad, were equivocal. As a means of solving the dilemmas involved in the expansion of slavery, the surveys were worse than useless. But as an elucidation of the botany, zoology, and geology of the West the railroad surveys were a glorious chapter in the history of American science. They were the culmination of two decades of steady effort and the result of a highly developed system of exploration in which the federal government took the lead, utilizing civilian collectors and scientists under the general supervision of the army.

American expansion in the 1850's had maritime as well as overland objectives. Manifest destiny carried beyond the bounds of United States territory, leading to filibusters in Central America, expeditions to the Amazon, and diplomatic gestures which suggested the acquisition of Cuba. Much of the pressure behind these efforts was Southern in origin, seeking more elbowroom for slavery. Hence Asa Gray was personally unsympathetic to overseas expansion. Referring to the Bahama Islands, he wrote to Sir William Hooker, "You can get information from there sooner than we can— till we annex it, with the rest of creation, and by the time that amount of annexation is accomplished I shall be glad to come and live at Kew." [23] Politics had nothing to do with using the vessels of expansion for the benefit of science. Almost without realizing it, Gray was on the verge of receiving the means of a pivotal scientific discovery—a gift which he received because he was an American and because his countrymen were carrying the stars and stripes to far places.

When Commodore Matthew C. Perry organized the United States Navy's attempt to open Japan for American commerce, he learned from the number and insistence of the applications from scientists, both foreign and domestic, that the hermit kingdom possessed unknown treasures in natural history as well as in trade.[24] Unique among American military officers of the nineteenth century, however, Perry saw in a civilian scientific corps a threat to security as well as discipline. He feared especially as a potential Russian spy Philipp Franz Siebold, the greatest living authority on Japan, whose plants had formed the basis of the *Flora Japonica* received by Gray as a present in Munich back in 1839. Accordingly Perry tried to keep all civilian scientists out of his ships and to encourage his officers to fill their places. Nevertheless, Dr. James Morrow, who went along to show agricultural implements to the Japanese, wished to collect plants. By incredible good luck S. Wells Williams, the missionary whom Perry engaged in China to act as interpreter, was Gray's old friend from the Utica Gymnasium. Morrow and Williams, then, made a small collection of Japanese plants, which they sent to Gray, who eventually published them in Perry's report.[25] This collection alone might have put him on the trail of the dynamic relationship between the floras of eastern Asia and eastern North America. Long before Perry's return and before the many jurisdictional difficulties which plagued the collection had been settled, the queer but great Charles Wright was on his way to the Orient with the expedition which had the duty of exploiting scientifically the way opened by Perry's diplomacy.

The North Pacific Exploring Expedition, under the command of Cadwallader Ringgold, who had served with Wilkes, set sail in 1853 from Norfolk, proceeding via Madeira and the Cape of Good Hope to Hong Kong, preparatory to beginning surveys. Gray considered this voyage "just the thing" for Wright, largely because he foresaw it would give an opportunity to supplement the Hawaiian Island collections of the Wilkes Expedition.[26] For his part Wright hoped to get to warmer regions, for he, like many of the western collectors, seemed to suffer more from cold than from heat and dreamed of the paradise of the tropics.

The actual course of the little vessels (the flagship *Vincennes* was not new when Wilkes had sailed her) fulfilled the expectations of neither Gray nor Wright. A long delay in Hong Kong, occasioned by the internal trouble in China and the "derangement" of Commodore Ringgold, gave Wright the unwelcome opportunity of collecting in the neighborhood of that oft-visited port. That the specimens he gathered here became the occasion and largely the basis for George Bentham's *Flora Hong-Kongiensis* is a concrete tribute to his world standing as a plant collector. Although he never reached Gray's primary target, the Hawaiian Islands at all, other opportunities opened.

John Rodgers, who succeeded the addled Ringgold in command, was so truly an officer and a gentleman that he had the genuine interest in science and the intelligence in administering it necessary to make the exploring expedition a success. Both Wright and William Stimpson, the able student of Agassiz's who served as zoologist, had their best support from the new commodore. Through the Ryukyu island chain and across to the Bonins, the expedition surveyed places whose names would one day loom large in American history. But the best chances for the naturalists came in Japan, where Wright, although confined to the areas about the ports of Shimoda and Hakodate, made leisurely collections which exhibited the main features of the flora of the country. The remainder of the cruise, into the Bering Strait and down to California, yielded nothing botanically, largely because Wright never had a chance to go ashore.[27]

The North Pacific Exploring Expedition lost much of the scientific fame it deserved in two accidents. Most of Stimpson's zoological specimens were burned in the great Chicago fire of 1871. Even before that the publication of the official reports foundered against Congressional antipathy and then sank permanently during the Civil War.[28] Fortunately Commodore Rodgers gave the scientists permission to publish their results in private journals, hoping with this device to secure priority and impress Congressmen. Although these scattered contributions soon lost their identity as a coordinated enterprise, they did enter the stream of science. As will appear later, Wright's collections gave Asa Gray the raw material for the most important paper he ever wrote.[29]

As if Gray were not already heavily enough engaged, the forces of American expansion and the whims of his collectors pushed him into dealing with specimens of American plants of the Caribbean area, Mexico, and southward. Augustus Fendler, unsuccessful in further western ventures and always restless, went off to a German colony called Colonia Tovar in Venezuela where he continued to collect dried specimens to be marketed through Gray.[30] Louis Cachand Ervendberg, a German who ran off to Mexico for highly personal reasons after several years in Texas, also sent in collections to be sold to other botanists.[31]

As usual, however, the greatest collector of all who made the trek southward was Charles Wright. Gray hoped he would work up his own collections from the exploring expedition and actually set him to work on them, but Wright's utter uselessness for anything except collecting became again apparent. By the fall of 1856 plans were afoot to cure the collector's "rheumatics" by sending him to Cuba. According to Sir William Hooker, "the mountains of E. end of Cuba are *terra incognita* for botany." Gray advised Wright, "Pray stay long enough to gather the harvest fairly." Despite the fleas and the occasional lapses in Gray's letter-writing Wright found Cuba so much to his taste that he harvested its plants almost uninterruptedly for nine years. Gray, realizing that he could not do justice to these collections, referred Wright to Professor H. R. A. Grisebach of Göttingen. "He is up to W. Ind. Botany, I am not." [32] Gray still had the responsibility he had always assumed for Wright—the transmission of money, books, supplies for pressing plants, and, to the collector's annoyance, the giving of advice. The total record, however, shows two men of disparate temperament and accomplishments teaming effectively for science. Neither one could do the other's job.

In a weird turn of events, another collection from south of the border came into Gray's hands in the 1850's. Jean Louis Berlandier had gone out to Mexico for the elder De Candolle in 1826. Gray had to determine and sort these specimens which should have been disposed of a generation before. Although he despised the collection and considered Berlandier a dishonest knave, the hard, almost menial labor which he performed provided Berlandier material for several herbaria and helped to reintroduce it into the stream of science. Herbarium botanists labor under a peculiar responsibility in that the omissions of one generation turn up in the next, for the rule of precedent renders the first collections in a region of almost eternal importance.[33]

The whole mass of plant material coming in from the explorations, both western and overseas, furnishes the key to many questions about the nature of Gray's scientific work. These bundles of dried specimens, and all that they entailed in writing and study, tyrannically governed the distribution of Gray's time, his choice of problems, and the miscellaneous results of his work during the 1850's. Joseph Hooker did not hesitate to berate his American friend. "What a pest, plague & nuisance are your official, semi-official & unofficial Railway reports, surveys &c. &c. &c. Your valuable researches are scattered beyond the power of anyone but yourself finding them. Who on earth is to keep in their heads or quote such a medley of books—double-paged, double titled & half finished as your Govt. vomits periodically into the great ocean of Scientific bibliography." [34] This confusion is eloquent witness that Gray was not planning his research, but simply struggling to keep up with the avalanche.

The press of Gray's daily duties and of the incoming collections shows how American society shaped the course of science. Those who ask why America has not produced great basic discoveries and scientists of the stature of Newton can find here a relevant case in which the forces are observable. Asa Gray had become America's leading botanist and in the 1850's was at the prime of life, health, and mental vigor. What prevented him from producing his *Principia*? The practicality of American society and the desire for the economic application of science played but a minor role, since his only gesture in their direction was the report on forest trees for the Smithsonian, which he always laid aside to do one of these days. The contempt of money-mad and success-mad countrymen played almost no role in hampering one who was affectionately received as a son-in-law by Charles Greely Loring. Physical isolation could not have been a deciding factor, for Gray not only spent a year abroad, but kept constantly in touch with the best of European science.

The answer lies rather in the multiplicity of duties which Americans heaped upon anyone who had proved his eminence at research. Neither he nor anyone else thought of releasing the nation's leading botanist to pursue philosophical studies in the nature of life. Protection which would have provided this leisure was completely foreign to the American civilization of the mid-nineteenth century. Any humble clergyman or schoolteacher in Alabama or Illinois considered it his inalienable right to collect some plants in his neighborhood, dry them, send them to Professor Gray of Cambridge—possibly the only botanist's name he had ever heard—and expect a letter by return mail which contained a list of names of his plants and words of encouragement and praise. More often than not, he got the letter. In a variation on this theme, the botanists of the country felt an obligation to place good textbooks in every schoolroom, thereby condemning Gray to writing progressively simpler versions, one after the other. Harvard College assumed that he was being paid to teach boys and to keep the garden alive. Only after that could he think of research. The government claimed him to work up its collections, bad as well as good, on its own time schedule, which involved waiting as well as working. Gray and the society about him agreed that he could not refuse to answer these calls. This inability to care for the institutional housekeeping of science without draining off research talent is one key to lack of scientific creativity in America.

The effect on his research of the pressures which held Gray almost enchained are obvious. In the first place, he could not leave the herbarium to go into the field and gain the insights which the observation of living plants can give. Modern botanists, equipped with jeeps, station wagons, and plane tickets to Havana, feel that they can gain a true picture of a plant population only by alternation between field and laboratory. Such a pleasant and instructive variation in routine was impossible for Gray. Collecting required months of time and the technique of survival in the wilderness. The men who did the collecting were a rare breed, able to keep the lamp of science alive in the most isolated mountain camp, but usually restive after a month or two inside the settlements. Even had Gray transcended this temperamental requirement, he had too much work stacked up to leave Cambridge for long journeys. Suppose he had gone himself with the North Pacific Exploring Expedition instead of sending Charles Wright. Who would have prepared the seven papers and five reviews a year—his average in this period— for three years?

The pressure of the collections coming in also dictated that he stick close to taxonomy. His regular notes in the *American Journal of Science* attest his continuing interest in the broader reaches of botany—in the chemistry of vegetation and plant physiology.[35] He followed with interest the discovery of the alternation of generations in the cryptogams which was gradually taking shape in the

213

works of Wilhelm Hofmeister. George Bentham paid him the compliment of asking him to summarize Hofmeister's work to demonstrate and clarify its larger significance. "You are too much up to the whole thing not to be able to give a clear idea of all that is essential in forty or fifty pages." [36] But in physiology Gray could not do much research, only follow the results. Tear open a bundle of specimens, examine them rapidly, study flowers under a simple microscope, compare with other specimens, straighten out the precedence in the nomenclature, and write it all up in clear but packed technical phrases—this process went on day after day. Taxonomy had to be for Gray the center of research.

Incidentally, the hurry of the period affords the best explanation of the lack of file-clerk nicety which characterized his herbarium. Data on labels was often sketchy and numbers were sometimes scrambled. Gray well knew what information should appear on labels. He complained to Wilkes on one occasion that "I experienced great difficulty from the want of information taken from the living plants . . . and also the particular stations of the plants: the labels attached to the specimens . . . usually giving only the name of the Island or district where they were gathered." [37] The many lapses from the ideal label were the product of adverse circumstances both in the field and the herbarium. They did not spring from a conscious policy.

However, the deflection of Gray's scientific efforts by the forces of American society and the enchainment of his research to the results of American exploration gave him an opportunity while they took away leisure and freedom. In the first place, the new collections crossing his table left him with no illusions that species were always easily discernible. In many cases the first sparse specimens from a region would represent two plants seemingly quite distinct, only to have fuller materials come in containing transitional forms. After making thousands of judgments on borderline cases, Gray developed a highly sensitive, almost intuitive grasp of the variations in the forms of plants and of the distinction between genetically controlled characteristics and ephemeral modifications produced by environment.

In the second place he was the first botanist ever to gain a simultaneous and accurate knowledge of the general outlines of the vegetation of eastern North America, western North America, and eastern Asia represented by Japan. No European could command the advantages which being an American had conferred upon him through the expansionist activities of the 1850's. Gray had in hand enough good material to be able to see the floristic relationships of the whole Northern Hemisphere. The thousands of seemingly insignificant dried specimens were, for the mind which could see them in global terms, the keys to a major scientific discovery.

XII

GRAY'S MIND AND THE
THREAT OF AGASSIZ

THE publication of Charles Darwin's *Origin of Species* in 1859, one of the great events in the history of science, took place within a few days of Asa Gray's forty-ninth birthday. Of all the scientists who have studied the processes of life since the sixteenth century, only a handful have experienced such a dramatic moment at the height of their careers. For the happy few of that generation, the question of species was the supreme test not only of their knowledge and judgment as scientists but also of all they knew and believed in the deepest recesses of their personalities. At least for the clearest headed and the best informed, the crisis did not arise unheralded in a single instant, nor did it spring full-grown from the brow of Darwin. The climax of the development of Asa Gray's mind came before November 1859, as did his greatest contribution.

Amid the daily grind of teaching and taxonomy, Gray had always lightly played with larger groupings of facts concerning the plants he studied, especially geographical distribution.

By the late 1840's an intriguing problem had broken into his consciousness. Charles Darwin, struck with the high percentage of peculiar species of animals on the Galápagos Islands when he visited them on the voyage of the *Beagle,* had observed not only that the peculiar species were of the same genera as animals on the mainland but that they were each limited to their own island. Such a distribution suggested that basic types, having migrated to the islands, had in their isolation diverged into new species. When Joseph Hooker showed a similar distribution of the plants of the Galápagos,

Gray was immediately interested, labeling the paper "important."
Then, using the Wilkes expedition collections, he came up with an
example of his own in the Hawaiian Islands.[1] Thus the stimulus of
Darwin already lay behind Gray's unfulfilled wish to undertake a
Hawaiian Island "Flora" and to have Charles Wright make ade-
quate collections there.

With larger problems of natural history coming home to him in
a concrete way, and with his own maturity as a scientist largely
achieved, Gray formulated in the early '50's a clearly defined concept of a species as the basic unit of taxonomy and as a description
of a genuine discontinuity in nature. His formal definition of a
species was the same as that he had taken from A. P. De Candolle's
Théorie élémentaire de la botanique when he read it back in the
1830's. Not only was a species made up of individuals which resembled one another, but they stood to one another as parent and
offspring. As time went on, the latter part of the definition, the assumption of a true genetic connection between all members of a
species, became by far the more important for him. Like breeds
like, was his primary article of faith. In comparison, special creation of the species in the beginning was of minor importance. He
believed it, yes, but the beginning was lost in the mist; no direct
evidence for it existed. What was crucial for him as the specimens
passed under his microscope was the question whether one species
could undergo a transmutation into another one between one generation and the next. Permanency of present species, not miraculous creation of primordial ones, seemed to him to be necessary if
natural history was to have any meaning. The vicissitudes of climate, soil, and environment made organisms vary, but an eventual
check was placed on variation by the inability of unlike species to
breed together. It was this inability which created the species
border, not that he or any other could find this border easily,
least of all by referring to an ideal type. The "choice of what to
take as the typical forms is not free. We take, e.g. . . . . the particular form . . . of which Linnaeus, say, happened to have a
specimen sent him, and on which he established the species; and I
know more than one case in which that is a rare form of a common
species." [2] The border could not be determined in advance, but

only by observation, by a study of the morphology of the plant. But how did this show the boundary? Here Gray could only refer to sound principles of classification and the experience of the naturalist. The weak point of the natural system and the morphological approach, which formed the scientific orthodoxy to which Gray adhered, lay in this inability to go beyond a description of the organs and a subjective judgment on them.

Gray's insistence on a genetic connection among all the individuals of a species was an important basis for his violent and abiding dislike of Lamarck's revolutionary ideas and those of the *Vestiges*. He was also a campaigner against that crude kind of popular transmutation theory which made farmers claim they had stalks on which two kinds of grain were growing simultaneously.[3] By implication, his idea of genetic connection led him to favor the doctrine that each species originated in a single locality. Likewise, he could not admit that the spontaneous generation of plants or animals from inorganic matter broke into the chain of parent to offspring. As a practicing naturalist, he felt he must assume, regardless of theories of original creation, that the characteristics of a plant lying on his table were determined, within rather broad limits, by the characteristics of some organic ancestor. In this important question of spontaneous generation he was siding with the great trend of evidence which would culminate in the experiments of Louis Pasteur which so discredited the advocates of spontaneous generation. Genetic boundaries had to encompass species on all sides to render taxonomy possible. To classify plants would be impossible if new kinds might spring up spontaneously or might appear transmuted from the familiar kind.

The emphasis on genetic connection as the basis of species led Gray to the problem of hybridization. Did the crossing of two different forms obscure species boundaries? Did crossing produce new species? Like most botanists of his day, Gray believed that crossing blended the two parents, and hence was a device for "obliterating, not creating, species." If hybridization were widespread and produced fertile offspring, all species lines would have been long since washed out. Gray pointed out, however, that if hybrids occurred in nature, they stood a good chance of being fertilized by their parents.

"In such cases they are said to revert to the type of the species of the impregnating parent; but would they return exactly to that type, inheriting as they do a portion of the blood of a cognate species?" [4] If Gray had been an Austrian monk instead of a busy American professor, he might have been able to experiment on plants with this question in mind. It was just such leads that he found hardest to get the leisure to follow.

Gray considered his ideas on species scientifically orthodox. While he had learned them in the first place from A. P. De Candolle, he had above all things British botanical practice in mind when he described his principles as "sound." He meant that he admired the monographs of Robert Brown, that he could go into the herbarium of Sir William Hooker or George Bentham and agree with them on which two of a series of specimens represented distinct species. Young Joseph Hooker perhaps had a tendency to throw too many species together, but his judgment, too, Gray highly admired.

Yet beliefs about species were but concrete examples of a man's general philosophy. Already by 1850, after the *Vestiges* uproar, there was such tension over the broader implications of the meaning of species that Gray's whole philosophy was involved, although neither his religion nor his philosophy appear in self-conscious theorizing in the 1850's. Part of it was reticence. Much more of the lack stemmed from that same press of work which hampered his entry into the more abstruse scientific problems. His education had provided him with no formal training in theology or philosophy. When did he ever have time to sit down and read the works of David Hume or Immanuel Kant? There is no convincing evidence that in these years he gave detailed study even to William Paley's *Natural Theology*, a book to which he owed much. In general, he absorbed his philosophical ideas from those around him, especially from the members of the Cambridge Scientific Club, where James Walker held forth on "Strauss's theological work—natural religion—Paley's argument imperfect," and Daniel Treadwell examined the *Ninth Bridgewater Treatise*.[5] Despite this lack of formal articulation, however, Gray's philosophical orientation was surprisingly well developed.

The same empirical cast dominated his approach as it had in the 1840's, and the same fidelity to evangelical Christianity persisted. The argument from design in nature was common to both patterns, and a limited vitalism cemented the whole together. Since he believed vital force a characteristic of all living beings, not just the higher animals, he early developed a lively interest in sensitive plants, insectivorous plants, and the coiling of tendrils, all of which seemed to show sensitivity and hence the rudiments of independent behavior in plants. Vitalism was one of the ways in which he sealed off a species from genetic contamination, in this case from the inorganic environment. Most of Gray's actual arguments on vitalism place heavy emphasis on the greater complexity of organic phenomena rather than on their being forever undecipherable by science. He sometimes seemed to be saying that the main function of the vital principle was to serve as the vehicle of purpose in nature, to counteract the randomness which characterized inorganic reactions.

Among the incidental results both of Gray's religious affiliation and his ideas on species was a definite opinion on man's place in nature, and more particularly on the difference among the races of man. Humans were a part of nature—"the longest-domesticated of all species." [6] It was the relation of the various subgroups to one another which gave the naturalist trouble. The evangelical emphasis on the moral worth of every member of the human race reached its greatest heights in the agitation against slavery which surrounded Gray on every side in the 1850's. Those scientists who were trying to prove the inferiority of the Negro, notably Josiah Nott and George R. Gliddon, combined their attack on the unity of the races with a bitter assault on orthodoxy. Since Gray's whole scientific orientation and all his ideas on species and hybridization pointed toward the unity of the human races, he found on this point his religion and his science were not merely reconcilable but in fundamental agreement.

Despite this example of community of interest, Gray was singularly detached from his co-religionists in this period. Surrounded as he was by Unitarians at home and at college, his only formal connection with orthodox Christianity was through the pastor of the

First Church in Cambridge. Even this church was not Presbyterian but Congregational. Aside from attending, and at times teaching a Sunday School class, Gray was not active. During all the years before 1859 he made no important public pronouncement on theology or on church affairs. His major intellectual intercourse with the clergy of the period was not with an American Presbyterian, but with R. W. Church, a member of the Oxford movement who, although in the 1850's only a country parson, was destined to be the Dean of St. Paul's. If he lived in Britain, he said, he would "be a churchman, although a pretty low one, at least in some respects; and I am a most hearty wellwisher to the Church of England." [7] Hence his whole direct influence on the community was by the example of his profession of faith alone.

A profound empiricism dominated his thinking about science. Gray not only trusted experience and observation as the basis of his scientific method but explicitly gave priority to their results over religion itself. He even trusted the experience of particular facts over large scientific generalization and theories which claimed their validity from idealistic constructions. To him, of course, facts were intimately tied up with dried plant specimens. It "is in me to sympathize more with & estimate higher the slow induction that leads step by step to sound conclusions so far as they go, than the bolder flights of the genius which so often leads the possessor to mount three pairs of stairs only to jump out of the garret window." [8] Gray had sat at a table for eight weeks in 1851 with the nephew of Jeremy Bentham, practicing a simple but persistent kind of empiricism on the plants of the Wilkes Expedition. His working intimacy with the Hookers was so strong that he even contemplated moving to Kew, Joseph generously offering him a hundred pounds out of a legacy to come over. [9] Thus Gray came close to thinking like a British botanist on most important subjects. Especially did he eschew mysticism and anything smacking of German idealism.

For a Britisher this dislike of German idealism would hardly have seemed unusual. But as an American Gray had to reckon with the fact that almost at his own back door transcendentalism was the most vigorous intellectual movement in the country. Is it possible that a botanist living in Cambridge, Massachusetts, was not aware of the flowering of New England? Ralph Waldo Emerson, Henry Thoreau, and the rest of the Concord group must often have passed the Botanic Garden. When Gray went out to the Shaker community to get their medicinal herbs for Sir William Hooker's museum, he must have passed through the village of the philosophers. But the suggestion that Thoreau's *Walden* described a proper attack on the secrets of nature would have left him unimpressed. Thoreau's fancy that he was exploring the farthest Indies while sitting on the shore of a pond would have seemed sheer nonsense to the sponsor of Charles Wright. Ironically, that queer individual came closer than the transcendentalists to fulfilling Emerson's call for an American scholar, the man of action thinking. The sage of Concord, if he ever met the explorer, would have been appalled at the form his own specifications took. Gray treated Emerson and Thoreau with a silence that the accident of acquaintance and the hostility of Harvard to the Concord group cannot fully explain away. He was hostile to their whole way of looking at nature, to their idealism, and to their German inspiration.

On the other side Thoreau saw in Gray only a disembodied *Manual of Botany* whose descriptions did not please him and who slavishly followed the rules of nomenclature. When Thoreau was struck by a passage in Gray, he read into it a symbolism which changed the matter-of-fact scientific prose beyond recognition. He pondered a statement by Gray that roots "not only spring from the root-end of the primary stem in germination, but also from any subsequent part of the stem under favorable circumstances, that is to say, in darkness and moisture, as when covered by the soil or resting on its surface." It is certain that Gray meant here exactly what he said, but for Thoreau these words meant that "the most clear and ethereal ideas (Antaeus-like) readily ally themselves to the earth, to the primal womb of things." [10] The discrepancy between these two ways of looking at the same phenomenon is the measure of the great gap between transcendentalism and Gray's empiricism. The essential connection between individuals which made them members of a species came from the actual fact of genetic kinship, not from an ideal concept either in the mind of the Creator or the naturalist. In resisting the idealism prevalent in American thought, Gray was starting on a lonely road which would set him off from the community more clearly than did his penchant for religious orthodoxy.

Sound and orthodox, both in science and religion, Gray could describe himself in the early 1850's. Such a position invited the charge that he repressed new insights, both in himself and in others. The author of the *Vestiges* had howled in his rebuttal that scientists were scorning him as unorthodox. Was science in the 1850's a conspiracy to keep down truth? Was it afraid to face the facts it dug up? Was it the service tool of the clergy? Asa Gray's career provides answers to all these questions. Having declared his fidelity to science he did not flinch at the path it made him follow. Indeed, his interest quickened as new vistas opened, the only deterrent being that incubus of routine work waiting for him in herbarium, garden, and classroom.

Gray was aware of dynamic possibilities lurking in the difficulties in the concept of species. A whole battery of unsolved problems in biology was gathered in the one word. That intriguing configuration of plants and animals in the Galápagos Islands had tickled his fancy, but it was hardly more than a query. The discovery of the alternation of generations in the lower plants had large implications concerning the unity of the plant kingdom, but it was only gradually unfolding beneath a thick layer of very technical papers. Geology, however, had been much in the mind of professional naturalist and popular lecture-goer for many years. The past not only stretched back for millions of years, but fairly definite periods had become discernible. Organic fossils, mostly animals, were the keys to the periods, and the doctrine of uniformitarianism—that the processes now observable and operating at their present intensity were the agents of change in the geological past—had been well publicized in Sir Charles Lyell's *Principles of Geology*.

Gray, having accepted the new geology without the slightest fanfare, was only lightly involved in the theorizing and the quarreling of the geologists, who were then the most numerous, the best organized, and best supported group of naturalists in America. He did, however, encourage the work of Leo Lesquereux, a Swiss who followed Agassiz to the United States but who, after working at the Botanic Garden for a little while, moved to Columbus, Ohio, where he was employed by Sullivant. Lesquereux was doing the first considerable body of work on paleobotany in the United States.[11] Gray also benefited from his old friendship with James Dwight Dana, which continued in their close cooperation on the publication of the *American Journal of Science,* of which Dana was the editor and Gray an associate editor with Agassiz and Wolcott Gibbs. Gray was thus near enough to know what was going on in geology without having to take sides often. So great were the gaps in geological evidence, however, that it had little relevance to practical taxonomy. And even though in retrospect the application of geology to the species problem is one of the essential steps leading to the revolution, Lyell's *Principles* was now an effective advocate of the fixity of species and a damaging critique of such early evolutionary theorists as Lamarck.

Gray gradually became aware in the early 1850's that his orthodox scientific position was facing a truly formidable challenge by a set of theories which, if allowed to carry the day, would completely smash his whole philosophy and many of his scientific generalizations. This threat was the more personal because it resided in a man whom he saw often and with whom he had cordial relations. The man was Agassiz.[12] In a surprisingly short time after his first arrival in the United States in 1846, Agassiz had clearly overshadowed his botanical colleague as well as all the other native-born scientists. He had captured the Lawrence Scientific School for his own uses. He had gained important research facilities by an alliance with the leading scientist in the government, Alexander Dallas Bache of the Coast Survey. He became the fount of authority for all the zoologists of the country, while his glacial hypothesis made the geologists bow down in awe. In launching his *Contributions to the Natural History of the United States* he had every Bostonian of any means at all lined up as a paying subscriber. His achievements in raising money made Gray's efforts to replace the 45-year-old pickets in the garden fence appear ridiculously inconsequential. Above all he used his glowing personality, his foreign accent, his Continental manners, and his exuberant energy to become in the American public eye the very model of a scientific man.

As the shadow of Agassiz spread over American science Gray

began to feel cramped. As early as 1849 a note of reserve had already appeared when he wrote to Engelmann, who had known Agassiz as a student in Germany, that "A. and I always get on perfectly well—tho' perhaps we might not if we worked in the same field; yet one who understands his impulsive character ought to have little or no difficulty.—We continue intimate friends and he remains very popular here." [13] Both of them belonged to the Cambridge Scientific Club, of course.

Agassiz's eminent social abilities soon found a wider sphere. In 1852, Emerson recorded in his journal, "I saw in the cars a broad-featured, unctuous man, fat and plenteous as some successful politician, and pretty soon divined it must be the foreign professor who has had so marked a success in all our scientific and social circles, having established unquestionable leadership in them all; and it was Agassiz." Soon afterward, the professor joined the *literati*—Emerson, James Russell Lowell, Richard Henry Dana, Jr., John Lothrop Motley, Oliver Wendell Holmes, and several lesser lights—to form the Saturday Club. At these regular meetings intimacy flourished in an atmosphere of good cheer and good conversation. The group was even sometimes called Agassiz's Club. Emerson listed Agassiz as second only to Thomas Carlyle as one of "my men." [14]

On a national scale Agassiz belonged to an equally remarkable group from whose association the exclusion of Gray can hardly have been entirely accidental. The Scientific Lazzaroni considered themselves the choicest spirits and the best brains of American science. Devoted to good food and wine, they usually met at the same time as the American Association for the Advancement of Science. Gray's friends Henry and Dana were members, but the dominating figures were Alexander Dallas Bache, who served as the beloved chief, and Agassiz and Benjamin Peirce of Harvard. This was the "Young America" movement among the scientists. They were determined to put down old-fogeyism and to build noble scientific institutions for themselves and the nation. Although their first major scheme, a privately supported national university at Albany, New York, had come to nothing, they were, through Benjamin Apthorp Gould, one of their members, deeply involved in the controversial Dudley Observatory at Albany. The group tended to work together in the politics of the AAAS and too on appointments to scientific positions.[15] Through the Lazzaroni Agassiz seemed much nearer the inner workings of the scientific profession as a whole in America than was Gray.

The shadow of Agassiz as a social lion could perhaps be borne. Even his outstanding success in attracting students and funds for science could hardly be objected to in terms which would not smack of jealousy. Gray nevertheless gradually came to realize that in his colleague's system of thought lay a threat to his whole conception of science and philosophy.

Agassiz came to the United States bearing the very essence of German idealistic philosophy. He had as a student at Munich deeply imbibed the prevailing *Naturphilosophie* directly from Friedrich W. J. von Schelling, Laurenz Oken, and especially Ignatius Döllinger. These idealists ran wild in trying to put all nature into a unified and absolute system of ideas.[16] Although their excesses quickly discredited the movement, it left an abiding mark on those who had embraced it. Agassiz always saw reality as plan, pattern, type imposed on matter. Where an empiricist might infer the Creator from the hand and the eye, the Germans had it the other way round. The Creator and the design were the ultimate reality, of which the hand and the eye were but manifestations. They could see evolution everywhere, but it took place in the mind of God.

In his Paris period Agassiz overlaid his *Naturphilosophie* with the science of his master, Cuvier. From the great French zoologist he gained comprehensive ideas of the classification of the animal kingdom, the understanding of which was greatly clarified by the comparative method. Cuvier as the student of the fossils of the Paris basin also led Agassiz back into the long time-span of geological history and encouraged him to do his master work, the *Poissons Fossiles*. Despite Cuvier's great labors in establishing the progression of organic beings from lower to higher geologic strata, he saw development as an idealistic connection, not a physical one. The various strata were sealed off from one another by catastrophes which destroyed all genetic connection between the organisms of two different eras. Agassiz's brilliant theorizing on a glacial age, the extension of great ice sheets over vast areas of the northern hemisphere, only served to deepen his commitment to Cuvier's catastrophic theory. Thus, the main sources of Agassiz's philosophical orientation steeped him in idealism. Indeed it served as his religion as well as his philosophy. For he was a member of no church and had a commitment to no creed except his belief in the Creator, whose mind he saw all about him as nature itself. No wonder that he found the company of Emerson and the atmosphere of transcendentalism in America congenial.

Agassiz's idealism was of course the basis of his concepts of species and their distribution. All systematic groupings were joined by "an ideal connection in the mind of the Creator." This plan of creation "which so commends itself to our highest wisdom, has not grown out of the necessary action of physical laws, but was the free conception of the almighty Intellect, matured in his thought, before it was manifested in tangible external forms. . . ." [17] He explicitly denied the genetic connection which Gray saw as basis of a species. Indeed, far from admitting that all individuals of a species had a common ancestor, he asserted that after each catastrophe, new species had been created in many individuals over approximately the same range they occupied until the next catastrophe. The Creator's all-embracing mind had been thinking such thoughts a long time, for "animal and vegetable life was as active and profusely scattered upon the whole globe, at all times and during all geological periods, as it is now." [18]

The twentieth-century mind finds this system of thought so foreign that it can only with difficulty reconcile it with the immense reputation Agassiz enjoyed in his prime, twenty years after the publication of his friend Lyell's *Principles of Geology*. Yet a general phenomenon in the biology of the middle years of the nineteenth century was the amazing amount of precise and brilliant research being done by those under the spell of *Naturphilosophie*, catastrophism, and idealism in general. Karl Ernst von Baer in Germany and Richard Owen in England are parallels to Agassiz in this respect. And the catastrophist geologists such as Adam Sedgwick and Sir Roderick Murchison had done more to unravel the sequence of strata and their fossils than had Lyell. These men had their share of authority in the scientific world of 1850, and they backed their positions no less with their grand generalizations than with their impressive research accomplishments.

When Agassiz had first arrived in the United States in 1846, during the excitement over the *Vestiges,* Gray had recognized the trend of Agassiz's ideas on species and had definitely disagreed, especially when they concerned the human species. Genetic connection had then seemed, however, less important than the fact that both men abhorred the transmutation of species as advanced by Lamarck and the *Vestiges.* They both also consistently referred to the Creator with reverence. And Gray could only rejoice that zoological research received from Agassiz an unprecedented stimulus.

Through the early 1850's Gray's mood toward Agassiz changed, reflecting both the social cramp which the rise of the colossus inflicted on him and his re-evaluation of the scientific factors. By 1854 Gray, realizing that "it often does more harm than good" to combat his colleague's views in public, had fully ranged himself in opposition. "I only, at the proper place & time put on record such views as I believe in, that it may not be afterwards supposed I had fallen in" with Agassiz. In talking with him "(a good genial fellow, and who bears contradicting as well as—could be expected) I confine myself to trying to show him that his own data do not at all necessitate the conclusions he sometimes draws from them." By the next year Gray, in a less amiable frame of mind, had singled out Agassiz's penchant for public lecturing as a most unfortunate activity. It "has greatly injured" him—"tampering with strict veracity for the sake of popular effect reacts on the mind . . . I fear." [19] In Gray's eyes Agassiz was telling American lecture audiences what they liked to hear, substituting their approval for that of the few qualified scientists—the only competent tribunal.

Two major factors form the background of Gray's reappraisal of Agassiz. One was that having denied that a species was genetically bound by descent from a common ancestor, Agassiz denied the unity of the human races. God had created separately large numbers of each of the races and meant them to remain apart. As a Swiss immigrant he may not have appreciated at first that he was very close to the pro-slavery argument, which had a scientific as well as a political and social side. But, when in 1854 he contributed an essay to Josiah

Nott's and George R. Gliddon's *Types of Mankind,* no doubt could remain that his theories were at the service of the defenders of slavery. This enormous and miscellaneous collection of evidence had but one purpose, to prove the inferiority of the Negro.[20] Such a performance was naturally displeasing to Gray. Because Nott and Gliddon found their main opposition in the South from clergymen, they also violently opposed organized religion. For instance, Gray's collaborator and correspondent, the Reverend Moses Ashley Curtis, was a leading opponent of Nott in the *Southern Quarterly Review.*[21] Thus Agassiz had a reputation as a dangerous infidel among the orthodox as well as a scientific ornament for the pro-slavery argument.

The influence of Agassiz's position on the unity of the races is easy to overemphasize. It did not phase his intimacy with an anti-slavery zealot such as Emerson. The religious odium which he aroused was not directly responsible for Gray's shift in attitude. "Agassiz has prejudiced (not scientific men but) the Orthodox against him by associating himself with Gliddon and Nott, and by his views on human species. To us they are merely unfounded: to many unscientific people they are offensive." The main effect on Gray of Agassiz's venture into the squalid company of the pro-slavery advocates was a further reduction of his respect for the man. "A. has a touch of the empiric about him, in that he is always writing and talking *ad populum*—fond of addressing himself to an incompetent tribunal." [22]

Agassiz had a much more ambitious project afoot which, breaking upon the Cambridge community in 1855, bode fair to threaten Gray even more profoundly. He issued a prospectus for ten volumes of contributions to the natural history of the United States. At the outset he had the backing of Francis Calley Gray of Boston (who was not kin to anyone born in Sauquoit, New York), and the very name of Agassiz had such magic that soon 2500 people had subscribed, "a support such as was never before offered to any scientific man for purely scientific ends. . . ." [23] Despite the joy with which all lovers of science in the United States greeted this announcement, one as familiar as was Gray with Agassiz's personality and ideas could easily predict that the zoologist would state his principles *a priori* as the essential first step. Nor was there any doubt about the philosophy he would announce. Natural history in America would be saddled with Agassiz's views of ideal species, of multiple creation, catastrophism, and static geographical distribution of plants and animals. If Agassiz's self-confidence, his undoubted popularity among nonscientific people, and his financial resources could establish a scientific doctrine, he was almost sure to carry the day. His forthcoming essay on classification might well influence the whole course of intellectual history of the late nineteenth century. Since self-assertion, fame, and money are not, however, the stuff of which scientific progress is made, Asa Gray looked for other resources.

The one other American scientist who had the knowledge, the intellectual vigor, and the breadth of experience to stand up to Agassiz was James Dwight Dana. The Wilkes Expedition had given him opportunities on a world scale in both zoology and geology which he had made the basis of distinguished research. He was, further, a devoutly religious man at home in the orthodox atmosphere of Yale. At the time of the *Vestiges* excitement, it was he who had cautioned Gray that it was unnecessary to believe that proof of transmutation of species would destroy religion. He made the same distinction that Gray made between scientific men who believed in orthodox religion and the uninformed people who attempted to read their Bibles as literal textbooks of natural history. His controversy with Taylor Lewis, for example, was a defense of science against the literal interpretation of the Bible. At the same time, as a staunch believer in the unity of the human species, he criticized Agassiz for putting the essay in the *Types of Mankind*. He dared suggest, in regard to Agassiz's ideal concept of a species, that in this area "science is far from a conclusion based on well established natural history facts." [24]

An old and true friend of Gray's, Dana gave him both help and comfort. His vast knowledge of geology was at the botanist's service in long letters as well as in published form. Gray would have been seriously handicapped between 1854 and 1859 had he been forced to dig out alone the geological facts he used as background. Dana also held open to Gray a continuous invitation to air his views in the *American Journal of Science,* not only in the regular botanical notes but in larger articles as well. Although Agassiz had superior means of reaching the lecture audiences of the country Gray had full opportunity to put his case before the scientific men.

Nevertheless, as discussion developed, Dana's usefulness to Gray became sharply limited because, in spite of differences with Agassiz, he too was an idealist who saw comprehensive laws of nature self-evident in every hillock. In his "Thoughts on Species" he based his argument on a comparison of "species" of inorganic substance with those of plants and animals. As he explained it to Gray, "there are mathematical constants at the basis of the inorganic kingdom, that is, fixed units under mathematical law, and hence the conclusion, in view of nature's unity, the *necessary* conclusion, as it seems to me, that there are fixed units in the organic kingdom." Although not disagreeing with the conclusion, Gray objected to this method of reasoning, which "comes only with the force of an *analogy*. . . ." And "all my experience makes me cautious and slow about building too much upon analogies. . . ." [25] Besides, Dana, working under his own load of cares as a prominent American scientist, was heading toward a physical collapse.

Gray's main support, then, in a test with Agassiz had to come from two sources—from Europe and from his own research. Among those friends he had been cultivating in Europe since his first visit in 1838 were two men who, working separately, were laying the foundations of the subscience of plant geography. Friendship with Joseph Hooker and Alphonse De Candolle was in the long run worth more than Agassiz's social success, and among those parcels of dried specimens ever piling up on Gray's table lay empirical data against which to test the imposing array of idealistic categories.

As Gray and Agassiz exchanged pleasantries in chance meetings in Cambridge in the mid-1850's they gave little external sign that between them lay a philosophical canyon cut deep in the history of Western thought. But their superficial agreement about the constancy of species and the existence of Creator became progressively less prominent than their basic differences. For how did each arrive at a belief in constant species and a Creator? Gray was the embodiment of British empiricism, of a rational religion based on materialistic arguments, of a muted vitalism that stressed organization rather than the presence of a soul, the disciple of induction who was sparing in the use of analogy in arriving at generalizations. He would have been perfectly at home in the late eighteenth century. Agassiz on the other hand embodied all those revolutionary forces which had transformed eighteenth-century rationalism into the German idealism of the nineteenth century—not only Kant and Goethe but also Schelling and his *Naturphilosophie*. Cuvier had merely added high scientific authority without changing the idealistic way of proceeding. When Gray looked at nature he saw questions. Agassiz saw only answers.

By 1855 Gray had clearly recognized this deep disagreement. He felt the threat to his whole way of thinking about nature and science. The evolutionists who had come and gone—Lamarck and the author of the *Vestiges*—gave him little cause for alarm, but the lengthening shadow of Agassiz was much in his thoughts.

XIII

DARWIN AND JAPAN— THE SUMMIT OF GRAY'S CAREER

As the results of the great explorations stacked up on Asa Gray's table, the possibility became ever brighter of a scientific comprehension of the distribution of plants over the earth. Significantly, it was at the centers of taxonomic study, Kew, Geneva, and Cambridge, Massachusetts, where men saw this hope most clearly. Joseph Hooker, on his return from India in 1851, had settled down near his father at Kew and devoted himself to elaborating both the flora of India and that of Australia and New Zealand. This was the same kind of taxonomic work Gray was doing, and the two soon fell into an easy and friendly correspondence, much of it technical discussion of particular familiar plants. But because Hooker had served as his own collector and because his travels had the global sweep of the British imperial enterprise, he was in a position to get a comprehensive view of the geographical distribution of plants. When in 1854 the lengthy introduction of his *Flora of New Zealand* appeared, Gray saw it as a "god-send." He used it at the Scientific Club on a night when "unfortunately Agassiz was obliged to be absent from Cambridge," and by reprinting much of it in the *American Journal of Science* he placed it on public record in the United States. The gist of Hooker's theories of geographical distribution appeared in his position on the limits of species, which were: (1) that all individuals of a species have proceeded from one pair, and that they retain their distinctive characters; (2) that species vary more than is generally supposed; (3) that they are more widely distributed; and (4) that their distribution has been affected by natural causes, although not necessarily the same ones to which they are exposed now. Hooker explicitly upheld the permanency of species, distinguishing this property from their origin, about which one "speculator" might differ from another.[1] Hooker knew, too, that what he said attacked, with a wealth of supporting data, the ideas of Agassiz, who he considered "had a prominent seat in judgment" before him. But the Swiss's "opinions are too extreme for respect and hence are mere prejudices. They are further contradicted by facts. Lyell and I have talked him over by the hour." [2] Indeed, the interposition of an article by Agassiz on "The Primitive Diversity and Number of Animals in Geological Times" between the two installments of Gray's summary of Hooker's Essay in the *American Journal of Science* might make a careful and knowing reader conclude that a debate was going on. However, evidence is lacking that Hooker's ideas on the New Zealand flora made any impression on the American scientific reading public.

Gray's own comments clearly outline the state of his thinking at the time. He saw all of Hooker's points as questions worthy of research, and on most of them he came close to agreement. Far from being upset, he found himself stimulated. Why, for instance, did Hooker after convincingly maintaining the probability that each species spread from a single locality, go on to conclude that it must originate in a single pair? To Gray the creation of a species was "exceptional, inexplicable, (we should call it impossible antecedently to the fact.)" Several pairs, created in a primordial area might avoid "the imminent risk of the premature destruction of a single individual." [3] Hooker seemed to be drawing on some hidden body of theory which gave his conclusions a support not visible on the surface. Certainly no connection appeared between the theories and the affectionate tribute he paid in his acknowledgments to his friend Charles Darwin.

Gray boldly formulated his ideas around "the general and fundamental law of genetic resemblance." Races, once originated, "show the strongest tendency to reproduce the parental features or peculiarities." This of course led again to the question of hybrids, and

Gray advanced the suggestion that unisexual trees should be less variable than others. He also revealed his interest in the problem of disjunct distribution—shown by the collection of a species from only two isolated localities half a world away from each other. Could they possibly have traveled so far? This in turn brought up methods of transport for seeds. If the individuals of a species were genetically related, these questions took on moment.

Hooker, less exposed to Agassiz, did not attach so much importance to the law of genetic resemblance, to which he admitted being accustomed, "like atmospheric pressure." He did, nevertheless, give his assent to it, quoting Gray, "the most able of Transatlantic botanists, who is no less sound as a generalizer than profound in his knowledge of details." When he had received the whole series of Gray's comments, he was even more impressed with "as pretty a specimen of admirable close, clear, and accurate reasoning as I ever wish to peruse." [4] From this time onward, Gray and Hooker were peers, with the Englishman somewhat the senior in concentrated experience and the American the senior in age, judgment, and sagacity.

In the late summer of 1855 Gray made his third visit to Europe. It was an emergency—the illness of his brother-in-law in Paris— and he had only twenty-one days in Paris and London between his ships. On the return voyage with his convalescent, however, Gray read, besides Hooker's introduction to *Flora Indica,* a hefty two-volume work entitled *Géographie botanique raisonnée*, written by his friend Alphonse De Candolle. Here he found a general summary of a whole field of knowledge which had not been clearly defined before. Although Humboldt had considered plant geography a generation before in his observations on life zones and the influence of climate, until De Candolle no connection existed between the mass of data gathered by the great explorations and any theory about why plants were distributed in the way they were found. As one would expect from a botonist engaged in the most ambitious taxonomic project of the age, the *Prodromus* of the flora of the world, De Candolle made full use of the systematic botany that had been the product of his and other herbaria for many years. In addition he felt that the time for generalizing had come, incidentally insisting that this was true largely because botany had surpassed zoology in both systems of classification and nomenclature.[5]

Gray immediately perceived that this was "one of the most important books of our day." He also saw that it brought into focus, not just taxonomic botany, but a "wide class of questions, highly and almost equally interesting to the botanist, the zoölogist, the geologist, the ethnologist, and the student of general terrestrial physics." [6] The old natural history had crumbled into specialties, but a new synthesis of disciplines was forming again in the 1850's around the dynamic relations of living organisms to each other and their environment, all set against the background of geological time. De Candolle dealt with the study of species from a geographical point of view—their limitation in area, their spread, means of transport, and disjoined species. Gray found clearly expounded the problems of migration in earlier geological periods and the statement of such tricky puzzles as the relation between the floras of North America and Asia.

Yet all the admirable statistical tables and lists of species gave De Candolle few answers to the questions he asked. He was the consummator of a period and the organizer of a mountain of data without being able to take the next steps. For instance, while he felt it probable that most species originated in a single locality, he felt that some disjunct distributions indicated the possibility that the creation of two individuals of the same species at widely separated places could occur at least once in a while. This conclusion was a highly unsatisfactory straddle between Hooker and Agassiz. Indeed, Hooker had little use at all for De Candolle's effort, calling it "pretentious & feeble." He asserted that the "really great problems are almost overlooked, simply because no one has put them forward, & he has no originality to conceive them himself. . . ." [7] Although in the long view Gray's evaluation of the epoch-making nature of De Candolle's book was more justified than Hooker's sneers, again Hooker seemed to be talking with a more comprehensive theory definitely in mind, some reason for taking his position, which he did not divulge and which his friend did not possess.

This mystery lurking in both the published works and the letters of Hooker came from a force outside himself. Amid the unusually pregnant scientific situation in the 1850's a genius had arisen. Hooker, Gray, and De Candolle were all first-rate scientists, capable of establishing a new sub-science of plant geography at the same time they contributed mightily to taxonomy. But Charles Darwin's horizons were already so much broader than theirs that even a single letter of his, written in haste, rearranged the facts of natural history into new and striking patterns. Hooker did not exaggerate when he confessed he would never have taken up the subjects of the distribution and variation of species but for the advantages he "had derived from his friendship and encouragement." [8]

Darwin in his own person recombined in a new pattern the special disciplines relating to life. He had begun his years on the *Beagle* as an old-time naturalist, an amateur who collected whatever came to hand in the field. But when he had returned to England and settled down to a quiet life at Down House to work up the results of his voyage, he became the foremost authority on the geology of South America and then, turning to his zoological collections, spent the years from 1848 to 1854 publishing a definitive monograph on the *Cirripedia,* the barnacles. This combination of fields, however, had an entirely different meaning to him than to earlier naturalists, because he organized his natural history around a single leading problem. Were species immutable? If not, how did they change? From the time of his observations on the peculiar species of animals on the Galapagos Islands the question had possessed him and transformed all his data from dry and discrete facts into a magnificent tissue of interrelated argument. Finally finished with the barnacles in 1854, Darwin was ready to bring his work on the variation of species together.

He attacked the problem simultaneously on three major fronts. The first was a study of the variation of organisms under domestication. Here he performed the signal service of bringing the practical lore of plant and animal breeders into the realm of science. His application of these data to the species problem, however, had all the weaknesses of the analogy between the conditions of the garden and those of nature. His second front of attack was on the geological record, which had been unfolding for a generation and which had stimulated the speculations of the author of the *Vestiges.* But the geological record contained so little evidence of transitional forms that Darwin was forced to insist on its imperfection to keep catastrophists such as Agassiz from using it against him. Fossil botany, especially, had as yet produced few meaningful results.

The third line of attack, and the one which had given him his original clue in the Galápagos Islands, was a study of the geographical distribution of species. A "species" was, whether real or not theoretically, a taxonomic unit—a definition by which practicing naturalists reduced the chaos of living organisms on the earth to some sort of order. Darwin here could use the results of scientific exploration which had been building up since the time of Linnaeus, a vast body of empirical evidence. If he could demonstrate the history of a species from its actual distribution he would more nearly approach the kind of direct proof which neither of his other lines of attack gave him.

Darwin was too distracted by his illness (as undefinable as Mrs. Gray's) to engage in the usual duties of a scientific man—no lecturing, no teaching, no learned society meetings or politics. Among the happy fruits of his Darwin and Wedgwood ancestry was enough money to live not only for research alone, but to do so without struggle. He was, nevertheless, far from being a recluse. His intimacy with Sir Charles Lyell was unbroken from the beginning of his studies on his return to England. His friendship with Joseph Hooker was in some ways even closer, since they were nearer in age, with Darwin the senior, and since they had both been well salted on exploring expeditions to the southern hemisphere. Beyond these two Darwin had a remarkable network of correspondence, based not on exchange of specimens or institutional trivialities, but solely on his desire for all the information possible on the problem which possessed him—species. Although his own research was respectable and although he was an ingenious if crude experimenter, it was his power of eclecticism, this ability to use other men's researches in his own patterns, that made him different from other mortals.

Asa Gray did not discover Darwin. On the contrary, Darwin discovered Asa Gray. It was a typical masterstroke by the genius of eclecticism. Shortly after Hooker had received Gray's opinion of the *Flora of New Zealand*, he sent the letter to Darwin, who immediately measured both Gray and Agassiz from it. As to the botanist, he responded to Hooker, "how very pleasantly he writes. To see his and your caution on the species question ought to overwhelm me in confusion and shame; it does make me feel deuced uncomfortable." Despite this obvious disagreement, he was "pleased and surprised to see A. Gray's remarks on crossing, obliterating varieties, on which, as you know, I have been collecting facts for these dozen years." Gray's views on Agassiz, Darwin called delightful, and he noted about the zoologist how very singular it is that "so *eminently* clever a man, with such *immense* knowledge on many branches of Natural History, should write as he does." [9] Thus Darwin immediately marked Gray as an observer whose opinion carried weight, while, in the most complimentary terms, he dismissed Agassiz's theorizing completely. That Darwin and Gray were both empiricists was a much stronger bond than the fact that Gray and Agassiz were both believers in the constancy of species.

In April 1855, Darwin tested directly his opinion of Gray's worth. With his scratchy but precise hand he wrote a letter which began in the depths of humility. "I hope that you will remember that I had the pleasure of being introduced to you at Kew." He wished to beg a favor which he hoped would cause no trouble. "As I am no Botanist, it will seem so absurd to you my asking botanical questions, that I may premise that I have for several years been collecting facts on 'Variation,' & when I find that any general remark seems to hold good amongst animals, I try to test it in Plants." The question concerned the range of Alpine plants in the United States. Darwin had copied a list of them from Gray's *Manual*. "I want to know whether you will be so very kind as to append from memory (I have not for one instant the presumption to wish you to look to authorities) the other habitats or ranges of these plants." Were they indigenous, or were they found also in Arctic America, Arctic Europe, Arctic Asia, or the mountains of Europe? And how high are the White Mountains? And had Gray published a list of North American plant species common to Europe? "Should you think it very presumptuous in me to suggest to you to publish (if not already done) such a list in some Journal?" [10]

The humble tone did not obscure the vigor of thought which these questions presupposed. They revealed that Darwin was already pushing at the frontiers of the new-born science of plant geography. They further revealed his surprising willingness to adopt a tool which was admittedly only a *Manual,* a student's handbook. But here alone he could get a comprehensive view. The descriptions might be incomplete and the treatment of synonyms inadequate for the botanical monographer. But let all that go. Start counting and comparing. In a few strokes of the pen he laid down a program of research for Gray which held obvious promise.

Darwin had written other such letters in his quest for information. Then a kind of natural selection operating on the correspondents allowed only the fittest to survive. Gray possessed two inherent advantages in that Darwin was less familiar with systematic botany than with any other science in his new synthesis and less familiar with North America than with any other continent. A man had to have more than mere opportunity, however, to gain the inner circle of Darwin's friends. That Gray, given the chance, showed the qualities of mind and character necessary to rise to Darwin's level is the clearest and most objective evidence of his greatness that his whole career affords.

In answering this first letter Gray felt the weight of his crushing routine. Darwin's investigations "relate to matters in which I take much interest, but can do no more than to furnish some few data when asked for, that others, who happily have leisure for such inquiries, may work up." He had always intended, when the *Flora of North America* was finished, to study "the geographical and climatic relations" of North American plants, comparing them with northern Europe and northern Asia. "I was more sanguine in former years. Now I doubt if I shall ever live to see this Flora finished. . . ." He had, however, besides the answer to Darwin's questions, a counterproposition to make. He was just beginning to revise the *Manual* for the second edition. If Darwin "will kindly give me hints as to what is needed, and how to do it, I will undertake the comparison of the plants of this moderate area (bounded by the Atlantic coast, New Brunswick, St. Lawrence, Great Lakes, Mississippi & Potomac or Chesapeake Bay) with the General N. amer. flora and with that of the northern part of the old world. . . ." [11] A wealth of experience enabled him to make this offer.

Besides the stimulation he felt from Darwin's questions, Gray immediately saw in him the antithesis of Agassiz. When he received Darwin's short published note on the question whether sea-water kills seeds—a bit of evidence which bore on the transport and distribution of species—Gray promised "I shall have it nearly all reprinted in Silliman's Journal as a nut for Agassiz to crack." Perhaps Darwin would soon be in a position to decide between Hooker and Agassiz on geographical distribution.[12] Thus began in a small way the presentation of Darwin's theories to the American public,[13] although, as in the case of Hooker's works reprinted in the *American Journal of Science,* the scientific audience had to draw its own conclusions and generally did not do so.

As the correspondence battened, Gray's analysis of the *Manual* data rapidly took shape, the first part of his "Statistics of the Flora of the Northern United States" appearing in the *American Journal of Science* in September 1856. He explained that while working on his revised edition, he was "requested by an esteemed correspondent, upon whose judgment I place great reliance, to exhibit . . . the elements of the flora I was occupied with." [14] This article, which was omitted from Gray's collected works and is seldom referred to by twentieth-century scientists, is a landmark in the history of American botany and one of the foundation papers in the science of plant geography. With some hints from De Candolle and with the guidance of Darwin's incisive questions Gray took the important step of applying statistics to the analysis of floristic units—the species and genera which had been stacking up in the taxonomic literature.

Statistics applied to the data of biology was one of the necessary tools which Darwin had to employ to convert the conventionally arranged information of the 1850's into a new pattern.[15] At base, the idea he had taken from Malthus of the struggle for life was a statistical concept. And statistics, through the work of such men as Quetelet, had coalesced into a method of wide applicability so recently that statistical support for an evolutionary theory was entirely unavailable even as late as the publication of the *Vestiges.* In the 1850's, however, a fascination with statistics was in the air.

Buckle's *History of Civilization,* an effort to reduce history to a statistical science, was one of the few nonbotanical books which Hooker made Gray read in these years. Joseph Henry, while unfamiliar with the currents swirling in natural history, was at this period reflecting on the possibility of applying Malthus's ideas on human populations to plants and animals.[16]

Gray's use of statistics was in many ways crude. For instance, to determine range of territory covered by a species, he turned through the *Manual* putting a figure "1" beside those which were very local, a "2" by those with a range of not more than an eighth of the territory, and "3" for widespread species. He then classified the last species into three other groups, those with few individuals, those not abundant in individuals, and those very abundant in individuals.[17] This process, based largely on Gray's experience with plants rather than on formal notes, could give only rough approximations. Yet he was making in his head exactly the kind of analysis a modern botanist uses when he plots the stations of a species on a map with his little colored dots. And he had reduced his data to a form in which he could manipulate it statistically.

Gray compared the flora of eastern North America to that of Europe, giving special attention to Alpine plants, to closely allied species, and to the range of large and small genera. He then briefly suggested the relations with western North America and with eastern Asia also, concluding with a statement on the key problems in his disagreement with Agassiz—whether species migrated in a single locality or not. He concluded that in analyzing all distributions the botanist had to suppose means of transport he could not demonstrate and to rely on judgments drawn from imperfect data. "We should therefore work in one and the same direction for the explanation of . . . extraordinary no less than of the ordinary cases of distribution. . . ." He described the choice as between Hooker and Agassiz. Of one theory, "the only question is whether it will sufficiently explain all the facts of distribution; the second supersedes the necessity of such explanation, by assuming the actual distribution to be essentially the original state." Only Hooker's theory was compatible with "the natural idea of species as consisting of kindred individuals descended from a common stock, which, whether demonstrable or not as a fact, gives us a clear and distinct conception of *species,* the only one we possess." [18] Thus Gray's case against Agassiz and his alliance with Darwin and Hooker was now complete, at least on the subject of geographical distribution of plants.

Darwin was above all things both polite and humble. These qualities may explain his telling Gray that only Hooker's New Zealand essay "makes any approach to the cleárness which your paper makes a non-Botanist appreciate the character of the Flora of a country." The same qualities might even account for his saying that "to be *simply* mentioned even in such a paper, I consider a very great honour." But they can hardly completely explain away his assertion that "you cannot appreciate your own work in the generalising line. —Good Heavens if I had written a paper half as good as yours, how conceited I should have been!" More significantly, he measured Gray's results by that same unrevealed scale which had appeared in Hooker's writings. "I have been eminently glad to see your conclusion in regard to species of large genera widely ranging: it is in strict conformity with the results I have worked out in several ways. It is of great importance to my notions." [19]

These notions also loomed up when Darwin said that one statement in the "Statistics" riled him dreadfully. He himself recognized the role of theory in eliciting such a remark, and it reminded him of a little story. "Lyell told me, that Agassiz having a theory about when Saurians were first created, on hearing some careful observation opposed to this, said that he did not believe it, 'for Nature never lied.' I am just in this predicament, & repeat to you that 'Nature never lies:' ergo, theorisers are always right." [20] This story clearly distinguishes the scientific method of the idealist from that of the empiricist. However much Darwin was a theorizer, his hypotheses were not the ideas of the devotees of *Naturphilosophie.*

Gray was aware that Darwin was drawing on a vast reservoir of theory. To Dana he wrote that, while he had a bias toward centers of radiation for each species, he did not believe in centers for groups of species. However, from "Darwin's questions to me I think I perceive some of the grounds on which he would maintain it." That he had to infer Darwin's larger views did not bother him particularly. "The right way to bring a series of pretty interesting questions towards settlement is perhaps in hand. . . ." A number of naturalists should work toward a common problem from all sides. "Such men as Darwin, Dr. Hooker, De Candolle, Agassiz, and myself,—most of them with no theories they are bound to support,—ought only to bring out some good results. And the less each one is influenced by the other's mode of viewing things the better." Gray fondly believed the right way was "to know no theory, but to see what the facts tend to show, when fairly treated." Nevertheless, on the subject of the distribution of plants, "certain inferences are slowly settling themselves in my mind. . . ." [21] The day for the unveiling of theories and for choosing sides on a grand scale was close.

In July 1857, Darwin, already deep in the business of writing his large book on species, felt he needed to let Gray in on his secret. To continue the stream of Gray's remarks, so valuable to him, required the risk of this revelation.[22]

Down   Bromley   Kent   July 20th

My dear Dr. Gray:

What you say about extinction, in regard to *small* genera & local disjunction, being hypothetical seems very just. Something direct, however, could be advanced on this head from fossil shells; but hypothetical such notions must remain. It is not a little egotistical, but I sh.ᵈ like to tell you, (& I do not *think* I have) how I view my work. Nineteen years (!) ago it occurred to me that whilst otherwise employed on Nat. Hist., I might perhaps do good if I noted any sort of facts bearing on the question of the origin of species; & this I have since been doing. Either species have been independently created, or they have descended from other species, like varieties from one species. I think it can be shown to be probable that man gets his most distinct varieties by preserving such as arise best worth keeping, & destroying the others,—but I shᵈ fill a quire if I were to go on. To be brief I *assume* that species arise like our domestic varieties with *much* extinction; & then test this hypothesis by comparison with as many general & pretty well established propositions as I can find made out,—in geograph. distribution, geological history—affinities &c. &c. &c. And it seems to me, that *supposing* that such hypothesis were to explain such general propositions, we ought, in accordance with common way of following all sciences, to admit it, till some better hypothesis be found out. For to my mind to say that species were created so & so is no scientific explanation, only a reverent way of saying it is so & so. But it is nonsensical trying to show how I try to proceed in compass of a note. But as an honest man I must tell you that I have come to the heterodox conclusion that there are no such things as independently created species—that species are only strongly defined varieties. I know that this will make you despise me. I do not much underrate the many *huge* difficulties on this view, but yet it seems to me to explain too much, otherwise inexplicable, to be false. Just to allude to one point in your last note, viz. about species of the same genus *generally* having a common or continuous area; if they are actually lineal descendants of one species, this of course would be the case; & the sadly too many exceptions (for me) have to be explained by climatal and geological changes. A fortiori on this view (but on exactly same grounds) all the individuals of the same species sh.ᵈ have a continuous distribution. On this latter branch of the subject I have put a chapter together, & Hooker kindly read it over. I thought the exceptions & difficulties were so great that on the whole the balance weighed against my notions, but I was much pleased to find that it seemed to have considerable weight with Hooker, who said he had never been so much staggered about the permanence of species.

I must say one word more in justification (for I feel sure that your tendency will be to despise me & my crotchets) that all my notions about *how* species change are derived from long-continued study of the works of (& converse with) agriculturists & horiculturists; & I believe I see my way pretty clearly on the means used by nature to change her species & adapt them to the wondrous & exquisitely beautiful contingencies to which every living being is exposed.

Thank you *much* for what you say about *possibility* of crossing of the grasses: I have been often astounded at what Botanists say on fertilisation in the bud: I have seen *Cruciferae* mentioned as instance, which every gardener knows how difficult it is to protect from crossing!

. . .

But my letter has been horribly egotistical: but your letters always so greatly interest me, & what is more they have in simple truth been of the *utmost* value to me.

Your's most sincerely & gratefully
C. DARWIN

This letter put Gray to a crucial test. Darwin felt it contained plenty to make Gray despise him, even though both of them saw clearly that their ideas of scientific method and of geographical distribution had much in common. To infer from Darwin's next letter, Gray opened his response with a vehement protest of affection and surprise that his friend would think grounds existed for a break. To have become heated in opposition to a doctrine, even an extreme one, which was based on valid evidence and close reasoning, would have violated Gray's code as a scientific man. He did state his objections to the transmutation of species. Darwin was all understanding. "The facts which kept me longest scientifically orthodox are those of adaptation— . . . the mistletoe with its pollen carrᵈ by insects & seed by Birds, the woodpecker with its feet & tail, beak & tongue to climb tree & secure insects. To talk of climate or Lamarckian habit producing such adaptations to other organic beings is futile." He had, however, surmounted this difficulty, and since Gray seemed interested, he would enclose "the briefest abstract of my notions on the *means* by which nature makes her species." He did put on one restriction. "You will, perhaps, think it paltry in me, when I ask you not to mention my doctrine; the reason is, if anyone, like the author of the Vestiges, were to hear of them he might easily work them in, & then I shᵈ have to quote from a work perhaps despised by naturalists & this would greatly injure any chance of my views being received by those alone whose opinion I value."

Gray thus entered the little circle of initiates who were sworn to secrecy. Although a few British naturalists were aware of the bearing of Darwin's ideas from having talked to him, only Sir Charles Lyell, Joseph Hooker, and now Gray had seen these ideas in the connected form of a written outline.[23] The paper Darwin sent his friend contained in most essentials the same argument he had shown to Lyell and Hooker in 1844. The main addition was a statement of the principle of divergence—"that the varying offspring of each species will try (only few will succeed) to seize on as many and as diverse places in the economy of nature as possible." Mainly it was a bare, unadorned statement of the argument that later appeared in the first six chapters of the *Origin of Species*. The first part discussed selection by man and what it can do. The second part applied selection to organisms in nature, expanding its time range to millions of generations. The third part described the struggle for life and the resulting natural selection, "the title of my Book." The fourth part, discussing variation, finally produced a statement on the formation of species themselves. "I cannot doubt that during millions of generations individuals of a species will be born with some slight variation profitable to some part of its economy." Gray queried the last phrases with a "?" Such "will have a better chance of surviving, propagating, this variation, which again will be slowly increased by the accumulative action of Natural selection; and the variety thus formed will either coexist with, or more commonly will exterminate its parent form." The word "propagating" draws another "?" from Gray, as well it might, for Darwin never did adequately explain how a variation was passed along to a new generation. This was a genetic theory of species with a vengeance, for not only were like forms descendants of a common ancestor, but unlike forms as well.

When Darwin called the sketch *"most* imperfect" he gave Gray an opening to object, not against the general bearing of the theory, but that it was "grievously hypothetical & large parts by no means worthy of being called inductive." This last charge Darwin translated by describing as "my commonest error . . . probably induction from too few facts." Gray also became the first of many critics to object to Darwin's assigning a positive role to natural selection. "I had not," wrote Darwin, "thought of your objection to my using the term 'Natural Selection' as an agent; I use it much as a geologist does the word Denudation, for an agent, expressing the result of several combined actions." [24]

Gray was definitely impressed. To Dana he prophesied that "before long there must be one more resurrection of the development theory in a new form, obviating many of the arguments against it, and presenting a more respectable and more formidable appearance than it ever has before." [25] The time had not yet arrived, however, to come to grips directly with Darwin's theory, even though its grand architecture was now dimly visible. Gray scarcely thought of himself as in the presence of a completed revolutionary doctrine. It was more like a spirited, only half-serious conversational swordplay between friends. Whether or not he completely agreed with all the implications of Darwin's theory of transmutation seemed at the time far less important than the fact that Darwin's and Hooker's ideas on plant geography cut directly against Agassiz, who still held the center of the stage as the great radical.

Of the two great reconstructions of the world of living organisms looming up on either side of Gray, that built by Agassiz seemed in the fall of 1857 the more imposing, the more loudly trumpeted, and the more dangerous. Agassiz threatened Gray's scientific method, his factual evidence, and his definition of a species as a succession of genetically connected individuals. Darwin threatened none of these, essentially changing Gray's interpretation only by extending genetic connection beyond species to higher groups and ultimately to all living organisms. Although this extension was stupendous, it left most of Gray's basic scientific beliefs strengthened rather than otherwise. Hence the story of Gray's major theoretical enterprise of the years 1857 to 1859 revolved about Agassiz rather than Darwin.

Agassiz erupted anew as an acute threat to Gray in 1857 by publishing Volume I of his *Contributions to the Natural History of the United States*. His essay on classification contained all the views of the idealist's natural history worked out by splendid logic and pompous self-assurance. Moreover, the book had the stamp of approval of the wealthy "Boston Public, which he bleeds freely. . . ." Somewhere along the line, too, Agassiz had invaded the one Boston organization about which Gray really cared, the American Academy of Arts and Sciences. On the strength of his popularity and "incited by an unmanageable disposition, he lately attempted to play the despot in the Amer. Academy, but got a quiet rebuff, which will teach him more conciliatory ways, I hope." [26]

Under the pressure from Agassiz, Gray found his position shifting even further from what it had been in 1846. Then, as the upholder of orthodoxy against the *Vestiges*, he had, with the help of Agassiz and others, blocked the appointment of Henry D. Rogers to a professorship at Harvard. Now he referred to Rogers's brother William as "perhaps the most distinguished geologist and physicist of the United States, the elder brother of a most distinguished family of savans who have made the name illustrious." [27] Significantly, the Rogerses were not included in the Scientific Lazzaroni, and William B. Rogers would eventually emerge as its enemy. As Agassiz went on from one social triumph to another Gray desperately needed an issue, a specific case with which he could pin Agassiz down and escape that all-explaining dictum—"a species is a thought of the Creator."

Gray found his issue—a problem for the solution of which his entire scientific career was relevant. His correspondence with Darwin and Hooker gave him a theoretical framework to use as a source of hypotheses. His laborious taxonomic research gave him the data. His knowledge of the flora of North America had been gained only through years of classification, correspondence, and administration of exploration. No one but Torrey could command this knowledge. Even Gray's early journeys to the southern Appalachians served well, giving him direct knowledge of some of the plants which were to figure most prominently in his study. He also had his data coming in, thanks to the expansive tendencies of the American republic, from Japan. Charles Wright's specimens, added to those collected by Williams and Morrow with Perry, were all in hand by 1857. They had to be worked up anyway. Even Torrey could not follow beyond the borders of North America. No European alive had the right combination of experience. The relation of the floras of eastern Asia and eastern North America was Gray's own problem, one which not even Hooker was in a position to answer. The plants of Japan and the United States held the balance between Agassiz and Darwin.

Gray had known for a long time that an unusual number of the plants of eastern North America were found also in eastern Asia and nowhere else. Indeed, he himself pointed out that this general observation had been made in the eighteenth century when Linnaeus' collector Thunberg had reached Japan. The question was, how had these species, either identical or very closely similar, arrived at a position on different continents without any representatives between the two places? If the Creator on some occasions made two magnolias exactly alike and put them down, one in North Carolina and one in Japan, the question was already answered. But Gray's pointing out this relation in both 1840 and 1846 in reviewing Zuccarini's *Flora Japonica* [28] indicates that he had never accepted the mere fact of disjunct distribution as its own sufficient explanation. He had pointed to it more insistently in his "Statistics of the Flora of the United States."

Darwin had been immediately struck by this reference. "Nothing has surprised me more than the greater generic & specific affinity with E. Asia than with W. America. Can you tell me . . . whether climate explains this greater affinity? or is it one of the many utterly inexplicable problems in Bot. geography?" [29] With the results of Charles Wright's labors on the North Pacific Exploring Expedition, Gray was hot on the trail of the inexplicable.

After he had classified the Japan collections in the usual way he arranged the results in tabular form, making the kind of statistical analysis he had introduced in his earlier paper. This enabled him to state definitely that of the 580 species from Japan fewer were present in western North America than in Europe, and far more were represented in eastern North America than in either of the other regions. Furthermore, some forty genera were alone found in eastern North America and Japan.[30] In postulating a reason for this distribution, Gray turned to the geological history of the northern hemisphere.

The sequence of events came out quite clearly. In the Tertiary period, when flowering plants had already become well established, a temperate flora covered much of northern extremities of all the continents, extending unbroken between Asia and North America in the Bering Strait region. With the advance of glaciers in the Northern hemisphere this homogeneous flora was driven southward and sundered into great branches, one in North America and one in Asia. After the glaciers receded, the temperate floras again moved northward, mingling across the Bering Strait, and with the cooling of the climate moved southward again to their present stations. Thus an unbroken series of causes and effects accounted for the striking disjunction of plants in eastern North America and eastern Asia. What had been an *a priori* case for the double creation of species was completely and convincingly destroyed. Common ancestry and a single center of creation was established as the more reasonable assumption.

An even more interesting question arose, however, because not all of the cases of disjunct distribution were identical species. With great caution but nevertheless with a full appreciation of what he was doing, Gray concluded that representative species may "in many cases be lineal descendants from a pristine stock, just as domesticated races are," that "variation in species is wider than is generally supposed, and that derivation forms when segregated may be as constantly reproduced as their original." In certain particular cases, then, Gray's work showed that Darwin was right about the transmutation of species. Sometimes, and at some places, one species did turn into another.

Gray's discovery could only be powerful support to Darwin's ideas and equally impressive refutation of those of Agassiz. Since its main distinction lay in tying for the first time a large number of taxonomic data to the great sweep of geological history, it is almost frightening to contemplate Gray's lack of experience in geology. While he had indicated his assent to Lyell's general point of view in the early 1840's, he had taken no part in the active development of the science in America in the 1850's. When he formed his theory he had to rely on others for his basic information at a period when the nature and timing of the glacial ice sheet in North America was still open to all sorts of questions. That he chose his informants well is a measure both of his judgment and his luck. For the geological processes he envisioned have proved in their major outlines if not their details essentially correct.

Significantly, Gray turned for geological help to Americans rather than to Hooker and Darwin. In spite of nearly a generation of work on the glacial ice-sheet that overspread the northern hemisphere, so little was actually known and agreed upon that Gray could take his choice between theories. Darwin told him that the temperature in northern regions was higher just before the glacial epoch, but between the glaciers and the present he only vaguely suspected a warm period. Gray's friend James D. Dana agreed that for the period before the glaciation in North America "the probability is that the climate was considerably warmer than now." But Dana maintained that after the glacial epoch there was another period of warmer climate.[31] Why did Gray risk displeasing his European correspondents to adopt Dana's idea of a postglacial warm period and to assert that "the temperate floras of North America and of Eastern Asia, after having been for long ages most widely separated, must have become a second time conterminous"? The first mingling of temperate floras over the Bering Strait was a brilliant deduction and is hailed as good science to this day.[32] But for Gray to say that they mingled a second time after the glaciation brought an immediate castigation from Hooker, who asserted that Lyell and Darwin also disagreed.

251

No modern geologist or plant geographer has any evidence to back Gray up on this point. Indeed he himself later admitted that he "had divined" the whole geological interpretation "long before I knew of fossil plants." [33] In his later work he dropped the idea of a second mingling after the glacial epoch. The explanation of this peculiar and soon abandoned position is found in the central theme of this story, the battle of world systems between Darwin and Agassiz. Gray's paper would be good science without the second mingling, but only with it included could he use his discovery against Agassiz.

By late 1858 Gray could clearly see that Darwin's theory must soon become generally known. The bars of secrecy were down. Wallace, having reached parallel conclusions to Darwin on variation and natural selection, had unwittingly forced the announcement of Darwin's theory in brief form before the Linnaean Society in July 1858. The short sketch which Darwin had sent to Gray in September 1857 was one of the two documents displayed to prove Darwin's priority.[34] To those very few who had followed with understanding the twistings and turnings of theory in botany, zoology, and geology through the 1850's the air was full of expectancy. Gray's whole spirit quickened at the thought of bringing Agassiz to bay with Darwin's tools.

The long years under the shadow of the splendid personality had galled him. The public acclaim, the adulation of the *literati,* the behind-the-scenes smugness of the Scientific Lazzaroni, the shoals of worshipping students, had all elevated Agassiz to the height of his fame. That Gray could at such a juncture come forward and publicly challenge the idol of American science gave him a sense of deep relief, satisfaction, and even amusement. He chose his ground deliberately to give himself every possible advantage. At the same time he took care to give Agassiz ample warning and opportunity to answer.

For a first try-out he informally outlined his new theory of the distribution of eastern North America-eastern Asia plants to the Cambridge Scientific Club on December 10, 1858. As usual, they met at the speaker's house, doubtless with the usual pleasant refreshment of food and drink. Three presidents of Harvard—past, present, and future—Jared Sparks, James Walker, and C. C. Felton, were there. Dr. Morrill Wyman and schoolmaster E. S. Dixwell joined professors Agassiz, Joseph Lovering, Daniel Treadwell, and Joel Parker to complete the group that evening. They were congenial, accustomed to one another and to hearing Gray, who had entertained them nearly every year since 1846. Lovering and Dixwell, who took notes, accurately grasped the main outlines of Gray's position. Agassiz "took it very well indeed." [35]

Having thus felt the ground, Gray was ready for a full-dress presentation at the American Academy, the organization which he had served diligently for many years as corresponding secretary and where Agassiz had recently met his rebuff. The scene of the Academy's meeting of January 11 was the house of Mr. Charles Greely Loring in Boston. On that spot he had courted Jane. There his brother George had died. Mr. Loring was of course present as a member of the academy and as host. Old Jacob Bigelow, the president and a botanist of an earlier day, was on hand despite his more than seventy years. In all twenty-two members were present, besides two Dartmouth professors who were down for the evening. The scientists in the group—Benjamin Peirce, Lovering, F. H. Storer, A. A. Gould, and Henry James Clark, were in general more closely associated with Agassiz than with Gray. The wealth of Boston had its representatives, especially John Amory Lowell, who still bore the air of the patron of both Gray and Agassiz even though the Panic of 1857 had temporarily embarrassed his financial position. Gray had invited Torrey to come up from New York to hear him "knock out the underpinning of Agassiz's theories about species and their origin; show, from the very facts that stumbled De Candolle, the high probability of single and local creation of species, turning some of Agassiz's own guns against him." Torrey could not come, but Gray was full of confidence nevertheless. The years under Agassiz's shadow were over.

After outlining his theory of the relation of the eastern Asian flora to that of eastern North America, Gray carefully defined his understanding of Agassiz's position. Each species "originated where it now occurs, probably in as great a number of individuals occupying as large an area, and generally the same area, or the same discontinuous areas, as at the present time." This hypothesis "is more difficult to test, because more ideal than any other." To refer the distribution by species as well as their origin "simply to the Divine will . . . would remove the whole question out of the field of inductive science." [36] This was the nub of their disagreement—nothing less than their whole way of approaching science. Agassiz's method began with an ideal category and fitted all observations to it. Gray began with his observations and organized them by tentative hypotheses. The two stood at a watershed in the history of the scientific method as applied to the problems of life. Agassiz spoke for the past, Gray for the future.

In his further criticisms of Agassiz, Gray emphasized his belief in the genetic connection of all individuals of a species. This was of course a necessary assumption if the distribution of identical species in Japan and eastern North America were to be explained as having come from one flora spanning the Bering Strait. Gray asserted the great antiquity of present species. Here he had to be very careful, for Agassiz believed that none of the species of the Tertiary period had survived to the present. This is the place where Gray must use that second mingling of the flora after the glaciers had receded. For even if Agassiz insisted that the glaciers were a great catastrophe which had wiped the earth clean, the second mingling would have taken place at so recent a period that he could not deny the existence of present species. Gray then concluded that the anomalies in actual distribution of species were "to be sought in the vicissitudes to which the species must have been subject in their earlier days." [37]

After Gray had spoken for over an hour in a "steady (if not smooth) stream," Agassiz "took up his parable for half an hour nearly. . . ." [38] He was not only polite; he acknowledged the great importance of Gray's statements. He avoided a direct examination of the botanical evidence, by saying that his opinions were "founded on observation of the animal kingdom." He even mentioned some turtles which followed a parallel pattern. His answer was merely a reaffirmation of his position and a denial that climate or other physical forces affected the distribution of animals. Even though he basked in great renown as the popularizer of the glacial epoch, he did not attack Gray's rather shaky geology at all. In one opportunistic shaft he came closer than he realized to unseating himself.

"With reference to the single origin of conspecific individuals . . . the warfare which so many species wage upon others was in itself an insuperable objection to the assumption that any one species could have originated in a single pair." [39] Did he realize he was here playing with Darwin's own tool—the struggle for existence? Old Dr. Bigelow from the chair asked a question which demonstrated how far behind the naturalists of the earlier generation had been left by the development of geology and plant geography. Gray neatly turned his answer to Bigelow against Agassiz, and with that the meeting was over.

Agassiz, without losing any of his self-assurance, felt that the debate still left something more to be said. At the next meeting of the academy, January 26, he moved that additional monthly meetings be held in February, March, and April, at the rooms of the academy "for scientific communications and discussions." Since no such show had developed among Boston scientists in years, Benjamin Peirce suggested that these extra meetings be opened to "persons not Fellows of the Academy who would be likely to be interested in the proceedings such as advanced students of science." The cozy advantage of Mr. Loring's parlor would not last. The president appointed Agassiz, Peirce, and Gray to plan the meetings.[40]

In February the genial gladiators took up arms again, with thirty members present and perhaps some outsiders. Gray restated his case, emphasizing his geological interpretation and introducing his fossil evidence which providentially had come in from Leo Lesquereux just a few days before. Agassiz again challenged the effect of climate on the distribution of plants, and, as Gray expected, denied the continuity of species between the Tertiary period and the present. He "could not but believe that, if Professor Gray were to exercise the same critical judgment upon the fossil Flora which he does with reference to the existing Flora, he would find differences between the species of the two epochs similar to those found in the animal world." [41] This sly aspersion on Gray's limited geological experience was one way for Agassiz to utilize his unrivaled reputation.

Actually Agassiz was having even more difficulty matching Gray in print than in the meetings. For the American Academy was a society of record, whose *Proceedings* carried the debate to the whole world of science. Gray insisted that Agassiz put his remarks "in black and white, that he might stand fairly committed on the subject." After Agassiz had stated his position *ex tempore* at the meeting of January 11, Gray had made his own manuscript available for reference, so that Agassiz's "remarks as printed . . . were his deliberate propositions written or dictated by himself afterwards." For the record of the second meeting on February 22, Agassiz had plenty of opportunity to prepare in advance, but again spoke *ex tempore*. "There the report—a very imperfect abstract, but quite as good as his actual remarks—was furnished by the Recording Secy. —it was supplied A., who promised to write out his remarks, but *did not* (bad health & want of time)—but he returned the notes as they are printed." [42]

Agassiz's inability to answer Gray effectively in these debates was partly a result of the pressures besetting a scientist in America. Gray was often hard-pressed by the demands made upon him. Agassiz, because he was lionized by multitudes of lecturegoers and literary people as well as naturalists, was simply overwhelmed by his position as the personification of science in America. In these early months of 1859 he was launching his Museum of Comparative Zoology, performing the political miracle of securing $100,000 from the Massachusetts legislature for a building as well as raising $71,-000 from private sources. These funds, added to $50,000 left by the will of Francis C. Gray and the collections which Agassiz had sold to Harvard for $12,000, gave the new museum a financial basis hitherto undreamed of in America. He was actively working with the architects on plans for the new building. Engrossed in building this empire, Agassiz doubtless found a challenge on scientific grounds irrelevant as well as annoying.

Beneath Agassiz's brilliant façade some signs of dangerous overextension were even then appearing. A sordid controversy between him and James D. Dana was, early in 1859, threatening to strain the decorum of the *American Journal of Science*. When Jules Marcou, a stormy protégé of the great man, had violently attacked Dana on geological matters, Agassiz came to his henchman's aid with a warmly laudatory statement which he prefaced with the remark, "I have not yet seen Marcou's latest publication on American

Asa Gray, taken about 1841.
From a very early daguerreotype.

Asa Gray, 1865

Asa Gray, 1873

Asa Gray, 1884. Bronze bas-relief by
Augustus Saint-Gaudens. Now at the
Harvard University Herbarium.

Louis Agassiz

Charles Darwin

Charles Lyell

Joseph Dalton Hooker

Alphonse De Candolle

John Torrey

Charles Wright, plant collector

George Engelmann

Joseph Henry

Amos Eaton

John Amory Lowell

James Dwight Dana

Dr. and Mrs. Gray and the garden house

Botanic Garden, with, left to right, the original house, herbarium, laboratory, and green houses.

Gray in his study

Sereno Watson in the herbarium

G. L. Goodale in the laboratory

Gray in the field. La Veta Pass, Colorado, 1877. Left to right, seated, Sir Joseph Hooker, Professor Asa Gray, Mrs. Strachey, Mrs. Asa Gray, Dr. Lamborn, General Strachey, and Dr. F. V. Hayden. Mr. James Stevenson is standing between Dr. Lamborn and General Strachey. (The other members of the party are unidentified.)

Geology, but. . . ." When Dana objected to publishing this "on the ground that *you had not read* the *book*," Agassiz wrote that if the *Journal* did not carry the article Dana "might take his name" from the list of editors on the cover. As editor, Dana then allowed the article to stand, writing a strong and detailed rejoinder. Thus, during the same months that Gray was using Dana's geology to confound Agassiz before the American Academy, Dana was anxiously consulting Gray about editorial policy with respect to Agassiz. They had a common problem in pinning the great man down to facts— and cases. Dana concluded bitterly that if "Agassiz prefers to befriend Marcou . . . to dealing fairly with me, there is a lack of *something* in him. I suppose there was no intentional wrong. But such double dealing is sure to betray itself & prove a double failure." [43]

With Agassiz too busy and bedeviled to make a record, the March and April supplementary meetings of the American Academy furthered the debate little. In March, Charles Pickering, whose career had reached its zenith during his years on the Wilkes expedition, spoke on geographical distribution in a vein easily reconcilable with Gray's position. At the April meeting, devoted to astronomy, Gray presided in the absence of the president and vice president. At the regular monthly meeting of the academy the same month, Agassiz made a curiously indirect counterattack. Henry James Clark, the microscopist who had left Gray to become Agassiz's favored assistant, made a statement hailing the revival of the doctrine of spontaneous generation by the French physiologist F. A. Pouchet and reported from his own observation that microscopic animals had arisen from dead and decomposed muscle. "Professor Agassiz corroborated Mr. Clark's statements most fully, and spoke of the discovery as one of the very greatest interest and importance." [44] Well he might welcome such a find, because his system of geologic catastrophes and the new creation of millions of individuals after them required an act of the creator indistinguishable from spontaneous generation. O unlucky Trojan. He had no escape in this direction. Within four years Pasteur would annihilate Pouchet's whole theory. One of the great advantages both Gray and Darwin enjoyed over Agassiz and over the *Vestiges* and Lamarck as well was their complete independence of any need for spontaneous generation as an essential part of their theories. They dealt solely with living, self-reproducing systems.

The Cambridge Scientific Club, which enjoyed the debate between its two members quite as much as did the American Academy, now gave both Agassiz and Gray a turn in the spring of 1859. Agassiz, although he had subsided before the academy, was still able to hold forth on the system of ideas he had spent his whole life developing. On March 10, he entertained the club, speaking on what one listener described as the "Plan of creation. In the first creations, predicting of what was to follow." This cosmic approach gave Gray his chance. Poor Mrs. Gray, unusually ill this particular spring, had to get up a lordly dinner twice in five months. When Gray entertained the club on May 12, he unveiled the ultimate bearings of his own work; that is, he introduced Darwin to Cambridge, Massachusetts.

Although the distribution of species and not their origin had been the subject of discussion between him and Agassiz, he was quite aware of the bearing his Japan paper had as evidence in favor of Darwin's theories. Not only did identical species follow the peculiar eastern Asia-eastern North America distribution, the same pattern appeared in the distribution of genera, and in many cases plants found only in the two regions were just barely different enough to be classified as separate species. Why did not these closely related species have a common ancestor as well as the identical species? And why did not the vicissitudes which produced the disjunct distributions also account for the slight differences between closely related species from the two regions?

In his cautious footnote to the published memoir, Gray clearly defined his position on Darwin not later than April 25, 1859.[45] Referring to the joint publication of the Darwin and Wallace papers in the Linnaean Society *Journal* he described his friend's theory as the "only noteworthy attempt at a scientific solution" of the "fundamental and most difficult question remaining in natural history"— aiming "to bring the variety as well as the geographical associations of existing species more within the domain of cause and effect." These views must bear "a prominent part in all future investigations into the distribution and probable origin of species. It will hardly be doubted that the tendencies and causes indicated are really opera- tive; the question is as to the extent of their operation." Gray was not yet willing to go the whole way. "But I am already disposed, on these and other grounds, to admit that what are termed closely re- lated species may in many cases be lineal descendants from a pris- tine stock, just as domesticated races are; or, in other words, that the limits of occasional variation in species (if by them we mean primordial forms) are wider than is generally supposed, and that derivative forms when segregated may be as constantly reproduced as their originals." This statement, eminently cautious as it is, re- flects a clear understanding of the workings of evolution, and in publicly jumping the barrier between species Gray took a step ahead of every botanist and zoologist in the world except Darwin and Wallace themselves. Even buried in a footnote—and hedged with qualifications—the action was bold and the direction unmis- takable.

In the intimacy of the Cambridge Scientific Club, Gray had no need to guard his statements against the future. He had no need to commit himself. He "expanded Darwin's views—to see how it would strike a dozen people of varied minds and habits of thought, and partly, I confess, maliciously to vex the soul of Agassiz with views so diametrically opposed to all his pet notions." Besides the primary target the company included the usual membership. A varied group indeed, one with intellectual weight in the United States, received a full-scale preview of an epoch-making idea. The record of their reaction shows a scant awareness of the historic oc- casion. E. S. Dixwell noted for the evening, "Gray's on some papers about the sporting of species & varieties—approaching Lamarck's theory." Joseph Lovering merely said, "Subject, Origin of Species &c. Read from Darwin." Benjamin Peirce wrote to his wife that Dr. Gray gave an account of "a Mr. Darwin's and a Mr. Wallace's speculations as to the possible changes of a species under the influ- ence of external agencies." He too mentioned Lamarck and the fa- miliar example of the giraffe's neck, indicating that Gray linked Darwin to earlier evolutionists but also gave an outline of the mechanism of natural selection.[46]

On the surface the gathering was, in Peirce's words, "pleasant enough." Afterwards he and Agassiz walked the streets of Cambridge together. They talked of the war between France and Austria, and of the threat to Switzerland's neutrality. Did they know that they stood on the knife-edge between two epochs in the intellectual history of the Western world? Did they know that the hesitant, eager tones of plain, familiar Asa Gray carried a message of more importance than Napoleon III, Franz Joseph, and all their legions rolled together? Peirce, secure in the abstractions of mathematics, would never fully grasp the import of Darwin.[47] Most of the others, despite their eminence or their preparation over the last few months through the analysis of the Japan Flora, had hardly the background to grasp the full implications of evolution before the popularizers, the explainers, and the rephrasers had done their work.

The issue at the garden house that spring evening cut between two men alone. Gray, enjoying himself, reported Agassiz "was worried a good deal." [48] And twenty years later Agassiz's very words were still etched in the memory of his host and adversary. "Gray, we must stop this." [49]

Stop it, indeed. No longer could Agassiz dismiss the new ideas as the crotchets of a botanist. No longer could he refuse to see, at least dimly, that all his beliefs about the nature of the organic world had been challenged. Moreover, that the notion even occurred to him to stop the course of science emphasized his idealistic rebellion against the extension of empiricism into natural history. Gray and Darwin both felt it their highest duty to follow chains of cause and effect through the facts of nature regardless of the unexpected direction the path might take. To one who saw the duty of the scientist as the unveiling of a perfect plan, the pursuit of truth in a direction which threw doubt on the plan itself was so obviously an error that it should be stopped.

Ranged behind Gray and Agassiz that pleasant spring evening was the whole structure of western thought. Behind Gray stood the tradition of empiricism and of medieval nominalism. Behind Agassiz stood romanticism, transcendentalism, *Naturphilosophie*, Goethe, and medieval realism. Which of these traditions would capture biology was the issue of 1859. Since the prize included not only the vegetable and animal kingdoms but man himself, nonscientists would soon be competing.

Agassiz's sailing for Europe in June 1859 closed the first debate in America on Darwin's theories. The country might have been fortunate had it been the last. The issues had been probed and the ultimate tendencies laid bare. Yet a punctilious civility prevailed. False appeals to prejudice were lacking, and no references to the *Book of Genesis* muddled the clarity of the disagreement. Scientifically speaking, the evolutionary system worked out by Darwin had in the Japan essay a firm lodgement powerfully buttressed by data of peculiarly American origin. The 1859 debate was complete, and it was a victory for Darwin and Gray, for empiricism over idealism in biology. It incidentally revealed an increased maturity in American science and its institutions.

The great limitation of the 1859 debates was the lack of a comprehending audience. The handful of the Cambridge Scientific Club and the two dozen or so more who heard the debates at the American Academy were in general unable to see the momentous issues in the midst of the details of Gray's statistical analysis of species and genera of plants. And Agassiz's very feebleness in meeting squarely the detailed issues robbed them of impact. Even had those who heard understood, they were only a small part of the Cambridge and Boston intellectual community. Especially missing were the literary giants. Emerson, James Russell Lowell, Longfellow, George Ticknor, Francis Parkman, and Charles Eliot Norton were not included in any audience. Bright Harvard students such as Oliver Wendell Holmes, Jr., did not feel its stimulation.

A few scientists in other cities soon saw the *Proceedings,* but they were not prepared to take up arms for Gray, and so great was Agassiz's prestige they felt no need to do so on his side. Elias Durand wrote Gray from Philadelphia that he was not able to agree with him and prepared a paper for the American Philosophical Society against him, but "fearing that my powers of elocution and want of spunk could not carry me through, I remain silent." [50] More important, he indicated that Joseph Leidy, the zoologist, also opposed Gray. Thus Philadelphia, as a second cultural center in the country, failed to react strongly to the debates. It was John Brown's raid on Harper's Ferry, not the polite thrust and counterthrust of Gray and Agassiz, which was capable of stirring up Americans in 1859.

Asa Gray's place in the Darwin circle is easier to judge from the vantage point of the calm summer of 1859 than later, when secondary issues began to obscure the view. To understand it, one must first ascertain what Darwin himself was trying to do. The philosophical arguments for evolution were reasonably complete, though mixed with trash, in the *Vestiges*.[51] Darwin's own leading assumptions were well formed even earlier. His problem in these long years was not to arrive at the idea of evolution but to adjust the idea to the great corpus of biological knowledge which was itself rapidly gaining weight and changing in the 1840's and 1850's. Here lay Darwin's task and his synthetic genius. To tie the great mass of classified knowledge of plants and animals together into a pattern was really his best hope for direct evidence for evolution. He could not make one species from another even in the garden or breeding pen. He could not find a record of the exact moment of transmutation preserved from past geologic ages. He could and did get his evidence of evolution from the way in which organisms were distributed over the earth. Far from discrediting the old taxonomy, Darwin consummated it and vindicated its essential validity. The creation of the new subscience of plant geography was a major precondition to giving the theory of evolution a valid scientific basis. This new subscience made the *Origin of Species* possible, not the other way round.

Four men shaped this essential prop to the theory of evolution, missing in 1846 and present in 1859. Gray, Hooker, and Alphonse De Candolle held the accumulated knowledge of a generation of unprecedented exploration of the whole globe. Together they organized the data, applied statistical methods, and reached some preliminary generalizations. To establish the probability of a single local area for the origin of a species over the supposition of a multiple creation established a clear path in Darwin's direction. Hooker and Gray showed great ability at forming their material into larger generalizations. They did so in part because of the fourth founder of plant geography—Darwin, the man, as distinguished from Darwin, the book. He was the one who forced them to ask the big questions, to analyze their data, to look beyond the deadening routine of the herbarium. Gray vaguely wanted to study plant geography in the 1840's; he might have got around to it in the 1880's under his own power; he actually did take it up in the 1850's, with such splendid and creative results, because of Darwin's probing, driving questions.

The "Statistics of the Flora of North America" is a fine fruit of the Darwin-Gray-Hooker cross-fertilization. Yet the Japan essay, with its global sweep, its setting in geological time, its statistical identification of a striking natural discontinuity, and its beautiful resolution of the problem has a certain autonomy. Although it owes its existence to Darwin and its peculiarities to Agassiz, its essentials bear the characteristic marks of the mind of Asa Gray. More than anything else he ever wrote this essay compressed the endless labor of his days and nights into the simple unity of a great and scientifically valid generalization. Save for details, this vision of the distribution of the flora of the northern hemisphere has remained almost unmodified in a century of great advances in the science.

As Gray neared his forty-ninth birthday in the fateful year of 1859 he knew that the Japan essay was no *Principia*. Had he not borne the burdens of being a scientist in America, would he have been a Darwin with an essay on species? Is America to blame? The speculation is idle, but because no *Principia* emerged, all was not lost. The Japan essay was a peculiarly American document. From Charles Wright and Commodore John Rodgers and the sailors of the North Pacific Exploring Expedition and from James D. Dana came the ingredients which a native of Sauquoit, New York, shaped into a classic scientific theory of pioneer importance to a section of a science. The achievement of gearing it to a revolution which was yet to happen put him in the vanguard internationally as well as at home. The moment is a bright one in the annals of science in America.

THE IMMEDIATE IMPACT
OF THE *ORIGIN OF SPECIES*

EVEN in the summer of 1859, Asa Gray knew that Darwin's book when published would far exceed the questions of geographical distribution and raise fundamental issues. To grapple with them, a man's whole being, his intellect and his emotions as well as his professional judgment, would be tested. His philosophy, his religion, his own position in the universe were the ultimate fields of the questioning he was about to undertake.

As early as 1857, while still concerned largely with geographical distribution and with the thrust of Agassiz's idealism, Gray had already found large philosophical questions. Hooker, challenging that muted vitalism which had a place in Gray's thought, had called in T. H. Huxley, "the most clever rising physiological zoologist we have & a very nice fellow; but without the bump of veneration & is throwing hot shot & shell into Cuvier, Owen, Ehrenberg & Agassiz, right & left!!!!" Huxley thought "Asa Gray does not fully apprehend a very important circumstance, viz. that vitality is not merely force, but a mode of operation of force." Gray, admiring Huxley's "perfectly clear conceptions," admitted his distinction, but he still had maintained a place for an "unknown something" which "controls physical & chemical forces, and directs their applications." [1] Thus Gray already had a serious place in the philosophical discussions as well as the scientific work of the Darwin circle. He differed much less from them—Hooker, Lyell, and the newcomer Huxley—than he did from Agassiz. But differences were there, in temperament as well as ideas, and the oncoming crisis, brought even nearer as Darwin slaved on the abstract of his "big work," required that Gray's position in the circle be thoroughly examined.

As soon as Agassiz had retired from the debate in May 1859, Gray warned Hooker that "You attack on one extreme flank. Agassiz, on the opposite. No wonder if the blows I strike at the latter are so many blows in your favor. When we come to fight you then we must choose proper weapons for that." The jumping of the species barrier on a few closely related species was the beginning, then, and not the end of his evaluation of Darwin's ideas. Hooker, by this time working on an introduction to his *Flora of Tasmania,* which was in effect an announcement of his adherence to Darwin's notions, was already in a state of continual excitement. Not content to let Gray hang on to any remnant of a special creation theory, he recommended to Gray the "private eating" of his own Japan essay. Hooker was careful to say that Darwin's theory could not be demonstrated directly and to label it a hypothesis. "All I ever aim to do is to put the Development hypothesis in the same coach as the creation one. It will only be a question of who is to ride outside & who in after all." [2] The figure of the coach is a useful one for defining Gray's position. He had admitted Darwin's development hypothesis to the coach, but unlike Hooker was still unwilling to have it ride inside.

Gray freely admitted that "we go side by side a good long way,—and then you go further—perhaps to fare worse. My position is perhaps only a temporary one,—i.e. the orthodox position." Assume the extinction "of any quantity of intermediate forms and you can then imagine the development of the present vegetable kingdom by excessive variation. But just consider what an enormous amount of sheer, gratuitous assumption this requires!" To extend the reasoning from closely allied species to genera, orders, and classes required an effort which was almost as hard for a naturalist to muster as that needed to get over the species barrier in the first place.

Furious long letters went back and forth during the whole summer and fall. Gray on one occasion implored Hooker, "I fear the variation hypothesis is worrying your soul. Take it easy." Out of all the disputation Gray made a final summary of his position to Hooker on October 18, 1859, less than a month before the publication of the *Origin of Species*. "Somehow I do not stagger so much at your conclusions as at your philosophy or fundamental principles. I am quite ready to believe that any particular cognate species so called originated by variation, wherever you say so." He had gone this far by the previous April. "But [I] still stick at the *progression,* and the development of the Vegetable kingdom by variation from a primordial something." The tendency to push cause and effect back *ad infinitum* beyond the bounds of time itself "is natural since physical science has to do with the series of effects & not with efficient cause at all." But Gray only wondered "if you carry out this view to its ultimate and legitimate results,—how you connect the philosophy of religion with the philosophy of your science. I should feel uneasy if I could not connect them into a consistent whole—i.e., fundamental principles in science should not be in conflict." [3]

This statement contained all the elements of Gray's position on the eve of the publication of the *Origin*. He was willing to accept as a scientific probability the fact that one species might vary into another. He recognized, however, that to extend this to the whole of organic life was a philosophical problem, and one which involved the whole relation of science and religion. He accepted the responsibility of attempting a solution of the metaphysical problem which the acceptance of Darwin's form of evolution posed.

It was this acceptance that set him off most clearly from Hooker, who wailed that "I am utterly destitute of power to understand metaphysics." He could not "conceive any conflict between the fundamental principles of my religion & science. There is far more in both than I can understand. To me it is all supernatural . . . I hope this is not pantheism but really I do not know." [4] And in the ensuing years he made no serious efforts to inquire into the matter. In somewhat the same way Huxley's agnosticism was a refusal to attack the metaphysical problem which Gray had undertaken. Darwin always protested that he was in a muddle.

Gray's orthodox religion, then, played a role in shaping his reception of Darwin. The role was not, however, that usually ascribed to religion at this juncture in history. It did not blind his scientific judgment. It did not force him to the least intellectual dishonesty.

It did set for him a metaphysical problem to be solved, one which he approached with a light heart and a joyous disregard for his own lack of formal philosophical training.

Darwin finished reading the proofs on the *Origin of Species* on October 1, 1859, and, completely exhausted, departed for a water-cure establishment. He had promised to send advanced sheets to Gray, as he in fact did to Lyell, but in the rush he forgot, as did John Murray, the publisher.[5] On November 11, Darwin wrote, "I have directed a copy of my book (as yet only an abstract) on the Origin of Species to be sent to you. I know you are pressed for time; but if you can read it, I shall be infinitely gratified. From its condensed state it is *indispensable* to read it *all* straight through." [6] The book appeared on November 24, the 1250 copies selling out within the day. But one copy was on the ship for Gray, and others made their way to America.

In London the reaction was immediate. Hooker reported, "Darwin's book is out & created a tremendous furore on all hands." Dr. Francis Boott, Gray's old friend and a confidant of the friends of Darwin around London, gave the first of his reports on the tide of opinion. "I have not seen Hooker. I suppose he has full faith. Lyell has not, nor Herschell nor Sedgwick. I hear that the last told Darwin he had to hold his sides with laughing." [7]

By the time Gray's copy arrived, about Christmas, Darwin was the name on the lips of all sorts of intellectual people, not just naturalists. Unlike the Japan essay or Hooker's introduction to his *Flora of Tasmania,* which was published at about this time, the *Origin of Species* made its ultimate implications plainer than it made its splendid and intricate skeins of scientific reasoning. The group which "grew warm discussing the new book of Mr. Darwin's" around the fire in Jeffries Wyman's work room in Cambridge the day after Christmas consisted not only of the anatomist but also of the poet James Russell Lowell, the historian Henry W. Torrey, and the aesthete Charles Eliot Norton. Thanks perhaps to Gray's efforts of the past year, these men did not have to be scientists to know that "if Darwin is right Agassiz is wrong." The book was already "exciting the admiration and the opposition of all our philosophers." These men around the fire believed Agassiz to be "busy in writing a review of the book in which he intends to refute Mr. Darwin's chief conclusions." In this same village and in this same atmosphere, Gray read the *Origin of Species* in the week between Christmas and New Year's.[8]

Asa Gray read the volume attentively, pencil in hand. Prominent in his mind was his difference with Agassiz as to whether the individuals of a species were genetically connected. When Darwin said, "Perhaps the correct subject, would be, to look at the inheritance of every character whatever as the rule, and non-inheritance as the anomaly," Gray noted "Yes!" [9] As he went on, the exclamation points outnumber the question marks, and even such compliments as "well put" occasionally appear. His questions often centered on the phenomenon of variation, so crucial to Darwin's system, yet admittedly "governed by many unknown laws." Gray queried, for instance, the statement, "I do not believe that variability is an inherent and necessary contingency, under all circumstances, with all organic beings, as some authors have thought." Gray definitely believed otherwise. He objected to "too much personification" of nature and felt part of the discussion of cross-fertilization "overdone! too fanciful." Without committing himself, he singled out the theme that nature never makes jumps, "Nature non facit saltum," as one worthy of extended analysis. The idea of sexual selection struck him as "sentimental." Darwin's statement that intercrossing "plays a very important part . . . in keeping the individuals of the same species, or of the same variety, true and uniform in character" Gray identified as "my old idea."

The sum of all the markings Gray made in his copy of the *Origin* point to the conclusion that he approved much of Darwin's reasoning and most of his individual examples. Neither the struggle for existence, nor the suggestion that all organic beings descended from one primordial form, nor the problem of the origin of man elicited any remonstrance from Gray.

He did not by any means accept the whole of Darwin's system. That one species passed into another was probable. That natural selection was at work was equally likely. However, Gray was alive to the dangers lurking in the least known factor of Darwin's case, variation. Why, if organisms normally breed true, do they sometimes diverge and pass the variation along to their progeny? Darwin himself, bedeviled by this question, fell back in part on the doctrine of use and disuse, also crediting external conditions with some effect on variation. Here Gray wrote in the margin, "and so it comes to *Lamark,* after all!"

A deeper philosophical reservation also bothered Gray, the same one which had emerged from his summer discussion with Hooker. When Darwin admitted that some difficulties "are so grave that to this day I can never reflect on them without being staggered," Gray wrote, "Nor I, put with 186!" This reference leads directly to the most crucial of Archdeacon Paley's examples of design in nature, the eye. Darwin said on page 186, "To suppose that the eye, with all its inimitable contrivances . . . could have been formed by natural selection, seems, I freely confess, absurd in the highest possible degree." Gray remarked, "So it does." He was not yet ready to throw Paley over, but the issue was fairly joined. Gray's religious doubts thus centered—not about *Genesis* or other scriptural objections—but squarely on the issue of design in nature. His reaction to the eye example is a fair indication that he intended to meet it on the same ground as had Paley in the eighteenth century.

To Hooker he wrote on January 5, 1860, that Darwin's book "is done in a masterly manner. It might well have taken twenty years to produce it. It is crammed full of most interesting matter, well expressed, close, cogent; and taken as a system makes out a better case than I had supposed possible." As long as Agassiz dominated the American scene, however, Gray's extensive agreement with Darwin had to take precedence over any ultimate disagreements with the tendencies of the *Origin.* Gray immediately perceived this. "Agassiz cannot abide it (of course) and so has publicly denounced it as atheism &c &c. I am bound to stick up for its philosophy, and I am struck with the great ability of the book, and charmed with its fairness." [10]

Agassiz's behavior was indeed that of a bitter and vindictive man. To Gray he said, when he had read only a part of the *Origin,* "it is poor—very poor!!" And Gray reported to Hooker that Agassiz "growls over it, like a well-cudgelled dog—is very much annoyed by it—to our great delight—and I do not wonder at it." Referring to a previous controversy Agassiz had had with a geologist, Gray continued that "to bring all ideal systems within the domain of pure science, and give good or natural explanations of all his capital points, is as bad as to have Forbes take the glacier-materials A. had long muddled over, and give scientific explanation of all phenomena."

Not all of Agassiz's behavior could have provided Gray with unalloyed amusement. On January 14, 1860, the zoologist went for a walk in the evening with one of his students. Discussing a book about the Andes, Agassiz "said that the practice of some artists of substituting their own fancies for real nature was the result of mere *laziness*. . . ." He compared them to "those naturalists who adopt some pleasing but false theory like that of Darwin instead of investigating the difficult points of Science." He also mentioned "that he was surprised to learn that Prof. Gray inclined to that theory. He mentioned some of his ideas in regard to the true classification of plants and said that Botanists were far behind Zoologists in regard to true classification." Undermining colleagues in the estimation of students is always despicable business, and doubtless such incidents were in Gray's mind when two days later he burst out that he wanted "to stop Agassiz's mouth with his own words, and to show up his loose way of putting things. He is a sort of demagogue, and always talks to the rabble." [11]

Gray's strategy, then, in the face of Agassiz's hostile tactics, was primarily to ensure that Darwin "shall have fair play" in America. To do so he had first to protect, if he could, Darwin's interest in the *Origin* from the depredations of piratical publishers who, because of the lack of an international copyright law, had a clear field to snatch an unexpectedly lucrative literary property. Second, he had to secure an impartial review in the *American Journal of Science*. He incidentally published there much of Hooker's pro-Darwin but wordy introduction to the *Flora of Tasmania*, which made no more impression than had Gray's earlier effort to forward anti-Agassiz views by this indirect method. [12] The new science of plant geography was rapidly being swamped in the general clamor.

The publishing problem required Gray to have the confidence of Darwin and the alertness to move quickly. Mending his oversight on the first edition, Darwin sent to Gray advance sheets of the second English edition and, aware now of the potential sale of the *Origin,* requested Gray to aid an American reprint and "to make, for my sake & Publisher's, any arrangement for any profit." [13] Gray immediately made a stir in Boston with Ticknor and Fields for an American edition.

However, since the United States recognized no foreign copyright and, as it turned out, could grant a copyright to American citizens only, the way was open for anyone with a printing press and a copy of the English edition to publish an American edition, paying the author nothing. A more serious aspect of this anarchy was the fact that Darwin was already introducing corrections and additions into the English edition, and unauthorized American publishers would soon be publishing an outdated, inaccurate version. As soon as word reached Boston that two New York houses were coming out, Gray "wrote asking them to give way to the author and his reprint of a revised edition. I got an answer from Harper's that they withdraw—from the Appleton's that they had got the book out . . ." but were willing to pay the author a royalty. The Boston house then withdrew and, on the principle that "all got is clear gain," Gray determined to accept Appleton's offer. Thus the New York publishers, pushed on by the enthusiasm of one of their authors, E. L. Youmans, began their career as the purveyor of Darwin in America.[14]

The new edition under this arrangement contained the first version of Darwin's historical preface and a great many minor corrections. Gray had, on behalf of Darwin, the choice between a flat fifty pounds, or a 5 percent royalty on sales. Gray took the royalty. Appleton's regretted the lack of copyright protection, "think it a monstrous shame, but we are obliged to take things as they actually exist." By May 1, 1860, the publishers had printed 2500 copies of the *Origin* and sold 1750, paying Darwin £22. Darwin professed to be so grateful to Gray for these business arrangements that he offered him part of the royalties, "as I *wholly & absolutely* shall owe all to you." [15] Gray's great accomplishment, however, was to provide the American public with an edition of the *Origin* in some respects even ahead of the current English edition. The 1750 copies sold by May 1 are evidence of the wide dissemination of Darwin's ideas in America in their most authoritative form. No amount of derision or opposition could prevent their spread.

Since James D. Dana had completely collapsed physically and gone off to Italy at this crucial juncture, the duty of reviewing the book for the *Journal* naturally fell on Gray as the next senior member of the board of editors. He was thus speaking for the *Journal* and not merely as a guest reviewer. Although he made no effort to disguise his identity, the review as printed was unsigned.[16] Agassiz, of course, as the editor next in line, would be free to express himself in the *Journal's* pages as he saw fit.

Gray began by predicting a controversy which "is not likely to be settled in an off-hand way," nor should it be. "A spirited conflict must ensue, which,—to borrow an illustration from the doctrine of the book before us—may be likened to the conflict in nature among races in the struggle for life, which Mr. Darwin describes; through which the views most favored by facts will be developed and tested by 'Natural Selection,' the weaker ones to be destroyed in the process, and the strongest in the long run alone survive." Gray was well aware that this was a mere analogy. However, by appealing to the facts rather than "the influence of received and favorite systems" he was specifically invoking the right to freedom of thought as applicable in this crisis and as the highest value in a scientific dispute. A later age would adopt the same type of analogy in the phrase, "free trade in ideas," but Gray had raised the standard at a crucial time. It is the key to his position on Darwin and to his influence on the controversy. The most important thing was not whether Darwin was right or wrong but rather the insistence that his theory be judged by the standard of reason and not by passion.

Although regretting the illness of Dana, who was so admirably equipped to judge the *Origin,* Gray frankly stated that his "idealistic" views "will not harmonize readily with a doctrine so thoroughly naturalistic as those of Mr. Darwin." Then Gray turned by name to Agassiz, "The other great Naturalist whose name adorns the title-page," to contrast his views with those of Darwin. Using his own idea of "similarity of progeny to parent" as fundamental to the idea of a species, he showed that Agassiz denied genetic connection altogether while Darwin, holding "the orthodox view," extended it further, making species descendants of others in the same way as varieties. Species "are varieties of a larger growth and a wider and earlier divergence from the parent stock: the difference is one of degree, not of kind." The ordinary view was that natural agencies were responsible for the distribution and perpetuation of species, a supernatural agency for their origin. "The theory of Agassiz regards the origin of species and their present general distribution over the world as equally primordial, equally supernatural; that of Darwin, equally derivative, equally natural."

Agassiz was, in Gray's eyes, "theistic to excess," while Darwin's aim "must be regarded as a legitimate attempt to extend the domain of natural or physical science." Gray, even while protesting that he "had no prepossession in favor of naturalistic theories" and did not have the presumption to decide between the extreme views, was in effect hailing Darwin as a brother empiricist. Running the comparison between Darwin and Agassiz still further Gray became one of the first to point out that the two systems had striking parallelisms. "Apparently every capital fact in one view is a capital fact in the other." Agassiz as a great researcher had indeed drawn out many skeins of evidence, in embryology, for instance, which could be woven by either pattern. It was this recognition that in the years ahead was to allow Gray to maintain a modicum of respect for Agassiz in the face of great provocation. It was this correspondence of ideas, too, which gave the students of Agassiz, emotionally tied to their master and intellectually tied to Darwin, the excuse to elaborate the absurd theory that "without Agassiz, Darwin could not have been." [17]

When Gray came to explain Darwin's system, his years of intense preparation paid off handsomely. Although he quoted copiously from the *Origin,* his account clearly indicated mastery both of Darwin's ideas and their implications. The review provided a clear and perceptive outline of the whole argument. What more can an author ask? The same mastery of the subject matter appeared in Gray's discussion of the objections to the theory. Some of these, such as the lack of intermediate forms in the geological record, Gray took from the *Origin* itself. Others reflected his own ideas. As

273

to hybridism, cross-breeding between two varieties produces in-creased fertility, "yet when they have diverged one degree more the whole tendency is reversed, and the mongrel is sterile. . . ." More important, Darwin in attempting to reconcile the unity of type among organisms and their adaptation to environment had failed to produce a mechanism for this. How do organisms, which nor-mally breed true to type, sometimes vary in such a way as to adapt themselves to their environment? "Whenever he attempts this he reminds us of Lamarck, and shows how little light the science of a century devoted to structural investigation has thrown upon the mystery of organization."

In short, Darwin's system had a piece missing, and Gray knew it. With hindsight it is easy to see that the missing piece was the science of genetics. Although Gregor Mendel was a contemporary of Darwin and Gray, his discovery would not relieve this flaw in evolutionary theory during their lives. Gray's not having the key piece did not prevent him from noticing its absence in the clearest possible terms. Given varieties, "natural selection might determine which should survive and where it would prevail," but "really, we no more know the reason why the progeny occasionally deviates from the parent than we do why it usually resembles it." All argu-ments which purport to prove that Gray "accepted" or "rejected" Darwin *in toto* must take account of the fact that the American had advanced a valid scientific objection which did credit to his wide knowledge and accurate powers of observation. Since genetics had long been the cornerstone of his own ideas of species, it is not too surprising that his questions were already calling for the next revo-lution in science. To have accepted Darwin on genetics would have been quite as obscurantist and anti-scientific as to have accepted the first chapter of *Genesis*.

Since Gray was entirely aware of religious objections beginning to stir against the *Origin,* he ended his review by examining the question "what would happen if the derivation of species were to be substantiated, either as a true physical theory, or as a sufficient hypothesis?" He was not surprised that the book was denounced as atheistical, but he was concerned "that it should be so denounced by a scientific man . . ." i.e., Agassiz, "on the broad assumption that a material connection between the members of a series of organized beings is inconsistent with the idea of their being intellectually connected with one another through the Deity. . . ."

Evolution was not then necessarily atheistic. "It would be more correct to say, that the theory in itself is perfectly compatible with an atheistic view of the universe. That is true; but it is equally true of physical theories generally." Gray, who had always had a sense of the history of science, saw the kinship between the question raised by Darwin and those already posed by Newton. Indeed, "the theory of gravitation and . . . the nebular hypothesis assume a *universal and ultimate* physical cause, from which the effects in nature must necessarily have resulted." Yet no one in 1860 seemed to consider Newton's theory a step toward atheism or pantheism. Gray even slyly quoted Agassiz's approval of the nebular hypothesis. Darwin's hypothesis "merely takes up a *particular, proximate cause,* or set of such causes, from which, it is argued, the present diversity of species has or may have *contingently* resulted. The author does not say *necessarily* resulted. . . ." Surely "Mr. Darwin's theory is none the worse, morally, for having some foundation in fact." This plea for the innocence of science of theological bearing was a doctrine with a future. Gray's friend and neighbor, Chauncey Wright, coined the term, "the neutrality of science," to cover it and through him it entered the philosophy of William James and John Dewey. Gray's word *"contingently"* is one with a twentieth-century flavor.

Had Gray stopped at this point, his review would have weighed heavily against those orthodox who were muttering about the tendencies of the new book. It would have weighed also against those philosophers such as Herbert Spencer who were placing a cosmic evolution in the center of their systems. But the neutrality of science, if it meant that scientific theories did not have an effect one way or another on ultimate philosophical questions, meant also that a scientist could adopt the new theory without destroying his previous religious orientation. Gray could not see in the results of adaptation "the atheism of fortuity" because the theory "undertakes to assign real causes for harmonious and systematic results." How could chance produce design? The way was still open to Paley. Gray did not know how Darwin "harmonizes his scientific theory with his philosophy and theology," but what "is to hinder Mr. Darwin from giving Paley's argument a further *a-fortiori* extension to the supposed case of the watch which sometimes produces better watches, and contrivances adapted to successive conditions, and so at length turns out a chronometer, a town-clock, or a series of organisms of the same type?"

The quotation from William Whewell's *Bridgewater Treatise* which Darwin placed opposite the title page of the *Origin* led Gray to think it probable that Darwin saw "the whole system of nature as one which had received at its formation the impress of the will of its Author. . . ." Indeed he had the choice of regarding the intervention of the Creator as *"done from all time,* or else as *doing through all time."*

Gray then produced his own view. Action of the Creator *"done from all time"* led to atheism because it suggested "an eternal sequence of cause and effect, for which there is no first cause." Action of the Creator *"doing through all time"* threatens with pantheism. "We feel safe from either error, in our profound conviction that there is order in the universe; that order presupposes mind; design, will; and mind or will, personality." This view left "us with the same mysteries in Nature as in Providence, and no other. Natural law . . . is the human conception of continued and orderly Divine action."

Gray's harking back to Paley and the design argument put him at a disadvantage. These were eighteenth-century relics open to the logical objections of anyone who, like T. H. Huxley, chose to read Hume carefully. In a real sense Gray by stressing a general Providence acting through time had left Paley's rather mechanical line of argument. But there seemed in the early days of 1860 a real chance that the exquisite design of evolution might fortify design in the old sense. Darwin lent encouragement by tacking on to the quotations in the front of the book a sentence from Bishop Butler, whose position in the eighteenth century was similar to Paley's. "The only distinct meaning of the word 'natural' is *stated, fixed,* or settled; since what is natural as much requires and presupposes an intelligent mind to render it so, i.e., to effect it continually or at stated times, as what is supernatural or miraculous does to effect it for once." If Darwin accepted a line similar to that of Gray's, the defenders of the derivative hypothesis would have a retort to religious objections.

In a broader sense Gray was pointing to one of the two possible ways of looking at the new theory. On the one hand, the assumption that the derivation of organic beings voided all previous theory and belief, leaving only materialism in its place, was a point of view shared by the extremes on both sides. The materialists accepted this point of view with jubilation; the devout believers, recoiling in horror, rejected the whole theory, but upon exactly the same premise as their adversaries. Gray attempted to say that another point of view was possible, that a scientific hypothesis was a system of ideas about observed phenomena which did not prove speculations about the universe or its relation to ultimate moral law. Neither Newton nor Darwin (how often the two names were coupled in those early months of 1860) made the truth of religion any more or less acceptable. Old beliefs, themselves fraught with difficulties, were still possible and still necessary. In becoming the spokesman in the English-speaking world for this second point of view, Gray found himself in the middle between the extremists who, agreeing on the other point of view, were doing battle with each other.

Gray's review was the occasion for rejoicing in the Darwin circle in Engand. Hooker immediately wrote, "You have succeeded *au merveille*—both with the Nat. Hist., Metaphysic, & above all the Theological aspect of the whole question." He detected, however, an "evident bias . . . to the old doctrine" and conjectured that "Darwin's work had made a deeper hole in your prejudices & preconvictions than you are yet aware of. . . ." Hooker also pointed out to Darwin that Gray's review had "produced great effect, in leading people to think" and had "greatly mollified opposition." Lyell thought it "the best thing that has appeared on the subject." [18]

Darwin's reaction was frank both in generosity and observation. In his opinion the review was "by far the most able which has appeared, & you will have done the subject infinite service." Those points directed toward proving design did not evoke his enthusiasm. Even "with the Eye, as numerous fine gradations can be shown to exist, the perfecting this wondrous organ by Nat. Selection I must look at as a difficulty to our imagination & not to our reason." As to an omnipotent and omniscient Creator, he granted that "to foresee is the same as to preordain; but then when I come to think over this I get into an uncomfortable puzzle *something* analogous with 'Necessity & Free-will' or the 'Origin of Evil,' or other such subjects quite beyond the scope of the human intellect." Darwin was quite anxious that the American edition of the *Origin* use Gray's review as a preface. "Please observe," he wrote, "that I do not class your Review by any means as opposed, though you think so yourself! It has done me *much* too good service to appear in that rank in my eyes." [19]

Some scientists who reacted against Darwin also gave the review careful attention. W. H. Harvey, professor at Dublin, a warm personal friend of Gray's and of most of the Darwin circle, had been thoroughly angered by Darwin even though "Hooker & Lyell and *all the nobs* go with him." He liked Gray's "view of the matter" and thought he saw in it an *"undercurrent"* against Darwin. Fortunately "there was *one* of my bot. friends at least, whose feet were not quite whipt from under him." Even Harvey, however, reported that those who did not know Gray "thought you had not *stated* objections to the theory broadly enough, but had rather written an apology." Francis Boott, who could see Darwin's system at work in his own specialty, the sedges, but who could not follow to a general application of it, called Gray's review "the best yet on the subject." He, too, was a good friend of Hooker and Lyell, and hence in a mood to sympathize with Gray's "tone," which he described as the "truest." [20]

The only other reviewer to grapple adequately with the crisis presented by the *Origin of Species* was Huxley. This zoologist overnight changed himself from a rising but junior member of the Darwin circle to the bulldog—the public defender and shaper of strategy. In many ways Huxley and Gray, the two major favorable reviewers, reacted alike to the *Origin*. They both praised its author and his ability, they both defended the propriety of the attempt Darwin had made, and the weight of their remarks told in his favor. They both recognized that even if the theory proved unfounded the book would be a landmark in natural history. They both, however, considered the case incomplete and voiced objections which had a prophetic validity. Gray had pointed out the absence of a science of genetics; Huxley questioned the universal applicability of the aphorism that nature never makes jumps. They both showed great tactical ability in shaping their arguments, and each in his way was a phrasemaker.[21] They both even adopted an analogous position on the neutrality of science.

Only at this final stage did the two part company. Huxley later remarked that "the materialistic position . . . is as utterly devoid of justification as the most baseless of theological dogmas." With this Gray would have agreed. "But," Huxley continued, "with a view to the progress of science, the materialistic terminology is in every way to be preferred." [22] Gray preferred, on the basis of the same logic, the terminology of the design argument and evangelical Christianity. The difference, a mere matter of language, was slight, but since it had to do with ultimates, it presaged a basic split in the Darwin circle. The man of Down would eventually have to make the choice.

The reaction among American scientists, while less crystallized than in England, indicated that Gray had made real progress in getting consideration for Darwin, although none of Gray's usual friends was able to accept the new idea. Moses Ashley Curtis saw Darwin as "only Rafinesquius redivivus, for old R. anticipated him in that notion of 'natural selection.' " He was willing to wait awhile before acceptance, but the fruit of Gray's work was his admission that "Darwin seems to write ably & well." Edward Tuckerman feared Darwin's ideas still "belonged to transcendental science, though an Englishman cannot treat even that in any other way than his own materialistic one." Arnold Guyot thought Gray's an "able review" but still insisted that what "unfolds itself is the Creator's plan." Leo Lesquereux thought Darwin's theory "contradicted by the only data which could afford reliable evidence," that is, geology. But he agreed with Gray that the system could not harm those "who are steeled by faith against harm," a view he later changed, and was even willing to toy with the idea that Christ was the "first specimen of a new species." [23] Since these latter two men were both Swiss who had followed the magnetic pull of Agassiz to America, their very consideration of the subject was an accomplishment for Gray.

Strangely, the old friend who most nearly warmed to the new theory was Joseph Henry. He had already been reflecting on such books as Buckle's history. Now he was "somewhat pleased to learn" that Darwin "had connected his speculations with the theory of Malthus and had gone into a line of speculation on which I had entered." [24] The friendship between Gray and Henry, a momentous one for science in America, thus found an additional bond in a sympathetic interest in Darwin.

Gray felt bound to explain to the Darwin circle in England the ambivalence of his review. To Darwin himself he had written that the review "does not exhibit anything like the full force of the impression the book has made on me." But Gray felt for strategy's sake that he would be safer to "stand noncommitted as to its full conclusion, than I should if I announced myself a convert; nor could I say the latter, with truth." To Hooker, Gray wrote, "I said that Darwin and you should have a *fair* hearing here, and have kept my word." Every day "I feel the advantage, and see the weight which my remarks have . . . a weight which would be lost very much had I come in as a convert." He could defend Darwin "against illogical attacks and absurd propositions." Besides, he could always move forward toward Darwin, "while to take the back track is not so pleasant." He wished "to fortify every position as I proceed, so as to *defy* attack, and be ready for any future sally I may make in defense of Darwin." The enemy was already in sight. "Agassiz is writing, at length, I hear, and Bowen, our metaphysical professor also. I watch for a chance if possible, to spit the two on one pen at one thrust." [25]

Through these remarks of Gray run two great figures of speech which in the Darwinian crisis were to take on almost literal meaning. The metaphor of war and the metaphor of church quickly overshadowed more subtle positions; especially the ideal of scientific detachment and of impartial evaluation of the evidence.

The all-pervasive metaphor of war found a congenial application in the central idea of the *Origin* itself. The struggle for life was the never-ending battle in which all organisms engaged. Gray was much less bemused by this phase of the metaphor than most of his contemporaries because he readily saw that plants did not pick up swords and slay one another. He meant rather the continuation of the battle within science between idealism and empiricism which had already developed in the debates over the flora of Japan. In this stage of the metaphor of war, Gray was practically and wholeheartedly on the side of Darwin and against Agassiz. What a time to be alive! The mild, stooped naturalists laid aside their microscopes and rallied to the colors. The mildest of them all, Charles Darwin, goaded by the review of Richard Owen, promised, "I will buckle on my armour & fight my best." [26] Gray was not only one of three or four general officers of Darwin's army, but the sole commander of the important American sector.

During the spring and summer of 1860 the metaphor of war entered a third stage. All sorts of people who sat mute and uncomprehending during the Japan debate fearlessly sprang into action when the *Origin* raised even larger issues. No longer did the metaphor refer to a battle within science, but to a battle between science on the one hand and theology on the other. In its most extreme form, the warring armies considered themselves fighting either for or against science itself, and for or against religion itself. Gray was just as much an orthodox Christian as ever. Indeed, at the height of the excitement over the *Origin* he wrote to Harvard's treasurer urging the appointment to the faculty of "some scholarly and genial clergyman of the more liberal wing of the orthodox Congregationalists." [27] The tendency of materialists to take over Darwin's idea and to go to war on religion Gray of course resisted. The tendency of the clergy and other defenders of the faith to attack Darwin and all science as atheistical not only filled him with dismay but struck him as very faulty tactics. He protested "against the folly of those who would . . . fire away the very ramparts of the citadel, in defense of needless outposts. . . ." [28] In the third stage of the metaphor of war, then, in the battle between science and religion, Gray had to attempt, not to mediate, but to change the positions of both groups of combatants. He had to make both reject the doctrine that Darwin's system was necessarily atheistic. As the metaphor of war gained strength in its third stage, Gray's position became harder and harder to maintain as the combatants nailed their flags to the mast.

Thus the metaphor of war led to the metaphor of the church. The word "conversion" had already made its appearance. In the early discussions, Gray and Hooker, for instance, had used it simply to indicate what main hypothesis a naturalist chose as a basis for further work. As Hooker had said, it was a question of who rode outside the coach and who inside. As the metaphor of war engulfed the imagination of the age and moved into its third stage of a battle between science and religion, conversion to Darwin's theory took on all the gravity of a solemn renunciation and repentance coupled with a profession of faith in a new dogma. The generation which had witnessed the agonies of Newman on the path to Rome understood what a conversion was. Huxley especially understood and used this metaphor, with his "church scientific" and his "lay sermons." It was he who described the positive philosophy of August Comte as "Catholicism without Christianity." [29] To fill the gap between the two extremes, he invented his own faith—agnosticism. Gray could not solve the problem so easily.

As the metaphor of the church gained sway, two militant bodies of the faithful increasingly lost touch with one another and began to feel that he who is not for us is against us. Solid scientific doubts about the complete adequacy of every detail of Darwin's theory became indications that a scientist harbored a secret belief in the old religion. On the other hand a kind word about Darwin's immense labor and ability became a token that the devil was at work and faith was corroding. Although Gray sometimes toyed with the metaphor of war he could not accept the metaphor of the church. In its place he attempted to substitute the neutrality of science.

The ambivalence of Gray's first review of the *Origin* becomes more understandable if it is viewed in some other context than the metaphors of war and the church. He was writing as a scientist for his peers, free to criticize without damnation, and free to praise without commitment. It was not the review, but the metaphors, which made it seem equivocal. After March of 1860 Gray had to enter the smoke of battle and undergo the perils of a warrior. He, no more than any other thinking man, could avoid commitment. Hooker remarked that "One of the most interesting studies that the book opens, is that of the kinds & qualities of mind that ignore, or sneer, or read, or mark, or learn, or inwardly object." [30] Gray, having already read and learned, responded with a vivacity and a flexibility which heightened the effectiveness of his keen intellect.

XV

THE CREST OF THE
DARWINIAN DEBATE

As all eyes in the intellectual world of Boston and Cambridge turned to the growing storm over evolution, from long habit they looked toward Agassiz. Gray's review had anticipated him but hardly displaced him from the center of the stage. Agassiz had the advantage in the growing tension because he was spoiling for a fight. He gladly accepted the battle metaphor, not only as a continuation of his scientific struggles, but in the sense of the battle against atheism as well. To his students he gave vivacious lectures on the folly of Darwinism. Yet he exhibited a distinct preference for a campaign in the flesh rather than in print. His long-awaited blast in the *American Journal of Science* did not appear while the oral debates were going on. When it did finally appear in July 1860, it was neither a review of Darwin nor an answer to Gray, but rather a warmed-over section from a manuscript volume of the *Contributions to the Natural History of the United States*. It accomplished little other than serve notice that Agassiz, far from backing down or modifying his earlier views, was confidently expecting that Darwin's "mere guesses" would soon pass away.[1] The true dimensions of his effort only emerged as the various scientific societies of the community worked through their winter schedule.

The Boston Society of Natural History was more Agassiz's ground than Gray's. Nevertheless, even here a champion of Darwin promptly arose in the person of William Barton Rogers, who forced the discussion into geological lines. Agassiz became increasingly discomfited as the points at issue gradually came down to the stratigraphy and geological history of New York state. In the labyrinths of detail Rogers clearly possessed not only the initiative but a superior grasp of facts.[2]

In the Scientific Club, Agassiz had another chance. On February 23, 1860, he reiterated his views on "the number of distinct periods in the geology of the earth." Since Agassiz emphasized the complete break between each stratum, Gray's paper to the club two weeks later on the axiom *Natura non agit saltatem* may be considered an answer and a flanking attack. At the same time it was also an original piece of reasoning which never worked its way into publication.[3]

Ascribing to Leibnitz the axiom that nature never makes jumps, he asserted that, while no one used it as a "*test* of the correctness of any theory," the facts which naturalists deal with might "favor or illustrate the *principle*. We may, perhaps, *infer* the principle from the phenomena." This statement epitomized the difference in his and Agassiz's concept of scientific method. He did not "suppose that Nature makes no distinct steps at all, but only *short steps*—not *infinitely fine* gradations!" The subtle distinction between this stand and that of Darwin put him closer than his friend to twentieth century science. But as he looked over possible breaks in the scheme of nature—between plants and animals, between different plant structures, in sexuality, sensitivity, individuality, in geological history, even in barriers between species—he found that "to the whole system the axiom applies." This discourse was a splendid blow for Darwin.

The real arena, however, was again the American Academy of Arts and Sciences. Here scientific Boston and the Boston of society and literature met. And, unlike during the debate of the previous year, the laymen were aroused. Agassiz had begun the attack on Darwin's geology here in January, but when this line of discussion had become the subject of debate with Rogers in the Boston Society of Natural History, he took up a new subject. On March 13 he maintained "the position that varieties, properly so called, have no existence, at least in the animal kingdom." [4] His friend Benjamin Peirce then called, as he had in 1859, for three special meetings "for scientific discussions."

The time had come for Agassiz's great effort. And when he came to the special meeting of March 27 it was clear that he was not alone. For the program featured his allies rather than himself. Francis Bowen, officially Harvard's professor of philosophy, was ready with the article he had prepared for the *North American Review*. He concluded that Darwin carried out "his theory to the entire denial of the doctrine of final causes." [5] His tone was on occasion derisive. "Mr. Darwin boldly traces out the genealogy of man, and affirms that the monkey is his brother,—and the horse his cousin, and the oyster his remote ancestor." [6]

The other nonscientist to enter the debate that evening was none other than John Amory Lowell. It was he who had been an enthusiastic amateur botanist, the source of funds for Gray's exploring enterprises in the 1840's, the close associate of Charles G. Loring, and a friend of Mrs. Gray. Now he stood up in the camp of the enemy, for he followed Agassiz in denying the existence of all varieties whatsoever. Using the botanical knowledge he had gathered in association with another, he attributed all seeming varieties to hybridization. He also attacked Darwin concerning the development of instinct, and concerning the definition of such loaded words as "accidental." Behind these objections he clearly objected to the religious implications he drew from Darwin. To him it seemed "at once more reverent, and more consonant to the feelings implanted in our nature, to believe in an ever-acting Providence,—to believe that not a sparrow falls to the ground without the Father,—to believe that all the adaptations so admirably fitted to the need or the gratification of His creatures are the direct act of the Creator." To prove that the design argument could be put to various uses, it is only necessary to contrast this view with that of Gray. After Agassiz added a few words of approval to a discussion of the subject of hybridization, Gray struck back very briefly at the end. [7]

The alliance which Gray faced that night was truly formidable. The points at issue with Agassiz were the same they had disputed in 1859. Bowen carried no great weight, and Gray had deplored his prolixity even when they had been allies against the *Vestiges* back in 1846. But John A. Lowell was more than just a defected friend. Besides embodying a considerable share of the wealth and

power of Boston, he was the leading member of the Harvard Corporation. Was a friend and defender of Darwin on the Harvard
faculty safe? Although the issue was not one to be discussed, it was
inherent in the situation. Lowell seemed to be following a course
which led to the condemnation of Darwin and all his works.

The faint scent of danger presented by the alliance facing Gray
only whetted his combativeness. To him Bowen's article was "very
poor and ill-mannered," Lowell was "put up by Agassiz." As for
that glorious man of science, "I really think his mind has much
deteriorated within a few years." [8] At the next meeting he took on
all three.

On the evenings of April 10 and May 1, Gray had the floor from
the beginning. He first made clear his independent judgment that
"variation and natural selection would have to be admitted as
operative in nature, but were probably inadequate to the work
which they had been put to." When he heard of it, Hooker was dis-
satisfied with Gray for using the word "probably." [9] The middle
ground of scientific objections was fast disappearing. But in the rest
of the rebuttal Gray stood up manfully for Darwin.

Gray mostly covered familiar ground—varieties, hybridization,
the influence of domestication. It was still in part a split between
idealism and empiricism because, against the charge that Darwin
was too speculative and metaphysical, Gray animadverted that the
theory "would generally be regarded as too materialistic and physical, rather than too metaphysical in character, and that, *a fortiori,*
physical geology and physical astronomy would on this principle be
metaphysical sciences."

Yet each time he went over the ground he brought out a few new
points and clarified a few others. For instance, he had to reconcile
somehow his old belief that all organisms breed true and the new
belief that they sometimes pass along variation. Here, while dealing
with the unfamiliar subject of animal instinct, he was driven to
admit "the fact of the heritability both of acquired habits and apti-
tudes, and of certain modified structures." [10] This was, however, a
reluctant concession against which his deep belief in the stability
of inheritance fought hard, and he was careful not to adopt it as a
general rule as applied to structure. The genetics of the Darwinian

generation was simply too crude to reconcile normal stability with heritable variations which were necessary if Darwin's system was to work. Gray never went nearly as far as Darwin in admitting the heritability of acquired characters.

More important to the nonscientific audience at the American Academy, Gray undertook to defend his attitude toward the doctrine of design. He was here faced with people who believed that Darwin's work threatened a belief in design and who insisted that Darwin must therefore be repudiated. Gray's tactic was not so much to argue that design existed in nature as to point out that the philosophical problems concerning it were those with which the "philosophical naturalist" was already familiar. The "establishment of this particular theory by scientific evidence would leave the doctrines of final cause, utility, special design, or whatever other teleological view, just where they were before its promulgation, in all fundamental respects. . . ."

Just as Agassiz emerged from these debates committed publicly against Darwin, Gray emerged committed to his defense of design in nature and to the possibility of a theist being a Darwinian. He insisted that the argument for design rested on "the adaptation of structure to use, irrespective of the particular manner in which the adaptation may be conceived to have been brought about." Darwinian natural selection was a secondary cause, whose operation might remove a particular phenomenon—the creation of a species—from the realm of the supernatural. But no theist can hold that only the supernatural "can be regarded as designed." Nor can he hold that "the so-called *accidental* element in natural selection negatives design, though it may render it more difficult to prove design in opposition to the atheist. . . ."

This very activity—disputation with so-called "atheists," became a major activity for Gray almost simultaneously with his debates before the American Academy. On the whole, he had a much more genial relation with them than he did with Agassiz. Indeed, one of the first to come forward was his old friend and neighbor Daniel Treadwell, one-time Rumford Professor at Harvard and a member of the Scientific Club. Their conversation promptly appeared anonymously as a "Discussion between Two Readers of Darwin's Treatise

on the Origin of Species." [11] The two disputants outdid themselves
in using figures of speech far more subtle than the usual carnage.
The designer here is a billiard player. Does the roll of a ball after
it has collided with another represent design on the part of the
player, or the blind necessity of physical laws? Gray upheld the
presence of design even when known secondary causes were at
work, concluding that if "the discussion had gone on, it might, perhaps, have been made to appear that the Darwinian hypothesis, so
far from involving the idea of necessity (except in the sense that
everything is of necessity), was based upon the opposite idea, that
of contingency." Here again he tried to put contingency—design
operating within the natural order—at the center of his system.

Privately he described this discussion as a mere "pendant" and
Treadwell as "a skeptical neighbor of mine, a man who hangs
doubtfully on the skirts of atheism, and thinks Darwin's book will
give him a firmer hold." Gray felt Treadwell "might have set me a
vastly harder task if he knew how. But he is old-fashioned, has no
doubt that design proves *personality* and does not appreciate the
subtle objections which may be raised and which are so difficult to
answer. . . ." [12] This comment hints that Gray did not think of
design in nature as the offshoot of the workings of the mind of a
personal God. He also clearly conceived himself to be engaged in a
search for a new philosophical formulation. Despite his self-confidence he shows none of the attitude of a man already convinced
he possessed the whole truth.

A far more important skeptic than Daniel Treadwell lived in
Cambridge and entered Gray's circle with the rising Darwinian
crisis. Outwardly, Chauncey Wright was an humble and eccentric
man who made his living at the Harvard Observatory, across the
street from the Botanic Garden, by making computations for the
United States *Nautical Almanac*. This particular winter he was also
teaching in Agassiz's school for girls. His real profession, however,
was that of village philosopher. He had already worked his way
through British empiricism to the point of becoming a disciple of
John Stuart Mill. The publication of the *Origin of Species* set him
on fire to accommodate Mill's philosophy to the new doctrine of
evolution. [13] At the age of thirty, Wright was just coming into his

own as a philosopher in 1860, having taken up the study seriously only about four years before. He was elected to membership in the American Academy of Arts and Sciences at the meeting of January 25, 1860, just in time to be present for the debate between Gray and his opponents. The succeeding meetings profoundly shaped his philosophy and his views on natural selection.

While he had no connection at all with orthodox Christianity or with the design argument of Paley, his reaction to Darwin's book immediately revealed the close correspondence between his and Gray's views. In February 1860, he wrote in a letter concerning the *Origin of Species* that "Agassiz comes out against its conclusions, of course, since they are directly opposed to his favorite doctrines on the subject; and, if true, they render his essay on Classification a useless and mistaken speculation." Wright already believed that "this development theory is a true account of nature, and no more atheistical than that approved theory of creation which covers ignorance with a word pretending knowledge and feigning reverence." [14] Even in this statement there is an echo of Gray's position.

Chauncey Wright gradually shaped his synthesis of Darwin with the British empirical tradition culminating in Mill around the doctrine he called the neutrality of science. By this he meant that science advanced piecemeal on the basis of observation and experiment, using general ideas as hypotheses. The investigator should be free from the domination of *a priori* systems at all times, keeping ethical sentiments separate from scientific knowledge. Thus Darwin's system was a scientific theory of biology, a hypothesis which had no necessary causal effect on religious, philosophical, or social matters. Although Asa Gray never used the phrase, he lived it. In his scientific practice and his ideas about Darwin, Gray provided Chauncey Wright with a model which was not lost upon the philosopher. Wright made explicit in philosophical terms the influence which shaped Gray and the conclusions he drew. The botanist in return made available to Wright a wealth of scientific experience and insight.[15]

A problem on which Gray set Wright to work was phyllotaxy— the study of the arrangement of leaves on a stem—one of the aspects of botany most thoroughly permeated with idealism. Goethe had launched the idea, and it had meshed well into *Naturphilosophie*. One of the two Germans who had developed the subject was Alexander Braun, whose brother-in-law, none other than Louis Agassiz himself, had stimulated interest in the mathematics of leaf arrangement among the professors at Cambridge when he first arrived in America. Gray had joined Benjamin Peirce in a short communication on it in 1849, but the practical botanist felt his mathematical colleague *"ran off into the sky, dementedly."* [16] Although Gray treated the subject more fully in his textbook in 1850 he really "never meddled with this mathematical stuff." It was just the kind of recondite subject which delighted Wright. The outcome of years of work on leaf arrangement was his complete recasting of an idealistic system into one derived by natural selection. Leaves were arranged about a stem to economize space and have good exposure to light, being based on two plans perhaps derived from fronds of *algae*.[17] Joined together, Gray and Wright thus proceeded with the destruction of the world of Agassiz and the erection of the world of Darwin in a brilliant and almost forgotten line of research.

By December 1860, Gray was attempting through Darwin to get Huxley to publish in his new *Natural History Review* an article by Chauncey Wright. Gray called it "a good philosophical discussion of Derivative Hypothesis." But Darwin feared it was "too metaphysico-theological for me." Huxley, while he was as anxious to have an anti-Darwinian article as a favorable one, also considered Wright's review "too general & not natural-historical enough." [18] Thus the high command of the Darwinian movement in England rejected Chauncey Wright despite Gray's position as one of their peers and his advocacy of Wright. Partly it was the anti-metaphysical bent of Darwin, Huxley, and the other leaders of the movement. Gray here stands out for his higher threshold of tolerance for philosophizing. But partly it was the hard lot of the men in between the warring sides. Chauncey Wright was a skeptic in the same way Gray was orthodox, but it was their attempt to stay in the middle which hurt them in the eyes of both sides.

Although the main stream of Darwinism rejected him and although he died in 1875 without producing a systematic body of work Chauncey Wright earned a place in American philosophy which has grown rather than shrunk. By word of mouth he influenced William James, Charles Saunders Peirce, Oliver Wendell Holmes, Jr., and the other young men of the evanescent Metaphysical Club of Cambridge in the 1870's. These philosophers were outside Gray's range, too young and uninterested in botany. But among them they made pragmatism an important American philosophy. And through Chauncey Wright, Asa Gray's science and his way of looking at science lay in the foundation of their thought. The main line of the history of empiricism in America runs from Gray, who absorbed his partly out of the Paley-laden American air but also imported it directly from Britain, to Chauncey Wright, to pragmatism.

After the death of the philosopher who was as queer in his way as his namesake the collector, Gray summarized their relationship in a letter to Charles Eliot Norton. "We always got on admirably as to our antagonisms, which came to play only as we reached the last question of all; and each understood the other's ground too well to entertain the idea that he could drive the other clear out of it." [19] The last question of all was theism—God, design, and revealed Christianity. Yet the extent of their agreement is the measure of Gray's progress in unconsciously forging the outlook of a scientist which would be compatible, not to the invective-ridden atmosphere of 1860, but to the pragmatic twentieth century.

Others besides the skeptics Treadwell and Wright focused their attention on Gray's ideas as a result of his appearances in the spring of 1860. William Barton Rogers, who was fighting Agassiz on the geological front, showed a new cordiality. Charles Eliot Norton, who had recently come to live in the ancestral home at Shady Hill in Cambridge, not only expressed interest but accepted Gray's "vindication of the theory from the charge of necessarily tending toward atheism" as "complete." Theophilus Parsons, law school professor and a neighbor of Gray's, tried to advance an intermediate interpretation of Darwin which told against Agassiz.[20]

By far the most important ally for Gray was his old friend and colleague Jeffries Wyman, who had founded zoological study in Harvard College and had kept it out of the reach of Agassiz. Gray described him to Darwin as "the person best prepared to criticize your book of anyone in America—for all matters of embryology, zoology, anatomy &c—and as cautious as possible—could give you many interesting facts and hints." Although he took no public stand, Wyman was soon placing his great store of scientific knowledge at Darwin's disposal. For instance, he joined Chauncey Wright in attacking idealistic notions of the formation of bees' cells, a problem raised by Bowen's remarks on instinct.[21]

While these acquisitions of strength centering around Gray in Cambridge by no means matched the powerful alliance centering on Agassiz, it was a respectable showing. And the very fact that Gray launched his current of opinion in the face of the opposition of wealth and power made his stand appear courageous as well as astute. This aspect of Gray's efforts was not lost on Darwin, whose many words of praise reached a climax immediately following the American Academy debates. "What a battle you do seem to have been fighting on the origin of species. I can most plainly see that whatever amount of truth my book may contain, the saving of it (as I told Hooker the other day) will surely be due to a very small body of men. Had it not been for Lyell, Hooker, yourself & two or three others, I am well convinced my book & the whole subject would have been mere flash in the pan." Later he described Gray's "generosity in getting my views a fair hearing, & not caring himself for unpopularity" [22] as "most unselfish,—I would say noble." After reading the American Academy *Proceedings,* he wrote, "I declare that you know my Book as well as I do myself; & bring the question new lines of illustration & argument, in a manner which excites my astonishment & almost my *envy!*" Still thinking in terms of the metaphor of the battle in its second phase, he said, "every word seemed weighed carefully & tells like a 32-pound shot." As a tangible evidence of his esteem, Darwin had the report of Gray's argument before the American Academy reprinted in England.[23]

This feeling of gratitude on Darwin's part was heightened by the events of June 1860. Agassiz was of course a name to conjure with in Europe as well as America, and Gray's engaging him was of great importance in itself. The crisis of opinion in England was more pressing, for there Richard Owen was playing the same role. Like Agassiz, he attacked Darwin from idealistic assumptions.

Like Agassiz, he asserted that Darwin's ideas were a fad which would soon pass away. Like Agassiz, he was continuing a scientific debate which stretched back to the mid-1850's, in his case with Huxley. Like Agassiz, he put up nonscientific men to argue his case in public. The result was the famous meeting of the British Association at Oxford. Both Hooker and Darwin wrote Gray of the clash with Bishop Samuel Wilberforce and of Owen's part in it. Incidentally, the fact that the speaker who touched off the fireworks at Oxford was an American held no interest for Gray, who had had his bout with John W. Draper a decade and a half before. To Hooker, Gray wrote, "I should have liked to bandy words a little with the bishop of Oxford." [24]

The encounter at Oxford between the bishop and the scientists transformed, by its dramatic circumstances, the whole nature of the conflict over Darwin's theory. Before, it had been, despite a growing concern among all sorts of laymen, essentially the old battle within science between idealism and empiricism. Darwin and his band faced Owen and Agassiz, but all were equally within the realm of science. The Bishop of Oxford accomplished what Bowen and Lowell, thanks in part to Gray, had failed to do in America. He made the conflict appear in the eyes of the world as one between religion and science, between a black-hooded and obscurantist priesthood of theologians on the one side and the scientific sons of light on the other.[25]

The metaphor of the battle now shifted from the phase in which Gray had entered with great zest as a combatant to the phase in which he stood squarely in the middle. In a warfare between science and theology the side which adopted Gray's view would automatically call off hostilities completely. Or would he be forced by the conflict to renounce either his religion or his science? As the scientists lost control of the controversy and passionate invective replaced the urbanity of the debates within science, the necessity of choosing sides seemed more eminent. Some members of the Darwin circle, especially Huxley, were content to accept the fight with theology. Others, notably Lyell, were unwilling to do so. The decision of strategy rested finally with Darwin himself, a sincere man as yet undecided as to how to answer the Bishop of Oxford. This was just the time that Gray's most comprehensive and most widely distributed effort to formulate his views on Darwin began to appear in the *Atlantic Monthly*.[26]

His article, which began in the July number of that eminently literary magazine and continued in the August and October numbers, ran over the whole ground of the argument. He drew on all of his previous formulation, going back even to the problem of the persistence of Tertiary species into the present, an echo of the argument over the Japan essay. He summarized his Scientific Club paper on the aphorism *natura non agit saltatem*. In the third part he gave explicit attention to Lowell and Bowen under the title of "Darwin and his Reviewers." Fortunately Agassiz's excerpt from his book had finally appeared in the *American Journal of Science,* so that he could get full treatment also.

Gray was insistent that his purpose in this "light-toned" article was, while directed against the critics of Darwin, to "show the futility and unreasonableness" of their attacks and "to remand the discussion to its proper field." It was directed to a general audience and was, Gray thought, what the public needed. "The argument is mainly *ad hominem,* and must I think shut up *our* reviewers' mouths." Much as he would like to take on Richard Owen, he could only give a "few hits" in passing. "On the principle and duty of washing dirty linen at home, I felt bound to attend to Lowell, Bowen, and Agassiz, my neighbors, & to do it particularly—not only to wash them but to *iron* them out as well as I could in a good natured way,—though they really deserved a savage treatment." Gray had to keep it light, for he knew he was lucky to get into the *Atlantic* at all. The editor at that time was James Russell Lowell, who was, as Gray put it, "a near friend of Agassiz, and a nephew of J. A. Lowell." [27]

Gray set his whimsical, easy tone in the very first sentences. "Novelties are enticing to most people: to us they are simply annoying. We cling to a long-accepted theory, just as we cling to an old suit of clothes. A new theory, like a new pair of breeches, ('The Atlantic' still affects the older type of nether garment,) is sure to have hard-fitting places. . . ." This elaborate pose of reluctance gave Gray a chance to show some of his real doubts. For instance, he carefully left a loophole for the special creation of man, relying on Wyman for evidence that intermediate links "between the *Bimana* and the *Quadrumana* are lacking altogether." Even here, however, he could not resist a sly slap at the social theories of Agassiz, pointing out that on Darwinian principle the "very first step backwards makes the Negro and the Hottentot our blood-relations;—not that reason or Scripture objects to that though pride may." Despite his continued protestations of judicial impartiality, the whole weight of his scientific argument was in favor of Darwin and the whole weight of the attack, both scientific and philosophical, was directed against his critics.

Indeed, buried in the cautious phraseology was a definite commitment to Darwin's evolution. It did not go all the way on natural selection and certainly not to any new cosmic philosophy. "But we may confess to an impression, thus far, that the doctrine of permanent and complete immutability of species has not been established, and may fairly be doubted. We believe that species vary, and that 'Natural Selection' works. . . ." The qualifications then tacked on did not lessen the commitment. "We are disposed to rank the derivative hypothesis in its fullness with the nebular hypothesis, and to regard both as allowable, as not unlikely to prove tenable in spite of some strong objections, but as not therefore demonstrably true." This would hardly satisfy a zealot. It seemed weak in the face of the metaphor of church, which demanded every man commit himself to an all-inclusive faith. To a believer in the neutrality of science, to one who appreciated the long history of scientific discovery and the relativity of scientific truth, this was both as far as Gray could go and as far as he needed to go.

In the argument for design in nature which he advanced here, not, be it remembered, against Darwin but against Agassiz and Company, Gray made one significant addition. He finally came up to the problem of how to introduce design into the Darwinian system. Variation was the point he seized upon. At least "while the physical cause of variation is utterly unknown and mysterious, we should advise Mr. Darwin to assume, in the philosophy of his hypothesis, that variation has been led along certain beneficial lines." Then followed a figure of speech which would reappear regularly in the debates of the next few years. "Streams flowing over a sloping plain (here the counterpart of natural selection) may have worn their actual channels as they flowed; yet their particular courses may have been assigned; and where we see them forming definite and useful lines of irrigation, after a manner unaccountable on the laws of gravitation and dynamics, we should believe that the distribution was designed." Here at last is a bridge between the Darwinian system which he so heartily appreciated and the Creator in whom he so devoutly believed. Streams of beneficent variation took the place of the muted vitalism which characterized his older thought as the cement by which he held his religion and his empirical science together.

Yet the figure of the stream of beneficent variation had in it not only the weakness of analogy. It also led backward to the difficulties, usually avoided by Gray, in which the philosophy of Paley was enmeshed. How could one infer a beneficent Creator purely from the mechanics of nature? How could one avoid an iron determinism through all nature regulating every detail? Gray himself when he shook himself free of the figure insisted only that "the derivation hypothesis leaves the argument for Design, and therefore for a Designer, as valid as it ever was. . . ." But could his figure of the beneficial stream impress the "English mind," which he saw as "prone to positivism and kindred forms of materialistic philosophy," a school for which he had no "predilection . . . but the contrary"? He was confident that his reasoning would not "play into the hands of positivists and materialists generally." Around the strength of this position on design lay the destiny of Gray's influence on the philosophical synthesis of the post-Darwinian world.

The style of the *Atlantic* article immediately attracted attention. Since it appeared anonymously, people in England immediately saw in it the hand of both Washington Irving and Oliver Wendell Holmes. A Cambridge worthy was so sure that the editor had written parts of it that he congratulated James Russell Lowell "and said that he could readily pick out the Lowellian passages. Whereupon Lowell told him that he read it only in proof and neither altered nor added a letter." [28]

Darwin outdid himself in praise, going behind the words to the man. "My conclusion is that you have made a mistake in being a Botanist, you ought to have been a Lawyer, & you would have rolled in wealth by perverting the truth, instead of studying the living truth of this world." As soon as he had seen the second installment of the article he went even further. "I am sure you are a poet. No by Jove I will tell you what you are, a hybrid, a complex cross of Lawyer, Poet, Naturalist, & Theologian! Was there ever such a monster seen before?"

Darwin, as he had done with the rebuttal in the American Academy, sent part of the *Atlantic* article to a British natural history journal for republication, offering to pay for it.[29] But he did not consider the editor very courteous, and the desire to have Gray's work widely distributed in England still haunted him. In the wake of the British Association meeting and the outbreak of open war between science and theology, however, Darwin saw even more than scientific understanding in Gray's article. It was a weapon to use against the enemy, an answer to the Bishop of Oxford which would disarm him. "I have been thinking of a larger scheme, viz. to get the whole . . . published with (as you permit) your name." Since a book and two pamphlets had just appeared against the *Origin,* "a pamphlet on our side (to a certain extent) might sell."

Darwin insisted that it was "very adviseable to have some remark or title, showing its bearing on Natural Theology or Design." [30] Hence his motive was perfectly clear—to capitalize on the calming effect Gray's design argument would have at least on the more amenable religious objectors.

It is particularly important that during the early fall of 1860 the only major member of the Darwin circle available to advise the suddenly famous naturalist was Sir Charles Lyell. Hooker had gone off to Lebanon, while Huxley was distracted by the death of his little son. Lyell of all the original Darwinians had reacted most nearly as had Gray. He had admitted much, but had recoiled at the tag of "convert." His doubts were heightened as he became preoccupied with the position of man in the evolutionary sequence. Hence, it is not surprising that he encouraged Darwin's strategy in this enterprise. Darwin reported that "Lyell has highest opinion of 'talent & science' in the review" and thought "it would be well worth while if a little Book could be got up by Asa Gray for the theological part is so admirable & would have many readers." Darwin and Lyell knew what to do with Gray's article. "Bishop of London was asking Lyell what he thought of the Review in Quarterly, & Lyell's answer was read 'Asa Gray in Atlantic.' " [31]

Although Lyell and Darwin were unable to arrange a reprint with John Murray in London, they did not let the project die. Gray was able to get Ticknor and Fields, the publisher of the *Atlantic,* to make up the pamphlet to be distributed by Trübner and Company in London. Unlike the original, the work now bore Gray's name. Ticknor and Fields, however, perhaps because James T. Fields was an ardent Agassizian, never sold any of the reprints in America. Fields about this time succeeded Lowell as editor of the *Atlantic,* and Gray's brief appearance as an author there was not repeated, while Agassiz became a regular contributor.[32] Thus, although actually printed in America, the pamphlet was in effect a British publication and received the impetus of Darwin's promotional efforts there. For many years to come the name of Asa Gray was more closely linked with his own views on Darwin in England than it was in the United States, where only a few people in Cambridge could identify him as the author of his series of anonymous papers.

The pamphlet bore the title, "A Free Examination of Darwin's Treatise on the Origin of Species, and of its American Reviewers." Across the top of the title page appeared in Gothic letters the motto, "Natural Selection not inconsistent with Natural Theology." Darwin took pains to send it, not only to the major British journals for review, but also to a long list of individuals, including, in addition to scientists, the "B. of Oxford," Charles Kingsley, and Robert Chambers, who would one day be revealed as the author of the *Vestiges.*

The response to Gray's pamphlet and the dent it made in the hostility of some waverers was indeed gratifying. W. H. Harvey wrote " 'Almost thou persuadest me to be a Darwinite'—not quite, but thou persuadest me to be a Grayite." J. H. Balfour of the University of Edinburgh took comfort in the fact that Gray only gave "a qualified adhesion to Darwin's views." Even some German scientists gave the pamphlet a careful reading.[33]

In religious circles Gray's pamphlet also made an impression. Charles Kingsley wrote to his fellow Christian socialist Frederic D. Maurice that "by far the best forward step in Natural Theology has been made by an American Dr. Asa Gray, who has said better than I can all that I want to say." Gray's old friend R. W. Church, already beginning to rise toward a position of influence in the Church of England, was at least willing to say that "you seem to have cleared the way for a fair discussion 'of the *Origin*' on its merits and evidence." Church, however, put his finger on a change of mood which was descending over the toiling campaigners fighting around the *Origin*. "The book, I have no doubt, would be the subject of a great row, if there were not a much greater row going on about *Essays and Reviews*." [34] Attention was already wandering; whole battalions were marching off for all sorts of irrelevant forays; some, as in this reference to higher criticism of the Bible, were hastening to fight the same war on another front entirely. By the spring of 1861 the metaphors of battle were having a hard time keeping up appearances. That plodding, moral naturalists and plodding, moral parsons were knights in shining armor suddenly began to appear slightly ridiculous. In an atmosphere of such rapidly dissipating tension, Gray's pamphlet had only a mildly soothing effect.

If Gray's argument for the compatibility of the Darwinian hypothesis with theism failed to win over the Bishop of Oxford, it failed equally to win over an even more important leader, Darwin himself. Even while heaping praise on Gray and distributing the pamphlet to all his friends, Darwin had gradually hardened his opinion against the design argument. At first he had protested that he was himself bewildered. "I had no intention to write atheistically. But I own I cannot see, as plainly as others do, & as I sh^d wish to do, evidence of design & beneficence on all sides of us. There seems to me too much misery in the world." [35]

Despite his protestations of perplexity, however, Darwin kept coming back to the problem of design in his letters to Gray and obviously put much effort into formulating his views. In the fall of 1860, just when the publication of the pamphlet was being arranged, Darwin in effect announced his decision. "I grieve to say

I cannot honestly go as far as you do about design." Concentrating on Gray's metaphor of the stream of beneficial variations, he said, "I cannot believe this; & I think you would have to believe, that the tail of the Fan-tail was led to vary in the number & direction of its feathers in order to gratify caprice of a few men. Yet if the fan-tail had been a wild bird & had used its abnormal tail for some special end, as to sail before the wind . . . everyone would have said what beautiful & designed adaptation." [36] While an amiable discussion continued between the two friends, it held from this time on a fundamental disagreement.

With Darwin's decision against the design argument, Gray lost his place as a shaper of strategy in the inner circle of friends. The assumption quickly grew up that Darwin had annihilated Paley's argument, and Huxley moved quickly forward to become the interpreter of Darwinism before the public. Gray's solution would obviously have been quite different. Later students have often puzzled over Lyell's hesitation and near estrangement from Hooker, Huxley, and Darwin without noting that Lyell alone of the inner circle in England adhered to Gray's position. Indeed, on the last pages of the *Antiquity of Man,*[37] he specifically adopted Gray's view of design in nature. Other factors, of course, entered into Lyell's later opinions on the *Origin,* but he and Gray stepped out of the inner circle together on the same issue. This time of decision, too, marked the climax of Huxley's ascendancy. His agnosticism, not Gray's argument from design, became the official policy of the Darwinian movement.

On his side Gray also made a momentous decision which set his course away from Huxley and the Darwin inner circle. The naturalists most concerned with the transmutation of species had suddenly discovered themselves immersed in the whole range of the problems of philosophy and theology. Gray and the rest had during the hectic year of 1860 attempted to cope with all these themselves. However, by fall definite signs of philosophical exhaustion were setting in among the original Darwinians. Joseph Hooker fled on a vacation to Lebanon and returned fully resolved to have nothing more to do with philosophizing about evolution. "The whole subject had gone as much out of my head & heart as was possible under any circumstances, & I positively looked at the 'Origin' with aversion on my return." [38]

With the old leaders panting for breath, newer and eager minds were anxious to take up the question, and they had ready-made a whole philosophy which would explain the universe in evolutionary terms. Herbert Spencer had been writing about evolution since 1851, had coined the phrase "survival of the fittest" which Darwin later adopted, and was well on the way to creating a complete philosophical system. His works had gone slowly before the publication of the *Origin,* but in 1860 definite signs appeared that Spencer's time had come. He provided the philosophy which would serve Darwinism.

Spencer had no more ardent admirer than Edward Livingston Youmans, the almost blind lecturer and chemist who was by his advice making the Appletons the publishers of evolution in America. By March 1860, Spencer was in touch with Youmans about an American edition of his works, suggesting a circular with the endorsement of Americans of note. "My friend Prof. Huxley has suggested Prof. Dana, Prof. Asa Gray, Prof. Leidy, and Dr. Draper as likely men. . . ." [39]

In December 1860, Gray lightly mentioned to Hooker his judgment on Spencer. "You think so much—you & Darwin—of Herbert Spencer that I subscribed for the new issue of his writings—and have just glanced at his 'principles.' Can't say I like his *principles.* and am amused to see him run 'the philosophy of the conditional' into *positivism.* . . ."

This dislike of Spencer, whose all-encompassing philosophy was open to many of the objections Gray had found to Agassiz's, deepened as time went on. It was one of his great bonds with Chauncey Wright, who spent much of his energy combatting Spencer. The neutrality of science meant that a hypothesis such as Darwin's served no better for Spencer than for any other all-inclusive philosophical or theological system. When Wright died, Gray said that "he points out clearly the essential difference between Darwinism, which is scientific, and Spencerism, which is 'philosophical.' Save the mark!" [40]

By turning his back on the alliance of Spencer and Darwin, Gray was refusing to give his assent to all extensions of evolutionary theory into the sphere of social and political development. Social Darwinism was to have a great vogue in America, but without Spencer it would have been a very different movement. Gray in disassociating himself from the philosophy of Spencer also cut himself off from social Darwinism. Instead of becoming the tame scientist in the service of propagandists such as Youmans and John Fiske he held himself politely aloof from them. That this decision hurt his prestige both in the Darwin inner circle and before the American people there is no doubt. But as social Darwinism moved farther from science and became a monstrous worship of blind competition and brute force, Gray and Chauncey Wright have gained a certain posthumous grandeur in resisting the rush to Spencer.

The year 1860, so unlike any other in the history of biology, ended with the rapid dissipation of the crisis atmosphere. Darwin had stirred up the mind with a vengeance, and the habits and definitions of a twelvemonth back already seemed ancient and outlandish. Agassiz's *Contributions* and Humboldt's *Kosmos* stood as mute and silent as Inca temples. Not least among the casualties had been, of course, the Darwin inner circle itself. The tight little band of Lyell, Hooker, and Gray, who had shared the secret and contributed their talent was torn asunder by the very fact of publication. They were further pushed from one another and from Darwin by the intrusion of new men and new issues. Gray split off on the issue of design and the philosophy of Spencer especially. And new giants were arising, men like Huxley who loved and used the public favor.

Yet even in the upheaval of 1860 the band of Darwin, Lyell, Hooker, and Gray showed one thing in common which would prove lasting. They were, above everything, devoted to science and to research. None of them succumbed to the spell of the metaphor of church to make the *Origin* a new bible. Plenty of lesser men would do that. But not these original Darwinians, especially not Darwin himself. Already in 1860, new problems of research were intruding on philosophy and publication arrangements in the correspondence between Darwin and Gray. Even as they disagreed on design, they formed a new and even more intimate friendship based on the search for new truth among plants. The *Origin* was the beginning of research on unimagined new paths, not the end of the quest. One of the most powerful corrosives of the metaphors of battle and the church, of the tense atmosphere of 1860, was science itself.

The program of research which Darwin took up in 1860 dealt almost entirely with plants. This choice was partly dictated by his ill-health and the availability of his garden. He designed his research, however, not as an amiable diversion but with a serious purpose. It was, as Gray called it, a "flank movement" on the enemy. The gradation of structure from plants which had both male and female organs in one flower to those which had separate male and female flowers was not an abrupt difference, but was rather represented by many intermediate forms. Hence the study of this polymorphism in plants was connected with Darwin's favorite aphorism that nature never makes jumps. One of the results of this gradation of structure was that even plants with hermaphrodite flowers proved to have elaborate structures to assure cross-pollination and to avoid perpetual self-fertilization, another of Darwin's favorite ideas which was essential to his over-all system.

Plants also provided a testing ground for adaptation. What could appear more useless to its possessor than the showy flower of the orchid? Yet when Darwin patiently investigated the relation of flower structure to the insects which visited them and incidentally effected the interchange of pollen, he showed that the delicate flower parts each served a definite purpose.[41]

Insectivorous plants opened up all the evolutionary problems revolving around sensitivity and the continuity of the plant and animal kingdoms. These strange fly-traps and catchers of small insects have extremely complicated mechanisms by which they attract and ensnare their prey, just the kind of beautiful adaptation which Darwin loved to prove with simple experiments.[42]

In every one of these endeavors Gray had as much to offer as any of Darwin's English friends, and in the total range of subjects he was probably better informed and more adaptable even than Hooker. Thus his relation with Darwin became almost uniquely intimate. They both lived with gardens at their doors, tried the same experiments and carefully compared their results both in publications and in lengthy letters.

At times Gray even briefly took the lead. Back in 1858 he had worked into his distractedly busy life some observations on the coiling of tendrils. Darwin used Gray's short paper as the starting point of a whole line of research on the movements in plants [43] which extended the idea of reaction and sensitivity far beyond the relatively rare insectivorous plants.

Even while this new botanical intimacy with Darwin flowered, Gray did not entirely lose sight of its possible bearing on the problem of design. Indeed, when the book on orchids appeared, Gray, admittedly with a vein of "petite malice," congratulated Darwin "for having brought back teleological considerations into botany." [44] What Gray meant was that Darwin's approach in searching for the use or survival value of each structure in plants had reintroduced a kind of naturalistic "purpose" which was unknown in the idealistic concept of Agassiz. To extend this kind of purpose to cover the operation of a final cause in nature was precisely the thing which Darwin would not do and which Gray hoped to imply from the delicate adaptations in orchids. Clearly the two friends had retired to positions so far apart on the question of design that they could only snipe at one another occasionally, a pastime which did not in the least disturb their collaboration on botany.

An even more insistent line of research was calling Gray away from the Darwinian melee. He had after all been a taxonomist all his life, and the great bundles of unexamined plants dating all the way back to the Wilkes expedition lay on his shelves to haunt him. Even while writing the *Atlantic* article Gray had complained, "I really have no time for it, and after commencement I must have done with it, and set about my proper work." In England, too, taxonomy was stirring. Hooker, besides telling Gray he "must do up the American Flora somehow," was embarking on his great work of re-examining all the generic boundaries among the higher plants. In this project he was joined by Bentham, who despite his early background in philosophy had let the whole furore of 1860 pass him by. "I am now too old," he wrote Gray, "and too lazy to enter into controversies so that I shall confine myself to the old systematic routine and go on describing species as if they were really distinct and grouping them into genera etc. for convenience of study." [45] Whatever the *Origin* had done to botanists' ideas about species, it had not relieved them of the necessity of the patient and unending exploration of the plants of the world. In turning from speculations on the derivative hypothesis back to his work table Gray was only saying that he, like Darwin and Hooker, was first of all a scientist who had the unknown before him.

The philosophical divergences and the revival of research had shattered the metaphor of the battle and removed Gray from the inner circle of Darwinism, the movement as distinguished from Darwin the man. Even had these forces not been effective, Gray faced an even more profound distraction in 1861. He alone of the original inner circle was an American. Although he had on occasion wished he could move to Kew and join physically the international group of which he rightly fancied himself a part, he now suddenly realized that he was and all along had been deeply committed to his nationality. He had to share great travail with the rest of these countrymen. The battle over Darwinism, a highly mannered and metaphysical affair, had been only a "storm in a Victorian teacup." [46] Americans now faced real conflict, real bloodshed, real warfare. Asa Gray, although now over fifty and beyond military age, became immediately and deeply involved.

XVI

YEARS OF WAR

THE political crisis which broke with the election of Abraham Lincoln in November 1860 brought out something new in Asa Gray. He was, of course, a Republican, as were most of the members of the Cambridge Scientific Club and the Loring clan. He had long upheld scientifically the unity of the human race, and his religious orthodoxy made the moral aspects of the slavery problem the more impressive to him. Yet when the specter of disunion rose over the land Gray discovered within himself an intense, passionate patriotism with which he did not hesitate to startle his friends over the world.

In October 1860, Gray was confidently expecting a Republican victory. "A worse administration than the present is impossible." He was "tired of living under threats, and such foolish ones—for secession would bring utter ruin on the South." A year of Lincoln's administration "will show the whole South that they have nothing to fear for their rights." By January 1861, with secession already begun, Gray took a darker, more strident view. "About the country, I have no heart to write—all looks so bad. Yet it must settle some way." The border states "ought to pronounce strongly against *secession* . . . It is wicked to calculate the value of the Union." [1]

By February, in the last fatuous days of James Buchanan's presidency, Gray was adopting the nomenclature which would serve him in political analyses for the next four years. "All reason and right and patience appears to be on one side: all madness, audacity, and folly on the other. The feeble administration was helpless in the hands of hoodwinking traitors & thieves."

At just this juncture Gray suffered in the garden another of his more serious physical accidents, in which his left thumb was cut off just at the base of the nail. To him it meant "My fighting days are over." [2] Nevertheless, after the shots at Fort Sumter had opened hostilities and the calls for volunteers began to stir Massachusetts, Gray vented his emotions by behaving as martially as possible. He joined a company whose duty was to guard the State Arsenal in Cambridge and drilled with them regularly. On scraping up $550 for government bonds, he expressed amazement "that people do not come forward with their money—those that can't go to fight. I wish I could do both." He favored taxes, "five per cent direct on property and income, and heavy indirect besides. What is property! I would fight till every cent is gone, and would offer my own life freely; so I do not value the lives or property of rebels above my own." He regretted having no children only in "that I have no son to send to the war." [3] The sight of Mrs. Gray's brothers and nephews in uniform must have stirred him deeply.

Coupled with his profession of military ardor, Gray expressed the more peaceful aspects of his patriotism with a new sensitivity. When he and Mrs. Gray went to Sauquoit in the summer of 1863 to visit his mother, he was conscious of a quickening pride in his native land. "We were among the people of a thriving region; a well-to-do set; no poverty near us for miles and miles, i.e., no hardship, except any that a drunken laborer might bring on his family. . . ." He saw as he drove around "a happy and comfortable country, more and more so every year, and perhaps a larger ratio of the population refined to a reasonable degree in feeling and life than I know of in any other part of the world." [4] This was the nation Gray was so ardently determined should be preserved.

His love of the Union shaped his attitude toward both Abraham Lincoln and the institution of slavery. In June 1861, with hostilities barely under way, he wrote to Joseph Hooker, "I am no *abolitionist,* but if the rebels & scoundrels persevere, I go for carrying the war so far as to liberate every negro, tho' what we are to do with this population I see not." Early in 1862, when the President was insisting on a war for the preservation of the Union in the face of violent criticism from anti-slavery groups, Gray wrote, "Lincoln is a trump, a second Washington, steady, conservative, no fanatical abolitionist." He early predicted that the fate of slavery depended on the length and bitterness of the war. After Lincoln's Emancipation Proclamation, Gray wrote to Darwin that "someday when you turn back to some early letter of mine you will see that I was a fairly good prophet; that the South might have delayed the abolition of slavery by giving up early in the conflict, but that every month of continued resistance hastened and insured the downfall of slavery." Thus Gray's affection for Lincoln and appreciation for his position spanned the whole war. "Homely, honest, ungainly Lincoln is the representative man of the country." [5]

The war wrought changes in Gray's life far more important even than his opinions as a reawakened citizen. Without being a total war in the twentieth-century sense, it was nevertheless a shattering experience for American social, political, and economic institutions. In such an upheaval, science, for all its façade of disinterestedness and internationalism, was involved just like any other institution.

The obvious and immediate effect of the outbreak of war was the abrupt sundering of the network of botanical information leading to Gray from the South. Even during 1860 the old exchange of letters had continued almost as if no crisis impended. Gray reviewed appreciatively two major additions to Southern botanical literature in the course of the year.[6] But as secession became the order of the day one after another of the Southern correspondents wrote to explain his position.

Some of the Southern botanists were sympathetic to the Union. A. W. Chapman wrote from Apalachicola, Florida, "We are in the midst of a revolution—entering into a war against the central government and into a war among ourselves—awful!" T. M. Peters wrote apologizing for his neglect of collecting because he had been campaigning for the Union.[7] These voices were soon to be hushed.

Others cordially upheld the Southern point of view. Massachusetts-born Moses Ashley Curtis, one of Gray's most important collaborators, condemned Massachusetts and South Carolina as equally fanatical and wrong-headed. Yet "we believe we are, in the main, right; & we *know* that in some things the North is wrong, has insulted & injured us . . . We all, to a man, look upon the election of Lincoln . . . as an *insult* & an outrage." In answer to Gray's question whether there were no Union men in South Carolina, Henry W. Ravenel wrote back, "I answer none." In his journal Ravenel recorded that although his correspondence with Gray had always been scientific "the state of the times warranted an allusion to politics." Just before the firing on Fort Sumter he finally threw down his challenge to Gray. "Reconstruction & re-union now are out of the question. *It is too late!* Coercion—subjugation! These have become trite phrases, but only fools who do not weigh their import can seriously urge them. Five millions of freemen fighting for their homes & their liberties can never be subjugated." [8] On this note of confidence the scientists of the South broke their ties with the remainder of the earth. From Gray's point of view, a whole botanical province was lost.

Even with old friends outside the Confederacy, Gray felt the strain on well-established lines of communication and friendship. Joseph Henry, for instance, believed that the Union could not be permanent and that peaceful separation was better than bloodshed. Gray's collector Charles Wright, who had imbibed Southern principles while in Texas, was fortunately in Cuba at the outbreak of the war. Gray kept him there out of harm's way and his own range of debate until 1864.

George Engelmann, a Democrat in the border slave state of Missouri, suffered all the anguish of genuinely divided loyalties. Gray wrote him glibly, "I believe in capital punishments. The life of a rebel is duly and justly forfeit." Engelmann's views, in contrast, clearly revealed the tension of the times. Gray's letters "I must confess, surprized, I might almost say, shocked me. I did not think you so bloody minded, harsh and onesided, but I suppose, hearing and seeing only one phase, one aspect, and being far removed . . . from the scenes and sorrows of fraternal war, you (I mean all your people) can well afford to indulge in this way of thinking." [9] Although Engelmann and Gray never completely broke their scientific ties and only occasionally lost a tone of good humor in their letters, the old bonds were weakened.

The smoothly operating network of communication which had served American science well during the 1850's was fundamentally strained by the war. The *American Journal of Science* found itself for the first time in ten years without a backlog of articles. Nobody felt like working. A few days after Fort Sumter, Gray wrote to Alphonse De Candolle, "we are now opening a war, upon the determination of which our very existence depends, and upon which we are to concentrate all our strength and soul, so I have no time nor heart to write of botany just now." [10] In the eighteenth century, wars had only slightly affected science. In the twentieth century they completely engulfed it. The Civil War stood midway between. It hurt science by breaking its communications but did not draft it to any great extent into the service of the military.

Because Gray was a patriot, and because he was one of the few Americans with extensive connections in England, he considered it his duty to inject the Civil War into his international correspondence. He must, he felt, convince his British friends that the Union was something real and necessary, that it was not only worth saving but that it had to be saved. In this enterprise he found a partner in Charles G. Loring, who not only wrote many letters but also engaged in trans-Atlantic debate in print.[11]

Through the various crises in Anglo-American relations during the war Gray valiantly upheld the Northern point of view. The first crisis was the *Trent* affair, in which Gray's old acquaintance Captain Wilkes removed from a British ship two Confederate agents, the "ineffable scamps" Mason and Slidell. Both the Bostonians and the British became very much excited. By the time of the crisis over the *Alabama* and the other Confederate ships built on British ways, Gray was mainly impressed by the "smallness of mind and largeness of gullibility of the British people." Nevertheless he did not allow himself to "suppose you will fight because you dislike us; and so conversely." [12]

It was this undercurrent of hostility, this heightened consciousness of national difference that affected Gray's relations with his English friends. Since they were all of the upper classes or closely allied to them, all the pressure on them at home tended to make them sympathize with the South or at best to consider the American Union an unimportant affair whose disruption was probably a blessing. Old Francis Boott in London, tied by family interests to the Massachusetts textile lords, pleaded for understanding and deplored Gray's animosity. W. H. Harvey expressed more of the same feeling. R. W. Church was sufficiently polite to receive lengthy dissertations from his American friend.[13]

With Joseph Hooker, the adjustment was more difficult. Since he believed that Darwin's theory of natural selection had provided a scientific underpinning for the British aristocracy, he had little use for American ideas or American problems. Early in the war he wrote to Gray "I think the less said the sooner mended about the war & your *slightly animated!* description of John Bulls opinions & notions. A nation at war is no longer in its senses; however just the cause." With this warning of fundamental difference, both attempted to stick to botany and leave politics alone, but neither succeeded. Hooker kept alluding to his sympathy for both sides and professing to be a Quaker. Gray, while elaborately expressing sympathy for this point of view, kept advocating the Union cause and praising war. Before "the war I was losing my hopes for my country, and indeed thinking that I might be glad to leave it. *The first gun raised my spirits;* and *they have never flagged since.* The war has made me intensely, even proudly *national* as well as hopeful. Already it has done us vast good—in spite of the evil—and I look for greater benefits." [14] They were indeed civilized gentlemen who could continue their scientific collaboration in the face of political differences. But an element of strain was there.

The man who drew out Gray's most intense efforts to present the American point of view was that great master at drawing people out, Charles Darwin. He reflected perfectly the upperclass British combination of hostility to the North and abhorrence of slavery. He made intense efforts to understand the war and its issues. Although they chaffed about their opinions "being entirely dependent on longitude," their animated exchanges had an overtone of high seriousness. Gray for the only time in his life applied a biological concept to men and nations. "If it is the old question of struggle for life, good feeling has not much to do with it: the weak must go to the wall . . . 'Blessed are the strong, for they shall inherit the earth.' " [15]

In contrast to the coolness which arose with Hooker, however,

Gray's lengthy letters to Darwin only lifted their relationship to a new intimacy. Gray could say, even in the earlier stages when war with England was still a possibility which weighed upon them, "Yes, I will promise not to hate you;—quite the contrary." Darwin on his side wrote "Here is an insult! I shall always think of you as an Englishman." To this Gray replied, "Your thinking of me 'as an Englishman' would once have been a compliment, and is what from my well-known feelings and expressions I have passed for among my friends here." By the end of the war, Gray, having largely given up his crusade among the English upper class, could still refer to Darwin as "the only Britisher I ever write to on this subject, and, in fact, for whose opinions about our country I care at all. So I hasten to rejoice with you over the beginning of the end." [16]

Gray's renewed patriotism was a part of his duty as a citizen rather than as a scientist. Hence his attitude toward a great event in the organization of American science which took place during the war—the founding of the National Academy of Sciences—was shaped by other factors than patriotism. Indeed, science was only hesitantly used as a support for military technology during the war and botany scarcely at all. A National Academy of Sciences was created by Congress on March 3, 1863, and Gray was named in the act as one of fifty incorporators. The expressed purpose of the new organization was "whenever called upon by any Department of the Government," to "investigate, examine, experiment, and report upon any subject of science or art. . . ." The real springs of Gray's actions with regard to the National Academy are found in a source which had already influenced his course for years. For in the midst of the little band who engineered the academy into existence was the familiar figure of Louis Agassiz. [17]

On the one hand the war had upset the irrepressible zoologist's plans. He could not understand why his students went off to join the army when they might have stayed on to share in the great work of building up the Museum of Comparative Zoology. His belief in the plurality of races led him to discourage any idea of the amalgamation of the Negro population with the white. [18] On the other hand, Agassiz's matchless social position in Boston and in American science was undiminished, and a combination of the war and the chances of Harvard University politics gave him unparalleled opportunities in the years between 1861 and 1863.

He was of course continuing his fight against Darwinism, speaking before the Lowell Institute and publishing freely in the *Atlantic Monthly*. His appeal was less to scientists than to the broad American populace, and the man once distrusted by the clergy now became increasingly popular with those same revered gentlemen who now needed scientific ammunition against Darwin.[19] The fact that he was no longer taken seriously by many naturalists both in America and abroad had not yet appreciably affected his reputation.

When C. C. Felton, who had been president of Harvard for only two years, died early in 1862, Agassiz had an excellent opportunity to influence Harvard policy. He and Benjamin Peirce wanted not only a man who would build up the sciences, but also one who would build up their kind of science. John A. Lowell as the leading member of the Corporation was their natural ally, and they succeeded in putting in their man. The Reverend Thomas Hill was a Unitarian, a Republican, an anti-Darwinian, and an amateur naturalist and mathematician whose ideas have a remarkable resemblance to those of Agassiz and Peirce.[20]

Immediately after Hill was confirmed as president in October 1862, a general re-examination of university policy began. To some it appeared to be an attempt by the scientists to win a larger place in the curriculum at the expense of the classics. However, the major agitation took place between two groups of scientists and took place not in the college but in the Lawrence Scientific School, where the classics did not exist anyway. Agassiz, aided by Peirce, was of course dominant, and he stood for the system by which the students became the personal protégés and almost personal property of the regnant professor. Gray and Wyman had in general carried the load of natural history instruction in the college and had been members of the staff of the scientific school only in name. Now Gray became involved in the school's reorganization.

In this effort he found an ally in Charles William Eliot, the young assistant professor of chemistry who had shifted to the scientific school from the college when Eben Horsford had resigned the Rumford professorship in order to forward some of his schemes for using chemistry in the war. Eliot had definite ideas about the reformation of the school and was by no means a tool of Agassiz or Peirce or even of his own former sponsor, the chemist Josiah Parsons Cooke, who taught the college classes in the subject.

In October 1862 the crisis began with deceptive harmony when Agassiz presented a preliminary report for a "general course" and Gray moved that it be accepted. On November 4, Eliot was delighted to draw up a detailed plan for a two-year general course to be followed by two years in a special department. Eliot's plan called for "a Course of Instruction extending through two years, and comprising a regular system of required recitations and exercises in Mathematics, Chemistry, Physics, Physiology, Botany, Zoology, Physical Geography, Rhetoric, French, German, & Drawing, preparatory to the prescribed studies of the special Departments. . . ." When Eliot presented his report a "discussion ensued between Profs. Agassiz and Peirce urging objections to the plan proposed, and Profs. Gray, Wyman, Lovering, and Eliot supporting the new scheme, but without passing any votes the Faculty adjourned." At the next meeting, Gray came forward with a series of proposals. But Agassiz was absent and Peirce objected, so the faculty after long discussion submitted the various plans to President Hill who "said that he should consult Prof. Agassiz and consider any plan he might suggest." Thus, even though at one point a majority of the faculty had supported Eliot's plan, Agassiz emerged in complete control with the help of a compliant president. His proposal amounted to a series of university lectures, which when later carried out proved a dismal failure as a foundation for a graduate school and which were certainly no solution to the ills of the Lawrence Scientific School.[21]

What Gray thought of Agassiz's policy and the Lawrence Scientific School is clearly reflected in a letter of advice he wrote to Engelmann strongly suggesting that his friend send his son to Harvard College rather than to the Lawrence Scientific School. "We have really—thanks to Agassiz and Peirce thwarting all good plans—no *Scientific School* at Cambridge. *They have one at Yale,* but here are separate schools: in one they teach Chemistry thoroughly, in one Engineering,—in another there are *lectures* on Zoology and

Geology—of no use to a young beginner, and very little to an older hand." This, then, was his opinion of Agassiz with his overpowering reputation as a teacher. "But no cooperation—no combination for general and elementary Nat. History instruction; though there is a fine field open here, and students would pour in, if there was any system." [22]

With the Lawrence Scientific School and the president of Harvard University well under control, Agassiz and Peirce looked for an even larger sphere of influence. One of the epoch-making effects of secession was the legislation, possible only when the Southerners had left Congress, providing grants of federal land in support of agricultural and mechanical colleges. The Morrill Act included shares for the old states as well as the new. In the last days of 1862 those learned men of Massachusetts who fancied they had political influence were swarming around Governor John A. Andrew to get the proceeds of the sale of 360,000 acres of land for their institutions. Agassiz and Peirce hoped to get the mechanical part of the grant for the Lawrence Scientific School. Their main stumbling block was the newly incorporated Massachusetts Institute of Technology, the brainchild so long nutured by William Barton Rogers.[23] Whether coincidence or not, this incursion of Agassiz into the arena of state politics tended to throw the two major defenders of Darwin in the Boston area doubly in alliance. Rogers and Gray had fought Agassiz in the debates of 1860, and now, without any particular intimacy having grown up between them, they again joined against him.

The Agassiz-Peirce combine did not stop at the boundaries of the state of Massachusetts. They were but one pole of that informal society, the Scientific Lazzaroni, which gathered the brightest and the gayest of America's scientists, definitely excluding Asa Gray, into a net of friendship. The other pole of strength was in Washington, where the chief of the Lazzaroni and of the United States Coast Survey, Alexander Dallas Bache, was a key figure in the scientific enterprises within the government. Throughout the 1850's the Lazzaroni had had two major aims. One was the creation of a national university which would be truly national and truly a university with adequate scope given to science. Their other aim was a national scientific organization close to the government which would serve as an adviser on scientific matters.

Since the first of the Lazzaroni aims, a national university, had been foiled in Albany and New York City successively, they now conceived the possibility of accomplishing their aims in Massachusetts. Harvard and the Lawrence Scientific School seemed a likely nucleus, especially with the friendly aid of President Hill. When the schemers thought of the land grant money for Massachusetts and a staff made up of the best scientists in the country, who often turned out to be fellow Lazzaroni, they envisaged the possibility of a true university in Cambridge. Hence their drive for the land-grant money. Hence also their effort to secure the Rumford professorship for one of their own members, Wolcott Gibbs of New York.

The plan for the Gibbs appointment, which was hatched in January 1863, had to surmount the normal ambitions of Charles W. Eliot, the assistant professor of chemistry whose plan for the scientific school had been supported by Gray and attacked by Peirce and Agassiz. So, in addition to Gray and Rogers, the Lazzaroni had a third target in young Eliot. It happened that Gibbs was a chemist of established reputation and European training, while Eliot's scientific education showed all the limitations of his having attended Harvard in the sterile 1850's. He could only offer as qualifications the local reputation he had already developed as an administrator and his thorough knowledge, even at twenty-nine, of the labyrinthine mysteries of the Cambridge and Boston mind. President Hill was thoroughly committed to Gibbs's appointment at least as early as February 1863. During the whole of the spring of 1863, Hill was putting forward one inadequate proposal after another aimed at keeping Eliot on the staff in a subordinate position while denying him the Rumford chair.[24]

In Washington the Lazzaroni were as active as in Cambridge. Agassiz was to have an expense-paid trip to the capital in February to become a Regent of the Smithsonian Institution and also to attend a meeting of the Lazzaroni themselves at Bache's house. Peirce and the astronomer Benjamin Apthorp Gould were already in Washington for the latter meeting, but it was Agassiz who produced the necessary final ingredient for the accomplishment of the Lazzaroni's second aim. To create a national scientific organization an act of Congress was necessary; Agassiz brought in the politician. Senator Henry Wilson of Massachusetts met with Agassiz, Peirce, Bache, and Gould at Bache's house on February 19, 1863, and came away with a list of fifty American scientists whom Congress would incorporate into a self-perpetuating National Academy of Sciences.

Although Bache had consulted his friend and fellow-Lazzaroni Joseph Henry about an academy, the secretary of the Smithsonian had expressed fears both of opposition in Congress and resentment from scientists who might be left out. Accordingly, Bache, Agassiz, and friends had been careful to get the whole scheme arranged without Henry's knowledge. He was amazed when he learned that Senator Wilson had managed the bill through Congress without debate on the last evening of the session, March 3, 1863. The rest of the scientific community, both those on the list and those excluded, were taken completely by surprise.

Gray was now, whether he wished it or not, locked in a full-scale political struggle. The issues blended into one another, and the key people shifted somewhat on different issues, but a line of cleavage had developed in which Gray and Agassiz were constantly divided. The cleavage began in the village of Cambridge and extended through the whole of the American scientific community. It extended from the realm of ideas, where the Darwinian fires smoldered, through high policy of the nation and the state, to the pettiest of back-fence gossip. On one side was the Lazzaroni group, with Agassiz, Peirce, Bache, Gibbs, B. A. Gould, and their allies working for their kind of science in a great Agassizian university at Cambridge and the National Academy in Washington. On the other side were Gray, Henry, Rogers, and Eliot, unorganized as a group with a common platform but in general standing for Darwinian science, reform of the Lawrence Scientific School, an unfettered institute of technology in Boston, and the older scientific societies of the country as against the mysterious upstart, the National Academy. Gray's long association with the American Academy made him especially conscious of the lack of adjustment between the new academy and existing organizations.

John Torrey, who had been staying with Joseph Henry, was the first to give Gray an inkling of the occurrences in Washington. He emphatically reported that the "whole matter was concocted by the party at the Coast Survey," and that Henry "was not one of the managers." That Gray's reaction was being closely watched by the Lazzaroni is clearly shown in Benjamin Peirce's report to Bache, back in Washington. "Gray is already showing the cloven hoof. He is trying to divide Henry from us . . . He asks Agassiz about the list and says that Henry says he was not consulted about the list. Agassiz says that he knows Henry was consulted, and took part in arranging it." A number of letters written by Henry show Agassiz mistaken here. Peirce, who had been in Washington and knew the facts for himself, nevertheless continued, "whatever be the true facts of the case; it is a nice peg to hang up a wet blanket upon. Ha! Ha! Ha! The botanist may find that [it] is possible to dig too deep for successful undermining. His questioning of Agassiz, did not aid him much—I guess. But we must keep our eyes open; and never forget that presbyterianism is a most mysterious form of concatenation." [25]

Gray's own account of his reaction to the National Academy was less Machiavellian than his enemies'. To Henry he wrote that the "list on the whole is good—a few names there which I should never have thought most worthy of it, and some significant and invidious exceptions. If others think as I do, they would make no outcry at being left out. My being in is the only thing that troubles me." He was deeply distressed by what Benjamin Apthorp Gould told him—that the government would pay the traveling expenses of members and print their papers as official documents. He need not have worried, because the National Academy never succeeded in getting money out of Congress for these things, but he nevertheless here showed a definite sensitiveness to government domination. His conclusion was "to do nothing but leave it for wiser heads to shape things as well as they can." This is precisely what Gray did, passing up the New York organization meeting while William Barton Rogers went down to fight the Lazzaroni almost alone.

A clear-cut test between the two factions arose in Boston, however, the first in which Gray's course could be judged by a segment of the community. Old Jacob Bigelow had retired as president of the American Academy of Arts and Sciences, and the choice of his successor gave the membership, so well prepared by the years of debate, a chance to vote on Asa Gray. Not only was he elected, but William Barton Rogers became corresponding secretary and Chauncey Wright recording secretary. "I could have succeeded in avoiding it," wrote Gray, "had it not been that Agassiz and his small clique set to work with all their might against me.—" The result "was a demonstration that made A. open his eyes, and has, I hear, mortified him exceedingly." [26]

The other camp did indeed take Gray's election as a vote against them. Peirce reported to Bache in Washington: "Yesterday met the American Academy, and to show their hatred of the National Academy, all its opponents combined to elect Gray . . . and William B. Rogers. . . ." Gray, according to Peirce, would "now feel untrammeled in giving support to the creatures who have given him possession of the highest object of his ambition. And these fellows are lower and meaner, and more unscrupulous than I suspected." Who were these unseemly characters among Boston's most genteel? "I always," continued Peirce, "had associated Eliot with the position of his family in Boston society and regarded him as a gentleman and a man of honor. But I grieve to write that he is far otherwise. . . ."

A week later Peirce professed to regret the election only in "the odious way in which it was done." But Gray's show of power gave him pause, for the appointment of Gibbs was still hanging fire. "I am anxious about the Rumford professorship—I fear that things are not going right." He asked Bache, "Suppose that the election is given to Eliot; what would you advise me to do? Is it worth while to be laboring to elevate the University standard, when we see that as soon as Agassiz and myself are gone, the whole thing must fall into the hands of imbeciles?" [27] Peirce would have despaired indeed had he dreamed that in only six years Eliot would succeed Hill as president of Harvard.

The Lazzaroni still had some victories ahead, however. They did secure the appointment of Gibbs, indirectly forcing Eliot's resignation. Bache went ahead vigorously with the National Academy.

Gray did not, at this time, publicly take issue with the National Academy's policy or attempt to organize an opposition. In September 1863, he wrote that the Academy "is strictly governed by the Coast Survey and Agassiz clique," but he and Wyman "have resisted all importunities, and concluded not to *join*, nor *decline*— to say and do nothing—at present, and *see*." [28]

At this juncture a long simmering quarrel suddenly erupted within Agassiz's own scientific household which involved Gray with Agassiz in a more personal way than had the far-flung political activities of the Lazzaroni or even than had Darwinian evolution. Henry James Clark, who had left Gray to study with Agassiz, had for years been the zoologist's favored student and assistant. In return for the master's blessing, Clark had not only taken over most of Agassiz's work at the microscope but had become, of all the students at the museum, the one most thoroughly imbued with Agassiz's idealism. According to Gray, Clark was "quite incapable of understanding what natural selection meant—as much so as Agassiz *himself*—only the former would like to understand it, and the latter wilfully would not." [29] In 1860 Clark had become an assistant professor in the Lawrence Scientific School.

The pressures on Clark were those of the nether regions of science. His salary was small, his family large and growing. His research, year after year, went into Agassiz's *Contributions to the Natural History of the United States*, and no one ever heard of Clark, nor did the master show any signs of ever introducing him to society as a mature scientist in his own right. In July 1863, Clark felt he could wait no more in patient subordination. Despite ten years' service since graduating from the scientific school, "it would seem as if I was so utterly incompetent to make an independent observation, that Professor Agassiz appropriates the whole without a word of credit for the discoverer." After vainly seeking to get Agassiz to agree to an arbitration, Clark published his pamphlet called *A Claim for Scientific Property*.[30]

Although in Agassiz's eyes, Clark had committed an unforgivable sin, Gray felt that Clark "was of the greatest use to Agassiz, and I can not but think that A. used him very unfairly as soon as he no longer wanted him or found it difficult to pay for his services." [31] On September 9, 1863, at a meeting of the faculty of the Lawrence Scientific School "Prof. Agassiz moved that Assistant Professor Clark be requested to retire from the Faculty meetings until his relation to the head of the Department in the Scientific School be regulated." The motion was lost. Clark was allowed to finish out his appointment, but he had no real future at the scientific school in the face of Agassiz's wrath, and indeed his subsequent career indicates that he never really recovered from this crisis before his death at the age of forty-seven. Yet the severity of the sting which Agassiz's colleagues in the scientific school had delivered is clearly shown by the fact that when he walked away from that faculty meeting, he did not attend another for nearly four years.[32]

Agassiz and Gray were coming to a parting of the ways. Throughout their scientific debates, throughout their wide-ranging differences over policy, they had to this point maintained a civil and friendly personal intercourse. In December 1863, Agassiz spoke against Darwin before the Scientific Club, with Gray attending.[33] They both attended three meetings in the spring of 1864.

Gray and Wyman decided to go to the National Academy meeting "to see how it works—whether the *clique* is going to rule and exclude worthy men—like *Bond* and *Baird*,[34] or not. If they are, then we shall withdraw from the concern. If not, then I will help do justice, and after that have as little to do with the concern as possible." Agassiz tried his best to block Baird and to stir up a quarrel between Gray and Leo Lesquereux, but in neither case did he succeed.[35] The failure to keep Baird out of the academy so chagrined Agassiz that Joseph Henry had to explain to him that Baird "was the choice of a large majority of the cultivators of Natural History; and although your opposition was honest in intention, and your position correct in general principle yet I think that had you prevailed in your opposition, a majority of all the naturalists would have resigned. . . ."[36] This meeting, as the election to the presidency of the American Academy had shown for Boston, marked Gray's political ascendancy over Agassiz in American science. While the Darwinian controversy did not ostensibly figure in the caucus atmosphere of a National Academy election, it is possible to sense Agassiz's increasing isolation. As even his students deserted him, his charm on the lecture platform no longer saved him; the grand Louis was no longer invincible. And, with the serious illness of Bache in 1864, the National Academy ceased to be the property of a clique. The Lazzaroni terminated their attempt to revolutionize the scientific institutions of the United States.

The one account of the actual break between the two men, despite the fact that it is anonymous and the admittedly fallible memory of a quarter century, is quite precise in placing it as taking place on the train returning from New Haven. There "the controversy was continued with such acrimony that Professor Agassiz made an end of it by calling Dr. Gray 'no gentleman.' " It is not necessary to credit the Cambridge legend that Agassiz challenged Gray, Heidelberg fashion, to a duel. As Mrs. Gray put it, "Agassiz used some violent language to Dr. Gray." [37] In Gray's code, to call him no gentleman was sufficient to insult him "foolishly and grossly."

The spectacle of Gray and Agassiz in open conflict had about it a certain morbid interest for their contemporaries. Leo Lesquereux, who knew both the principals well, lamented, "what pains me much indeed is the violent hatred and jarring spite openly proclaimed by men of high standing whose influence should be only good and productive of a higher tone. . . ." Yet as Lesquereux contemplated the two men engaged in what to him was an indecent quarrel he saw as few had before him Gray's character in its full dimensions. "Like Agassiz he well knows that he is a prince of science and if he does not openly despize small men and poor things, he keeps his whole regard for high standing subjects. But he is certainly frank and honest and despizes every kind of duplicity." [38]

The story of these years amply shows that scientists, like other men, are incurably political animals. Some of them, however, tend to be political by necessity and not by choice. The next logical step for Gray, having taken Agassiz's measure, was to form a coalition with Rogers, Eliot, and Henry to rule American science in place of the vanquished, leaderless, and disintegrating Lazzaroni. By hard work in the Cambridge wards he might have taken over the Lawrence Scientific School and even tried for Harvard University. He did no such thing. He took no more interest in the National Academy, resigning in 1867. He let the Lawrence Scientific School go its own way. He was indifferent to Eliot as a potential president of Harvard. He took no direct interest in Rogers's Massachusetts Institute of Technology. His *de facto* coalition disappeared as quickly as the Lazzaroni themselves.

A key to Gray's reluctance to play scientific politics permanently appears in his attitude toward his break with Agassiz. "I have always acted on the rule that personal quarrels should be rigidly kept down to the parties themselves as far as was honorably possible—so that they might work the least possible mischief. During the long period in which I had to cut Agassiz entirely—for gross offense . . . I prevented my personal friends from breaking with him or noticing it—insisting that the break should be simply between us two." [39]

From scientific politics Gray turned to his own botanical establishment, in the development of which the Civil War years offered significant opportunities. The 1850's had been years of intellectual ferment but institutional sterility. In the 1860's the ascendancy of Darwinism predetermined the main lines of speculation, but the rapidly increasing economic power of the newly self-conscious nation of the North both demanded and gave the opportunity for new institutional arrangements in science. After the first shock the Civil War by no means absorbed all of the North's energies. Indeed it seemed to stimulate them.

Gray remarked to Darwin, who wondered how one could think of science in the midst of war, "Well, first, we get used to it. Second, we need something to turn to, and happy are they who, forbidden to engage personally in the war (as I am ever itching to do), have something to turn to. Third, I do not do much, do nothing, in fact, except my college duties now for months. . . ." When Gray was having trouble getting money to Charles Wright in Cuba because of exchange rates he asked if there was "not some Yankee product that I could ship to you" which some Cuban friend wanted, "sewing-machines, agricultural implements, chairs . . . I will send you anything, from a mousetrap to a wheelbarrow!" [40] Only soldiers were wrapped up in the war; civilians were busy building a new industrial America.

An instance of the new impulse and the new energy showed results in a new type of western exploration. Although the South was cut off as a field for collecting, the West was more accessible than ever. The topographical engineers of the army were recalled for war duty, breaking up the soldier-civilian teams who had brought in the bulk of the plant collections before 1860. Their place was taken by collectors who benefited not only by the easier transportation to the West but also by the growth of a society sufficiently stabilized to allow season-long collecting without military escort. In the late 1850's a few collections had come in from California made by people living there. Their activity indicated that a thorough re-exploration of the western half of the continent had begun.[41]

The real watershed in Rocky Mountain botanical exploration, long Gray's target area, came in 1862 when C. C. Parry, veteran of the Mexican Boundary Survey, wrote to Gray about an expedition. "I think I shall be less anxious to go over a wide scope of country than to *explore thoroughly* the region of special interest as indicated by you." He would devote several growing seasons to it "so as to collect material for a complete botanical survey" of a well-marked district. This was a fair statement of the collecting philosophy of the new period. The botanists on the railroad surveys, dashing in a single season from the plains to the Pacific, naturally had obtained only the conspicuous plants which happened to be flowering as they passed along. By staying in the Colorado mountains for several whole seasons, Parry could collect with a completeness unknown before.

Why he could do in Colorado what others before him had not done was directly attributable to the social and economic push into the territory just before and during the Civil War. For discovery of gold deposits in this portion of the mountain range "has attracted thither an adventurous and enterprising population, settling with wonderful celerity its picturesque valleys and introducing into its wild recesses many of the arts and comforts of civilized life." [42]

Gray performed his usual service of sorting the collections and publishing accounts of them as they came in. Parry had collected alone in 1861, and with Elihu Hall and J. P. Harbour in 1862. The team had the kind of dispute so common among both old and new field botanists. Hall and Harbour made many sets of each species, while Parry took pains with a smaller number, opening himself to the charge of being lazy. Gray was the one who heard their case and decided on the disposition of the joint collection, apparently to the satisfaction of all concerned.[43] In general the new style collector required less personal service from Gray than had earlier explorers such as Charles Wright. However, the responsibility of the head-quarters botanist remained unchanged, and the unique value of Gray's herbarium and library increased with each passing year.

Another phenomenon which illustrated the growing power and wealth of the country was the appearance, even in wartime, of advanced students of botany in Cambridge. Joseph Trimble Rothrock came to the scientific school in 1860, and, "brave fellow as he is," took some time out to serve in the army before receiving a degree of Bachelor of Science in 1864. His first collecting effort, on the Kennicott expedition to Alaska in connection with a telegraph line which was one more evidence of expanding American wealth—was not successful, and for a few years thereafter he seemed to have no possibility of making his living as a botanist. His eventual return to science and his distinguished career in Pennsylvania indicate that the students of the 1860's were not wrong in sensing larger opportunities in science.[44]

William James Beal, who had already graduated from the University of Michigan, came to the Lawrence Scientific School in 1862 and received his degree in botany in 1865. Significantly, both Gray and Agassiz painted a gloomy picture of opportunity in natural history to Beal, but his later career at Michigan Agricultural College indicates that the Morrill Act for land-grant colleges had already laid the basis of increased employment of botanists.[45]

Gray also attracted another student to botany. Horace Mann, Jr., son of the educator, was the first Bostonian of substantial family to take up the subject professionally—a delay of some twenty years from the time Gray began to teach at Harvard. After two years in Lawrence Scientific School he went, with Gray's encouragement but at his own expense, to that most intriguing of collecting grounds for a Darwinian—the Hawaiian Islands. On his return, Mann finished his course at the scientific school and gave every promise of being what Gray had long sought but never found, a true professional assistant.

The need for assistance became more pressing because of a noteworthy event in the history of botany at Harvard which occurred in 1864. Until that time Gray's herbarium and library had been his own personal property, maintained by his own money and piled high in the wing of the garden house which had been added in 1848. In the midst of the war, however, he was able to institutionalize his personal holdings by giving them to the university. This step was possible because, despite the inflation of the 1860's and the many calls for donations to the United States Sanitary Commission and other war relief, more money was available for scientific purposes in Boston than ever before. William Barton Rogers found this so in establishing M.I.T. The severe financial difficulties in which Agassiz's museum found itself in these years is a reflection on the management rather than on the generosity of Boston donors.[46]

One of Asa Gray's most recurrent nightmares involved the loss of his herbarium by fire. It was a well justified fear in nineteenth-century America; witness the loss of John Carey's herbarium by fire in New York in the 1840's, the threat to Dr. Torrey's collection during the draft riots of 1863, and the loss of Stimpson's zoological collections in the great fire in Chicago. To a burly expressman who persisted in coming into Gray's quarters smoking a pipe, the little botanist did not hesitate to say with finger wagging, "if you come in here smoking again, I'll heave you outdoors." [47]

Gray had for a long time made an offer of his herbarium to the university in return for a fireproof building and a fund for maintenance. Late in 1863, Nathaniel Thayer, a wealthy man of Boston and large donor to the university, somehow heard of this offer, even though Gray scarcely knew him, and came forward with the money for the building. Old Jacob Bigelow, "who has lots of money and loves to keep it," led off with a subscription for the $10,000 maintenance fund. Gray estimated that his own contribution in books and specimens was worth $15,000, but both George B. Emerson and John A. Lowell said it was worth at least $20,000.[48] The reappearance of Lowell among Gray's and botany's supporters is a measure both of the rapidity with which the Darwinian passions of 1860 had cooled and of Gray's success in maintaining and even improving his standing in the community during these tempestuous years.

An early spring in 1864 allowed a good start on the new building, which was well along when Grant began the steady grind before Richmond. Immediately adjoining the old garden house, from which it was separated by a double set of wrought-iron doors, the new brick building was one and one-half stories high with dimensions of 32 × 56 feet. The summer was largely "frittered away" in details. In the fall, the move, even to the better quarters, left Gray "very much *at sea* yet,—all the old associations—places for books &c.—broken up." [49]

The opening of the herbarium was a proud and happy time. Of course the moving went on almost until the very moment "(wife and I half dead)" that the members of the American Academy arrived to see the new quarters. John Torrey, almost Gray's oldest friend alive, came up especially for the occasion. And, in his formal letter of presentation to President Hill, Gray mentioned some statistics which measured his own accomplishment. "The Herbarium is estimated to contain at least 200,000 specimens, and is constantly increasing. From the very large number of typical specimens it comprises, its safe preservation is very important." The library "contains about 2200 botanical works. . . ." A particularly gratifying extra gift was Mr. Lowell's donation of 335 volumes of very rare and costly botanical books.

By early 1865, Gray was settled in his new building, relieved of a burden of about $500 a year in upkeep. Several minor difficulties remained. The maintenance fund lacked $1000 of being filled. Gray could not find a curator, and for this job he was still thinking in terms of his old explorers, Fendler and Wright. The building was *"perfectly satisfactory."* Although he did not realize it, this satisfaction had in it the seeds of danger. For, unless the building were vastly too big—of Agassizian dimensions—in 1864, it would have difficulty lasting much longer than Gray's own time.

The creation of the University Herbarium made clear the gradual decline of the Botanic Garden as the center of Gray's interest. The fund for the garden had long been inadequate, and Gray during these years managed to keep it going only with the help of extra funds provided by a Boston doctor, George Hayward.[50] Speaking to the Cambridge Scientific Club in January 1865, Gray made explicit this change of emphasis, basing it on scientific rather than financial grounds. "The Herbarium is the *Liber veritatis* of the Botanist—the only certain record of species." It was far "more important than Botanic Gardens—which can contain but a small part of known species, and can preserve and *keep alive* for a long while, few of them, —and at much cost, and great risk.—Annuals & biennials only by sowing the seed annually.—so are precarious." Perennials were also precarious, for "even when seemingly hardy, they *die out!*" He also stressed "cross-impregnations" and "the variations and abnormalities developed under domestication." [51] This attitude, which summed up twenty-two seasons of struggle with the garden, foreshadowed the future development of Gray's researches. A botanic garden to him was still a place for preserving wild species, not for experimenting on them. One might almost blame Darwin for Gray's loss of confidence in the garden. The *Origin of Species* had heavily emphasized variation under domestication and the effects of cross-pollination in the hands of man.

In the spring of 1865, Mrs. Gray went to Washington to visit her brother Charles, by then a general in the army, who took her up close to the lines. She "had the honor of having a rebel shell thrown at her!" How deeply they all "felt, rejoiced, and suffered" during those spring months. "Slavery is done away, and we now have the task of establishing a new better order of things at the South. . . ." Lincoln's assassination filled the "whole land with the deepest and tenderest grief, like that of a personal bereavement. . . ." Through some of the letters of these days runs the unmistakable refrain of "Hang Jeff Davis on a Sour Apple Tree," but Gray professed not to hate even the rebels.[52]

As the months went by for Gray in his improved surroundings, he was living in a vibrant country in which he had full faith. His Southern botanical friends made a sorry contrast as one by one they reported in to him. T. M. Peters, the staunch Unionist, emerged with a tale of the "terror that menaced Union men" in Alabama, and a fierce desire to hang not only Davis but *"all* his traitorous set." In contrast, Henry Ravenel, humbled and shorn of his property, wanted to take up botanical collecting for a livelihood. Moses Curtis hoped to catch again "a glimpse of my old correspondent, Prof. Gray, still perched upon the Floral tripod in all his ancient dignity and importance, & as ready as ever to extend his friendly hand as far as N. Carolina." Curtis had done nothing on botany for four years except on "one subject, towards which my stomach urged me in times of scarcity. . . . I mean the eatable mushrooms." [53] Although Gray welcomed them back heartily in the name of science, he can hardly have overlooked the tremendous drain on the human resources that were available for science in the South which showed in letters that he received.

The final scene in the drama of the Civil War years took place for Gray in Cambridge in the fall of 1866. The great Agassiz came straight out with an apology. To Engelmann, Gray wrote, "As to Agassiz, 2½ years ago, he insulted me so foolishly and grossly that we have had no kind of intercourse—till—a month ago—he sought thro' a friend a reconciliation—he professed a most complete and satisfactory apology, and now we are on hearty pleasant terms—to his great relief. I think he means to *avoid trouble* now—and get on smoothly, I hope so—I have none but pleasant and kind feelings towards him." Joseph Henry, jubilant at this news, paid Gray one of the compliments of a lifetime. "I am sure he is a happier man on this account and that you are none the less comfortable. I hope in future he may be guided by a little more of your wisdom and a little less by that which has of late years directed him." [54]

While returning to the civility which had characterized their relations before 1863, the two men tacitly agreed that the scientific and political issues over which they had fought for so long now belonged to the past. And on every count Gray could shake hands with great satisfaction. The idealism of Agassiz had ceased to be a major force in biology even among his own students. Darwin's popularity had proved to be no fad of the moment. The Lazzaroni were no longer active either in Cambridge or in American science. Although the Museum of Comparative Zoology loomed larger physically than the Herbarium, the imbalance in support by Boston of Gray's and Agassiz's work had been largely redressed. These issues of the past were as dead as slavery. A newer urban and industrial America provided unheard-of opportunities as well as the challenge of greater problems. Agassiz's few remaining years in the postwar United States, tinged as they were with bitterness, formed an anticlimax. Unlike his illustrious colleague, Asa Gray could look at both past and future with confidence.

XVII

TRANSITION FROM PROFESSOR TO PATRIARCH

EVEN during the war, Gray had begun to speak of retirement with passion. He dreamed of release from his professorship and a return to work on the *Flora of North America,* already stalled for more than twenty years. After the war, some kind of relief became his major objective. Still in his fifties and in the best of health, he nevertheless saw too little time stretching ahead. The things he had undertaken "when I foolishly thought there was no end of work in me" [1] now loomed too large even for one without rapidly increasing teaching and administrative duties. With dogged patience Joseph Henry did not let him forget even the report on forest trees, still hanging over from 1850. And, besides the *Flora,* the Wilkes expedition plants, the *Genera Illustrata,* the western collection of Wright and others after *Compositae* were all hopelessly bogged.

Personally, retirement meant securing enough income to make up for his professor's salary. An aunt of Mrs. Gray's, one of the country kin in Connecticut, left a small legacy in 1863, which whetted Gray's appetite without quite solving the problem. By the summer of 1866 he wrote, "Well I have given our University Corporation warning that I would resign tomorrow if I could possibly afford it, and I could keep the occupancy of this house, and that I shall do so anyhow some day if they do not . . . give me an assistant for the weary college work and care of this poverty-stricken little garden. . . ."

The real problem lay in these Harvard activities which Gray had cared for since 1842 and for which he had, despite momentary discouragement, too much regard to abandon. The garden was in an especially perilous state. Gray called it his "bête noire." At the end of 1865 the deficit stood at $600 and "I was cooly told by the Treasurer I must pay the difference out of my own pocket—and I should have been obliged to had not Mr. Lowell come forward and given the sum." A small fund raised among the usual friends such as Mr. Lowell prevented a recurrence of a crisis and the carrying out of Gray's wish that the university "drop our garden altogether, or let me be quit of it." [2] The problem remained.

In the classroom, Gray felt not only the pressure of greater numbers but also the weight of endless repetition. The invitation to interested students to come to herbarium and garden for special instruction became more frequently accepted in the postwar years, a reflection of a definite increase in interest in science. Although Gray was glad to have them, they "add to my botheration." Furthermore, since the new herbarium had no room for instruction, he urgently needed a new building for classroom and laboratory work in botany. The old quarters in the Harvard Yard were inadequate, and other departments increasingly usurped them. A few simple microscopes for students no longer sufficed in the postwar world, and as early as 1866 Gray recognized the need for an addition to his string of buildings at the garden. [3]

To meet the problems and opportunities of expanding scientific instruction at Harvard and at the same time to put Gray's own research program on a sound basis required a complete re-evaluation of the botanical institutions of the country. With John Torrey already seventy years old and Daniel Cady Eaton at Yale the only fulltime botanical professor besides Gray, the multiple responsibilities on Harvard were great. Support of an entirely new order both in money and personnel was needed, and quickly.

Gray was entirely aware of the institutional implications of his personal position. Although he tried all the old ways of raising money, such as editing a new edition of the *Manual,* he was thinking in larger terms. His experience with explorations and with the National Academy made him feel that the democratic governments in the United States, either federal or state, are "good for nothing" in supporting either exploration or museums. "Neither our Congress nor our executive department can be depended on for attending to any such thing wisely or honestly." Agassiz had depended extensively on the state of Massachusetts for his museum, and the new United States Department of Agriculture was beginning to think of a department of botany and a national herbarium. Gray saw as the proper support for science in America gifts made by individuals to *"institutions* corporate." The people expect to support science themselves, "and feel they can manage them better than a political government." To Hooker, Gray ruefully conceded that "we cannot trust *officials;* there are more knaves and jobbers among them than with you." [4]

The question was, where in the United States could one find a donor with sufficient resources to put Harvard botany and Asa Gray on a secure financial base. Clearly John A. Lowell's handy and timely $600 here and there were not enough. Gray thought he saw his man. George Peabody, born in South Danvers, Massachusetts, had made his fortune in the city of London. As early as July 1865, Gray had heard that Peabody "means to come back to his own country before long" and saw him as a source of money. [5] Early in 1866, Peabody's nephew, Othniel C. Marsh, a Yale graduate who had laid the basis for a promising scientific career in study abroad, appeared in Cambridge talking of a gift to Harvard. He consulted Gray, who fell in with his plan to found a professorship and museum of archaeology and ethnology. Marsh talked in terms of $100,-000 for Harvard, but Gray "told him $150,000 would be necessary." [6] While helping form such large-minded plans for another department than his own, Gray could scarcely have avoided reflecting that his personal and institutional problems in botany could be solved with a much smaller amount.

Two powerful friends then came to Gray's aid in the effort to gain a grant from Mr. Peabody. Joseph Hooker, who was becoming more and more concerned about the disarray of Gray's research projects, wrote a letter, probably through the former American minister, Charles Francis Adams, designed for Mr. Peabody's eye. And Joseph Henry, who was concerned with Peabody's large plans for an institute in Baltimore, tried to further the negotiations from his vantage point in Washington.

Gray's requests for himself were, in contrast to his advice to Marsh, almost too modest. "An endowment of $20,000 or $25,000 would not only set me up for the work, but also the *Herbarium*— which, for Botany, is worth 10 Botanic Gardens." Joseph Henry spotted a difficulty in this modest request. While Peabody "is a man of noble purpose, and desires to do good, I think he would all things being equal, prefer to perform those acts which will give the most renown." [7] Gray could call the money the Peabody fund, which furnished renown hardly equal to a building or a self-perpetuating institute.

Although his hopes ran high for some months, Gray began to sense he waited in vain for a sign of favor from Mr. Peabody. A number of small things went wrong. Peabody and Robert C. Winthrop, with Hooker's letter in hand, went up to the Botanic Garden, but Gray was not in. Henry was out of town when Mr. Peabody came to Washington. In the spring of 1867, Mr. Peabody, having set up funds and institutions of unheard of proportions, was about to return to England. When Gray was appointed to the board of trustees of the Essex Institute, he was tantalized by the uncertainty of omen. But he thought "it not improbable that the whole matter has passed out of Mr. Peabody's mind. He has certainly done enough in this country, and has done it remarkably well." [8] Thus the first great philanthropist of the post-Civil War era proved a wholesale rather than a retail giver.

Gray had made no progress. He tried an old technique to increase his income. Writing his *Field, Forest and Garden Botany*, he hoped to "raise my stipend from publisher from $700 to $1400 or 1500 per annum—which, so far as money goes would serve my purpose." Mrs. Gray objected to this effort, for she "well knows that every job, counted at 3 months, takes 6 or 9." [9] He had only a casual interest in cultivated plants and had to draw their descriptions largely from the literature rather than from specimens or living material. Driven as he was by need for money on which to retire, he always considered this his poorest work. Yet so skilled had he become that, despite his motive and fatigue, he could not possibly write a bad book.

The man who made a great career out of this minor phase of Gray's work asserted, concerning *Field, Forest and Garden Botany,* "it is remarkable how accurately he indicated the species which have been chiefly concerned in the evolution of garden forms, and how comprehensively he covered the field of the domestic flora." [10] Though he wrote a better book than he would admit, it failed to win him financial independence.

Even had money been available, Gray faced another even more serious problem. Where would he find trained botanists to relieve him of teaching, garden administration, and herbarium routine? Here the lean teaching years from 1842 to 1860 showed their effects. During all that time Gray had produced at Harvard, either in the college or the scientific school, not a single professional botanist, much less one capable of taking over part of his own work. In the whole country the recruits during these years had been very few. American botany had lost a generation. Gray tried out Augustus Fendler as a curator and had various arrangements with Charles Wright. But these men were both undomesticated frontier collectors who had acquired neither training nor temperament for sedentary work when age had sapped their legs of strength. In the late 1860's these queer, charming wanderers of another era could not save American botany. Gray had to depend on young boys thirty years his junior.

In postwar America the boys were coming into science as their older brothers had not. And these lads were not collectors before they were scientists, but rather the opposite. The need to give them instruction was indeed a part of the increasing load that made Gray's lot unbearable. He would have been at home at Harvard in 1946, when in many departments there was no intermediate between senior professor and untrained graduate student. The increasing number of students, beginning with Eaton, Rothrock, and Beal, indicated that nothing was essentially wrong with Gray as a guide for budding botanists, despite his lack of glamor in the classroom. The poverty of the 1850's was a combination of forces in American society which made science universally unattractive and of forces at Harvard which made real advanced study almost impossible. In the 1860's the forces in American society, aided perhaps by the *Origin of Species,* made more young men available for scientific study, and Harvard would soon have to change or lose its place in American education.

Among the new crop coming up Gray spotted a likely prospect. Horace Mann, Jr., fresh from collecting in the Hawaiian Islands, seemed to have the qualities necessary to take over as a curator. Of course, over the gap of a generation in their ages, Mann seemed to Gray slightly feckless—"slow-minded, not over well prepared." In the garden "he hardly knows beans from peas, a sage from a Foxglove." Yet he "is bent on being a botanist, and will succeed, I think. . . ." Besides being a gentlemanly young man, he "takes the severe drill I put him through well." [11] Thus Mann, representing the hope of the future, could lift a small part of the weight Gray's shoulders had carried so long alone.

Although solving the institutional problems which surrounded him was still beyond his powers, Gray determined in 1868 that some temporary pause was necessary. Charles G. Loring had died in the fall of 1867 and Mrs. Gray's always delicate health was worse than usual. In May 1868, Gray wrote to Charles Darwin, "I am half dead with drudgery, half of it at least for other people; see no relief but to break up, and run over, with wife, who needs a change, to your side of the water for a good long while." [12] Leaving Cambridge early in September 1868, the Grays were settled in a house near Kew within two weeks, a great contrast to the month's voyage required in 1839.

This sojourn in Europe was subtly different from the earlier ones. Botany was still present, of course. Gray worked at Kew alongside Joseph Hooker, who was now the director, following the death of Sir William. More than before botany played a secondary role to both society and travel. In England, life was a round of visits, many to the country. They stayed with the Reverend Mr. Church in Somersetshire, and, with the Hookers and John Tyndall, they visited Down House. [13]

When they left England the Grays were almost unreservedly tourists, since they shepherded various young Lorings and Putnams, especially two young ladies, in a quest for culture. The fashionable winter vacation in those years was a cruise on the Nile. The Prince of Wales was doing it this same season of 1868–69. As the dahabeahs plied leisurely up and down, more than one impromptu meeting of pleasure-seeking Americans occurred—even such unlikely encounters as the philosopher Emerson and a little boy named Theodore Roosevelt. For the Grays, Egypt afforded little botany, much sunshine, and much rest—a genuine change of pace for Gray. The M.D. after his name brought him briefly back to the practice of medicine after nearly forty years, for "a hakim or doctor is a great godsend to the people, and you have to give medicine all day long." Three months on the Nile occupied all the cold part of the winter.

Spring on the continent brought only more sightseeing. In Switzerland, Gray eagerly raced up the same mountain passes he had crossed thirty years before and pronounced his wind as strong as ever. Hooker, watching the Grays "wasting . . . substance & animal tissues all over the continent," was aghast. "You Americans are fearful and wonderful people—curious exaggerations of our good & bad qualities, with a few differentials of your own. We look on you as the Spanish & Portuguese in the tropics look on the English— Ergo we are in decadence, you in the ascendant." [14] Paradoxically, however, Gray's health was buoyant, and Jane's great weakness diminished in proportion to the frantic pace of travel.

The visit to England was important from a Darwinian point of view. For the first time since the great events of the year following the publication of the *Origin of Species,* Gray was able to talk face to face with the other members of Darwin's inner circle, both old and new. Socially it was a great triumph. On their weekends at Down, the Grays fitted in easily among the numerous guests, cousins, and casual callers who flowed continuously in and out. Mrs. Gray saw Darwin as "entirely fascinating." He was "tall & thin, though broad framed, & his face shows the marks of suffering and disease . . . He never stayed long with us at a time, but as soon as he had talked much, said he must go & rest, especially if he had had a good laugh." Less than two years older than his American friend, his "hair is grey, & he has a full grey beard cut square across the upper lip, but the sweetest smile, the sweetest voice, the merriest laugh! and so quick, so keen!"

In London, Dr. Gray came home delighted "with his dinner at the little Club of gentlemen where he went by Dr. Hooker's invitation." At this gathering, the famous *X* Club, he met Spencer, Tyndall, and Sir John Lubbock, among others. Huxley was not there on that particular evening. Gray must have made a good impression on these men. When John Fiske was in London a few years later talking to Herbert Spencer about Agassiz, the philosopher said, "to put him as high as Dr. Asa Gray or Jeffries Wyman is to put him too high. . . ." Indeed, Fiske found "the unanimous opinion to be that the great American is Dr. Gray. Over here they regard Gray as the greatest botanist in the world, even a little bigger than Hooker." [15]

In the midst of social triumph, however, a note of discord appeared under the surface. For the year 1868 marked the end of Gray's long effort to prevent the complete demise of the doctrine of design in its new Darwinian setting. In 1860 a strong possibility had existed that Gray's adaptation of design to Darwinism, or at least the neutrality of Darwinism in its bearing on ultimate questions, might be the major answer put forth to counteract the onslaughts of Bishop Wilberforce. Darwin had, however, rejected Gray's argument privately. In 1868, Darwin took the final step not only of rejecting the design argument in a very conspicuous place but specifically of linking the rejection to Gray. On the last page of *Variation of Plants and Animals under Domestication,* he concluded, "However much we may wish it, we can hardly follow Professor Asa Gray in his belief" in lines of beneficent variation. As usual Gray had cheerfully arranged for publication in America, and in a review in the *Nation,* he answered briefly, seeking to refute a metaphor Darwin used about the builder of a stone house who selected stones of random shapes and sizes.[16]

In their letters the two maintained the good humor of men who had long since argued themselves to a stand-still. Darwin paraphrased an Edinburgh reviewer as saying "that Prof. Asa Gray could with the greatest ease smash me into little pieces." Gray admitted that he "was put on the defence by your reference to an old hazardous remark of mine"—the reference to the stream of beneficent variations. "I found your stone-house argument unanswerable in substance (for the notion of design must after all rest mostly on faith, and on accumulation of adaptations, &c.—); so all I could do was to find a vulnerable spot in the shaping of it, fire my little shot, and run away in the smoke." [17]

Despite the easy way Gray and Darwin joked about this difference, the American in Europe could scarcely avoid the feeling that the decision had gone against him and that Darwinism had come close to merging with materialism and the philosophy of Herbert Spencer. Although Huxley's real position was not impossibly far from Gray's and much more subtle and sensitive than that of many of the new dogmatists, his language was so pungent that he seemed to be the proponent of the union between Darwinism and a rigid materialism. To R. W. Church, Gray wrote from London in August 1869 that he could not attend the meeting of the British Association at Exeter. "I am on the whole glad enough to keep away, especially from *Darwinian* discussions—in which I desire not to be at all 'mixed up' with the Huxley set, and the prevailing and peculiarly English Materialistic-positivistic line of thought—with which I have no sympathy—while in natural history I am a sort of Darwinian." [18]

With the completion of his isolation from the main current of British Darwinism, Gray fully realized almost for the first time his basic community of interest with Lyell, and the aging geologist reciprocated. In presenting a copy of a new edition of the *Antiquity of Man* to Gray, he wrote, "I hope you will accept a copy from me in acknowledgement on my part of the very great advantage I derived from your writings when I was writing the 'Antiquity of Man' & had to consider how far I should go with Darwin in the direction of 'Creation by Variation.'" [19]

Gray responded not only with appreciation for the book but with an explicit recognition that Lyell alone of all the prominent Darwinians had been a staunch supporter of the Union cause during the Civil War. He thanked Sir Charles and Lady Lyell "for being such fast friends of our country when *in extremis,* as well as for your kind attention to us." [20] Thus at a series of dinner parties, after Sir Charles had reached the age of seventy, two of the original Darwinians celebrated both their community of interest and the fact that they formed a minority rejected by the reigning high priests of Darwinism. The cliché was already well-formed that the *Origin of Spe-*

cies had killed the argument of Paley, but two men whose contribution to the evolutionary movement outshone almost everyone save Darwin himself could still trust their faith in an ordered world of nature. It was a melancholy satisfaction for Gray to know that his line had been followed by the great Lyell.

Gray brought back from Europe one possession which he did not have when he had left America. During the lazy winter in Egypt he raised a "venerable white beard." The dictate of fashion was doubtless behind his decision. Other mature men had cultivated beards in the 1860's—Lincoln, Darwin, Longfellow, Jeffries Wyman. When Gray had left Cambridge in 1868 approximately half of the faculty wore them. The cruise on the Nile simply gave him an opportunity to catch up with the mode. Not all of his friends approved. Joseph Henry felt it would "forever as long as it is worn change to me a face which from long association has become a source of pleasure for me to look upon." He doubted whether "a man over the age of 45 has a moral right to so change his appearance that his friends cannot recognize him."

Nearing his sixtieth year, Gray felt he had earned his beard.[21] Although it was indeed a symbol of advancing age, it certainly indicated no physical decline. His quick step carried him over the Wingern Alp to Grindelwald as quickly with the beard as it had thirty years before. The transformation was more subtle than mere senescence. The beard was a symbol of a new position in society, the assumption of the role of a patriarch who still had many years left to look down from the heights he had attained.

The beard, however, solved none of the problems which he had left unsolved in Cambridge. Indeed, the Grays returned home in the fall of 1869, somewhat earlier than they had intended, because of a tragedy such as those with which Bostonians of the nineteenth century were all too familiar. Horace Mann, Jr., on whom rested so much responsibility for the present and so much hope for the future, declined rapidly and died of tuberculosis. To his mother it was a crowning personal sorrow. To botany it was the breaking off of a promising professional career. Gray felt the death of his assistant on both these counts, but he was also affected in another way as well. "The loss of Mann has frustrated all my hopes and expectations. I had intended my absence to establish him in the work, so that the laborious detail at least might be hereafter taken by him. Now I see no one to replace him.—the work here doubling in amount & hardship, and I too old & too little patient to do it as well as I formerly could." [22]

Thus at the end of 1869 Gray had to start all over again building a botanical establishment at Harvard to replace the one he had served so long. Fortunately, at this point he began to display a largeness of vision in realizing that biology was moving so rapidly into so many new fields that simple replacement for himself was not the answer. Indeed, the relatively unspecialized point of view of Gray's earlier years made it easier for him to plan a new program involving a group of specialists. Fortunately, too, Harvard University had, during the Grays' absence in Europe, appointed a new president who could be counted on to end the drift which had characterized university policy for a quarter of a century.

Charles W. Eliot had of course stood with Gray in the crises of 1862 and 1863 and had suffered the great defeat of his life when Wolcott Gibbs was appointed to the Rumford professorship. Less than six years later Eliot's return to Harvard showed clearly how far and how quickly the world had moved beyond the once mighty Agassiz. Gray, however, appears to have had no part in the selection of Eliot and, indeed, as one of the older faculty members, probably would have preferred Andrew Preston Peabody. The issues raised by Eliot's ideas on education were not ones in which Gray had much interest.

Yet when he found his "young friend" in the presidency, he immediately recognized an ally in solving his own pressing problems. "He understands and appreciates," Gray wrote to Hooker, "and if we could light upon a fit person or persons—anyone promising to be a good professor, there would be nothing to prevent my throwing off all . . . work . . . and I could secure at least the house here *rent-free*—which would serve." Admitting the existence of the lost generation of botanists and the seeming absence in America of any real successor, Gray told Hooker that to "save time and the risk in the making of a man, we will *import* from you, if there is any one fit and really promising, whom we could tempt." Eliot's determination to transform Harvard from a school for boys to a real university was already apparent. "Our present Praeses.," wrote Gray a little later, "will be sharp on getting not only a first-class teacher, but a strong man—to take position in science." [23] For three years the search was to go on, in both Europe and America, without success. Eliot on his side described the situation bluntly. "To illustrate the failure of the system of the last 40 years to breed scholars, let us take the most unpleasant fact which I know for those who have the future of this University to care for—Asa Gray, Benjamin Peirce, Jeffries Wyman and Louis Agassiz are all going off the stage and their places cannot be filled with Harvard men, or any other Americans that I am acquainted with. This generation cannot match them. These men have not trained their successors. This is a very grievous fact which had better not be talked about—it is altogether too significant." [24]

Meanwhile the financial horizons of the University with respect to botany broadened considerably. The will of Benjamin Bussey had left a fund and a farm in Jamaica Plain, Massachusetts, for the establishment of an agricultural school. In 1870 and 1871 the Harvard Corporation took steps for a building and an instructional staff. Although the Boston fire of 1872 hurt the Bussey fund badly and although Gray had nothing to do with the program of instruction, the Bussey Institution added a potential resource to Harvard's institutional assets in botany.

Much more important was a bequest in the will of James Arnold, a New Bedford, Massachusetts, merchant who died in 1869. The leading trustee to whom this estate went for "the promotion of Agricultural, or Horticultural improvements, or other Philosophical, or Philanthropic purposes " [25] was George B. Emerson, the man responsible for Gray's appointment at Harvard back in 1842 and the author of the report on the trees of Massachusetts. Late in 1871, with litigation cleared up and with Emerson disposed toward an arboretum under the care of Harvard, Gray saw the possibility of an income of $5000 to $6000 a year. "I am laboring to have the thing annexed to the Botanic Garden here—administered as one concern and to have somebody got to take charge of tree-raising & planting . . . and superintend the whole garden &c.—here." One serious problem was "whether we can find room for the arboretum" in Cambridge. However, a possibility existed that a group led by the poet Longfellow, whose view from his front steps was at stake, could buy some seventy acres along the Charles River.[26]

On the strength of the Arnold bequest, Gray notified the Harvard Corporation that at the end of the academic year in the summer of 1872 he would resign the oversight of the garden and his professorship, offering to continue to look after the herbarium in return for the rent of the house. The extra money for the garden would leave his conscience free to give up the "incubus," and perhaps at long last the way would be clear for concentrated botanical work and the *Flora of North America*. The weakness of Gray's scheme was that its real aim was to relieve him of the necessity of leadership rather than to furnish leadership for a new and expanded institution.

On January 18, 1872, Gray talked to Emerson so long that he developed a bad cough. By late February he began to chafe at the delay. The "three trustees are rather at cross-purposes, and though agreeing to offer the concern to our University Corporation, will hardly get it done, I fear this spring." Emerson, "too old" to be reliable, had at first felt "the importance of getting work & care off my hands," but then he took "another tack," deciding to visit European arboreta to "see *what he shall see*." [27]

The matter dragged on another month, until the Arnold trustees made an agreement with the Harvard Corporation. The income of the Arnold fund was to accumulate to $150,000, the net income from which was to be devoted to the maintenance of an arboretum located on part of the Bussey land at Jamaica Plain, on the other side of Boston from the botanical establishment in Cambridge. Once again Gray had suffered a major disappointment. To Hooker he wrote, "Well,—as to our prospective arboretum, I have got it off my mind . . . Our University Corporation allowed the trustees of Arnold's bequest to get the better of them, and impose conditions & restrictions that reduce my interest in it to 0." He was thinking primarily of his own problems, for the arboretum "will be a good thing in its time—not soon enough to do any good here." Clearly Gray could not retire in the summer of 1872.

344

These years of enforced teaching were not by any means lost. The classes were large, but their interest had a new depth. To Torrey, Gray wrote in the fall of 1870, "I have an *advanced class* this year, and they come up here, and take up a vast deal of my time. But it is enjoyable work as they are the pick of a dozen out of 50 or 60 of the preceding year." [28]

In 1871, having found a donor who was genuinely interested in his botanical pursuits—Mr. Horatio Hollis Hunnewell—Gray supervised the building of a "much-needed botanical lecture-room and laboratory for students." This structure completed the physical plant strung across the Botanic Garden. "Mrs. Gray may walk in winter, from her dining room, through our little drawing room-entry —library or parlor—my study—greenhouse corridor—herbarium —lobby—laboratory—lecture-room—passage—stove—and cool house, into conservatory, of 3 compartments—a long affair—but don't imagine anything at all grand." [29] Thus Gray had finally gathered at one place a complete botanical establishment. He had the outdoor gardens, the indoor gardens, the herbarium, the library, and the rooms for instruction all at the Botanic Garden. The students instead of the professor had to walk the distance of nearly a mile from the Harvard Yard, but otherwise everything was close at hand, every phase of botany virtually under one roof.

Because of the availability of his new lecture-room and laboratory, Gray experimented in the summer of 1871 with a special class for schoolteachers. This effort was in response to the general demand for teacher education which was growing rapidly after the Civil War, and the summer school was an obvious device to meet it. Agassiz would soon be founding his summer course at Penikese Island. Professor N. S. Shaler was doing much the same thing in geology.[30] For Gray it only added to the urgency of some relief from his teaching and administrative load.

In the summer of 1872, even though Gray's hopes for retirement had to be deferred, he enjoyed a triumphal tour of the country. Not only was he president of the American Association for the Advancement of Science, but the completion of the transcontinental railroad opened to easy access the lands his collectors had struggled so long to reach. At first the association hoped to meet in San Francisco, but its inability to secure free passes on the railroad forced the meeting back to Dubuque, Iowa. Since the Grays nevertheless were determined to see California, late in June they set out. Their company included besides the Grays a couple of Lorings, an English friend with her maid, and others for some legs of the journey. It might conceivably have been a far larger and more lively party, for Gray had issued invitations to Hooker, Tyndall, Huxley, and his friend the Reverend Mr. Church.[31]

As the Union Pacific train with its palace car made its way westward from the plains into the intermountain plateau, Gray made every stop a sortie for flowers. On one such his hand clutched the genus *Grayia,* named in his honor by Sir William Hooker when he was but a stripling visitor in Glasgow. These original specimens had been gathered by a Hudson's Bay Company fur trapper only some forty years before, yet the whole relation of civilization to the high western country had completely changed in that interval. Gray's whistle-stop efforts were of no particular botanical importance. Such vague location entries on his herbarium tags as "Utah-Nevada desert" reflected more a tourist's confused effort to keep up with the speed of modern transportation than a collector's indifference to geographical considerations. "I suspect I shant collect much. Younger men (like Torrey!) must do that.—I go to *rest* and *loaf,* and *see* plants *in situ.*"[32]

In California, Gray saw the redwoods which he had tried to visualize twenty years before. And in the Sierra he had as a guide to Yosemite valley John Muir. This young man was a naturalist in a sense that Emerson would have approved,—a lover of nature who felt her presence so vividly that he almost personified her—a transcendental position. Muir had eagerly awaited the arrival of the "first botanist of the world," whom he felt "to be a great, progressive, unlimited man like Darwin and Huxley and Tyndall." The old chasm between transcendentalist and empiricist had become scrambled since 1859, but when the two met, Muir still felt its presence. Sizing up Gray, the great nature enthusiast reported, "He is a most cordial lover of purity and truth, but the angular factiness of his pursuits has kept him at too cold a distance from the spirit world."

Nevertheless, the visit not only established cordial relations between the two, but inspired Muir to undertake botanical explorations in the Sierra.[33]

On the return journey the Grays went to Denver, whence they were able to go up into the Rockies, through the towns of Idaho Springs and Georgetown, to a region explored by C. C. Parry in 1862. The collector had named two of the highest peaks there Torrey's Peak and Gray's Peak. With Parry as the host and a whole party of local citizens in attendance, both Dr. and Mrs. Gray ascended Gray's Peak to take possession of one of the loftiest spots in Colorado.[34] It was, of course, an easy climb, but "such a sea of peaks, north, south, east & west,—patches of snow, little green vallies, mountain sides, the South Park a long stretch of green far away to the S. E., below us a blue-green little lake in a mass of snow, close around us the sharp base mt. ridges, & far away on the horizon, the misty *plains,* reaching away to the East." What greater honor could come to a man than to have his name attached to such a spot? An old settler presided at the summit, where the local newspaper editor made "a most ornate & complimentary speech." Gray responded almost fluently enough to please his wife, who recorded that he spoke "uncommonly well I thought, for him, so little given to extempore speaking." Resolutions were passed confirming the name, and since one of the party was the son of the author of the words of "America," they all joined in singing it before beginning the descent.[35]

From Colorado the Grays descended into the heat of Iowa in August to receive the more formal honors of the presidency of the AAAS at the meetings in Dubuque. The title of his presidential address, "Sequoia and Its History," might have been more appropriate had the meetings been held in San Francisco as scheduled. Nevertheless, it was a specimen of Gray's prose at its best. Although written in off moments between trains and at hotels, the address was a polished version of the Japan essay of 1859 with all the crotchets removed which the controversy with Agassiz had introduced. In addition, Gray examined more explicitly the relations between the flora of western North America and those of eastern North America and eastern Asia. The continental view induced by actual travel was

347

congenial to the intercontinental view already arrived at in the Darwinian studies of the late 1850's. Thus Gray chose his greatest theme for his presidential address, and in doing so improved his formulation of it.

Back in Cambridge in the fall of 1872 Gray's long-sought retirement took shape at last. The money and the men he had sought so long now seemed suddenly to materialize, although he continued some duties, including his classes, until the summer of 1873. Still as vigorous as ever and only a little over sixty, he nevertheless felt, because of the big tasks he wished to be doing, that retirement had delayed too long. Others interested in botany generally thought so too. One of his new California acquaintances wrote he "was glad to hear of Prof. Gray's Relief—Don't believe in human Atlases! all very pretty in Poetry & Mythology. E'en Ulysses bow needs to be unstrung anon." [36]

The reason for the breaking of the log jam was implicit in an appointment made in the fall of 1872. Charles Sprague Sargent became director both of the Botanic Garden and the new Arnold Arboretum. He would relieve Gray of his greatest single administrative burden in Cambridge, and at the same time he would undertake to build a new institution in Jamaica Plain. On the surface Sargent had no professional qualification for the task. A graduate of Harvard in 1861, he had fought in the Civil War and traveled in Europe without showing any particular bent for science. Nor does he seem before 1872 to have had any particular connection with Asa Gray. He was simply, as Gray described him, a "gentleman of ample means," who "has a vast deal to learn." [37]

Sargent had grown up among the great estates stretching west of Boston from Brookline out through Wellesley. He was the heir of a tradition of horticultural practice and experiment which went back through his relative Henry W. Sargent to Andrew Jackson Downing, Gray's old acquaintance and one of the earliest landscape gardeners in the country.[38] Thus Sargent's interests were horticultural with especial emphasis on the ornamental trees and shrubs which made some of the great estates west of Boston far outshine the Botanic Garden in Cambridge.

Behind young Sargent stood the imposing figure of Horatio Hollis Hunnewell. A Boston banker in close touch with the financing of the burgeoning railroad network across the nation, Hunnewell partook of the opportunities of the era of Vanderbilt and Gould and the Big Four. Yet his fortune was so conservatively managed that even a blow like the great Boston fire of 1872 left him unruffled. Although Hunnewell had lost half a million dollars, Gray "met him at dinner yesterday, as quiet and pleasant as possible—seemingly less put out by the fire than he was by the bad winter which killed his Rhododendrons & Pine-trees." The same age as Asa Gray, Hunnewell had also been inspired by Henry Sargent, who was his relative, to take up horticulture after the age of forty, and he had made his estate at Wellesley a show place which, among other things, had the finest collection of coniferous trees in America.[39]

Hunnewell's hand in support of botany at Harvard had first appeared when he gave the money for Gray's lecture room and laboratory. In the fall of 1872, with Sargent taking up his duties, the connection between the estate horticulturists and Harvard became suddenly much closer. In November 1872, Gray wrote to Joseph Hooker, "Do not speak aloud; but I hear that somebody, or somebodies, have fix[ed] me out a little pension of $1000 a year, if I will resign here—& give myself to Flora N. America . . . Sargent has mainly instigated it, & has just told me." The final arrangement provided that Hunnewell and Ignatius Sargent, Charles's father, should each contribute $500 a year for Gray in return for "undivided attention" to the *Flora of North America*.[40] Thus, after thirty years of vain searching, Gray achieved almost without asking for it the continuous financial support which could liberate him from the dead hand of routine.

The appearance on the scene of Sargent and the substantial financial and horticultural interests he represented was of course a signal addition to the botanical resources at Harvard and a genuine relief to Gray. That Sargent eventually became a first-rate scientist as well as an institution builder was an unanticipated boon. It was natural, too, given the place of residence and interest in ornamental plants of Sargent, Hunnewell, and their friends, that the Arnold Arboretum rather than the Botanic Garden in Cambridge became the focus of their efforts and affections. Jamaica Plain was handy to the great estates; results in landscape gardening rather than the training of students in botany were the center of their attention; and socially their bonds were with the wealthy people of Boston's suburbs rather than with the university community.

Gray therefore still had to get someone to take his classes at Harvard. As late as January 1873, President Eliot was "disposed to try hard for a man of already assured position. He is wanted to work hard in instruction—but in very much such lines as he likes, and also to make or maintain a name in research." Since these specifications fitted no American, the net widened to Europe. Gray thought especially of A. De Bary of Strasbourg, who had made a name in studies of the flowerless plants. Gray really thought "the safest course is to build up with bricks from the native soil." [41] Whether by choice or necessity Harvard chose the native bricks. And because the pre-Civil War generation had produced no botanists of established reputation, the staff which Gray gathered came by paths which, although different from the one which had so unexpectedly delivered Sargent, were equally fortuitous.

The first new staff member was George Lincoln Goodale. A graduate of Harvard Medical School in 1860, he had received his initial impetus to botany from Edward Tuckerman at Amherst and had become an instructor of natural history at Bowdoin College. From there in 1870 he wrote to Gray complaining that "study by ones' self is unsatisfactory" and proposing that he work on plant physiology at his home, submitting himself to periodic examination by Gray. From this beginning Goodale quickly came into Gray's field of vision, and in the fall of 1872 he came to Cambridge to take over some of the regular classes so long taught by Gray. By the summer of 1873 he had proved capable of assuming the entire burden of instruction. At the end of June of that year Gray could write that on "Saturday I gave the last lecture that I mean ever to deliver!" [42]

Goodale immediately proved himself not so much a successor to Gray as an effective faculty member in Eliot's new university. His emphasis on the study of plant physiology was fortunate. In Gray's younger days physiology had been relatively much less well developed than taxonomy. After 1860 it was rapidly forging ahead as the most active area of study of all the plant sciences. Gray, for all his interest in the subject, had never been able to give it concentrated attention. Goodale was able to develop this latent side of Gray's earlier career and even take over the writing of the physiological portion of the *Botanical Textbook*. He also inherited the miscellaneous collections of tree sections, palmetto fronds, and the like which Gray had gathered and stored in the cabinets of the laboratory. From these Goodale gradually created the Botanical Museum and arranged for its famous collection of glass flowers.

The successor of Gray who came nearest to following what was to become the conventional approach to a professional scientific career was William Gilson Farlow. A graduate of Harvard College in 1866, he had taken Gray's standard advice to get a medical degree and had then returned to become Gray's assistant in 1870. Two years later, equipped with letters of introduction signed "A. Gray" to eminent scientists, this small gamecock of a man went to Europe for study in his special subject, cryptogamic botany. After the *Origin of Species* and the work of Pasteur, studies of lower forms of life, especially those of microscopic size, suddenly assumed vast theoretical and practical importance. Gray had cultivated this field largely by encouraging his team of experts—M. A. Curtis, Tuckerman, and Sullivant. Farlow learned the latest European techniques and prepared to make a career of this one study.

Because Farlow had some independent means, he was able to buy Curtis's collection of fungi, and Gray arranged for Sullivant to leave his moss collections to Harvard. Hence when Farlow returned to the Harvard staff in 1874 he was able to carry the cryptogamic studies of the previous generation to new heights. He also shared with Goodale the major burden of undergraduate teaching. Through Farlow another side of Gray's work which he himself had had to neglect was brought to a new height of perfection.

With this great influx to the staff Gray had only one nightmarish problem to solve. The bane of taxonomy is the limitless amount of tedious but skillful drudgery necessary to keep a herbarium going and to publish comprehensive works. The immense number of individual groups and the staggering quantity of individual bits of information which must be handled daily put a tremendous strain on both systems and personnel. To maintain a broad scientific vision and to get the necessary routine done at the same time is never easy. Gray desperately needed a curator for his herbarium who had the patience and humility to handle much of the routine and who at the same time had sufficient scientific attainment to work as a taxonomist. Almost simultaneously with the arrival of the teaching staff Gray found the perfect herbarium curator.

Sereno Watson differed in every way possible from the other recruits. He was oldish, only sixteen years younger than Gray. Although he graduated from Yale he spent his time until his fortieth year in a succession of unsuccessful teaching, business, and farming ventures. Then, suddenly, in the space of two years, he attended Sheffield Scientific School at Yale, where he studied chemistry and metallurgy, and, on going to California, joined Clarence King's Survey of the Fortieth Parallel, which with government money represented the new era of season-long western collecting. With King, Watson soon got his chance when the botanist became ill, and he collected with both skill and energy. On his return east Watson soon requested Gray's help,[43] and he was invited to come to Cambridge to work on his collection. Soon Gray had him preparing a bibliographical index to North American botany. By the spring of 1872, Watson was already on hand and taking over some of Gray's immense correspondence. A painfully shy bachelor who lived in a modest part of Cambridge and who, though a Congregationalist, belonged to a less stylish church than the one Gray attended, Watson refused all teaching and all larger scientific and social activities. But he was a hard worker, mastering the highly mannered rules of taxonomic botany. That one with such a narrow background should do such eminently satisfactory work indicated that taxonomy was taking a more modest sector of the scientific front in the post-Civil War world. Yet if Watson had been more responsive to the newer and more fashionable currents in science, he would have been less useful to Gray.

Taken as a whole the reorganization of botany at Harvard in 1872–73 was one of Gray's remarkable achievements. It showed that, despite years of scarcity of human material and only modest institutional results, he was an ingenious and far-sighted organizer and handler of men. Botany became one of the first departments at

Harvard to convert itself from the old college way of pre-Eliot days to the new university way. Gray did not, as did Francis Bowen, block progress by hanging on. He did not try to perpetuate his own method of teaching. He did not, like Agassiz, leave a void in the instructional staff which required a complete rebuilding by other hands. He gave ample room for new specialties to arise with the changing currents of science.

The one weakness of the new situation was not of his making and was not immediately apparent. None of the four individuals who succeeded Gray, for all the energy and drive within the separate fields that each displayed, could take the lead for the coordination of the whole enterprise. Gray himself served this function from his post as director of the Herbarium for the remainder of his life. All four men respected him, sought his advice, and allowed him to shape the continuous compromises necessary to keep unbearable friction from developing. The one aspect of himself that Gray could not duplicate in his staff was his own moral ascendancy over them and his position of undisputed leadership. But the harmful fruits of this entirely understandable failure did not become apparent until after his time.

The year of Gray's retirement, 1873, marked a great change in his life not simply because it ended a phase of his career. His image before the world changed, too, because of the death, within a short time, of many whose careers had impinged on his. John Torrey died early in the year, then William Starling Sullivant. Jeffries Wyman was near death with tuberculosis. Above all, Agassiz came to his end in December. He had long been a sick and bewildered man. Gray, who wrote of him graciously if also elliptically in the *Nation,* felt real grief at the time of his death. It was less for Louis than for the young wife of Alexander, who died within a few days of her father-in-law.[44]

As these men passed from the scene Gray seemed to increase in symbolic stature. Especially had he always seemed junior to Torrey and Agassiz. Now he was alone—the first botanist of the United States and a peer of the greatest patriarchs of Cambridge. In the year 1873 Emerson was the one who wrote the letter inviting Gray to join the Saturday Club. The Congress of the United States named him to succeed Agassiz on the Board of Regents of the Smithsonian. For years he had been a close confidential adviser to Joseph Henry, but the formal recognition came only with the death of Agassiz.

In 1873, too, Gray was elected a foreign member of the Royal Society of London, his greatest international recognition up to that time. To Hooker he wrote, "I may enjoy such honors in all simplicity when they come—be it late or early—as I never, even in the most remote way, *fished* for any. . . ." [45] After ten years of service, he resigned the presidency of the American Academy of Arts and Sciences in favor of Charles Francis Adams, one of the most eminent of Americans.

The time for the harvest of rewards had come. For the rest of his life Gray would enjoy the privilege of an unagitating but unsullied fame. With his white beard, he looked the part of a patriarch, and in botany he was to prove that he was one in fact. He was henceforth serenely above the small duties and responsibilities of a working professorship without giving up a life of intense activity in the science he loved.

XVIII

A THEIST IN THE AGE
OF DARWIN

As Gray entered his years of retirement he was, despite the rejection of his religious ideas by the younger members of Darwin's inner circle, necessarily linked with his English friend, by this time one of the world's most famous men. Their early association and their continuing collaboration were insurance that Gray was in a broad sense a Darwinian. When the British magazine *Nature* wanted a sketch of the life of Darwin in 1874, the editor invited Gray to write it as "one whom all would trust" to estimate his subject "absolutely free from local colouring & 'cliquism.' " [1]

The 1870's were the high point of Gray's and Darwin's mutual efforts on botanical subjects. Insectivorous plants probably attracted their attention most steadily. Gray had two other Americans as well as himself—W. M. Canby and Mrs. Mary Treat—observing *Dionea, Drosera,* and other genera whose behavior in trapping and digesting insects suggested interesting problems in evolution. The coiling of tendrils and the lengthy observations on self-fertilization also continued to appear in their exchanges and in Gray's published notes in American journals as well as in Darwin's books.

One of Gray's more popular books for young people was a simple exposition on this kind of Darwinism called *How Plants Behave: How They Move, Climb, Employ Insects to Work for Them, etc.,* which appeared in 1872. In simple language Gray described sensitive plants, twining plants and their tendrils, mechanisms in flowers for cross-fertilization, insect cross-pollination in orchids, and the capture of insects by plants. It is doubtful that many of the multi-

tudes who used this book had any inkling they were imbibing pure
Darwinism. No mention of the origin of species or of the descent of
man appeared in it. Yet it was on these botanical subjects that Darwin and Gray continued their intercourse, and it was discoveries
made on them by which Darwin continued to elicit Gray's enthusiastic admiration. In return, Darwin in 1877 dedicated his *The Different Forms of Flowers on Plants of the Same Species* to Gray "as
a small tribute of respect and affection."

Despite his close and continued association with Darwin, Gray
maintained a studied reserve concerning some main lines of Darwin's later work. When the *Descent of Man* was finished, Darwin
predicted "I shall probably receive a few stabs from your polished
stiletto of a pen." Gray's reaction was, "Almost thou persuadest me
to have been 'a hairy quadruped, of arboreal habits, furnished with
a tail and pointed ears' &c." Since Gray genuinely considered the
whole subject as out of his line,[2] he made no public comment on
the book in print. Any defense of Darwin or any disagreement by
Gray had to exclude the most notorious if not the most important
inference from Darwin's main thesis.

Pangenesis received much the same treatment. Gray discussed
this ingenious and unfortunate theory of the mechanics of genetics
before the Cambridge Scientific Club in 1868. Reporting to Darwin, Gray was careful to say that in the group, which incidentally
included Agassiz, "pangenesis seemed to strike all of us as being as
good an hypothesis as one can now make." [3] Nevertheless, pangenesis did not figure prominently in Gray's later thinking on hybridization.

Ironically, Gray had played a part in leading Darwin to pangenesis. One of the little jewels of observation which Gray had tossed
off in the 1850's had been his recognition of the direct action of
pollen on the female parts of certain plants, especially cucumbers
and *Zea mays*. This phenomenon, later named *Xenia* and explained
in genetic terms as double fertilization, still figures in the literature of genetics, although Gray's role in recognizing the nature of
the problem has only recently received recognition by Conway
Zirkle. Yet Darwin did see Gray's little paper and used his evidence
in developing a line of argument that "pollen includes gemmules,

derived from every part of the organisation, which diffuse themselves and multiply by self-division; hence it is not surprising that
gemmules within the pollen . . . should sometimes be able to affect the same parts . . . in the mother plant." Darwin's gemmules have not stood the test of later research, however accurate
the observations on the direct action of pollen which led him to it.[4]

Indeed, in most respects, Gray's basic ideas about his science
showed marked continuity with his views in the early 1850's. "We
still hold that genealogical connection, rather than mutual resemblance is the fundamental thing. . . ." The processes of the organic world were still walled off from inorganic nature. Spontaneous generation, at least under present conditions, seemed even less
a possibility than it had twenty years earlier. And Gray, despite his
occasional weakening when talking about instinct, never felt that
the influence of environment directly produced variation. "It would
be very like a chemist," he once wrote, "to think that *external influences* will explain everything.—But I presume he believes that peculiarities are heritable. If he does, then he thinks he can explain, or
will be able to explain, the origination of variations. I cannot—that
is, to any extent, and do not expect to. When he will show us *how*
external influences actually worked to change a *peach* into a *nec-
tarine,* I will consider his proposition." [5] Thus the law of genetic resemblance, which had been at the center of Gray's pre-Darwinian
thought, still had an important role to play. Like still begat like. He
could no longer say forever, but he did say they did so for a very
long time. And when plants did vary, the cause was to him unknown.
This insistence on ignorance on this point rather than a resort to
some facile generalization was in itself important.

Not only did Gray reject Darwin's pangenesis, but also, along
with his denial of acquired characteristics, he rejected the neo-
Lamarckians, who had many advocates in America in the 1870's
and 1880's. On one occasion he referred to the Hyatt-Cope school
as "people who have got hold of what they call a *law*—tho' I do
not see that they contribute any *vera causa* at all." Thus Gray
turned his back on a belief in acquired characters, differing from
both Darwin and the neo-Lamarckians. His position, conservative
in the sense that it closely resembled his pre-Darwinian view, nev-

ertheless placed him by the gatepost of the road that led to modern genetics.[6]

Some changes, it is true, were necessary to adapt to the new era. Species, instead of being eternal, were now groups which were "at present & for our time—distinct. Intermediate forms were the *plague,* now they are *guides* & aids." [7] Although he still talked of Darwin's hypothesis rather than his theory, Gray became less and less equivocal about giving his adherence to the general idea both of natural selection and the derivation of species from earlier forms.

Although he gave Darwin more and more unqualified scientific adherence, their familiar differences over teleology and design in nature became more deeply entrenched. Gray continued to assert, in season and out, that Darwin had re-introduced teleology into natural history. He meant by this that Darwin had shown the utilitarian purpose of many exquisite mechanisms which, under older forms, had remained simply inexplicable. "A bur in the light of morphological botany may be seen to be a seed, a fruit or a portion of one, a calyx, an involucre, or what not. Under the teleological aspect, which was once thought to be expelled from natural history, but which has come back in full force, a bur is one adaptation for the dissemination of seeds by cattle or other animals." [8]

Darwin and Gray agreed on this kind of utilitarian teleology to be found in nature, and their delighted discoveries in orchids, insectivorous plants, and the rest only bore them out. Gray went on, however, to say that many "who clearly perceive that man inevitably will and must read Purpose in or into Nature, conceive of Unconscious Purpose. This to most minds seems like conceiving of white blackness. To most minds Purpose will imply Intelligence." [9] Thus the old disagreement about design in nature still separated Gray's teleology from Darwin's.

As he entered the final great period of activity after his retirement in 1873, Gray was able to put down with some precision his own idea of his religious position and his relation to Darwin.[10] He was still "a humble member of the Christian church, & as for orthodoxy, I receive & profess, *ex animo,* the Nicene creed for myself, though with no call to deny the Christian name to those who receive less." His view of Darwin he re-emphasized by telling a story about

Charles Kingsley when he visited the Botanic Garden. "I think he called partly to compliment me upon being, in my own way, a sort of defender of the faith." Kingsley said that after he had read the *Origin of Species* "he wrote Mr. Darwin to tell him that in his opinion he had not damaged the grounds of natural theology at all, though the superstructure would need reshaping in a way that it would delight the heart of Paley, if he were alive,—indeed that the new arguments & explanations of old difficulties would improve instead of injuring natural theology." Darwin had replied "he certainly had not meant to do any harm, & was very glad to hear that he had not done any."

Gray could thus conclude, "I dare say I am much more orthodox than Mr. Darwin; also that he is about as far from being an atheist as I am." Did Darwin "deny the existence of a Creator?" Gray's answer was, "certainly not." Was he an infidel? "Can't say till you tell me what you mean by an infidel—and perhaps not then." Did he disbelieve the Bible? "I don't believe the Bible teaches science, or makes various claims that many good people have been in the habit of making for it." Even in giving these answers, Gray still held to the neutrality of science. "I don't think it of much consequence to raise the question about Darwin's or my own personal belief." To say that Darwinism was itself a religious belief "seems much the same as saying my belief is Botany, or Prof. Peirce's Mathematics." Doctrines of evolution "can be held theistically or atheistically. Of course I think the latter wrong & absurd."

Despite his confidence that Darwin was no atheist, Gray could not forget his sharp defeat on the design argument in 1868 nor his realization that the Darwin circle in England under Huxley's leadership was moving in another direction, supported by a deep tide of opinion. Since atheistic doctrines of evolution "are prevailing & likely to prevail, more or less, among scientific men, I have thought it important & have taken considerable pains to show that they may be held *theistically*." In his heart he knew he was waging uncertain battle for a cause growing all the time less popular. "Indeed, I expect that a coming generation will give me the credit (which I am content to wait for) of being one of the few who fought manfully for the very citadel of natural theology when misguided friends were hurling away its bulwarks, insanely thinking them proper missiles with which to crush those who are attacking unimportant outworks." This appeal to the judgment of history, the only one Gray ever made, is in itself a measure of his poor opinion of the prospects of success for his mission in 1874.

The plight of a Darwinian theist and a believer in the doctrine of design was rendered bad enough by the rise of agnosticism, so powerfully driven home by the eloquence of Huxley. But it was rendered truly desperate by the thunder of theologians, who, in rejecting Darwin and all his works, joined with the most radical of the evolutionists in insisting that natural selection and the resultant derivation of new species knocked the props from under Paley's argument. The Reverend Charles Hodge, professor of theology of Princeton Theological Seminary, published in 1874 a book called *What Is Darwinism?* [11] in which he took the view that Darwin's natural selection was inimical to all forms of the design argument and hence was atheistical. His intent, of course, was to carry forward the war against Darwin in the name of theology. Gray, having nearly despaired of converting scientists to the possibility of evolution and theism dwelling together, now tried to convince a theologian of the same thing. He was here re-entering the argument in which the metaphor of battle still held sway. No longer did it refer to battle between scientists but rather to the long-drawn-out war between science and theology. Defending Darwin as strongly as the record would possibly allow, he reasserted his position that "evolution may be as profoundly and particularly theistic as it is increasingly probable. The taint of atheism which, in Dr. Hodge's view, leavens the whole lump, is not inherent in the original grain of Darwinism—in the principles posited—but has somehow been introduced in the subsequent treatment." [12]

A modern student of the relations between evolution and theology concluded that after 1874, when Hodge wrote his book, "no one undertook seriously to reconcile natural selection with design." [13] On the level of rigorously logical, formal philosophy such a conclusion sets the date much too late, because the design argument had had hard going at least since the time of Hume. On a second level of the rough-and-ready philosophizing indulged in by scientists and theologians such as Gray and Hodge, who were forced to take up the problem of design although they were not strictly speaking philosophers, the conclusion may possibly be reached by matching the points in the debate. Perhaps Gray had been argued down and ruled out on points by 1874. But on this level, the formal logic—the debate—is of much less importance than the influence the various arguments exerted, not on the other protagonists, but upon a wide public. In this latter sense Gray's arguments for the compatibility of evolution with theism were full of life in 1874. Indeed, his influence on Protestant theology in America had scarcely begun.

From the point of view of 1874, the most striking fact about Gray's writings on Darwinian subjects and their relation to theism, a considerable and ever-growing stock of literature, was the complete anonymity under which he clothed its appearance in print. The *Atlantic* article of 1860 had appeared with Gray's name only in England. None of the others was signed, and the reviews which he was contributing to the *Nation* with increasing regularity were not generally known to be by him. The fact of his authorship was not exactly a secret; his name simply had no marked impact in connection with his views. A survey of the literature of Darwinism in 1872 in a magazine whose general position was sympathetic to that of Gray does not even mention him.[14]

During the whole period from 1859 until 1874, Gray had had little to do with the organized clergy in the United States. His friendship with R. W. Church, by the 1870's the Dean of St. Paul's, had flourished, but rather more in a personal than in a theological way. He often indulged in half-serious exchanges of opinion with Mrs. Gray's relative, Charles Loring Brace, whose real business was social work with the underprivileged children of New York but who had had a preacher's education. It was probably Brace who introduced Gray to certain writers who would not ordinarily have come his way and whose views as a whole he did not necessarily accept. For instance, the quotation with which Gray ended his "Sequoia and Its History" is from Francis Power Cobbe, who was a correspondent of Brace's and was most widely known as an anti-vivisectionist.[15] But again Gray's interchange of ideas with Brace was more a personal affair than a channel of communication with Protestant church circles.

Only a very observant and patient reader could have seen in Gray's scattered and anonymous articles on Darwinism and religion a considered and consistent viewpoint which might serve the Protestant church well, despite such extreme conservative warnings as Hodge's. Unless someone took the trouble to pull together Gray's contributions to the subject and present them forcefully in church circles, Gray's impact might have remained as diffuse as it had been in the decade and a half after 1859. But just such a person did appear in 1874 and did launch Gray on a new career as a theist and Darwinist combined. The Reverend George Frederick Wright was not related to either Charles Wright or Chauncey Wright, and he resembled these two very different men only in that like them he played an important role on the same stage with Asa Gray.

George Frederick Wright was a thorough Congregationalist. Educated at Oberlin College and Oberlin Theological Seminary, he was in 1874 the pastor of the Congregational Church in Andover, Massachusetts, hard by that center of conservative Calvinist theology, the Andover Theological Seminary. During a country pastorate in Vermont some years before, he had begun to geologize as a hobby, gradually developing sufficient proficiency to make studies, which had real scientific merit, of the glacial deposits in the neighborhood of Andover. Since this background turned Wright to pondering the relation of religion to science with a good deal more understanding than a theologian of the stamp of Hodge could muster, Wright was predisposed to look for some kind of middle ground. Gradually he found that the anonymous author of the *Atlantic* article and other reviews on Darwinian subjects was "guiding my own thoughts and convictions concerning the readjustments in the arguments for natural theology made necessary by recent scientific discoveries. . . ."

In the afterwash of Gray's anonymous review in the *Nation* of Hodge's *What Is Darwinism?*, G. F. Wright wrote a letter to the editor on a point of theology upon which it touched. Gray answered courteously, and Wright was surprised to find that the celebrated botanist "had made special inquiries about me, and sent his kind regards, and soon after I was permitted to meet him in person. . . ." [16] At last Gray had a real ally in the clergy, one who genuinely wished to introduce a better understanding of science among them at the same time he was building a redoubt against the infidels.

Wright contributed to the discussion the idea that the tenets of Calvinistic theology had much in common with Darwinism. For instance, he said that the "Calvinistic doctrine of the spread of sin from Adam to his descendants has also its illustrative analogies in the Darwinian principle of heredity." Also, the "adjustment of the doctrines of fore-ordination and free-will occasions perplexity to the Calvinist in a manner strikingly like that experienced by the Darwinian in stating the consistency of his system of evolution with the existence of manifest design in nature." [17] Gray was perhaps the example of the Darwinian enmeshed in difficulties. Certainly he had often asserted that all the old difficulties remained where they were even after Darwin. But he had never pursued, despite his orthodoxy, the analogy with Calvinism. Indeed, the name of Calvin and any explicit mention of the more characteristic doctrines such as predestination are even more conspicuously absent from Gray's writings than are the usual Darwinian catch-phrases which he sedulously avoided. Gray remained the scientist; Wright remained the theologian. They nevertheless formed an effective alliance.

In June 1875, Wright wrote to Gray that "a fresh perusal of your Atlantic Monthly articles impresses me anew with the great value not only of them but of what else you have written on that subject. The infidel class of Darwinian expositors have had the ear of the public entirely too much, and have needlessly added to the alarm of orthodox people. And such opponents as Hodge and Dawson [18] have made matters still worse." Would not Gray "confer a great favor on the world" and allow his essays to be collected and republished? Wright cited his own case as a measure of the possibilities. "It was your Christian faith and your clearness of conception and statement that, when once I had access to a library where I could find what had been written on the subject, were the most important factors in leading me to my present views." Other ministers might do likewise. "There is yet an immense amount of prejudice and misconception upon this subject to be removed." [19]

While Gray felt the scholar's uneasiness at seeing fifteen-year-old articles on an explosive subject reawakened with new ink, he showed a certain amount of gratification at the suggestion. "At present, I think I should let them alone, unless there comes what you ministers recognize as a call, and such a call I should defer to." It would mean, of course, the end of anonymity, and "you don't know how I dislike to have my name bruited about." [20]

The question of a publisher had yet to be settled, but when the rumor went around that Gray was to republish he got an immediate reaction. It did not come from the religious press but from E. L. Youmans, the disciple of Spencer who worked for the Appletons. Gray must have been something of a puzzle to those apostles of evolution in America, Youmans and John Fiske. He was closer to Darwin than they. And each time they went to Europe they heard his praise sung loudly in the Darwin circle itself. Yet Gray's attitude toward them was cool.

John Fiske had made a real effort to put Gray on a Darwinian pedestal by contrasting him with the unmerciful portrait he drew of Agassiz. Gray's reaction was anything but warm. The article "seems to me remarkable for the truths which it were better not to say, at least in the tone adopted. It seems to me in rather bad taste, and the writer—not being a naturalist—does not know what Mr. A's good work and strong points are." Once Gray spoke of Youmans as "a great admirer and useful friend of Herbert Spencer— I imagine a *dilletante* sort of man." [21]

The basis of Gray's coolness to these Spencerians was more than that they were a generation younger than he and publicists rather than scientists. In the great shifts of opinion following the publication of the *Origin of Species,* the followers of Spencer had replaced Agassiz as the American idealists, the allies of transcendentalism, and the believers in nature as the reflection of an immanent deity. Evolution had a central place with them, but the *a priori* method of reasoning belonged to the tradition of Agassiz rather than to that of Darwin. Gray was against closed ideal systems of philosophy, regardless of the place they gave to evolution. Both Spencer and his followers and the German evolutionists by then on the rise were in Gray's eyes speculative rather than scientific.[22] It was in a letter to G. F. Wright in 1875 that Gray paid his last respects to Chauncey Wright by referring to the latter's article, "German Darwinism," in the *Nation* and emphasizing the difference between Darwinism and Spencerism.[23] Later Gray specifically made the same point against John Fiske's Christian cosmic evolutionism when he said that the "wonder is, not at this climax of Christian hope, but as to how it can be legitimately attained from the underlying scientific data." [24] A humble belief in the mysteries of orthodox Christianity seemed to Gray more scientific than a dogmatic adherence to any philosophy old or new.

Despite Gray's coolness to them and their inability to appreciate his philosophical stand, the Spencerians could not afford to snub the friend of Darwin. Hence through Youman's efforts the Appletons—publishers of Darwin and Spencer—agreed to bring out Gray's *Darwiniana*. It was a queer combination—the impetus from a conservative Congregationalist clergyman of Andover and the vehicle provided by the friend of Spencer. In view of Gray's beliefs the enthusiasm of both made a certain amount of sense. But Gray added a chapter on teleology which left no doubt that he intended the book to serve the ends of George Frederick Wright.

The collection contained Gray's first review of the *Origin of Species,* the dialogue with Daniel Treadwell, the *Atlantic* series, "Sequoia and Its History," and reviews and other articles, such as the 1874 sketch of Darwin. This massive reprinting of old material was the greatest possible tribute to the clarity of Gray's thinking during the excited days of 1860. James D. Dana, possibly thinking of the contrast to himself, admitted that Gray had "nothing to take back, which is much to say or have said of you." [25]

In the introduction Gray described himself as "one who is scientifically, and in his own fashion, a Darwinian, philosophically a convinced theist, and religiously an acceptor of the 'creed commonly called the Nicene,' as the exponent of the Christian faith." Although he had used essentially this description in 1874, his specification of the Nicene Creed as his form of belief is a late addition, appearing nowhere in the 1860 literature. Was it an addition to emphasize unflinching orthodoxy as opposed to more liberal brands of Christianity, as is often implied when Gray's self-description is quoted? On the contrary, it was a careful differentiation from the Apostles' Creed to protect the integrity of a scientist's belief in observed data. The Nicene Creed states, "I look for the Resurrection of the dead." The Apostle's Creed changes this to "I believe in . . . the Resurrection of the Body." Gray felt that the Nicene Creed was "remarkable for its complete avoidance of conflict with physical science" and was a worthier interpretation than "the crude notion of the revivification of the human body." [26]

In his final chapter on teleology, written especially for *Darwiniana,* Gray intended to "present the argument for design in such a way as to tell on both sides." On one hand he wished to reach "Christian men, that they may be satisfied with, and perchance may learn to admire, Divine Works effected step by step, if need be, in a system of nature. . . ." On the other hand, he aimed at "the anti-theistic people, to show that without the implication of a superintending wisdom nothing is made out, and nothing credible." [27] In executing this intention Gray rather heavily overlaid his argument with closely reasoned and relevant refutations of ephemeral articles in the *Westminster Review* and the *Contemporary Review,* the total effect of which was unfortunately to slow and somewhat obscure the main argument. The influence of G. F. Wright appeared here and there, as in a reference to St. Augustine and a footnote which contained Gray's lone nod to David Hume.

At base, however, Gray's reasoning ran something like this. Darwin had reintroduced teleology into natural history by showing that every organ had a useful purpose to the plant or animal which possessed it, either in the past or the future if not at present. This did not necessarily imply the existence of a God. "Darwinian evolution (whatever may be said of other kinds) is neither theistical nor non-theistical." Hence Darwin's kind of teleology did not prove design. But if "all Nature is of a piece—as modern physical philosophy insists—then it seems clear that design must in some way, and in some sense, pervade the system, or be wholly absent from it." Difficult as it was to conceive design "in a whole of which the series of parts appear to be contingent, the alternative may be yet more difficult and less satisfactory." A belief in a general and all-comprehending design as the alternative to chaos was the position which Gray had reached, and the adaptations in nature seemed to suggest a basic order, belief in which was important to the scientist. Gray then went on to equate design with its "theological synonym," Providence. Thus Gray's religion and science rested on an unproved but profound belief in a basic order in nature.

Noteworthy in its absence from Gray's 1876 formulation was the figure of the stream of beneficent variation, which was reprinted in its place in the *Atlantic* article, but which Gray had long before come to realize was hazardous. Now he tried another figure of speech. "Natural selection is not the wind which propels the vessel, but the rudder which, by friction, now on this side and now on that, shapes the course . . . Variation answers to the wind. . . ." He did not even hint now that the wind followed some beneficent direction. But he did insist that variations, "the differences between individual plants and animals, however originated, are evidently not from without but from within—not physical but physiological." With this one blow Gray separated himself from both Darwin and the neo-Lamarckians on the issue of acquired characteristics, but he now hazarded no guess as to the direction of variations. He rested his case that "the *Divine* it is which holds together all Nature." [28]

Darwiniana's appearance in 1876 dispelled immediately the anonymity with which Gray has so carefully cloaked his role as a philosopher and commentator on religion and science. "The appearance of this volume," remarked the reviewer in Youman's *Popular Science Monthly,* "will take many people by surprise." G. F. Wright was overjoyed at the result of his scheme. "It seems to me most timely," he wrote to Gray, "that your views are made accessible just now. Prof. Huxley's lectures are centering attention upon the scientific attitude." As the main speaker at the opening of the Johns Hopkins University, Huxley was indeed having a triumphant tour of the United States. Whether or not Wright considered Gray as a possible antidote, he could scarcely avoid some satisfaction at having a theistic scientist's testimony appear at just that moment. Actually, Gray tried hard to entertain Huxley when he was in New England, but a trip of his own interfered, and John Fiske managed to monopolize the eminent Britisher's time while he was in and near Boston.[29]

The reception of *Darwiniana* by reviewers was highly favorable. Both *Popular Science Monthly* and the *New York Times* approved. The religious press, especially that under Congregational influence, raised a chorus of praise.[30] A view so carefully designed to follow the middle way, however, had to expect frowns from more extreme positions on both sides. The religious paper *Independent,* one of the most influential, would only admit that "Prof. Gray simply says that development is harmonious with theism. But we want what will prove theism." This reviewer correctly asserted that Gray had made no such proof and that he had stated the question of the cause of variation "as produced under some internal force, which force it is hardly worth while to imagine to be anything other than some law or laws yet occult, but which are liable to be discovered one of these days." If the development theory were accepted, the reviewer insisted that "the commonly-received argument from design will have to be very much modified. . . ."[31]

On the other side, the review in the *Nation* was sure to be read by a broad segment of liberal opinion. This magazine was doubly important in that it had already become Gray's main vehicle for his anonymous articles on science and religion. To Wright, Gray wrote, "I had rather—for the subject's sake, merely, it fell into orthodox than into heterodox hands." And although he realized that an author has no business picking his own reviewer, he hinted to his friend Charles Eliot Norton that he should "do what is needful."[32] Norton, while certainly not orthodox, could be depended on to be thoughtful and fair. However, the book actually fell into the hands of Henry Ware Holland, who had in the past already reviewed Fiske's *Cosmic Philosophy* and Chauncey Wright's *Philosophical Discussions.*

Holland, representing the fully ripened conviction that Darwin had indeed damaged the argument from design, charged Gray with not understanding the slips in its logic. "His mind is candid and direct, he has thought at length upon the subject, and indeed, his whole book turns upon it; yet, strange to say, he does not seem familiar with Paley's argument or the way in which it has been affected by the evolution theory." In Holland's opinion Gray never fully answered Daniel Treadwell's line of reasoning which he included in the old 1860 dialogue. "It is not a sufficient answer to say that the variation of species by law instead of miracle does not *dis*prove design, or that complicated results produced by simple means *may* have been planned as fully as if caused by direct volition." This was true, but was a mere negative. The old argument had "turned on the complexity, and that is now otherwise accounted for." [33] Thus, on the level of formal philosophy, Gray had failed to construct an argument for theism from design in nature which had compelling force to those of his contemporaries who were willing to examine his work rigorously. The argument from design was, after all, a proper philosophical problem of the eighteenth century. The eighteenth century was gone, and Asa Gray could not single-handedly bring it back.

The publication of *Darwiniana* nevertheless coupled the name of an eminent and clear-headed scientist with theism, and Gray's influence in church circles emanated from this coupling, not from the internal logic of his work. He found that his collaboration with George Frederick Wright was a continuing one, and together they felt a responsibility at the same time to correct the ignorance which attached itself to science.

One of the more flamboyant personalities in Boston in the late 1870's was Joseph Cook, a graduate of Harvard and Andover Theological Seminary, who used a smattering of scientific learning gained in two years in Germany to launch an anti-evolution crusade. Sponsored by a committee compounded of Massachusetts governors and clergymen, his Boston Monday lectures drew to the Tremont Temple, at least by his own account, throngs of representatives of "the first intellectual culture" of New England. Stenographic reports appeared in the Boston *Daily Advertiser* and later in a series of volumes, the 1877 one carrying the subtitle *Biology*.[34] It was a clever combination of extravagant rhetoric, high-sounding scientific terms such as "bioplasm," and a narrow, scurrilous attack on Darwinian evolution.

George Frederick Wright was much alarmed at "Mr. Cook's remarkable rhetorical display" and feared it was "likely to raise up a harvest of bigotry and self assurance of which we shall soon be made ashamed." Not only did Wright redouble his efforts to show the compatibility of science with the main truths of Christianity,[35] but he stimulated Gray to stoop to notice Mr. Cook.

Cook's excesses were so great that Gray had fun knocking him down. What else could he do when the "merits of these lectures are in a degree peculiar; their faults are still more so"? Gray made much, for instance, of the fact that the stenographer had interjected through the text "applause," "sensation," and "laughter." He concluded that in "serious earnest we think that this production is not one for orthodoxy to be proud of, and that it is best to declare this opinion plainly, and promptly." John Fiske, who later took his turn at tilting with Joseph Cook, was glad to claim Gray as an ally.[36]

On the scientific flank of Gray's and Wright's middle position an adversary arose who was as formidable as Cook had been ludicrous. The astronomer Simon Newcomb touched in his address as president of the American Association for the Advancement of Science on the problem of science and religion. His proposition was "that science concerns itself only with phenomena and the relations which convert them, and does not take account of any questions which do not in some way admit of being brought to the test of observation." That this "is the whole universe we should all be very sorry to suppose, and none more so than he who has the honor to address you. But, should I pretend to a scientific knowledge of what lies behind this visible frame, I should be acting the part of the rash speculator, rather than that of the cautious thinker." [37] While Newcomb's statement was very close in its general bearings to Gray's own temperament, the astronomer so baldly divorced the sphere of science from a sphere in which Providence might operate that one with even a lingering partiality for the argument from design could only feel uncomfortable.

Since Newcomb's address was reprinted in a religious paper, the *Independent,* Gray answered there in a letter in which he feigned the ingenuous role of a "Country Reader." As usual since *Darwiniana,* he consulted Wright about his strategy. Gray questioned whether it might not be a legitimate hypothesis, on the analogy of man's manipulation of nature, to suppose "an intelligent cause which may (not does) modify to ends the operations of natural laws. . . ." He was unwilling to banish Providence (which he had equated with design) completely from the sphere of science. He supposed that men could alter the course of nature in particular ways. Is then the inference that another being "of a higher order may also modify the particular course of nature without infraction of its laws" completely unscientific? [38]

When both the editor of the *Independent* and Newcomb took Gray's answer to mean that science could show the intervention of Providence on a large scale, he returned to the charge, and then yet again. Much of it was the familiar argument. At least some parts of nature showed purpose, as in the mechanism of the insectivorous plant, and this teleology in the individual organism oft repeated added up to an analogy of a mind working on a nature made of laws. Because his adversary was an astronomer, Gray framed his argument with more precise logic than usual, giving prominence to the concept of nature as a mechanism in the physicist's sense. Here he revealed, underneath, the ever-present distinction between the living and the nonliving world which had figured in a quiet way in his thought since the 1840's. When he said that definite ends show themselves "notably in the animal and vegetable kingdoms" he left no doubt that his argument was based on the presence of life. The editor of the *Independent* finally summed up Gray as saying, "My idea is that the doctrine of Providence is identical in its grounds with that of the adaptation of means to ends in Nature. . . ." [39]

Newcomb remained unimpressed, the controversy eventually coming to an indecisive impasse. Gray had had fun disposing of Joseph Cook, whose point of view was rapidly losing favor. Newcomb on the other hand presented in bald terms what scientists were increasingly coming to feel. Science and religion were completely distinct spheres—a man could be comfortable in either or both as long as he insisted that no connection joined the two. Gray was explicitly unwilling to admit this complete divorce, but his argument that the two spheres did interact was too complex to follow easily. He had to establish the analogy between the mind of man and the supreme intelligence at the same time he had to deny that the supreme intelligence followed human patterns of thought. He had to deny that crude interruptions in the course of nature, miracles, had occurred at any rate since biblical times while he was affirming that if they happened the method of science could not detect them. Newcomb could not follow him.

By 1879, Gray himself was describing the discussion of evolution as "now a little threadbare." [40] The terms of the argument about design, about the implications of natural selection, and about Darwin's view of his own work had not changed essentially in the nearly two decades since that memorable year of 1860. Agassiz and his resplendent idealism seemed impossibly ancient. The old Darwin circle now had little influence and no cohesion. Lyell was dead. Hooker and Gray were intimate collaborators on taxonomy. Gray and Darwin still had interests in common as long as tendrils twined and Venus's fly-traps caught their prey. But on the great issues of science and religion, on the ultimate philosophical implications of their work, the old friends had completely talked themselves out. Other, younger, more strident voices, often speaking German, were now the ones heard shouting of evolution. Even Huxley seemed elderly by 1879.

Nevertheless, since George Frederick Wright had unveiled him to the American public as a theist and evolutionist combined, Gray felt a new and different responsibility to a larger public. His almost unique personal position as a botanical authority, a friend of Darwin, and now as a reconciler placed new demands upon him. The arguments were the same, but the circumstances gave his words an oracular quality. His audience was no longer the bench of the high court of scientific opinion, as in the days when he flayed Agassiz for courting popular applause. The audience was now those conscientious people who had a yearning for both science and religion but who had somewhere become confused by all the diatribe. What they wanted was to see, not to hear or to reason with, but just to see a first-rate scientist who professed himself to be a theist and a Christian. Gray took on a new importance as an exhibit, not as a logician.

Recognition of his new role prompted Gray to break his ancient rule of never giving public lectures to accept an invitation to go to

New Haven to address the Yale divinity students. G. F. Wright's friend Professor G. P. Fisher gave him the assurance of a sympathetic and receptive audience. Gray took the assignment seriously, for it meant a real interruption in his botanical labors. What would Hooker say? Sir Joseph, out of sympathy with Gray's philosophical ideas anyway, was always driving him to complete the *Flora of North America*.[41] With the feeling that he would do some good Gray made extensive preparations once he started. A tryout before the Cambridge Scientific Club tested his ideas on the changes in science in the past thirty years. He wrote to Charles Loring Brace inquiring what doubts about science troubled him and what doubts were most current among clergymen. Since Gray and Brace almost never agreed on anything, the answer from New York that "the old argument from design has lost something of its force" was hardly surprising.[42] In Cambridge, Gray submitted the manuscript to his pastor at the First Church for comment. As if for balance, he also showed it to his Saturday Club friend, Dr. Oliver Wendell Holmes.

The audience at Yale had in it distinguished people. Outstanding among the theologians was old President Noah Porter, his heart hardened against the agnostics. O. C. Marsh was also there. In the fifteen years since Gray had tried to get money from George Peabody through him, Marsh had become a leading student of evolution as a paleontologist and had risen to the presidency of the National Academy of Sciences. Although Gray's two lectures were especially designed for theological students, the first belonged in Marsh's world, and the second, if not in President Porter's, at least in Professor Fisher's.

Practicing investigators seldom take time off for a sober, thirty-year view of the course of science as a whole, measuring it both against the trends of the times and their own personal experiences. The first of the New Haven lectures gave Gray this rare opportunity. Later botanists have often overlooked this summary of Gray's scientific beliefs, so replete with clues to his own changing judgments before and after Darwin. They have been put off, perhaps, by the apologetic title of the whole book which resulted from the lectures, *Natural Science and Religion*. Gray confidently asserted that the problems raised by evolution were not new, that geology and the nebular hypothesis had posed the same philosophical questions in their day. Tortured constructions of Scripture had not succeeded then. Now "we may take it to be the accepted idea that the Mosaic books were not handed down to us for our instruction in scientific knowledge." [43]

His catalogue of changes in the thirty years since 1850 stressed the continuity of his own views as often as their disruption. The animal and plant kingdoms—once separate and distinct, capable of precise definition—now appeared to him as one continuum. Protoplasm now appeared as the one essential common denomination of all living things. Nevertheless, the organic world was still a self-contained, self-perpetuating system. "Thus far, spontaneous generation, or abiogenesis,—this incoming of life apart from that which is living,—is not supported by any unequivocal evidence, though not a little may be said in its favor." In the shadow of Pasteur, this was brave caution and an indication that Gray's mind had a flexibility that would have stretched all the way to the biochemical discoveries of the mid-twentieth century. He even emphasized that the single cell was in itself a "very complex structure." Far from being simple, the cell had already developed a greatly sophisticated structure and behavior. "It is an illusion to fancy that the mystery of life is less in an amoeba or a blood-corpuscle than in a man."

In discussing species Gray referred to the older view that they had no genetic connection as having "died a royal death with Agassiz." The new view was that all plants and animals have a genetic connection with one another. Gray's own insistence that he was not governed by any worshipful devotion to ideal species he illustrated with a little story. "Some one when asked if he believed in ghosts, replied, No, he had seen too many of them. So I have been at the making and unmaking of far too many species to retain any overweening confidence in their definiteness and stability." Are species then mere shadows, not substantial things? "I do not exactly agree . . . but I believe that they have only a relative fixity and permanence." Here was good soil for pragmatism.

All plants and animals vary more or less. "Now this simple principle,—extended from races to species; from the present to geological ages; from man's domesticated animals to all animals and plants;

from struggle with disease to struggle for food, for room . . . this is *Darwinism*." Natural selection was a "truth,—a *catena* of facts and direct inferences from facts." The open question was, however, what do its operations amount to? By 1880, general confidence, including Darwin's, in natural selection had been shaken. Gray's caution can only be called good judgment. "No doubt it may account for much which has not received other scientific explanation; and Mr. Darwin is not the man to claim that it will account for everything." Gray hammered once again at his old insistence that the nature of variation was completely unknown. "There is of course a cause for the variation. Nobody supposes that anything changes without a cause; and there is no reason for thinking that proximate causes of variation may not come to be known; but we hardly know the conditions, still less the causes now." This insistence, in the face of Darwin's pangenesis theory, was the open invitation Gray left for the development of the science of genetics. Gray even went so far as to deny that the purely accidental nature of variation had been proved, though he knew enough now not to suggest any benevolent direction taming variations for benign ends.

In the second lecture, "The Relations of Scientific to Religious Belief," Gray ceased to labor his point about design in nature. Nevertheless, constantly before him loomed the skeptics of his point of view. He sought a way to carry conviction in spite of their criticisms. In 1860 it had been Daniel Treadwell. It might have been Huxley; it might have been Newcomb. It might even have been Hodge or Charles Loring Brace. Whatever their bias, agnostic or orthodox, they had in common one insistent idea—that Darwin had destroyed the argument from design in nature as a logical basis for religious belief. Gray carefully recast his argument. Evolution adds no "new perplexity to theism." Many scientists (and here he made a bow to his old friend James Dwight Dana in the audience) held evolutionary ideas which were theistic and yet not very different in essentials from Darwin's hypothesis.

Gray's old doubt about whether the sum of many minute variations could produce a functioning, seeing eye crept in. While "I see how variations of a given organ or structure can be led on to great modification, I cannot conceive how non-existent organs come thus to be. . . ." Nor "am I at all helped in this respect by being shown that the new organs are developed little by little." He may have been indulging in an element of wishful thinking, the reliance on complexity to give some new Paley a chance to say that since no one can imagine how it came to be, Providence must have done it. Yet in 1880 this doubt about gradual steps was brave, scientifically well-grounded, and almost forward-looking.

Other familiar strains appeared. That which "science removes from the supernatural to the natural" is not "lost to theism." Here the Newcomb controversy came grating in. The "business of science is the course of Nature, not with interruptions of it, which must rest on their own special evidence." This skirted dangerously close to the divorce between science and religion which had been at the heart of Newcomb's contention. Gray was not able to maintain in a convincing way a role for Providence to play in the course of nature without violating some of her fixed laws. There was another side to this perplexity, however. What was the alternative to design? The true issue is "not between Darwinism and direct Creationism, but between design and fortuity, between any intention or intellectual cause and no intention nor predictable first cause." Having reached this point, Gray equated design with the basic belief shared by almost all scientists, either consciously or unconsciously, in the basic orderliness of nature.

On the place of man in nature, which the Victorian public took to be the greatest one raised by Darwin, Gray guardedly broke a long-standing reticence. Mediate creation was to him a secondary phenomenon, no less divine because it could be explained by natural causes. But as to the actual origin of man, Gray answered, "We do not know at all." He admitted "traces of his existence up to and even anterior to the latest marked climatic change in our temperate zone: but he was then perfected man; as no vestige of an earlier form is known." These views fitted more closely to Alfred Russel Wallace's ideas on the origin of man than they did to the gradual evolution envisaged by Darwin.[44]

Gray ended his lecture with a personal and confessional statement. "I accept Christianity on its own evidence." By saying "the revelation on which our religion is based is an example of evolution"

Gray reticently gave his approval to the higher criticism of the Bible then growing up. But it is also the echo of his early position of the 1840's. The stream of Scripture "brings down precious gold; but the water—the vehicle of transportation—is not gold." Despite this light dismissal of biblical authority, Gray was still no Unitarian. Revelation essentially culminated in "the advent of a Divine Person, who, being made man, manifested the Divine Nature in union with the human, and . . . this manifestation constitutes Christianity." In black and white, as few men ever dare to do, Gray had made his scientific and religious confession.

The reaction to Gray's lectures was entirely predictable. All sides paid their respects to the scientific eminence of the author. President Porter rumbled conservative protests which the *Presbyterian Review* echoed. Wright and his allies at New Haven otherwise fully controlled the majority opinion among the clergy in applauding, and they were joined by a scientist in O. C. Marsh. A liberal clergyman, William G. Eliot of St. Louis, was equally enthusiastic, and an outright freethinker, Boston variety, found the lectures a starting point for a statement of his own agnostic point of view.[45]

The complaisance of these comments, however, failed to mask the lack of real stir from the lectures. They fortified the rapid trend of American Protestantism toward an accommodation with Darwinism. So too, as Wright pointed out, "numbers of the younger scientific men whom I know are drinking in the spirit of these lectures and the harvest will be by and by." But influential opinion in the English-speaking world of 1880 doubted an easy accommodation, and Gray had failed to provide for genuine doubters a middle way. No one recognized this failure more clearly than Julia Wedgwood, who felt more than most people the need for a way to be a Darwinist and a theist at the same time.

As a niece of Darwin's, Julia Wedgwood saw the warfare of science and religion as a family matter. Her loyalty to her uncle fought directly with her cherished convictions. "Physical science at its present stage is hostile to the beliefs that seem to me more important than all that Physical Science has to teach." She was convinced that the general tendency of her uncle's influence, "or rather of the influence of the body of men of which he is, somewhat accidentally, the eponymous hero" was "distinctly atheistic." Hence she took comfort in the fact that Darwin from his first association with Gray "felt a degree of respect for your views, with which I think no other person sharing his interests has been able to inspire him." Or rather, she continued, thinking of the old disagreement about design, "perhaps it would be truer to say that you are the only person who shares his interests & holds the views which he fails to share, others bound to him by common tastes are so also by common negations." [46]

Despite the "real consolation" which Gray's example gave her, however, Miss Wedgwood saw that *Natural Science and Religion* was too mild to breast the tide of agnosticism which was running strong in British scientific circles. "We know of no one so distinguished as Professor Gray in the scientific world who retains any share of the conviction that all which we sum up in the name of *science* is but a part, and the least important part, of that which it imports to treat as reality," but "we must allow that this conviction is not here set forth with all the distinctness and force which characterise what is directly scientific." She also spotted one of the weakest parts of Gray's case, the identification with the reasoning of Paley, whose works she thought "raised as many difficulties as they solved." [47] Under the clear, cold light of Huxley and the publicists of Darwin in England, the slim book of Yale lectures had little chance.

During his last years, Gray, giving only fitful attention to Darwinism and to his religious position, changed few of his arguments. In 1881 he paid an affectionate last visit to Down House and its master. When in the spring of 1882 Darwin died and his remains went to rest in Westminster Abbey "near those of Newton," Gray paid his respects in a memoir.[48] He compared his old friend to Galileo. The writings of both "conflicted with similar prepossessions," and the Darwinian theory, "legitimately considered, bids fair to be placed . . . upon the same footing with the Copernican system." Incidentally, Gray recalled the intellectual climate of the 1850's in which many naturalists had "worked up to, or were nearly approaching, the question of the relation of the past inhabitants of the earth to the present . . . in such wise as to suggest inevitably that, somehow or other, descent with modification was eventually to be the explanation." Gray was here describing his own position, the importance of which he implied when he speculated that if "Lyell had known as much at first hand of botany or zoology as he knew geology, it is probable that his celebrated chapter on the permanence of species in the 'Principles' would have been reconsidered before the work had passed to the ninth edition in 1853."

Occasionally Gray sallied forth against his opponents on both sides, alike against the theological objectors to Darwinism and the materialist critics of theism. In 1882 he insisted to a group of ministers in Boston that "with the rise and development of astronomy, physics, geology, and later of biological science, the tables were turned, and now many religious beliefs—or what were taken for such—are controlled and modified by scientific beliefs—none more so than in the matter of 'biblical creation.' " Where he felt the evidence clear he had been willing to listen to science first and religion second at least since the 1840's, and he now explicitly reaffirmed that "settled scientific belief must needs control the religious." [49]

On the other hand he sortied to meet one of the latecomers to the Darwin circle who had made the problems of science and religion a specialty. George J. Romanes had been orthodox in 1873 but by 1878 had published anonymously the skeptical *Candid Examination of Theism*. By 1883 he had just begun a long swing back toward orthodoxy, although he had not gone far enough to escape a challenge by Gray in *Nature*. Romanes in Gray's eyes asserted that "the theory of natural selection has destroyed the evidence of special design in organic nature, so that now the facts of organic nature furnish no other and no better evidence of design than do the facts of inorganic nature." Gray's answer showed that thin line of vitalism which had always separated him from the British empirical tradition: "Doubtless in a certain sense all nature is of a piece. But in another sense—the very one we are concerned with—it is of at least two pieces; no matter how it came to be so. One of them is pervaded by an element of its own—that of *direction of actions to ends*—which is more and more manifested as we rise in the scale of being, but is characteristic of all organisms."

379

This distinction ultimately led Gray back to his assertion of the complete ignorance of the nature and mechanism of variation and genetics. He understood "that the particulars in which progeny differs from parent are potential in the germ or in the cells of which the germ consists, and therefore wholly beyond observation." He might have said it was beyond the observation of the biology of the 1880's. "The upshot is, that, so far as observation extends, it does not warrant the supposition of omnifarious and aimless variation; and the speculative assumption of it appears to have no scientific value." [50] Darwin had disagreed with Gray on this point in 1860, and the dominant Darwinians disagreed with him in 1883.

To Sir Joseph Hooker the Gray-Romanes debate was "much beating of the air." Hooker, who had followed Huxley and Herbert Spencer and his own Tory political predilections in what he disparagingly called metaphysico-logical matters, had lost all interest in Gray as a philosopher despite their close personal friendship. Indeed, when Huxley raised the question whether Gray really understood Darwin, Hooker only partly defended his fellow botanist. Gray had understood the *Origin* clearly in "the first few years of his active promulgation of it," but had "sought to harmonize it with his prepossessions, without disturbing its physical principles in any way." In later years "he got deeper and deeper into theological and metaphysical wanderings, and finally formulated his ideas in an illogical fashion." [51] Thus did Gray fail to penetrate even when the target was close at hand.

In November 1886, Gray entertained the Cambridge Scientific Club for what proved to be the last time. As a special guest, Alfred Russel Wallace described how Spencer, Lamarck, the *Vestiges,* and particularly Malthus had led him to his own view. Gray then exhibited his letters from Darwin, especially those received before the publication of the *Origin.*[52] In Gray's own lifetime, his relation with Darwin had already become a part of history, the letters had become documents, and two of the leading survivors of the Darwin circle spoke of the events of 1859 and 1860 as if they belonged to the ages.

A parallel exists between Gray and Wallace beyond the close proximity of their names in the first publication of the theory of evolution. Both had continued an affectionate friendship with Darwin to the end of his life. Yet both had come to differ with the later Darwinians about the existence of an area of value outside of science in the realm of religion. And because of this disagreement both were able to spot shortcomings in the dominant Darwinian synthesis. Neither was completely taken in by an excessive gradualism or by many of the dubious applications of the struggle for existence to human society. Wallace saw something as yet unexplained in the development of the human brain, while Gray eschewed pangenesis and was content to leave the cause of variation so completely unexplained that he left an open invitation for the development of a new science of genetics.

The parallel is less close on the side of their religious beliefs. Wallace went off into spiritualism, at which Gray doubtless scoffed with the best of the positivists. Gray on the other hand persisted in identifying himself with a species of Christianity which had long historic roots and thus by implication a future. He helped to guarantee its future by assisting its accommodation with Darwinism, a less startling but more significant movement than the warfare which some clergymen waged against it. Gray's great accomplishment in his thinking and writing on science and theology was to provide an example which made it easier for Protestants to accept Darwin and to readjust their beliefs to accept what was most worth accepting of nineteenth-century science.

Because of the accomplishment of his example, the label of failure on Gray's career as a Darwinian theist needs careful definition. He failed to provide for the best minds of his generation a way out of the dilemma on which they fancied Darwin had impaled them. He failed to prevent the plunge to obscurity of the eighteenth-century argument from design associated with the name of Paley. Julia Wedgwood was right in seeing that he did not feel the full force of logic which drove the men of the later Darwin circle to agnosticism. Because he rejected the extension by analogy of Darwinian figures of speech to the entire universe, he did not really appreciate the specter of the materialistic determinism which Darwin evoked for so many of his contemporaries. Gray did not feel the horror, as did his friend Jeffries Wyman, who shuddered when he contemplated the struggle for existence as "an *awful* spectacle—not one perfect form on earth, every individual, from crystal up to man, imperfect, warped, stunted in the fight." [53]

If Gray was untypical of the scientists of his age, he was also untypical of orthodox Christian thinkers. The questioned authority of the Scriptures and the lost uniqueness of man never bothered him. Science when it could reach a consensus had clear priority over religion as a source of truth where the two entered the same territory. The task of reconciliation was thus so much easier for him than for others that his case lacked the sharpness to sway the minds which were more genuinely disturbed. It should give pause to the judge who wishes to dismiss Gray's case, however, that the dominant Darwinian synthesis of the 1880's has itself suffered from the ravages of time. Not only did it foster grotesque misapplications to human problems, not only did it in the work of such men as Herbert Spencer revive idealism in an evolutionary guise to be a target for the pragmatists of the next generation, but much of what it insisted was absolute scientific truth has joined the fragments of its own iconoclasm in the discard heap. Those parts of Darwinism which survive—the great fact of evolution itself and the working of natural selection—were precisely those parts which Gray accepted when he called himself a Darwinist.

When Gray is compared neither to the dominant Darwinians nor to the theologians but to the pragmatists, it becomes clear that the general tendency of his thought as well as his example had a living future. Chauncey Wright, whom Gray had aided and guided in 1860, had developed in the concept of the neutrality of science a description of what science could and could not do for Gray. Science was not a religion or a description of the universe to which one must be converted and which one must worship. It was a limited and useful instrument which had nothing to say about questions which could not be asked of it. That Gray and Wright disagreed about what was beyond science is incidental. They agreed in condemning Spencer and the German Darwinians. Gray knew he was making a joke when he said that Darwin had reintroduced teleology into natural history. But the kind of teleology he pointed to here, the purpose which an organ served for the organism which developed it, is pure pragmatism as the younger Americans developed it. Gray is the most clearly identifiable link in American intellectual history between the Providential utilitarianism which was so pervasive in the early nineteenth century and the standard of usefulness which was the keystone of pragmatism at its end. Gray provided a straight highway from Paley to Chauncey Wright and William James.

XIX

THE PATRIARCH OF
NEW PLANT SCIENCES

I N the fall of 1873 Gray watched ninety Harvard botany students troop by the windows of his study and reflected "with
a constant sense of comfort" that "I need not bestow a thought on
them!" He was happy as a king so nearly "free from outside cares &
worriment, and working therefore without distraction." [1] After
thirty years he turned again to his basic task, the *Flora of North
America*. To his own generation of botanists, as to those coming
later, the friendship with Darwin was a legend and the argument
from design an enigma. Asa Gray was to them a taxonomist, a
classifier who reached his full powers, his full potentiality, only in
the act of classifying plants. At last, freed by the silent largesse of
Hunnewell and Sargent, Gray took his place as a premier taxonomist. The great years had begun.[2] Liberty Hyde Bailey, looking
back in 1949, still felt the thrill. "I like the heading in Rodgers's
book, 'Asa Gray—the Great Years Begun.' He was fortunate in his
period. It was the time of the great explorations. Torrey was gone.
There was no other place to determine the plants from the expeditions except Gray." [3]

No one working in America, and few elsewhere, had such a stock
of memory of the thousands of names, the complexes of floral characters, the ranges and habitats, the tangled nomenclatural relationships, the bibliographical references, the new discoveries and
would-be discoveries, knowledge of the strengths and weaknesses
of hundreds of botanists all the way back to Linnaeus. No American
had seen so many herbarium specimens in the European centers,

knew the wanderings of type specimens as collections had dispersed and congregated into new hands over the past fifty years. No one had so much of the literature in a working library at his elbow. Gray's herbarium, while not senior to Engelmann's or Torrey's, was just reaching full effectiveness when those two were entering a period of difficulties. The National Herbarium in Washington was scarcely underway and, because of a controversy with the Commissioner of Agriculture, under a cloud with Gray and the other botanists anyway.

Hence Gray's house was the unchallenged headquarters of all that went on in American botany. "Everyone who had any idea of going into botany," remembered Bailey, "had to come to see Gray, even if they just stood around and looked at him through the window." He was a sight to see. Coming into the herbarium on a half-run, he would attack a bundle of plants brought in by some collector, calling off their names without hesitation and perhaps without absolute accuracy, laying aside the few which were interesting and merited further study.[4] "He received everyone *very* graciously" and often put the visitors up for bed and board. Despite the appearance created by his beard, he was light on his feet. At seventy-two he jumped from a moving horsecar once too often and broke his collar bone. Two years after that, on coming out of the garden house, he found Mrs. Gray and the young Baileys sitting on the flight of stone steps which led down the bank. Rather than disturb them, he leaped over their astonished heads and landed at the bottom of the flight. From his retirement at sixty-three until the last months of his life after his seventy-seventh birthday, Gray combined youthful vigor, mental alertness, and a venerable appearance in almost unchanged proportions.

The object of Gray's retirement, the *Synoptical Flora of North America,* had highest priority of all his activities throughout the remainder of his life. In one sense, Gray was taking up again in earnest the burden which had been his since his first collaboration with John Torrey in the 1830's. His work avowedly built upon that part of Torrey and Gray, *Flora of North America,* which had appeared between 1838 and 1842. He understood, of course, that the very interruptions of thirty years, the special reports on explorations, rendered the parts already published "antiquated," and that he would ultimately have to cover the old ground as well as new. The passage of thirty years had changed more, however, than just the number of species and specimens to be considered. It had changed the relative place of taxonomy in the family of plant sciences. Gray, in welcoming Darwinism, had had his share in creating this change, and as a member of the generation whose span of years fell about equally before and after the publication of the *Origin* he was in a position to recognize the true significance to taxonomy of the most important book of the nineteenth century.

Although Darwin had seemingly destroyed the constancy of species, the *Origin* was really a culmination of the quest for a natural system of classification. Not only did it explain, by community of descent, the meaning of affinity and relationship, but it was based, as friends of Darwin such as Gray and Hooker well knew, in very important respects on taxonomic data. Without the great quest for classification on a world scale, the *Origin* would have lacked that connection with empirical evidence which gave it most strength. Hence the taxonomists who survived beyond the 1850's felt no call to change the techniques which had helped to produce such a triumph. They could not change greatly anyway, because both before and after the *Origin* the only reliable guide to the relations of plants was the structure of their parts—their morphology. The same old dry specimens collected by men who climbed mountains and crossed deserts continued to provide the data. Ernst Haeckel might coin the word phylogeny and the popularizers of Darwinism might evoke the awe-inspiring picture of the great branching tree of life. The first Darwinian botanists fortunately knew, however, that this vision did not easily fit the realities of the data. A century after Darwin has not progressed very far toward a comprehensive placing on an evolutionary tree even of all the great groups of flowering plants. The goal of a phylogenetic arrangement Darwin firmly set, but the ability to realize it was so far away that the botanist with a respect for data had no choice but to continue to practice his craft almost unchanged. "When we talk," wrote Gray, "about which is *species* and which *variety,* we don't venture to suppose we can tell which came from the other, or first divided from some common stock." [5]

The 1870's and 1880's were an Augustan age for taxonomic botany. In England basic reference tools which still stand out as guideposts were taking shape. Bentham and Hooker were bringing to completion their *Genera Plantarum*, an effort to marshal by a single set of standards an authoritative description of the genera of flowering plants, using direct examination of specimens. They ignored the phylogeny of larger groups not because they rejected evolution but because it was irrelevant to the task they had in hand. In the 1880's a bequest of Darwin himself set in motion the compilation of the *Index Kewensis*, which has become the basic bibliography of the publication of plant names.

Gray's continuing friendship with Hooker and his genuine respect for George Bentham meant that his *Synoptical Flora* would be an American extension of the British effort. From the beginning he and Torrey had based the botanical independence of the United States on cooperation with European centers rather than on competition with them. Hooker, father and son, and De Candolle, father and son, had freely granted the North American field to one who had by 1873 become an authority in his own right.

The *Origin* had wrought a great change for plant taxonomy less by changing the study itself than by stimulating allied sciences. The lower plants now took on a heightened interest, not excluding the micro-organisms which Pasteur was already connecting with such important practical matters as fermentation and disease. The physiology of plants seemed now more clearly than before a chemical and physical key to the phenomena of life. The adaptation of host and parasite gave a clue to plant pathology. Taxonomy, which had long reigned as the dominant plant science, now began to find its kingdom crowded. Its very success and stability now worked against it. With Darwin, biology had become a great science, on a footing with physics and chemistry. It was easy to forget that the collector, the plant press, the herbarium ticket, the simple microscope, and lots of observation of nature in the field had wrought the revolution! By the 1870's and 1880's taxonomy was undergoing a relative loss of prestige at the same time it was building some of its most durable monuments.

Asa Gray did not express his attitude toward the new developments by a shift in his own work but by the encouragement he gave to the younger generation of American botanists. Except for Engelmann and Edward Tuckerman, the key men of the Torrey and Gray team of headquarters experts on the various groups of plants had gone the way of the early field collectors. For the *Synoptical Flora*, Gray had to put together a new team of younger men who lived in a different institutional setting and responded to different interests. Although Gray continued to tell young men to study medicine to assure themselves a livelihood and take up botany only later, the changes in American institutions after 1873 opened up new opportunities. The new universities were now willing to hire specialists in science. The staff which replaced Gray—Goodale, Watson, Farlow, and Sargent—is a handy example. Perhaps more typical was the series of posts held by John Merle Coulter, who was able to follow botany even while teaching, first at Wabash College and then at the University of Indiana.[6]

The greatest difference in opportunity, beginning in the 1870's, came from the rise of the land-grant colleges. These institutions, many of them direct responses to the federal land subsidy for agricultural and mechanical colleges provided for by the Morrill Act of 1862, gradually worked toward more advanced training in botany and horticulture. William James Beal found a fruitful career at Michigan Agricultural College at East Lansing. Beal made crossbreeding experiments which brought him into direct correspondence with Darwin. He was later the man who arranged for his student Liberty Hyde Bailey to work with Gray as a herbarium assistant. Following Beal's pattern, Charles E. Bessey studied with Gray and went on to a land-grant career, first at Iowa Agricultural College and later at Nebraska. J. C. Arthur found a place at the University of Wisconsin, and Charles R. Barnes caught on at Purdue. The Middle West became the land of opportunity for professional botanists.

Meanwhile, in the western and southwestern reaches of the country, the target areas of previous years, scientific collecting was undergoing important transitions. In the first place, settlements were becoming sufficiently stable that residents could take on a part of the responsibility for collecting. In the second place, the elaboration of the railroad network made it possible for collectors to move rapidly over the area, independent of military escort. In the third place, and reflecting the more basic changes, government scientific enterprise was shifting from the military expedition to the permanent multipurpose scientific survey as the basic organization for exploration.[7] The older, blurred picture of the flora of western North America drawn from the collections of Charles Wright, Fendler, and the railroad surveys was giving way to clearer and more detailed knowledge produced by the re-exploration. The same thing was going on in geology and the zoology of the vertebrates. Gray clearly recognized this new kind of collecting. North American plants, he admitted, "continue to come in faster than I can study and dispose of them. This comes from the increasing number of botanical explorers, and the new facilities offered to them by new railroads along our southwestern frontiers and other out-of-the-way places."[8]

The resident collectors in the West naturally centered in California. Edward Lee Greene was an Episcopal clergyman who had a number of parishes in Colorado, New Mexico, and finally California before he began to teach at the University of California in Berkeley. J. G. Lemmon, a veteran of the "hateful stockade" at Andersonville, was so disturbed by his war experiences that he found botanical collecting his only occupation and release. Many more such as these not only fed a continuous stream of collections to Gray but also formed a nucleus for organized scientific life on the West Coast, the California Academy of Science soon boasting a herbarium of its own.

C. C. Parry, who had learned his collecting on the Mexican Boundary Survey and who had pioneered in intensive independent collecting in Colorado in the 1860's, was a transitional botanical collector in this transitional period. Headquartering in Davenport, Iowa, he traveled over the whole West and Southwest, reporting faithfully to Gray. Like his predecessors Wright and Fendler, he proved unsuited to the life of a civilized botanist. When Gray and others tried to domesticate him by securing his appointment as botanist at the Department of Agriculture, he found the political necessities of government service intolerable. After 1871, Parry again became a roving collector. Gray was responsible for his taking an interest in the anthropological opportunities afforded by the Indians as well as in plants, for during these years Gray was acting as the head of the Peabody Museum in Cambridge. Parry found it hard to adjust to the new era. Yet his day was not entirely over, for beyond the southern border lay unexplored lands where the plants still had no Latin names.

In 1878, Parry joined forces with Edward Palmer,[9] another of the frontier breed, to collect in the neighborhood of San Luis Potosí, Mexico. "A good *active* collector," he reported to Gray on his return, "could make a *splendid haul* by putting in a season between Monterey and Saltillo including the high Mt. valleys not hard to reach but involving hard work and some risks." Northern Mexico would be "the choice collecting ground for the next 25 years!" Who could attack this new target area, which was to supplant the southern Rockies as the primary goal of American botanical effort? "I was in hopes," continued Parry, that "Palmer might do, but I find like all us old *codgers* he knows how to *shirk hard work.*" Parry was right about Mexico as the coming field but wrong about Palmer's energies. In the 1880's and afterward the quiet, frail-looking former army surgeon did important work in Mexico. Cyrus Guernsey Pringle won almost equal fame in the same region.[10] The work of John Macoun in Canada during the same years was, with the Mexican collections, making a reality of the concept of a flora of North America as distinct from a flora of the United States.

In the midst of this teeming botanical scene, Asa Gray had to choose a course that would allow him not only to complete the *Synoptical Flora of North America* but that would enable him to make it the capstone of his own career and the whole botanical effort of the United States. To do so he had to keep taxonomy in the forefront of an increasing family of plant sciences. He had to keep a band of collectors whose composition was changing in character as well as numbers at work in the field. He had to have prompt access to the specimens which came from their explorations. Almost singlehandedly he had to adjust the effort of American botany to that of Europeans. Understandably, any large change in the frame of reference would be a catastrophe. If such a change came from an altered scientific view, Gray could bear it, especially since taxonomy had already ridden through the Darwinian change of goal. If, however, Gray's work ran into trouble from the artificial direction of the man-made rules of nomenclature, Gray could not be expected readily to delay for them.

Although Gray worked steadily through these years, progress was slow. In 1878 he published volume II, part 1, which took up where the old Torrey and Gray *Flora* had left off at the end of *Compositae*. Here he added thirty-two families to those covered by one or the other of the works and, as it turned out, proceeded as far toward the end of the list of families as he was ever to get. For he then went back to the groups covered by Torrey and Gray, reworking the second part of volume I. The part which he published in 1884 thus included once again the great family of the *Compositae* and allowed him to say his final word on it. After 1884 he was working on volume I, part 1, which would have completed the updating of Torrey and Gray.

Despite the freedom of his retirement Gray soon found that the task of maintaining himself at the center of the American botanical profession made a prison for him. His resolve to move steadily ahead on the *Synoptical Flora* he found constantly frustrated by the routine of naming plants, assigning numbers to specimens, corresponding with the collectors, and publishing preliminary papers to establish priority of discovery until he could, perhaps years later, include the description in its proper place in the *Synoptical Flora*. At first Gray had hoped that Sereno Watson could take over this drudgery. But Watson, who did indeed shoulder a large burden of correspondence, could not help Gray in the elaboration of the *Flora* if he were himself inundated with routine. Many would not accept a substitute for Gray. As one of them mentioned in a letter of thanks for Gray's having named his plants, "the value of the collection will be much increased thereby." When Goodale handled Gray's mail for a season, he reported, "you would smile if you could know how many letters of absolutely trivial importance come every day; just to get your autograph I think." [11]

Good reasons prevented Gray from dropping his onerous functions as the clearinghouse of all American botanical information. He had to see all the collections made in North America, and, given the status of other herbaria and libraries in the United States, the likelihood that a plant already once described might be published again was greater in the hands of other botanists than in Cambridge. "It is necessary that I should have every thing collected over our wide regions come to my hands," Gray explained to Hooker, and "that would not long be if I did not promptly report & name up." Here was the basic exchange between Gray and the collectors. He received the fullest sets of specimens in return for his services of sorting and naming. The completeness and value of his herbarium as well as the *Flora* depended on this service. As to the consequences of his letting go the reins, "half a dozen of our fellows would be publishing here & there & everywhere. It requires much tact to prevent it. And if I did not attend to these collections, in a way, as they come in—there are 4 or 5 men in the country—all unfit, who would catch at them at once, and only add to a confusion which I should have in the long run to clear up." [12]

This necessity required Gray to take an interest in the systematic publications of other botanists. If they were only to make new names which he would ultimately have to reduce to synonyms, he had better make his suggestions while the article was still in manuscript. Gray gave this advice in a friendly manner, and most of the botanists thought too highly of his knowledge to disregard it, although some of them grumbled. On occasion a botanist even suppressed an article at Gray's suggestion.[13] If this was censorship, it had its base alone in the moral force of Gray's position in the profession and the immense and undoubted value of the advice he freely gave.

Even if other botanists with good libraries and herbaria took over routine examination and naming, a further barrier prevented Gray from letting go his function of clearinghouse. He simply had no money with which to buy collections. Personally he made ends meet only with the Hunnewell-Sargent subsidy and the royalties from his textbooks. Mrs. Gray's family, for all its position in Boston, was in a period of business reverses which engulfed Charles G. Loring's "handsome" patrimony. "Blessed are they who do not expect anything." The funds available at Harvard for the herbarium barely paid Sereno Watson's salary. President Eliot in calling for funds, which incidentally never came, stated bluntly that "two such learned men as Dr. Gray and Dr. Watson ought not to be giving their precious time to the examination of the multifarious collections which are incessantly poured in upon them." [14] Either money or service was necessary to keep the system going. Caught in this treadmill, Gray's eminence was both an achievement and a cause of tension. The patriarch received his honor, but he could not entirely escape the desire of youth to throw off the yoke of venerable ways.

One source of tension came from the young academics of the Middle West. They had grown up under the spell of evolution, which was only a late addition to the system of botanical education enthroned in Gray's line of textbooks. Furthermore, they, like scholars in many fields in the embryonic universities of the United States, had come under the influence of German scholarship. If they were vaguely encouraged by Gray's friendship with Darwin, they filled their minds and found their fighting faith in Julius von Sach's *Lehrbuch der Botanik*. Here the lower forms of plant life came into their own as guides to phylogeny and the realm of the newly significant micro-organisms. Physiology and not taxonomy seemed to hold the key to life. The laboratory with its high-powered microscopes and staining techniques became the habitat of the botanist in place of the field and herbarium. Not just the morphology of the adult plant but its whole life history became the object of interest.

In one sense none of this "new botany" was new to Gray. He had followed the work of such great Germans as Hofmeister and had published notices of it when none in America had eyes to see it. Moreover the format of his basic textbook allowed for both physiology and the lower plants. The very fact that he could call on Goodale and Farlow to join him in a four-volume effort was evidence of the encouragement he gave younger men to go in these new directions. But Farlow never completed his part of the new *Gray's Botanical Textbook,* and Gray's own projected fourth volume on the natural orders never materialized. The two volumes which did appear—Gray, *Structural Botany,* and Goodale, *Physiological Botany*—did much to bring the contents up to date without changing in any way the implied order of a botanical education. Structural and morphological botany not only equipped the taxonomist but "furnished needful preparation to those who proceed to the study of

Vegetable Physiology." This order of emphasis was precisely what the new botanists, dominated by German models, wished to change.

Charles E. Bessey led off the campaign with an American version of Sachs's *Lehrbuch*. Gray praised Bessey for a "timely gift to American students of a good manual of vegetable anatomy and of the structure and classification of the lower cryptogamia, which was very much needed." [15] When the Midwesterners followed up, however, with the so-called ABC book of the laboratory—Arthur, Barnes, and Coulter, *Handbook of Plant Dissection*—Gray put in a pleasant demurrer to the new fashion. He questioned "whether, for common education, there is not a tendency to introduce histology too early into the course; also to treat it too technically and so to say Germanically." The last word was meant to be derogatory, for the "Germans of our day excel in investigation and supply excellent material. But they seem to lack the gift of exposition and sense of proportion; and so, for educational purposes, their writings need something more than translation." [16] The difference between Gray and the "new botany" of the Midwest was the difference between two generations, the earlier centered on Britain and France, with the younger centered on the new Germany. To the end, however, age and youth respected one another. Gray could take a share of credit for the accomplishments of his students and protégés in the new botany.

One specific issue which agitated some of the younger men, especially a paleobotanist like Lester Ward, was Gray's stand on the position of the gymnosperms. This great group of cone-bearing plants, so conspicuous in the North American flora with its pines, firs, and spruces, had customarily appeared in classificatory systems bracketed with large groups of flowering plants. Now the vision of phylogeny and the record of fossil plants suggested that the gymnosperms were more primitive than the flowering plants. Hooker, with characteristic bullheadedness, had fought this line of reasoning since the 1850's. Gray had always left the gymnosperms to Engelmann or somebody else. This was not a question on which he had a strong independent position, and he wished to avoid a stand. By 1877, however, he could no longer ignore the American clamor. "Engelmann is urging the *class Gymnospermae,* to stand next the cryptogams."

Not only was Engelmann the great American authority, but, Gray admitted, the "general tendency is in that direction: early appearance in time, peculiarity in embryo-formation, and adaptation of development doctrines being the leading ideas." Indeed Gray leaned toward placing the gymnosperms in a subclass parallel to the other great divisions of flowering plants—the dicots and monocots. In view of Hooker's insistence that gymnosperms were dicots, however, to adopt such a scheme would endanger the great alliance with British botany on which Gray had based his career. Hooker's authority overrode all the American critics rolled into one, including even Engelmann. "I should wish, of course, to follow" Hooker. Accordingly Gray soon came out in favor of a subordinate position for the gymnosperms [17] and stood the criticisms of the Americans for the rest of his life. In the light of twentieth-century research the phylogenetic position of the gymnosperms is much more complicated than either side in the 1880's saw it, but Gray's adherence to the dicoyledenous position of the gymnosperms was not one of his most perceptive decisions. This one unpopular stand was a small price to pay for the alliance with Hooker. Lester Ward, for one, could still look on Gray as a pioneer evolutionist despite the gymnosperms. Because Ward's enduring place in American intellectual development stems from his sociology rather than his paleontology, Gray's acknowledged general influence with him is of more basic importance than the mechanical differences of opinion.

A far different spirit, based on assumptions entirely foreign to the progressive Midwesterners, arose on the Pacific Coast. There taxonomy reigned supreme among the resident collectors. They had scarcely heard of Darwin, much less of the new botany emanating from Germany. They gloried that they lived in the field, close to the growing plants. Their normal reward was to have their name on a species—*Bolanderi, Nevinii, Greenei, Parryi, Palmeri, Lemmoni*. The greater honor was a whole genus, but the early collectors had done their job well enough that new genera did not turn up every day. The California Academy of Sciences in San Francisco provided a convenient place for matching honors, while the mails from the East allowed plenty of time for brooding. Gray had a double connection with this hypersensitive coterie. He depended upon them, of course, for botanical exploration in California and perforce had to name their collections. Besides, because he and Watson had played the major roles in completing the botany of the California Geological Survey, the two stood as the authorities on that particular flora. They were in this case not only the distant generalizers but also local experts *in absentia*.

Sometime in the 1870's, Gray became aware that a distinctive California botanical attitude existed in the California Academy of Sciences, where that "good-hearted and impracticable fellow" Albert Kellogg was the leader of the resident botanists. C. C. Parry visited the herbarium of the academy in 1875 and reported to Gray that "they are keeping back a number of nice things that ought to be in the Flora." He wished "they would take a reasonable view of things and put their material in the right hands but the old jealousy crops out." In 1879 a San Francisco teacher who needed a local flora for his classes of girls explained to Gray that he did not seek Kellogg's help because "he had expressed himself as much displeased with me on account of my sending plants to you instead of my giving them to him for determination." [18]

This smouldering resentment of California's colonial status in botany received a marked impetus when the Episcopal church transferred the Reverend Edward Lee Greene to California. Greene had long corresponded with Gray and had met and liked him in Colorado in 1872. As early as 1876, however, Greene evinced the attitude that Gray was a closet botanist who knew only dried specimens and did not possess the field man's intimacy with living plants. "The proposed specific name of 'carneum,' " he wrote Gray concerning a new *Polemonium,* "is better for the dried than for the fresh specimens. You might drive along a mountain ride where the plants were in full bloom without seeing anything of the color which suggests that name." [19]

By 1881, Greene reached the point of a declaration of independence for California botany. The opportunity came from Gray's absence from Cambridge for a year to study in Europe. Greene sent his season's collection to Cambridge as usual in September 1880. In February 1881, however, Greene published a new *Asclepias* in the *Bulletin* of the Torrey Botanical Club in New York despite Gray's advice that it was not new. Greene had felt "quite confident that it was only the old story of which there are a score of examples in our correspondence, of your referring a new species of my finding, to our old one and insisting on it for a year or so, then admitting it new." [20]

Publishing independently not only added the fame of authorship to the botanical immortality gained in plant names, it had practical advantages of speed and hence of priority. If a collector had to wait a year or so for Gray to get around to publishing he might lose credit for a discovery of a new plant to a collector who was in the field after him but who published immediately in California. Hence Greene's independence—and he began publishing not only his own collections but those of others—immediately put pressure on all the collectors. J. G. Lemmon in particular felt the lash of Greene's activity. "Wrecked Andersonville prisoner" that he was, he had always been deeply involved emotionally in the honorifics of botanical names. When Gray honored Lemmon's wife with a new genus, *Plummera,* the grateful husband described the scene. "We have just held a grand celebration, mother & I dancing around the room with 'amabilis' as the central figure alternately shouting for joy and weeping with gratitude." Greene disquieted him. "You see I come upon quite a lot of plants that were new until Greene got them. Cannot you give me credit on the new genus of Greenella (since my specimens help to confirm it) by writing *Greenella Lemmonii* in publishing?" Gray expostulated, "Why you have Lemmoni's as thick as locusts all round! I *hate* the combination of two personal names. Green & Lemmon don't match." [21]

In December of 1881 Lemmon confessed to Gray that "there is so much pressure brought to bear upon me here that I have begun to describe plants—just a few—before the Acad. to be published in our 'Mining & Scientific Press' of San Francisco." The kind of pressure he described was in the form of accusations by Greene "that to send my plants East to have them named after he has indicated the new species is 'a species of meanness'—(He did not finish the sentence)." He further quoted Greene as saying on the same occasion at the California Academy, "Rusby, Parish, & Pringle send me things that were growing last August and now they are published."

And again, "Why, I publish more new things than Watson, Engelmann, Eaton, Porter, Vasey and all the other botanists have for the last four months." [22]

Gray was always understanding of Lemmon, but his reaction to the others was definite. "The people who 'sting' you are great fools. It does not require any knowledge of botany and only a little of rules to name a plant—hit or miss, it may stick, good if it does, no matter if it does not." Lemmon should not worry about his reputation. "If you knew what a nuisance in the science Dr. Kellogg's name is— good meaning soul though he be, you would not envy his botanical reputation." [23]

Greene on his part labeled Lemmon untrustworthy and denied that he had ambitions as an author, laying to "your own & Mr. Watson's long absence" the "several scores of n. sp. I have published within a year." Thus Gray and Greene for the moment avoided a direct showdown, but the word was out in the profession that a revolt was stirring. Old George Engelmann commiserated with Gray. "So you have your troubles with aspiring botanists! It is a state of things which had to come sooner or later, and is certainly unpleasant enough, and will make a good deal of annoying labor." He chaffed Gray that "you are somewhat to blame for this chase after botanical notoriety, as you 'to encourage aspiring collectors' stick their names to innumerable new species and there is no end to Wrightii, Parryi, Lemmoni, etc. etc." He had always favored descriptive names anyway. But Engelmann, who had lived in St. Louis when it was the raw West, had an eye for basic causes. "It is amusing to see State Pride cropping out in these Western botanists, they seem to want their flora for themselves! And still there is something in it, if they can only do it well." [24]

Not the validity of the idea of a Western regional autonomy in botany, but the condition that the work be well done, was the heart of Gray's case. With Torrey he had led a regional revolution in the 1830's, shifting the center for the study of North American plants from one side of the Atlantic to the other. The great tactic of that revolution was cooperation with Europe, not competition. The very journey to Europe which Gray made in 1880–81 was a part of his continuing effort to see all of the European types of the *Compositae*

Gray had won a continent by adopting European standards and meshing his enterprise with the world effort. Nothing of such a spirit animated Greene. He did not show any desire to make a journey East which would have corresponded to Gray's 1838–39 tour of the herbaria of Europe. As time went on Greene gradually revealed the personal wellsprings of his rebellion. Others were field-men, contemptuous of the closet. Almost all the Westerners had an emotional commitment to some kind of regional autonomy. From these sources Greene derived most of his support, but his own dislike of Gray sprang also from sources peculiar to himself.

In the first place, Greene not only believed that species were immutable,[25] he also believed that they existed in much greater number than botanists had been willing to admit. To Gray, intermediate forms had become since Darwin guides and aids. In Greene's sharp eyes they appeared as potential species, if he could detect any differences at all. This view ran counter not only to the practice of the masters of the day but also counter to the goal of a taxonomy which would ultimately reflect evolutionary relationships. Furthermore, Greene's criterion of a species was his own insight into the form of the living plant, without regard to external influences such as climate and soil. Few of the three thousand or so new species which Greene made have won the approval of botanists, though the names remain, and later workers must often pick them up.

In the second place, Greene had no use at all for the Europeans with whom Gray had worked for half a century. "I do not believe anything will teach me to reverence a certain British trait which expresses itself so strongly in the *Genera Plantarum;* or to be tolerant of it," he wrote to Gray. On another occasion, when Gray referred him to European discussions he answered, "I have not read the discussions by Bentham and by De Candolle. They are probably inaccessible to me any way. I have simply followed what seems to me *to be* the *only* way, which is not subversive of all rights of priority." [26] Among the points which worried Greene was the so-called Kew rule, a practice followed by Bentham and Hooker which allowed a botanist moving a plant name from one genus to another to ignore if he desired the species name given in the old genus. Thus on some occasions a known early name could be passed over. This modification of the rule of priority has been the bone of much honest contention, and the International Rules no longer allow it. To Greene it was a personal insult, a form of larceny by which closet botanists robbed field men as surely as if they had taken money from their pockets. Since many of Greene's genera did not stand up in Gray's hands, he took this practice as a fiendish criminal trick aimed directly at him.

In the third place, Greene extended the sense of injury which he felt concerning the reigning authorities back into history. He said, speaking of Linnaeus, "It was bad enough for the brilliant, sprightly and highly gifted Swede to go on so recklessly ignoring, as he often did (whether he meant it or not) his predecessors and contemporaries, some of whom appear to have been, in some points, his betters." But in comparison, Bentham and Hooker, "in order to save themselves trouble, have done more deliberate and unpardonable injustice to great names, than Linnaeus ever meant to do." This point of view led Greene into long-range research in the history of botany, which, if he had his way, would produce early names which under a law of absolute priority would unseat those familiarly used for many years. He championed not only such American workers as Nuttall and Rafinesque, but also that host of botanists who had worked before Linnaeus. "Surely, my judgment would be that, ante-Linnaean generic names ought *all* to be restored to their proper authors." Nomenclature was a means of rendering historical justice even posthumously, rather than a necessary convenience for scientists whose primary interest lay in the plants.

In the fourth place, Greene in the 1880's was going through a religious crisis only dimly perceived by his botanical contemporaries. C. C. Parry reported to Gray in 1883 that Greene, still an Episcopal clergyman, was "involved in a disagreeable church squabble in which the bishop sided against him but since has been *honorably reconciled. . . .*" At about the same time Greene began to teach botany at the University of California. In 1886 he added a postscript to a letter to Gray, "I am plain Mr. E. L. G. &c.; not 'Rev.' having some months since taken the place, which I mean to keep, of lay member of the Roman Catholic communion." That some connection between this conversion and his antiquarian interests in botany existed in his mind, he at least hinted at in a remark that may have been an attempted joke: "I am a worshipper of 'saints and relics.' Hence my desire to have this specimen, with Nuttall's autograph." [27]

With this series of tensions driving him on, Greene not surprisingly reached the point of accusing Gray of dishonesty. Mentioning various genera at issue, he charged that "you are not likely to attribute to me such meekness as to remain unaffected by so grave a violation of the very fundamentals of scientific justice and good faith." He concluded this charge with the assertion that "it is in your power to exalt a man, in the estimation of the scientific public, to very high rank as a botanist; and that you can easily relegate him to the limbo of conceited 'cranks.' You appear to have decided how you will dispose of me."

Gray showed his agitation by preserving a copy of his answer, "I cannot make it very detailed, but I mean to make it explicit." He outlined his motives for giving Greene advice, stated his version of the facts on the genera involved, and concluded, "I mean to treat you with complete consideration. I shall save valuable time & your temper, by avoiding for the future all 'tiresome discussion.' I am convinced that I should have done so long ago." Gray did wish "you had informed me in advance of your Kumleinia," for "I thought I might have saved you from what you could have seen—on a survey of the Genus—is ill judged. But why should you not have your own way unmolested?" [28] For the short remaining period of his life Gray made no more effort to give Greene advice.

Gray was guilty of Greene's charge of being a "conservative" in only a limited way. He wished to follow the rules of botanical nomenclature to which he and his friends, the great authorities of the day, had been accustomed. In every other way, as a biologist, as an evolutionist, an internationalist, and as a man, Greene was more conservative than his elder. Even in nomenclature, Greene's insistence on an absolute rule of priority revolutionized settled practice by bringing up old names. This insistence must bear some responsibility for divorcing taxonomy from the rest of botany. In Gray's middle years he had personified a synthesis of the various approaches to plant life. In the 1880's this synthesis was breaking down, and taxonomy was drifting out of the main stream of the plant sciences. The increased emphasis on nomenclatural legalities accentuated the drift.

Among Eastern botanists, some of the younger ones who had little in common with Greene took essentially his attitude toward absolute priority in botanical nomenclature. The ablest and best placed of these rebels was Nathaniel Lord Britton, a geologist who had come into botany under the protection of the paleontologist John S. Newberry at Columbia. Only twenty-eight years old when Gray left the scene in 1887, Britton was already beginning to make New York a center of plant taxonomy for the first time since the death of Torrey. As one trained outside of botany, he had no feeling for the elegant traditions of the Hookers and De Candolles and Benthams. To him absolute priority for the first published name was a way of reducing an art to a mechanical certainty. His drive in this direction produced some name changes during Gray's lifetime, and by 1892 Britton led a full-fledged revolt in drawing up the so-called Rochester Code, which led eventually to a distinctive American Code of nomenclature. Gray had to leave to another generation the quelling of this revolt against the internationalism on which he had built his whole career. He had supported the International Rules drawn up by De Candolle in 1867. His students and Harvard successors followed the International Rules even at the height of the American Code's popularity.

These tensions underneath the surface all point, however, to Gray's essentially unchallenged position as patriarch. The times conspired with his capabilities to create his personal domination of the science. The great reorganizations going on in American life after the Civil War were usually personified. Andrew Carnegie and steel, John D. Rockefeller and oil, the Big Four of the railroads were but the most conspicuous of these couplings. In a quieter way and in a quieter field Gray was a captain of botanical industry. The botanists themselves recognized this pre-eminence in 1885 when, on Gray's seventy-fifth birthday, they presented him with a silver vase entwined with plants associated with him. The cards of one hundred and eighty botanists accompanied the tribute. Practically all of them had some kind of personal tie with Gray to make their contribution appropriate. With so many botanists active in the country, however, the personal organization was at its farthest limits.

The captain of botanical industry had an *ex officio* role in the world at large. In an age when railroads bought influence with rebates and free passes, Gray negotiated with the presidents of lines to see that science receive its share of the bonanza in the form of free passes for collectors. Yet his more important duties involved advice on larger issues of scientific policy.

After Gray succeeded to Agassiz's place on the Regents of the Smithsonian Institution, he was one of the few scientists on the board. This duty took him often to Washington and made him the familiar acquaintance of those rare politicians of the period who took an interest in science—for instance, James A. Garfield. Because of the death of Henry in 1878, Gray's term covered a difficult period of transition for the institution, leaving him finally the sole link with the era of the founding. Among the projects to which he lent his hand was the recapture of the government's herbarium from the Department of Agriculture. In the National Museum the botanical curator would work "under an intelligent and scientific head" instead of being a clerk "liable to be dismissed on a month's notice at the mere will of the Agricult. Commissioner, who has mostly been either an ass or a political partisan, or a mule between the two." [29] The transfer eventually took place several years after Gray's death.

One of the most serious needs of scientific institutions in America in the 1880's was some means of channeling the burgeoning personal fortunes of the day into effective means of financial support. Few of the moguls of the age of organization saw any connection between their wealth and science. Hence the captains of science had to be on the lookout for opportunities to harness the fortunes of the captains of industry. Gray, as always better at advising the gifts of large sums for other institutions than his own, entered into this duty with enthusiasm. On Engelmann's death in 1884, Gray became a principal adviser to the aged Henry Shaw. He not only saw to the drawing of Shaw's will in favor of the Missouri Botanical Garden, but he picked William Trelease as the first director. Had Gray lived longer, he might have provided the same kind of advice to Leland Stanford, who was just beginning to build his university.[30]

An advisory activity of Gray's which never bore fruit has, nevertheless, a pivotal place in the direction American plant science was to take. In the 1870's he was part of a movement to preserve some of the California redwoods for posterity by having the federal government set aside land. Enlisting the aid of his old friend Frederick Law Olmsted, he attempted to get the President and the Secretary of the Interior to reserve lands both in the Sierra and near the Coast. In January 1878, Gray called on Carl Schurz, the Secretary of the Interior, and arranged for the geologist Clarence King to see him on the matter also. Olmsted ultimately reported, however, that Schurz "had come to the conclusion that it was not expedient to take land upon the President's action alone. . . ." In later years Gray continued to urge the desirability of the preservation of trees in California.[31] This modest effort foreshadowed a great alliance between American biologists and conservationists which would reach major proportions within fifteen years after Gray's death.

Gray's interest in tree preservation and his role as adviser on policy both figured prominently close to home in the reorganization of Harvard's botanical establishment. By 1879 some readjustments of the settlement of 1872–73 clearly seemed needed. Charles Sprague Sargent was too ambitious to trouble himself indefinitely with the old, small garden in Cambridge as soon as his arboretum was ready for full development. His plans evidently rubbed a number of people wrong—including Goodale and President Eliot. Furthermore, among his schemes was the removal of the whole botany operation of the university, including garden and herbarium, to the Bussey Institution in Jamaica Plain. At the same time Farlow was discontented with the treatment he was receiving and was about ready to decamp for Johns Hopkins.

Gray's influence was probably decisive in making the rearrangements which kept all these able and strongminded young men in Harvard's service. The garden and herbarium stayed in Cambridge, where with Gray's help Goodale not only took over the garden but began to build up the botanical museum which was to be his most lasting monument. Farlow was mollified even though Gray had to offer to put up $200 of his own money to do it. These two men carried on botanical instruction at Cambridge for a generation, their energies focused on their own institutions and on the college. A price which Gray had to pay for the vigor he stimulated in them was the beginning of a shift of teaching activity away from the row of buildings in the Botanic Garden which he had built. In 1883 instruction formally shifted from the garden buildings to Harvard Hall.[32] The site which William Dandridge Peck had inaugurated back in 1810 had waxed as a botanical center for seventy years. Beginning with the reorganization of 1879 it began the slow wane which finally ended in 1954. Gray saw only the very first stage of this decline. He well knew the problems of the garden itself, and he could take pride in the institutions Goodale and Farlow were building.

Sargent presented the greatest problem and the greatest opportunity. When, early in 1879, Gray found that ideas to move to Jamaica Plain, "which I supposed had only very vaguely possessed Mr. Sargent's mind were assuming the form of propositions with practical bearing I had to undertake to disperse them." Sargent took this rebuff "like the real gentleman that he is" and in return received Gray's backing to begin to develop the Arnold Arboretum in earnest, despite President Eliot, "who likes him not." Having long since given up his own project on forest trees for the Smithsonian, Gray now gave Sargent an added push in the direction of forestry by getting him "the position of expert agent for the census of *Forest & forest products*—pay rather small, but allows any amount of travel all paid for, and all needful assistance." The result was Sargent's *Report on the Forests of North America*. By 1881 Gray reported with pride that Sargent "seems to have made a mark in his Census forestry work. He has developed not only a power of doing work, but of getting work done for him by other people, and so can accomplish something." [33] Gray had forged his link with the future conservation movement.

The critics of Gray who, in calling him a closet botanist, implied that he disliked the out-of-doors and far places were profoundly wrong. In retirement Dr. and Mrs. Gray became great travelers. They spent a year in Europe in 1880–81, carrying on the pattern Gray had set as a young man—much botany, but also art and architecture. In addition, they became regular visitors to the American

West. They were a late example of the British traveling tradition of the mid-nineteenth century which produced the men who discovered the sport of mountain-climbing and which combined sightseeing and empire all the way to the Himalayas. Gray's friends Hooker and John Ball had performed their botanical exploits in this tradition. The Grays were at the same time the first of the tourists, for they waited until the railroads took them in comfort to the places where collectors had had serious adventure only a few years before.

The journey which transcended mere tourism most clearly occurred in 1877, when Gray's repeated entreaties to Sir Joseph Hooker to come to America bore fruit. To have the President of the Royal Society of London and a Himalaya veteran for a traveling companion was a triumph in itself. To have the whole thing financed by F. V. Hayden, then riding high as head of one of the rival surveys of the western territories, was also convenient. Since Hayden was trying to establish himself in competition with Major J. W. Powell, the army engineers, and the Coast Survey as the scientific surveyor of the West, the presence of Hooker and Gray augmented his prestige measurably.[34] For Gray and Hooker it meant a chance to make a comprehensive survey of the flora of North America and to test against this overview their respective theories of geographical distribution. Hence, theirs was not a mere collecting trip but an offshoot of their earlier Darwinian studies.

As usual Hooker left his wife at home, but Mrs. Gray, also as usual, accompanied the party, which consisted of Hayden himself and various companions for parts of the way. Major General Sir Richard Strachey of the Royal Engineers and wife went as far as Salt Lake City. Joseph Leidy and wife and daughter went as far as Colorado. The vice president of the Denver and Rio Grande Railroad joined them in his part of the territory, and at every stop the local naturalists were on the alert.[35]

While by no means a dangerous journey in 1877—Hooker reported "not a ghost of an adventure"—the energies of the two sexagenarian botanists drove them until they themselves complained. After botanical stops at Philadelphia and St. Louis the party began work in earnest in Colorado, penetrating the Rockies at La Veta Pass, at Colorado Springs, and of course at Gray's Peak above

Georgetown. When at Fort Garland beyond La Veta Pass, they climbed Sierra Blanca. Although it was not, as they believed possible, the highest mountain in the Rockies, it gave ample proof that sixty-seven years rested lightly on Gray. The plant presses were busy all the time, for when they left Colorado Hooker had specimens of about five hundred species. While none of these plants was new, they provide an answer to those who felt that Gray never collected in the West at all and to those who felt he did not document geographical distributions with specimens.

After a brief stop in Utah to view the Wasatch Mountains and Brigham Young, the party moved on to California, over the Sierra to Yosemite. Using General John Bidwell's Rancho Chico as a starting point, Gray and Hooker also penetrated the Mount Shasta region of northern California. They had the benefit of the enthusiasms of John Muir on this journey. At a campfire one night Gray asked why *Linnaea borealis* had not been discovered in northern California. The next morning Hooker and Muir found it. According to one of Muir's transcendentalist outlook, "Gray had felt its presence the night before on the mountain ten miles away." [36] A knowledge of the ranges of hundreds of genera may have had quite as much to do with it. The gulf between the tradition of the nature lover which descended on Muir from Emerson and the tradition of the botanist represented by Gray was never more clearly demonstrated than at these campfires of the Bidwells in northern California. Muir would build up the fire "to display the beauties of the silver fir, which in the glow . . . assumed the appearance of enormous pagodas of filigree silver. Mr. Muir would wave his arms and shout: 'Look at the glory! Look at the glory!' " For this demonstration the botanists returned only silence. When Mrs. Bidwell asked them if they did not think it beautiful they responded, "Of course it is. But Muir is so eternally enthusiastic, we like to tease him." [37]

By the time he had reached the Pacific Coast, Hooker was willing, despite some minor complaints about American civilization expected in one of his station, to admit that he could not "fancy any route over which a European would get more accessible Botany new to him than a railroad trip across N. America." And "A. Gray is a trump in all senses." The cementing of friendship and the impression made on Americans was only part of the result of the journey. Gray and Hooker wrote an essay on the geographical distribution of the plants of the Rockies which Hayden pushed into print despite his defeat in the struggle for supremacy over the other surveys.[38]

Although Gray may have seemed dry to an enthusiast like Muir, he showed in his journeys a kind of sentiment of his own. The Southern travels which interspersed his years of retirement gave him ample scope for feelings which were no less sentimental for being attached to the things with which he worked most, taxonomic units. The reason for the Southern travels was a persistent cold and cough which regularly developed in Cambridge winters and springs. Instead, however, of following "the beaten track to east Florida," Dr. and Mrs. Gray began a series of journeys whose objectives sprang from botanical sentiment.

In 1875 they made their "pious pilgrimage to the secluded native haunts of that rarest of trees, *Torreya taxifolia.*" What emotions welled up at the thought of his old friend, who had gone to his grave with a sprig of *Torreya* on his coffin! Memories returned, too, of Hardy Croom, whom he had seen many years before, bringing to John Torrey the types of both *Torreya* and *Croomia*. Soon afterward Croom had vanished in a shipwreck in the Atlantic. The railroad journey into the byways of the deep South required long delays, poor quarters, and "ablutions made at the tank of the locomotive." But to see *Torreya* growing in its unique locality on the Apalachicola River was a thrill. Gray had some eye for a romantic landscape as he passed on a steamboat "down the brimming river, bordered with almost unbroken green of every tint, from the dark background of the Long-leaved Pines to the tender new verdure of the Liquidambar . . . interspersed with the deep and lustrous hue of *Magnolia grandiflora.*" The names were there, but so was the landscape.[39]

In 1876 the Grays went to the mountains of Virginia, North Carolina, and Tennessee, "where I used to roam and botanize more than thirty years ago." It was a journey of botanical reminiscence to the regions where Gray had once searched for *Shortia galacifolia*. In 1878 the word filtered up from a North Carolina herb-collector that *Shortia* had at last been found. "Now let me sing my nunc dimittis." [40] Vindication had come for the young botanist daring to make a find in the great *Jardin des Plantes* in that far-off day in 1839. When at last it bloomed in the garden he caressed it with real feeling.[41] Nothing would do now but a pilgrimage to *Shortia* for 1879. The Gray party arrived too late to see the rare flower, but they saw the habitat and had another gay and strenuous season of tramping through the mountains. A railroad accident during their return left them unscathed. In 1884 the Grays made a last short journey to their beloved Roan Mountain in North Carolina.

Even at seventy-four Gray still longed to see the botanical frontier, which had already reached Mexico. In February 1885, the Grays were doing their duty by the exposition in New Orleans "(I hate such)," but the weather was bitter cold. When Farlow came down armed with passes on the Mexican railroad, they decided to go to Mexico City. The excursion was not a success. Gray coughed so continually that the American embassy doctor ordered them immediately down to Orizaba and a lower altitude. Not until they fled to California did the cough get better.

When they arrived in Santa Barbara the mayor was at the wharf to meet them, driving them "to the fine watering-place kind of hotel, and on being shown at once to our rooms we found them all alight and embowered in roses, in variety and superbness such as you never saw the beat of, not to speak of Bougainvilleas, Tasconias, and Cape-bulbs in variety. . . ." Mrs. Gray "was fairly taken off her feet." [42] Santa Barbara was only responding naturally to the visit of one of America's celebrated men, the leader who stood for botany in the age of titans.

LAST DAYS 1886–1888

I N the summer and fall of 1886 life had for Gray an unclouded serenity. He was making James Russell Lowell's poem about him almost a reality:

> Just Fate: prolong his life, well spent,
> Whose indefatigable hours
> Have been as gaily innocent
> And fragrant as his flowers.

He had recently achieved immortality for his physical features by sitting for a bronze plaque by Augustus Saint-Gaudens. He thought it a "good representation to go down to posterity." Of course he was still grinding away at the *Flora* but "probably shall be found so doing when I am called for." Mrs. Gray's years of illness were but a memory. They both enjoyed "life with a zest, being in all respects happily situated, particularly in having plenty to do." [1]

Even the shadow of death seemed farther away than it had when, in his twenties, he had feared the fate of his namesake Asa, who had died young of tuberculosis. He would not as a young man allow himself the kind of remark he made about the assurance he gained from his seventy-sixth birthday. "I have always observed that if I live to November 18, I live the year round." He had at that time one more circle of seasons to make.

The holiday of 1886 to Oneida County revived all his earliest memories. The valley of Sauquoit, little changed in sixty years, still showed its "beautiful rolling hills and valleys, fertile and well cultivated . . . like much of rural England. . . ." Gray was not unmindful that he was patriarch of the Gray family as well as of botanists. A half-century at the great centers of learning and travel to far places had never alienated him from his brothers and sisters and their numerous children who now gathered round. In his will he provided, should Mrs. Gray die before him, for the bulk of his estate to go to "the surviving children, grand-children, and great-grand-children of my late father Moses Gray and mother, Roxana Gray. . . ." [2]

In the spring of 1887, when he realized that Hooker was not likely to come to the United States that year, Gray decided to go to Europe. Although he felt obliged to "feign a scientific necessity," this was clearly a journey of pleasure, "positively Dr. Gray's last appearance on your shores." [3]

The whole six months in Europe was a triumph. Tours on the continent were of course necessary, even though only De Candolle, "aged, but fairly cheerful," of old friends were left there. Instead of botany the Grays had a holiday of art galleries and cathedrals from Vienna to Normandy. Almost every stop had a memory—Vienna, changed since Endlicher, dead nearly forty years now, had played the host; Geneva in 1881; a steamer on the Danube opening views seen forty-eight years ago. The journey down the Rhine to the Netherlands was the same as 1850.

On the continent Gray was, as he had always been, mostly tourist. In England he was a part of society. During this year of the golden jubilee of Victoria, not everyone who cheered could remember with Gray the London of the late 1830's which had seen the Queen's accession. Among the books of the jubilee year was the *Life and Letters of Charles Darwin,* in which no reader could mistake the warm esteem with which Darwin addressed Gray in some of the most revealing letters in the volumes. Gray's place in the Atlantic community demanded he should be honored, and the British answered handsomely. Gray himself had a definite idea of what was fit for the occasion. When Cambridge proposed to award him an honorary Doctor of Science, he was careful to inquire what it meant. Only Alexander Agassiz had one as far as he knew, "and I do not care to be cut simply on that pattern—the more, as I suppose our Pres. Eliot will be there for L. L. D., & he was a pupil of mine. . . ." [4] All was adequately explained, and Cambridge brilliantly honored "the venerable priest of Flora." The Grays were guests of Mrs. Darwin, with Lord Acton providing pleasant conversation at lunch. If Gray really wanted an LL.D., Edinburgh provided it; Oxford added a D.C.L.

Gray's defense of religion paid a final dividend in opening to him a number of country seats, with invitations to social gatherings which science alone would scarcely have gained him. Sir Edward Fry entertained him, as did Lord Blachford in Devon. The Grays' friend of over thirty years, Dean Church, welcomed them at the Deanery of St. Paul's and made it possible for that embodiment of Victorian Christianity, W. E. Gladstone himself, to satisfy an expressed desire to meet Dr. Gray. The honored visitors even had to make a choice between the Archbishop of Canterbury's garden party at Lambeth Palace and one at the Gladstones'. Mrs. Gray went to Lambeth while Dr. Gray gave vent to his long-standing admiration by going to Dollys Hill, "the pleasant country house, which some one . . . has lent to the G. O. M." The opportunity could hardly have turned better. It is tempting to imagine the American thinker on science and religion having a most revealing conversation with the gladiator who had recently tilted with Huxley about *Genesis*. But, alas, "Gladstone said he was very glad to see me in the flesh, and we had pleasant talk, of nothing in particular."

The climax finally came at the meeting of the British Association in Manchester, where Gray posed as one of the elders, "nearly, if not quite, the oldest member" on the list of Corresponding Members. He spoke ceremonially, which was not his custom, in behalf of the foreign guests of the association. If he used some conventional phrases like "blood is thicker than water," he nevertheless managed to say with feeling that in "the forum of science we ignore" the term foreigner. In a last few days at Kew Gray entertained the younger British botanists with tales of their own forebears in science. He who had coaxed information from Robert Brown and talked with Menzies of Vancouver's voyage could tell stories out of a British past that they had lost. Everything was a last time. When crossing the channel from the continent Gray did it "probably not to be again on this side." The same was true of the Atlantic.

October 1887 meant coming home "after long play" to more work than ever. Perhaps Gray might write up some of his reminiscences. The *Vitaceae* of the *Synoptical Flora* beckoned toward the seemingly endless road through the plant kingdom. Darwin's *Life and Letters* required a review. The Cambridge Scientific Club meeting at E. S. Dixwell's on November 5 devoted the evening to honoring Gray and welcoming him home. Baird of the Smithsonian had died, entailing a special meeting of the Regents in Washington to choose Samuel P. Langley as the new secretary. Gray prepared the usual botanical necrology for the *American Journal of Science*. He had served, besides all else, as the almost official eulogist and, incidentally, recorder of elusive biographical information for American botanists since the 1840's. He had presided bibliographically at the graveside of more than three hundred and twenty. "Such things are a great drawback to the privileges of old age. You get left so alone, especially childless people, like Mrs. Gray & I. But we slip away all the easier for it when the time comes." [5]

At Thanksgiving dinner with the Loring family in Boston on November 24, 1887, Gray had a slight cold, nothing more. On Friday, November 25, he took things easy, although he set a Miss Murphree straight about a plant from the southern Alleghanies. Friday evening he had two slight chills, and the doctor ordered him to bed on Saturday.

On Sunday at noon he was so much better that he came downstairs, past the tall grandfather clock into the cluttered tidiness of the lower floor. He went into the study, where the bay window, source of light for many hours at the microscope, looked out over the Botanic Garden. The autumn had been the most beautiful in many years in eastern Massachusetts. He knew the source and kind of every leaf that drifted down before him.

When we think of a man's life we are apt to isolate him from his surroundings and consider only his individuality. It is well sometimes to have the fact brought before us that a man's surroundings—what he has seen and known—in the course of it—make up a great part of the man, tho' they do not make the *core*. But it is well to take into view how much of the natural world, of history, of experience of other minds and of the fruits thereof a man open to it all receives into his own being in the course of 80 years, or less.[6]

Gray's individuality as a scientific discoverer had a clear definition. His theory of the relation of the floras of eastern North America and east Asia was a discovery of importance, considered all by itself. In addition, its elaboration marked a milestone in setting the method of approach for a whole new subscience, plant geography. It was a discovery with originality and ingenuity, neat and clear. It gave Gray's name a prominent place in the literature, a place that would last indefinitely. Every now and then he had struck off additional small discoveries—on the coiling of tendrils or the direct action of pollen on the seeds of maize. When followed up, these amounted to something in the hands of others. More important, he had made in the daily course of his taxonomic labors countless discoveries, all duly reflected in descriptions and revisions.

Gray's position in science was not fully measurable, however, in individual discoveries. He had from first to last smoothly and without loss of motion added his work to the stream of science. Many of his names and concepts would fall in the hands of later workers, an outcome he confidently expected. It was not the end product but the continuing enterprise that carried the full life of science. In 1830 the stream had moved past Gray only slowly and in small volume. Now, this Sunday in 1887, the stream went by him as a rushing torrent. His contribution had helped to change both the volume and the velocity of the moving stream.

Science deals with facts, but it is a human enterprise. Without communication among men, science has no existence. Gray had grasped this from the first. His net was always widening and carefully tended, from his teachers and his friends, to his correspondents, to the readers of the *American Journal of Science,* to the learned men of the Western world gathered in the solemn communion of universities and academies. He had sent on to others what he knew and had gathered in what others knew. On this net of knowledge he built his institutions. The herbarium and library were by-products of the net. His educational enterprises as teacher and textbook writer added to its dimensions. The net stretched. Its fringe reached into Southern hinterland and Western wild. It converged on Gray from all over North America and fanned out again across the Atlantic. Each strand carried its two-way freight of information.

Those who manned the stations on Gray's net had not been

ciphers; they were friends. A scientist was a brother, a man with whom to break bread—the Baron Jacquin at Vienna or Charles Wright just in from the Rio Grande. In memory John Torrey stood out as the best of friends. He had started weaving the net and had shown Gray where the center was. At that time Sir William Hooker, "my beau-ideal," had held the skeins from the whole world. Joseph had carried on his father's place at Kew. Although he had been dead wrong about the Civil War, one could ask for no finer friend. Robert Brown could have been even greater than he was if he had only tried, but the Hookers had faithfully tended the net. Augustin-Pyramus De Candolle had provided the link with the century of Linnaeus, and Alphonse, good soul, had carried on the great *Prodromus*. One could go on naming them all afternoon.

The young American botanists would soon become too numerous to remember. But not yet. Gray could see them all as friends too. Manufactured botanists are seldom worth the trouble. Professional education was essentially a matter of communicating with colleagues. True, some had studied at Cambridge, despite the long dry spell at first. Eaton and Rothrock had come first. Then they were too thick to count. Some worked for degrees. Some had jobs in the herbarium. Some just stayed around for a while. Gray's students were not registered for Ph.D.'s. What did one of the greatest of them think of the man to whom they came perforce with all their affairs? "I was in and out of Gray's study and became in a way quite unusual for a young man and an old one intimate with him." "He would like to torment me, largely for my ignorance." "He was very good at Latin." "I have no contrary opinion of Gray at all. He was a superior person in every way." "Asa Gray was our greatest botanist." [7]

The country in which Gray lived had changed in his seventy-seven years. He had measured the geographical change by the boundaries of plants, by the dried specimens which crossed his table. He had helped give scientific meaning to the growth of the United States. It could have expanded both in size and number without science, unless someone made a conscious effort. Someone had to see that collectors went out to the frontier and beyond. Someone had to see that the labors of these rough-hewn intellectuals entered the world stream of science. They could not do that part of the job themselves. Someone had to see that children in the common schools had botany books which represented the best science of their day. Easy shortcuts and watered down exercises were not the true demand of democracy. Once Gray had taken the whole scene of the United States for granted. One might even get more research done by moving to Kew. But the specter of losing it all in the Civil War opened his eyes. The greatest glory of advancing years was the ability to travel the length and breadth of the continent by rail. From Van Buren to Grover Cleveland, Gray had seen Presidents and participated in decisions which shaped public policy toward botany. Joseph Henry had shown him much of the inner workings of more general scientific policymaking by leaning on him for intimate advice.

Science has its data, which are vain without the agency of men and institutions. All three together, nevertheless, fall short of being the whole of science. Ideas too must play their part. Gray knew this as a young man, when the great chain of being still structured natural history. His conviction of the important role philosophy had to play remained unchanged after the rise of evolution. If someone had told him that a historian in the twentieth century would divide the two halves of the nineteenth century into the age of philosophy and the age of science, he would have denied that such a line crossed his career. Looking at the anti-metaphysical bent of a friend like Hooker, he might conceivably have grasped what the historian meant. A man's science had to be informed and organized by his philosophy. He had early shaped this course within the framework of British empiricism. This he had absorbed directly from his botanical friends and indirectly from the utilitarianism of Paley which had replaced so much of the theological content of the Protestantism to which he had been converted by the Torreys in New York. Fortified in empiricism by both science and religion, he had proved impervious to idealism, either German or American transcendental. This orientation had made him less popular than Agassiz in the America of the 1850's, and it had furnished the philosophical basis of their clash.

Empiricism had made Darwin appear as a savior in the midst of the clouds of transcendentalism in which Agassiz gloried. The additional material connections which Darwin's thought made possible in the organic world, supplanting ideal ones, was profoundly congenial to Gray's whole philosophy. In accepting Darwin, he felt no need to revolt against either metaphysics or religion. It was his metaphysical interest which prompted him to play midwife to a philosophical movement which in 1887 still had no name and lived a hidden life, mostly in Cambridge. Gray would doubtless have objected to being called a pragmatist. Yet he had, through the queer fellow Chauncey Wright at the observatory across the street, helped pragmatism on its way. One of the things he contributed was an understanding of Darwin's theory as it stood in science, unencumbered by the new idealism which Herbert Spencer attached to it. The other thing he bequeathed was an embodiment of Chauncey Wright's concept of the neutrality of science. When Chauncey Wright made much of the complete lack of moral and ethical overtones in the neutrality of science, he had before him a perfect example in Gray. They disagreed only when it came to ultimates, but it was because science left the old problems where they had been before that Gray still considered himself able to accept the Nicene creed.

Science changed religion not at all, when all about cried revolution. Science was not a substitute religion. A humble believer in the Christian faith in 1846 or 1858, he was the same in 1887. Since one still had to choose world views, the orthodox belief had as much to recommend it as ever. In choosing this route Gray had parted company with many who shared his empiricism. Chauncey Wright himself, Huxley, Hooker, and dear old Darwin himself went another way. But the fight had been worth something. One Darwinian had been a theist. One orthodox Christian had been a first-rate scientist. The example itself had an effect on men.

Although botany is the amiable science and to the poet the flowers seem innocent, it would be the all-stifling tragedy if controversy were banished from the life of the botanist. Gray had been in this as in other ways peculiarly blessed. From Amos Eaton to E. L. Greene, Gray had punctuated his career with continuous thrust and counterthrust. He had reveled in it in the brashness of youth, challenging the Linnaean system as an obscurantist conservatism. In turn he had patiently taken the part of age, meeting Greene as if called by duty. In the midst of necessary and continuous controversy the important thing was never to wage battle for personal gain, for personal glory, for petty spite, or for wrathful revenge. Towering above all the other opponents loomed the ample image of Agassiz. Gray had taken the measure of the dominant figure of his generation. Gray felt in his heart he had won. He felt Agassiz had gone to his grave knowing he had lost. It was a sweet and famous victory.

Darkness blotted out the last light of the Sabbath, and the Botanic Garden no longer appeared through the bay window. Life was not yet done; controversy was not yet over. The clockwork of the mind ticked on at its accustomed pace. Those young botanists were tearing up nomenclature faster than a man could mend it. Britton, that young man at New York, had made a quite unnecessary name in the last issue of the Torrey Botanical Club *Bulletin*. One could not take off half a year in Europe without everything getting out of hand. Mrs. Gray protested it was time to rest. No, sit down and write Britton a letter, which "was important and must be written." [8]

"I want to liberate my mind by insisting that the process adopted violates the rules of nomenclature by giving a superfluous name to a plant, and also that in all probability your name is an incorrect one." The name which Britton had superseded, *Conioselinum Canadense,* had had after it T. & G., Torrey and Gray. Torrey had good reasons for what he did. "Besides, the preface of that 'Flora' states that Walter's herbarium had meanwhile been inspected by Dr. Torrey's colleague, who may now add that the Apium bipinnatum is not there." In London, forty-eight years before, that fact had slipped into its place in his mind. "I am sure that you will not take it amiss when I say that very long experience has made it clear to me that this business of determining rightful names is not so simple and mechanical as to younger botanists it seems to be, but is very full of pitfalls." Rather, it was a humane art, which required a lifetime of loving practice. "We look to you and such as yourself, placed at well-furnished botanical centres, to do your share of conscientious work and to support right doctrines . . . the high authority of Bentham . . . maxim of the elder De Candolle. . . ." He had seen De Candolle in the flesh; he had worked with Bentham as a friend and peer.[9]

Monday, November 28, Gray started down for breakfast. Everything seemed the same. The wallpaper on the bedroom wall was the same which Gray had seen most days since 1848, when he brought his bride to the newly decorated house in the garden. On the stairs, suddenly he could no longer move his hand and arm. At the breakfast table he was worse, an "ill turn" he called it. Yet afterward he addressed legibly two copies of his review of Darwin's *Life and Letters*. Goodale came in at nine o'clock and found him lying on the sofa. "He spoke of the attack and then passed on to other subjects." He could only have spoken of botany. Goodale was alarmed at what he saw, for he cut the conversation short and went for a physician. "By and by the numbness passed partly off, and, after a while, he went up stairs. . . ." [10] The rest is postlude.

On Thursday Gray had lost the power of connected speech. Only Mrs. Gray, the nurses, and doctors saw him. Young Pat Jackson from the numerous tribe of Lorings came to stay in the house to run for the doctor in a sudden emergency.[11] No call was ever sent, for the doctor could do nothing. All December the word went out that there was no hope. "He does not seem to suffer pain and is very quiet. It is sad to think of him thus, who was but a few days ago so active & bright and hopeful." [12] Mrs. Gray, who had known so many years of weakness, was now all strength "under fearful strain." The newspapers began their editorials and summaries. The year 1888 belongs to the life of Asa Gray only in a formal sense. He lay quiet and speechless until January 30, when at seven-thirty in the evening he died.

The end of an era in American botany was also the end of an era in Cambridge. The community which gathered in Appleton Chapel at Harvard was essentially the one which within a few years had buried Emerson and Longfellow. They felt at Gray's funeral that more had ended than just one life. "He is the last of my own elder Cambridge friends," Charles Eliot Norton reflected. "My pleasant memories associated with him date back to my earliest

College years. He was one of the few surviving friends of my Father and Mother." [13]

Francis Greenwood Peabody, as University preacher, read the verses of Scripture. "Consider the lilies of the field, how they grow." "Every tree is known by his own fruit: a good man out of the good treasure of his heart bringeth forth that which is good." As he read, Peabody kept thinking of a verse which he did not read, Paul's reference to "the simplicity which is in Christ." What gave "this great man of science an almost unique power over students, fellow-scientists, neighbors, and friends, was the impression of his single-mindedness and his simplicity." [14]

Alexander McKenzie, pastor of the First Church in Cambridge, who had pondered deeply on the meaning of Gray's career, including the correspondence with Darwin, made a few remarks. He was well aware of Gray's preference for the Nicene Creed, with its phrase, "I look for the resurrection of the dead." He doubtless had chosen the words of the ninety-second psalm which appeared on the black-edged cards that announced Gray's death. "For thou, Lord, has made me glad through Thy work; I will triumph in the works of Thy hands." [15]

The funeral party went through the whiteness of fresh snow to Mount Auburn Cemetery. Years before, Gray had helped old William Darlington with the Latin for an elaborate epitaph for his tombstone. "But *entre nous,* I should not fancy such an one on my own." [16] Mrs. Gray put on the headstone simply a cross and "Asa Gray 1810–1888."

NOTE
ON THE SOURCES
NOTES

The Gray Herbarium collection also contains manuscripts of many of Gray's addresses and both his and Mrs. Gray's travel journals. The manuscript of the unpublished Wilkes Expedition volume and Charles Wright's unpublished botany of the North Pacific Exploring Expedition are the most important of the botanical manuscripts. Some field notes of collectors in Gray's period remain, but they are less numerous than those for later times.

Using Gray's incoming mail as a guide, one can find many collections of Gray's letters to others in manuscript repositories all over the United States and western Europe. The more important collections consulted for this biography were found at the Academy of Natural Sciences, Philadelphia; the American Philosophical Society; the Public Library, Beverly, Massachusetts; the Boston Society of Natural History (housed in the Boston Museum of Science); the Conservatoire botanique de Genève, Switzerland; Fairfield Alumni and Historical Society (housed in the Herkimer County Historical Society); First Church, Cambridge, Massachusetts; Hamilton College Library, Clinton, New York; Houghton Library, Harvard University; Harvard University Archives; Historical Society of Pennsylvania; Jepson Herbarium, University of California, Berkeley; Royal Botanic Gardens, Kew; Library of Congress; Library of the Museum of Comparative Zoology, Harvard; Massachusetts Historical Society; Missouri Botanical Garden; New York Botanical Garden; New York Historical Society; New York State Library, Albany; Oberlin College Library; Smithsonian Institution; Yale University Library. Individuals who hold Gray papers and generously allowed their use included Mrs. D. W. Brown, Romulus, New York; Mrs. Nathaniel Clapp; General Harris Jones; Edgar W. Owen; and Mrs. Joseph N. Robbins.

The key to Gray's published writings is [Sereno Watson and G. L. Goodale], "List of the Writings of Dr. Asa Gray, Chronologically Arranged, with an Index," *American Journal of Science*, XXXVI (1888), appendix 3–67. This list contains approximately 780 entries, an indication of the size of Gray's publication effort. Although this bibliography is essentially complete, a number of publications cited in the notes written by Gray do not appear in the list. The major collections of Gray's papers are Charles S. Sargent, ed., *Scientific Papers of Asa Gray* (2 vols.; Boston, 1889), which is regularly cited in the following notes as *Scientific Papers,* and Asa Gray, *Darwiniana* (New York, 1876). Jane Loring Gray, ed., *The Letters of Asa Gray* (2 vols.; Boston, 1893), the major published collection of letters, is regularly cited as *Letters.* Mrs. Gray, while changing punctuation, was usually a faithful copier who exercised her editorial powers largely in leaving things out, sometimes with an indication and sometimes not. Where I have seen the original and found the variations unimportant, I have cited the published version.

The library of the Gray Herbarium provides a kind of physical guide to the vast botanical literature in which Gray was immersed throughout his life. Both books and reprints reveal the sources of his ideas. In some cases, notably the first editions of the *Vestiges of the Natural History of Creation* and Darwin's *Origin of Species,* the Gray copies are of double value because of extensive marginal notation. That this library is one of the outstanding collections for taxonomic botany in the United States is an indication of the general importance of Gray's efforts to exchange the works of his pen for the botanical literature of Europe and America. The Grayana collection of the library is almost complete in holdings of books written by Gray, and in addition the fact that they were often his working copies is important.

As guides to botanical literature, G. A. Pritzel, *Thesaurus Literaturae Botanicae* . . . (Leipzig, 1872), and the Royal Society of London, *Catalogue of Scientific Papers,* proved most useful. The two outstanding special bibliographies which aided this study have been D. C. Haskell, *The United States Exploring Expedition, 1838–1842, and Its Publications, 1844–1874* (New York, 1942), and Max Meisel, *A Bibliography of American Natural History: The Pioneer Century, 1769–1865* . . . (3 vols.; New York, 1924–1929).

Among the large mass of secondary literature of a historical nature which has gone into the making of this book, biographies have loomed large as sources of information. Some of these are really collections of biographies, for example, Joseph Ewan, *Rocky Mountain Naturalists* (Denver, 1950), S. W. Geiser, *Naturalists of the Frontier* (Dallas, 1937), M. A. DeW. Howe, *The Later Years of the Saturday Club, 1870–1920* (Boston, 1927), and A. D. Rodgers III, *American Botany, 1873–1892: Decades of Transition* (Princeton, 1944). A list of the individual biographies which have proved most useful is rich in those large Victorian lives and letters which sometimes tell infuriatingly little of their subject and hence of ours, but which by the prodigality of their quotations from the sources have nevertheless done an indispensable service. Among the more important of these are Elizabeth Cary Agassiz, *Louis Agassiz: His Life and Correspondence* (2 vols.; Boston, 1885); Emma Brace, ed., *Life and Letters of Charles Loring Brace* (New York, 1894); Francis Darwin, ed., *The Life and Letters of Charles Darwin* . . . (3 vols.; London, 1887), and *More Letters of Charles Darwin: A Record of His Work in a Series of Hitherto Unpublished Letters* (2 vols.; New York, 1903); D. C. Gilman, *The Life of James Dwight Dana* . . . (New York, 1899); Leonard Huxley, *Life and Letters of Sir Joseph Dalton Hooker* . . . (2 vols.; London, 1918); B. D. Jackson, *George Benthan* (London, 1906); Catherine Lyell, ed., *Life, Letters and Journals of Sir Charles Lyell, Bart.* (2 vols.; 1881). Among the few recent biographies of people close to Gray are Andrew D. Rodgers III's books on John Torrey, William Starling Sullivant, John Merle Coulter, and Liberty Hyde Bailey, and Ethel M. McAllister, *Amos Eaton, Scientist and Educator, 1776–1842* (Philadelphia, 1941). If this biography of Asa Gray leads to fresh appraisals of other figures in nineteenth-century science, it will have accomplished something of value.

4 2 5

NOTES

I

EARLY YEARS

1. Asa Gray, "Autobiography," Jane Loring Gray, ed., *The Letters of Asa Gray* (Boston, 1893), I, 13–14, hereafter referred to as *Letters;* David Brewster, ed., *The Edinburgh Encyclopaedia* (Philadelphia, 1832), IV, 1–343 *passim;* William Williams of Utica, N.Y., whose edition Gray probably read, was engaged in a serial publication of the *Encyclopaedia* in the 1820's.

2. *Edinburgh Encyclopaedia*, IV, 26.

3. William Lincoln, *History of Worcester, Massachusetts*. . . . (Worcester, 1862), 48, 49n; Robert Gray was twenty at the time of the immigration, and he is "supposed to be one of [the] sons" of a John Gray. The farm was on Lincoln Street. John Gray was one of five men furnished by the town to a company of scouts in 1722. The inscription on the tombstone in the Old Burial Ground in Worcester Common reads: "Here Lyes Buried the Body of Mr. Robert Gray, who died Jany 16th 1766. Aged 69 years. One of the company of Scotch Emigrants, who settled here in 1718." Worcester Society of Antiquity, *Collections,* I, No. 3 (1878), 37.

4. Spencer Miller, *Joseph Miller of Newton, Massachusetts* (New York, 1942), 29; Gray, "Autobiography," *Letters,* I, 2.

5. Gray in his "Autobiography" positively states that Joseph Howard was born March 8, 1766, at Pomfret, Connecticut (*Letters,* I, 3). However, in 1848 Howard told Mrs. Gray that he was born in Beverly, Massachusetts. Jane Loring Gray, Sauquoit, N.Y., to Charles G. Loring, July 21, 1848, Harvard University Archives. Mrs. Charles A. Weatherby examined for me the village and church records at Pomfret without finding a trace of his birth.

6. Henry C. Rogers, *History of the Town of Paris and the Valley of the Sauquoit* (Utica, 1881), 168, 178, 274.

7. Gray, "Autobiography," *Letters,* I, 1–28, contains Gray's own version of his first thirty years.

8. Alice A. Gray, MS Gray Family Record, in possession of Mrs. Joseph H. Robbins of Sauquoit, N.Y.

9. Gray, "Autobiography," *Letters,* I, 11; quotations in this chapter not otherwise noted come from this source.

10. Alice A. Gray, copy from the Records of the Presbyterian Church of Sauquoit, MS Gray Family Record.

11. Alice A. Gray, MS Gray Family Record, 46, gives his estate at the time of his death as $12,000 to $15,000.

12. A. D. Gridley, *History of the Town of Kirkland, New York* (New York, 1874), 134.

13. Gray gives his age as "twelve, or near it." If he had had Charles Avery as a teacher he would surely have mentioned the fact. The Avery family had no remembrance of Gray at this period. See Walter Avery, Clayville, N.Y., to Mrs. Asa Gray, n.d. [c. 1888]. Hence Asa could not have gone to Clinton before September 1822, and 1823 is the more likely year because of his positive assertion of 1825 as the date he went to Fairfield.

14. For example, the many letters of Elias Fries to Asa Gray. Latin continues to be used today for plant descriptions.

15. MS Log Book of the Phoenix Society, Hamilton College Library.

16. William Smith, Arlington, Mass., to F. L. and D. D. Warne, Christmas 1890, Fairfield Alumni and Historical Society, Herkimer, N.Y. (housed in the Herkimer County Historical Society), hereafter referred to as FAHS.

17. Franklin B. Hough, *Historical and Statistical Record of the University of the State of New York, during the Century from 1784 to 1884* (Albany, N.Y., 1885), 387n, 388.

18. William Smith, Arlington, Mass., to F. L. Warne and D. D. Warne, Christmas 1890, FAHS. Smith said that he was a classmate of Gray's in 1825–26 and told the stories of Asa and Eli Avery painting a cow and eating the principal's chickens. The latter story Gray himself ascribed to a slightly later period, but on the whole he disclaimed these yarns.

19. MS Minutes of the Calliopean Society, 31, 34, FAHS. MS Treasurer's Account Book, Calliopean Society, 1818–39, FAHS, lists among initiation fees paid on February 14, 1826, the entry: "A. Grey, for ditto, 1.50."

20. Asa Gray, Cambridge, to Othniel S. Williams, August 15, 1860, Hamilton College Library, Clinton, N.Y.

21. Hamilton College, *Catalogue of the Corporation, Officers, and Students* (Clinton, 1834–35), 17, gives total expense for a freshman as $72 to $91.50; College of Physicians and Surgeons of the Western District of the State of New York in Fairfield (Herkimer County), *Catalogue of the Faculty and Students* (Albany, N.Y., 1826), 5, places the cost at about $100. Copy in New York State Library; Joseph D. Ibbotson and S. N. D. North, eds., *Documentary History of Hamilton College* (Clinton, N.Y., 1922), 198.

22. Asa Gray, Cambridge, to Moses Gray, June 24, 1844, Hamilton College Library. Discussing the education of his younger brother, Asa considers Hamilton and Yale as the immediate alternatives. This letter indi-

cates that Moses Gray consulted his children on matters of their education but definitely reserved decision for himself.

23. Harvey Cushing, "The Pioneer Medical Schools of Central New York," *The Medical Career, and Other Papers* (Boston, 1940), 123–151.

24. MS Catalogue of Students, FAHS; Olaf Larsell, "Fairfield Medical School and Some Early Oregon Physicians," *Oregon Historical Quarterly,* XXXVII (1936), 102–110.

25. MS Copy of Report of the Trustees to the Regents, January 1828, FAHS.

26. Hough, *Record,* 391–392; MS Records of the proceedings of the Trustees, Jan. 21, 1826, FAHS.

27. MS Copy of Report of the Trustees to the Regents, Jan. 7, 1828; Jan., 1829, FAHS.

28. D. D. Warne, Fairfield, N.Y., to Mrs. Asa Gray, Feb. 22, 1888, quotes Dr. William Mather, then past ninety, who remembered Gray at the medical school.

29. The lack of interest shown when he attended an anatomical lecture in Paris might indicate such a feeling. *Letters,* I, 179.

30. Journal entry, July 4, 1818, quoted in Mary Hamilton Hadley, "An Old Time Pilgrimage in Pursuit of Science," *New England Magazine,* n.s., XXV (1902), 766.

31. See William Martin Smallwood and Mabel Sarah Coon Smallwood, *Natural History and the American Mind* (*Columbia Studies in American Culture,* VIII; New York, 1941), 228.

32. Dixon Ryan Fox, "The Vanished Naturalist," Association of the History Teachers of the Middle States and Maryland, *Proceedings,* XXVIII (1930), 58–67.

33. The work slightly earlier had a pivotal effect on the career of Albert Barnes, a Fairfield Academy graduate and student at Hamilton College who later became a most influential clergyman. Charles Noble, "Albert Barnes," *Dictionary of American Biography* (1st ed.), I, 628.

34. *Edinburgh Encyclopaedia,* IV, 1–343; for comparison, see William J. Hooker, "On the Botany of America," *American Journal of Science,* IX (1825), 263–284.

35. Amos Eaton, *A Manual of Botany for the Northern and Middle States* (4th ed.; Albany, N.Y., 1824.)

36. MS Daybook of Dr. John F. Trowbridge, Bridgewater, 1822–23, Oneida Historical Society, Utica, N.Y.

37. Lyman F. Kobler, "Lewis Caleb Beck," *Dictionary of American Biography* (1st ed.), II, 116.

38. Lewis C. Beck, Albany, N.Y., to Asa Gray, May 3, 1830.

39. Lewis C. Beck, Albany, N.Y., to Asa Gray, Aug. 3, 1831.

40. Note, John Torrey to James Hadley, suffixed to letter, John Torrey, New York, to Asa Gray, dated September 1830, postmarked Nov. 25, 1830.

41. D. D. Warne, Fairfield, N.Y., to Mrs. Asa Gray, Feb. 22, 1888; Asa Gray, Bridgewater, N.Y., to N. W. Folwell, Jan. 5, 1832, in possession of Dr. L. H. Bailey, Ithaca, N.Y., expresses himself on theses: "Old Mc. threatens to examine the theses himself & straiten them up does he? He threatens as much every year, but don't be concerned about him."

II

FROM MEDICINE TO SCIENCE

1. Asa Gray, Bridgewater, N.Y., to N. W. Folwell, March 14, 1831, in possession of Dr. L. H. Bailey, Ithaca, N.Y.
2. (Salem, Mass., 1828). There is a London edition of 1822, and the preface is dated Feb. 8, 1819.
3. Asa Gray, Bridgewater, N.Y., to N. W. Folwell, April 17, 1831, from a copy furnished by Mrs. D. W. Brown, Romulus, N.Y.; Gray to Folwell, March 14, 1831.
4. Lawrence, *Lectures*, 15, 17, 20, 24.
5. Conway Zirkle, "Natural Selection before the 'Origin of Species,'" American Philosophical Society, *Proceedings*, LXXXIV (1941), 109–110.
6. Asa Gray, New York, to N. W. Folwell, Feb. 25, 1836, from copy furnished by Mrs. D. W. Brown, Romulus, N.Y.; Gray to Folwell, March 14, 1831; Asa Gray, Bridgewater, N.Y., to N. W. Folwell, Jan. 5, 1832, from a copy furnished by Dr. L. H. Bailey, Ithaca, N.Y.
7. Gray to Folwell, March 14, 1831; Gray to Folwell, April 17, 1831.
8. James Hadley, Fairfield, N.Y., to John Torrey, Jan. 5, 1841, New York Botanical Garden Library; MS Notebook of Dr. William Mather, FAHS.
9. Asa Gray, New York, to N. W. Folwell, Oct. 4, 1834, from a copy furnished by Mrs. D. W. Brown, Romulus, N.Y.
10. Gray to Folwell, Jan. 5, 1832.
11. I. Bernard Cohen, *Some Early Tools of American Science: An Account of the Early Scientific Instruments and Mineralogical and Biological Collections in Harvard University* (Cambridge, Mass., 1950), 23; Edward S. Dana, ed., *A Century of Science in America with Special Reference to the American Journal of Science 1818–1918* (New Haven, 1918), 13–59.
12. John Torrey, New York, to L. D. von Schweinitz, May 1, 1830, C. L. Shear and N. L. Stevens, eds., "The Correspondence of Schweinitz and Torrey," Torrey Botanical Club, *Memoirs*, XVI (1921), 244.
13. Karl F. W. Jessen, *Botanik der Gegenwart und Vorzeit in culturhistorischer Entwickelung. Ein Beitrag zur Geschichte der Abendlandischen Völker* (Leipzig, 1864, republished Waltham, Mass., 1948), 464, gives in

a summary of statistics of botanical literature 2983 systematic works between 1801 and 1847 as compared to 647 devoted to anatomy and physiology.

14. A typical attitude is shown in William J. Hooker, "On the Botany of America," *American Journal of Science,* IX (1825), 263–284.

15. Augustin-Pyramus De Candolle, *Théorie élémentaire de la botanique, ou exposition des principes de la classification naturelle et de l'art de décrire et d'étudier les végétaux* (2nd ed.; Paris, 1819), 22.

16. Ralph L. Rusk, *The Life of Ralph Waldo Emerson* (New York, 1949), 187–188.

17. Ethel M. McAllister, *Amos Eaton: Scientist and Educator 1776–1842* (Philadelphia, 1941), 229.

18. Amos Eaton, *Manual of Botany for North America.* . . . (6th ed.; Albany, N.Y., 1833), vi.

19. John Torrey, *A Flora of the Northern and Middle Sections of the United States; or, a Systematic Arrangement and Description of All the Plants Hitherto Discovered in the United States North of Virginia* (New York, 1824).

20. John Lindley, *An Introduction to the Natural System of Botany.* . . . (1st American ed., John Torrey, ed.; N.Y., 1831).

21. Asa Gray, "Chester Dewey," in Charles S. Sargent, ed., *Scientific Papers of Asa Gray* (Boston, 1889), II, 345–346, hereafter cited as *Scientific Papers.*

22. John Torrey, New York, to Asa Gray, Oct. 6, 1831.

23. Gray to Folwell, Jan. 5, 1832; Asa Gray, Bridgewater, N.Y., to John Torrey, April 6, 1832, *Letters,* I, 37.

24. Gray to Folwell, Jan. 5, 1832.

25. Asa Gray to John Torrey, April 6, 1832; Jan. 2, 1833, *Letters,* I, 36–37.

26. M. M. Bagg, *The Utica High School* (Utica, N.Y., 1886), 3, copy in the Gray Herbarium with annotation by Asa Gray.

27. *The Utica Directory* (Utica, N.Y., 1832, 1838), copy in Utica Public Library.

28. Gray to Torrey, Jan. 2, 1833, *Letters,* I, 38–39.

29. S. Wells Williams, Ship *Morrison,* East Indian Ocean, to Asa Gray, September 3, 1833. Williams mentions Dana in a familiar way to Gray, but Dana in old age had no remembrance of "hearing of [Dr. Gray] at that time." James D. Dana, New Haven, Conn., to M. Miller Gray, Feb. 20, 1888.

30. Bagg, *Utica High School,* 7.

31. The fragment of a herbarium in FAHS, Herkimer, N.Y., contains plants labeled in Gray's writing, some of them dated July 1832. A direct tradition, almost certainly correct, has this collection the work of a student. The specimens discovered in Little Falls, N.Y., and described in [Homer D. House], "A Small Collection of Plants from Central New York, Collected by Asa Gray, 1832," New York State Museum, *Bulletin,* No. 205–206

(1918), 10–13, probably stems from this class activity as the dates on the tags are May and June 1832.

32. Albert G. Rau, "Lewis David von Schweinitz," *Dictionary of American Biography* (1st ed.), XVI, 483–484; Francis W. Pennell, "The Botanist Schweinitz and His Herbarium," *Bartonia,* No. 16 (1934), 1–8.

33. Asa Gray, Utica, N.Y., to L. D. von Schweinitz, Nov. 15, 1832, from copy in the Historical Society of Pennsylvania.

34. Asa Gray, "Characteristics of the North American Flora," *Scientific Papers,* II, 275.

35. Regents of the University of the State of New York, *Forty-sixth Annual Report* (New York State Senate Document No. 70, Jan. 1, 1833), 57–65.

36. Gray to Torrey, Jan. 2, 1833, *Letters,* I, 38.

37. *Ibid.*; "John Torrey," *Scientific Papers,* II, 362.

38. Gray to Torrey, Jan. 23, 1833, *Letters,* I, 40–41.

39. Asa Gray, New York, to N. W. Folwell, Oct. 4, 1834, from a copy furnished by Mrs. D. W. Brown, Romulus, N.Y.

40. J. F. Solierol, Metz, France, to Asa Gray, March 1, 1833; Asa Gray, Utica, N.Y., to N. W. Folwell, July 25, 1833, from a copy furnished by Dr. L. H. Bailey, Ithaca, N.Y.

41. J. G. C. Lehmann, Hamburg, to Asa Gray, Oct. 6, 1833.

42. Asa Gray, Hamilton College, to N. W. Folwell, June 2, 1834, from copy furnished by Mrs. D. W. Brown, Romulus, N.Y.

43. J. B. Crawe and Asa Gray, "A Sketch of the Mineralogy of a Portion of Jefferson and St. Lawrence Counties N.Y.," *American Journal of Science,* XXV (1834), 346–350.

44. A. D. Rodgers III, *John Torrey: A Story of North American Botany* (Princeton, N.J., 1942), 104–105.

45. Asa Gray, "Benjamin D. Greene," *Scientific Papers,* II, 310–311; see M. A. DeWolfe Howe, ed., *The Articulate Sisters: Passages from the Journals and Letters of the Daughters of President Josiah Quincy of Harvard University* (Cambridge, Mass., 1936), 82–83.

46. Shear and Stevens, Torrey Botanical Club, *Memoirs,* XVI (1921), 280.

47. John Torrey, Medical College, New York, to Asa Gray, March 1, 1834.

48. John Torrey, New York, to Joseph Henry, Aug. 29, 1838.

49. Mercer Street Presbyterian Church in the City of New York, *Manual* (New York, 1862), 26, lists the Torrey family as members. The connection with the New School branch is established through the views of Thomas Skinner, pastor of the Mercer Street Church, 1835–47. P. P. Faris "Thomas Harvey Skinner," *Dictionary of American Biography* (1st ed.), XVII, 201–202.

50. C. Bruce Staiger, "Abolitionism and the Presbyterian Schism of

1837–1838," *Mississippi Valley Historical Review,* XXXVI (1949), 391–414.

51. John Torrey, Princeton, N.J., to Asa Gray, July 28, 1836.

52. John H. Redfield, Philadelphia, to Jane Loring Gray, November 1888.

53. George Gray, Cambridge, to Lucy Ann Cobb, Aug. 9, 1845, courtesy of General Harris Jones, West Point, N.Y.

54. John Torrey, Medical College, N.Y., to Asa Gray, March 1, 1834.

55. Asa Gray, *North American Gramineae and Cyperaceae* (New York, 1834), Part I. There are two intact copies of this work at the Gray Herbarium. For a detailed discussion of the problems arising in connection with this mode of publication, see Harold W. Rickett and C. Gilley, "Asa Gray's Earliest Botanical Publications (1833–1836)," Torrey Botanical Club, *Bulletin,* LXIX (1942), 461–470.

56. Records of the Secretary of War, Register of Letters Received, XXXIV (Item L55), National Archives, lists the following letter: Major LeConte to Secretary of War, New York, Feb. 6, 1834, request that Asa Gray accompany an expedition to the West. Letter itself not located; Torrey to Gray, March 1, 1834.

57. Asa Gray, Utica, N.Y., to "Dear Chum" [N. W. Folwell], April 13, 1834, published in *Herkimer Citizen,* Jan. 6, 1903 (clipping in scrapbook at Herbarium). The addressee is certainly Folwell, indicated by references to his marriage.

58. Asa Gray, Utica, N.Y., to John Torrey, March 22, 1834, *Letters,* I, 43.

59. A copy of the first edition (Paris, 1813) remained in Gray's library, but it is dated 1841.

60. Asa Gray, Hamilton College, to John Torrey, June 9, 1834, here quoted from original in New York Botanical Garden Library. Published in part in *Letters,* I, 45–47; Gray to Folwell, June 2, 1834.

61. Gray to Torrey, June 9, 1834.

62. Anson Dart, Delta, N.Y., to Charles Avery, March 25, 1834, Hamilton College Library, is addressed to Clinton, Oneida County; James Hadley, Fairfield, N.Y., to B. W. Dwight, June 27, 1834, Hamilton College Library, mentions a Mr. Avery in this capacity.

63. Asa Gray, Utica, N.Y., to N. W. Folwell, Aug. 29, 1834, copy furnished by Mrs. D. W. Brown, Romulus, N.Y.

64. Gotthilf Heinrich Ernst Mühlenberg (1753–1815); Thomas Nuttall (1786–1859); William Baldwin (1779–1819).

65. Gray to Folwell, Oct. 4, 1834.

66. Asa Gray, New York, to Moses Gray, Nov. 21, 1834; Asa Gray, New York, to Roxana Gray, Feb. 7, 1835, *Letters,* I, 49; Gray to Folwell, Oct. 4, 1834.

67. Asa Gray, "A Monograph of the North American Species of Rhynchospora," Lyceum of Natural History, New York, *Annals,* III (1835),

191–219; Asa Gray, "A Notice of Some New, Rare, or Otherwise Interesting Plants, from the Northern and Western Portions of the State of New York," Lyceum of Natural History, New York, *Annals,* III (1835), 220–236; for a detailed discussion of subsequent editions of these papers see Rickett and Gilley, "Gray's Earliest Publications," Torrey Club, *Bulletin,* LXIX (1942), 466–470.

68. Shirley Gale, "Rhynchospora, Section Eurhynchospora, in Canada, the United States and the West Indies," *Rhodora,* XLVI (1944), 90.

69. Asa Gray, New York, to William J. Hooker, April 4, 1835, *Letters,* I, 51; William J. Hooker, *Companion to the Botanical Magazine. . . .* I (1835), 14, refers to the grass book as "among the most beautiful and useful works of the kind that we are acquainted with."

70. Gray to Roxana Gray, Feb. 7, 1835, *Letters,* I, 49.

71. John Torrey, New York, to Joseph Henry, Jan. 16, 1835; Feb. 2, 1835; Feb. 18, 1835.

72. MS note in the handwriting of Jane Loring Gray, Reminiscence File, Gray Herbarium, gives the date as February 6; Robert E. Thompson, *A History of the Presbyterian Churches in the United States (American Church History Series,* VI; New York, 1895), 91, 119.

73. Asa Gray, Bridgewater, N.Y., to N. W. Folwell, June 15, 1835, from copy furnished by Mrs. D. W. Brown, Romulus, N.Y.

74. Asa Gray, New York, to N. W. Folwell, April 28, 1835, from copy furnished by Mrs. D. W. Brown, Romulus, N.Y.

75. Asa Gray, New York, to N. W. Folwell, May 3, 1836, from copy furnished by Mrs. D. W. Brown, Romulus, N.Y.

76. Gray to Folwell, April 28, 1835.

77. Lucy A. Cobb to Jane Loring Gray, Nov. 7, 1888; Horace Smith and James Smith, *Poetical Works* (Epes Sargent, ed., New York, 1857), 8.

78. Jane Loring Gray in *Letters,* I, 30.

79. C. Bruce Staiger, "Abolitionism and the Presbyterian Schism of 1837–1838," *Mississippi Valley Historical Review,* XXXVI (1949), 395n.

80. Asa Gray, New York, to Moses Gray, April 6, 1835; Charles Noble, "Albert Barnes," *Dictionary of American Biography,* I, 627–629.

81. Gray to Folwell, April 28, 1835.

82. Asa Gray, *Elements of Botany* (New York, 1836), x.

83. John Torrey, Princeton, N.J., to Asa Gray, May 29, 1835; Gray to Folwell, June 15, 1835.

84. Asa Gray, Sauquoit, N.Y., to John Torrey, *Letters,* I, 52–53.

85. Asa Gray, New York, to N. W. Folwell, Sept. 29, 183[5], from copy furnished by Mrs. D. W. Brown, Romulus, N.Y.

86. Asa Gray, New York, to Moses Gray, Sept. 28, 1835, *Letters,* I, 54–55, original in Hamilton College Library.

87. Gray to Folwell, Sept. 29, 183[5].

88. Asa Gray to Moses Gray, Sept. 28, 1835; Asa Gray, New York, to

Moses Gray, Nov. 17, 1835, *Letters,* I, 55–56. Original in Hamilton College Library.

89. Asa Gray, New York, to Elsada Gray, Nov. 16, 1835; Asa Gray to Moses Gray, Nov. 17, 1835.

90. Regents of the University of the State of New York, *Annual Report* (Albany, 1836), 40.

91. Almira Hart Lincoln [Phelps], *Familiar Lectures on Botany* (2nd ed.; Hartford, Conn., 1831), 98; the same wording is used in *ibid.,* (7th ed.; New York, 1838), 79; see also Emma L. Bolzau, *Almira Hart Lincoln Phelps: Her Life and Work* (Philadelphia, 1934), 72–78.

92. Amos Eaton, New York, to John Torrey, Nov. 4, 1835, New York Botanical Garden Library, quoted in part in MacAllister, *Eaton,* 238–239.

93. Gray, *Elements* (1836), x, 304–305.

94. S. Wells Williams, Macao, to Asa Gray, Dec. 10, 1836.

95. Gray, *Elements* (1836), vi, 286.

96. De Candolle, *Théorie élémentaire,* 22, 55, 193–194.

97. Gray, *Elements* (1836), 289.

98. Asa Gray, "John Carey," *Scientific Papers,* II, 417–418.

99. Gray to Folwell, May 3, 1836.

100. Chester Dewey, Pittsfield, Mass., to John Torrey, April 6, 1836, New York Botanical Garden Library.

III

GOVERNMENT AS A PATRON

1. Lyceum of Natural History in the City of New York, *Charter, Constitution, and By-Laws* (New York, 1835, 1837). Copy in the library of the New York Historical Society.

2. Asa Gray, New York, to N. W. Folwell, May 3, 1836, copy from Mrs. D. W. Brown.

3. Asa Gray [New York], to John Torrey, July. 1836 (answered July 30, 1836), Gratz MSS, Historical Society of Pennsylvania; John Torrey, Princeton, N.J., to Asa Gray, July 12, 1856; July 18, 1836.

4. Gray to Torrey, July, 1836; William B. Shaw, "James Ellsworth De Kay," *Dictionary of American Biography* (1st ed.), V, 203–204.

5. Quoted in Daniel C. Haskell, *The United States Exploring Expedition, 1838–1842 and its Publications 1844–1874; a Bibliography* (New York, 1942), 2, hereafter cited as Haskell, *U.S. Exploring Expedition.*

6. Harley H. Bartlett, "The Reports of the Wilkes Expedition, and the Work of the Specialists in Science," American Philosophical Society, *Proceedings,* LXXXII (1940), 603–608; R. F. Almy, "J. N. Reynolds: a Brief

Biography with Particular Reference to Poe and Symmes," *The Colophon,* n.s., II (1937), 227–245.

7. J. N. Reynolds, *Voyage of the U.S. Frigate Potomac, under the Command of Commodore John Downes, during the Circumnavigation of the Globe, in the Years 1831, 1832, 1833, and 1834. . . .* (New York, 1835), v, 519.

8. J. N. Reynolds, *Address on the Subject of a Surveying and Exploring Expedition to the Pacific Ocean and South Seas. Delivered in the Hall of Representatives on the Evening of April 3, 1836* (New York, 1836), 70–74, hereafter cited as Reynolds, *Address.*

9. Max Meisel, *A Bibliography of American Natural History* (New York, 1924–29), II, 459; Bartlett does not seem to consider this scientific work when discussing Reynolds.

10. Reynolds, *Address,* 106, 111, 112, 128, 149–152.

11. E. G. Conklin, "Connection of the American Philosophical Society with our First National Exploring Expedition," American Philosophical Society, *Proceedings,* LXXXII (1940), 519, 520, 538.

12. Charles Pickering, Philadelphia, to Asa Gray, Sept. 23, 1836; Mahlon Dickerson, Washington, D.C., to Asa Gray, Oct. 3, 1836.

13. Asa Gray, New York, to Moses Gray, Oct. 8, 1836, *Letters,* I, 61–62.

14. R. Harlan, Philadelphia, to John Torrey, Oct. 8, 1836.

15. Asa Gray, New York, to W. J. Hooker, Oct. 10, 1836, *Letters,* I, 58–59; William Darlington, West Chester, Penna., to John Torrey, Oct. 11, 1836, Gratz MSS, Historical Society of Pennsylvania; Darlington to Gray, Oct. 10, 1836.

16. Louis N. Feipel, "The Wilkes Exploring Expedition: Its Progress through Half a Century: 1826–1876," U.S. Naval Institute, *Proceedings,* XL (1914), 1329–1330.

17. Mahlon Dickerson, Washington, D.C., to Asa Gray, Nov. 5, 1836. Asa Gray, New York, to Moses Gray, Jan. 4, 1837; Feb. 10, 1837, typed copy at Gray Herbarium.

18. Asa Gray, New York, to Moses Gray, March 21, 1837, *Letters,* I, 63; J. P. Couthouy, Boston, to Asa Gray, March 17, 1837; Charles Pickering, Philadelphia, to Asa Gray, March 20, 1837.

19. Asa Gray, New York, to N. W. Folwell, April 4, 1837, Cornell University Library; Asa Gray, to John Torrey, March 31 [1837], New York Botanical Garden Library.

20. J. N. Reynolds and Mahlon Dickerson, *Exploring Expedition. Correspondence between J. N. Reynolds and the Hon. Mahlon Dickerson under the Respective Signatures of "Citizen" and "Friend of the Navy" Touching the South Sea Surveying and Exploring Expedition; Wherein the Objects of the Enterprise and the Causes Which Have Delayed Its Departure Are Canvassed* [New York, 1838]. Originally published in the *New York Times* of

July, August, and September 1837, and in the *New-York Courier and Enquirer* of December and January 1837–38.

21. Charles Pickering, Washington, D.C., to Asa Gray, April 27, 1838; Asa Gray, New York, to John F. Trowbridge, Nov. 9 and Dec. 5, 1837, *Letters,* I, 64–65; [Joel R. Poinsett], "The Exploring Expedition," *North American Review,* LVI (1843), 258.

22. *American Gardener's Magazine (Hovey's Magazine),* II (1836), 421–424; *American Journal of Science,* XXX (1836), 399.

23. Gray to Folwell, April 4, 1837; William Darlington, West Chester, Penna., to Asa Gray, July 11, 1836; Lewis Tice, Meridian, Cayuga County, N.Y., to Asa Gray, Feb. 24, 1837; Charles W. Short, Lexington, Ky., to Asa Gray, June 23, 1836.

24. Asa Gray, "A Translation of a Memoir Entitled 'Beitrage zur Lehre von der Befruchtung der Planzen.' (Contributions to the Doctrine of the Impregnation of Plants;) by A. J. C. Corda," *American Journal of Science,* XXXI (1837), 308–323.

25. Asa Gray, "Remarks on the Structure and Affinities of the Order Ceratophyllaceae," Lyceum of Natural History, New York, *Annals,* IV (1837), 41–60.

26. Asa Gray, "Melanthacearum Americae Septentrionalis Revisio," Lyceum of Natural History, New York, *Annals,* IV (1837), 105–140.

27. Asa Gray to John F. Trowbridge, Nov. 9, 1837, typed copy in the Gray Herbarium.

28. Harley H. Bartlett, "Asa Gray's Nonresident Professorship; the Beginning of the University in Ann Arbor," *Michigan Alumnus Quarterly Review,* XLVII (1941), 217–219; Board of Regents of the University of Michigan, *Proceedings* (1838), 37–38.

29. Reynolds and Dickerson, *Correspondence,* 38–41.

30. Charles Pickering, Washington, D.C., to Asa Gray, April 27, 1838.

31. Stevens T. Mason, New York, to Asa Gray, May 18, 1838.

32. C. S. Rafinesque, Philadelphia, to John Torrey, April 10, 1838, New York Botanical Garden Library. The eccentric Rafinesque, ending a life of great labor for natural history penniless and forgotten, complained bitterly to Torrey concerning the *Flora* that "I am told you wait for the help of Dr. Gray and dont ask mine. Where is he? Well paid to go to Europe for the Univy of Michigan. You never recommended me for anything . . . but young men step up & gather the dollars." The position of this letter in the file suggests it was misdated, the year actually being 1839, when such knowledge would more likely have reached Philadelphia.

33. Asa Gray, "The Flora of North America," *Scientific Papers,* II, 250.

34. Gray to J. F. Trowbridge, July 18, 1838, *Letters,* I, 66.

35. Michigan Regents, *Proceedings* (1838), 50, 56; E. Farnsworth, Detroit, Mich., to Asa Gray, July 30, 1838.

36. Asa Gray, New York, to Moses Gray, Aug. 6, 1838, *Letters*, I, 67.

37. Asa Gray, Cleveland, Ohio, and Detroit, Mich., to Mrs. John Torrey, Aug. 10, 12, and 14, 1838, *Letters*, I, 67–68, 71–76; F. Paul Prucha, ed., "Reports of General Brady on the Patriot War," *Canadian Historical Review*, XXXI (1950), 56–68.

38. Gray's account of his visit to Detroit appears in a series of letters to Mrs. Torrey, *Letters*, I, 73–83.

39. John Torrey, New York, to Joseph Henry, postmarked Aug. 29, 1838.

40. Asa Gray, New York, to Joseph Henry, Nov. 6, 1838; Joseph Henry, Princeton, N.J., to Asa Gray, Nov. 1, 1838; John Carey, New York, to Asa Gray, Nov. 5, 1838; Asa Gray, New York, to S. G. Morton, Oct. 23, 1838, Morton Papers, American Philosophical Society.

41. Michigan Regents, *Proceedings* (1838), 56.

42. Russell E. Bidlack has made a definitive analysis of Gray's relationship to the University of Michigan Library in an unpublished doctoral dissertation on the history of the University of Michigan Library, prepared at Ann Arbor.

43. Stevens T. Mason, New York, to Asa Gray, Oct. 31, 1838; Zina Pitcher, Detroit, Mich., to Asa Gray, Sept. 17, 1838.

IV

ENVOY TO EUROPE

1. Asa Gray, New York, to Moses Gray, Nov. 7, 1838, and Asa Gray, Ship *Pennsylvania*, to Roxana Gray, Nov. 9, 1838, *Letters*, I, 84; William J. Hooker, Glasgow, to John Torrey, Sept. 3, 1838, New York Botanical Garden Library; Joseph Henry to Asa Gray, Nov. 1, 1838.

2. Quoted in Andrew D. Rodgers III, *"Noble Fellow" William Starling Sullivant* (New York, 1940), 109.

3. John Torrey, New York, to Joseph Henry, Nov. 9, 1838.

4. Asa Gray, "Journal," *Letters*, I, 265, is the basic source quoted. Gray's journal took the form of letters to John Torrey, his wife, and occasionally to the Misses Torrey. Some passages not published there are quoted from the MS journal in the Gray Herbarium.

5. Leonard Huxley, *Life and Letters of Sir Joseph Dalton Hooker . . .* (London, 1918), I, 32.

6. John Torrey and Asa Gray, *Flora of North America* (New York, 1838), I, 413.

7. Identification of McLeod is made in Susan D. McKelvey, *Botanical Exploration of the Trans-Mississippi West* (Jamaica Plain, Mass., 1955), 627–635.

8. William J. Hooker and G. A. Walker Arnott, *The Botany of Captain Beechey's Voyage* (London, 1841), 315, 387–388.

9. Asa Gray, "Brown and Humboldt," *Scientific Papers,* II, 283–286.

10. Asa Gray, "Notices of European Herbaria, Particularly Those Most Interesting to the North American Botanist," *American Journal of Science,* XL (1840), 11.

11. B. Daydon Jackson, "George Bentham," in J. Reynolds Green, ed., *English Men of Science* (London, 1906); Asa Gray, "George Bentham," *Scientific Papers,* II, 451–464.

12. M. L. Fernald, "Some Early Botanists of the American Philosophical Society," American Philosophical Society, *Proceedings,* LXXXVI (1942), 70; Bernice G. Shubert, Photographs of the Herbarium of Thomas Walter at the British Museum, 1946–1947, bound and deposited in the Gray Herbarium, opposite page 65; M. L. Fernald and Ludlow Griscom, "The Identity of Lobelia Glandulosa Walt," *Rhodora,* XXXIX (1937), 497.

13. George Haven Putnam, *George Palmer Putnam: A Memoir Together with a Record of the Publishing House Founded by Him* (New York and London, 1912), 33, states that Wiley & Putnam was founded in 1840 and makes no mention of G. P. Putnam's presence in London in 1839, but Gray's references both to the man and the firm are explicit.

14. Francis Boott, London, to John Torrey, Oct. 30, 1839, New York Botanical Garden Library.

15. Huxley, *Joseph D. Hooker,* I, 180–181.

16. Asa Gray, "Botanical Necrology (Matthias Jacob Schleiden, Theodore Schwann)," *American Journal of Science,* 3rd ser., XXIII (1882), 333–334.

17. Asa Gray, "Notes of a Botanical Excursion to the Mountains of North Carolina, &c. with Some Remarks on the Botany of the Higher Allegheny Mountains, in a Letter to Sir Wm. J. Hooker," *American Journal of Science,* XLII (1842), 3–9.

18. Asa Gray, Munich, to George Bentham, June 20, 1839, Library of the Royal Botanic Gardens, Kew.

19. Mariana Starke, *Travels in Europe: for the Use of Travellers on the Continent, Including the Island of Sicily, Where the Author Had Never Been Till the Year 1834. Including an Account of the Remains of Ancient Italy, and Also the Roads Leading to Those Remains* (9th ed.; London, 1837).

20. Augustin-Pyramus De Candolle and Alphonse De Candolle, *Prodromus systematis naturalis regni vegetabilis . . .* (Paris, 1824–70).

21. Asa Gray, "Augustin-Pyramus De Candolle," *Scientific Papers,* II, 289–309.

22. Asa Gray to G. P. Putnam, July 23, 1839, *Letters,* I, 265–266.

23. Asa Gray, London, to George Bentham, Sept. 30, 1839, Royal Botanic Gardens, Kew, reprinted without date in *Letters,* I, 267; Asa Gray, London, to William J. Hooker, Sept. 13, 1839, *Letters,* I, 268–270.

24. State of Michigan, *Documents Accompanying the Journal of the Senate* (Detroit, 1841), I, 420–487, lists the title of each book. Russell Bidlack has analyzed these purchases carefully, identifying and marking the books still extant in the University of Michigan Library and also determining in most cases which books were selected by Putnam and which by Gray.

25. Asa Gray, New York, to Moses Gray, Nov. 5, 1839, *Letters,* I, 270.

V

LAST YEARS OF UNCERTAINTY

1. Michigan Regents, *Proceedings,* July 12, 1839, p. 93, shows the money authorized. John Carey, acting as Gray's agent, had prodded Governor Mason in a letter written May 23, 1839, and after the regents' vote he received a promise of immediate payment. S. T. Mason, Detroit, to John Carey, July 14, 1839. It was not actually charged off the University books until April 1840.

2. Michigan Regents, *Proceedings,* April 8, 1840, p. 129.

3. Russell Bidlack's dissertation thoroughly examines the reaction of the authorities to the books and also their subsequent fate.

4. James Constable, New York, to Asa Gray, Dec. 31, 1842; Asa Gray, New York, to William J. Hooker, March 17, 1840, and May 30, 1840, MS copy at Gray Herbarium.

5. Asa Gray, New York, to George Bentham, Dec. 28, 1839.

6. Asa Gray, New York, to William J. Hooker, March 17, 1840, May 30, 1840, May 20, 1841, *Letters,* I, 274–275, 279, MS copy.

7. Alphonse De Candolle, Geneva, Switzerland, to Asa Gray, July 26, 1840; Asa Gray, New York, to Alphonse De Candolle, Sept. 15, 1840, *Letters,* I, 276–277.

8. John Torrey and Asa Gray, *Flora of North America* (New York, 1840), I, xi–xiii.

9. This unusually large number resulted from the fact that most of the United States Army was concentrated in Florida for the Seminole War, and doctors in service and one officer sent plants.

10. Asa Gray, "Botanical Excursion to North Carolina," *American Journal of Science,* XLII (1842), 48; Moses Ashley Curtis, Wilmington, N.C., to Asa Gray, May 21, 1841; June 21, 1841.

11. Asa Gray, "George Engelmann," *Scientific Papers,* II, 439–441; George Engelmann, St. Louis, Missouri, to Asa Gray, November 26, 1840; Asa Gray, New York, to George Engelmann, Sept. 12, 1841, typed copy.

12. Torrey and Gray, *Flora of North America,* I, 553; Francis W. Pennell, "Travels and Scientific Collections of Thomas Nuttall," *Bartonia,* XVIII (1936), 35–39; Asa Gray, New York, to William J. Hooker, May 20, 1841, MS copy.

13. For a detailed account see A. Hunter Dupree, "Thomas Nuttall's Controversy with Asa Gray," *Rhodora,* LIV (1952), 293–303.

14. Asa Gray, "The Longevity of Trees," *North American Review,* LIX (1844), 193. One authority, Pennell, *Bartonia,* XVIII, 44n, considers this judgment unjust because "in 1844 Gray had not grasped what a remarkable proportion of endemism [plants peculiar to the region] characterizes every portion of western North America."

15. Asa Gray, "Remarks Chiefly on the Synonymy of Several North American Plants of the Orchis Tribe," *American Journal of Science,* XXXVIII (1840), 306–311.

16. A[sa] G[ray], "Notice of the Botanical Writings of the Late C. S. Rafinesque," *American Journal of Science,* XL (1841), 221–241. For a recent thorough appraisal of Rafinesque's scientific work see Elmer D. Merrill, *Index Rafinesquianus* (Jamaica Plain, Mass., 1949), 1–64.

17. Spencer F. Baird, Carlisle, Penna., to Asa Gray, Feb. 7, 1849; M. L. Fernald, "Overlooked Species, Transfers and Novelties of the Flora of Eastern North America," *Rhodora,* XLVI (1944), 20n.

18. *American Journal of Science,* XXXIX (1840), 168–181.

19. George Lincoln Goodale, "The Development of Botany Since 1818," in E. S. Dana, ed., *A Century of Science in America, with Special Reference to the American Journal of Science, 1818–1918* (New Haven, 1918), 447.

20. *American Journal of Science,* XXXIX (1840), 175–176; XL (1841), 176–177.

21. *Ibid.,* LXII (1841), 184–185; Amos Eaton, Rensselaer Institute, Troy [N.Y.], to Benjamin Silliman, Feb. 10, 1842, with note on back in handwriting of Benjamin Silliman, Sr., and letter, Benjamin Silliman, Jr. [New Haven, Conn.], to Asa Gray, Feb. 14, 1842; Eaton to Gray, Feb. 18, 1842.

22. *American Journal of Science,* LXII (1842), 377–378; LXIII (1842), 215–216; Chester Dewey, Rochester, N.Y., to Asa Gray, April 15, 1842.

23. Moses Ashley Curtis, Hillsborough, N.C., to Asa Gray, March 14, 1842.

24. J[ohn] C[arey], "Notice of a Flora of North America," *American Journal of Science,* LXI (1841), 275–283.

25. Josiah Quincy, *The History of Harvard University* (Cambridge, Mass., 1840), II, 452.

26. MS Minutes of the Massachusetts Professorship, 15.

27. Ernest Ingersoll, "Harvard Botanic Garden and Its Botanists," *Century Illustrated Magazine,* XXXII (1886), 237; Benjamin L. Robinson, "The Removal of an Old Landmark," *Harvard Graduates Magazine,* LXXV (1911), 419.

28. I. B. Cohen, *Some Early Tools of American Science* (Cambridge, Mass., 1950), 108; Harvard University, *Catalogue of the Officers and Students of the University in Cambridge* (Cambridge, Mass., 1823), 6.

29. William Smellie, *Philosophy of Natural History* (1st ed.; Edinburgh,

441

1790); John Ware, ed., *Philosophy of Natural History, with an Introduction and Various Additions and Alterations, Intended to Adapt It to the Present State of Knowledge* (Boston, 1824).

30. President of Harvard University, *The Annual Report . . . to the Overseers on the State of the Institution* (Cambridge, Mass., 1826–1831).

31. Thomas Nuttall, *An Introduction to Systematic and Physiological Botany* (Cambridge and Boston, 1827), a modest work based on the Linnaean system. It appears not to have been used widely.

32. President, *Annual Reports*, 1833–1837.

33. Walter Channing, *A Brief Memoir of Joshua Fisher, M.D., Late President of the Massachusetts Medical Society, from the Annual Discourse before the Society, June 6, 1833* [Boston, 1833], 1–8; Josiah Quincy, Cambridge, Mass., to Asa Gray, March 26, 1842.

34. Thaddeus William Harris, Cambridge, Mass., to D. Humphreys Storer, June 14, 1838, Library of the Boston Society of Natural History.

35. [Thaddeus William Harris], *Report on the Insects of Massachusetts Injurious to Vegetation* (Cambridge, Mass., 1841); Students' Notebooks, Harvard University Archives; Thaddeus William Harris, Cambridge, Mass., to Asa Gray, Feb. 28, 1850.

36. [J. Marcet], *Conversations on Vegetable Physiology; Comprehending the Elements of Botany, with Their Application to Agriculture* (New York, 1830).

37. Thomas Wentworth Higginson, MS Notebooks of Flowers, 1841–42; *Dictionary of American Biography* (1st ed.), VIII, 321; Thomas Wentworth Higginson, Introduction to S. H. Scudder, ed., *Entomological Correspondence of Thaddeus William Harris, M.D.* (Boston Society of Natural History, *Occasional Papers*, I; Boston, 1869), xi–xxxvii.

38. Harris to Storer, June 14, 1838.

39. Asa Gray, "Francis Boott," *Scientific Papers*, II, 317; Benjamin D. Greene, Boston, to Asa Gray, Dec. 24, 1841.

40. Benjamin D. Greene, Boston, to Asa Gray, Nov. 30, 1841; William Oakes, Ipswich, Mass., to Asa Gray, Jan. 31, 1842; Asa Gray, New York, to B. D. Greene, Dec. 14, 1841; Edward Tuckerman, Boston, to John Torrey, April 16, 1841, Library of the New York Botanical Garden.

41. Gray to B. D. Greene, Dec. 14, 1841; Asa Gray, New York, to William J. Hooker, March 30, 1842, *Letters*, I, 282.

42. Benjamin D. Greene, Boston, to Asa Gray, Dec. 24, 1841.

43. This was Gray's opinion. George Gray [Asa's brother], Cambridge, to Elsada Gray, July 15, 1845, in the possession of General Harris Jones, of West Point, N.Y. "Dr. says he probably owed his appointment here to his (Emerson's) influence."

44. Oakes to Gray, Jan. 31, 1841.

45. Gray to Hooker, March 30, 1842, *Letters*, I, 284. Gray here ascribed these views to his first letter to Greene, of which the original does not bear

him out. Such a position is based on more accurate information than he had before going to Cambridge.

46. George B. Emerson, Boston, to Josiah Quincy, March 25, 1842, Harvard College Papers, 2nd ser., XI (1842–1843), 33–35, Harvard University Archives.

47. Harvard College Records, VIII, 160, Harvard University Archives.

48. Josiah Quincy, Cambridge, to Asa Gray, March 26, 1842, Gray Herbarium "Official" box.

49. Gray to Hooker, March 30, 1840, *Letters*, I, 284; Asa Gray, New York, to Josiah Quincy, March 31, 1842, Harvard College Papers, 2nd ser., XI (1842), 39–40, Harvard University Archives; Josiah Quincy, Cambridge, to Asa Gray, April 5, 1842, Beverly, Mass., Public Library; Zina Pitcher, Detroit, Mich., to Asa Gray, April 26, 1842.

50. Michigan Regents, *Proceedings,* May 3, 1842, 235; Asa Gray, New York, to Josiah Quincy, April 26, 1842, Harvard College Papers, 2nd ser., XI (1842), 60, Harvard University Archives.

51. Thaddeus William Harris, Cambridge, to D. Humphreys Storer, April 26, 1842, Boston Society of Natural History.

52. Josiah Quincy, Cambridge, to Asa Gray, May 4, 1842.

53. S. E. Morison, *Three Centuries of Harvard, 1636–1936* (Cambridge, Mass., 1936), 257–258.

54. William Oakes, Ipswich, Mass., to Asa Gray, May 2, 1842.

55. For example, Francis Boott, London, to Asa Gray, Jan. 1, 1843; William Darlington, West Chester, Penna., to Asa Gray, May 9, 1842.

56. Asa Gray, *The Botanical Textbook for Colleges, Schools, and Private Students* (New York, 1842), ix.

57. Gray to Hooker, July 30, 1842, *Letters*, I, 291.

VI

THE PROFESSOR AT CAMBRIDGE

1. Asa Gray, Boston, to John Torrey, July 25, 1842, *Letters*, I, 288.

2. *Ibid.*, 287; Isabella James to Mrs. Asa Gray, Oct. 25, 1895.

3. William J. Hooker, Kew, to Asa Gray, Nov. 10, 1842, MS copy; Asa Gray, Cambridge, Mass., to Lewis R. Gibbes, July 26, 1842, Gibbes Papers, Library of Congress.

4. Asa Gray, Cambridge, to John Torrey, Sept. 15, 1842, *Letters*, I, 292–293.

5. Asa Gray, Cambridge, to Josiah Quincy, Sept. 16, 1842, Harvard College Papers, 2nd ser., XI, 163–169, Harvard University Archives; Gray to Torrey, Sept. 15, 1842, *Letters,* I, 292–293.

6. John Torrey, Princeton, N.J., to Asa Gray, Sept. 6, 1842; Asa Gray, Cambridge, to George Engelmann, Sept. 26, 1842, typed copy.

7. Asa Gray, Cambridge, to George Engelmann, Nov. 14, 1842, typed copy.

8. John Carey to Gray, Aug. 16, 1842.

9. Asa Gray, Cambridge, to Mrs. John Torrey, Dec. 14, 1842, *Letters,* I, 296.

10. S. E. Morison, *Three Centuries of Harvard, 1636–1936* (Cambridge, Mass., 1936), 275.

11. Alexander McKenzie, *Lectures on the History of the First Church in Cambridge* (Boston, 1873), 228; MS Records, Dec. 30, 1842, First Church in Cambridge.

12. Gray to Mrs. Torrey, Dec. 14, 1842, *Letters,* I, 295–296.

13. John Carey, Buffalo, to Asa Gray, July 28, 1843.

14. Boston Society of Natural History, *Proceedings,* I (1842), 81, 90, 180.

15. American Academy of Arts and Sciences, *Proceedings,* I (1846), 3.

16. Cambridge Scientific Club, Records, Sept. 24, 1846, Jan. 28, 1847, and March 10, 1847, Harvard University Archives.

17. Harvard College Records, VIII, 192, Harvard University Archives.

18. Asa Gray [Cambridge], to Mrs. John Torrey, March 2, March 18, 1843, *Letters,* I, 300–302.

19. E. Q. Sewall, MS Diary, April 16, 1844, Harvard University Archives.

20. Jason Martin Gorham, MS Diary, May 11, May 23, May 30, 1848, Harvard University Archives.

21. Edward W. Emerson, "Asa Gray," M. A. DeWolfe Howe, *Later Years of the Saturday Club 1870–1920* (Boston, 1927), 62; James K. Hosmer, *The Last Leaf* (New York, 1912), 278–281.

22. John Mead, MS Journal, April 19, May 30, May 31 [1848], 38, 41–42, Harvard University Archives; also reported in Gorham, Diary, 32, 34, Harvard University Archives.

23. Mead, Journal [March] 30 [1848], 35–36, Harvard University Archives.

24. Gray to Mrs. Torrey, March 18, 1843, *Letters,* I, 302–303.

25. On Nov. 30, 1844, the Corporation raised Gray's salary to $1500 and made him "liable to all the duties incumbent upon the Fisher Professorship. . . ." MS copy of record, Gray Herbarium, "Official" box.

26. President, *Annual Reports,* 1842–1848.

27. See Charles Lyell, *Travels in North America in the Years 1841–2; with Geological Observations on the United States, Canada, and Nova Scotia* (New York, 1845), I, 86–88.

28. Ferris Greenslet, *The Lowells and Their Seven Worlds* (Boston, 1946), 210–211; see also, Harriette K. Smith, *The History of the Lowell Institute* (Boston, 1898), 15–16.

29. Smith, *The History of the Lowell Institute,* 49–94, contains a complete list of speakers, 1839–98.

30. Lyell estimated the scale as more than three times as high as that paid in London for the best lectures. *Travels, 1841–2,* I, 89.

31. Gray to Mrs. Torrey, Dec. 14, 1842, *Letters,* I, 295.

32. Asa Gray, Cambridge, to William J. Hooker, Feb. 28, 1843, MS copy; William J. Hooker, Kew, to Asa Gray, June 30, 1843.

33. Isabella James to Mrs. Asa Gray, Nov. 16, 1893.

34. Asa Gray, Cambridge, to Moses Gray, Nov. 18, 1843, *Letters,* I, 314.

35. Asa Gray, Cambridge, to John Torrey, Feb. 17, 1844, I, 314–315; Gray, *Botanical Textbook* (2nd ed.; New York, 1845), 162, gives what probably was the same diagram.

36. Gray to W. J. Hooker, April 1, 1844, *Letters,* I, 324; Asa Gray, Cambridge, to John Torrey, March 1, 1844, *Letters,* I, 315–316, corrected in some details by the original in the library of the New York Botanical Garden.

37. *Ibid.,* I, 319.

38. Gray to W. J. Hooker, April 1, 1844, *Letters,* I, 324.

39. Mrs. James Freeman Clarke [Boston], to E[lizabeth] G. H[indekoper], [Jan.?] 22, 1846, Clarke papers, Houghton Library, Harvard University, called to my attention by Dr. Stanley Bolster.

40. Gray to Torrey, March 25, 1844, *Letters,* I, 319. The letter from Torrey which prompted these remarks has not been located.

VII

THE PATTERN OF A YOUNG MAN'S THOUGHTS AND DEEDS

1. George Gray, Cambridge, to Elsada Gray, Nov. 14, 1845, in the possession of General Harris Jones, West Point, N.Y.

2. Harvard College Records, VIII, 214, Harvard University Archives.

3. W. S. Sullivant, Columbus, Ohio, to Asa Gray, July 12, 1843.

4. *Ibid.*; Gray to W. J. Hooker, Aug. 11, 1843, *Letters,* I, 307; Earl L. Core, "Travels of Asa Gray in West Virginia, 1843," *Rhodora,* XLII (1940), 344–351.

5. W. S. Sullivant, *Musci Alleghanienses* (Columbus, Ohio, 1845).

6. MS copy of record, Nov. 30, 1844, Gray Herbarium, "Official" box; MS bills, Gray folder, Hamilton College Library, Clinton, N.Y.; Francis Boott, London, to Asa Gray, Dec. 3, 1844.

7. Asa Gray, Cambridge, to Parker Cleaveland, Aug. 7, 1844, Norcross Papers, Massachusetts Historical Society.

8. Asa Gray, "Lindley's Natural System of Botany," *Scientific Papers,* I, 7.

9. Asa Gray, "Spiritual Life in Plants," *American Journal of Science,* XL (1841), 170.

10. *Letters,* I, 321; Soame Jenyns, *A View of the Internal Evidence of the Christian Religion* (C. N. Cole, ed., *The Works of Soame Jenyns,* IV; London, 1790); A. H. Bullen, "Soame Jenyns," *Dictionary of National Biography,* X, 769–770.

11. William Paley, *Natural Theology: or, Evidences of the Existence and Attributes of the Deity, Collected from the Appearances of Nature* (John Ware, ed.; Boston, 1854), Walker's annotated copy in Harvard College Library.

12. See Wendell Glick, "Bishop Paley in America," *New England Quarterly,* XXVII (1954), 347–354; Leslie Stephen, *English Thought in the Eighteenth Century* (London, 1927), I, 413–414; II, 125.

13. See C. C. Gillispie, *Genesis and Geology* (Cambridge, Mass., 1951), 209–216.

14. A. N. Whitehead, *Science and the Modern World* (2nd English ed.; Cambridge, England, 1932), 95.

15. See John T. Merz, *History of European Thought in the Nineteenth Century* (London, 1903), II, 368–464.

16. Asa Gray, MS Lecture on Vegetation and the Sun, in Gray Herbarium, delivered before the Lowell Institute in 1853–54. Dated from American Academy of Arts and Sciences, *Proceedings,* III (1854), 87.

17. Paul B. Sears, *Charles Darwin: the Naturalist as a Cultural Force* (New York, 1950), 17, points out that special creation fitted the facts of its day.

18. [Asa Gray], "Review of *Explanations: A Sequel to the Vestiges of the Natural History of Creation,*" *North American Review,* LXII (1848), 471.

19. [Asa Gray], "The Chemistry of Vegetation," *North American Review,* LX (1845), 3–42.

20. John W. Draper, *A Treatise on the Forces Which Produce the Organization of Plants; with an Appendix Containing Several Memoirs on Capillary Attraction, Electricity, and the Chemical Action of Light* (New York, 1844).

21. See Donald Fleming, *John William Draper and the Religion of Science* (Philadelphia, 1950), which, however, unfortunately omits consideration of Gray's review of Draper's book.

22. Asa Gray, MS marginal note in Draper, *Treatise,* 8, Gray Herbarium copy.

23. *Ibid.,* 14; the printed version, Gray, *North American Review,* LV, 40–41, is more obscure if not more polite, substituting "intumescence" for *"sugar* and *wind."*

24. Asa Gray, Cambridge, to John Torrey, Feb. 12, 1845, Library of the New York Botanical Garden.

25. G. J. Mülder, *The Chemistry of Vegetable and Animal Physiology* (Fromberg, trans.; Edinburgh [1845]).

26. Asa Gray, Cambridge, to John Torrey, Feb. 12 and March 8, 1845, *Letters,* I, 328–330.

27. Lyell, *Travels in North America, in the Years 1841–2* . . . , I, 25–27, 42.

28. L. C. Eiseley, *Darwin's Century: Evolution and the Men Who Discovered It* (Garden City, 1958), 97–115.

29. Asa Gray, Cambridge, to John Torrey, Friday morning [December 1845], Library of the New York Botanical Garden.

30. (Edinburgh, 1844; New York, 1845); Robert Chambers was not identified as the author until many years later.

31. *Vestiges* (New York, 1845), 269, Gray's copy. Capitals the author's, but italics Asa Gray's.

32. Francis Boott, London, to Asa Gray, Dec. 23, 1844; Gray to Torrey, Feb. 12 and March 8, 1845, *Letters,* I, 328–330.

33. Asa Gray, Lowell Institute MS Lecture No. 7.

34. [Francis Bowen], "Review of *Vestiges of the Natural History of Creation,*" *North American Review,* LX (1845), 438; Asa Gray, Cambridge, to John Torrey, March 30, 1845, Library of the New York Botanical Garden.

35. *American Journal of Science,* XLVIII (1845), 395; James D. Dana, New Haven, to Asa Gray, June 17, 1845.

36. [Asa Gray], "Review of *Explanations: A Sequel to the Vestiges of the Natural History of Creation,*" *North American Review,* LXII (1846), 465–506.

37. *American Journal of Science,* I (1846), 250–254; James D. Dana, New Haven, to Asa Gray, April 27, 1846.

38. Asa Gray, MS marginal note in *Vestiges,* 122.

39. Asa Gray, Cambridge, to John Torrey, [Jan. 26, 1846], [Feb. 20, 1847], Library of the New York Botanical Garden.

40. James D. Dana, New Haven, to Asa Gray, July 12, 1848; John Torrey, New York, to Asa Gray, Jan. 22, 1846; A. A. Gould, Boston, to Jeffries Wyman, Feb. 21, 1847, typed copy in Library of Museum of Comparative Zoology, Harvard University.

41. Jeffries Wyman, "Experiments on the Formation of Infusoria in Boiled Solutions of Organic Matter, Enclosed in Hermetically Sealed Vessels and Supplied with Pure Air," *American Journal of Science,* XXXIV (1862), 79–87; A. Hunter Dupree, ed., "Some Letters from Charles Darwin to Jeffries Wyman," *Isis,* XLII (1951), 104–110.

42. Elizabeth Cary Agassiz, ed., *Louis Agassiz: His Life and Correspondence* (2 vols.; Boston, 1885), I, *passim.*

43. Asa Gray, Cambridge, to Jared Sparks, Dec. 11 [1846], Sparks Papers, Houghton Library; E. C. Agassiz, *Agassiz,* II, 437.

44. Asa Gray, Cambridge, to John Torrey [spring of 1847?], Library of the New York Botanical Garden. Agassiz doubtless drew from the researches of Alexander Braun on this subject—phyllotaxis. Here, rather than any evolutionary interest as Wiener suggests, is the probable source of Gray's information which appeared in the 1850 edition of his *Textbook*. See P. P. Wiener, *Evolution and the Founders of Pragmatism* (Cambridge, Mass., 1949), 258n.

45. George Gray, Cambridge, to [Lucy Ann Cobb], April 17, 1847, in possession of General Harris Jones, West Point, N.Y.

46. Gray to Torrey [Feb. 20, 1847], Library of the New York Botanical Garden.

47. Asa Gray, "Louis Agassiz," *Scientific Papers,* II, 484.

48. Asa Gray, Cambridge, to John Torrey, Jan. 4, 1847, Library of the New York Botanical Garden.

49. John Torrey, New York, to Asa Gray, Jan. 11, 1847; Asa Gray, Cambridge, to John Torrey, Jan. 24, 1847, *Letters,* I, 345–347, quoted here from original in the New York Botanical Garden.

50. *Letters,* I, 346–347; M. A. Curtis, Hillsborough, N.C., to Asa Gray, Jan. 6, 1845.

51. Abbott Lawrence to Samuel A. Eliot, Jan. 7, 1847, President, *Annual Report,* 1846–47, 27.

52. Asa Gray [Cambridge], to John Torrey [Feb. 20, 1847], Library of the New York Botanical Garden.

53. Asa Gray [Cambridge], to J[ane] L. L[oring], Monday evening, 9 o'clock, 1847, *Letters,* I, 349.

VIII

"WHERE PLANTS HAVE NO LATIN NAMES"

1. George Gray, Cambridge, to [Mrs.] Lucy [Cobb], Jan. 12 [1847], May 4, 1847, in possession of General Harris Jones, West Point, N.Y.

2. The subject is treated compendiously in Susan D. McKelvey, *Botanical Exploration of the Trans-Mississippi West* (Jamaica Plain, Mass., 1955); of immense value also is Max Meisel, *A Bibliography of American Natural History* (3 vols.; New York, 1924–29).

3. For a discussion of the psychological problems of a collector, see Paul Horgan, introduction to Josiah Gregg, *Diary & Letters* (M. G. Fulton, ed.; Norman, Oklahoma, 1941), I, 20–21, 33–37.

4. Asa Gray, Cambridge, to John Torrey, Dec. 5, 1842, *Letters,* I, 294.

5. G. Engelmann, St. Louis, to Asa Gray, June 4, 1843; G. Engelmann, St. Louis, to Asa Gray, Dec. 6, 1844; Asa Gray, Cambridge, to G. Engelmann, March 22, 1845, typed copy; Asa Gray, Cambridge, to John

Torrey, Oct. 1, 1844, *Letters,* I, 327–328, reflects Gray's attitude before Wyman was rejected.

6. G. Engelmann, St. Louis, to Asa Gray, Aug. 6, 1849.

7. G. Engelmann, St. Louis, to Asa Gray, July 27, 1843.

8. Asa Gray, Cambridge, to G. Engelmann, June 22, 1843, *Letters,* I, 305; A[sa] Gr[ay], "Notice of Botanical Collections," *American Journal of Science,* XLV (1843), 225–226.

9. Asa Gray, Cambridge, to G. Engelmann, February 13, 1843, and July 15, 1846, *Letters,* I, 298, 342.

10. G. Engelmann, St. Louis, to Asa Gray, March 9, 1843.

11. Joseph Ewan, *Rocky Mountain Naturalists* (Denver, 1950), 254; Engelmann to Gray, Dec. 6, 1844.

12. Asa Gray, Cambridge, to W. J. Hooker, Oct. 14, 1845, MS copy; Asa Gray, Cambridge, to W. J. Hooker, Feb. 28, 1846, MS copy.

13. See S. W. Geiser, *Naturalists of the Frontier* (Dallas, Texas, 1937), 159–180.

14. G. Engelmann, St. Louis, to Asa Gray, March 20, 1842, and Jan. 18, 1843; Asa Gray, "Notice," *American Journal of Science,* XLV, 226.

15. G. Engelmann, St. Louis, to Asa Gray, Jan. 11, 1845.

16. Asa Gray, Cambridge, to G. Engelmann, Nov. 20, 1845, and Feb. 27, 1846, typed copy.

17. Asa Gray, Cambridge, to W. J. Hooker, Aug. 16, 1845, MS copy.

18. Asa Gray, Cambridge, to G. Engelmann, Feb. 3, 1845, typed copy.

19. Gray to Engelmann, Feb. 27, 1846, typed copy.

20. Gray to Engelmann, May 30 [1846], *Letters,* I, 341; Engelmann to Gray, June 25, 1846.

21. Augustus Fendler, "An Autobiography and Some Reminiscences," W. M. Canby, ed., *Botanical Gazette,* X (1885), 285–290.

22. Gray to Engelmann, July 15 [1846], *Letters,* I, 342; G. Engelmann, St. Louis, to Asa Gray, Aug. 2, 1846.

23. G. Engelmann, St. Louis, to Asa Gray, Sept. 1, 1846, gives August 11; Asa Gray, "Plantae Fendlerianae Novi-Mexicanae. . . ." American Academy of Arts and Sciences, *Memoirs,* IV (1849), 2, gives August 10. The troops were Colonel Sterling Price's Second Missouri Regiment. Ewan, *Rocky Mountain Naturalists,* 147, is incorrect in saying he went with Lieutenant J. W. Abert.

24. G. Engelmann, St. Louis, to Asa Gray, July 27, 1847; Augustus Fendler, St. Louis, to Asa Gray, July 25, 1848.

25. G. Engelmann, St. Louis, to Asa Gray, Oct. 31, 1847; Asa Gray, Cambridge, to William J. Hooker, Aug. 22, 1848, MS copy.

26. Asa Gray, Cambridge, to William J. Hooker, April 2, 1849. MS copy; Asa Gray, Cambridge, to G. Engelmann, Nov. 30, 1848, and March 24, 1849, typed copy; G. Engelmann, St. Louis, to Asa Gray, March 28, 1849; Aug. 6, 1849; Sept. 26, 1849.

27. G. Engelmann, St. Louis, to Asa Gray, Oct. 26, 1849.

28. Asa Gray, Cambridge, to Parker Cleaveland, April 26, 1848, Washburn Papers, Massachusetts Historical Society.

29. Asa Gray, "Charles Wright," *Scientific Papers,* II, 468; Geiser, *Naturalists of the Frontier,* 215–252.

30. Charles Wright, Rutersville, Texas, to Asa Gray, March 14, 1845, and Aug. 8, 1846.

31. Charles Wright, San Antonio, Texas, to Asa Gray, Sept. 20, 1848.

32. Asa Gray, Cambridge, to W. J. Hooker, Nov. 11, 1857; Wright to Gray, Sept. 20, 1848; Asa Gray, Cambridge, to G. Engelmann, Dec. 4, 1848, typed copy.

33. *Letters,* I, 329–330; *Garden and Forest,* VIII (1895), 130; J. F. McDermott, ed., *Up the Missouri with Audubon: The Journal of Edward Harris* (Norman, Okla., 1951).

34. Asa Gray, Cambridge, to W. J. Hooker, Dec. 1, 1846, MS copy.

35. Joseph Prestele, Ebenezer, N.Y., to Asa Gray, January 1845.

36. Asa Gray, Cambridge, to W. J. Hooker, Feb. 28, 1843, MS copy.

37. Asa Gray, "Chloris Boreali-Americana. Illustrations of New, Rare or Otherwise Interesting North American Plants, Selected Chiefly from Those Recently Brought into Cultivation at the Botanic Garden of Harvard University," American Academy of Arts and Sciences, *Memoirs,* n.s., III (1846), 1–56 plus 10 plates.

38. Asa Gray, *Genera Florae Americae Boreali-Orientalis Illustrata. The Genera of the Plants of the United States Illustrated by Figures and Analyses from Nature, by Isaac Sprague* (2 vols.; Boston, 1848–49).

39. Asa Gray, Account Book, 1838–50, back of book; Asa Gray, Cambridge, to G. Engelmann, Feb. 29, 1848; Asa Gray, Cambridge, to John Torrey, July 20, 1847, *Letters,* I, 347.

40. Gray to Torrey, July 20, 1847, Library of the New York Botanical Garden.

41. E. D. Merrill, "Unlisted New Names in Alphonso Wood's Botanical Publications," *Rhodora,* L (1948), 104.

42. Alphonso Wood, *A Class-Book of Botany, Designed for Colleges, Academies, and Other Seminaries Where Science Is Taught* (1st ed.; Boston, 1845), 3–4.

43. Quoted in Merrill, *Rhodora,* L, 114.

44. Asa Gray, Cambridge, to John Torrey, n.d. [fall 1844], Library of the New York Botanical Garden.

45. [Asa Gray], "Chemistry of Vegetation," *North American Review,* LX, 4.

46. Wood, *Class-Book,* (1st ed.), 4.

47. Edward Hitchcock, president of Amherst College.

48. Asa Gray, Cambridge, to John Torrey, Nov. 13 and 21, 1845, *Letters,* I, 334–336; Asa Gray, *A Manual of the Botany of the Northern United*

States, *from New England to Wisconsin and South to Ohio and Pennsylvania Inclusive (the Mosses and Liverworts by Wm. S. Sullivant), Arranged According to the Natural System* (1st ed.; Boston and Cambridge, 1848).

49. M. L. Fernald, *Gray's Manual of Botany* (8th ed.; New York, 1950), vi, is grossly misleading in making the statement that Gray "specially acknowledged the help of three active botanists of the period. . . . Hundreds of enthusiastic coöperators, about 400 of them . . . have stimulated the present work." In the *Manual* (1st ed.), vi, Gray apologizes that he cannot make "acknowledgments which are justly due to many attentive and zealous correspondents throughout the country; and their daily increasing number renders this appropriate expression more difficult. . . ." Using the acknowledgments in the *Flora* as a base, an estimate of one hundred contributors seems nearer the mark than three.

50. Tuckerman's part appeared in American Academy of Arts and Sciences, *Proceedings*, I (1847), 195–285.

51. John Carey, New York, to Asa Gray, Aug. 25, 1845.

52. John Carey, New York, to Asa Gray, Saturday morning, n.d.

53. Asa Gray, Cambridge, to John Torrey, Sept. 28, 1847, and Asa Gray, Cambridge, to G. Engelmann, Dec. 20, 1847, *Letters*, I, 348–349, 351.

54. Asa Gray, Cambridge, to Charles Wright, Jan. 17, 1848, *Letters*, I, 352–353.

55. *Manual* (1st ed.), iii.

IX

THE PERSONAL REVOLUTION OF 1848

1. The view of Gray's household during these years is found in a scrapbook of letters of George Gray lent to me by General Harris Jones.

2. John Carey, New York, to Asa Gray, May 22, 1848, March 20 [1849?].

3. Eliza Torrey to Mrs. Asa Gray, Dec. 29, 1888, reprinted in *Letters*, I, 323.

4. Asa Gray, Cambridge, to Mrs. Roxana Gray, May 6, 1847.

5. Jane Loring [Gray], Hartford, Conn., to Mrs. Charles G. Loring, June 10, 1841, and Aug. 3, 1843, courtesy of Mrs. Nathaniel Clapp; Jane Loring [Gray], Lebanon [Conn.], to C. W. Loring, Aug. 16, 1844.

6. Isabella Batchelder James, Exeter, England, to Jane Loring Gray, Nov. 16, 1893.

7. See Theophilus Parsons, *Memoir of Charles Greely Loring* (Cambridge, Mass., 1870); Charles H. Pope and Katharine Peabody Loring, *Loring Genealogy* (Cambridge, Mass., 1917).

8. Asa Gray to Mrs. Roxana Gray, May 6, 1847.

9. Asa Gray to Mrs. Roxana Gray, May 6, 1847; Asa Gray to John Torrey, Sept. 28, 1847, *Letters,* I, 348.

10. See Katharine P. Loring, *The Earliest Summer Residents of the North Shore and Their Houses* (Salem, 1932).

11. Charles G. Loring to Asa Gray, March 27, 1846.

12. [W. G. Farlow], *Memorial of Asa Gray* (Cambridge, Mass., 1888), 19.

13. Charles G. Loring to Asa Gray, March 4, 1847, courtesy of Mrs. Nathaniel Clapp.

14. Asa Gray [Cambridge], to Elsada Gray, Dec. 17, 1847, George Gray scrapbook; Jane Loring [Gray], Boston, to Mrs. Roxana Gray, Jan. 9, 1848, George Gray scrapbook.

15. Asa Gray, Cambridge, to Charles Wright, Jan. 17, 1848, *Letters,* I, 353.

16. Asa Gray, Cambridge, to Mrs. Roxana Gray, May 6, 1848; John Mead, Journal, 39, May 4 [1848], Harvard University Archives.

17. Asa Gray to Mrs. Roxana Gray, May 6, 1848.

18. Asa Gray [Cambridge], to Jared Sparks, Feb. 3, 1852, Sparks Papers, Houghton Library.

19. Jane Loring Gray to Charles G. Loring, Tuesday afternoon [n.d.], Harvard University Archives.

20. Jane L. Gray, Cambridge, to Mrs. C. G. Loring, July 10, 1852; Oct. 9, 1860, Harvard University Archives.

21. Jane L. Gray, Cambridge, to Mr. and Mrs. C. G. Loring, July 12, 1853, Harvard University Archives.

22. Jane Loring Gray, Cambridge, to Charles G. Loring, April 11, 1853; March 13, 1853, Harvard University Archives.

23. Jane Loring Gray, Cambridge, to Charles G. Loring, Feb. 20, 1853, and May 1, 1853, Harvard University Archives.

X

AN AMERICAN IN WORLD BOTANY

1. Jane L. Gray, Washington, D.C., to Charles G. Loring, June 8, 1848, Harvard University Archives; Asa Gray [Cambridge], to John Torrey, June 1848, *Letters,* I, 358–359.

2. W. J. Hooker, Kew, to Asa Gray, Feb. 28, 1843, and Aug. 30, 1843, MS copy.

3. Joseph D. Hooker, *The Botany of the Antarctic Voyage of H. M. Discovery Ships 'Erebus' and 'Terror' in the Years 1839–1843, under the Command of Captain Sir James Clark Ross. Part I. Flora Antarctica* (2 vols.; Lon-

don, 1844–47); Asa Gray, "Review of J. D. Hooker, *Botany of the Antarctic Voyage . . . ,*" *American Journal of Science,* XLVIII (1844), 205.

4. A. Hunter Dupree, *Science in the Federal Government* (Cambridge, Mass., 1957), 60–61, 70–76.

5. Asa Gray, "Scientific Results of the Exploring Expedition," *North American Review* (July 1846), 211; Asa Gray, Cambridge, to J. D. Hooker, Dec. 31, 1845, *Letters,* I, 337, and original, Kew.

6. Daniel C. Haskell, *The United States Exploring Expedition, 1838–1842, and Its Publications, 1844–1874. A Bibliography* (New York, 1942), 84–85.

7. John Torrey, Princeton, N.J., to Asa Gray, May 30, 1848; W. S. Sullivant, Columbus, Ohio, to Asa Gray, April 29, 1848; Asa Gray, Cambridge, to John Torrey, June 1848, *Letters,* I, 358–359.

8. Asa Gray, Kew, to James A. Pearce, April 2, 1851, copy in Wilkes Publication folder, Gray Herbarium.

9. Joseph Henry, Washington, to Asa Gray, Oct. 5, 1848.

10. Joseph Henry, Washington, to Asa Gray, May 23, 1848.

11. Asa Gray, Trees of the United States, MS fragment; Asa Gray, *The Forest Trees of North America. Plates Prepared between the Years 1849 and 1859* (Washington, 1891); Joseph Henry and Asa Gray, contract dated April 15, 1850.

12. Asa Gray, Appendix to Smithsonian Institution, *Annual Report for 1850* (Washington, 1851), 23; Joseph Henry, Washington, to Asa Gray, Feb. 19, 1850; John Torrey, New York, to Asa Gray, Jan. 11, 1850.

13. For a brief account of this year, see *Letters,* II, 369–388. A detailed account exists in MSS in the form of 50 letters preserved at the Gray Herbarium from Mrs. Gray to members of her family.

14. Emma Brace, ed., *Life and Letters of Charles Loring Brace* (New York, 1894), 89–121; [F. L. Olmsted], *Walks and Talks of an American Farmer in England* (2 vols.; New York, 1852).

15. William Irvine, *Apes, Angels, and Victorians* (New York, 1955), 28–29; Leonard Huxley, ed., *Life and Letters of Thomas Henry Huxley* (London, 1913), I, 126.

16. Haskell, *Bibliography,* 22; Charles Wilkes, Washington, to James A. Pearce, April 23, 1852; Charles Wilkes to John Torrey, March 16, 1851.

17. Jane L. Gray, Kew, to Charles G. Loring, April 4, 1851, Harvard University Archives; Asa Gray, Kew, to James A. Pearce, July 15, 1851, copy; W. S. Sullivant, Columbus, Ohio, to Asa Gray, July 8, 1852; Joseph Henry, Washington, to Asa Gray, May 23, 1852, and May 27, 1852.

18. Asa Gray, Cambridge, to Charles Wright, Sept. 20, 1854.

19. Asa Gray [Cambridge], to Charles Wright, Aug. 1, 1862, *Letters,* II, 484; Charles Henry Davis, Washington, to Asa Gray, Dec. 10, 1863.

20. *United States Exploring Expedition,* XVII. *Botany.*

21. MS in Gray Herbarium.

XI

THE WAKING HOURS OF AN OVERLOADED BOTANIST

1. James C. White, "An Undergraduate's Diary," *Harvard Graduates' Magazine* (1913), 642.
2. James K. Hosmer, *The Last Leaf* (New York, 1912), 278–281.
3. See S. E. Morison, *Three Centuries of Harvard 1636–1936* (Cambridge, Mass., 1936), chap. XII.
4. Edward Wagenknecht, *Longfellow: A Full-Length Portrait* (New York, 1955), 51–52.
5. Harvard College Records, X, 64, Harvard University Archives.
6. President of Harvard University, *Report for 1859–1860, Treasurer's Statement*, 2.
7. Jane L. Gray, Cambridge, to John Amory Lowell, April 28, 1856, Gray Herbarium.
8. Asa Gray, Cambridge, to James Walker, Dec. 13, 1858; President of Harvard University, *Report for 1857–1858*, 15–16.
9. Frederick Tuckerman, "Henry James Clark," *Dictionary of American Biography,* IV, 131–132.
10. Asa Gray, Cambridge, to Daniel C. Eaton, Feb. 23, 1858, *Letters,* II, 438–439 (corrected by typescript).
11. Asa Gray, Cambridge, to George Engelmann, Jan. 14, 1856, typed copy.
12. John Torrey, New York, to Asa Gray, April 27, 1850; M. A. Curtis, Hillsborough, N.C., to Asa Gray, March 26, 1857.
13. Asa Gray, *How Plants Grow: A Simple Introduction to Structural Botany* (New York, 1858), 3, 7, 41, 49.
14. Asa Gray, Cambridge, to R. W. Church, May 15, 1857, *Letters,* II, 429; Ivison and Phinney, New York, to Asa Gray, Dec. 29, 1857; Asa Gray, Cambridge, to George Bentham, April 26, 1858, *Letters,* II, 438.
15. Asa Gray, *Plantae Wrightianae Texano-Neo-Mexicanae: An Account of a Collection of Plants Made by Charles Wright . . . ,* Parts I and II (Washington, 1852 and 1853).
16. For Parry see Joseph Ewan, *Rocky Mountain Naturalists* (Denver, Colo., 1950), 34–44; H. H. Rusby, "A Biographical Sketch of Dr. George Thurber," Torrey Botanical Club, *Bulletin,* XVII (1890), 204–210; A. E. Waller, "Dr. John Milton Bigelow, 1804–1878, An Early Ohio Physician-Botanist," *Ohio Archaeological and Historical Quarterly,* LI (1942), 313–331.
17. C. C. Parry, John Torrey, and George Engelmann, *The Botany of the Boundary,* Part I of Volume II of William H. Emory, *Report on the United States and Mexican Boundary Survey. . . .* (Washington, 1859).

18. John M. Bigelow, Lancaster, Ohio, to Asa Gray, April 19, 1853, Sept. 2, 1856; Asa Gray, Cambridge, to G. Engelmann, July 14, 1853, typed copy.

19. Asa Gray, Cambridge, to G. Engelmann, Sept. 27, 1854; Nov. 21, 1854, typed copy.

20. See A. Hunter Dupree, *Science in the Federal Government* (Cambridge, Mass., 1957), 91–114.

21. Gray to Engelmann, Nov. 21, 1854.

22. John Torrey, "Report on the Botany of the Expedition," Secretary of War, *Reports of Explorations and Surveys, to Ascertain the Most Practicable and Economical Route for a Railroad*, IV (Washington, 1856), 59.

23. Asa Gray, Cambridge, to Sir William J. Hooker, June 21, 1854.

24. A. Hunter Dupree, "Science vs. the Military: Dr. James Morrow and the Perry Expedition," *Pacific Historical Review*, XXII (1953), 29–37.

25. Asa Gray, "List of Dried Plants Collected in Japan by S. Wells Williams, Esq., and Dr. James Morrow," Matthew C. Perry, ed., *Narrative of the Expedition of an American Squadron to the China Seas and Japan, Performed in the Years 1852, 1853, and 1854. . . .* (Washington, 1856), II, 301–322.

26. Allan B. Cole, *Yankee Surveyors in the Shogun's Seas: Records of the U.S. Surveying Expedition in the North Pacific Ocean, 1853–1856* (Princeton, N.J., 1947); Asa Gray, Cambridge, to Charles Wright, Oct. 28, 1852.

27. The Gray Herbarium has seventeen letters, Charles Wright to Asa Gray, written during the expedition, and Wright's day-by-day journal. It also has a manuscript report of the botany, largely in Wright's hand, describing plants from Madeira, Cape of Good Hope, Sydney, Hong Kong, Arctic Asia, Loo Choo (Ryukyu), Bonins, Japan, California, and Nicaragua.

28. John Rodgers, Washington, to Asa Gray, March 21, 1860.

29. Asa Gray, "Diagnostic Characters of New Species of Phaenogamous Plants, Collected in Japan by Charles Wright, Botanist of the North Pacific Exploring Expedition . . . ," American Academy of Arts and Sciences, *Memoirs*, n.s., VI (1859), 377–452.

30. For example, Asa Gray, Cambridge, to Sir William J. Hooker, March 24, 1856; A. Fendler, Colonia Tovar, Venezuela, to Asa Gray, July 1, 1857.

31. Asa Gray, "A Cursory Examination of a Collection of Dried Plants Made by L. C. Ervendberg around Wartenberg, near Tantoyuca, in the Ancient Province of Huasteca, Mexico, in 1858 and 1859," American Academy of Arts and Sciences, *Proceedings*, V (1861), 174–190; S. W. Geiser, *Naturalists of the Frontier* (Dallas, 1937), 95–131, presents almost all that is known of Ervendberg, but in accusing Gray of unfair dealing he overlooks three things. (1) Ervendberg chose Mexico as a field at a time when Gray was not working on plants from that area. (2) The arrangement between them was a business proposition—selling specimens—and not philanthropy. (3) Ervendberg himself admitted the fairness of the arrangement and the

generosity of Gray's treatment in a letter to Asa Gray from Colonia de Wartenberg, Mexico, Oct. 24, 1860. This letter, in the autograph collection at the Gray Herbarium, Geiser does not cite.

32. Asa Gray, Cambridge, to Charles Wright, Monday, 27th (no month or year); Jan. 10, 1857; April 24, 1863.

33. Geiser, *Naturalists of the Frontier*, 30–54, is a militant defender of Berlandier. The story of the purchase and distribution of the collection had a prominent place in Gray's correspondence. See especially Asa Gray, Cambridge, to Sir William J. Hooker, July 31, 1854, typed copy; Asa Gray, Cambridge, to G. Engelmann, Dec. 10, 1855, typed copy; C. W. Short, Louisville, Kentucky, to Asa Gray, April 7, 1855; May 9, 1855.

34. Joseph D. Hooker, Kew, to Asa Gray, March 26, 1861.

35. See especially Asa Gray, "Von Mohl's Vegetable Cell," and "Boussingault on the Influence of Nitrates on the Production of Vegetable Matter," *Scientific Papers*, I, 51–58, 100–104 (first published in 1853 and 1858).

36. George Bentham, London, to Asa Gray, Oct. 15, 1862.

37. Asa Gray, Cambridge, to Charles Wilkes, July 17, 1852.

XII

GRAY'S MIND AND THE THREAT OF AGASSIZ

1. MS note in Lowell Institute Lectures, Folder 6; Asa Gray, "Note on Transactions of the Linnaean Society," *American Journal of Science*, 2nd ser., V (1848), 451–452; Asa Gray, "On Some Plants of Order Compositae from the Sandwich Islands," American Association for the Advancement of Science, *Proceedings*, II (1849), 397–398.

2. Asa Gray to Charles Darwin, received Aug. 20, 1856, Francis Darwin, ed., *More Letters of Charles Darwin*. . . . (New York, 1903), I, 429.

3. Asa Gray to R. F. Johnston, July 18, 1855, reprinted in the *Boston Cultivator* (from a clipping in the Gray Herbarium).

4. Asa Gray, "Hooker and Thomson's Indian Flora," *Scientific Papers*, I, 64–65 (first published 1856).

5. Cambridge Scientific Club, MS Records, Dec. 13, 1855, May 13, 1858, Harvard University Archives.

6. Asa Gray, "Notice of Dr. Hooker's Flora of New Zealand," *American Journal of Science*, XVII (1854), 336

7. Asa Gray, Cambridge, to R. W. Church, Feb. 7, 1853, *Letters*, II, 396.

8. Asa Gray, Cambridge, to J. D. Hooker, Sept. 28, 1858, Kew.

9. J. D. Hooker, Kew, to Asa Gray, Dec. 24, 1857.

10. B. Torrey and F. H. Allen, eds., *The Journal of Henry D. Thoreau* (Boston, 1949), II, 204; IX, 67, 252; XII, 208.

11. A. D. Rodgers III, *"Noble Fellow" William Starling Sullivant* (New York, 1940), 191–211.

12. For the main facts in Agassiz's life, the source is still Elizabeth C. Agassiz, *Louis Agassiz: His Life and Correspondence* (2 vols., Boston, 1885).

13. Asa Gray, Cambridge, to G. Engelmann, Aug. 28, 1849, typed copy.

14. E. W. Emerson, *Early Years of the Saturday Club 1855–1870* (Boston, 1918), 11–19, 31; Bliss Perry, ed., *The Heart of Emerson's Journal* (Boston, 1926), 331.

15. Richard J. Storr, *The Beginnings of Graduate Education in America* (Chicago, 1953), 82–93; see A. Hunter Dupree, *Science in the Federal Government* (Cambridge, Mass., 1957), 118–119, 135–136. I am indebted to Edward Lurie for information on this subject.

16. Josiah Royce, "Some Relations between Philosophy and Science in the First Half of the Nineteenth Century in Germany," *Science,* n.s., XXXVIII (1913), 567–584.

17. Louis Agassiz, *Contributions to the Natural History of the United States* (Boston, 1857), I, 9.

18. Louis Agassiz, "The Primitive Diversity and Number of Animals in Geological Times," *American Journal of Science,* XVII (1854), 324.

19. Asa Gray, Cambridge, to J. D. Hooker, Feb. 21, 1854, Kew; Asa Gray, aboard the *SS Canada,* to J. D. Hooker, Oct. 6, 1855, Kew.

20. Edward Lurie, "Louis Agassiz and the Races of Man," *Isis,* XLV (1954), 238–239.

21. [M. A. Curtis], "Unity of the Races," *Southern Quarterly Review,* VII (1845), 372–448; M. A. Curtis, Hillsborough, N.C., to Asa Gray, Jan. 6, 1845; Society Hill, S.C., March 15, 1850.

22. Asa Gray, Cambridge, to J. D. Hooker, July 13, 1858, Kew.

23. Agassiz, *Contributions,* I, viii.

24. [J. D. Dana], "Agassiz's Contributions to the Natural History of the United States," *American Journal of Science,* XXV (1858), 328–329.

25. J. D. Dana, New Haven, to Asa Gray, Nov. 13, 18⁙; Asa Gray, Cambridge, to J. D. Dana, Nov. 7, 1857, *Letters,* II, 431.

XIII

DARWIN AND JAPAN—THE SUMMIT OF GRAY'S CAREER

1. Asa Gray, Cambridge, to J. D. Hooker, Feb. 21, 1854, Kew; Asa Gray, "Notice of Dr. Hooker's Flora of New Zealand," *American Journal of Science,* 2nd ser., XVII (1854), 243.

2. J. D. Hooker, Kew, to Asa Gray, Jan. 26, 1854, Leonard Huxley, *Life and Letters of Sir Joseph Dalton Hooker* (London, 1918), I, 475.

3. Asa Gray, Cambridge, to J. D. Hooker, Feb. 21, 1854, Kew; Gray, "Hooker's New Zealand Flora," *American Journal of Science,* XVII, 244.

4. Asa Gray, Cambridge, to J. D. Hooker, Feb. 21, 1854, Kew; J. D. Hooker, Kew, to Asa Gray, March 24, 1854, Huxley, *Hooker,* I, 477; J. D. Hooker, *Flora Novae-Zelandiae* (London, 1853), I, xii.

5. A. De Candolle, *Géographie botanique raisonnée* (Paris, 1855), I, xiv–xv.

6. Asa Gray, "De Candolle's Geographie Botanique," *Scientific Papers,* I, 67 (first published 1855).

7. J. D. Hooker, Kew, to Asa Gray, Dec. 10, 1856; Ronald Good, "Plant Geography," California Academy of Sciences, *A Century of Progress in the Natural Sciences 1853–1953* (San Francisco, 1955), 748–749.

8. Hooker, *Flora Novae-Zelandiae,* I, xxii.

9. Charles Darwin, Down, to J. D. Hooker, March 24 [1854], Francis Darwin, ed., *Life and Letters of Charles Darwin* (New York, 1887), I, 403–404.

10. Charles Darwin, Down, to Asa Gray, April 25, 1855, only partly reprinted in F. Darwin, *Life and Letters,* I, 420.

11. Asa Gray, Cambridge, to Charles Darwin, May 22, 1855, Cambridge University Library.

12. Asa Gray, Cambridge, to Charles Darwin, June 30, 1855, Francis Darwin, ed., *More Letters of Charles Darwin* (New York, 1903), I, 422.

13. Asa Gray, "Darwin, Does Sea-Water Kill Seeds?" *American Journal of Science,* XX (1855), 282.

14. Asa Gray, "Statistics of the Flora of the Northern States," *American Journal of Science,* XXII (1856), 204.

15. See Philip Wiener, *Evolution and the Founders of Pragmatism* (Cambridge, Mass., 1949), 3–5, for an appreciation of the role of statistics in the period 1846–59.

16. J. D. Hooker, Kew, to Asa Gray, Dec. 24, 1857; Joseph Henry, Washington, to Asa Gray, Oct. 22, 1859.

17. Gray's copy of the *Manual* [1856] carries a series of numbers in the margin in red pencil for the family *Cyperaceae.*

18. Gray, "Statistics," *American Journal of Science,* XXIII, 388–389.

19. Charles Darwin, Down, to Asa Gray, Oct. 12 [1856]; November 24 [1856]; January 1 [1857].

20. Darwin to Gray, January 1 [1857].

21. Asa Gray [Cambridge], to J. D. Dana, Dec. 13, 1856, *Letters,* II, 424–425.

22. Taken from the original; partly printed in F. Darwin, *Life and Letters,* I, 437–438.

23. Charles Darwin, Down, to Asa Gray, Sept. 5 [1857]; printed in

F. Darwin, *Life and Letters,* I, 477–482; the copy sent to Gray is in another hand than Darwin's but corrected by him. It varies in detail from the version published at the Linnaean Society.

24. Charles Darwin, Down, to Asa Gray, Nov. 29 [1857], F. Darwin, *More Letters,* I, 126, but here quoted from the original.

25. Asa Gray, Cambridge, to J. D. Dana, Nov. 7, 1857.

26. Asa Gray, Cambridge, to J. D. Hooker, July 13, 1858, Kew.

27. Asa Gray, Cambridge, to Sir W. J. Hooker, July 27, 1857, typed copy.

28. Asa Gray, "Review of *Flora Japonica,*" *American Journal of Science,* XXXIX (1840), 175–176; Asa Gray, "Analogy between the Flora of Japan and That of the United States," *American Journal of Science,* II (1846), 135–136.

29. Darwin to Gray, Oct. 12, 1856, F. Darwin, *More Letters,* I, 434.

30. Asa Gray, "Diagnostic Characters of New Species of Phaenogamous Plants, Collected in Japan by Charles Wright, Botanist of the U.S. North Pacific Exploring Expedition," American Academy of Arts and Sciences, *Memoirs,* n.s., VI (1859), 437, 442.

31. Charles Darwin, Down, to Asa Gray, Aug. 11 [1858], F. Darwin, *Life and Letters,* I, 491; J. D. Dana, New Haven, Conn., to Asa Gray, Jan. 11, 1858.

32. Hui-Lin Li, "Floristic Relationships between Eastern Asia and Eastern North America," American Philosophical Society, *Transactions,* n.s., XLII (1952), 371–429.

33. Asa Gray, "Forest Geography and Archaeology," *Scientific Papers,* II, 227.

34. Charles Darwin and Alfred Russel Wallace, "On the Tendency of Species to Form Varieties; and on the Perpetuation of Varieties and Species by Means of Natural Selection," Linnaean Society, *Journal* (Zoology), III (1858), 45.

35. Cambridge Scientific Club, MS Records, Dec. 10, 1858, Harvard University Archives; Asa Gray, Cambridge, to John Torrey, Jan. 7, 1859, *Letters,* II, 450.

36. Gray, American Academy of Arts and Sciences, *Memoirs,* VI, 445.

37. American Academy of Arts and Sciences, *Proceedings,* IV (1860), 132–133.

38. Asa Gray, Cambridge, to Daniel Cady Eaton, Jan. 12, 1859, Yale University Library.

39. American Academy, MS Minutes, Jan. 11, 1859, III, 57; American Academy, *Proceedings,* IV, 134.

40. American Academy, MS Minutes, Jan. 26, 1859, III, 59.

41. Leo Lesquereux, Columbus, Ohio, to Asa Gray, Jan. 24, 1859; American Academy, *Proceedings,* IV, 178.

42. Asa Gray, Cambridge, to J. D. Hooker, May 30, 1859, Kew.

43. Louis Agassiz, "On Marcou's 'Geology of North America,'" *Amer-*

ican Journal of Science, XXVII (1859), 134; J. D. Dana, New Haven, to Asa Gray, June 14, 1859; J. D. Dana, "Reply to Prof. Agassiz on Marcou's Geology of North America," *American Journal of Science,* XXVII (1859), 137–140.

44. American Academy, *Proceedings,* IV, 199–201.

45. The reprints of Gray's Botanical Memoirs from the American Academy, *Memoirs,* have a printed title page bearing the inscription, "Boston and Cambridge: Published April 25, 1859."

46. Cambridge Scientific Club, Records, May 12, 1859, Harvard University Archives; Benjamin Peirce to Mrs. Benjamin Peirce, May 13, 1859, Harvard University Archives.

47. See Sven R. Peterson, "Benjamin Peirce: Mathematician and Philosopher," *Journal of the History of Ideas,* XVI (1955), 89–112.

48. Asa Gray to J. D. Hooker, May 16, 1859.

49. Asa Gray, "Differences in Science in 21 Years," MS dated Oct. 24, 1878.

50. Elias Durand, Philadelphia, to Asa Gray, April 16, 1859.

51. For a persuasive exposition of this point of view, see A. O. Lovejoy, "The Argument for Organic Evolution before the 'Origin of Species,'" *Popular Science Monthly,* LXXV (1909), 499–514, 537–549.

XIV

THE IMMEDIATE IMPACT OF THE *ORIGIN OF SPECIES*

1. J. D. Hooker, Kew, to Asa Gray, June 26, 1856; enclosure in J. D. Hooker, Kew, to Asa Gray, Feb. 14, 1858; Asa Gray, Cambridge, to J. D. Hooker, July 6, 1857, Kew.

2. J. D. Hooker, Kew, to Asa Gray, May 31, 1859.

3. Asa Gray, Cambridge, to J. D. Hooker, June 21, 1859, July 19, 1859; Oct. 18, 1859, Kew.

4. J. D. Hooker, Kew, to Asa Gray, Nov. 27, 1859.

5. Charles Darwin, Down, to Asa Gray, Jan. 28 [1860], F. Darwin, ed., *Life and Letters of Charles Darwin* (New York, 1887), II, 63–64, hereafter referred to as F. Darwin, *Life and Letters.*

6. Charles Darwin, Down, to Asa Gray, Nov. 11 [1860], F. Darwin, *Life and Letters,* II, 13, last sentence in MS only.

7. J. D. Hooker, Kew, to Asa Gray, Nov. 27, 1859; Francis Boott, London, to Asa Gray, Dec. 9, 1859.

8. C. E. Norton, Shady Hill, to Elizabeth C. Gaskell (Dec. 27, 1859), Jane Whitehill, ed., *Letters of Mrs. Gaskell and Charles Eliot Norton 1855–*

1865 (London, 1932), 42–43; Asa Gray, Cambridge, to Francis Boott, Jan. 16, 1860, Lyell Autograph Collection, American Philosophical Society.

9. Charles Darwin, *On the Origin of Species by Means of Natural Selection, or the Preservation of Favoured Races in the Struggle for Life* (London, 1859), 13, Asa Gray copy in the Gray Herbarium, with notes on margins and back end paper.

10. Asa Gray, Cambridge, to J. D. Hooker, Jan. 5, 1860, *Letters*, II, 455; Gray to Boott, Jan. 16, 1860.

11. A. E. Verrill, Diary, entry for Jan. 14, 1860, Harvard University Archives; Gray to Boott, Jan. 16, 1860.

12. J. D. Hooker, "On the Origination and Distribution of Species:— Introductory Essay to the Flora of Tasmania," *American Journal of Science*, XXIX (1860), 1–25, 305–326.

13. Charles Darwin, Down, to Asa Gray, Dec. 21 [1859], F. Darwin, *Life and Letters*, II, 40.

14. Asa Gray, Cambridge, to Charles Darwin, Jan. 23, 1860; *Letters*, II, 456; D. Appleton and Company, New York, to Asa Gray, January 19 [1860]; see John Fiske, *Edward Livingston Youmans: Interpreter of Science for the People* (New York, 1894), 111.

15. D. Appleton and Company, New York, to Asa Gray, Feb. 17, 1860; enclosure in Charles Darwin, Down, to Asa Gray, May 22 [1860]; Charles Darwin, Down, to Asa Gray, Feb. 1 [1860].

16. [Asa Gray], "Review of Darwin's Theory on the Origin of Species by Means of Natural Selection," *American Journal of Science,* 2nd ser., XXIX (1860), 153–184, reprinted in Asa Gray, *Darwiniana: Essays and Reviews Pertaining to Darwinism* (New York, 1876), 9–61.

17. Joseph Le Conte, in Daniel C. Gilman, *The Life of James Dwight Dana* (New York, 1899), 255.

18. J. D. Hooker, Kew, to Asa Gray, March 16, 1860; Charles Darwin, Down, to Asa Gray, Feb. 24 and April 3 [1860].

19. Charles Darwin, Down, to Asa Gray, Feb. 24 [1860]; Charles Darwin, Down, to Asa Gray, April 3 [1860], F. Darwin, *Life and Letters*, II, 91.

20. W. H. Harvey, Dublin, to Asa Gray, Feb. 9 and May 20, 1860; Francis Boott, London, to Asa Gray, April 20, 1860.

21. For Huxley's reviews, see his *Darwiniana: Essays* (London, 1893), 1–79.

22. T. H. Huxley, "On the Physical Basis of Life," *Lay Sermons, Addresses, and Reviews* (New York, 1871), 144, 146.

23. M. A. Curtis, Hillsborough, N.C., to Asa Gray, March 13, 1860; Arnold Guyot, Princeton, N.J., to Asa Gray, April 20, 1860; Leo Lesquereux, Columbus, Ohio, to Asa Gray, March 25, 1860, April 7, 1861.

24. Joseph Henry, Washington, D.C., to Asa Gray, Jan. 9, 1860.

25. Asa Gray to Charles Darwin, Jan. 23, 1860, *Letters*, II, 457; Asa Gray, Cambridge, to J. D. Hooker, March 26, 1860.

26. Charles Darwin, Down, to Asa Gray, May 18 [1860].

27. Asa Gray, Cambridge, to Amos A. Lawrence, March 3, 1860, Lawrence Papers, Massachusetts Historical Society.

28. Asa Gray, Cambridge, to R. W. Church, May 7, 1861, *Letters,* II, 464.

29. T. H. Huxley, "Scientific Aspects of Positivism," *Lay Sermons,* 147–173.

30. J. D. Hooker to Asa Gray, March 16, 1860.

XV

THE CREST OF THE DARWINIAN DEBATE

1. Louis Agassiz, "On the Origin of Species," *American Journal of Science,* 2nd ser., XXX (1860), 142–154.

2. Meetings of Feb. 15, March 7, March 21, and April 4, 1860, Boston Society of Natural History, *Proceedings,* VII (1860), 231–235, 241–245, 246–252, 271–275.

3. Cambridge Scientific Club, Records, Feb. 23, 1860, Harvard University Archives; Asa Gray, Discourse from the Axiom, *Natura non agit saltatem,* MS dated March 8, 1860, Gray Herbarium.

4. American Academy of Arts and Sciences, *Proceedings,* IV (1857–60), 410.

5. American Academy, MS Minutes, March 27, 1860, III, 101.

6. Francis Bowen, "Darwin's Theory of Evolution," *North American Review,* XC (1860), 477.

7. American Academy, *Proceedings,* IV, 428–430; John Amory Lowell, "Darwin's Origin of Species," *Christian Examiner,* LXVIII (1860), 464; American Academy, MS Minutes, III, 104–105.

8. Asa Gray, Cambridge, to J. D. Hooker, March 31, 1860, Kew.

9. American Academy, *Proceedings,* IV, 411; J. D. Hooker, Kew, to Asa Gray, July 5, 1860.

10. American Academy, *Proceedings,* IV, 413, 426.

11. *American Journal of Science,* XXX (1860), 226–239. When it was reprinted in Asa Gray, *Darwiniana* (New York, 1876), 62–86, Gray substituted the initials "D. T." and "A. G." for the disputants. The identification is confirmed by Morrill Wyman, "Memoir of Daniel Treadwell," American Academy of Arts and Sciences, *Memoirs,* XI (1888), 473.

12. Asa Gray, Cambridge, to J. D. Hooker, Aug. 21, 1860, Kew.

13. See especially Philip Wiener, *Evolution and the Founders of Pragmatism* (Cambridge, Mass., 1949), 31–69, 213–220; also J. B. Thayer, ed., *Letters of Chauncey Wright* (Cambridge, Mass., 1878); Chauncey Wright, *Philosophical Discussions* (C. E. Norton, ed.; New York, 1877).

14. Chauncey Wright, Cambridge, to Mrs. Susan Lesley, Feb. 12, 1860, Thayer, ed., *Letters*, 43.

15. Wiener, *Founders of Pragmatism*, 253, suggests that Wright's doctrine owes much to Gray and Jeffries Wyman, a valid conclusion despite several mistakes in regard to Gray.

16. Asa Gray, Cambridge, to Charles Darwin, June [1863], typed copy; see Benjamin Peirce, "Mathematical Investigations of the Fractions Which Occur in Phyllotaxis," and Asa Gray, "On the Composition of the Plant by Phytons, and Some Applications of Phyllotaxis," American Association for the Advancement of Science, *Proceedings*, II (1849), 444–447, 438–444.

17. Asa Gray, *Botanical Textbook* (3rd ed.; New York, 1850), 141–149; see Chauncey Wright, "The Uses and Origin of the Arrangement of Leaves in Plants," *Philosophical Discussions*, 296–328; Asa Gray, *Structural Botany* (*Botanical Textbook*, I, 6th ed.; New York, 1879), 119–131.

18. Asa Gray, Cambridge, to J. D. Hooker, Dec. 10, 1860, Kew; Charles Darwin, Down, to Asa Gray, March 12 [1861]; Charles Darwin, Down, to Asa Gray, April 11 [1861]; see also Charles Darwin, Down, to Asa Gray, Dec. 14 [1860], with enclosure, Huxley to Darwin.

19. Asa Gray, Cambridge, to C. E. Norton, Aug. 9, 1876, Houghton Library.

20. W. B. Rogers, Boston, to Asa Gray, Jan. 28, 1860; C. E. Norton, Shady Hill, to Gray, Feb. 21, 1860; American Academy, *Proceedings*, IV, 415.

21. Asa Gray, Cambridge, to Charles Darwin, Jan. 23, 1860, Cambridge University Library; A. Hunter Dupree, "Some Letters from Charles Darwin to Jeffries Wyman," *Isis*, XLII (1951), 104–110; A. Hunter Dupree, "Jeffries Wyman's Views on Evolution," *Isis*, XLIV (1953), 243–246; Jeffries Wyman, "Notes on the Cells of the Bee," American Academy of Arts and Sciences, *Proceedings*, VII (1865–1868), 68–83.

22. Charles Darwin, Down, to Asa Gray, May 18 [1860]; Charles Darwin, Down, to Jeffries Wyman, Oct. 3, 1860, Dupree, *Isis*, XLII, 107.

23. *Athenaeum*, 1860, part 2, 161.

24. Charles Darwin, Down, to Asa Gray, July 3 [1860]; J. D. Hooker, Kew, to Asa Gray, July 5, 1860; Asa Gray, Cambridge, to J. D. Hooker, Sept. 17, 1860, Kew.

25. For the Oxford debate, see F. Darwin, *Life and Letters*, II, 322; Leonard Huxley, *Life and Letters of Thomas Henry Huxley* (London, 1913), I, 259–274; Donald H. Fleming, *John William Draper and the Religion of Science* (Philadelphia, 1950), 68–73; William Irvine, *Apes, Angels, and Victorians* (New York, 1955), 3–8.

26. Asa Gray, "Darwin on the Origin of Species," *Atlantic Monthly*, VI (1860), 109–116, 229–239; "Darwin and His Reviewers," 406–425, reprinted separately and in *Darwiniana*, 87–177.

27. Asa Gray, Cambridge, to J. D. Hooker, July 6, 1863, Kew; Asa Gray, Cambridge, to J. D. Hooker, Aug. 21, 1860, Kew.

28. J. D. Hooker Kew, to Asa Gray, July 23, 1860; W. H. Harvey, Dublin, to Asa Gray, Nov. 3, 1860; Gray to J. D. Hooker, Aug. 21, 1860.

29. Charles Darwin, Down, to Asa Gray, Sept. 26 [1860]; the second part of the *Atlantic* series appeared under Gray's name, as contributed by Charles Darwin and specifically as an answer to Agassiz in the *Annals and Magazine of Natural History*, 3rd ser., VI (1860), 373–386.

30. Charles Darwin, Down, to Asa Gray, Oct. 19 [1860].

31. Charles Darwin, Eastbourne, to Asa Gray, Oct. 24 [1860]; Charles Darwin, Down, to Asa Gray, Dec. 11 [1860].

32. Asa Gray, Cambridge, to Charles Darwin, May 18, 1862; James C. Austin, *Fields of the Atlantic Monthly* (San Marino, Calif., 1953), 164–165.

33. W. H. Harvey, Dublin, to Asa Gray, Nov. 3, 1860; J. H. Balfour, Edinburgh, to Asa Gray, Dec. 12, 1860, April 11, 1861; see, for example, J. Steetz, Hamburg, to Asa Gray, Oct. 19, 1861.

34. Mrs. Charles Kingsley, ed., *Charles Kingsley: Letters and Memories of His Life* (London, 1877), II, 171; R. W. Church, Whately, to Asa Gray, March 28, 1861, Mary Church, ed., *Life and Letters of Dean Church* (London, 1894), 188.

35. Darwin to Gray, May 22 [1860], F. Darwin, *Life and Letters*, II, 105.

36. Darwin to Gray, Nov. 26 [1860].

37. Charles Lyell, *The Geological Evidences of the Antiquity of Man with Remarks on Theories of the Origin of Species by Variation* (London, 1863), 502–506.

38. J. D. Hooker, Kew, to Asa Gray, Dec. 25, 1860.

39. Herbert Spencer, London, to E. L. Youmans, March 26, 1860, John Fiske, *Edward Livingston Youmans: Interpreter of Science for the People* (New York, 1894), 109.

40. Asa Gray, Cambridge, to J. D. Hooker, Dec. 10, 1860, Kew; Asa Gray, Cambridge, to G. F. Wright, Sept. 14, 1875, *Letters*, II, 657.

41. Darwin's voluminous work on these subjects are most conveniently gathered in *The Different Forms of Flowers on Plants of the Same Species* (London, 1877), *The Effects of Cross and Self Fertilization in the Vegetable Kingdom* (London, 1876), and *On the Various Contrivances by Which Orchids Are Fertilised by Insects* (London, 1862).

42. See Charles Darwin, *Insectivorous Plants* (London, 1875).

43. Asa Gray, "Note on the Coiling of Tendrils of Plants," American Academy of Arts and Sciences, *Proceedings*, IV (1858), 98–99; Charles Darwin, "On the Movements and Habits of Climbing Plants," Linnaean Society, *Journal* (Bot.), IX (1865), 1–118.

44. Asa Gray, Cambridge, to Alphonse De Candolle, Feb. 16, 1863, *Letters*, II, 497; Asa Gray, "Fertilization of Orchids through the Agency of Insects," *American Journal of Science*, XXXIV (1862), 428.

45. Asa Gray, Cambridge, to C. E. Norton, June 9, 1860, Houghton Library; J. D. Hooker, Kew, to Asa Gray, Aug. 9, 1860; George Bentham to Asa Gray, undated but probably April 1, 1861.

46. C. E. Raven, *Science, Religion, and the Future* (Cambridge, England, 1943), 33.

XVI

YEARS OF WAR

1. Asa Gray, Cambridge, to G. Engelmann, Oct. 11, 1860; Oct. 30, 1860; Jan. 7, 1861, typed copies.

2. Asa Gray, Cambridge, to J. D. Hooker, Feb. 18, 1861, Kew; Asa Gray, Cambridge, to G. Engelmann, Jan. 25, 1861, *Letters,* II, 466.

3. Asa Gray, Cambridge, to Daniel Cady Eaton, Oct. 4, 1861, *Letters,* II, 470; Asa Gray, Cambridge, to G. Engelmann, Feb. 20, 1862, *Letters,* II, 471; Asa Gray, Cambridge, to Charles Darwin, July 7, 1863, *Letters,* II, 508.

4. Asa Gray, Cambridge, to Charles Darwin, Sept. 1, 1863, *Letters,* II, 511–512.

5. Asa Gray, Cambridge, to J. D. Hooker, June 10, 1861, Kew; Asa Gray, Cambridge, to Charles Wright, April 17, 1862, *Letters,* II, 483; Asa Gray, Cambridge, to Charles Darwin, Sept. 1, 1863 and Feb. 16, 1864, *Letters,* II, 513, 523.

6. A. W. Chapman, *Flora of the Southern United States,* and M. A. Curtis, *Geological and Natural History Survey of North Carolina, American Journal of Science,* 2nd ser., XXX (1860), 137–138, 275–276.

7. A. W. Chapman, Apalachicola, Fla., to [Asa Gray], Dec. 24, 1860; T. M. Peters, Moulton, Ala., to Asa Gray, Dec. 23, 1860.

8. M. A. Curtis, Hillsborough, N.C., to Asa Gray, Dec. 5, 1860; H. W. Ravenel, Black Oak, S.C., to Asa Gray, Dec. 11, 1860; A. R. Childs, ed., *The Private Journal of Henry William Ravenel, 1859–1887* (Columbia, S.C., 1947), 43; H. W. Ravenel, Aiken, S.C., to Asa Gray, March 21, 1861.

9. Asa Gray, Cambridge, to G. Engelmann, June 9, 1862, typed copy; G. Engelmann, St. Louis, Mo., to Asa Gray, Dec. 9, 1861.

10. Benjamin Silliman, Jr., New Haven, to Asa Gray, July 31, 1861, Beverly, Mass., Public Library; Asa Gray, Cambridge, to Alphonse De Candolle, April 26, 1861, *Letters,* II, 481.

11. Charles G. Loring correspondence in Houghton Library; C. G. Loring, *England's Liability for Indemnity: Remarks on the Letter of 'Historicus'*. . . . (Boston, 1864), which originally appeared in the *Boston Daily Advertiser,* in March 1864.

12. Asa Gray, Cambridge, to Charles Darwin, Feb. 18, 1862 and Sept. 1, 1863, *Letters,* II, 477, 513.

13. Francis Boott, London, to Asa Gray, June 27, 1861, Jan. 21, 1862, and May 27, 1862; W. H. Harvey, Dublin, to Asa Gray, Dec. 19, 1861; Asa Gray, Cambridge, to R. W. Church, Dec. 25, 1863; April 4, 1864, *Letters,* II, 518, 526.

14. J. D. Hooker, Kew, to Asa Gray, July 5, 1861; Asa Gray, Cambridge, to J. D. Hooker, Dec. 27, 1863, Kew.

15. Charles Darwin, Down, to Asa Gray, Dec. 11 [1861], F. Darwin, ed., *Life and Letters of Charles Darwin* (New York, 1887), II, 174; Asa Gray, Cambridge, to Charles Darwin, Feb. 18, 1862, *Letters,* II, 477.

16. Asa Gray, Cambridge, to Charles Darwin, Jan. 22 [1862], March 31, 1862, and April 11 [1865], *Letters,* II, 480, 503, some redated from internal evidence.

17. A. Hunter Dupree, *Science in the Federal Government* (Cambridge, Mass., 1957), 141–148.

18. Dorothy G. Wayman, *Edward Sylvester Morse: A Biography* (Cambridge, Mass., 1942). See Agassiz's correspondence with Samuel Gridley Howe, E. C. Agassiz, ed., *Louis Agassiz: His Life and Correspondence* (Boston, 1885), II, 591–618, originals in Houghton Library.

19. Louis Agassiz, *Methods of Study in Natural History* (Boston, 1863).

20. S. E. Morison, *Three Centuries of Harvard, 1636–1936* (Cambridge, Mass., 1936), 304–305; William G. Land, *Thomas Hill: Twentieth President of Harvard* (Cambridge, Mass., 1933), 213–223.

21. Henry James, *Charles William Eliot: President of Harvard University 1869–1909* (Boston, 1930), I, 95; Lawrence Scientific School, Faculty Records, Sept. 30, 1862; Oct. 7, 1862; Nov. 4, 1862; Nov. 18, 1862; Dec. 2, 1862; Jan. 6, 1863, Harvard University Archives.

22. Asa Gray to G. Engelmann, March 18, 1865, typed copy.

23. Emma Savage Rogers, ed., *Life and Letters of William Barton Rogers* (Boston, 1896), II, 140–145.

24. Benjamin Peirce [Cambridge], to A. D. Bache, Feb. 5, 1863, Peirce Papers, Harvard University Archives; James, *Eliot,* I, 98–112.

25. John Torrey, New York, to Asa Gray, March 9, 1863; Benjamin Peirce, Cambridge, to A. D. Bache, March 27, 1863, Peirce Papers, Harvard University Archives.

26. Asa Gray, Cambridge, to Joseph Henry, April 18, 1863; Rogers, *Life and Letters,* 161–162; American Academy of Arts and Sciences, *Proceedings,* IV (1863), 141; Asa Gray, Cambridge, to J. D. Hooker, July 6, 1863, Kew.

27. Benjamin Peirce to A. D. Bache, May 21, 1863, and June 7, 1863, Peirce Papers, Harvard University Archives.

28. Asa Gray [Cambridge], to G. Engelmann, Sept. 2, 1863, typed copy.

29. Henry James Clark, *Mind in Nature* (New York, 1865); Asa Gray, Cambridge, to Charles Darwin, Aug. 7, 1866, typed copy.

30. H. J. Clark, *A Claim for Scientific Property* (July 1863), 3, photo-

stat in Museum of Comparative Zoology, Harvard University; see Jules Marcou, *Life, Letters, and Works of Louis Agassiz* (New York, 1896), II, 52–55.

31. Asa Gray to Charles Darwin, Aug. 7, 1866, typed copy.

32. Lawrence Scientific School, Faculty Records, Sept. 9, 1863, and following years, Harvard University Archives.

33. Cambridge Scientific Club, Records, Dec. 3, 1863, Harvard University Archives.

34. George P. Bond, astronomer at the Harvard Observatory, and Spencer F. Baird, zoologist and assistant secretary at the Smithsonian.

35. Asa Gray, Cambridge, to G. Engelmann, July 20, 1864, typed copy; Leo Lesquereux to J. P. Lesley, Jan. 21, 28, 30, 1865, American Philosophical Society Library.

36. Joseph Henry, Washington, to Louis Agassiz, Aug. 13, 1864; A. Hunter Dupree, "The Founding of the National Academy of Sciences —A Reinterpretation," American Philosophical Society, *Proceedings,* CI (1957), 439–440.

37. *Boston Evening Transcript,* Jan. 31, 1888; handwritten sheet at front of Mrs. Gray's copy of Marcou, *Agassiz,* I.

38. Leo Lesquereux, Columbus, Ohio, to J. P. Lesley, Jan. 21, 28, 30, 1865, March 21, 1866, American Philosophical Society Library.

39. Asa Gray, Cambridge, to J. D. Hooker, Aug. 27, 1874, Kew.

40. Asa Gray, Cambridge, to Charles Darwin, July 2, 1862, *Letters,* II, 486; Asa Gray, Cambridge, to Charles Wright, Nov. 14, 1862, *Letters,* II, 495.

41. See, for example, Gray's publications on the collections of Emanuel Samuels and L. J. Xantus, Boston Society of Natural History, *Proceedings,* VII (1859), 142–149.

42. C. C. Parry, Davenport, Iowa, to Asa Gray, Jan. 3, 1861; C. C. Parry, "Physiographic Sketch of [a] Portion of the Rocky Mountain Range . . . ," *American Journal of Science,* 2nd ser., XXXIII (1862), 231.

43. C. C. Parry, Mt. Vernon [Colorado], to Asa Gray, July 14, 1862; Parry, Davenport, Iowa, to Gray, Nov. 18, 1862; Elihu Hall, Denver, Colorado Territory, to Asa Gray, Sept. 1, 1862; G. Engelmann, St. Louis, to Asa Gray, Oct. 8, 1862.

44. Asa Gray, Cambridge, to William Darlington, Sept. 29, 1862; Joseph T. Rothrock to Asa Gray, June 22, 1865, Dec. 14, 1869, Dec. 28, 1869, June 3, 1873.

45. Ray Stannard Baker and Jessie Beal Baker, eds., *An American Pioneer in Science: The Life and Service of William James Beal* (Amherst, Mass., 1925), 3–6, 54–57.

46. For a graphic description of Agassiz's administrative methods, see Lesquereux to Lesley, March 21, 1866.

47. Liberty Hyde Bailey, interview, May 19, 1949.

48. Asa Gray, Cambridge, to J. D. Hooker, Feb. 22, 1864, Kew; Asa Gray, Cambridge, to Joseph Henry, Dec. 10, 1863.

49. Asa Gray, "Harvard University Herbarium," *American Journal of Science,* XXXIX (1865), 226; Asa Gray, Cambridge, to G. Engelmann, Oct. 14, 1864, typed copy.

50. President of Harvard College, *Report for the Year 1862–1863,* 4.

51. Asa Gray, De Herbariis, MS dated Jan. 12, 1865, Gray Herbarium Library.

52. Asa Gray, Cambridge, to G. Engelmann, March 29, 1865, *Letters,* II, 531; Asa Gray, Cambridge, to R. W. Church, May 1, 1865, *Letters,* II, 533–534; Asa Gray, Cambridge, to Charles Darwin, May 15, 1865, typed copy.

53. T. M. Peters, Moulton, Ala., to Asa Gray, June 17, 1865; Ravenel, *Journal,* 289; M. A. Curtis, Hillsborough, N.C., Sept. 1, 1865.

54. Joseph Henry, Washington, to Asa Gray, Oct. 31, 1866.

XVII

TRANSITION FROM PROFESSOR TO PATRIARCH

1. Asa Gray, Cambridge, to J. D. Hooker, Nov. 21, 1865, Kew.

2. Asa Gray, Cambridge, to J. D. Hooker, July 6, 1863; Dec. 6, 1865; and June 3, 1866, Kew.

3. Asa Gray, MS Notes for Lectures, 1864, Gray Herbarium Library; Asa Gray, Cambridge, to Charles Wright, May 19, 1866, *Letters,* II, 546; President of Harvard University, *Annual Report,* 1866–67, 4.

4. Asa Gray, Cambridge, to J. D. Hooker, May 10, 1866, and June 3, 1866, Kew.

5. Asa Gray, Cambridge, to J. D. Hooker, July 12, 1865, Kew.

6. C. Schuchert and C. M. LeVene, *O. C. Marsh: Pioneer in Paleontology* (New Haven, 1940), 75, 229; Asa Gray, Cambridge, to J. D. Hooker, Oct. 9, 1866, Kew.

7. Asa Gray, Cambridge, to Joseph Henry, Nov. 12, 1866; Joseph Henry, Washington, to Asa Gray, Oct. 31, 1866.

8. Asa Gray to J. D. Hooker, Oct. 9, 1866, Kew; Joseph Henry, Washington, to Asa Gray, March 8, 1867; Asa Gray, Cambridge, to Joseph Henry, March 17, 1867.

9. Asa Gray, Cambridge, to J. D. Hooker, May 20, 1867, Kew.

10. L. H. Bailey, *Cyclopedia of American Horticulture* (New York, 1900), II, 684.

11. Asa Gray, Cambridge, to J. D. Hooker, March 19, 1866, Kew; Asa Gray, Cambridge, to J. D. Hooker, May 20, 1867, Kew.

12. Asa Gray, Cambridge, to Charles Darwin, May 25, 1868, *Letters,* II, 562.

13. For a detailed account of this year in Europe, see *Letters,* II, 565–599; see also Mrs. Gray's letters to her sister in the travel journal in the Gray Herbarium Library.

14. J. D. Hooker, Kew, to Asa Gray, July 20, 1869.

15. Ethel F. Fiske, ed., *The Letters of John Fiske* (New York, 1940), 275.

16. Charles Darwin, *Animals and Plants under Domestication* (New York, 1868), II, 516; *Nation,* No. 142 (1868), 236.

17. Charles Darwin, Down, to Asa Gray, May 8 [1868]; Asa Gray, Cambridge, to Charles Darwin, May 25, 1868, *Letters,* II, 562.

18. Asa Gray, London, to R. W. Church, Aug. 22, 1869, typed copy. The version in *Letters,* II, 592, silently omits the reference to Huxley.

19. Sir Charles Lyell, London, to Asa Gray, Nov. 11, 1868, Autograph Collection, Gray Herbarium.

20. Asa Gray, Kew, to Lady Lyell, Nov. 15, 1868, American Philosophical Society Library.

21. Joseph Henry, Washington, to Asa Gray, May 29, 1870; Asa Gray, Cambridge, to Joseph Henry, Oct. 18, 1870.

22. Asa Gray, Cambridge, to Joseph Henry, Dec. 18, 1869.

23. Asa Gray, Cambridge, to J. D. Hooker, Jan. 22, 1870, March 1, 1870, Kew.

24. Henry James, *Charles W. Eliot: President of Harvard University 1869–1909* (Boston, 1930), II, 12–13.

25. Samuel E. Morison, ed., *The Development of Harvard University since the Inauguration of President Eliot 1869–1929* (Cambridge, Mass., 1930), 357, 508–517.

26. Asa Gray, Cambridge, to J. D. Hooker, Dec. 27, 1871, Kew; Edward Wagenknecht, *Longfellow: A Full-Length Portrait* (New York, 1955), 98.

27. Asa Gray, Cambridge, to J. D. Hooker, Jan. 18, 1872 and Feb. 27, 1872, Kew.

28. Asa Gray, Cambridge, to J. D. Hooker, May 6, 1872, Kew; Asa Gray, Cambridge, to John Torrey, Nov. 4, 1870, typed copy.

29. Asa Gray, Cambridge, to R. W. Church, Feb. 27, 1871, *Letters,* II, 614.

30. President, *Annual Report,* 1871–72, 15; 1872–73, 20; J. L. Love, *The Lawrence Scientific School in Harvard University 1847–1906* (Burlington, N.C., 1944), 23–24.

31. For accounts of this journey, see *Letters,* II, 625–633; MS letterjournals by Mrs. Gray in Gray Herbarium Library.

32. Asa Gray, Cambridge, to W. M. Canby, June 7, 1872, typed copy.

33. John Muir, *Letters to a Friend: Written to Mrs. Ezra S. Carr 1866–*

1879 (Boston, 1915), 125, 128; William Frederic Badé, ed., *The Life and Letters of John Muir* (Boston, 1923–24), I, 253.

34. A recent survey records the altitude of Gray's Peak as 14,274 feet.

35. *Colorado Miner,* Georgetown, Colo., Aug. 22, 1872. A clipping is in the Gray scrapbook at the Gray Herbarium.

36. Albert Kellogg, San Francisco, to Sereno Watson, Nov. 25, 1872.

37. Asa Gray, Cambridge, to J. D. Hooker, May 6, 1872, Kew; Gray to Hooker, October 24, 1872, Kew.

38. Emma W. Sargent and Charles S. Sargent, eds., *Epes Sargent of Gloucester and His Descendants* (Boston, 1923), 192–193; A. Hunter Dupree, "Asa Gray and Andrew Jackson Downing—A Bibliographic Note," *Rhodora,* LVIII (1956), 243–245.

39. Asa Gray, Cambridge, to J. D. Hooker, Nov. 16, 1872, Kew; H. H. Hunnewell, ed., *Life, Letters and Diary of Horatio Hollis Hunnewell* (Boston, 1906), 3 vols.

40. Asa Gray, Cambridge, to J. D. Hooker, Nov. 2, 1872, Kew; C. J. Sprague, Boston, to Asa Gray, Aug. 16, 1873 and Dec. 27, 1873.

41. Asa Gray, Cambridge, to J. D. Hooker, Jan. 4, 1873, Kew.

42. G. L. Goodale, Bowdoin College, to Asa Gray, June 25, 1870; Asa Gray, Cambridge, to J. D. Hooker, July 3, 1873, Kew.

43. Sereno Watson, New Haven, Conn., to Asa Gray, Dec. 9, 1869.

44. Asa Gray, Cambridge, to Alphonse De Candolle, Jan. 16, 1874, typed copy.

45. Asa Gray, Cambridge, to J. D. Hooker, July 7, 1873, Kew.

XVIII

A THEIST IN THE AGE OF DARWIN

1. J. N. Lockyer, London, to Asa Gray, March 30, 1874; Asa Gray, "Charles Robert Darwin," *Nature,* X (1874), 79–81.

2. Charles Darwin, Down, to Asa Gray, Feb. 5 [1871]; Asa Gray, Cambridge, to Charles Darwin, April 14, 1871, *Letters,* II, 615; Asa Gray [Cambridge], to Charles Darwin, Nov. 21, 1870, Cambridge University Library.

3. Cambridge Scientific Club, Records, Feb. 13, 1868, Harvard University Archives; Asa Gray, Cambridge, to Charles Darwin, Feb. 24, 1868, *Letters,* II, 561.

4. Charles Darwin, *The Variation of Plants and Animals under Domestication* (New York, 1868), I, 480; II, 437–441, 463–464.

5. Asa Gray, "Species, Considered as Variation, Geographical Distribution, and Succession," *American Journal of Science,* 2nd ser., XXXV (1863), 443; Asa Gray, Cambridge, to Charles Loring Brace, July 6, 1863, *Letters,* II, 462–463.

6. Asa Gray, Cambridge, to Charles Darwin, March 7, 1872, *Letters,* II, 624; for detailed statements of Gray's genetic ideas see Asa Gray, "Naudin on the Nature of Heredity and Variability in Plants," *American Journal of Science,* 3rd ser., XI (1876), 153–154; Asa Gray, "Review of W. K. Brooks, *The Law of Heredity,*" *American Journal of Science,* XXVII (1884), 156–157; Asa Gray, "Review of Francis Parkman, *The Hybridization of Lilies,*" *American Journal of Science,* XV (1878), 151–152.

7. Asa Gray, Differences of Science in 21 Years, MS of talk before Cambridge Scientific Club, Oct. 24, 1878, Gray Herbarium Library.

8. Asa Gray, "Burs in the Borage Family," *American Naturalist,* X (1876), 1; for a typical general statement of this theme, see Asa Gray, *Darwiniana* (New York, 1876), 288.

9. Asa Gray, "Relation of Insects to Flowers," *Contemporary Review,* XLI (1882), 609.

10. Asa Gray, Cambridge, to Clara ———, March 3, 1874, from copy in Hamilton College Library.

11. (New York, 1874), especially pp. 174–177 for comments on Gray.

12. Asa Gray, "What Is Darwinism?" *Nation,* May 28, 1874, reprinted in Gray, *Darwiniana,* 271.

13. Stow Persons, "Evolution and Theology," in Persons, ed., *Evolutionary Thought in America* (New Haven, Conn., 1950), 426.

14. F. Gardiner, "Darwinism," *Bibliotheca Sacra,* XXIX (1872), 240–289.

15. Asa Gray, "Sequoia and Its History," *Scientific Papers,* II, 164; see Emma Brace, *Life and Letters of Charles Loring Brace* (New York, 1894), 386.

16. G. F. Wright, "Professor Asa Gray," *The Advance* (Chicago, Ill., Feb. 9, 1888), clipping in Gray scrapbook, Gray Herbarium Library.

17. G. F. Wright, "Some Analogies between Calvinism and Darwinism," *Studies in Science and Religion* (Andover, Mass., 1882), 224, 230–231.

18. J. W. Dawson of McGill University, whose violently anti-Darwin stand Gray had combated anonymously in his "Attitude of Working Naturalists toward Darwinism," *Nation,* Oct. 16, 1873, and *Darwiniana,* 236–251.

19. G. F. Wright, Andover, Mass., to Asa Gray, June 26, 1875.

20. Asa Gray, Cambridge, to G. F. Wright, July 1, 1875, *Letters,* II, 655–656.

21. E. L. Youmans to Asa Gray, Dec. 7, 1875, autograph collection; John Fiske, "Agassiz and Darwinism," *Popular Science Monthly,* III (1873), 692–705; Asa Gray, Cambridge, to Joseph Henry, Oct. 17, 1873; Asa Gray, Cambridge, to J. D. Hooker, Oct. 29, 1866, Kew.

22. An indication on the Germans is given where Gray wrote "Good!" in the margin of the proof sheets of Francis Darwin, ed., *Life and Letters of Charles Darwin* (London, 1887), II, 186, at the point where T. H. Huxley says that the German biologists "were evolutionists, *a priori,* already and

they must have felt the disgust natural to deductive philosophers at being offered an inductive and experimental foundation for a conviction they had reached by a shorter cut."

23. Chauncey Wright, "German Darwinism," *Nation,* Sept. 9, 1875, 168–170; Asa Gray, Cambridge, to G. F. Wright, Sept. 14, 1875, *Letters,* II, 657.

24. Asa Gray, "Review of John Fiske, *The Destiny of Man Viewed in the Light of His Origin,*" *Nation,* XXXIX (1884), 426.

25. J. D. Dana, New Haven, Conn., to Asa Gray, Aug. 10, 1876.

26. Asa Gray, *Natural Science and Religion* (New York, 1880), 109. In the presentation copy to Mrs. Gray, preserved in the Gray Herbarium Library, the word "material" appears in Gray's handwriting opposite the phrase "human body."

27. Asa Gray, Cambridge, to G. F. Wright, Aug. 14, 1875, *Letters,* II, 656.

28. Quoted from Aristotle in *Darwiniana,* 390.

29. "Review of *Darwiniana,*" *Popular Science Monthly,* IX (1876), 624; G. F. Wright, Andover, Mass., to Asa Gray, Sept. 29, 1876; Asa Gray, Cambridge, to J. D. Hooker, May 19, 1876; Aug. 1, 1876; Sept. 25, 1876, Kew.

30. *Popular Science Monthly,* IX (1876), 624; *New York Times,* Sept. 18, 1876; "Darwinism in America," *Congregationalist,* Sept. 6, 1876; *Vermont Chronicle,* Sept. 16, 1876; *The Advance,* Sept. 21, 1876; *Christian Register,* Oct. 28, 1876; G. F. Wright, "Review of *Darwiniana,*" *Bibliotheca Sacra,* XXXIII (1876), 773–778.

31. *Independent,* Oct. 5, 1876.

32. Asa Gray, Cambridge, to G. F. Wright, Aug. 8, 1876, Wright Papers, Oberlin College Library; Asa Gray, Cambridge, to C. E. Norton, Aug. 8, 1876, Houghton Library, Harvard University.

33. [H. W. Holland], "Review of *Darwiniana,*" Nation, XXIII (1876), 358.

34. Joseph Cook, *Boston Monday Lectures: Biology, with Preludes on Current Events* (Boston, 1877).

35. G. F. Wright, Andover, Mass., to Asa Gray, July 5, 1877 and April 8, 1878.

36. Asa Gray, "Cook's Lectures on Biology," *New Englander,* XXXVII (1878), 100, 113. Gray continued the controversy in a letter to the *Independent,* May 9, 1878; John Fiske, *A Century of Science* (Boston, 1899), 349.

37. Simon Newcomb, "Simplicity and Universality of the Laws of Nature," *Independent,* Sept. 5, 1878, 5.

38. Asa Gray, Cambridge, to G. F. Wright, Oct. 24, 1878, *Letters,* II, 684; Asa Gray, Letter to the Editor of the *Independent,* No. 1555 (1878), 16.

39. Asa Gray, *Independent,* No. 1558 (Oct. 10, 1878), 1; No. 1562 (Nov. 7, 1878), 1–3, 16.

40. Asa Gray, "Plant Archaeology," *Nation,* No. 742 (Sept. 18, 1879), 195.

41. Asa Gray, Cambridge, to J. D. Hooker, March 27, 1880, Kew.

42. Emma Brace, ed., *The Life of Charles Loring Brace,* 367.

43. Asa Gray, *Natural Science and Religion* (New York, 1880), 8. Subsequent quotes are from the same source.

44. Loren C. Eiseley, *Darwin's Century: Evolution and the Men Who Discovered It* (Garden City, N.Y., 1958), 287–324.

45. *Presbyterian Review,* I (1880), 586; G. F. Wright, "Review of *Natural Science and Religion,*" *Bibliotheca Sacra,* XXXVII (1880), 390; G. F. Wright, Andover, Mass., to Asa Gray, May 18, 1880 (2 letters); W. G. Eliot, Jefferson, N.H., to Asa Gray, July 4, 1884; C. J. Sprague, Boston, to Asa Gray, March 3, 1880.

46. Julia Wedgwood, London, to Asa Gray, Oct. 19, 1881, Feb. 3, 1882, and June 11, 1882.

47. [Julia Wedgwood], "A Botanist on Evolution," *Spectator,* LV (1882), 536–538.

48. American Academy of Arts and Sciences, *Proceedings,* XVII (1882), 449.

49. "Evolution versus Evangelical Religion," *Boston Evening Transcript,* Sept. 13, 1882.

50. Asa Gray, "Natural Selection and Natural Theology," *Nature,* XXVII (1883), 527–528; XXVIII (1883), 78.

51. J. D. Hooker to Asa Gray, April 6, 1883; J. D. Hooker to T. H. Huxley, March 27, 1888, Leonard Huxley, *Life and Letters of Thomas Henry Huxley* (New York, 1900), II, 205–206.

52. Cambridge Scientific Club, Records, Nov. 17, 1886, Harvard University Archives.

53. A. Hunter Dupree, "Jeffries Wyman's Views on Evolution," *Isis,* XLIV (1953), 245.

XIX

THE PATRIARCH OF NEW PLANT SCIENCES

1. Asa Gray, Cambridge, to J. D. Hooker, Nov. 4, 1873, Kew.

2. A. D. Rodgers III, *American Botany 1873–1892: Decades of Transition* (Princeton, 1944), chap. I, is headed "Asa Gray—the Great Years Begun." This work covers in detail the subjects of the following chapter.

3. L. H. Bailey, interview, May 19, 1949.

4. J. M. Coulter, "Asa Gray," D. S. Jordan, *Leading American Men of Science* (New York, 1910), 220.

5. Asa Gray, Cambridge, to John Muir, Feb. 5, 1878.

6. See A. D. Rodgers III, *John Merle Coulter: Missionary in Science* (Princeton, 1944).

7. A. Hunter Dupree, *Science in the Federal Government* (Cambridge, Mass., 1957), 194–214.

8. Asa Gray, Cambridge, to Sir Edward Fry, Feb. 26, 1882, *Letters,* II, 731.

9. See Rogers McVaugh, *Edward Palmer: Plant Explorer of the American West* (Norman, Okla., 1956).

10. C. C. Parry, Davenport, Iowa, to Asa Gray, Oct. 29, 1878; May 2, 1879; Helen B. Davis, *Life and Work of Cyrus Guernsey Pringle* (Burlington, Vt., 1936).

11. M. W. Harrington, Ann Arbor, Mich., to Asa Gray, Jan. 14, 1873, autograph collection; G. L. Goodale, Cambridge, to Asa Gray, Nov. 18, 1880.

12. Asa Gray, Cambridge, to J. D. Hooker, Dec. 6, 1875, Kew.

13. C. C. Parry, Davenport, Iowa, to Asa Gray, April 21, 1884.

14. Asa Gray, Cambridge, to J. D. Hooker, Feb. 12, 1875, and July 27, 1875, Kew; President of Harvard University, *Report, 1882–1883,* 36.

15. C. E. Bessey, *Botany for High Schools and Colleges* (New York, 1880); *American Journal of Science,* XX (1880), 337.

16. *American Journal of Science,* XXXI (1886), 478.

17. Asa Gray, Cambridge, to J. D. Hooker, Feb. 27, 1877, Kew; Asa Gray, "Organogeny of the Female Flower of Gnetum Gnomon," *American Journal of Science,* XIII (1877), 470; L. F. Ward, "Asa Gray and Darwinism," *New Monthly Magazine,* August 1888, 85–92.

18. C. C. Parry, San Bernardino, Calif., to Asa Gray, Nov. 18, 1875; Volney Rattan, San Francisco, to Asa Gray, April 24, 1879.

19. H. H. Bartlett, "The Botanical Work of Edward Lee Greene," *Torreya,* XVI (1916), 161; Rodgers, *American Botany,* 55; E. L. Greene, Yreka, Calif., to Asa Gray, July 18, 1876.

20. E. L. Greene, Silver City, N.M., to Sereno Watson, Sept. 28, 1880; to Asa Gray, Feb. 2, 1881.

21. Asa Gray, Cambridge, to J. G. Lemmon, Aug. 9, 1880, Jepson Herbarium, University of California.

22. J. G. Lemmon, Oakland, Calif., to Asa Gray, Dec. 21, 1881; July 31, 1880; Dec. 10, 1881; Dec. 1, 1881.

23. Asa Gray, Cambridge, to J. G. Lemmon, Jan. 15, 1882, Jepson Herbarium, University of California.

24. E. L. Greene, Berkeley, Calif., to Asa Gray, Dec. 19, 1881; George Engelmann, St. Louis, Missouri, to Asa Gray, Dec. 24, 1881.

25. W. L. Jepson, "Edward Lee Greene," *Dictionary of American Biography,* VII, 565.

26. E. L. Greene to Asa Gray, Jan. 5, 1886; E. L. Greene, Berkeley, Calif., to Asa Gray, Oct. 2, 1885; Rodgers, *American Botany,* 253–254.

27. C. C. Parry, Davenport, Iowa, to Asa Gray, July 3, 1883; E. L. Greene, San Francisco, to Asa Gray, April 26, 1886; E. L. Greene, Berkeley, Calif., to Asa Gray, Jan. 5, 1886 and Dec. 16, 1886.

28. E. L. Greene to Asa Gray, Feb. 1, 1886; Asa Gray to E. L. Greene, draft answer to Greene's letter of Feb. 1, 1886.

29. Asa Gray, Cambridge, to J. D. Hooker, May 1, 1883, Kew.

30. Henry Shaw, St. Louis, to Asa Gray, April 19, 1884; William Trelease, St. Louis, to Asa Gray, Oct. 12, 1885; Asa Gray, Cambridge, to J. D. Hooker, June 9, 1884, *Letters,* II, 752; C. C. Parry, Davenport, Iowa, to Asa Gray, Feb. 27, 1885; Dec. 28, 1885; March 14, 1886.

31. Asa Gray, Cambridge, to J. D. Hooker, Dec. 3, 1878, Kew; Asa Gray, Cambridge, to F. L. Olmsted, Jan. 3, 1879, Olmsted Papers, Library of Congress, furnished me through the courtesy of Mrs. Laura W. Roper; F. L. Olmsted, New York, to Asa Gray, March 1, 1879; Asa Gray, "A Redwood Reserve," *American Journal of Science,* XXXIII (1887), 425–426; "The Monterey Pine and Cypress," *Science,* VI (1885), 433–434.

32. Asa Gray, Cambridge, to J. D. Hooker, April 28, 1879, Kew; President of Harvard University, *Report, 1878–1879,* 42; Asa Gray, Cambridge, to J. D. Hooker, Dec. 26, 1879, Kew; Asa Gray, Cambridge, to Alexander Agassiz, Aug. 29, 1880, copy in Goodale's hand in possession of Mrs. Nathaniel Clapp, Beverly Farms, Mass.; Harvard College Records, April 23, 1883, XIII, 208, Harvard University Archives.

33. Asa Gray, Cambridge, to J. D. Hooker, April 28, 1879; July 15, 1879; Asa Gray to [Francis] Parkman, Feb. 21, 1879, Washburn Papers, Massachusetts Historical Society; Asa Gray, Cambridge, to J. D. Hooker, Nov. 20, 1879, Kew; Dec. 25, 1881, *Letters,* II, 729.

34. Dupree, *Science in the Federal Government,* 195–208.

35. Standard accounts of this journey are found in *Letters,* II, 670–676; Leonard Huxley, *Life and Letters of Sir Joseph Hooker* (New York, 1918), II, 205–217.

36. W. F. Badé, *The Life and Letters of John Muir* (Boston, 1924), II, 82.

37. Mrs. John Bidwell, quoted in Linnie M. Wolfe, *Son of the Wilderness: the Life of John Muir* (New York, 1945), 194.

38. Huxley, *Hooker,* II, 216, 217; Asa Gray and J. D. Hooker, "The Vegetation of the Rocky Mountain Region and a Comparison with That of Other Parts of the World," U.S. Geological and Geographical Survey of the Territories, *Bulletin,* VI (1880), 1–77.

39. Asa Gray, "A Pilgrimage to Torreya," *Scientific Papers,* II, 189–196.

40. *Letters,* II, 682.

41. L. H. Bailey, interview, May 19, 1949.

42. Asa Gray, Lathrop, California, to J. D. Hooker, May 1, 1885, *Letters,* II, 768.

XX

LAST DAYS 1886–1888

1. Asa Gray, Cambridge, to J. D. Hooker, June 30, 1885, Kew; Asa Gray, Cambridge, to J. D. Dana, Sept. 20, 1886, *Letters,* II, 785; Asa Gray, Cambridge, to A. De Candolle, June 29, 1886, *Letters,* II, 784.

2. Asa Gray, Cambridge, to J. D. Hooker, Sept. 15, 1886, *Letters,* II, 786; Asa Gray, Will, County of Middlesex, Massachusetts, Registry of Probates, Cambridge, Massachusetts.

3. Asa Gray, Cambridge, to Sir Edward Fry, Nov. 13, 1886; Asa Gray, Cambridge, to J. D. Hooker, Jan. 25, 1887, *Letters,* II, 790, 791.

4. Asa Gray, Geneva, to J. D. Hooker, May 24, 1887, typed copy.

5. Asa Gray, Cambridge, to J. D. Hooker, April 21, 1882, Kew.

6. Asa Gray, Cambridge, to R. C. Waterston, April 1, 1884, Boston Society of Natural History.

7. L. H. Bailey, interview, May 19, 1949.

8. *Letters,* II, 812.

9. Asa Gray, Cambridge, to N. L. Britton, Nov. 27, 1887, *Letters,* II, 813–815.

10. G. L. Goodale, Cambridge, to J. D. Hooker, Jan. 2, 1888, Kew.

11. Patrick Tracy Jackson, interview, April 6, 1954.

12. Sereno Watson, Cambridge, to W. T. T. Dyer, Dec. 12, 1887, Kew.

13. Charles Eliot Norton, Cambridge, to Sir John Simon, Feb. 2, 1888, M. A. DeW. Howe, ed., *Letters of Charles Eliot Norton,* II, 187.

14. F. G. Peabody, in *In Memoriam: Asa Gray* (Cambridge, Mass., 1888), 45.

15. Alexander McKenzie, in *In Memoriam: Asa Gray,* 9–30, 38–41.

16. Asa Gray, Cambridge, to Mrs. T. P. James, April 30, 1863, *Letters,* II, 501.

INDEX

INDEX

College of Physicians and Surgeons, New York, 15

College of Physicians and Surgeons of the Western District of the State of New York, 9; chartered, 10; faculty, 11; confers degree on Gray, 18; decline of, 23

College of Surgeons, London, 81

Colonia Tovar, Venezuela, 210

Colorado, plants, 325–326; Greene collects in, 389; 1877 visit, 406–407

Colorado, plateau, 76

Colorado River of Texas, 160

Colorado Springs, Colorado, 406

Columbia River, 75, 76

Columbus, Ohio, 223–224

Committee on the Library, Joint, 186, 195

Commons, House of, 82

Compositae, 29, 139; first interest in, 16; Gray borrows from W. Hooker, 95; Nuttall's, 98; completed for *Flora*, 117; from Frémont, 157; Gray's stopping place, 170, 205, 332; in *Synoptical Flora*, 391; types on 1880 journey, 398

Comstock, J. L., 51; writes elementary botany, 48

Congregational Church, 37; in Sauquoit, 3; Gray attends, 115; in Cambridge, 119; Mrs. Gray does not join, 182; Gray's activities in, 220–221; Watson and, 352; G. F. Wright and, 362; reaction to *Darwiniana*, 368. See also Orthodoxy

Conioselinum Canadense, 418

Conservation, Gray and, 404

Constable, James, 97

Contemporary Review, 366

Conway, New Hampshire, 116

Cook, James, 58

Cook, Joseph, 369–370, 371

Cooke, Josiah Parsons, 130, 192, 315

Cooper, James Fenimore, 8

Cooper, Sir Astley, 81

Cooperstown, New York, 8

Cope, Edward Drinker, 357

Corda, A. J. C., 64, 83, 88

Corn Laws, 190

Corporation, Harvard, 178; and Gray's appointment, 109–110; and garden, 117; appoints Wyman, 149; adds to house, 181; grants leave, 190; authorizes microscopes, 199; Gray

gives notice to, 332; Bussey Institution, 343; and plans to retire, 344; agreement with Arnold trustees, 344; on Gray's salary and duties, 444. *See also* Harvard University.

Corsica, plants of, 35

Coulter, John Merle, 388, 394

Couthouy, J. P., 67, 68

Crawe, J. B., 35

Crawford Notch, 116

Croom, Hardy, 408

Croomia, 408

Cruciferae, 245

Crystal Palace, 190, 191

Cuba, 208, 324

Curtis, Moses Ashley, 201; letter from, 102; gives information on collecting, 96; and Wilkes fungi, 194–195; on Wood, 202; opposes Nott, 229; on Rafinesque and Darwin, 279; and secession, 309–310; after war, 330; collections to Harvard, 351

Cutler, Manasseh, 106

Cuvier, Baron Georges, 20, 140, 150, 226

Cyperaceae, 42, 89. *See also* Sedges

Dahabeah, 338

Dana, James Dwight, 263, 431; letter to, 243, 247; attends Utica Gymnasium, 31; Gray recommends, 60; and U.S. Exploring Expedition, 67; sails on exploring expedition, 68; on *Vestiges*, 145; on transmutation and religion, 148; and Harvard, 149; *Zoöphytes*, 186; helps Gray with geology, 224, 230–231; member of Lazzaroni, 225; stature, 230; idealism, 231; "Thoughts on Species," 231; on postglacial warm period, 251; controversy with Marcou and Agassiz, 256–257; collapse, 272; on Gray and *Darwiniana*, 365; at Yale lectures, 375

Dana, Richard Henry, Sr., 119

Dana, Richard Henry, Jr., 225

Danube River, 89, 411

Darby, John, 201

Darlington, William, 61, 117, 420

Dartmouth medical school, 11

Darwin, Charles, 2, 21, 68, 79, 147, 420; letter to, 280, 309, 324, 337; letter from, 244–245, 267; background compared to Gray, 5; first